W9-COB-382

Marketing Globally

Marketing Globally: Planning and Practice

A. Coskun Samli

University of North Florida

John S. Hill

University of Alabama

NTC Business Books
a division of NTC/CONTEMPORARY PUBLISHING GROUP
Lincolnwood, Illinois USA

Acquisitions Editor: Lynn Mooney
Product Manager: Judy Rudnick
Design Manager: Ophelia M. Chambliss
Cover design: Ophelia M. Chambliss
Interior design: Megan Keane DeSantis
Production Manager: Margo Goia
Production Coordinator: Denise Duffy

ISBN: 0-8442-3308-0

This book is dedicated to Bea, Evan, and Ayla

Linda, Christopher, and Richard

and to the memory of Richard R. Still (1921–1991)

Brief Contents

Contents

4   CHAPTER   The Financial Environment of International Marketing   84

2 PART
Assessing the International Marketing Environment 117

7   C H A P T E R   International Market Segmentation   155

3 PART
Implementing International Marketing Strategies   221

12 CHAPTER Marketing Industrial Products Internationally   267

13 CHAPTER International Marketing Channels   291

---

16 C H A P T E R   International Personal Selling and Sales Force Management   357

---

17 C H A P T E R   International Pricing   388

4 PART
Coordinating and Controlling Marketing Programs   409

18 CHAPTER   International Market Research and Information Systems   411

Preface

In the short period of three years, the total volume of world trade has gone up from about $7.5 trillion to $10.2 trillion, an increase of over 35 percent. With such a growth rate, the role of global marketing is bound to become more and more important.

These are exciting times for global marketing. In almost every part of the world, there is constant change favoring international marketing. European economic and, perhaps, political unification is still in negotiation; the North American Free Trade Agreement (NAFTA) is now a reality; the economic liberalization of Eastern Europe has great promise; the surging economies in the Pacific Rim are playing a key role in international trade; and ongoing economic and cultural developments everywhere in the world are causing the emergence of new and exciting markets throughout the globe. As a consequence, international marketing opportunities abound; never has the reason to be global been more compelling. We hope the authors' enthusiasm for their subject spills over onto you—our readers—and that you will find our text informative and interesting reading.

In this age of specialization, international topics buck prevailing trends. Our aim in writing this book has been to broaden student appreciation of world markets. Combined, our 50-plus years of global marketing experience has shown us that once a student's international curiosity is piqued, it remains globally focused thereafter. Hence, our objective has not been to prepare regional specialists in North America, Western Europe, Eastern Europe, and so on.

Rather, it has been to prepare students to be world marketers. Companies can and do specialize their international functions, but good executives know not only their product and market specialties but also how they fit into the broader global spectrum. Thus, they are capable of taking advantage of emerging global opportunities. The Chapter 1 geopolitical overview, therefore, provides valuable background to bring everyone "up to speed," and our first four chapters (comprising the world environment of global marketing) provide basic instruction in global cultures and environments.

We have found that the most effective international operators are those who understand the whys and wherefores of global behaviors. This belief is reflected in the approach of Chapter 2 to political, economic, and cultural institutions and their effects on human behavior (unlike other texts that tell you that such institutions influence behavior but don't say how). Then, because political, economic, and cultural change is the one constant in world markets, Chapter 3 deals with developmental issues, the emphasis here being again not just on what happens, but why.

Our environmental assessment concludes in Chapter 4 with a look at financial aspects of international marketing. All transactions have monetary considerations, and the international executives we know all have good groundings in foreign exchange rates and related financial factors.

Recognizing and evaluating world market opportunities is the focus of the second section. Overall, the authors rarely have been impressed by corporate recognitions and assessments of international marketing opportunities. The aim of Chapters 5 through 7, therefore, is to establish a bedrock of principles by which companies (both small and large) can evaluate their own global potential and assess foreign markets as scientifically and thoroughly as possible. Chapter 6 shows how to quantify international or global market opportunities, and Chapter 7 illustrates how the market segmentation process can be applied internationally. Also included in this section are exporting (Chapter 8, which includes export market assessment) and market entry strategies (Chapter 9), which are directly affected by perceptions of market opportunities.

Managing global (or international) marketing activities is the subject of Part Three. While much global trade and investment occurs because of similarities in consumption patterns and in values and attitudes among nations, effective international marketers know when to fine-tune their products, services, promotions, and distribution to fit local environments. The aim of Chapters 10 through 17 is to help students recognize when it is feasible to standardize some or all marketing activities, and when there needs to be manipulations in product, promotion, pricing, and distribution options. In other words, these chapters also indicate when to multilocalize. Chapter 10 is a strategy overview that highlights the major internal and external considerations in strategy formulation. Next, we discuss consumer product policies and practices (Chapter 11), and then we move on to industrial products and marketing mixes (Chapter 12). Distribution is tackled in Chapter 13, logistics in Chapter 14, and advertising in Chapter 15. In all cases, we have strived to link theory and practice and to illustrate principles with real,

corporate examples. Next in this section, Chapter 16 emphasizes personal selling, negotiation, and sales management in cross-cultural contexts. Much of this material is intended to reinforce and dovetail with material presented in Chapters 2 and 3.

Our final section, Part Four, deals with coordinating and controlling marketing programs. The task of planning, coordinating, and controlling business and marketing activities over many different country environments is complex. These topics are covered in Chapters 18, 19, and 20. First of all, because world markets constantly change, top managements place premiums on obtaining good information in a timely manner. Chapter 18 deals with marketing information issues. Then, organizational structures used in marketing globally are scrutinized in Chapter 19, and marketing control functions are reviewed in Chapter 20. Finally, in Chapter 21, the reader is placed in the position of chief executive officer of a large international concern and is introduced to the complexities of integrating the marketing function into global corporate planning. As Marvin Mann, CEO of IBM spin-off Lexmark, remarked a few years back, "In the future, there will be two types of CEOs—global CEOs and unemployed CEOs!" The message is clear: For those aspiring to reach high corporate management levels, global is the way to go, and international marketing is the field in which future leaders must show competence.

This text could not have been brought to a happy conclusion without the help of many others. To our students—past, present and future—we owe a debt of gratitude for stimulating our thoughts and providing a platform for testing many of the concepts in this text. Our respective deans, Earle Traynham at the University of North Florida and Barry Mason at the University of Alabama, provided encouragement and support. The secretarial staffs at both institutions did miraculous jobs in converting our non-Palmer-like scripts into meaningful prose, and we thank each one: Trish Lowery and Gwen Bennett, Barbara Woods and Brenda Patterson. We are also indebted to our research assistants, Mehmet Ongan and Thomas Jedlik, and Sean Dwyer and Jason Lueg—heroes behind the scenes.

Not least, we are indebted to colleagues at other universities who read and contributed to this book at various stages and who helped shape the authors' thinking and views. These include James Littlefield of Virginia Tech, James Wills of the University of Hawaii, Dhruv Grewal of the University of Miami, Attila Yaprak of Wayne State University, Tamer Cavusgil of Michigan State University, Jagdish Sheth of Emory University, Lawrence Jacobs of the University of Hawaii, Erdener Raynak of Pennsylvania State University, M. Joseph Sirgy of Virginia Tech, Tansu Barker of Brock University, Salah Hassan of George Washington University, Michael J. Thomas of Strathclyde, E. Stuart Kirby of the University of Aston, David M. Andrus of Kansas State University, Douglas N. Behrman of Florida State University, Jeffrey L. Bradford of Bowling Green University, David R. Decker of Youngstown State University, Joseph O. Eastlack, Jr., of Saint Joseph's University, M. Krishna Erramilli of the University of North Texas, Mushtag Luqmani of Western Michigan University, James Masulka of Youngstown State University, Agnes Olszewski of Seton Hall University, Gerald D. Sentell of Tennessee Associates, Inc., Theodore F. Smith of Old Dominion University, Adel El-Ansary of the University of North Florida, and Tunc Erem of Marmara University.

To these colleagues and many others, we are indebted. To all of you, we say thank you. Naturally, the responsibility for errors and incorrect interpretations belongs solely to the authors. To those who read this book, we hope you emerge from the experience with a sense of understanding of global markets and a desire to maintain high levels of interest in global events. Please, let us hear from you, and let your suggestions be the basis for future editions.

A. Coskun Samli

John S. Hill

The World Environment of International Marketing

The objective of Part 1, the first four chapters, is to provide you with a background to help you study and understand world markets. Chapter 1 offers a geopolitical overview of North America, Western Europe, Eastern Europe, the Middle East and Africa, Asia, and Latin America. It briefly describes the geographical and historical forces that have shaped developments in these regions and notes present-day commercial characteristics. This overview will allow you to relate daily world events to text material and to sharpen your geographic awareness.

Chapter 2 shows how economic, political, and social factors influence human behavior. Specifically, it discusses how economic systems (such as capitalism, communism, and mixed systems) mesh with social and religious elements to produce broad patterns of behavior, which are then modified by the particular idiosyncrasies of various countries. This treatment should contribute to your understanding not only of what behavioral variations exist throughout the world but also why they exist.

World markets are characterized by continuous change. Chapter 3 examines how and why economic, political, and social changes occur and, just as important, why change has not occurred in many nations. In particular, it studies the role of trade and investment as catalysts for cultural change.

For all international marketing transactions, foreign exchange rates are involved. For this reason, Chapter 4 discusses what foreign exchange rates are; what helps determine the values of foreign currency; and the effects of fluctuating exchange rates on trade, investment, and other commercial activities.

CHAPTER 1

Geopolitics of World Markets

Learning Objectives

When you have mastered the contents of this chapter, you will be able to do the following:

1 Discuss the diversity of the international marketplace and the relative economic significance of different regions of the world.

2 Explain the impact of geography and history on cultural development in various countries.

3 Contrast and compare the cultural characteristics of the Americas, Eastern and Western Europe, the Middle East, Africa, and Asia.

4 Analyze each region's commercial characteristics and environmental development as they affect world business.

THE WORLD: AN OVERVIEW

The world has more than 230 countries and more than 5 billion people. Of these, fewer than 30 countries are fully industrialized, most of them in North America and Western and Northern Europe. In the rest of the world (Eastern Europe, Latin America, the Middle East, Africa, and Asia), only Japan stands out as an economic powerhouse, though South Korea, Taiwan, Singapore, and Hong Kong are powering the Asian industrialization push.

Most of the world's countries, then, are in the process of industrializing. But development is slow, and enormous differences still exist between highly developed and still-developing countries with respect to industrial output and the populations that output must support. Some of these differences are shown in Table 1–1.

North America, Western Europe, and Australasia (Australia and New Zealand) together account for over 60 percent of the world's gross domestic product (28.7 percent, 30.0 percent, and 1.5 percent, respectively), but they have only about 14 percent of the world's population. At the other end of the spectrum, Latin America, Africa, and Asia account for just over one-third of world gross domestic product (34.6 percent, but only 16.6 percent without Japan), but they have more than 77 percent of the world's population (more than 4 billion people).

TABLE 1–1 ▪ *World and Regional Analyses: Gross Domestic Products and Population*

	Gross Domestic Product ($bn)	Average GDP per Capita ($)	Range per Capita ($)	Population Projections (millions)		
				1994*	2010	2020
Africa	$326 1.3%	$634	$12 (Zaire) to $3,087 (Mauritius)	514 9.7%	1,009	1,230
Middle East	$496 1.9%	$2,319	$841 (Iraq) to $16,247 (UAE)	214 4.0%		
Asia	$6,898 27.1%	$2,210	$10 (Bangladesh) to $36,739 (Japan)	3,122 58.8%	4,075	4,495
North America	$7,288 28.7%	$25,138	$18,778 (Canada) to $25,852 (U.S.)	290 5.5%	330	358
Latin America	$1,587 6.2%	$3,404	$242 (Haiti) to $8,182 (Argentina)	466 8.8%	583	642
Western Europe	$7,636 30.0%	$17,220	$2,144 (Turkey) to $37,259 (Switzerland)	443 8.3%	523	521
Eastern Europe	$845 3.3%	$3,543	$1,190 (Bulgaria) to $4,282 (Russia)	239 4.5%	307	317
Australasia	$375 1.5%	$17,584	$14,681 (NZ) to $18,152 (Australia)	21 0.4%	33	37
Totals	**$25,451 (100%)**			**5,309 (100%)**	**6,862**	**7,601**

Source: Adapted from "Indicators of Market Size for 115 Countries," *Crossborder Monitor*, 28 August 1996, 1–12; and *World Almanac 1997* (Mahwah, N.J.: World Almanac Books), 1996, 838–39.

*actual figures

Population projections in Table 1–1 suggest that this situation is not likely to change much before 2020. Africa and Asia, in particular, show steep increases in population. Their excess labor supply situations make them attractive to multinational corporations as manufacturing sites, especially for labor-intensive operations. Marketers, therefore, are most interested in industrially advanced countries because of their immediate market potential, their advanced technology, and their educated populations. Interest in developing countries focuses on their attractiveness as production sites and potential for long-term market growth.

Successful international marketers know their way around the world's markets, and they know how to evaluate marketing opportunities wherever they appear. Consequently, it is appropriate here to examine first the world's major regions—North America, Western Europe, Eastern Europe, the Middle East and Africa, Asia, and Latin America—and, in the process, look at their geographic, historical, and cultural characteristics.

NORTH AMERICA

Geographic Characteristics

North America, for the purposes of this book, consists of the United States and Canada (see Figure 1–1). Although Mexico and the Central American countries are technically part of North America, their culture and history make them part of Latin America. Geographically, Canada and the United States extend from the frozen Arctic south to the semitropical states of Florida, Texas, and California. The two countries share a 3,000-mile border, and because of the rigorous climate in northern Canada, almost 80 percent of Canadians live within 100 miles of the U.S. border.

Historical and Cultural Perspectives

Prior to colonization in the fifteenth and sixteenth centuries, North America was inhabited solely by Indian tribes and Inuit. Although Columbus "discovered" what is now the United States in 1492, serious colonization did not begin until the seventeenth century, with the landing of the *Mayflower* in 1620. From that time on, the continent attracted immigrants of many nationalities—French, English, Scots, Irish, Dutch, Scandinavian, Belgian, Polish, Russian, German, Czech, Italian, and Greek, among others. From this assemblage emerged the United States, which, having liberated itself from the British in 1776 and settled internal problems in the Civil War of 1861–1865, went on to become a world industrial power in the early twentieth century.

The richly varied ethnic composition of the United States reflects its history. It includes around 1.5 million Native Americans, more than 5 million Hispanics, and about 30 million African Americans. Its economy, the strongest in the world, is based largely on the principles of competition and free trade. The United States accounts for approximately 5 percent of the world's population, but it is responsible for a quarter of the world's gross domestic product (GDP). The nation's 260 million consumers have an average income of over $25,000 per person, making the United States the world's largest national mass market. Its currency, the dollar, is widely used and accepted around the world in commercial transactions of every description.

In terms of area, Canada is the second largest country in the world (smaller than

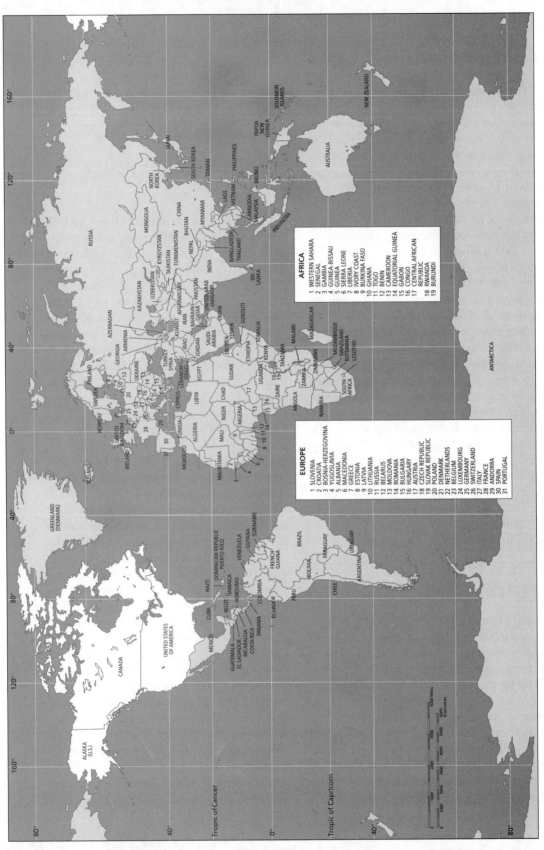

FIGURE 1-1 *North America in its Global Context*

Russia but larger than China). It has abundant raw materials and is the world's second largest gold and uranium producer. It ranks third largest in silver, and fourth in copper, and it has good supplies of nickel, zinc, lead, potash, and wood-related products.[1] The French were the first to colonize parts of Atlantic Canada in 1604, while the British came in 1755. Today, these two groups comprise Canada's major ethnic segments. About one-fourth of Canada's 29 million population are French speaking and live mainly in the province of Quebec. Differences between French-speaking and English-speaking Canadians have resulted in movements to separate Quebec from Canada.

Commercial Characteristics

1. U.S. direct investments in Canada in 1995 were in excess of $81 billion, mainly in manufacturing ($41 billion) and finance ($13 billion). Canadian sensitivity to foreign commercial influences, especially American (which accounts for about 80 percent of foreign investment in Canada), has been an important issue since the 1970s. Former Prime Minister Pierre Trudeau once commented: "When the U.S. sneezes, Canada catches the cold." Canadians, by contrast, are the fifth biggest group of foreign investors in the United States, with over $26 billion.

2. U.S.-Canadian trade, at about $276 billion in 1995, is the biggest trading relationship in the world. The United States accounts for about 70 percent of Canada's total exports and imports.

3. The United States has the most direct investment overseas of any country, totaling $796 billion in 1996. Its strong economy also has attracted over $600 billion of foreign direct investment, with

the United Kingdom accounting for over $132 billion of this total.

4. In 1988, the United States and Canada signed a free trade agreement. The aim of this agreement was to gradually remove barriers to trade and investment for most industrial, agricultural, and service sectors. In response to this creation of "North America, Inc.," numerous companies have consolidated their North American holdings to exploit the $7.3 trillion market. Mexico was admitted to the North American Free Trade Agreement (NAFTA) in 1994, and Chile's application to join the group was on NAFTA's 1997 agenda.

5. Although the United States is the world's largest industrial economy, agricultural products are among its biggest exports. In 1995, agricultural products accounted for more than $54 billion of the export total of over $583 billion. The U.S. trade deficit (how far import values exceeded export values) is of considerable concern. In 1995, the deficit was over $170 billion, with 1996 figures expected to top $180 billion.

WESTERN EUROPE

Geographic Characteristics

Western Europe extends from the Scandinavian countries of the north (which are on the same latitude and have similar weather patterns as Alaska) to the Mediterranean coastlines of Spain, France, and Italy (see Figure 1–2). From west to east, the region extends from Iceland (Greenland is Danish but has only 55,000 people over a huge, largely frozen area) to the borders of Poland, the Czech and

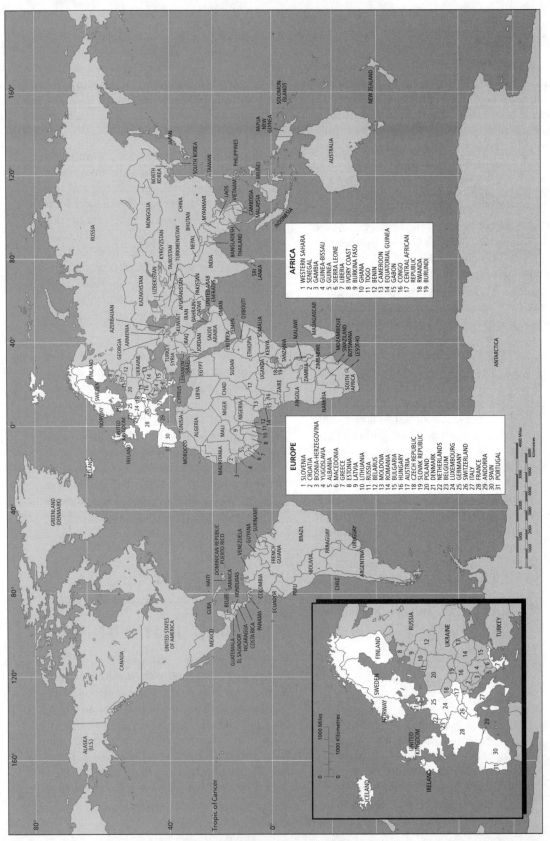

FIGURE 1-2 *Western Europe in its Global Context*

Slovak republics, Hungary, and Yugoslavia (now comprising Serbia and Montenegro). The major economic powers of Western Europe—the United Kingdom, France, and Germany—have temperate climates, with moderate winters (by Scandinavian standards) and warm (60–70 degrees Fahrenheit) rather than hot summers (unlike the southern United States and North and Central Africa, where temperatures are typically in the range of 80–90 degrees Fahrenheit). Historically, Western Europe's clement conditions have encouraged the year-round pursuit of economic activities. These activities resulted in early and fairly continuous commercial development. The trade and financial infrastructures upon which the Western European Industrial Revolution was founded evolved between the fifteenth and seventeenth centuries.

Today, for the most part, Western European countries are highly developed and heavily urbanized, with upwards of 60 percent of their populations concentrated around major urban areas. Public transportation systems (buses, subways, trains) are common within cities, and there are extensive train and bus networks between urban areas. The proximity of most European countries makes international travel easy and contributes greatly to the interrelatedness of European economies.

Historical and Cultural Perspectives

An early unification of Europe was brought about by the Romans, who, in the 500 years from about 100 BC to 400 AD, established an empire spreading over western and central Europe, parts of the Middle East, and the northern African coast from Egypt in the east to Morocco in the west. The Romans extended their civilization over the lands they conquered, building roads, formalizing trade routes, making laws, and establishing a common currency (the dinarius). The overthrow of the Romans by land-hungry barbarian tribes from the east caused chaos in the Roman Empire. Not until the eleventh century did real stability emerge through a form of political organization known as feudalism, in which kings gave lands to loyal vassals, who formed a military aristocracy. The lands were worked by the common people, who were bound to the feudal lords in an economic system known as manorialism.

Throughout their history, Europeans have been important traders, especially in the Mediterranean. As sea going ships became more reliable, European traders wandered farther afield. By the end of the sixteenth century, Ferdinand Magellan of Spain and Sir Francis Drake of England had circumnavigated the globe, and the rush to colonize the newly discovered lands was on. Over the next three centuries, the major European powers colonized and dominated most of the lesser-developed world, including North and South America until the nineteenth century (the United States until 1783), Africa until the 1960s, and the Middle East and parts of Asia (especially coastal areas and the Indian subcontinent) into the twentieth century.

Britain was the first country to industrialize (between 1750 and 1830), with iron, steel, steam power, electricity, and the factory system playing key roles in its economic growth. From the British lead, technology and economic growth spread to the continent (France, Germany, Belgium, and the Netherlands) during the nineteenth century, and through their colonizing activities, to the world's other continents. Economic progress was interrupted during World War I (1914–1918) and World War II (1939–1945). With the development of atomic weaponry and rivalry between the superpowers, the United States and the Soviet Union, Western Europe's political role in the world declined.

To compensate for its post-1945 loss of colonies, and to ensure that Europeans would never again go to war with one another, Western Europe began to integrate economically. In 1952, the Coal and Steel Community was founded. In 1957, the Treaty of Rome established economic blueprints for a "United States of Europe," known as the European Economic Community (EEC). Signatories to the initial agreement were France, West Germany, Italy, the Netherlands, Belgium, and Luxembourg.

Not long afterward, in 1960, the European Free Trade Association (EFTA) was founded in Stockholm. EFTA's intentions were to abolish trade tariffs between member countries (Austria, Iceland, Norway, Portugal, Sweden, Switzerland, Finland, Ireland, Denmark, and the United Kingdom). In 1973, the United Kingdom, Denmark, and Ireland joined the European Economic Community. In 1976 all tariffs were abolished between the EFTA and the EEC, making Western Europe the world's largest free trade area. Greece joined the European Community (EC, formerly the EEC) in 1982, and Spain and Portugal were added in 1986. In 1995, Sweden, Austria, and Finland entered what became the European Union.

The next step in European unification was the abolition of nontariff barriers within the EC. Initially laid out in a 1985 White Paper and later formalized in the 1987 Single Europe Act, a 1992 target date was set to harmonize diverse industry standards and to promote Europe-wide movements of products, labor, and capital. In 1991, EFTA countries agreed to adopt the EC's 1992 economic unification guidelines while maintaining their political independence. The creation of a 380-million-person consumer market (including EFTA) and the 1990s collapse of the Soviet Union resulted in a resurgence of Western Europe's importance.

From a cultural perspective, Western Europeans continue to maintain national distinctions, but there are sufficient similarities in their historical backgrounds and economic circumstances to give meaning to the term *European*. Fifteen of the 19 Western European countries have per capita gross domestic products of more than $15,000. Most have mixed economies; that is, there is some government ownership of key industries (utilities, telecommunications, energy-producing industries, and transportation systems), alongside private ownership of most other industries.

Most European countries feature extensive social welfare and retirement systems, a reflection of the socialist doctrine that the state should provide "womb-to-tomb" benefits for its people. Table 1–2 shows employer contributions in 14 countries with 1994 hourly labor costs broken down by direct wages and nonwage benefits (such as health, social security, paid leave, and other benefits). Notice that the United States provides nonwage benefits at 42 percent of direct wages. This is lower than Switzerland (53 percent), the Netherlands (75 percent), Germany (81 percent), Austria (101 percent), and Italy (99 percent).

Western Europe's personal tax rates are also high compared to those of non-European countries. Progressive taxes run at over 50 percent of personal income for the top income brackets in the Netherlands, Spain, Italy, and Germany. But in return, Western European enjoy extensive public transportation systems (e.g., rail and buses, many of them subsidized), free medical and hospital facilities, and mostly free education, up to and including university level.

Many West European countries (including Britain, France, Germany, the Netherlands, and Sweden) still have aristocracies whose members have strong economic holdings. In Germany, for example, the Quandt family has controlling interests in BMW and Daimler-Benz; the Flick family has large interests in pulp, paper, metals, iron,

TABLE 1–2 ■ *Worker Wages and Benefits: An International Comparison*
1994 Hourly Labor Costs (manufacturing in selected
industrialized countries, in U.S. dollars)

Country	Direct Wages	Nonwage Benefits	Percentage of Nonwage Benefits to Direct Wages
Italy	$8.13	$8.03	99%
Austria	10.82	10.90	101
France	9.23	7.80	85
Germany	15.10	12.20	81
Belgium	12.01	10.95	91
Netherlands	11.92	8.99	75
Sweden	11.25	7.56	67
Greece	4.23	2.70	64
Switzerland	16.20	8.64	53
Norway	14.95	5.96	40
UK	9.90	3.72	38
Ireland	9.04	3.13	35
U.S.	12.06	5.05	42
Denmark	16.84	3.60	21

Source: Adapted from: "Labour Costs: 1995 League Rankings," *Business Europe*, 2 October 1995, 2.

and steel; and the Klockner family has extensive interests in machinery and metals. In Sweden, the Wallenberg family owns Asea, Ericsson, Saab, SKF, and Swedish Match.[2]

The heredity monarchies and aristocracies of Europe have contributed to maintaining a strong class system based mainly on lineage ("family pedigree"). Europeans are born into specific social classes and generally stay there unless they are recognized for significant educational or professional achievements. Otherwise, social mobility (the ease in moving between social classes) is limited.

Politically, Europe is more left-wing than the United States, although there have been some prominent right-wing leaders, such as John Major of the United Kingdom and Helmut Kohl of Germany. European politics are complex. Many countries have multiparty systems, including left-wing socialist parties (left of center but not communist). Socialists favor high government involvement in industry and high taxes to finance broad social-welfare programs. Right-wing conservative parties favor low taxes, low government involvement in the economy, and less extensive welfare programs. The diversity of political interests results in multiparty coalitions forming governments in countries such as Switzerland, Italy, and Germany. Political instability is common—Italy, for example, has had over 50 different governments since 1945.

Commercial Characteristics

1. The 1992 economic unification of Western Europe involved the dismantling of all nontariff economic barriers between European Community members. To achieve this goal, 279 pieces of legislation were passed, most at the European parliamentary level. This was

followed by further movements toward political integration through the Maastricht Agreement, which set target dates for a common currency (the "Euro") in 1999 and for further joint political involvements on a European scale (e.g., common foreign and security policies).[3]

European economic consolidation (through EC '92) and political unification movements had many commercial implications:

- Some non-Europeans feared the emergence of a "fortress Europe" where the United States, Japan, and other non-EC nations would have their products "frozen out" of European markets. As a result, many U.S. and Japanese companies set up new investments within the European Union (as the EC was renamed in 1995 following the passage of the Maastricht Agreement). Over 1994–95, U.S. foreign direct investment (FDI) in Europe increased from $310 billion to $363 billion, or just over half of all American FDI worldwide.

- Economic unification led to the adoption of Europe-wide standards in many industries, including automobiles (emissions, wheelbases, and wiring, for example), pharmaceuticals (labeling and testing requirements), and other industries. This has enabled companies to create Europe-wide products and reap the benefits from manufacturing on a large scale. The harmonization of European industry standards made them acutely aware of the need to rationalize and consolidate their regional manufacturing and marketing bases. The EFTA countries adopted EC '92 industry guidelines, giving firms a 400-million-person target market. This further sensitized companies to the need

for Europe-wide operations. As a result, cross-border coalitions and joint ventures were formed to increase production and distribution capabilities. Asea of Sweden joined Switzerland's Brown-Boveri to form a multi-billion-dollar electrical equipment combine. Philips of the Netherlands linked with Britain's GEC to create a medical electronics giant. Other cross-border coalitions occurred in semiconductors (SGS of Italy with France's Thomson), consumer electronics (France's Thomson with Britain's Thorn-EMI-Ferguson), typewriters (Triumph-Adler of Germany with Italy's Olivetti), and autos (Germany's Volkswagen with Spain's SEAT).[4] American multinational corporations (MNCs) have also responded. Reynolds Metal initiated "Eurobases" to obtain resources more efficiently, speed up decision-making, and coordinate Europe-wide marketing strategies.[5]

- Europe-wide advertising media emerged. These ranged from Rupert Murdoch's London-based Sky Television Channel to the late Robert Maxwell's launch of Europe's first English-language daily, *The European*. Some English-language magazines were "taken European"; and the French publisher Hachette launched European-language editions of several U.S. magazines, such as *Car and Driver* and *Stereo Review*.[6]

2. European multinationals, while not as high profile as their U.S. counterparts, are just as active in world markets. Unilever is one of the world's largest manufacturers of consumer goods. The United Kingdom's British Petroleum (BP) took over the United States' Gulf to become a major player in the American retail gasoline market. Shell (a Dutch-British concern) is currently the biggest gasoline

retailer in the United States. Many European companies have global brand names and reputations, including the Dutch electronics giant Philips; Britain's Rolls Royce; Germany's BMW, Mercedes, Porsche, and Volkswagen; Sweden's Saab and Volvo cars and Ericsson electronics; Swiss-owned Nestle and Hoffman-Laroche; and Germany's chemical giants Bayer (the aspirin-chemical conglomerate), Hoeschst, and BASF.

3. The trends toward privatization (i.e., turning over government-controlled industries such as telecommunications to private ownership) and deregulation (permitting industries to compete openly against one another), picked up pace during the 1990s. More than $24 billion of government assets were turned over to the private sector in 1995, with the 1996 figure expected to exceed $40 billion. Industries affected include the French banking industry, German and Spanish telecommunications companies, British Rail, and health care sectors throughout Europe.[7] Deregulation has brought about increased competition in Europe's insurance, telephone services, and energy sectors, as companies previously sheltered under national monopolies have begun to compete across and within country markets.[8]

EASTERN EUROPE

Geographic Characteristics

Eastern Europe, for the purposes of this book, includes the Central European countries of Poland, the Czech and Slovak republics, Hungary, the Balkan countries, Russia, and the other states of the former Soviet Union (see Figure 1–3). Its northern shores touch the Arctic Circle. The largest part of the region comprises the states of the former Soviet Union, which together take up one-sixth of the world's land mass, span 11 time zones, and are about two and one-half times larger than the United States.

Throughout its history, Russia, the strongest of these states, tried to maintain control over this vast geographic expanse, but it has had problems.[9] One reason for the difficulty is the inhospitable climate of large parts of the region, which varies from subarctic temperatures in the north to desert-like temperatures in the south—a "climate to try the spirit." Figure 1–4(a) illustrates this variability. Only the western and southern borders of Russia are free from long, severe winters. Hungary, Poland, and the Balkans all enjoy moderate climates, but northwestern Russia bordering Finland is on the same latitude as Alaska and has similar severe weather.

Russia and the other former Soviet states are well endowed with natural resources. As Figure 1–4(b) shows, during the late 1980s, the Soviet Union was a prime producer of iron ore, coal, oil, diamonds, and gold. Only its inability to sustain agricultural output (because of climatic problems) prevented it from being self-sufficient in resources.

Historical and Cultural Perspectives

For most of the twentieth century, Eastern Europe was dominated by the Soviet Union. The Union of Soviet Socialist Republics (U.S.S.R.) originated in the Russian Revolution of 1917–1918—engineered by Vladimir Ilyich Ulyanov, known as Lenin, and Leon Trotsky—which caused the downfall of Czar Nicholas II. Lenin ruled the

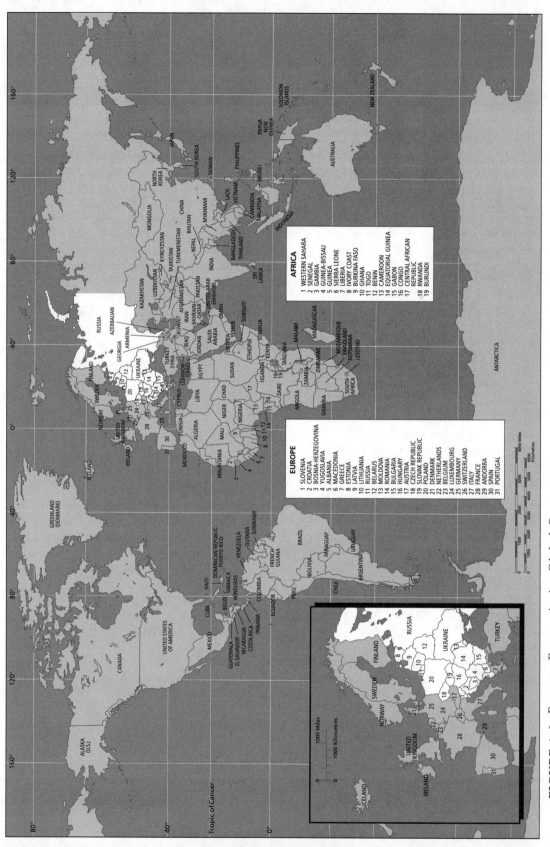

FIGURE 1-3 *Eastern Europe in its Global Context*

FIGURE 1–4(A) *Climatic Profile of the Former Soviet Union*
Not only does the former U.S.S.R. span eleven time zones, it also has great climatic variability. Many of its northern shores are on the Arctic Circle and are rarely free of snow and ice. In particular, the Siberian Peninsula at the northern and eastern end of Russia is climatically harsh. At the other end of the climatic spectrum, arid desert conditions are common in the states of Kazakhstan and Uzbekistan. Only in the western and southern parts of the region is the climate hospitable enough to support regular harvests in Ukraine and Turkmenistan. Even then, only small climatic changes are necessary to damage agricultural efforts.

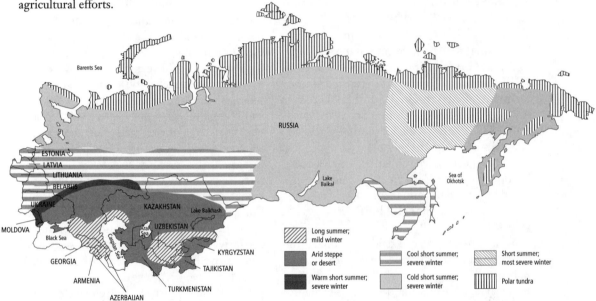

FIGURE 1–4(B) *The Former Soviet Union: Resource Endowments, late 1980s*
The former Soviet Union was among the world's leaders in mineral and fossil fuel energy production at the end of the 1980s. The region led in iron ore production and equaled the U.S. and China in coal production. The chart below compares the region's mineral and fossil fuel production in the late 1980s with its nearest competitors.

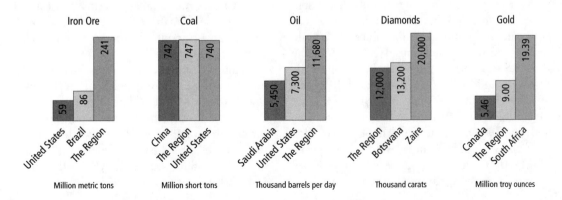

U.S.S.R. until his death in 1924. Joseph Stalin, who succeeded him, collectivized agriculture (that is, he placed privately held land under state ownership) and initiated comprehensive industrialization programs. Many people objected, but Stalin was merciless in eliminating opposition. Millions were executed or died in labor camps during the Great Purge of 1936–1938.

The U.S.S.R. was pulled into World War II in 1941 when, despite Stalin's having signed a nonaggression pact with Germany's Adolf Hitler, the country was attacked by the Germans. This resulted in the "Unholy Alliance" between the United States, Britain, and the U.S.S.R., which eventually forced Germany to capitulate in 1945.

The postwar boundaries of Eastern Europe, or the Eastern Bloc, as it was called, were determined in 1945 at the Yalta Conference by Franklin D. Roosevelt, Winston Churchill, and Joseph Stalin. This arrangement gave Stalin a sphere of influence in Europe extending over Romania, Bulgaria, Poland, Hungary, Czechoslovakia, Yugoslavia, Albania, and East Germany. These countries were controlled by communist governments and had state-run economies. In the postwar period, U.S.-Soviet tensions increased as both countries used their global influence to encourage noncommitted countries to adopt capitalistic or communistic philosophies. The wars in Korea, Vietnam, Nicaragua, and Afghanistan all grew out of East-West conflicts over economic and political philosophies. The Cold War between the United States and the U.S.S.R. continued until the break-up of the Soviet Union in 1991 and included the building of the Berlin Wall in 1961 to separate Berlin into Eastern and Western sectors. The Iron Curtain separating the Eastern Bloc from Western influences lasted over 40 years.

After years of government control and repression, the seeds of reform in the Soviet Union were sewn in 1985, when three aging Soviet ex-revolutionaries (Andropov, Chernenko, and Brezhnev) died within the space of three years and Mikhail Gorbachev emerged as the Soviet leader. Intent on reform, Gorbachev initiated restructuring of the Soviet economy (perestroika), which reduced governmental interference in economic matters and allowed greater "openness," or freedom of expression (glasnost). Censorship was almost eliminated, and for the first time in 70 years, elections were held in 1989. Perestroika and glasnost spread to most other Eastern Bloc countries. Poland and Hungary both held elections in 1989 and began to transform their state-controlled economies to allow more influence by market forces. East Germany and West Germany were reunited in July 1990. The 1990s has seen the countries of Central and Eastern Europe implement democratic reforms, free up prices, cut back state subsidies to industry, and privatize state enterprises. Results have been mixed, but the seeds of capitalism appear to have been sewn.[10]

In Russia, Gorbachev's reforms encouraged the expression of the great cultural diversity of the Soviet Union. The U.S.S.R. comprised more than 100 ethnic groups, speaking 80 different languages and writing in 5 different alphabets.[11] The Russians were the dominant ethnic group, with 140 million out of 270 million people. Taking advantage of glasnost, the smaller groups protested their domination by the Russians and the central government. Protest surfaced in all 15 republics.[12]

Amid negotiations within Russia and between Russia and former U.S.S.R. republics, a new order was created. The provinces within Russia came together (after considerable turmoil in some cases, notably Chechnya) to become the Russian Federation. The former U.S.S.R., minus Latvia, Lithuania, and Estonia, reconstituted itself as the

Commonwealth of Independent States (CIS) in 1992, and through the Treaty on the Creation of the Economic Union, has pushed toward economic integration, though many obstacles remain to be overcome.[13]

Commercial Characteristics

1. With glasnost and perestroika as driving forces, the economic reform of Eastern Europe is underway. In 1992, Hungary, Poland, and the Czech and Slovak republics signed a Central European Free Trade Agreement covering industrial and agricultural products and drawing together 85 million consumers. Under this arrangement, trade barriers were slated to be eliminated by the year 2000.[14]

2. Eastern-Western European integration plans have slowly moved forward. In 1994, the EU completed free trade agreements with the Baltic states of Latvia, Lithuania, and Estonia. In the same year, partnership agreements were also concluded to normalize trade relations between the EU, Russia, and the Ukraine.[15]

3. Privatization of former state-owned businesses has been brisk, with an estimated $200 billion of assets returned to private shareholders, which now accounts for 55 percent of regional GDP.[16] Privatization methods have included sales to strategic owners (foreign companies, or grouping firms in the same industries to gain scale economies and synergies). This has occurred in Estonia and Hungary. Insider buyouts to managers and workers have been used in Russia and Slovenia. Financial intermediaries were created in the Czech Republic, Slovakia, and Poland to market and manage privatized portfolios.

Finally, voucher schemes have been used, whereby citizens pay nominal sums for vouchers that are then cashed in for company shares. This method has been used in Moldova, Belarus, Romania, and Bulgaria.[17]

4. Operating conditions remain difficult for companies committing resources to Eastern Europe. This is reflected in $100 billion of investments pledged to Russia, of which just $3.5 billion had been actually invested by 1995. Problems encountered by Western companies included fluctuating economic fortunes, deficient physical infrastructures (which affect distribution and logistics), a lack of commercial legal infrastructures (affecting contract enforceability, for example), and crime problems (hooliganism, pilfering from work, corrupt bureaucracies, and racketeering/extortion). Nevertheless, companies have been attracted there for many reasons: PepsiCo to stay with its arch global rival, Coca-Cola; Teledyne to market its Cesna and Piper aircraft, the product life cycles of which have run their course in Western markets; Estée Lauder to consolidate the lead market position it had held since the early 1980s; Conoco to exploit Russia's tremendous oil reserves; and Hewlett-Packard to get a competitive jump on rivals such as IBM, Digital, and Olivetti.[18]

5. Hungary, the Czech Republic, Slovakia, and Poland have emerged as some of the more robust of the Eastern European economies. In Poland's case, economic reforms have been successful. Inflation, which hit the 600 percent mark over 1989–90, steadied to 28 percent in 1995. Economic growth in real terms was 6.5 percent in 1995. Poland has emerged as a low-cost manufacturing center (especially compared to Western Europe).

The country is ideally situated between Eastern and Western Europe, and it has a thriving private sector of over 2 million companies, of which 200,000 are active exporters. The U.S.'s Pepsi Co., Korea's Daewoo, and Western Europe's Asea-Brown-Boveri have upped their investments in anticipation of upsurges in the consumer products, auto, and heavy industry sectors.[19]

6. Companies have had problems changing the business habits built up during communist years. GE's experience was typical with Tungsram, the Hungarian light bulb manufacturer. In came GE: Order-delivery items were cut from 90 to 32 days; manufacturing time was reduced by 50 percent; breakages went from one in two products to world-class levels; management levels were cut from 11 to 3. The workforce of 18,000 was cut in half through relocation and early retirements, but problems were encountered adapting to team concepts and workplace freedoms.[20]

MIDDLE EAST AND AFRICA

Geographic Characteristics

Geographically, the Middle East is comprised of countries between the Mediterranean and Afghanistan (see Figure 1–5). Culturally, the term includes the North African countries from Morocco to Egypt, because they, like the Middle Eastern countries, are predominantly Muslim. Turkey is also considered part of the Middle East, although it is militarily allied with Western Europe.

Most of the Middle East has a harsh desert climate. In Saudi Arabia, daytime temperatures often reach 130 degrees Fahrenheit. The flat rock surfaces that dominate Arabian landscapes often are too hot to touch, but in winter, freezing temperatures are normal at night. In most of the Middle East, rainfall is low (except in Yemen, whose mountains catch the Indian monsoons and receive around 20 inches of rain per year). Hence, obtaining sufficient water for drinking and crop irrigation has been an important objective of most Middle Eastern states. Egypt has the River Nile; others (e.g., Saudi Arabia, Kuwait, and United Arab Emirates) have plans for national irrigation systems, including dams for rivers and desalination plants to take the salt out of seawater.[21]

Poor in water resources, the Middle East is rich in petroleum—it contains about 60 percent of the world's oil reserves. During the 1980s, in oil-producing Arab countries, a gallon of gasoline sold for the equivalent of U.S.$0.20, but the price of a gallon of bottled drinking water was $2.40.[22] The Middle Eastern oil-producing states took the lead in organizing OPEC (Organization of Petroleum-Exporting Countries) in 1961.

Of the roughly 50 countries in Africa, only the Republic of South Africa is reasonably well developed. Many parts of Africa are characterized by droughts and poor crop-growing soils. It also suffers from soil erosion and poor management of what agricultural land there is.[23] On going famines in Ethiopia and the Sudan have resulted from trying to farm in these less-than-ideal environments.

Africa, however, has other resources. In northern Africa (i.e., Africa north of the Sahara), there is oil in Libya, Morocco, and Algeria. In central and southern Africa, there are diamonds, copper, and other valuable minerals. These resources, discovered in the nineteenth and early twentieth centuries, prompted the European colonization of Africa.

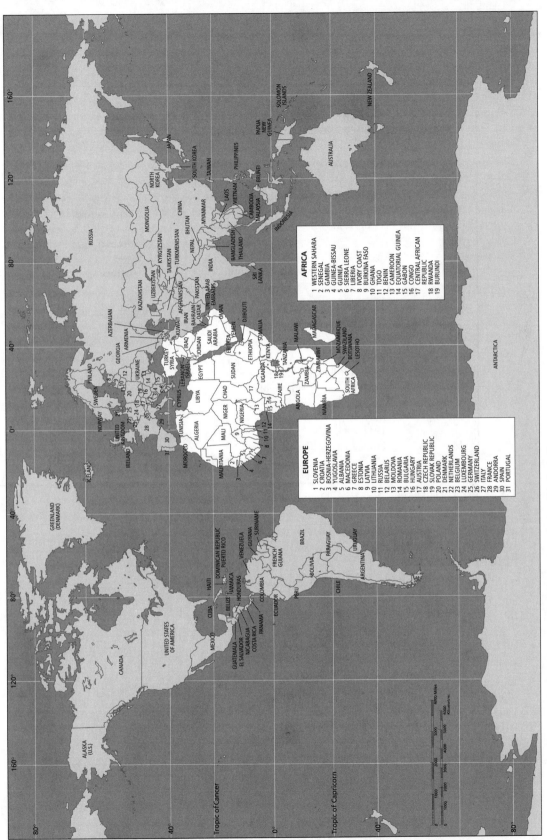

FIGURE 1–5 *Middle East and Africa in their Global Contexts*

Country	Foreign Domination	Present Form of Government	Number of Political Parties
Algeria	France 1848–1962	Republic, socialist oriented	1
Bahrain	Britain 1861–1971	Monarchy (emirate), capitalist oriented	None
Egypt	Britain 1914–1922	Republic, socialist oriented	7; 2 represented
Iran	—	Islamic Republic, indeterminate	12; 2 represented
Iraq	Britain 1924–1932	Republic (military), socialist oriented	2; 1 represented
Israel	Britain 1923–1948	Republic, socialist oriented	Over 20; 15 represented
Jordan	Britain 1923–1946	Monarchy, capitalist oriented	1
Kuwait	Britain 1899–1961	Monarchy (sheikhdom), state-capitalist	None
Lebanon	France 1923–1946	Republic, capitalist oriented	14
Libya	Italy 1912–1947	Republic (military), socialist oriented	1
Morocco	France 1912–1956	Monarchy, capitalist oriented	10

FIGURE 1–6(A) *Foreign Domination of Middle East and North America*

Historical and Cultural Perspectives

The development of both the Middle East and Africa has been affected by colonization by the major European powers. Figure 1–6(a) and Figure 1–6(b) show that these areas were dominated primarily by French and British interests, whose aim was to secure access to their mineral and oil supplies. This colonial grip was broken after 1945, when most of Africa and the Middle East gained independence. But many of the newly independent nations were unable to maintain themselves as democracies.

Today, democratic institutions are slowly emerging in Africa, where countries histori-cally have been run by one-party governments and presidents-for-life. Many of Africa's politi-cal problems relate to its ethnic fragmentation. The Republic of the Congo (formerly Zaire), for example, has more than 200 cultural groups, and South Africa has over 20 major tribal groupings. In many countries, such as Nigeria, voting trends have tended to be along tribal rather than political party lines. Although this pattern is changing, Africa continues to show political instability. Figure 1–7 shows dates of African independence and principal coups d'état (political and military takeovers).

Though Middle Eastern countries had fewer problems making the transition to independence—in part due to some degree of cultural uniformity, such as in language

Country	Foreign Domination	Present Form of Government	Number of Political Parties
Oman	Britain 1853–1951	Monarchy (sultanate), state capitalist	None
Qatar	Britain 1916–1971	Monarchy (emirate), state capitalist	None
Saudi Arabia	—	Monarchy, state capitalist	None
Sudan	Britain 1898–1946	Republic (military), socialist (?) oriented	1
Syria	France 1923–1946	Republic (military), socialist oriented	5
Tunisia	France 1881–1956	Republic capitalist oriented	1
UAE	Britain 1853–1971	Federation of emirates, state capitalist	None
Yemen AR	—	Republic (military), capitalist oriented	None
Yemen PDR	Britain 1893–1967	Republic (military, socialist oriented	3

Source: Elias H. Tuma, *Economic and Political Change in the Middle East* (Palo Alto: Pacific Books, Publishers, 1987).

(Arabic) and religion (Islam)—there are trouble spots in both the Middle East and Africa. In the Middle East, religious tension between the Sunnis and Shi'ites (both factions within the Islamic, or Muslim, religion) contributed to the 1980–1988 Iraq-Iran war. In Lebanon, religious struggles between Christian militants (to whom the French gave majority political power in 1946) and the numerically superior Palestinian-Muslim groups resulted in decades of urban warfare in the Lebanese capital of Beirut. Elections were held in 1996, though direct pressure, patronage, intimidation, and fraud prevented effective parliamentary opposition to the ruling government. In 1990, tensions escalated again when Saddam Hussein of Iraq invaded neighboring Kuwait.

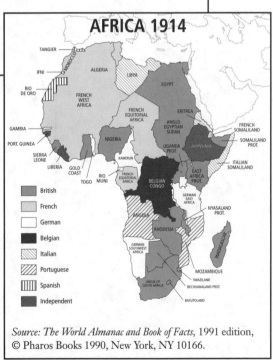

Source: The World Almanac and Book of Facts, 1991 edition, © Pharos Books 1990, New York, NY 10166.

FIGURE 1–6(B) *Foreign Domination of Colonial Africa*

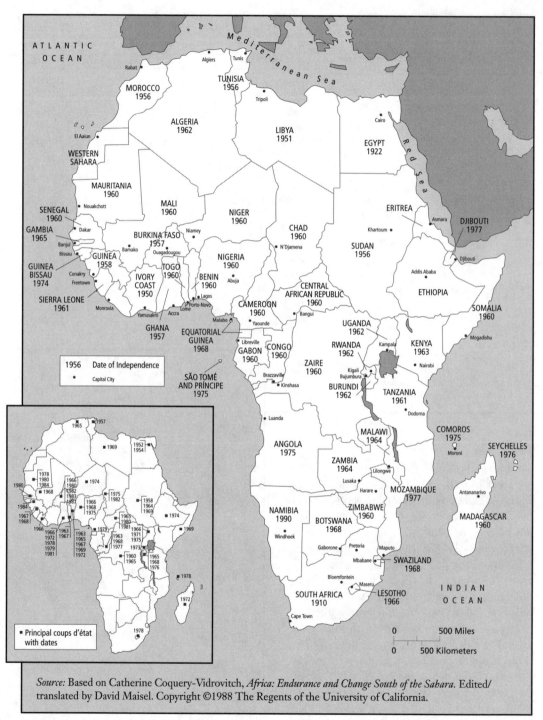

FIGURE 1–7 *Africa: Independence Dates and Principal Coups d'état*

Oil prices rose and a United Nations force was dispatched to protect Saudi Arabia (see the case "Oil Crisis, 1990s Style" at the end of this chapter for details).

The greatest friction in the Middle East, however, has been between Israel and the surrounding Arab world. In 1947, the United Nations (with U.S. and British backing) divided Palestine (as it was then known), into Jewish and Arab states. In 1948, the state of Israel was officially created. Since then, numerous disputes have occurred, especially over the proposal for an independent Arab homeland in Palestine, and a number of wars have been fought (notably in 1956, 1967, and 1973). Tensions eased somewhat with the U.S.-initiated peace accord between Egypt and Israel in 1979. More recently, the creation of the state of Gaza next to Israel has given the Palestinians a homeland. This has alleviated a major cause of Middle Eastern conflict.

Commercial Characteristics

1. Political and religious conflicts in the Middle East have complicated the task of Western firms doing business there, though there are signs that the region is becoming more attractive to international firms. Lebanon has emerged as a market with significant opportunities, especially for infrastructure projects where the Lebanese government has allocated $17 billion for telecommunications and civil engineering projects up to the year 2010. Still, however, the specter of political conflict hangs over the region, with Lebanon's commercial potential still dependent on Israeli-Palestinian relations and on its relations with neighboring Syria.[24] On the consumer side, changing preferences and rising disposable incomes have fueled an emerging franchise market in Morocco, where a new investment code has made licensing businesses more feasible and attractive to local investors.[25]

2. But emerging modernization and Westernization trends in the Middle East and North Africa have been met with resistance from fundamentalist Islamic groups. Turkey, Algeria, Afghanistan, Pakistan, Iran, Libya, Bahrain, and Sudan are among the countries most affected by the resurgence of extremist philosophies favoring strict interpretations of Muslim doctrines.

3. Democratic institutions have taken hold in sub-Saharan Africa, though many are fragile. Of the 42 mainland states in the region, only 4 had military rulers in 1996, with 30 having had elections.[26] Still, in many African countries, the military has been but a telephone call away from power, and this has affected business confidence in the area.

4. South Africa elected Nelson Mandela in 1994 to end decades of apartheid (separate racial development) rule. This ended 20 years of international isolation, as South Africa rejoined the world economy. The year 1995 saw economic growth of 3.5 percent, but problems remained as the country sought to overcome high black unemployment (estimated at over 40 percent) and make progress toward redressing massive inequalities in education and physical infrastructure development.[27] The transition to a more competitive economy, combined with a lasting legacy of apartheid, has resulted in an upsurge in crime and interethnic troubles.[28]

5. Many Middle Eastern and African countries have undeveloped infrastructures (ports, railroads, highways, telecommunications systems) and have little except

natural resources to contribute to the world economy. Their dependency on resources is a problem because as commodity prices change, the economic fortunes of these countries fluctuate. For example, petroleum went from $1 a barrel in the early 1970s to $40 by the late 1970s. Oil-export economies prospered during the 1970s but suffered during the 1980s as oil prices dropped to as low as $13 per barrel. Iraq's invasion of Kuwait then caused prices to rise past $30 per barrel. Such fluctuations make economic planning difficult because imports bought with oil dollars are essential to the industrialization process.

3,000 miles, is very wet in its western parts and arid in its eastern parts. The three inner islands of Java, Bali, and Lombok (where most of the country's 170 million people reside) have some of the most fertile soils in the world, so fertile that wooden gate posts grow roots.[29] Thailand, Malaysia, Indonesia, and many other areas of southern Asia have tropical rain forests as their major vegetation, with monsoons (heavy rains) occurring daily for six months of the year. In these areas, wet rice cultivation is the major agricultural pursuit. Parts of Asia along the Pacific are volcanic and subject to earthquakes. Japan, for example, averaged two earth tremors a day somewhere in the country during the late 1980s.

ASIA

Geographic Characteristics

Asia, for the purposes of this book, begins with Afghanistan and continues east to Japan. It extends from Mongolia in the north through the countries of south and east Asia, including the island states of Indonesia and the Philippines. Rounding out the Asian group are the Pacific islands and the mainly English-speaking nations of Australia and New Zealand (see Figure 1–8).

Geographically, Asia is diverse, ranging from the People's Republic of China (which has 1.2 billion of the world's 5.3 billion population), the world's third-largest land mass, down to the small states of Brunei and Singapore. In between, there is India (with one-sixth of the world's population, over 900 million people) and the sprawling countries of Indonesia and Philippines (which comprise more than 13,000 and 7,000 islands, respectively).

Asia has varied climates. Indonesia, for example, whose islands stretch more than

Historical and Cultural Perspectives

Much of Asia, like Africa and the Middle East, was colonized by Europeans between the sixteenth and nineteenth centuries. Only Thailand (formerly Siam) has never been occupied. The saying "the sun never sets over the British Empire" originated during the nineteenth century when Britain ruled India (until 1947), Malaysia (until 1957), and Singapore (until 1965). Australia and New Zealand were also under British influence as part of the British Commonwealth of Nations. The Netherlands ruled Indonesia until 1949. The Philippines, after 300 years of Spanish rule and 48 years of U.S. rule, gained its independence in 1946.

Asia has a diverse set of religions, which are causes of ongoing friction. India is a Hindu state, but it borders Pakistan to the northwest and Bangladesh to the northeast, both Muslim countries. Feelings run high because both Pakistan and Bangladesh were formerly part of India. First, West and East

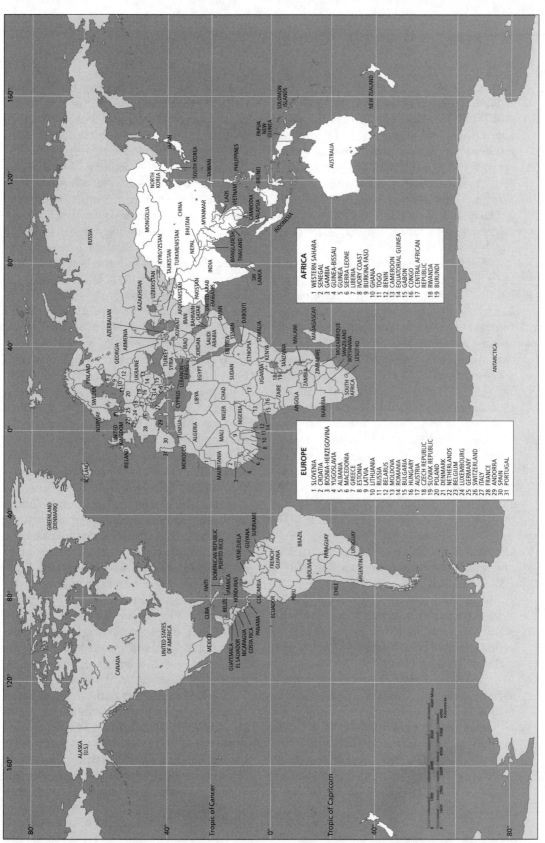

FIGURE 1-8 *Asia in its Global Context*

Pakistan were created as Muslim states in 1947, then East Pakistan became Bangladesh in 1971. There are also problems in Sri Lanka (the island formerly called Ceylon off southern India), where conflicts exist between the Tamils (Hindus who make up 18 percent of the population) and the majority Sinhalese, who are Buddhists. Tensions exist in Malaysia between Malay Muslims and the descendants of Chinese immigrants, who are largely Buddhist.

Mainland China (the People's Republic of China, not to be confused with the island state of Taiwan, which is the Republic of China), of all the Asian nations, has undergone the most change during the twentieth century. An ancient country ruled by successive imperial dynasties until 1911, China was governed from 1911 until 1925 by Dr. Sun Yat-Sen, a Western-educated physician who choreographed the downfall of the emperor. In the mid-1920s, military leaders struggled for power, and Chiang Kai-shek came to power. The 1930s were characterized by a "creeping" Japanese invasion until Japan formally invaded China in 1937. Chiang fought alongside the British and Americans against the Chinese communists led by Mao Tse Tung, who overthrew Chiang in 1949. Chiang and his Chinese nationalists fled out of China to establish their own Republic of China—Taiwan.

Over the next 25 years, Mao collectivized industry and agriculture on a massive scale. Mao died in 1976, and after a brief period of rule by the "Gang of Four" (which included Mao's widow), Deng Xiaoping took over in 1981. In 1985, he initiated reforms aimed at returning China to a more market-oriented economic system.[30]

Japan was an ancient feudal state whose modern history began in 1853, when the U.S. Admiral M.C. Perry sailed into Tokyo Bay and "opened up" the country to Western influences. Anthropologically, this long isolation resulted in making the Japanese today ethnically one of the world's purest racial groups. The Meiji Restoration in 1868 brought Japan out of its feudal past and led to the importation of Western ideas and methods. Gradually, the country industrialized. After military successes against Russia in 1905 and the annexation of Korea in 1910, Japan became a world power. Japan fought alongside Britain and the United States in World War I (1914–1918), and then revealed its imperial aspirations with the 1937 invasion of mainland China. In 1941, Japan attacked the U.S. base at Pearl Harbor, Hawaii, leading to the United States' entry into World War II (1939–1945). Atomic bomb attacks by the U.S. Air Force on Hiroshima and Nagasaki forced Japan's surrender in 1945. Following a period of American occupation (1945–1952), the Japanese, in spite of meager natural resources, rebuilt their country to become the second strongest free-market economy in the world.[31]

Asia is characterized by religious and ethnic diversity. China is mainly Buddhist, as are Burma, Thailand, and Tibet. India is Hindu. Japan's traditional religion is Shinto, but many Japanese are Buddhist, and a small percentage are Christian. Indonesia is the largest Islamic country in the world; while the Philippines is mainly Roman Catholic.

Another element of Asian cultural diversity is language. India alone has 15 major languages and 97 dialectic variations of Hindi, one of the principal languages. China has dozens of regional and local dialects. Indonesia has more than 250 languages and dialects, while the Philippines has more than 30.

Australia and New Zealand, in the South Pacific, were originally inhabited by native peoples, the Aborigines and Maoris, respectively. Both countries became part of the British Empire after Captain James Cook claimed them in 1769–1770. Australia was a penal colony until the mid-nineteenth century, when gold discoveries in the state of Victoria accelerated immigration by free citizens in the 1850s. New Zealand was one of the first nations to create a comprehensive welfare state in 1898. There were conflicts between natives and the British settlers in both nations.

Both countries are sparsely populated. Australia has about 17 million people, and New Zealand has less than 4 million. Both economies have substantial agricultural bases of livestock and crops, which are exported. Australia also has many natural resources, including iron ore, petroleum, natural gas, coal, and gemstones.[32]

Commercial Characteristics

1. Japan, Australia, and New Zealand are already well developed. Many smaller countries are industrializing at impressive rates. The four Tigers, South Korea, Taiwan, Hong Kong (which reverted from British to Chinese rule in 1997), and Singapore, are expanding aggressively and have used export-based growth to propel their economies toward developed-market status.

2. Trading blocs have taken on new importance as Asian countries have pushed toward increased commercial interdependence. The Association of Southeast Asia Nations (ASEAN), formed in 1967, comprises Thailand, Malaysia, Indonesia, the Philippines, Vietnam, Brunei, and Singapore. The group brings together 450 million consumers and a combined GDP of $400 billion.[33] A second major grouping, the Asia-Pacific Cooperation group (APEC), was established in 1989 to manage the growing trade links within the region. It is made up of 18 countries, including the United States and Chile from the Western Hemisphere. The group's aim is free trade by the year 2020.[34] On a smaller scale, an Australian-New Zealand free trade area was established in 1990; and the late 1990s has seen movements toward increased harmonization of these countries' trade practices and commercial laws.[35]

3. The dominant commercial powers in Asia are the People's Republic of China (China PRC) and Japan. Japan, in particular, rebuilt its economy in the 1950s, and in the 1970s and 1980s, it became the world's second largest free-market economy. Key success factors have been its ability to blend Oriental and religious values into a work ethic unrivaled in the Western world. Indeed, much of the Japanese management style (decision-making by consensus, lifetime employment, company rather than industry unions, market-share orientations, and quality circles) has been the polar opposite of traditional Western management styles. The Japanese approach has brought Japan considerable success in world markets. Major Japanese brands, including Sony, Honda, Toyota, Nissan, Citizen, Seiko, Canon, Hitachi, Panasonic, Toshiba, and Mitsubishi, are world renowned.

China has emerged as a force to be reckoned with in world commerce in the 1990s. Its 1.2-billion-person market has been a magnet to businesspeople worldwide. Foreign companies and governments have found the Chinese to be tough bargainers. The United States, in particular, has clashed with China over its trade surplus with the United States (about $35 billion to 40 billion in 1995–96); human rights and trade; protected markets; counterfeit goods (software, music, and movies); and what the United States perceives to be the blatant playing off of companies and countries against each other.[36]

LATIN AMERICA

Geographic Characteristics

Latin America encompasses Mexico, the countries of Central America, the island states of the Caribbean, and South America (see Figure 1–9).

Climatically, much of Latin America is affected by its proximity to the equator. Central America, the Caribbean, and northern South America have predominantly subtropical climates. The countries to the south (e.g., Argentina, parts of Brazil, and Chile) are more varied. Argentina is mainly temperate, but its northern regions (such as the Chaco) are hot and humid, while its southern parts (such as Patagonia) are on the cold side (subantarctic). Brazil is subtropical in the north and center but temperate in the south and east. Chile, which runs nearly 4,000 miles along South America's west coast, is subtropical in the north and subantarctic in the south.

Topographically, South America is similar to those parts of Asia that are on the same latitude. Earthquakes are common. Much of the area is made up of rain forests (Brazil is over 60 percent rain forest; Bolivia, 40 percent). There are also some very fertile lands, and coffee, cocoa, corn, and livestock are principal exports from these regions.[37]

South America has considerable natural resources. Chile is a world-class producer of copper, which is extracted from the mineral-rich Andes Mountains. Bolivia is a major source of tin, zinc, and silver; and Peru is an important source of silver and copper. Venezuela is an oil producer, as is Colombia, which also produces 90 percent of the world's emeralds and has the largest coal reserves in Latin America.[38]

Historical and Cultural Perspectives

Many Latin American countries had Indian civilizations predating the arrival of Europeans in the fifteenth and sixteenth centuries. The Mayas in Guatemala and Mexico, the Aztecs in Mexico, and the Incas in Peru and adjacent areas all had advanced forms of social and economic organization many years before the European conquests.

Modern Latin American history dates from the early 1500s, when the Spanish colonized most of the region and the Portuguese occupied Brazil. It remained under Spanish and Portuguese rule for over 300 years. Independence was won from 1810 to 1824, when all of the major Spanish colonies simultaneously rebelled against Spain—Mexico, Honduras, Peru, Panama, Nicaragua, Venezuela, and Colombia in 1821; Ecuador in 1822; Costa Rica in 1824; and Bolivia in 1825.[39] Brazil became independent from Portugal in 1822.

After independence, the newly formed nations were politically unstable throughout the nineteenth and twentieth centuries, with frequent periods of military governments and revolutions. Instability continued up to the 1980s.

The Spanish influence in most of Central and South America is evident in the wide prevalence of the Spanish language and the Roman Catholic religion. (Portuguese and Catholicism predominate in Brazil, the region's largest country.) Ethnically, Latin Americans are mixed. Many are descendants of the Spanish and Portuguese conquerors, but there are large groups of native Indian peoples, mixed groups of Indian and white ancestry (called mestizos), and blacks. Many dialects are spoken; Guatemala, for instance, has more than 20.[40]

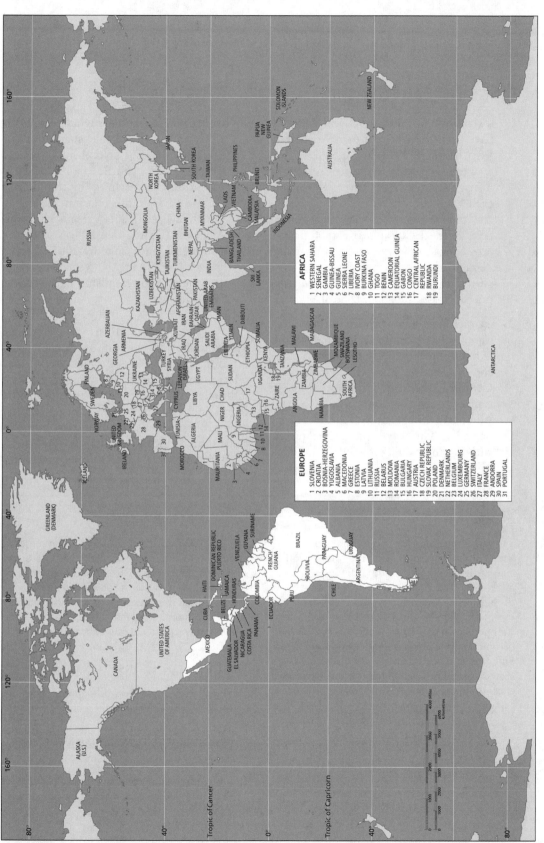

FIGURE 1-9 *Latin America in its Global Context*

Commercial Characteristics

1. Two major problems in Latin America have been foreign debt (which stood at $465 billion in 1994) and inflation. Two countries in particular, Mexico and Brazil, manage external debts of over $100 billion each.[41] Inflation has also been problematic, though the hyperinflationary conditions of the 1980s appear past. Inflation projections to the year 2000 place major markets in the 3–15 percent range, suggesting that, at least by Latin standards, price increases are under control.[42]

2. Market blocs and privatization have followed the democratization trends of the 1980s to open up Latin markets to trade and investment. The year 1993 saw the Central American Common Market replaced by the System of Central American Integration (Honduras, El Salvador, Guatemala, and Nicaragua, with Panama joining in 1996). This consolidated the regionalization of Latin American trade that started with Mercosur in 1988 (Brazil and Argentina, with Paraguay and Uruguay joining in 1991) and the 1992 rejuvenation of the Andean Pact bloc (Colombia, Venezuela, Ecuador, Peru, and Bolivia). In 1994, a blueprint was drawn up by the United States and 33 Latin American leaders to initiate a Free Trade Agreement of the Americas (FTAA) to establish a North-South free trade zone by 2005.[43] Talks are also occurring between Mercosur and the EU to establish a pan-Atlantic free trade area.[44]

Privatization trends are also apparent throughout much of Latin America. Airlines, banking, energy, metals, public works, and telecommunications are among the many industries being placed into private hands. Increasingly, though, the region's privatization programs must compete for international funds with similar programs in Western Europe, Eastern Europe, and Asia.

SUMMARY

The world marketplace is dynamic and diverse, with cultural, political, and economic profiles constantly changing. In 1985, the international marketplace was dominated by the Triad nations of Northern America, Western Europe, and Japan. In one decade, Latin America, Eastern Europe, and Asia have come on-stream and become major contributors to world commerce. Still, the developed Triad nations have the lion's share of global trade and investment. But the balance of global commercial power is shifting toward the industrializing world, whose low costs and growing markets make them attractive propositions to international corporations.

Understanding the world marketplace is a gargantuan task given the 200-plus nations that comprise it. This initial review of geographic, historic, political, economic, and commercial trends is only an appetizer. It sets the stage for an in-depth evaluation of international marketing topics and allows readers to place current events and corporate strategies into their proper geopolitical contexts. Without this background, you can learn only facts about international markets (the "whats"); you cannot understand them (the "whys").

DISCUSSION QUESTIONS

1. Which regions of the world appear to be the most attractive? Why?

2. What trends do you see in the world marketplace? Which do you think is the most important? Why?

3. Do you see your country/region's position in the world as becoming more or less important? Why?

Oil Crisis, 1990s Style

The Short-Term Problem:
Oil Prices and the World Economy

When Iraq's Saddam Hussein marched his armies into Kuwait on August 2, 1990, starting the Gulf War, the world held its breath. Although the Middle East (especially Saudi Arabia) produces only about 40 percent of the world's oil, the region contains almost 60 percent of world reserves. Turmoil and instability had contributed mightily to the 1973–1974 quadrupling of oil prices (from $3 to $13 per barrel) and to the 1979–1980 rise from $13 to $40 per barrel. In 1973, war between Egypt and Syria against Israel led to other countries taking sides with the United States and the Netherlands against the Arabs and caused OPEC to limit the sale of oil supplies to certain countries. The price of oil rose and stayed high.

In 1979, after the fall of the shah of Iran, the Ayatollah Ruholla Khomeini came to power and initiated a "holy war" against Iraq. The United States' previous support of the shah resulted in the captivity of over 50 Americans for more than a year (1980–1981).

Oil prices fell in the early 1980s and went down as low as $10 a barrel. Slowly, they rose to a tolerable price of $18 a barrel in 1989. The overall reduction in oil prices over the decade damped down worldwide inflation and encouraged nations (especially the United States) to expand economically.

In the wake of Kuwait's invasion by Iraq in 1990, oil prices moved inexorably up to and past the $30-per-barrel mark by August 1990, and world stock markets panicked. In the United States, the Dow Jones average fell 200 points in four days. Japan's Nikkei stock average fell 3383 points, or 11 percent of its total value. In 1973–1974, the oil price spiral had soaked up about 2 percent of developed countries' gross national products. Price increases doubled from 7 to 14 percent each year. There followed a period of inflation and economic stagnation, which came to be known as "stagflation." In 1979–1980, world inflation rates, having barely descended from the 1973–1974 war, doubled again, this time from 8 to 14 percent.

But the world was better prepared in 1990. The 1973–1974 and 1979–1980 price hikes had caused some nations to rethink their energy-related policies. They had adopted such measures as the following:

- Smaller, more fuel-efficient cars became more widely available, courtesy mainly of the Japanese. American manufacturers, with the exception of the makers of the Ford Escort, were not successful in building and marketing compact and subcompact cars.

- Offshore drilling gave the oil and gas industries new energy sources.

- European governments encouraged the upgrading of their public transportation systems. High-speed trains began to actively compete with auto and airline companies. Governments also discouraged private transportation by continued heavy taxing of petroleum. Petrol prices of $3 to $4 a gallon were not uncommon in Western Europe.

Japan's approach was to make more efficient use of its oil imports. It has been said that if Americans used oil as efficiently as the Japanese, they would need only 9.2 million barrels per day instead of the 16.6 million actually consumed. The United States accounts for over one-fourth of the world's 61 million barrel daily consumption.

Long-Term Problems: Reducing Tensions in the Middle East

As 400,000 American troops moved into Saudi Arabia as part of the United Nations force in the Gulf War of 1991, it became apparent that over the long term, some new approaches were needed to ensure stability in this economically vital region. Some of the problems that needed to be addressed were the following:

1. Were $18-per-barrel oil prices sufficient to sustain the modernization program in the Middle Eastern countries? Just before his invasion of Kuwait, Saddam Hussein had demanded $25 per barrel. This price would have helped Iraq's $70 billion external debt. Middle Eastern producers had experienced prices of more than $40. Should oil prices keep pace with global inflation, which usually averages 2 to 3 percent a year?

2. Should the United States and the United Nations continue to support feudal monarchies such as Saudi Arabia's while encouraging democracies elsewhere in the world (e.g., in Latin America and Eastern Europe)? Even the most ardent supporters of Middle Eastern monarchies would admit that oil revenues tend not to be evenly distributed among their peoples.

3. Israel's position in the Middle East needed to be clarified. While President Carter's Camp David Accords in 1979 were a start (it was the first-ever peace treaty between an Arabic state—Egypt—and Israel), there needed to be a permanent solution, especially with respect to the Occupied Territories taken and held by Israel since the 1967 war.

4. While the Middle East is mainly Muslim, there are ongoing rivalries between the more moderate Sunni Muslims and the more militant fundamentalist Shi'ites. Saudi Arabia, Kuwait, and Iraq are mainly Sunni. Iran is Shi'ite.

5. The Middle East has generally resisted outside attempts to change its traditional lifestyle, although it welcomes modernization in the form of hospitals, roads, and new infrastructures. The amount of economic and social change that can be introduced is therefore limited, making it difficult for Middle Eastern countries to keep pace in a rapidly developing world.

QUESTIONS

1. Do you think the 1990 oil price hike affected the world as much as the price rises of 1973–1974 or 1979–1980? Support your conclusions.

2. Do you think Americans could have done more during the 1980s to reduce their reliance on oil? If your answer is yes, think about what would have happened if European- or Japanese-style solutions had been applied in the United States.

3. Discuss each of the five long-term problems. For each, identify a solution and then consider its consequences.

Source: Case adapted from reports in *The Economist*, 11 August 1990 and 25 August 1990, and *Business Week*, 20 August 1990; plus television and radio news reports.

Where to Allocate Corporate Resources to the Year 2000

Your company, General Widgets, Inc., is exploring the world marketplace for the first time. You are the newly appointed international marketing director. You send your assistant, a newly minted economics graduate, out to get some data on world markets. Here's what (s)he came back with.

EXHIBIT 1–1

Country	1997	1998	1999	2000
USA				
GDP ($bn)	7,918	8,289	8,694	9,138
Growth Rate (%)	2.1	2.0	2.2	2.4
Inflation rate (%)	3.0	3.0	3.0	3.0
Canada				
GDP	654	701	736	777
Growth	2.6	2.4	2.6	2.9
Inflation	2.3	2.4	2.4	2.6
Mexico				
GDP	308	348	395	433
Growth	3.7	3.5	3.7	3.5
Inflation	17.6	13.4	10.0	7.3
The Netherlands				
GDP	423	443	468	496
Growth	2.8	2.6	2.8	2.8
Inflation	1.8	1.9	2.0	2.1
Belgium				
GDP	284	296	315	335
Growth	1.7	1.8	2.2	2.5
Inflation	2.0	1.9	2.4	2.3
UK				
GDP	1,271	1,335	1,438	1,549
Growth	3.3	2.0	2.6	2.8
Inflation	4.0	3.7	3.8	3.3
France				
GDP	1,670	1,760	1,870	1,980
Growth	2.6	2.5	2.4	2.5
Inflation	1.8	2.0	2.2	2.3

Country	1997	1998	1999	2000
Germany				
GDP	2,583	2,737	2,907	3,083
Growth	2.3	2.8	2.4	2.3
Inflation	1.8	2.0	2.2	2.3
Bulgaria				
GDP	14.4	15.1	16.1	17.2
Growth	3.8	4.3	4.5	4.8
Inflation	25.0	20.0	15.0	12.0
Romania				
GDP	38	43	49	55
Growth	3.8	4.3	4.5	4.8
Inflation	-	-	-	-
Russia				
GDP	600	705	771	864
Growth	4.0	5.0	5.0	5.0
Inflation	50.0	40.0	25.0	20.0
Argentina				
GDP	292	303	319	340
Growth	1.4	2.0	2.5	3.5
Inflation	1.6	1.9	2.5	3.2
Brazil				
GDP	802	904	1,013	1,123
Growth	4.2	5.8	5.5	4.5
Inflation	25.5	20.2	18.0	15.0
Chile				
GDP	79	87	97	105
Growth	5.5	6.7	6.4	5.3
Inflation	6.4	5.1	4.1	3.7

Country	1997	1998	1999	2000
India				
GDP	340	398	431	420
Growth	5.3	5.5	5.7	5.9
Inflation	7.5	7.0	7.0	7.0
Indonesia				
GDP	260	296	338	387
Growth	7.3	7.7	7.8	8.0
Inflation	8.0	8.0	8.5	8.5
Malaysia				
GDP	95	105	113	123
Growth	7.8	8.4	8.2	8.0
Inflation	4.0	4.3	4.0	3.7
Thailand				
GDP	194	215	245	280
Growth	7.5	7.4	7.9	8.4
Inflation	4.6	4.5	4.6	4.9

QUESTIONS

1. Widgets are supplied to major industries as parts of their manufacturing process equipment. Based on these statistics, which markets would you short-list for further evaluation? Why?

2. What other information would you gather to aid your selection of what markets to enter?

3. What other world markets would you consider (i.e., other than those listed)? Why?

Source: Based on data from *Crossborder Monitor*, 10 April 1996, 7; 28 February 1996,11; 6 March 1996, 7; 24 April 1996, 7; 3 April 1996, 7; 13 March 1996, 11; and 27 March 1996, 11.

ENDNOTES

1 *Culturgram for Canada* (Provo, Utah: Brigham Young University, 1996).

2 Lawrence G. Franko, *The European Multinationals* (Stamford. Conn.: Greylock Publishers, 1976).

3 "The European Institutions," *European Trends*, Second quarter 1996, 91–104.

4 "How Business Is Creating Europe," *Business Week*, September 1987, 40–41.

5 "Reynolds Metals Selects Lausanne as Werne Center for its European Operations," *Business International*, 20 March 1989, 83–88.

6 "European Satellite TV: Just So Much Pie in the Sky," *Business Week*, 24 October 1988, 30–42; John Rossant, "Magazines for the Global Village," *Business Week*, 9 May 1988, 91; and "The Press Barons Duke it Out across Europe," *Business Week*, 3 October 1988.

7 "Polish Off the Family Silver," *Economist*, 29 June 1996, 64–69; and Stewart Toy, "Who'll Snap Up the State Jewels of Europe?" *Business Week*, 3 July 1995, 86E–86H.

8 Peggy Salz-Trautman, "Tectronic Stirrings in European Insurance," *International Business*, June 1995, 56–59; and Nilly Landau, "A Call Center to Call Your Own," *International Business*, September 1994, 22–26.

9 *Culturgram for Russia* (Provo, Utah: Brigham Young University, 1996)

10 Fred Luthans, Richard R. Patrick, and Brett C. Luthans, "Doing Business in Central and Eastern Europe: Political, Economic and Cultural Diversity," *Business Horizons* 38, no. 5 (September–October 1995): 9–16.

11 *The Soviet Union* (Alexandria, Va.: Time-Life Books, 1985).

12 Peter Galuszka and Bill Javetski, "Can Gorbachev Control the Nationalism Glasnost Unleashed?" *Business Week*, 28 March 1988, 43.

13 V. Kirichenko, "The Status and Problems of Economic Relations in the CIS," *Problems of Economic Transition*, July 1996, 6–18.

14 "Central European Free Trade Agreement," *Eastern European Business Law*, August 1993, 2–5; and Alice Enders and Ronald J. Wonnacott, "The Liberalization of East-West European Trade: Hubs, Spokes and Further Complications," *World Economy*, May 1996, 253–272.

15 Enders and Wonnacott, "The Liberalization of East-West European Trade."

16 David Roche, "It Depends on What You Mean by Privatization," *Euromoney*, February 1996, 26–27.

17 Cheryl W. Gray, "In Search of Owners: Privatization and Corporate Governance in Transition Economies," *World Bank Research Observer*, August 1996, 179–97.

18 Alexia Bayer, "Hugging the Bear," *Journal of Business Strategy*, July–August 1995, 43–46.

19 Karen Lowry Miller, Frank J. Comes, and Peggy Simpson, "Poland: Rising Star of Europe," *Business Week*, 4 December 1995, 64–66, 70.

20 Michel Syrett and Klari Kingston, "GE's Hungarian Light Switch," *Management Today*, 15 April 1995, 52–58.

21 *Arabian Peninsula* (Alexandria, Va.: Time-Life Books, 1986), 100–04.

22 Ibid., 100.

23 Catherine Coquery-Vidrovic, *Africa: Endurance and Change South of the Sahara*, (Berkeley: University of California Press, 1988), 18, 148–61.

24 "Investment in Lebanon: Garden or Jungle?" *Crossborder Monitor*, 30 October 1996, 1, 8.

25 "Franchising in Morocco: Economic and Social Changes Fuel Spectacular Market Growth," *Middle Eastern Executive Reports*, September 1996, 16–17.

26 "Guns and Votes," *Economist*, 29 June 1996, 41.

27 Stephen R. Brent, "South Africa: Tough Road to Prosperity," *Foreign Affairs*, March–April, 1996, 113–126.

28 Mark Allix, "Key Players Forge Road Ahead," *Asian Business*, October 1996, 62-69.

29 *Southeast Asia*, (Alexandria, Va.: Time-Life Books, 1987), 35.

30 *China*, (Alexandria, Va.: Time-Life Books, 1989), 93–94, 145–46.

31 *Japan*, (Alexandria, Va.: Time-Life Books, 1985).

32 J.W. Wright, ed., *The Universal Almanac 1990* (Kansas City: Andrews and McMeel, 1989), 389–90, 461; and *The Far East and Australia 1989* (London: European Publication, Ltd., 1988), 191–93, 710–12.

33 Martin Evans, "Southeast Asia's Path to Continuing Growth," *World Trade*, February 1996, 26–30.

34 "Just Do It," *Far Eastern Economic Review*, October 1996, 5.

[35] Jeremy Carr, "Trade Practices," *Chartered Accountants Journal of New Zealand*, March 1996, 68–70.

[36] Amy Borrus, Pete Engardio, and Dexter Roberts, "China: The New Trade Superpower," *Business Week*, 16 October 1996, 56–57.

[37] *Culturgrams for Argentina, Brazil*, and *Chile* (Provo, Utah: Brigham Young University, 1996).

[38] *Culturgrams for Venezuela* and *Colombia* (Provo, Utah: Brigham Young University, 1996).

[39] *Culturgrams for Bolivia, Costa Rica, Mexico, Honduras, Peru, Panama, Nicaragua*, and *Ecuador* (Provo, Utah: Brigham Young University, 1996).

[40] *Culturgram for Guatemala* (Provo, Utah: Brigham Young University, 1996).

[41] "Status Report on Foreign Debt," *Business Latin America*, 20 February 1995, 5.

[42] "Latin America Forecast: 1996–2000," *Crossborder Monitor*, 3 April 1996, 7; and "Latin America Forecast: 1996–2000," *Crossborder Monitor*, 7 February 1996, 7.

[43] "Ripping Down Walls across the Americas," *Business Week*, 26 December 1994, 78–79.

[44] Pablo Maas, "Doing Deals," *Business Latin America*, 18 December 1995, 2.

CHAPTER **2**

Cultural, Political, Economic Systems and Their Interaction

Chapter Outline

Learning Objectives

When you have mastered the contents of this chapter, you will be able to do the following:

1 Define *culture* and name some of its key components.

2 Recognize cultural similarities and differences and explain their importance in world marketing.

3 Discuss how different methods of resource allocation (capitalist, centrally planned, and mixed) affect a society.

4 Assess the impact of culture and its religious, legal, and social components on societal behavior.

5 Describe how the characteristics of cultural and economic systems vary among the United States, traditional societies, Western Europe, and Japan.

CULTURAL AND POLITICAL SYSTEMS

Culture, in general terms, is the human-made part of the environment; it has three main characteristics. First, any given culture is shared by a number of people. A culture may be composed of small tribal communities, such as the Bushmen of Africa or Yanamamo of South America, or it may consist of larger national units, such as the British, the French, or the Japanese. Cultures may even be extended to multi-country groups like the Europeans, the Latin Americans, or the Arabs. Multicountry groups usually have one or more cultural dimensions in common (for example, shared language, religion, or political structure) but differ in other cultural characteristics (for example, local values or folklore).

Second, all culture is learned; it is passed from generation to generation through governments, customs, religions, laws, families, and education. Third, culture changes slowly unless precipitated by revolutions, trade, investments, and other influences. Even then, change is resisted by some or by many.

Components of Culture

To understand culture, one must know what elements it comprises and how they interrelate. In this text, we have adapted Terpstra's nomenclature to define the essential components of culture:[1]

1. Language is the means through which communication occurs within a culture. Language transmits ideas, concepts, and rules from one generation to the next.

2. Religion is the guiding force defining humankind's relationship with supernatural forces (for example, God or Allah) and in determining a culture's values and attitudes. Religion, by defining the values of the ideal life and the behaviors appropriate to achieving that ideal, shapes the attitudes that result from the underlying value system and are reflected in the culture's practices and personalities. Major world religions include Hinduism, Buddhism, Islam, Judaism, and Christianity.

3. Social organizations include the family, social class systems, and business and nonbusiness organizations.

4. Education is the means of passing on knowledge to the young. Through education, a new generation learns traditions, attitudes and values, and scientific and technological information.

5. Political elements consist of two features: (1) the processes for attaining community leadership, and (2) the actual political structures. Community leaders may be elected, born into roles, or may obtain power through military or other means. The political structure may stress single-person rule, government by a few, or government through single- or multiple-party systems.

6. Economic elements are concerned with the level of material culture and technology and include the means by which goods and services are allocated, (e.g., capitalism and communism).

7. Societal control mechanisms are the means cultures use to control individual and group behavior. They include social customs ("appropriate behaviors") and law.

8. Attitudes and values reflect the individual's and group's outlook toward government, economic systems, laws, and other people.[2]

TABLE 2–1 ▪ *Principal Spoken and Commercial Languages by Select Countries*

Country	Spoken Language(s)	Commercial Language(s)
Afghanistan	Pashto, Dari	Pashto, Dari, English
Albania	Albanian, French, Italian	Albanian, French
Belgium	French, Dutch, German	French, Dutch, German, English
People's Republic of China	Mandarin	Mandarin, English, Japanese
Czechoslovakia	Czech, Slovak	Czech, Slovak, English
Denmark	Danish	Danish, German, English
Finland	Finnish, Swedish	Finnish, Swedish, English, German
Hungary	Hungarian	German, English, Russian
The Netherlands	Dutch	German, French, English
Switzerland	German, Italian, French	German, Italian, French, English
Uganda	Kiswahii	English

Source: International Trade Center, *The Export* 3, nos. 2, 3, (Tuscaloosa, Ala.: University of Alabama, 1990).

CULTURAL SIMILARITIES AND DIFFERENCES

Identifying Cultural Similarities

Cultural similarities facilitate the movements of goods and services among countries. Where similarities exist at the consumer level, there are opportunities for international marketers.

LANGUAGE COMMONALTIES ▪ These commonalties make trade between nations easier. Shared languages enable the transferring of usage instructions, labeling, servicing requirements, and training manuals. They facilitate negotiation on order specifications and travel arrangements. Table 2–1 shows the principal spoken and commercial languages used in various major world markets. English is the most widely used nonlocal language, although French, Spanish, Arabic, and German also have multicountry usage. The widespread use of European languages in the developing world reflects Europe's earlier colonizing activities.

POLITICAL AND ECONOMIC SIMILARITIES ▪

These similarities are factors for categorizing countries into economic groups (generally according to the level of market development); and for organizing countries into multicountry units (e.g., the European Union).

There are many ways to classify countries according to economic development. One way organizes nations into five different "world" classifications. These categories comprise the following.[3]

- First World countries are affluent nations such as Canada, the United States, the countries of Western Europe, Japan, Australia, and New Zealand. The gross national product per capita in First World countries is usually over $10,000, and their income distributions are fairly even. These countries also have growing numbers of middle-income consumers.

- Second World countries comprise what were the socialist countries of Eastern Europe—Hungary, Poland, the former Soviet republics, Bulgaria, Yugoslavia, the Czech and Slovakian republics, Romania,

1. *Regional cooperation groups:* Regional cooperation groups aim to establish infrastructures in preparation for trade and development.

2. *Free trade areas (FTAs):* Free trade areas aim to establish free trade among members. Mercosur (Brazil, Argentina, Paraguay, and Uruguay) established an FTA by 1994. The U.S.-Canada Free Trade Agreement of 1989 was designed to reduce most tariffs by 1999. FTAs currently being established include: Southern Africa Development Community, by 2005; Free Trade of the Americas (North, Central, and South America), by 2005; and Association of Southeast Asian Nations (ASEAN), by 2005.

3. *Customs unions:* Customs unions aim to establish free trade among members and a common external tariff. An example is Mercosur (by the year 2000).

4. *Economic unions:* Economic unions are customs unions plus the free movement of labor and capital, and common economic policies.

5. *Political unions:* Political unions are economic unions plus a common parliament, civil service system, legal system, currency, and balance of payments, and a totally free movement of peoples and resources. The European Union by 1999?

The European Union (EU) began as the Coal and Steel Community in 1952. The European Economic Community was formed in 1957; it included France, West Germany, Italy, the Netherlands, Belgium, and Luxembourg. Britain, Denmark, and Eire (southern Ireland) joined in 1973. In 1976, it changed its name to European Community (EC). In 1977, EC merged with the European Free Trade Association (EFTA), comprising Iceland, Norway, Portugal, Sweden, and Switzerland, to establish the world's largest free trade area for nonagricultural products. In 1982, Greece joined the EC; in 1986, Portugal and Spain became members; and in 1995, Austria, Finland, and Sweden entered the EU. The Maastricht Agreement was ratified in 1993, establishing 1999 as the target date for the single currency.

Sources: "East African Community Resurrected—At Last," *Business Africa*, 15 April 1996, 6; Salah M. Nsouli, et al, "The European Union's New Mediterranean Strategy," *Finance and Development*, September 1996, 14–17; and "Thailand," *Crossborder Monitor*, 17 April 1996, 6.

FIGURE 2–1 *Multicountry Economic and Political Grouping*

and Albania. Although each of these countries previously had centrally planned economies, they all moved toward becoming market economies in the 1990s.

- Third World countries are the rapidly industrializing developing countries, such as Brazil, South Korea, Hong Kong, Singapore, and Taiwan. These countries are presently realizing their economic development potential.

- Fourth World countries are poor countries, but they have the resources and potential for development. Examples of Fourth World countries include Malaysia, People's Republic of China, Thailand, the Philippines, and Indonesia.

- Fifth World countries are mainly undeveloped and have few resources to aid industrialization. Chad, Ethiopia, Mali, Niger, and many other African nations are in this category. In everyday language, the term "third world countries" is used to refer to underdeveloped countries.

Similarities in economic status enable countries to be grouped into segments for market targeting (see Chapter 7). For example, economically advanced countries account for most of the world's demand for autos, consumer durables, high-tech products, and sophisticated consumer goods. Developing markets have different priorities; their aims are to build basic economic amenities such as roads, ports, telecommunications systems, and other industrial infrastructure needs.

The trend toward multicountry units reflects the desires of countries to have closer economic and (in some cases) political ties. These blocs succeed when countries have similar outlooks and philosophies. The outstanding current example is the European Union (EU), whose objective is to function as a single economic unit rather than as 15 nations. The EU aims to have one ruling body (the European Parliament), one civil service (the European Commission), and common laws and economic policies.

Multinational blocs (as they are also known) use economic linkages to provide foundations for political cooperation. Figure 2–1 shows the current status of a number of multinational blocs. Most such groups start out as regional cooperation groups, which aim to build infrastructure (ports, roads, and communication systems) capable of sustaining trade among member states. Then, a free trade area is formed, enabling tariffs between members to fall (though each country maintains its own external tariff). The third stage establishes a customs union that enables free trade but that also applies a common external tariff to imports from nonmembers.

The fourth and fifth stages go beyond groupings and move toward economic and political integration. At stage four (economic union), there is free movement of capital and labor. Member countries also integrate individual agricultural, economic, and energy schemes into meaningful region-wide policies.

The fifth stage—political union—is the one in which member countries sacrifice some national political sovereignty to a region-wide political body. In the case of the EU, the European Parliament makes regional laws that ultimately will supersede national laws. The free movement of resources, products, money, and people was scheduled for 1992 (see Figure 2–2). The anticipated results—increased trade, travel, and communication among EU members— were expected to reduce remaining European cultural differences.

SPECIFIC RELIGIONS ▪ Religions are rarely confined to a single nation or region. When countries share a religion, they also tend to

By 1992, the European Community had passed more than 94 percent of the 279 regulations to create a single internal market.

The following specific changes represented a part of the 1992 program:

- Harmonizing packaging, labeling, and processing requirements.

- Harmonizing rules pertaining to the free movement of labor and the professions within the EC, including mutual recognition of higher-education diplomas and comparability of vocational-training qualifications

- Elimination and simplification of national transit documents and procedures for intra-EC trade.

- Liberalizing capital movement (short- and long-term capital and stocks).

- Creating consumer protection regulations.

- Changing government procurement regulations.

- Harmonizing of standards for construction products, toys, heavy equipment, food products, medical devices, telecommunications, and detergents

- Harmonizing regulations in the health industry for high-tech medicine, medical devices, and pharmaceuticals.

- Harmonizing the regulation of services for finance, communication, and transport,

- Harmonizing the laws regulating company behavior for trademarks, company law, taxes, bankruptcy, copyrights, and mergers and acquisitions.

Source: Adapted from "1992 at a Glance," *Business America*, 15 January 1990, 12.

FIGURE 2-2 *Key Characteristics of the European Economic Integration Program, 1992*

have similar outlooks and philosophies. While a few religions or religious philosophies are country or region specific, most have spread around the world. Though Hinduism is found mainly in India, it is also practiced in Trinidad; however, Confucianism, as a religious philosophy, is specifically Chinese. Islam (the Muslim religion) dominates religious practices in Middle Eastern and North African countries; Judaism and Christianity are practiced throughout the world. While there are always different forms even within religions (Sunnis and Shi'ites within Islam; various

TABLE 2–2 ▪ *Estimated Religious Populations (in thousands), 1995*

Religion	Africa	Asia	Europe	Latin America	North America	Oceanic	World
Christians[a]	348,176	306,762	551,892	448,006	249,277	23,840	1,927,953
Muslims	300,317	760,181	31,975	1,329	5,450	382	1,099,634
Hindus	1,535	775,252	1,522	748	1,185	305	780,547
Buddhists	36	320,691	1,478	569	920	200	323,894
Jews	163	4,294	2,529	1,098	5,942	91	14,117
Other[b]	77,847	1,290,777	137,603	30,255	30,067	3,731	1,570,280
Totals	728,074	3,457,957	726,999	482,005	292,841	28,549	5,716,425[c]

[a] Includes Roman Catholics, Protestants, Orthodox, and Anglicans.
[b] Includes atheists, Chinese folk religionists, Confucians, ethnic religionists, Jains, Sikhs, Shintoists, and many others.
[c] Totals more than total world populations because of overlaps and shared religions.

Source: Adapted from *World Almanac 1997* (Mahwah, N.J.: World Almanac, 1997), 646.

congregations within the Christian faith), the general similarities in religious outlook promote cultural uniformity among country markets. Table 2–2 depicts the geographical distribution of the world's major religions.

EDUCATIONAL SIMILARITIES ▪ Such similarities among nations facilitate the movement of ideas, technologies, and lifestyles. All countries, including developing nations, have groups of well-educated consumers who share the tastes, lifestyles, and consumption patterns that are prevalent in developed countries. Indeed, these consumers often have more in common with their counterparts in other nations than they do with their own compatriots. Such well-educated consumers are said to have "high-profile" consumption patterns. The term "triadians" (or universal users) has been coined for those United States, Western European, and Japanese consumers sharing high-profile consumption patterns.[4]

AGE GROUP SIMILARITIES ▪ Age group similarities lend themselves to business opportunities. Similarities of age groups in different countries—among babies (special foods, toys), teenagers (fashions, music), and senior citizens—all facilitate the trade and transfers of products, ideas, and techniques.

Cataloguing Cultural Differences

Cultural differences are important. It is necessary to recognize cultural differences between buyers and sellers. Successful personal interactions between people of different nationalities involve appreciating differences in mannerisms, behaviors, and attitudes. In addition, marketing strategy is most effective when executives know when to adapt products and services to individual cultures.

Cultural mistakes are easy to make (for Americans this is particularly true in Middle Eastern, Asian, and Latin American countries) and are not easily forgiven (especially for repeat offenders). It is important for the businessperson to know not only what is acceptable behavior but also why it is acceptable. Similarly, managers need to know what is forbidden and why.

There are four stages of cultural perception.

1. Cultural ignorance exists when individuals have no knowledge of cultural differences. Businesspeople at this stage are liabilities to their companies and may do more harm than good on overseas assignments.

2. Cultural awareness takes place when people know there are cultural differences and are looking for them. A visitor at this stage is less likely to commit social or cultural blunders. He or she observes, catalogs, and attempts to make sense of foreign behaviors.

3. Culture knowledge is an extension of culture awareness. The visitor knows how to offer appropriate greetings (i.e., the bow in Japan) and other behaviors.

4. Cultural understanding occurs when a visitor not only knows what behaviors are appropriate but also *why* those behaviors are occurring. Individuals at this stage often are fluent in the local language and are aware of the behavioral and attitudinal subtleties of a culture.

Cultural Differences: Factors Shaping Worldwide Variations in International Behaviors

All societies, whether tribal communities or advanced economies, are composed of a variety of cultures. Anthropologically, language or dialect defines individual cultures. Multilingual societies (e.g., Congo, Indonesia, Philippines, Guatemala, and much of the developing world) are multicultural. Language not only distinguishes one cultural group from another, it also denotes a unique outlook on the world that is shared by group members. Many modern societies have cultural subgroups. For example, Native American tribes in the U.S. are distinguished by language and cultural differences.

All societal and cultural group behaviors are affected by the economic, religious, and legal systems they adopt. Figure 2–3 diagrams how these systems interact to affect behavior patterns on a worldwide basis. To survive, all societies develop economic systems to produce and distribute goods and services. These vary from centralized systems used in traditional tribal communities and in the former communist countries to the decentralized market-force-based system used in many advanced countries. Then too, all societies regulate the behaviors of their citizens through religion and through formal legal frameworks. In industrializing societies where legal systems are undeveloped, social and religious rules regulate behaviors. Economic, religious, and legal factors impact behaviors at the social and business levels. Further modifications of these behaviors occur at the country level, where eating habits, gestures, dietary, and other behaviors give nations degrees of cultural distinctiveness. Finally, individual differences play a part, with introversion-extroversion, and modern-traditional orientations affecting behaviors at the personal level.

ECONOMIC EFFECTS ON BEHAVIOR

Economics and Politics

The allocation of resources depends on the political philosophies of those in power. Only about 40 to 50 of the world's roughly 200 countries have freely elected democracies. The remainder consist of tribal communities,

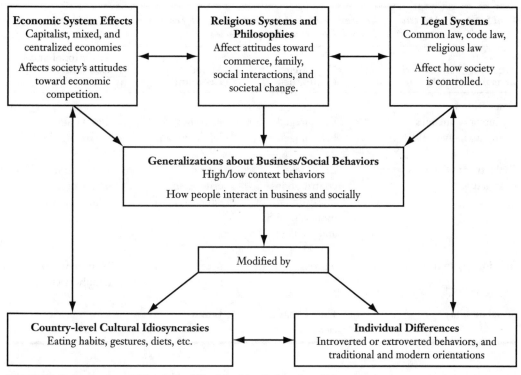

FIGURE 2–3 *Factors Shaping Worldwide Behavior Patterns*

dictatorships, one-party democracies, authoritative monarchies, and the like.[5]

Democracies prevail in most economically advanced nations, where parties representing the many prevailing political philosophies exist. Typically, one or more parties represent right-wing (conservative) interests. Conservative groups favor minimal government interference in national economies and prefer allocation of resources through supply and demand. Right-wing parties support private enterprise and do not discourage investment by foreign enterprises. Free trade is valued. The Republican Party in the United States and the Conservative Party in the United Kingdom exemplify such a philosophy.

At the opposite end of the political spectrum are the left-wing parties. These parties encourage governmental intervention in the economy, including ownership of strategic industries, such as energy, transportation, and the media. Socialist parties favor extensive welfare provisions for under-represented minorities, such as the unemployed, the chronically sick, and senior citizens. To finance these programs, left-wingers demand high rates of corporate and personal taxation. Hence, left-wing politicians are often labeled as "anti-big-business" and are prone to protect domestic industries with tariffs and to limit foreign involvement in the domestic economy. The Labour Party in the United Kingdom, some factions of the Democratic Party in the United States, and numerous socialist movements throughout Europe exemplify this philosophy.

Between these two extremes are numerous individual political philosophies.

TABLE 2–3 ▪ *Attitudes, Values, and Behaviors Derived from Capitalist, Mixed, Traditional, and Command Economies*

Attitudes, Values, and Behaviors with Respect to:	Capitalist Economies	Mixed Economies	Traditional and Command Economies
Competition			
Among companies	Encouraged	Encouraged	Discouraged
Among individuals	Encouraged	Discouraged	Discouraged
Evaluating individual's worth to society	Economic contribution (measured by money, wealth, and the like)	Hereditary criteria and education level	Hereditary; seniority and ethnic criteria
Individual advancement	Through merit	Merit and non-merit criteria	Non-merit criteria (family, friends, etc.)
Social mobility	High ("rags to riches")	Limited	Low

Switzerland, for example, has a small population of 6.5 million but over a dozen political parties. Both Sweden and Italy have multi-party systems covering the entire political spectrum.

Types of Economies

The three dominant political systems today are monarchies, democracies, and dictatorships. Each format establishes rules and objectives for foreign policy and trade. No matter which political structure a country adopts, it must allocate resources to further economic and political goals. There are two methods of allocating national resources: through supply and demand or through central allocation. *Capitalist philosophy* favors supply and demand and is encouraged by right-wing politicians. By contrast, the *socialist method*, favored by left-wing politicians, stresses central alloca-

tion. It should be noted that many countries find neither extreme attractive. Consequently, in Western Europe, both governments and market forces allocate resources. These countries are said to have *mixed economies*.

The resource allocation philosophy gives executives valuable clues about company behavior and attitudes within those markets. The qualities of capitalist, mixed, and command economies are summarized in Table 2–3.

CAPITALISM ▪ Capitalism emphasizes the free market system, with supply and demand forces determining prices, profits, and resource allocation. Competition in market-driven economies is intense, and the desire to compete and to win permeates society. In the United States, this philosophy was captured by the famous American football coach Vince Lombardi, who said: "Winning isn't everything, it is the only thing."

Market-driven economies like that of the United States rank individuals according to their economic usefulness. Social security and retirement systems are spartan.[6] Income, education, and material possessions (car, house) are primary indicators of social status. Individuals compete for social position, and fluctuations in economic fortunes are reflected in rises and falls in the social hierarchy.[7] Extreme, or "cutthroat," competition is not unethical. Merit is the major means of advancement, and objective means of personal assessment (e.g., numbers, performance) are preferred over subjective, or personal, biases.[8]

MIXED ECONOMIES ▪

Mixed economies are found in Scandinavia, the United Kingdom, France, Germany, and Italy. Such economies are market-based but often have key industries under government control, including postal services, telecommunications, utilities, broadcast media (e.g., television or radio), transportation (railways, public transit systems), and other "vital" industries (e.g., coal, shipbuilding, health services). Governments provide "womb-to-tomb" welfare systems in the form of free or heavily subsidized social security, health, and education facilities.[9] Tax rates are high to finance these programs. Firms compete, but not as vehemently as in the United States. Profits are made, but they are not necessarily at the level that would be found in a more competitive environment.[10]

In mixed economies, social causes preempt the emphasis on individual competition. Employment maintenance is a legitimate concern both at the company and national levels; worker participation is mandated in most major European economies.[11] On a personal and social level, individuals do not compete against each other. Results occur because of "teamwork" rather than maximization of individual efforts (the American way).[12] There are fewer incentives providing motivation for

individual achievement. Consequently, economic criteria have much less influence on social status in Europe than in the United States. Hereditary criteria (family background) are primary indicators of social position, with educational attainment the major means of social advancement. Social mobility is therefore limited. Individuals are assessed on both objective and subjective criteria (i.e., results obtained and personal qualities exhibited).[13]

SOCIALIST AND TRADITIONAL ECONOMIES ▪

Socialist and traditional economies centrally allocate resources. Countries that followed this increasingly less-influential mode included the former Soviet republics and the left-wing regimes of Eastern Europe that collapsed in the late 1980s and the early 1990s. Self-sufficient rural communities that provide central allocation of resources still exist in developing countries. Socialism is the dominant form of government in Zimbabwe, Angola, North Korea, and Cuba. All of these governments play primary roles in resource allocation.

By the 1980s, the disadvantages of these "command" economies had become overwhelming, enabling perestroika to occur and initiating movements toward free-market methods of resource allocation. These disadvantages included the lack of incentives to be efficient producers, the long times for decision making, bureaucratic inefficiencies, unrealistic price levels, foreign exchange rates, and the problems in translating societal needs into products and services.[14]

Centrally planned economies have other characteristics. They encourage cooperation and discourage competition between both companies and individuals. In return, individuals benefit from extensive welfare and social security systems. Social mobility is low, as there are few criteria to evaluate individual social positions. There is also limited social mobility in tribal communities, where hereditary and seniority criteria ensure slow social progress.[15]

CULTURAL CONTROL: RELIGIOUS AND LEGAL FACTORS

To function effectively in foreign countries, marketers must understand what cultural controls a society imposes on its members. All societies, whether they be tribal units, small communities, nations, or supranational entities such as the European Union, have three major regulators of behavior: religion, social customs, and laws. In many countries, one or more of these regulators dominates in given situations, but at times, conflicts result. For example, in the United States, laws are major regulators, but there are conflicts between laws and religion on issues such as abortion, school prayer, and the place of religion in education. In the Middle East and North Africa, legal and religious beliefs are combined, as in the legal framework of Saudi Arabia. Muslim law is based on religious concepts from the Koran as given by the prophet Mohammed.

All countries, to greater or lesser extent, have social rules defining acceptable behaviors. However, because religious and legal elements affect behavior to varying extents around the world, each needs to be reviewed.

Christianity

Christianity has its basis in the life and teachings of Jesus Christ, who was born a Jew in what is today Israel. As Table 2–2 shows, Christians make up the world's largest religious group—about one-third of the world's population, or almost 2 billion people. Christianity has three branches: Roman Catholicism, with about 970 million followers; Protestantism, with nearly 400 million; and Eastern Orthodoxy, with over 200 million members. Christianity is the major religion in Europe, the Western Hemisphere, and Australia, but many Christians also live in Asia and Africa.

Historically, Christianity grew out of Judaism, and its sacred teachings spring both from the Jewish Old Testament and from the New Testament of the Bible, which records the life and teachings of Jesus. Most Christians believe that Jesus is God incarnate, sent to the world to enable people to gain salvation by repentance of their sins. As in Judaism, the Ten Commandments form the basis of moral law for Christianity; various creeds express Christian doctrines.

The Western world, largely Christian by faith, has spearheaded the development of modernization for reasons outside the scope of this text. An important factor, however, in the development of modernization was the formulation of civil law, the work of jurists in seventeenth century France as a result of the religious strife between Catholics and Protestants. This development was important in creating the secular society that has been a mark of developed countries. Important also was the Protestant emphasis on reading the Bible, thus encouraging education for the purposes of literacy, another mark of developed nations.

It has been claimed that the Protestant faith, by motivating its adherents to the values of hard work and thrift, has instigated movement toward capitalism and economic development (the "Protestant work ethic"). But other nations that are not Protestant, nor even largely Christian, such as Japan, have also had enormous economic development through capitalism. Direct connections between religious doctrines and development are not easy to make, though marketers are aware that certain characteristics of a society, such as literacy and a market economy, are favorable to the business climate.

Judaism

Judaism, the religious faith of the Jews, is the oldest living religion in the Western world. According to tradition, sometime between the fifteenth and thirteenth centuries BC, the patriarch Abraham moved with his flocks north and west from Mesopotamia into the area later called Palestine. Eventually, his descendants moved into Egypt, where they were held in bondage. In the thirteenth century BC, the prophet Moses led them out of Egypt and unified them in the worship of Yahweh, the God who had chosen them as His people. Judaism was the world's first religion to teach monotheism, or belief in one God, and two other major world religions—Christianity and Islam—drew on its tenets in their development. Today, it claims over 14 million adherents across the world, mainly in North America, Europe, and Israel.

The Hebrew Bible, especially the first five books, which are called the Torah, is the basic source of Jewish beliefs. It contains the divine revelations received by the patriarchs Abraham, Isaac, and Jacob, as well as the Ten Commandments received by Moses, an important cornerstone of Jewish law. These laws are codified in the Talmud, a fifth- and sixth-century compendium of Jewish religious life and legal decisions, often couched in parables, fables, sermons, and homilies.

Judaism today has four major branches—Orthodoxy, Conservatism, Reform, and Reconstructionism. Orthodox Jews are least likely to assimilate into secular society, but they are important influences in Israeli politics and in Jewish communities worldwide. The other movements practice varying levels of adherence to the laws and traditions of Judaism. Jews, like Muslims, shun pork and do not mix meat and milk.

Because Jewish law and tradition disdain ignorance and sloth, education and industry have been emphasized and encouraged. Historically, Jews were persecuted in Christian countries for not recognizing the tenets of the Christian church. For example, Jews in medieval Europe were not allowed to hold property; many consequently settled in the growing cities, where they became active in commerce. Today, Jewish communities in many countries occupy a prominent place in world commerce.

Islam

The Muslim religion—Islam—dates back to the early seventh century AD and was established during the lifetime of the prophet Mohammed. It is practiced in about 30 countries, mainly in North Africa and the Middle East, and has over 1 billion adherents. Indonesia has the largest Muslim population of any nation in the world, with about 180 million worshipers. Islam is split into two major groups, the result of a disagreement over who should succeed Mohammed as leader. They are the Sunnis (about 90 percent) and the Shi'ahs or Shi'ites (about 10 percent).

The major precept of Islam is submission to the will of Allah (*Islam* means "to submit"). Its primary text is the Koran, which contains the divine revelations of the prophet Mohammed. The Koran is the source of the various legal and social codes that constitute Islamic law. These codes are strict, and Muslims typically do not eat pork, drink, or smoke. In the strictest Islamic societies—such as Libya and Iran—there are no nightclubs, bars, or casinos.

Muslims have five main duties:

1. To profess the faith, that there is no God but Allah, and Mohammed is the prophet of Allah.

2. To pray five times each day at specific times, no matter where one is.

3. To abstain from food, drink, and any worldly pleasure from dawn until dusk during the month of Ramadan.

4. To give to the poor. Because Mohammed was himself a poor orphan, the Muslim faith dictates that all followers should give 2.5 percent of their annual incomes to the poor, a practice known as "Zakaat." (Jews also have a strong tradition of giving charity, "Tzedekah.")

5. To make a pilgrimage to Mecca. Every able-bodied Muslim is encouraged to make at least one trip in his or her lifetime to Mecca in Saudi Arabia, the birthplace of Mohammed.

Islam dictates not only religious behavior but also social etiquette. Islamic societies are male dominated. In Shi'ite countries (for example, Iran), women must cover themselves from head to foot and must wear veils when they go outside. In Saudi Arabia, women are not allowed to drive cars. Westerners who do business in Muslim countries must try different marketing strategies to accommodate the needs of Islamic women and other Islamic traditions. Some types of technological change are welcomed, but other types of behavior (for example, habits of conspicuous consumption) are viewed with suspicion.

Hinduism

Hinduism had its beginnings in 1500 BC when Aryan invaders swept into what is today India and conquered its people. With them, they brought their beliefs in many gods and goddesses who rule nature, and these beliefs over time were blended with local practices to produce Hinduism. Today, Hinduism claims about 780 million adherents and 85 percent of India's population.

At the heart of Hinduism are the sacred texts of the Vedas and the Upanishads, which Hindus believe reveal the basic truths of life and the individual's place in the universe. The unifying philosophy is that birth, life, and death are all passing events in a cycle of births and rebirths, and that individual status is determined by how well or ill one lived in previous lives (karma).

The Aryans established the Hindu practice of caste, a system by which all Hindus are born into a specific social and occupational class. Movement from one caste to another is forbidden. These castes originally were three in number: the Brahmins or priestly caste, at the top; followed by the Kshatriya, or warrior caste; and the Sudra, or peasants and laborers, at the bottom. Beneath these three castes are the lowest of the low, then and today, who are the "outcasts" (out of the caste system)—the untouchables. Officially abolished in India in the mid-twentieth century, many castes nevertheless exist now. The caste system is very intricate and affects all relationships.

Hinduism does not have a body of authoritative doctrine, but it does provide a guide for correct conduct. Hindu society is strongly oriented toward family. Members of family units tend to be strongly loyal to each other, shielding each other during difficult times, and sharing benefits during good times. A businessperson contemplating a project in India should also keep in mind the dietary habits of Hindus: Because they venerate the cow, many Hindus are vegetarian. The businessperson should also be aware of the diversity of Indian society. Not all Indians are Hindus, and while Hindi is the official language of the country, many other languages are prominent.

Buddhism

Buddhism was founded in the early sixth century BC by Siddhartha Gautama, a member of a wealthy warrior-caste family in India. His search for spiritual enlightenment took him beyond the sacred Hindu texts and into a harsh life of self-mortification, where he denied himself nearly to starvation. After long meditation, he achieved an understanding of life contained in what came to be called the "Four Noble Truths":

1. Everything in life is suffering and sorrow.

2. The cause of suffering and sorrow is desire and attachment to worldly goods and goals, which bring disappointment, more sorrow, and more desire.

3. The way to end pain is to avoid desire.

4. The way to reach this end is by following a Middle Way that falls between self-indulgence and self-mortification. It is called the Eightfold Path, and it is like a staircase with eight steps: right knowledge, right purpose, right speech, right action, right living, right effort, right thinking, and right meditation. This path leads to *nirvana*—the total release of selfish cravings and desires and the achievement of release from the cycles of rebirths (Buddhism started out as a reform of Hinduism).

Today, Buddhism has over 300 million followers who have split into two major groups, the Theravada and the Mahayana sects. Among the fastest growing economies in the world (Japan, Hong Kong, Korea, Singapore, and Taiwan), Mahayana Buddhism is an important, if not the dominant, religion. Theravada Buddhism is the stricter of the two sects, and it is strong in Sri Lanka and in the Southeast Asian nations of Vietnam, Laos, Cambodia, Burma, and Thailand. Theravada Buddhism—like Hinduism—stresses traditional class structures; heredity has a major role in determining a person's social status, and family ties are strong.

In addition to Hinduism and Buddhism, Asia has many folk religions. For example, Shintoism is the state religion of Japan, but Buddhism has contributed significantly to Japanese lifestyles, just as Taoism and Buddhism have to Chinese lifestyles.

This brief overview of religious cultures suggests to the international marketing manager that specific religious practices and beliefs affect business practices. Religious holy days and seasons affect production patterns. Consumption patterns affect what products may be marketed successfully. Religious heterogeneity impacts business behavior and has potential destabilizing effects (as in Northern Ireland and India).

Effects of Religion: Some General Conclusions

Religious effects on behavior vary. In the developing world, Islam, Buddhism, and Hinduism tend to be pervasive influences on lifestyles. They affect attitudes toward materialism (as in Buddhism, when suffering ceases when desires cease); the family (Hinduism emphasizes family obligations and indirectly encourages nepotism, the granting of favors to those in family and close social circles); social class (Hinduism and the caste system); attitudes toward commerce (whether religion or making money should be an individual's top priority).

Within these religions, there are groups that are devout (Shi'ites in Islam; Theravadan Buddhists), and those whose religious principles are challenged by encroachments from modernization and Westernization and who recognize the developmental benefits these trends bring. Sunni Muslims and Mahayanan Buddhists recognize (though often warily) these benefits and are more tolerant toward them. Fundamentalist groups often initiate backlashes against Westernization because its materialist influence is viewed as an unwelcomed distraction to religion-based lifestyles.

Protestantism (and to a lesser extent, Catholicism) are less pervasive influences on everyday behaviors. The Protestant work ethic encourages industry, commerce, and frugality. Christianity places fewer impediments to modernization and Westernization and can be said to have contributed to development in Western Europe and North America.

LEGAL CONSTRAINTS ON INTERNATIONAL BEHAVIOR

Codes of Behavior

Most societies combine legal and social conventions to control individual and group behavior. In small-scale and developing societies, social customs prevail because populations are small and homogeneous and legal frameworks are still evolving. In these societies, codes of behavior are passed from generation to generation.

In large-scale traditional communities, social expectations are often woven into religious laws. Shari'ah, the body of Islamic law, seems by Western standards to be strict in dealing with the death penalty, with female adulterers, and with thieves. While only more strict Islamic societies such as those of Iran, Libya, and Pakistan currently prosecute individuals to the full extent of Muslim law, the Shari'ah serves as a code for religious and social activities.

As societies industrialize and develop their economies, social controls and religious laws generally become inadequate to police the greater varieties of behaviors found in modern societies. At some point, communities and countries opt for formal legal systems that go beyond religious doctrine. *Common law* has become established in countries with long histories of legal decisions. Common laws are based on precedents and interpretations. The United States and Great Britain have this kind of law. Other countries, especially those with shorter histories, base their legal system on *code law*, which has more tightly defined rules. Countries in Western Europe, in Latin America, and in Africa use this type of system.

Companies operating in foreign markets are subject to varieties of commercial laws. These laws cover approvals for new investments or expansions; the formation of new companies (involving capital requirements, shareholders, directors, disclosures, taxes, fees, types of shares, and so on); competition (over monopolies, market dominance, freedom to sell, resale price maintenance); patents and trademarks; taxation; and labor laws. Commercial information services, such as Business International (BI), supply such data—in BI's case, through its *Investment, Licensing and Trade* (ILT) service. Examples of national commercial laws are shown in Figure 2–4.

How far national legal systems define acceptable behavior varies. In the United States—a market-driven, competitive society—individuals generally are adjudged to have acted responsibly if they do not break the law. But in many other parts of the world, the law only partially defines acceptable behavior; instead, social customs (which are rarely laid out in the formal manner) define expected behaviors. Violations are initially viewed as antisocial actions, but if they are repeated, the offender receives

New investment approval: Egyptian law requires official approval for all foreign direct investment. Under Investment Law 230, the General Authority for Investment allocates land, obtains necessary licenses, approves customs exemptions, carries out tax registration, and monitors capital flows and profit remittance. There are different requirements for joint ventures, which are authorized under Companies Law 159.[a]

Local content requirements: As part of the Andean Pact agreement, local components must comprise 40 percent of the value of automobile output in Ecuador. This requirement will be phased out by the year 2000 to comply with World Trade Organization rules.[b]

Termination of employment: India's laws require government permission for closing down an operation or laying off workers.[c]

Competition policies: In Japan, antirecession cartels are legal and allow firms to cut back production jointly to cope with downturns in demand.[d]

Price controls: Malaysia's Price Control Act controls prices of essential foods, commodities, and manufacturers, such as building materials.[e]

Labor law: Germany's 1976 Co-Determination Act provides for 50 percent labor representation on supervisory boards of companies with over 2,000 workers. A similar law was being enacted at the EU level at the end of 1996.[f]

[a] Business International, "Egypt," *Investment, Licensing and Trade*, July 1996, 11.
[b] Business International, "Ecuador," *Investment, Licensing and Trade*, December 1996, 13.
[c] Business International, "India," *Investment Licensing and Trade*, November 1996, 54.
[d] Business International, "Japan," *Investment Licensing and Trade*, July 1996, 27.
[e] Business International, "Malaysia," *Investment Licensing and Trade*, May 1996, 28.
[f] Business International, "Germany," *Investment Licensing and Trade*, September 1996, 46.

FIGURE 2-4 *Examples of National Commercial Laws*

harsh penalties. "Reasonable behavior" is hence what is consistent with societal norms. In developing countries, unreasonable corporate behaviors often include (1) depriving others of jobs and livelihoods; (2) competing too vigorously and disturbing the status quo of an "orderly society"; (3) using market power to "bully" smaller firms; and (4) taking advantage of legal loopholes to further company or individual goals (for example, taking advantage of lax anti-pollution laws to contaminate foreign market environments).

Social laws also affect individual behavior and social relationships. Commercial relationships must, for example, take into account the status accorded to age and to women. But what sorts of social rules apply in which countries? The *high-low context* culture typology provides valuable clues.

HIGH-LOW CONTEXT CULTURES: A FRAMEWORK FOR UNDERSTANDING SOCIAL RULES

The high-low context classification, first developed by E. T. Hall, offers one framework for understanding intercultural differences in social rules.[16] The terms *high* and *low context* are used to define the level at which a spoken statement conveys a total message. In a low-context society such as the United States, what is said is what is meant. In high-context cultures, such as China or the Arabic countries, what is said is only part of what is meant. The context of the message—who makes the statement, his or her social standing, and his or her background—is as important as what is said. In low-context societies, written agreements and contracts abound. In high-context societies, the personal bonds and relationships between business partners are of greater importance. Table 2–4 shows a partial listing of high-, medium-, and low-context countries. Asian, Middle Eastern, and Latin American countries are high-context countries. By contrast, the Swiss, German, Scandinavian, and North American countries are low-context countries. In between, there are some medium-context European countries (England, Italy, Greece, and Spain).

Perhaps the only enigma on the economic spectrum is Japan. Unlike other countries that share its economic level, its cultural characteristics are considered high-context by Hall.

Differences between high-, medium-, and low-context behaviors are shown in Table 2–5. Their important contrasts are as follows:

1. Individuals are strongly valued in high-context societies. Their social status, backgrounds, and experience must be evaluated alongside the message content to derive its full meaning. By contrast, messages in low-context societies are presumed to be self-contained and complete ("the information speaks for itself").

2. In low-context countries, businesspeople prefer to do business "at arm's length," so that if a situation necessitates severing the commercial relationship, the break can be achieved cleanly and objectively, usually through legal mechanisms. But high-context cultures emphasize the social side of commercial relationships. Trust rather than legal contracts becomes the bonding element between parties. Much time is taken up in negotiations, so that high-context businesspeople can evaluate the trustworthiness and integrity of prospective partners.

TABLE 2–4 ▪ *Social Rules: High-, Medium-, and Low-Context Societies*

High Context	Medium Context	Low Context
Chinese	Greek	North American
Korean	Spanish	Scandinavian
Japanese	Italian	Swiss
Vietnamese	French	German
Arab	Dutch	
Latin American	English	

TABLE 2–5 ▪ *Social Interrelationships and Codes of Behavior in High-, Medium-, and Low-Context Societies*

Socially Based Attitudes, Values, and Behaviors Toward:	Low Context (e.g., U.S., Switzerland)	Medium Context (e.g., UK, France, Spain)	High Context (e.g., Middle East, Latin America, Asia)
Meeting people	Informal	Formal	Formal
Getting acquainted	Fast	Moderate	Slow
Depth of relationship	Shallow	Moderate	Deep
Trust in relationship	Little trust	Trust	Much trust
Limits on individual behavior	Legal	Legal/Social	Social
Reliance on lawyers	High	Moderate	Low/Zero
Meetings	Efficiency oriented	Mixture of business and social	Lengthy; much socializing
Business relationships	"At arm's length," preferably objective and nonsociable	Some mixing of social/business through contacts and networking	Business an extension of social relationship
Tolerance for mistakes	High	Medium	Low
Accountability for mistakes	At lowest level	At highest level	At highest level
Competition between individuals	Encouraged	Discouraged	Considered antisocial

Source: Adapted from E.T. Hall, "How Cultures Collide," *Psychology Today*, July 1976, 67–74.

3. High-context societies are tradition and status quo oriented. Change, readily accepted in low-context countries, occurs slowly in high-context societies, and is scrutinized carefully before implementation. Uncertainty is avoided at all costs, and cutthroat competition is avoided.

4. High-context cultures are unforgiving to both insiders and outsiders when mistakes are made. Foreigners are allowed few mistakes before their integrity (and hence their ability to do business) is brought into question.

This disciplined intolerance applies within high-context societies also. When mistakes are made, responsibility is accepted at the highest level. By contrast, a low-context society would likely find a scapegoat at a lower level to bear responsibility. Social rules dictate appropriate behaviors in high-context countries, reducing the need for lawyers.

Country-Based Social Etiquette Practices

While the high-low context classification provides a number of useful guidelines, all nations in reality have unique systems of social etiquette. These systems dictate behaviors for greeting people, visiting, eating, and dressing appropriately. Most countries also have distinctive attitudes about how formal one should be and how open, expressive, and individualistic one is "allowed" to be. Rules govern family behavior and duties, dating, diet, recreation, work, and holidays. The best way to learn about national social etiquette is through personal observations. However, where business is conducted through short visits, executives can read up on individual country cultures. One excellent source is Brigham Young University's *Culturgram* series, which portrays social customs in individual countries.

Similarly, all countries have their own folklore, arts, crafts, and customs. Colors, for example, have different connotations from country to country. Mourning, for instance, is symbolized by black in the United States but by white in Asia and purple in Latin America. Marketing techniques must take into account the connotations of colors and other symbols when products are to be packaged and advertised. Similarly, a company conducting business in a different culture must consider the meaning of brand names and the mood implied by musical tunes used in advertisements.

INTEGRATING CULTURAL AND ECONOMIC SYSTEMS

The U.S. Profile

The United States is a modern, industrialized society. Its economic system is based on the competitive allocation of resources with minimum government intervention. It is a dynamic, change-oriented society dominated by economic competitive activity. Merit is a major means of individual progression, and success is rewarded economically and with unhindered movement up the social ladder. The United States is a prime example of a country where individuals can go from the lowest to the highest social positions (from "rags to riches") in a single generation ("the American dream").[17]

Driving the U.S. economy is a strong work ethic that has emerged both from early Protestant roots and from the determination of later immigrant groups who aimed for better economic and working conditions. Change is viewed as improvement. The acquisition of material possessions is encouraged and is a means of achieving social status. Women are not shackled by religious restrictions and are increasingly contributing to U.S. economic progress. Americans also believe that people rather than religious deities control their destiny (i.e., the individual "makes things happen").

The low-context nature of U.S. society means that the law defines what is and is not permissible behavior. Competition brings about strong reliance on lawyers in commercial and other activities, and lawsuits are often the first recourse rather than the last, as in other societies. The American orientation toward efficiency also applies to social situations; brief acquaintances and informality are normal. The competitive nature of U.S. society also extends into social activities. Americans develop fewer deep social relationships than do people in other societies.

The Profile of Traditional Societies

Competition, the cornerstone of the American economy, is encouraged only to a limited extent in Asia, the Middle East, and Latin America. Until the late 1980s, competition was nearly nonexistent in Eastern Europe. Tradition in such societies is important, and change in most cases is evaluated cautiously. Social status changes slowly. Family background is an influential factor. Limited social movement occurs during an individual's lifetime.

In traditional societies, religious activities often take precedent over commerce and the pursuit of personal wealth. De-emphasizing material possessions, for example, is central to the Buddhist, Hindu, and Muslim religions. The emphasis is instead on the extended family as the major societal group. Religious philosophies define social rules.

In traditional societies, social customs and interpersonal relationships are extremely important. Much time is taken up in getting to know people and in determining their trustworthiness and integrity. Once established, relationships run deep; personal trust rather than legal contract determines the nature of business relationships.

Europe and Japan

Despite sharing economically privileged situations, Western Europe and Japan differ from the United States in two important respects. First, a major priority of European governments has been to support all of their citizens. Hence, there are extensive social welfare systems to look after senior citizens, the sick, and the unemployed. In Japan, companies provide for employees and their retirement.

Second, both Western Europe and Japan have much longer histories than has the United States. Consequently, the past exerts a much stronger influence on the present. Hereditary criteria determine social class, and there is little social movement between generations except through educational achievement. In Japan's case, seniority is also important, especially in companies. Both of these factors contribute to socially harmonious societies in which there is little competition between individuals. In Japan, the Shinto-Confucian-Buddhist philosophy makes the country a cohesive society with a strong work ethic. In Western Europe, interpersonal competition is viewed as antisocial behavior (as it is also in Japan), and teamwork is considered the key to progress.

In social behavior, Europe and Japan show characteristics similar to both American and traditional societies. The low-context Swiss, German, and Scandinavian peoples follow the U.S. style of socializing, while the medium-context countries of Britain, France, Italy, and Greece are more formal initially. People take time to make acquaintances, and they view trust as an integral part of business relationships. Premiums are placed on social formalities. Legal contracts confirm rather than define business relationships.

SUMMARY

This chapter describes the characteristics and the many components that comprise culture. Individual nations may be multicultural, monocultural, or part of a wider grouping, such as the European Union or Latin America. Multicountry blocs share culture similarities in language, religion, economic development level, and other dimensions. These similarities aid the flow of products and technologies among nations.

While international business is facilitated by cultural similarities, commercial deals are best consummated when cultural differences are acknowledged and necessary adaptations are made. Differences among nations are attributed to resource allocation methods (capitalist, mixed, and command economies) and to the means used to control behavior (through religious, legal, and social means). Finally, the cultural characteristics of the United States, Western Europe, Japan, and traditional societies have been profiled. Differences are most noticeable between industrialized and traditional countries. Europe and Japan, however, despite being fully industrialized, maintain a number of characteristics found in traditional societies.

DISCUSSION QUESTIONS

1. Americans have been characterized as "outgoing, friendly, loud, extravagant, wasteful, not class-conscious, disrespectful of authority, wealthy, generous, always in a hurry. . . ."[18] Explain these perceptions, using the framework developed in this chapter.

2. Again, using the framework, explain why:
   a. Latin Americans are stereotyped as fatalistic (with fortuitous events occurring by luck or by the grace of God), not time or efficiency oriented, nepotistic (i.e., favoring family and relatives in official appointments), aware of social differences, autocratic decision makers, competition shy, and socially sensitive.[19]
   b. Japanese are generalized as being formal, social status-conscious, male-dominated, patient, group rather than individually oriented, and preferring harmony and certainty to uncertainty and surprise.[20]

3. Perestroika, the economic restructuring of the former Soviet Union and Eastern Europe, involved moving from a communist to a market-forces or mixed economy. What sorts of economic changes would you expect to have occurred?

4. "EC '92 is pushing Western Europe toward U.S.-style market-forces competition." Using the economic systems framework, what sorts of changes might the region expect if this occurs?

5. "Low-context social relations are associated with market-forces economies and high-context behaviors with village economies." Discuss the pros and cons of this statement.

European Economic and Political Unification— What Should Companies Do?

The idea of a united Europe was suggested in a 1985 White Paper. In 1987, the Single Europe Act was passed; in it were procedures and a timetable for the economic unification of the European Community by 1992. American and European companies have adapted to the new, competitive European environment.

You have been asked to evaluate how American companies can best respond to the 1992 European challenge, which includes the following provisions:

1. Harmonization of product standards, testing, and certification for a variety of industries. How will this affect European manufacturing and product strategies?

2. In many industries, companies themselves monitor compliance with the new Europe-wide standards. EC regulators only check adherence at periodic intervals.

3. Harmonization of packing, labeling, and processing requirements, especially for food and chemical-based products.

4. Changes and harmonization of government procurement procedures and the "opening up" of government contracts to Europe-wide bids rather than the customary favoring of national suppliers (i.e., Italian government contracts going to Italian suppliers).

One cause of concern has been the EUs Reciprocity Provision, which simply states that if European companies are restrained in a foreign market, then similar restraints will apply to that country's activities in the EU. The Europeans argue that this provision should ensure a "level playing field," especially with respect to Japan (which has been a notoriously difficult market to penetrate for both Americans and Europeans).

5. The deregulating of Europe's financial environment has had a profound impact on companies. Distinctions between different financial institutions have fallen. Banks are allowed to offer greater varieties of services, including mortgages, underwriting, and investment counseling. What used to be a gentlemanly industry is being transformed into a highly competitive sector that makes the American financial services market seem languid by comparison.

6. The elimination and simplification of national transit documents and procedures. This action has meant that transporting goods within the EU has been greatly facilitated. Instead of 35 or more pages of documents and often 2- to 3-hour waits at borders, the trucking industry can get products from one side of the community to the other on a 2-page document, with substantial time-saving at the borders.

7. While not all European countries are part of EC '92, they are still affected by its economic fallout. Nonmembers, inside and outside the EU, all plan to follow the Community's 1992 initiative. In establishing standards for over 400 million consumers, European companies are expected to be front-runners in establishing world standards for new technologies.

8. Promotional strategies are expected to be affected by the following: (a) pan-European branding strategies for some types of consumer goods; (b) harmonization of standards pertaining to "fraudulent" promotions; (c) increasing numbers of pan-European media, including Skychannel television, the "European" newspaper, and cable services such as Cable News Network (CNN).

9. The Maastricht Agreement, ratified in 1993, set 1999 as the target date to introduce the common European currency (the "Euro").

QUESTIONS

1. If you were the CEO of a company that had many subsidiaries and branch plants throughout Europe, what would be some of your key concerns?

2. If your company (a medium-sized industrial firm) were considering entering European markets, what would be your primary considerations?

■

CASE **2-2**

Islamic Law: The Case of Gaza

Gaza Strip justice is dominated by Islamic philosophies and laws. Sheik Ahmed Matar is a typical "cadi." He administers the law for his extended family clan, which numbers about 5,000. He has only five years of primary school education, but he is an expert in applying Islamic laws and the unwritten precedents that have been handed down through generations of cadis.

There are persistent allegations of corruption against the cadis, but they have been the preferred settlement systems for legal disputes for hundreds of years. When a problem arises, the cadi first goes to the victim's family and obtains a cease-fire to let tempers cool. Then they negotiate, with money often becoming the ultimate settlement factor.

Typical punishments include the following:

Murder: A $91,000 fine or a percentage thereof, plus a bride to replace the victim.

Theft: A fine of four times the value of the stolen object plus $13 for every step the thief took from his house to that of his victim.

Sex-related crimes: Winking at a woman brings a fine of $2,600 or the eye is gouged out.

Rape: Rape brings a large fine, or the rapist strips and rides an oiled camel to the female's house. Every part of his body that touches the soil is cut off.

Wife-beating: The fine is determined by the severity of the injuries. The fine is quadrupled if the wife is publicly beaten.

QUESTIONS

1. In what ways is Gaza's cadi-based legal system similar to Western legal systems? In what ways is it dissimilar? What aspects of the system (if any) do you favor? Why?

Source: Adapted from Donna Abu-Nasr, "Religious Courts Try to Fill Legal Void Left in Strife-Torn Gaza," *Birmingham News,* 7 January 1994, A4.

ENDNOTES

1 Vern Terpstra and Kenneth David, *The Cultural Environment of International Business* (Cincinnati, Ohio: South Western Publishing, 1991).

2 Ibid.

3 Adapted from Richard D. Steade, "Multinational Corporations and the Changing World Economic Order," *California Management Review*, Winter 1978, 5–12.

4 Kenichi Ohmae, *Triad Power: The Coming Shapes of Global Competition* (New York: Free Press, 1985).

5 *Britannica Book of the Year* (Chicago: Encyclopedia Britannica, 1989), 379–81.

6 H. Stephen Gardner, *Comparative Economic Systems* (Chicago: Dryden Press, 1988); and Howard J. Sherman, *Foundations of Radical Political Economy* (Armonk, N.Y.: M.E. Sharpe, Inc. 1987).

7 Ludwig von Mises, *The Anti-Capitalist Mentality* (Chicago: Libertarian Press, 1972); and Bryce F. Ryan, *Social and Cultural Change* (New York: Ronald Press Company, 1969).

8 William G. Ouchi, *Theory Z* (New York: Avon Books, 1981).

9 Joop Den Uyl, "Democratizing the Social Structure," in *Eurosocialism and America*, ed. Nancy Liber (Philadelphia: Temple University Press, 1982), 107–117.

10 John Vaizey, *Capitalism and Socialism* (London: Weidenfeld and Nicolson, 1980).

11 F. Furstenberg, "Recent Trends in Collective Bargaining in Federal Republic of Germany," in *Collective Bargaining in Industrial Market Economies: A Reappraisal*, ed. F. Furstenberg (Geneva: International Labor Office, 1987).

12 R. Nath, *Comparative Management: A Regional View* (Cambridge, Mass.: Ballinger Publishing Company, 1989); and V. Marsick, E. Turner, and L. Cederholm, "International Managers as Team Leaders," *Management Review*, March 1989, 46–49.

13 T.N. Gladwin, "Strategic Management across Cultures: Some American, European, and Japanese Comparisons," in *Comparative and Multinational Management*, ed. A. Simcha Ronen (New York: John Wiley & Sons, 1986), 438–39.

14 E.D. Domar, *Capitalism, Socialism and Serfdom* (New York: Cambridge University Press, 1989), 15–28; and Andrew Zimbalist and Howard J. Sherman, *Comparative Economic Systems* (New York: Academic Press, Inc., 1984), 8–12.

15 Bryce F. Ryan, *Social and Cultural Change* (New York: The Ronald Press Company), 428–36.

16 E.T. Hall, *Beyond Culture* (Garden City, N.Y.: Anchor Press, 1976); and "How Cultures Collide," *Psychology Today*, July 1976, 66–74.

17 Zhenek Suda, "Modernization or Americanization: The Concept of Modernity and American Culture," in *Directions of Changes, Modernization Theory, Research, and Realities*, ed. Mustafa O. Altir, Burkhart Holzer, and Zdenek Suda (Boulder, Colo.: Westview Press, 1981), 249–61.

18 L. Robert Kohls, *Developing Intercultural Awareness* (Washington, D.C.: The Society for Intercultural Education, 1981), 12.

19 This list adapted from Robert T. Moran, "Cross-Cultural Dimensions of Doing Business in Latin America," in *Reference Manual on Doing Business in Latin America*, ed. Donald R. Shae, et al. (Milwaukee: University of Wisconsin, 1979).

20 Philip R. Harris and Robert T. Moran, *Managing Cultural Differences*, 2nd ed., (Houston, Tex.: Gulf Publishing Company, 1987), 390–98.

CHAPTER 3

Economic, Political, and Social System Changes

Chapter Outline

Change in Economic, Political, and Social Systems

Why Cultural Change toward Modernization Occurs

Effects of Cultural Change on Marketing

Learning Objectives

When you have mastered the contents of this chapter, you will be able to do the following:

1   Identify and explain changes occurring in a country's economic, political, and social institutions and in its citizens' values.

2   Discuss the relationship between modernization and economic, political, and social change; explain how these cultural changes are initiated and sustained; and name and analyze those factors impeding industrial progress and cultural change.

3   Name and evaluate what changes occur in marketing activities and consumer behaviors as countries develop.

Cultural change occurs as economic, political, or social institutions or behaviors are transformed through internal or external forces. Most often, changes in one sector cause changes in others. Thus, as countries develop economically and upgrade their technological and material aspects of life, political and social changes occur. Conversely, changes in political life (forms of government) and social life (including family, religion, education, and class structure) affect economic development. Institutional change and changes in personal values go hand in hand.

In most countries, the interplay of economic, political, and social change is a dynamic process. In the 80 or so percent of the world's countries that are in the process of industrialization, such change is especially significant. The markets in these countries are mainly tradition oriented, but there are small modernization sectors that spearhead the push from traditional to modern lifestyles.

In the 10 percent of the world's countries that are fully industrialized, institutions and behaviors are primarily modern, though traditional elements survive in rural areas

TABLE 3–1 ■ *Modernization and Cultural Change in Political, Economic, and Social Institutions*

From	To
Political Institutions	
Autarchy (dictatorships, president-for-life, tribal chiefs, general secretary of Communist party)	Democracy: Multiparty systems and philosophies
Economic Institutions	
Type of economy	Large-scale industrial economies with international dependencies (trade)
Small-scale: self-sufficient agricultural economies	Free-market (decentralized) economies
Command centralized economies	
Level of economic activity: Low-level subsistence economies	
Social Institutions	
Religious influence: pervasive, high	Lower religiosity
Control over community behavior (custom; religious precepts)	Civil, commercial laws
Societal ranking (social class): Heredity and seniority	Economic criteria (income, economic achievement, or mixed)
Familial obligations: extensive (major social grouping)	Weak (one of many social groups)
Education: Knowledge passed on orally (word of mouth) and contained within individuals' experience	Knowledge passed on through written word, books, and computer disks
Linguistic and ethnic backgrounds: Countries often multilingual and comprised of numerous ethnic communities	Countries linguistically homogenized, with ethnic communities bonded together by infrastructure

and among older age groups. International marketers must understand how and why these changes occur and know how they affect consumers' tastes so that they can formulate appropriate strategies to cater to the diverse needs they encounter both between countries and within individual markets.

CHANGES IN ECONOMIC, POLITICAL, AND SOCIAL SYSTEMS

Economic, political, and social systems consist of institutions and individuals. Institutions comprise organized, goal-directed groups of people who influence behavior patterns in political, economic, and social settings. Governments, political parties, religious bodies, companies, and families are some of the institutions molding individual behavior. For countries to industrialize, not only must institutions change (for example, from centrally controlled economies to economies controlled by market forces) but the values and attitudes of its citizens must change also.

Changes in Institutions

Table 3–1 shows the basic types of institutional change. Some institutional changes occur quickly, such as political coups d'état. Others evolve more slowly, such as the change from agricultural to industrial-based economies. Consequently, agricultural communities, even in industrial countries, usually retain traditional orientations.

CHANGES IN POLITICAL INSTITUTIONS ▪

Political institutional changes occur as economies modernize and populations become more educated. Autocracies ruled by a single absolute leader (such as tribal chieftains or dictators) over time give way to elected representatives and rulers having more democratic tendencies. Even Middle Eastern monarchs, who combine religious and political functions, have come under pressure, and in 1989, the king of Jordan allowed that nation to hold its first elections. Given the volatility of national political situations, it is difficult for international marketers to monitor and predict political change. Table 3–2 shows how corporations respond to this challenge.

To monitor political events over perhaps 150 countries would require tremendous resources if it were done on an individual market basis; hence, many MNCs subscribe to political-risk services. Table 3–2 is an excerpt from a Political Risk Services newsletter. Such services cover major markets and show what political party (or dictator) is in power, the extent of political turmoil, who is likely to be in power 18 months and 5 years hence, and present and future prospects for foreign investments (including such problems as restrictions and ownership questions), trade (tariffs, taxes, import restrictions), and financial transfers (availability of currency; foreign exchange restrictions). Finally, these services note key economic indicators because inadequate economic growth or excessive inflation are primary causes of political turmoil. Additional expert commentaries provide in-depth coverage for individual markets.

CHANGES IN ECONOMIC INSTITUTIONS ▪

Economic institutional changes occur in two ways. First, as societies develop, they tend to move away from the centralized distribution of resources, found in self-sufficient tribal communities and in the recently dismantled state-controlled economies of Eastern Europe, to market economies. This shift

TABLE 3–2 ▪ *Political and Economic Forecast Table*

Next to each country name is the date of our last update or report, followed by the 18-month (2nd line) and five-year (3rd line) political forecasts: the REGIMES most likely to hold power and their PROBABILITIES, risk ratings for TURMOIL (low to very high) and risk ratings (A+ the least to D-the most) for financial TRANSFER, direct INVESTMENT, and EXPORT to the country. Parentheses indicate a changed forecast. An asterisk means a non-incumbent regime. The list of ECONOMIC INDICATORS contains our most recently issued economic data and forecasts, including a previous five-year average, a one-year forecast or estimate, and a five-year forecast average. REAL GROWTH of GDP and INFLATION are expressed as percentages, and CURRENT ACCOUNT figures are in billions of U.S. dollars.

Country Regimes and Probabilities		Turmoil	Trans-fer	Invest-ment	Export		Real GDP Growth	Inflation	Current Account
ALGERIA	1/97					1992–1996	1.3	26.0	+0.08
Military 55%		High	B	B+	B-	1997	4.0	12.0	-1.50
Military 45%		High	C+	B	B-	1998–2002	4.5	8.0	+0.50
ANGOLA	10/96					1992–1996	-1.6	741.2	-0.63
MPLA 70%		Moderate	D+	C+	C-	1997	2.5	200.0	-0.60
*MPLA-led Coalition 60%		Moderate	C	C+	C+	1998–2002	3.0	50.0	-0.50
ARGENTINA	12/96					1992–1996	4.2	8.6	-5.14
Menem Reformist 50%		High	B	B	B-	1997	3.5	2.0	-2.00
*Reformist 50%		High	C+	B+	B	1998–2002	5.0	2.5	-5.00
AUSTRALIA	2/97					1992–1996	3.6	2.6	-14.81
Liberal-National 75%		Low	A	A	A+	1997	2.8	2.4	-16.00
Liberal-National 50%		Low	A-	A	A	1998–2002	3.2	2.6	-10.00
AUSTRIA	3/97					1992–1996	1.6	3.0	-2.40
SPO-OVP 70%		Low	A+	A	A+	1997	1.5	1.8	-3.50
SPO-OVP 60%		Low	A	A	A+	1998–2002	2.2	2.3	-2.50
BANGLADESH	7/96					1992–1996	4.4	3.7	-0.33
Awami League 45%		High	C	C+	C	1997	5.5	5.0	-1.50
*Military 40%		High	B-	C+	C	1998–2002	5.0	5.0	-1.00
BELGIUM	6/96					1992–1996	1.2	2.1	+11.84
Center Left 55%		Low	A+	A	A+	1997	2.4	1.8	+16.00
Center Left 40%		Low	A-	A	A-	1998–2002	2.5	2.2	+8.00
BOLIVIA	2/97					1992–1996	3.8	9.5	-0.52
*Centrist Coalition 45%		Moderate	B	A	B	1997	3.5	8.0	-0.75
*Populist Right 45%		Low	B	B+	B+	1998–2002	3.8	10.0	-0.70

requires the building of reliable infrastructures, which enable manufacturers to produce goods on a mass scale and to distribute them over wider market areas. Market systems also require a free flow of information. Communications (such as telephones, mail, and computers) are crucial in relaying market information between suppliers, producers, retailers, and consumers. Advertising agencies facilitate information flows to customers.

Second, economic changes occur as countries attain higher levels of economic activity. Manufacturing capacities expand as people move out of agricultural areas and

Country Regimes and Probabilities		Turmoil	Trans-fer	Invest-ment	Export		Real GDP Growth	Inflation	Current Account
BOTSWANA	5/96					1992–1996	4.1	13.3	+0.30
BDP 60%		High	B+	A-	B+	1997	4.8	11.0	+0.18
BDP 60%		Moderate	B+	B+	B+	1998–2002	5.0	15.0	+0.10
BRAZIL	2/97					1992–1996	3.3	1202.5	-6.64
Cardoso Coalition 50%		Moderate	C	B	C+	1997	4.5	12.0	-18.00
*Center-Right Coalition 50%		Low	B	B+	B-	1998–2002	4.0	10.0	-15.00
BULGARIA	3/97					1992–1996	-1.9	94.6	-0.12
Center Left 65%		Moderate	B-	A	B	1997	1.8	30.0	0.00
Center Left 55%		Low	B+	B-	B-	1998–2002	2.8	25.0	+0.50
BURMA	1/97					1992–1996	7.2	25.0	-0.38
SLORC 55%		Moderate	B	B	B-	1997	5.8	26.0	-0.28
SLORC 45%		Moderate	B	B	B-	1998–2002	6.8	24.0	-0.24
CAMEROON	3/96					1992–1996	-2.4	10.7	-0.43
Biya 60%		Moderate	C+	B+	C+	1997	3.5	8.0	-0.30
*RDPC 50%		Moderate	B-	C+	C	1998–2002	3.0	4.0	-0.30
CANADA	11/96					1992–1996	2.3	1.4	-14.99
Liberals 60%		Moderate	A	A	A+	1997	2.5	1.8	-3.00
Liberals 45%		Low	A-	A	A-	1998–2002	2.4	1.8	-10.00
CHILE	10/96					1992–1996	7.5	10.8	-0.96
Center Left 60%		Low	A	A	A+	1997	7.0	6.5	-1.80
Center Left 55%		Low	A	A+	A+	1998–2002	6.0	6.0	-1.50
CHINA	3/97					1992–1996	11.8	13.6	+1.56
Pragmatists 75%		Low	B	B+	B+	1997	10.5	6.5	+5.00
Pragmatists 65%		Low	A-	B+	B	1998–2002	9.0	6.0	+4.00
COLOMBIA	11/96					1992–1996	4.5	23.1	-2.66
Samper 45%		Very High	B	B	B	1997	2.8	20.0	-3.00
*Liberals 40%		Very High	C	B-	C+	1998–2002	4.5	18.0	+1.00
CONGO	8/96					1992–1996	0.5	15.6	-0.52
Lissouba 60%		Moderate	B	B	B-	1997	3.0	5.0	-0.30
Lissouba 60%		Moderate	B-	C+	B-	1998–2002	4.0	4.5	-0.25

Source: Reproduced with permission. Political Risk Services, Syracuse, NY, March 1, 1997, p. 8.

into industrial sectors. Agriculture becomes mechanized and less labor intensive. Modern factory systems, incorporating specialization and the division of labor, become common. Manufacturing surpluses make international trade viable. Some countries, such as Singapore, Japan, Korea, Taiwan, and Hong Kong, have based their economic development on export growth. As international trade has grown, many other countries, including those in Latin America and Eastern Europe, have reoriented their economies to take advantage of export-based growth.

CHANGES IN SOCIAL INSTITUTIONS ▪ Changes in social institutions are of five types.

The first social change is the movement from religion and tradition-based social rules to legal frameworks. In traditional societies, customs and religious rules govern behaviors between individuals and the sexes, lay out family obligations, and create expectations regarding commercial relationships. These are usually dictated by religious laws (as in Islamic societies) or social customs and are passed on orally from generation to generation. As countries modernize and people move from rural to urban areas, their lives become less influenced by tradition and are governed more by local and national laws.

The second social change is the tendency to rank people by achievement rather than by family pedigree. This change is slow. In developing countries and many developed countries, family name and status ("hereditary criteria") determine social standing, along with seniority (e.g., tribal elders with "accumulated wisdom" or "experience"). In traditional (but also industrialized) societies like Japan, both heredity and seniority are important. Seniority also is highly regarded in traditional institutions, such as trade unions, fraternal organizations, and academic societies, in advanced countries.

As countries develop, populations gain geographic and social mobility. People lose track of their family origins, and economic achievement rather than seniority usually determines an individual's place in the social order.

In practice, few societies adhere strictly to seniority, heredity, or economic criteria in assigning social status. For instance, in the United States, in most cities, there are families whose names signify both hereditary and economic status, notably the Kennedys in Massachusetts and the Bushes in New England. Worldwide, in tradition-based societies, there are emerging pockets of middle-income consumers ("yuppies") who base their social standings on income and other economic criteria. In the former Eastern Bloc, young, upwardly mobile Marxists ("yummies") emerged as an economic group in the 1990s.

The third social change is the shift from the traditional extended family (parents, children, uncles, aunts, and grandparents) to the nuclear family (parents and offspring). As economic growth and development occurs, the extended family becomes less useful. Social security and retirement plans replace the economic support systems provided by the family, and social activities outside the family, such as clubs and professional affiliations, tend to replace the kinship network.

Fourth, as countries grow, they need more efficient means of passing on information. Word-of-mouth, which works well in small-scale, rural communities, cannot cope with the information needs of technological, urban societies. Books and computers, which can be more standardized and objective, become the dominant methods of storing and passing on knowledge.

Fifth, and last, over long time periods, development tends to weld multilingual, geographically and ethnically fragmented communities into more unified, linguistically homogeneous societies. Infrastructures provide the means to exchange goods and services and enable travel and media services to broaden rural outlooks. (Nevertheless, where there are critical masses of particular ethnic groups, French Canadians for example, cultural diversity is maintainable.)

Changes in Values

For economic, political, and social change to happen, individual values as well as institutions must change. The transition from traditional to modern values (illustrated in Table 3–3) is slow, often taking place over

TABLE 3–3 ■ *Changes in Individual Basic Values as Societies Modernize*

Individual Values	Traditional	Modern
Economic		
Role of the individual	Accepts life as preordained	Believes life can be influenced by our skills and abilities
Direction of attention	Oriented to past	Oriented to future
Attitude toward risk	Avoids risk	Takes risk
Political-Social		
Social class	Determined by family and seniority	Achieved by individual effort
Difference of opinion and breadth of interest	Dislikes differing opinions; interested chiefly in immediate environment	Respects differing opinions; interested in national and international news
Family	Regards family as chief focus of life; attached to extended family	Regards family as one of many social groups in life; seeks broader social set outside extended family
Location	Prefers small towns	Prefers urban centers
Self-help tendency	Feels unable to achieve individually, as events are immutable	Depends on own skills and abilities to influence the future

Source: Jose F. Medina, "The Impact of Modernization on Developing Nation Consumption Patterns—The Case of Mexico" (Ph.D. diss., University of Alabama, 1989). Used with author's permission.

generations. Typically, the older members of society are the more conservative, and younger people are more progressive. In all countries, there are people with traditional values, those with modern values, and those with both. In fully developed countries, traditional values persist, especially in rural areas. Most value changes are associated with institutional changes and, like them, take place during the rural to urban population shifts that occur during industrialization. Changes in values fall into two categories— economic, and social.[1]

CHANGES IN ECONOMIC VALUES ■ An
important change in economic values is a shift of emphasis from community effort to individual effort. After leaving traditional rural communities, migrants to cities find themselves solely responsible for finding a job and income rather than relying on community efforts. As individuals realize that their lot in life depends on their own efforts, they begin to perceive that self-improvement is the key to success.

A second change is being more active and efficient in planning and using time. The change from traditional to modern lifestyles, especially in cities, where efficiency is stressed, makes individuals more aware of the usefulness of planning ahead and using time to the best advantage. This includes anticipating problems and looking for solutions. Traditional peoples usually do not anticipate future events, and solve problems only when they become immediate.

A third change is a willingness to take economic risks and accept new ideas. Traditional peoples generally avoid risk and penalize unconventional behavior. Modern individuals tend to have more economic resources and can afford to take risks. They are more likely to accept new products and ideas readily and to see them as a means of improving their social standing.

CHANGES IN SOCIAL VALUES ■ One of the greatest changes in social values in advanced urban societies is the emphasis on an individual's economic worth instead of on his or her family or seniority. As individuals realize they can influence their social rank by acquiring material possessions, they tend to value economic achievement more highly then family connections or years of service. As they associate individual achievement with personal effort and economic results, they tend to spend more time at work. As their economic position improves, individuals believe more in their abilities to shape their own destinies.

Another change in social values is a greater degree of tolerance. As people move from rural communities with rather narrow views, they alter their outlook on life and grow more tolerant of the wide diversity of opinions found in cities. They gain access to television, radios, newspapers, magazines, and books, which expose them to a wide range of regional, national, and international concerns. For example, urban dwellers are more willing to accept sexual equality than are people in rural areas.

The emphasis on individual economic worth also tends to weaken family values. As people move into cities and find jobs, the kinship patterns of the extended family built up in rural communities tend to fall apart. People no longer feel obliged to live with rel-

atives and to respect and financially support their elders. As kinship ties loosen, obligations to share rewards within the extended family weaken. For example, nepotism (giving jobs to relatives because they are "family") becomes less acceptable. Husbands, wives, and children begin to value social activities outside the family, such as clubs or professional associations.

Overall, the shift to modern values tends to make individuals more tolerant, broad minded, and economically motivated. Tolerance, broad-mindedness, and superior economic motivation are all desirable characteristics in managers.

WHY CULTURAL CHANGE TOWARD MODERNIZATION OCCURS

Cultural change in the direction of modernization is either internally or externally induced. In some countries, internal pressures predominate. For example, the political and economic reforms instituted by Mikhail Gorbachev in the Soviet Union started with a period of open discussion (glasnost, 1985–87). This period was followed by a series of institutional reforms that substituted some free-market principles for centrally controlled market mechanisms and moved one-party rule toward democratic processes. Finally, political and economic change gained momentum.

In other countries, personal values precipitated change. In Poland, Czechoslovakia, and East Germany, populations whose modern political and economic aspirations had been repressed since 1946 demanded and gained economic and political reform during the 1980s.

For most developing countries though, cultural change stems from external sources such as transfers of technology. International businesspeople are heavily involved in this process, because traders and multinational corporations are major vehicles through which production, marketing, and financial technologies are transferred between markets.

Initiating Cultural Change

Cultural change toward modernization is closely tied to transfers of technology and the industrialization that results.

TRANSFERS OF TECHNOLOGY ▪ When developing countries open their borders to trade and investment, they expose their traditional cultures to new consumer and industrial products and services; large-scale, efficiency-oriented manufacturing processes; sophisticated marketing practices (branding, sizing, packaging, promoting, advertising); widespread distribution of products; new technologies; and (through expatriate businesspeople) the consumption patterns of developed markets. Other effects include the advent of vocational training for industrial jobs, and the stimulation of local industries through competition and needs for local sources of raw materials and components.[2] MNC financial institutions contribute by creating local capital markets which enhance savings and make credit available to companies and consumers.

INDUSTRIALIZATION ▪ Cultural change occurs in developing societies as traditional lifestyles come into contact with modern lifestyles during the industrialization and urbanization processes.[3] MNCs and local businesses establish themselves in metropolitan areas because of proximity to seats of government, economically significant consumers, electric power sources, telecommunications

facilities, and labor markets. These urban centers—Buenos Aires, Argentina; Lagos, Nigeria; Bangkok, Thailand; and Sao Paulo, Brazil, for example—attract rural immigrants who settle on the outskirts, often in shanty dwellings. During the rural-to-urban move, old traditions get left behind and new lifestyles are substituted. The extended family is trimmed to the nuclear family, (although extended families often reassemble in towns). The result is overcrowded suburban slums, such as those in Soweto, South Africa, and in Manila, the Philippines. The migrants' economic prosperity becomes dependent on their success in finding employment.

In fast-paced urban societies, there is less time to examine people's family backgrounds, and seniority is often not revered because it is associated with decreased economic productivity. Individual advancement depends on workers making smooth transitions from timeless, agricultural subsistence economies, which require a diversified range of skills, to efficiency-oriented, profit-seeking factory systems, which require a few repetitious specialized skills. These are dramatic, often difficult, changes for migrants.

Sustaining Cultural Change

While industrialization and the resultant cultural change can originate either internally or externally, sustaining these processes depends upon the values of the local population. For ongoing development to occur, a majority of people must desire to change and be motivated to achieve. Ragnar Nurkse summarized this truth in his "Demonstration Effect" theory of economic development:

> When people come into contact with superior goods or superior

patterns of consumption, with new articles or new ways of meeting old wants, they are apt to feel after a while a certain restlessness and dissatisfaction. Their knowledge is extended, their imagination stimulated; new desires are aroused, the propensity to consume is shifted upward. . . . New wants . . . can be important as an incentive, making people work harder and produce more.[4]

In industrializing countries (as happened in the United States from 1870 to 1910), rural dwellers migrate to cities to become part of the urban industrialized system. Migration occurs because rural youths seek to break away from tradition-laden communities (where their futures are fixed by circumstance) to cities, where it is possible for them to gauge their true potentials. Inspired by day-to-day exposures to affluent lifestyles (through advertising and observing conspicuous consumers firsthand), these youths strive to become part of the "monied" society. If all goes well, their commitment produces sufficient financial reward to allow them to purchase the luxury goods and lifestyles that are the hallmarks of economic success. With success acting as positive reinforcement, individuals adjust their sights to the next level of conspicuous consumption. Emulation of economic superiors becomes the prime motivating force for change, for both developing and already-developed societies.[5]

All countries would industrialize if obstacles did not stand in the way. These obstacles are of three types: (1) those concerned with the industrialization process itself, (2) natural conditions preventing industrialization, and (3) human resistance to cultural change.

Impediments in the Industrialization Process

Industrialization does not occur smoothly. First, as has happened in many urban areas of developing countries, the influx of rural migrants occurs too rapidly for their easy absorption into the workforce. In this situation, governments act. In Indonesia, for example, authorities limited migrant flows into Djakarta during the rapid industrialization of the 1960s and early 1970s.[6]

Even when workers find jobs, generally they are not the hoped-for, high-paid jobs, because most migrants are uneducated and qualify only for unskilled work. Although some can upgrade their skills by on-the-job training, most migrants remain in unskilled jobs. As increasing numbers of rural migrants compete for places in the urban workforce, pay levels stay at or near subsistence levels. But throughout this time, television and other media expose migrants to modern lifestyles. Frustration mounts, and violence, alcohol, drug abuse, and vandalism often result.[7]

The regimented discipline of the factory system creates further problems. The cooperative efforts of tribal economies contrast with the urban workforce's rules and penalties for noncompliance, making adjustment difficult. Morale also is hurt by the long work hours and poor working conditions.

Natural Impediments to Industrialization

Two sets of natural problems make industrialization difficult in many countries. The first is the country's geographic makeup; the second is its ethnic and linguistic composition.

GEOGRAPHIC OBSTACLES ■ Countries need two types of resources for industrial development. First, they need *renewable resources* such as crops and other agricultural resources. A good climate (no extreme temperatures, tropical rains, or severe droughts) is essential for orderly transitions from agricultural to industrial economies, and the loss of farm populations in rural-to-urban migrations must be offset by mechanized farming processes.

Relatively few countries, however, have the temperate climates that produce consistent crops year after year. African countries, notably Ethiopia and the Sudan, find it difficult to sustain good harvests. The Middle East and much of central Asia also lack climates suitable for crops, often because of insufficient rain. Excessive rainfall also ruins most grain crops. Countries adapt, however, and in Asia's monsoon climates, wet rice cultivation is the major agricultural pursuit.

Second, countries need *nonrenewable resources* such as coal, energy, and minerals to aid economic development. Countries without such resources have two options. Either they develop very slowly (for example, Chad, Ethiopia, Sudan, Gabon, and Upper Volta), or they secure needed resources through colonization or trade. Raw materials from colonies contributed greatly to Europe's development between the seventeenth and twentieth centuries. Today, trade and investment give countries access to needed raw materials.

It is not enough for countries just to possess mineral resources; these resources must be accessible. Many developing countries have abundant resources, but they are unable to extract them without outside help. Multinational corporations, with their technology, fill this void and have made many natural resources available to world markets. The exploitation of these resources by developed country corporations continues to be a controversial topic in international politics and commerce.

Country size also affects a nation's ability to industrialize and to use market forces to distribute resources. The People's Republic of China and India historically suffered through their inability not only to produce goods and services but also to distribute them over their larger geographic areas. Emergent countries (especially those in geographically spacious Africa) have also had problems coordinating supply and demand because of weak infrastructures. To offset this difficulty, many countries, including Ethiopia and Mozambique, started off with socialist governments, which centralized organization of supply and demand.

Climate and terrain are also important. Inhospitable weather conditions and topographical features (such as deserts and rain forests) affect a country's ability to build infrastructures suitable for local, regional, and international trade. Island economies are special cases. In Britain's and Japan's cases, their island locations encouraged them to go abroad to seek markets and resources. For other countries, such as Indonesia and the Philippines, island status hampers industrialization efforts because of problems in coordinating many thousands of islands.

ETHNIC AND LINGUISTIC OBSTACLES ■ The other natural obstacle to industrialization is cultural diversity within a country's boundaries. Most of the world's lesser-developed countries are multilingual, while most advanced countries are linguistically homogeneous. For multilingual countries to industrialize, there are needs for common means of communication to facilitate the manufacture and distribution of products and services. At the company level, communication is essential in order to coordinate corporate activities. For example, South African mines generally are worked by single tribal and ethnic groups to facilitate coordination. On the national level, in India, and elsewhere in many parts of the world, English is used. Colonial languages are also used in Latin America (Spanish and Portuguese), Africa (French, English, and German) and Asia (English). In other countries, various dialects are blended into a common language. In Zaire, a hundred or so local dialects have been reduced to four major dialects.[8] In still other countries, the dialect of the dominant cultural group becomes a national tongue (Mandarin in China, Shona in Zimbabwe).

Human Resistance to Change

All societies have political, economic, and social power bases. In developing countries, modernization and cultural change threatens traditional power structures. Consequently, some resistance to cultural change is always present.

POLITICAL RESISTANCE ■ The political power base is undermined when countries move away from autocracies and dictatorships and move toward democratic styles of government. Rejected politicians still retain influence, even in democracies. The Philippines experienced these sorts of problems when Corazon Aquino supplanted Ferdinand Marcos. Political backlashes against change have been noticeable elsewhere, too, for example in Russia, where a left-wing Parliament has resisted President Yeltsin's reform efforts.

ECONOMIC RESISTANCE ■ The change from a centrally controlled economy to a market-force economy creates problems for consumers. In Eastern Europe, unrealistic, state-supported prices, which had been stable for decades, rose and created discontent, resulting in anti-reform sentiments. The

lifting of price controls in Poland in 1988 resulted in over 1,000 percent inflation rates during 1988–89.[9]

SOCIAL RESISTANCE ■ One form of social resistance to change is *religious resistance*. Religious resistance is most notable in traditional societies such as those of the Middle East and India. There, religious values stress family cohesiveness, somewhat impeding the rural-to-urban population flow, and urge continuity with the traditions of the past. This tends to weaken the motive for individual economic advancement and make individuals doubt their ability to influence their own destinies.

Another form of social resistance is where *regrouping of extended families in urban settings* takes place, so that wage earners use money to support grandparents and other relatives instead of buying washing machines and other luxury goods that nuclear families can.

Education systems can either resist or encourage change. If the educational system in a developing country stresses science and technology, change can occur at an accelerated pace. If it emphasizes the more traditional subjects of history, literature, philosophy, and music, not only are there shortfalls in developing adequate skills in science and technology, but preoccupation with the past (rather than the future) persist.

A *rigid class system* can also make development difficult. Where family position rather than economic achievement determines personal status, individual motivation to excel economically is downgraded.

Pronounced ethnic or tribal divisions can make it difficult not only to move toward national unity and democratic processes but also to sustain them once they are achieved. Africa's problems have been typical, with much political unrest following the national independence movements of the 1960s. In the mid-1990s, of the 42 mainland states in sub-Saharan Africa, 30 had held democratic elections and only four military rulers remained. Nevertheless, these young democracies have been deemed fragile because of their lack of ethnic unity.[10]

A Look At Japan

In 1945, Japan had been devastated and the future looked bleak.[11] Its geographic characteristics were not encouraging. The country was 65 percent rain forest, it was volcanic, and it had a long history of earthquakes. Only 17 percent of its land was cultivable. It had few energy resources. Traditional religions predominated, and people were ranked mainly according to family background and seniority. Yet despite its unfavorable profile for development, Japan, within three decades, grew to be the world's second largest free-market economy while still maintaining many of its traditions. Its success suggests that there are ways of developing an industrialized, modern society without forsaking national traditions. Some of the keys to Japan's success have been the following.

1. Home market demand was protected by tariffs until the 1970s, by nontariff barriers until the mid-1980s, and thereafter by an impenetrable distribution system. Today, Japanese trading companies (keiretzus) still control import access to the domestic market and hold the keys to the distribution system, which is dominated by small mom and pop stores controlling up to half of Japan's retail sales.

2. Japan industrialized using domestic rather than outside capital (such as capital from MNCs and the World Bank). Tremendous amounts of resources were required, which came from Japanese banks. The sources of these funds were

individual savings. Because Japan has never had a workable retirement system, companies paid annual bonuses to employees, averaging three to six months of annual salary. These were banked, giving Japan the highest per capita savings in the modern world and giving Japanese business plentiful supplies of capital to invest in expansion.

3. Competition within Japan is more product oriented than price oriented.[12] This keeps profit margins high and enables companies and distribution channels to pay (by Western standards) exorbitant employee bonuses. Other forms of competition are also scrupulously managed. The labor market is noncompetitive because of the prevalence of lifelong employment with one firm. The capital market has been noncompetitive, ensuring that savings yield only minimum interest (which is passed on to companies in low interest rates on loans). In 1996, the prime interest rate in Japan dropped to just 1/2 percent to keep capital costs low for companies with capital structures heavily biased toward debt rather than equity. The bias against internal competition is a reflection of the Buddhist and Shinto philosophies emphasizing social harmony and national cohesion.

4. Finally, to plan and integrate national economic efforts, the Ministry of International Trade (MITI) and the Ministry of Finance combined to choreograph Japanese industrial policy. They replaced natural market forces and the stock market in determining the allocation of financial resources.

Nevertheless, the Japanese economy, while robust, is vulnerable. Severe price competition has the potential to reduce company bonuses and personal savings, boost interest rates, and create chaos among debt-laden Japanese companies, whose equity and stocks account for only one-fourth to one-third of company capital. However, Japanese economic development is an excellent example of internally generated growth. This type of development explains why Japan, though industrialized, still manages to maintain many traditional behaviors.

EFFECTS OF CULTURAL CHANGE ON MARKETING

Intercultural or Intracultural Marketing?

Growth, development, and cultural change characterize virtually all societies. Awareness of cultural change provides international marketers with insights on cultural differences *within* countries. For example, in most countries, modern values are associated with urban centers, and traditional values are most frequently found in rural areas. In fact, the major difference between developing and advanced countries is the proportion of modern and traditional populations. Populations of developing nations are about 60 percent rural, 0–20 percent urban, and 20 percent in transition.[13] Less-developed infrastructures (roads, rails, telecommunications) impede the spread and adoption of new technologies. Developed countries are more urban based and have developed infrastructures that speed the diffusions of new products and technologies throughout markets.

Most marketing activities focus on adjustment problems as products and marketing move between cultures (between nations, or intercultural marketing). Often, in urban markets worldwide, sufficient similarities between consumers of different nations exist for marketers to standardize some marketing strategies worldwide ("global marketing"). In *intracultural marketing*, however, dealing with modern and traditional sectors poses problems for marketers within countries, especially when product sales expand into rural areas, where cultural diversity is greatest. Intracultural marketing is of the greatest importance for companies offering a mix of products and services to all segments within a market. These companies must manufacture products to appeal to both modern and traditional segments. Since rural populations are the more culturally diverse, customized products (and heavy adaptation of transferred products) become necessary (multilocal marketing). Urban markets, on the other hand, require fewer product changes to make them compatible with market and customer preferences.[14]

Changes in Marketing Institutions and Practices

Marketing processes become more sophisticated as countries develop. As Table 3–4 shows, economies based on agriculture and production of raw materials perform mainly a single marketing function—exchange. As economies mature and markets expand to regional, national, and international dimensions, marketers concern themselves more with physical distribution. Up to this point, national aggregate demand outstrips a country's supply capacity (as in developing countries and in Eastern Europe), and marketers are able to sell whatever they produce. This is typically called a *seller's market*. As mass production appears, the need for mass-market promotions emerges.

Modern marketing has its origins in economies where supply potential exceeds

TABLE 3–4 ▪ *Ranges in Marketing Functions as Countries Industrialize*

	Stage	Substage	Examples	Market Functions
Preindustrial economies	Agricultural and raw materials (Mk. (f) = prod.)*	Self-sufficient	Nomadic or hunting tribes	None
		Surplus commodity producer	Agricultural economy, such as coffee and bananas	Exchange
Industrializing economies	Manufacturing (Mk. (f) = prod.)	Small scale	Cottage industry	Exchange; physical distribution
Fully industrialized economies	Marketing (Prod. (f) = mk.)**	Commercial-transition	U.S. economy 1915–1929	Demand creation; physical distribution; market information
		Mass distribution	U.S. economy 1950 to present	Demand creation; physical distribution; market and product planning and development

*Mk (f) = prod.: Marketing is a function of production.
**Prod. (f) = mk = Production is a function of marketing.

*Source:*Philip R. Cateora, *International Marketing*, 6th ed. (Homewood, Ill.: Richard D. Irwin, 1987), 307. Reproduced with permission.

existing demand. This is typically called a *buyer's market*. Competition intensifies as rival producers compete for customer patronage. Tailoring output to customer needs becomes essential. Market information and the planning of markets and products become important.

Company marketing functions increase with economic development. When modern corporations venture into developing countries, they bring with them sophisticated marketing techniques. Some of these methods are beneficial in developing a country's marketing strategies. One study of product strategies in less-developed countries found that 7 out of 10 adaptations made to non-durable consumer goods were nonessential

and were made to make products fit prevailing market conditions better.[15]

However, some marketers misuse modern marketing methods. Nestle was one of many MNCs distributing infant formula in developing countries. Controversy arose about whether it was appropriate to market the product in poor economies, where breast-feeding not only was customary but also provided superior infant nutrition. Also, infant formula mixes required water, and contaminated water in some developing countries caused infant deaths.[16]

Creating demand in undeveloped markets has also been subject to criticism. Ritz cracker advertisements in Mexico encouraged illiterate, shoeless peasants to buy the product.[17] In many countries, governments protect consumers from overzealous marketers. In Europe, numerous media restrictions protect special consumer groups such as children. In India, there are laws guarding against sizing descriptions such as "giant," "jumbo," or "king" size. Similarly, to prevent consumer confusion over multiple sizings of products, governments in Kenya, Singapore, Malaysia, and Ecuador require manufacturers to produce standard-sized goods (for example, 250 cc and 500 cc bottles and 100-gram and 250-gram packets.)[18]

Changes in Consumer Behavior

As consumers become modernized, their consumption patterns change.[19] They come into contact with mass retailers, branded products, mass-media promotions, and greater varieties in stores and products.

There are pressures to change their consumption behaviors. Table 3–5 summarizes consumer adjustments to shopping and consumption habits.

Purchasing roles change as families acquire more purchasing power and buy more products. Instead of males making most purchasing decisions, women become more involved in day-to-day decisions (for food items) and in big-ticket decisions (such as refrigerators and stoves). Where women work outside the home, husbands may become involved in routine grocery shopping.

Sources of information change as consumers are exposed to more mass media. Commercial media become sources of useful information on the ever-increasing number of products and brands. Personal sources of information diminish in importance.

Brands, unimportant in traditional societies, increase in importance as manufacturers seek to differentiate similar products.

TABLE 3–5 ▪ *Changes in Consumption Habits and Behaviors*

	Traditional	Modern
Purchasing roles	Female dominant on day-to-day items; male dominant on big-ticket items	Joint decision making on most products and services
Sources of information	Personal sources	Commercial sources
Branding	Not important in product choice (waste of resources)	Important in discriminating among products
Labor-saving products	Unimportant; adversely considered (home cooking is best)	Very important
Product purchasing and retail habit	Mostly at local stores	Mostly at mass merchandisers (supermarkets, department stores)
Merchandising (advertising, point-of-purchase displays, "specials")	Unimportant	Very important
Packaging	Wasteful, excessive, not important	Important

Source: Jose F. Medina, "The Impact of Modernization on Developing Nation Consumption Patterns—The Case of Mexico" (Ph.D. diss., University of Alabama, 1989). Used with author's permission.

Initially, product variety and multiple sizes confuse traditional consumers. As consumers become more experienced, their ability to distinguish between brands sharpens.

Labor-saving household durables (such as refrigerators, stoves, and microwave ovens) and nondurable items (such as canned goods, dried "instant" foods, and frozen goods) become popular as numbers of working women increase. These goods change shopping habits and consumption patterns and give women time to become wage earners. Traditional homemakers have less need for labor-saving gadgets and generally regard home-cooked meals as superior to commercially prepared foods.

Retail outlets develop and consumption patterns change as consumers begin to shop at supermarkets, department stores, and specialty shops. Increased ownership of refrigerators and cars makes for less frequent shopping. Fewer trips are made to the local store, and socializing becomes less important in shopping.

Merchandising and packaging, basic components of modern retailing, are no longer viewed as superfluous. Whereas traditional consumers see in-store promotions, displays, and prepackaged products as expensive and unnecessary expenditures, modern consumers look upon merchandising and package displays as sources of useful information.

Differences in the purchasing habits of developing countries have been examined. In a study of upper-class and lower-class consumption patterns in Sao Paulo, Brazil, it was found that the upper classes (who are generally modern consumers) are more likely to buy durable goods from specialty stores, department stores, and supermarkets; use cash and credit cards; gain product information from print media; and use cars as their primary mode of transportation. Lower classes (who are generally traditional consumers) buy most of their durable goods from street vendors and discount houses and gain product information chiefly from television advertising and friends. They value credit as the most important retailer service, and they use buses and streetcars as their primary modes of transportation.[20]

SUMMARY

The majority of countries in the international marketplace are classified as "developing," a fact that makes cultural change a vital topic in world marketing. The fact that change is not uniform means that in any given country, marketers must understand both traditional and modern consumers. In developing markets, traditional consumers are the more numerous, and in advanced countries, modern consumers dominate.

Cultural change includes changes in political systems (from autocracies to democracies) and changes in economic systems (from centrally controlled economies to market economies) and in the level of economic development (from developing to developed status). Cultural change also includes social changes, such as the shift from customs and religious laws to legal codes as major controls over personal behavior. Changing multilingual societies develop means of communication among ethnic groups (such as colonial languages and dialects of the dominant cultural group). These institutional changes are accompanied by changes in economic, political, and social values.

Cultural change toward modernization may be internally generated through changes in political and economic philosophies (as with glasnost and perestroika in Eastern Europe) or in values (for example, popular demands for democratic processes and market economies). Change is frequently initiated through multinational corporations and technology transfers (trade, investments, and lifestyles).

In developing countries, change usually occurs slowly and is resisted. Some obstacles are natural, such as geographical characteristics (size, climate, terrain) and ethnic composition (many cultural groups). Other obstacles are human, as people object to the erosion of traditional political, economic, and social power bases. Economic change affects marketing functions, such as those creating demand and planning products, and modern marketing techniques sometimes confuse less-sophisticated consumers. Social change affects religion, the family, education, and the class system.

DISCUSSION QUESTIONS

1. Using Table 3–3, discover your own values. Are you predominantly modern, traditional, or a mixture of both orientations?

2. Compare and contrast urban-rural attitudes and behaviors in a country of your choice. (In the United States, you might contrast behaviors in New York with those of a small town in the South).

3. Do you think that cultural differences between nations are more or less important than cultural variations within nations? Under what circumstances is each important?

4. What do you think will happen if or when the Japanese market is truly opened up to foreign influences?

Westernization and Islamic Societies: Iran

Iran has been an Islamic country for hundreds of years, even when it was known as Persia. It became a fundamentalist Muslim Shi'ite society in 1979 when the shah was overthrown and the Ayatollah Khomeini became Iran's leader. The shah and the ruling elite had allowed women to throw off their veils and black headcoverings; alcohol was consumed openly; and immodest western apparel became permissible.

Declaring, "There is no fun in Islam," the Ayatollah Khomeini unleashed the powerful Ministry of Islamic Culture and Guidance to purge Iran of unwanted western influence. The years 1980–88 saw a holy war against Sunni-dominated Iraq.

But slowly, and especially under reform-oriented president Hashemi Rafsanjani, the culture pendulum swung back away from the religious hard-liners. Technology began to assert itself. VCRs were targets for outright bans but then survived, as the government set up a video store chain to distribute mullah-approved videos. But the biggest challenge to Shi'ite philosophies came in the form of Beavis and Butthead, as satellite television and MTV came to Iran. "The enemy's culture blitz is more dangerous than guns, tanks and missiles," declared Mahmood Mohammedi-Araqi, the head of the Islamic Propagation Origination. Technology, wrote Iran's highest ranking cleric, the Grand Ayatollah Mohammed Ali Araki, spreads "the family-devastating diseases of the West" and infects Islam with "cheap alien culture." Ayatollah Khomenei feared "the absence of moral restraints," and pointed the finger at the U.S. as "the big Satan" initiating the all-out offensive against Islam.

Change is occurring. The general consensus has been that the mullahs have allowed more self-expression and political participation, especially of the press and the parliament, than did the shah. In the trend-setting capital, Tehran, satellite dishes are common, and many Iranians are fascinated by American sitcoms; racy Turkish, Indian, and Israeli films; and rap videos. Teenagers in particular have been influenced by MTV, and some have gotten themselves arrested deliberately by flaunting western fashions and doing "western things" (such as being alone with a member of the opposite gender).

The mullahs do what they can to arrest the tide of westernization. Crowd scenes from the U.S.-based World Cup soccer tournament were censored, and winter soccer-fan scenes (with mufflers and winter coats) were substituted for miniskirts and halter tops.

QUESTIONS:

1. To what extent do you think that Western sitcoms, soap operas, and rap videos corrode societal values in your country? In Iran?

2. Are there any domestic religious groups you know that have similar views to those of Islamic Fundamentalists?

Source: Adapted from Peter Waldman, "Iran fights a New Foe: Western Television," *The Wall Street Journal*, 8 August 1994, A10.

Social Change in Indonesia

Indonesia is an industrializing nation, and it is plagued by the social upheavals brought about by economic change. It has been estimated that 2.1 million people enter the job market each year. Of that number, only 300,000 of them find jobs. Social problems abound in and around the capital of Jakarta as repressed aspirations of the younger generation are channeled into urban crime and violence. For example:

- Tobacco farmers torched 25 warehouses belonging to the state-owned plantation company, PTP.

- Anti-Muslim riots rocked East Timor after a prison official allegedly called Catholicism "a nonsense religion."

- Protesters burned 100 houses and a radio station owned by paper-maker Indorayan Utama after rumors of a company gas leak. MSG maker Cheil Samsung had similar problems after allegations of polluting local shrimp ponds. A carbon manufacturing plan in West Jakarta was burned to the ground following allegations of polluting the local neighborhood.

Many Indonesians have benefited from industrialization. But the 14 million middle class is dwarfed in the context of the 190 million total population. Over half of the 7 million unemployed are between 15–25 years old. What makes matters worse is the increasing concentration of wealth. About 80 percent of the country's top 400 companies are controlled by 20 conglomerates, many owned by ethnic Chinese groups that constitute just 3 percent of the Indonesian population. Riots followed after rumors that a Muslim girl accused of shoplifting had been manhandled at a Chinese-owned department store. There were similar problems after an ethnic Chinese man was fatally beaten for tearing pages out of the Koran. Indonesia is predominately Muslim.

The farming community was upset when 2,000 hectares of government land, previously farmed by rural peasants, was transferred to a state-run plantation company. In 1995, a local government decision to double land taxes aroused severe discontentment. Problems related to land tenure and labor relations accounted for 75 percent of grievances addressed to the Indonesian Parliament.

A root cause of discontent has been the lack of government responsiveness to the problems caused by rapid industrialization. President Suharto has been in power for over 30 years. The May 1997 elections were seen as a referendum on government handling of the situation.

QUESTIONS

1. If you were President Suharto, what pre-election measures would you take to try to rectify the situation?

2. To what extent do you think these upheavals are inevitable parts of the industrialization process?

Source: Adapted from John McBeth, "Indonesia: Social Dynamite," *Far Eastern Economic Review,* 15 February 1996, 20–22.

ENDNOTES

1. This discussion is based on the following works: Alex Inkeles, "The Modernization of Man," in *Modernization: The Dynamics of Growth*, ed. M. Weiner (New York: Basic Books, 1966); Alex Inkeles and David M. Smith, *Becoming Modern: Individual Change in Six Countries* (Cambridge, Mass.: Harvard University Press, 1976); Joseph A Kahl, *The Measurement of Modernism: A Study of Values in Brazil and Mexico* (Austin, Tex.: University of Texas Press, 1969); Leonard W. Doob, "Scales for Assaying Psychological Modernization in Africa," *Public Opinion Quarterly* 30 (1967): 414–21; Alan Peshkin and Ronald Cohen, "The Values of Modernization," *Journal of Developing Areas* 2 (1967): 7–22; Daniel Lerner, *The Passing of Traditional Society: Modernizing the Middle East* (London: Collier-MacMillan Ltd., 1958); Alejandro Porter, "The Factorial Structure of Modernity: Empirical Replication and a Critique," *American Journal of Sociology* 79 (1973): 15–44; and Everett M. Rogers, *Diffusion of Innovations* (New York: Free Press, 1962). The material was brought together in Jose F. Medina, "The Impact of Modernization on Developing Nation Consumption Patterns—The Case of Mexico" (Ph.D. diss., University of Alabama, 1989).

2. James Brian Quinn, "Technology Transfer by Multinational Companies," *Harvard Business Review* 47 (November–December 1969): 146–61; H.B. Thorelli, "The Multinational Corporation as a Change Agent," *Southern Journal of Business* 1 (July 1966): 1–9; and Harry G. Johnson, "The Multinational Corporation as a Development Agent," *Columbia Journal of World Business* 5 (May–June 1970): 25–30.

3. Much of the following section is taken from John S. Hill and Richard R. Still, "Cultural Effects of Technology Transfer by Multinational Corporations in Lesser Developed Countries," *Columbia Journal of World Business* 15 (Summer 1980): 40–51.

4. Ragnar Nurkse, *Problems of Capital Formation in Underdeveloped Countries* (New York: Oxford University Press, 1953), 58–59, 63.

5. It should be noted that Duesenberry's original application of the demonstration effect was to economically advanced societies. See James Duesenberry, *Income Savings and the Theory of Consumer Behavior* (Cambridge, Mass.: Harvard University Press, 1949).

6. Richard Critchfield, "The Plight of the Cities: Djakarta The First to Close," *Columbia Journal of World Business* 6, no. 4 (July–August 1971): 89–93.

7. Hill and Still, "Cultural Effects of Technology Transfer," 43. See endnote 3.

8. Vern Terpstra and Kenneth David, *Cultural Environment of International Business*, 3rd ed. (Cincinnati, Ohio: South Western Publishing, 1991), 27.

9. International Monetary Fund, Poland, *International Financial Statistics* 43, no. 2 (February 1990): 432–33.

10. "Guns and Votes," *Economist*, 29 June 1996, 41.

11. Adapted from John S. Hill, "The Japanese Business Puzzle—or Why the Japanese Market is Protected, and Likely to Stay That Way," *Journal of General Management* 15, no. 3 (Spring 1990): 20–38.

12. Raphael Elimelech, "Pricing Japanese Success," *Management Today*, May 1980, 84–89.

13. Based on John S. Hill, "Targeting Promotions in Lesser-Developed Countries: A Study of Multinational Corporation Strategies," *Journal of Advertising* 13, no. 4 (1984): 39–48.

14. John S. Hill and Richard R. Still, "Effects of Urbanization on Multinational Product Planning: Markets in Lesser-Developed Countries," *Columbia Journal of World Business* 19 (Summer 1984): 62–67.

15. John S. Hill and Richard R. Still, "Adapting Products to LDC Tastes," *Harvard Business Review* 62 (March–April 1984): 92–102.

16. Richard J. Barnet and Ronald E. Muller, *Global Reach* (New York: Simon and Schuster, 1974), 173; also see their Chapter 6, "The Global Corporations and the Underdeveloped World."

17. Ibid.

18. Hill and Still, "Adapting Products to LDC Tastes," 95. See endnote 15.

19. This section was adapted from Jose F. Medina, "The Impact of Modernization on Developing Nation Consumption Patterns—The Case of Mexico" (Ph.D. diss., University of Alabama, Tuscaloosa, 1989).

20. William H. Cunningham, Russell M. Moore, and Isabella Cunningham, "Urban Markets in Industrializing Countries: The Sao Paulo Experience," *Journal of Marketing* 38 (April 1974): 2–12.

CHAPTER

4

The Financial Environment of International Marketing

Chapter Outline

Exchange Rates

Balance-of-Payments Principles and Supply and Demand for Currencies

Effects of Currency Realignments on World Marketing Practices and Global Business Strategies

Foreign Exchange Controls

Other Financial Forces Affecting International Marketing Operations

Case 4–1: Marketing in Adverse Economic Climates: Procter and Gamble in Latin America

Case 4–2: Transfer Pricing Controversies

Learning Objectives

When you have mastered the contents of this chapter, you will be able to do the following:

1 Explain what exchange rates are, their importance to world marketing, the types of exchange rate arrangements between countries, and how and why exchange rates change.

2 Describe the effects of currency alignments on international marketing strategy and on global business strategy generally, and the ways managers can protect their companies from exchange-rate losses.

3 Discuss the different forms of foreign exchange controls and how these affect the marketing function.

4 Analyze the impact of financial forces such as taxation and inflation on world marketing.

EXCHANGE RATES

What Are Exchange Rates?

Exchange rates, simply put, are the prices of currencies in terms of other currencies. The U.S. dollar is the world's most dominant currency, reflecting the importance of the United States in international business affairs. Exchange rates are expressed in one of two interrelated ways. The first (and most usual way in the American context) is the number of foreign currency units that one U.S. dollar will buy. This number varies by country and over time. For example, in Table 4–1, 34 Belgian francs or 122 Japanese yen may be exchanged for 1 U.S. dollar.

The international marketer must be knowledgeable about exchange rates, because all products and services bought and sold on international markets have "two prices or costs." These are the price of the product in the home-market currency and the product's price in foreign currency. Movements in exchange rates therefore directly affect foreign market prices. When a Japanese company, for instance, is contemplating selling in the U.S. market, it must consider not only the price of its product in yen but also what the price will be in U.S. dollars. This consideration involves understanding how the yen's value rises and falls vis-à-vis the U.S. dollar.

Consider the following example. Assume that Toyota makes cars in Japan and exports them to the United States and that it costs 600,000 yen to make a stripped-down Tercel in Japan. Assume now at time T_1 that U.S.\$1.00=¥150 and that the landed cost in the U.S. is \$4,000. What happens if the yen changes (indeed appreciates) in value against the U.S. dollar? Assume that at time T_2, U.S.\$1.00 = ¥100. If at T_1, the Tercel had been priced at \$8,000 on the U.S. market, this would yield a \$4,000 margin, or 600,000 yen at 150 yen per dollar. At T_2, the landed cost would be \$6,000 (600,000/100 yen per dollar), and the car would have to be priced at \$12,000 to get the same return in yen. Thus, the marketing decision makers at Toyota must decide whether to maintain the price around \$8,000 and reduce their profit (in yen) by ¥400,000, or raise the price to \$12,000 to maintain the same ¥1,200,000 return, or perhaps go partway, for example by raising the price to \$10,000 (¥1,000,000). The point is clear—Toyota's potential profits in the U.S. export market are affected dramatically by fluctuations in the dollar-yen exchange relationship.

The second way to express exchange rates is how many U.S. dollars one unit of a foreign currency will buy. For example, £1 (British pound) in early 1997 equaled about U.S. \$1.63. International financiers deal currencies in both ways, depending on the currencies being exchanged. Table 4–1 shows exchange rate quotations as they appear daily in *The Wall Street Journal*.

Exchangeability of Currencies: Convertible (Hard) Currencies and Inconvertible (Soft) Currencies

Not all currencies are freely exchangeable (convertible) into all other currencies. The majority of country exchange rates have only limited convertibility into other currencies. Some currencies, like the Russian ruble as of 1996, have limited convertibility outside of their national borders. Currencies that are not acceptable to nonresidents of the country issuing them are big obstacles to all commercial transactions. One major objective of Eastern European states is to make their

TABLE 4–1 ■ *Selected Exchange Rates, 7 February 1997*

The New York foreign exchange selling rates below apply to trading among banks in amounts of $1 million and more, as quoted at 4 PM Eastern time by Dow Jones Telerate, Inc., and other sources. Retail transactions provide fewer units of foreign currency per dollar.

Country	U.S. $ Equiv		Currency per U.S. $	
	Fri	Thurs	Fri	Thurs
Argentina (Peso)	1.0012	1.0012	.9988	.9988
Australia (Dollar)	.7620	.7646	1.3123	1.3079
Austria (Schilling)	.08561	.08595	11.681	11.634
Bahrain (Dinar)	2.6525	2.6525	.3770	.3770
Belgium (Franc)	.02922	.02935	34.225	34.075
Brazil (Real)	.9550	.9552	1.0471	1.0469
Britain (Pound)	1.6300	1.6341	.6135	.6120
30-Day Forward	1.6291	1.6332	.6138	.6123
90-Day Forward	1.6270	1.6312	.6146	.6131
180-Day Forward	1.6241	1.6281	.6157	.6142
Canada (Dollar)	.7404	.7409	1.3506	1.3497
30-Day Forward	.7417	.7423	1.3482	1.3471
90-Day Forward	.7448	.7453	1.3427	1.3418
180-Day Forward	.7490	.7495	1.3352	1.3343
Chile (Peso)	.002396	.002395	417.35	417.60
China (Renminbi)	.1202	.1202	8.3216	8.3216
Colombia (Peso)	.0009339	.009329	1070.80	1071.88
"	"	"	"	"
Germany (Mark)	.6030	.6053	1.6583	1.6522
30-Day Forward	.6040	.6063	1.6555	1.6494
90-Day Forward	.6065	.6088	1.6488	1.6426
180-Day Forward	.6103	.6126	1.6385	1.6324
Greece (Drachma)	.003842	.003853	260.26	259.55
Hong Kong (Dollar)	.1291	.1290	7.7470	7.7490
Hungary (Forint)	.005824	.005845	171.70	171.09
India (Rupee)	.02788	.02787	35.872	35.875
Indonesia (Rupiah)	.0004205	.0004204	2377.88	2377.25
Japan (Yen)	.008135	.008079	122.93	123.78
Jordan (Dinar)	1.4094	1.4094	.7095	.7095
Kuwait (Dinar)	3.3047	3.3047	.3026	.3026
"	"	"	"	"
Poland (Zloty)	.3317	.3332	3.0152	3.0015
Portugal (Escudo)	.005959	.006020	167.81	166.10
Russia (Ruble)(a)	.0001774	.0001775	5636.00	5634.00
Saudi Arabia (Riyal)	.2666	.2666	3.7505	3.7505
SDR	1.3852	1.3897	.7219	.7196
ECU	1.1710	1.1754		

Note: Special drawing rights (SDR) are based on exchange rates for the U.S., German, British, French, and Japanese currencies. The European Currency Unit (ECU) is based on a basket of community currencies. *Source:* International Monetary Fund.

Source: The Wall Street Journal, 10 February 1997, C13.

currencies acceptable to foreign states (that is, to make them convertible into foreign currencies) by the year 2000.

Hard, or *convertible*, currencies are those that are acceptable to sellers as means of payment for goods and services. Generally, these are the most popularly traded world currencies, such as the dollar, yen, pound sterling, French franc, Swiss franc, and deutsche mark. These are the currencies of countries that are prolific traders and that have generally strong economies. Few or no problems are met in changing dollars for yen, pounds into deutsche marks, or Swiss francs into French francs.

Soft, or *convertible*, currencies are those that one party to an international transaction refuses to accept in exchange for its own. Developing countries often have inconvertible currencies; for example, the Ecuadorean sucre and Thai baht are inconvertible currencies. One reason why currencies of these and other countries are unacceptable to foreigners is that domestic inflation constantly causes the local currency to lose its value. That is, increasing amounts of the currency must be exchanged against the dollar (with the dollar being worth "more" and each unit of the local currency being worth "less"). Being paid in local currencies means that if any delays are encountered in exchanging into dollars (or other hard currencies), losses are likely to be incurred.

Some currencies become partially convertible as governments allow some exchange of local currencies back into hard currencies (at currency auctions, as Russia had, or for government-blessed projects). Currencies become fully convertible under two conditions: first, as they become prolific traders in world markets; second, as their exchange rates stabilize against world currencies. The year 1996 saw efforts by both Poland and China PRC to make their currencies (the zloty and reminbi) convertible.

Inconvertible currencies produce many problems for international business people.

Most soft currencies belong to industrializing countries that import more than they export. If these countries cannot consistently pay their import bills in hard currencies, they build up chronic debts (for example, Brazil and Mexico). The hard currencies these countries earn from exports to the United States, Europe, and Japan are consistently insufficient to pay their bills for goods imported from those trading partners. When U.S., Japanese, and Western European companies export to developing countries, those nations often do not have enough hard currency to pay the invoices. When this happens, companies desiring prompt payment have three options:

1. Accept the inconvertible currency and either keep it in the importing country (in banks or in investments), or try to exchange it using unofficial channels such as foreign banks. Using unofficial intermediaries, even if currencies are convertible, often means exchanging at a loss.

2. Wait in line with other foreign traders (sometimes for weeks or months) until enough hard currencies are earned so that payment can be made.

3. Accept local goods in payment as part of a barter arrangement. To determine the acceptability of goods (for example, to a U.S. exporter unable to get payment out of Malaysia), the exporter would scrutinize U.S. imports from Malaysia and identify an item that could be easily disposed of in the United States, such as agricultural produce or commodities such as tin, copper, or oil. Then, the Malaysian debtor would buy a quantity of the item equal to the value of the debt and ship it to the United States, where it would be sold for dollars and the exporter would then be paid.

Exchange-Rate Arrangements: Fixed or Floating Exchange Rates?

Most international business deals result in exchanges of currencies. Agreement on specific exchange rates is necessary to complete an international transaction. This is determined by the relevant exchange rate arrangement under which the transaction falls. Today there are 10 major types of exchange rate arrangements. Each arrangement has a fixed and a floating component, depending on the currencies being exchanged.

1 CURRENCIES FIXED TO THE U.S. DOLLAR

■ As of 30 September 1996, 20 countries pegged their currencies to the U.S. dollar. As Table 4–2 shows, most of these are in the Caribbean and Central and South America, but some are in Africa (Nigeria, Djibouti, and Liberia), the Middle East, and Asia (Syria, Iraq, and Oman). These countries peg their currencies to the U.S. dollar either because the United States is their major trading partner or because the countries prefer the security of being attached to a premier world currency. In financial dealings with the U.S., there are no exchange-rate uncertainties.

Fixed exchange rates help to stabilize commercial relations with major trading partners, but they also affect trade with third-party nations. When a currency appreciates in value (as the U.S. dollar did in early 1997), export prices rise, and it is more difficult to sell American-made products abroad. Likewise, nations with currencies pegged to the U.S. dollar have problems exporting to countries against whose currencies the U.S. dollar has appreciated. On the other hand, when the dollar weakens against European and Japanese currencies, not only is it easier for the United States to export to these countries, but also, all countries pegged to the dollar find their export prices becoming more competitive in the European and Japanese markets.

2 CURRENCIES FIXED TO THE FRENCH FRANC

■ Fourteen countries, all in formerly French-dominated North and West Africa, have currencies pegged to the French franc. This arrangement minimizes exchange-rate uncertainties between these countries and their major trading partner, France. It also lends some stability to exports to other markets in the European Community, as the French franc is, to varying degrees, itself pegged to other European currencies.[1]

3 CURRENCIES PEGGED TO OTHER CURRENCIES

■ A few countries are so closely linked to others (often geographically and commercially) that they peg their currency to that country. Kiribati relies so heavily on the Australian market for trade that it pegs its currency to the Australian dollar. Similarly, the undeveloped economies of Swaziland, Namibia, and Lesotho direct most of their external trade either to South Africa or through South African ports, and their currencies are pegged to the South African rand.

Many countries, however, have multiple trading partners with whom they prefer to maintain stable exchange rates. These countries are in a *composite currency arrangement*. This type of arrangement entails pegging a currency's value to a number of other currencies and weighting those values according to how much trade occurs between them and the host country. This process is illustrated in the fourth and fifth arrangements.

4 CURRENCIES PEGGED TO SPECIAL DRAWING RIGHTS (SDRS) ▪ The special drawing right (SDR) is a general composite currency made up of five other currencies, weighted according to their importance in world trade and finance. SDRs are comprised of the following: 40 percent U.S. dollar; 22 percent German deutsch mark; 17 percent Japanese yen; and 11 percent each the French franc and British pound. Countries such as Libya and Myanmar peg their currencies to the SDR because the "Big Five" are their major trading partners. The SDR also is fairly stable. For example, when the dollar's value fluctuates against the values of other major currencies, such as the yen or the pound, these often partially offset each other (that is, when one appreciates, another depreciates). The result is little movement in the home currency's value.

5 CURRENCIES PEGGED TO OTHER COMPOSITES ▪ There has been a steady decrease in the number of countries pegging their currencies to baskets of currencies of their own choosing (from 35 in 1990 to 20 in 1996). Countries use this arrangement because it gives them some flexibility in which nations it selects to be part of its currency-basket arrangement. It is easy to change both the composition of the currency basket and the relative weightings of currencies; Thailand's basket, for example, comprises the dollar, some European currencies, and the Japanese yen. But, as with the SDR, movements within the basket have helped to stabilize the Thai baht's value in international markets.

6 FLEXIBILITY LIMITED IN TERMS OF A SINGLE CURRENCY ▪ Values of four Middle Eastern currencies have shown limited flexibility in U.S. dollars. These countries (Bahrain, Qatar, Saudi Arabia, and United Arab Emirates) are all oil producers. Because the international price of oil is quoted in U.S. dollars, oil revenues can be calculated in local currencies, and economic planning (which depends very much on imports) is made easier. The only recent adjustments these countries have made against the U.S. dollar occurred during the strong-dollar period in the early 1980s, when adjustments were made to maintain these countries' international purchasing power against other world currencies and to offset the strong rise in import prices.

7 FLEXIBILITY LIMITED IN TERMS OF A GROUP OF CURRENCIES' COOPERATIVE ARRANGEMENTS: THE "EUROPEAN SNAKE." ▪ The aim of the European Union is to foster trade between member countries, so it is important for exchange rates to be fairly predictable. Hence, in the Cooperative European Arrangement, the 10 currencies involved maintain fixed values relative to one another, values that respective host governments are pledged to uphold through currency buying and selling. The European Monetary System (EMS as it is known) suffered some setbacks during 1992–93 when high German interest rates attracted much foreign capital to aid the industrialization of the former East Germany. These capital insurges increased demand for the mark and caused it to appreciate in value. This put pressure on other European currencies to maintain their agreed upon ± 2.25 percent parity value with the mark. The UK and Italy were unwilling to have their currencies increase in value to keep pace with the mark, so both withdrew from the EMS in 1992. The appreciating German mark continued in 1993,

TABLE 4–2 ■ *Exchange Rate Arrangements for 181 World Currencies*

Currency Pegged to a Single Currency or Basket of Currencies

US $ (20)	French Franc (14)	Other Currency (9)	SDR (2)	Other composite (20)
Antigua & Barbuda	Benin	Bhutan (India rupee)	Libya	Bangladesh
Argentina	Burkina Faso		Myanmar	Botswana
Bahama	Cameroon	Bosnia and		Burundi
Barbados	C. African Rep	Herzegovina		Cape Verde
Belize	Chad	(Deutsche mark)		Cyprus
		Brunei Darussalam		
Djibouti	Comoros	(Singapore		Czech Republic
Dominica	Congo	Dollar)		Fiji
Grenada	Cote d'Ivoire	Estonia		Iceland
Iraq	Equatorial	(Deutsche mark)		Jordan
Liberia	Guinea	Kiribati		Kuwait
	Gabon	(Australian		
Lithuania		Dollar)		Malta
Marshall Island	Mali			Morocco
Micronesia	Niger	Lesotho		Nepal
Fed. States of	Senegal	(South African		Seychelles
Nigeria	Togo	rand)		Slovak
Oman		Namibia		Republic
		(South African		
Panama		rand)		Solomon
St. Kitts & Nevis		San Marino		Islands
St. Lucia		(Italian lira)		Thailand
St. Vincent				
and the		Swaziland		Tonga
Grenadines		(South African rand)		Vanuatu
Syrian Arab				Western Samoa
Rep.				

*Source:*Adapted from International Monetary Fund, *International Financial Statistics*, (Washington, D.C.: International Monetary Fund, 1997), 8.

Flexibility limited to one or few currencies		More Flexible		
Single (4)	**Multiple (10)**	**Adjusted for inflation (2)**	**Managed Float (46)**	**Independently Floating (54)**
Bahrain	Austria	Chile	Algeria	Afghanistan Islamic State
Qatar	Belgium	Nicaragua	Angola	
Saudi Arabia	France		Belarus	Albania
United Arab Emirates	Denmark		Brazil	Armenia
	Germany		Cambodia	Australia
				Azerbaijan
	Ireland		China, P.R.	
	Luxembourg		Colombia	Bolivia
	Netherlands		Costa Rica	Bulgaria
	Portugal		Croatia	Canada
	Spain		Dominican Rep.	Ethiopia
				Finland
			Equador	Gambia, The
			Egypt	Ghana
			El Salvador	Guatemala
			Eritrea	Guinea
			Georgia	Guyana
			Greece	Haiti
			Guinea-Bissau	India
			Honduras	Italy
			Hungary	Jamaica
			Indonesia	Japan
			Iran I.R. of	Kazakstan
			Israel	Kenya
			Korea	Lao P.D. Rep
			Kyrgyz Rep.	Lebanon
			Latvia	Madagascar
			Macedonia (FYR of)	Malawi
			Malaysia	Mauritania
			Malaysia	Mexico
			Maldives	Moldova
				Mongolia
				Mauritius
			Norway	Mozambique
			New Zealand	
			Pakistan	Papua New Guinea
			Poland	Paraguay
			Russia	Peru
			Singapore	Philippines
			Slovenia	
			Romania	Rwanda
			Sri Lanka	Sao Tome and Principe
			Sudan	Sierra Leone
			Suriname	Somalia
			Tunisia	South Africa
			Turkmenistan	Sweden
			Turkey	Switzerland
			Ukraine	Tajikistan
			Uruguay	Rep. of Tanzania
			Uzbekistan	Trinidad and Tobago
			Venezuela	Uganda
			Vietnam	United Kingdom
				United States
				Yemen
				Republic of Zaire
				Zambia
				Zimbabwe

causing the European monetary authorities to allow ± 15 percent deviations from the agreed-upon par values. Still, some members (notably France) have strained to maintain close stable relationships between their currencies and the German mark.

8 ADJUSTMENTS ACCORDING TO A SET OF ECONOMIC INDICATORS ▪ Chile and Nicaragua have historically had inflation problems. Chile, for example, was expected to bring its inflation rate down to 7 percent in 1996.[2] Because steadily rising prices ruin a country's international price competitiveness, governments periodically devalue currencies to keep export prices at reasonable levels and to prevent imported goods from becoming too price competitive. While the economic indicator used may vary, most indicators are connected to price levels, usually the consumer price index.

9 OTHER MANAGED FLOATS ▪ A managed float occurs when the exchange rates of a currency float against other major currencies but are "managed" through fiscal and monetary controls that a government applies to its domestic economy. Although not officially a managed currency, the U.S. dollar acts like one. When there is good economic news, the dollar strengthens as people buy and increase the demand for dollars. When there is bad economic news, dollar values fall as the currency is sold on the foreign exchange market. The number of countries using this arrangement increased from 23 in 1990 to 46 in 1996.

10 INDEPENDENTLY FLOATING CURRENCIES ▪ Increasing numbers of currencies (including all-important currencies such as the dollar and the yen) float independently against other world currencies, their values being determined by market supply and demand. Under this arrangement, trade, investment, and money flows between two countries determine the exchange rate for their currencies.

BALANCE-OF-PAYMENTS PRINCIPLES AND SUPPLY AND DEMAND FOR CURRENCIES

What constitutes supply and demand for currencies? To understand market forces in currencies, we have to know something about the balance of payments and how it affects currency supply and demand.

Balance of Payments

The balance of payments of a country, simply stated, is an "accounting record of all economic transactions between residents of that nation and foreign residents during some specified time period" (usually a year).[3] The major component of the balance is the International Monetary Fund's (IMF) standard balance-of-payments presentation. It has three sections: (1) current account, (2) capital account, and (3) reserves.

The *current account* consists of four parts. The first part is the *merchandise trade balance* made up of exports and imports. When a country exports more than it imports, it has a trade *surplus*. When it imports more than it exports, it has a trade *deficit*. Generally, the crude trade balance (as it is known) is the most important indicator of a country's competitiveness in international trade.

The second part of the current account is the *goods, services,* and *income balance*, which includes not only exports ("credits," or "inflows" of money) and imports ("debits," or "outflows" of money) but also freight, insurance, and shipping charges [paid out by a country's residents (debits) or received by its residents (credits)]. These two sections comprise the goods and services account.

Third is the income accounts. These are made up of corporate and individual earnings repatriated from the resident country to foreign sources (outflows, or debits); and profit and income repatriations from foreign-based companies and individuals back into the resident country (inflows or credits).

Fourth and finally, there are unrequited (one-time) transfers by governments into and out of the resident country (credits and debits, respectively). Together, these four items comprise the balance of payments on current account.

The *capital account* consists of outflows and inflows of capital for purposes of investment. There are four parts. The first is the capital account. This comprises payments for fixed assets such as machinery and equipment. Credit items are foreign companies bringing equipment into the resident country. Debit payments are resident firms sending machinery from resident to foreign markets. *Direct investments* made in a resident country by foreigners are credits, or inflows; investments abroad made by country residents are debits, or outflows. *Portfolio investment* comprises purchases of securities or corporate equities but without the intent to participate in the company's management. These are usually stock market investments made in foreign markets (outflows, or debits); and those made by foreigners in the resident country (inflows, or credits). Finally, there are currency transactions, such as deposits and loans (generally, money movements among financial institutions). The financial account (item 78bjd on Table 4–3) comprises direct investment, portfolio investment and "other" invest-

ments (i.e., excluding capital account transactions, n.i.e.). Note that capital account items are labeled "assets" and "liabilities." Outgoing investments are capital outflows, which then become "assets" in foreign markets. Incoming investments are inflows but represent foreign "liabilities" in capital accounts.

Net errors and omissions are items that cannot be accommodated under traditional current and capital account labels. The balance of payments on current account (trade + services + income + government transfers) plus capital accounts n.i.e. (machinery and equipment transactions) plus financial accounts (direct, portfolio investments, money movements) plus net errors and omissions comprise the overall balance of payments. Positive balances of trade signify net inflows of foreign payments ("surpluses"); negative numbers are net outflows of money ("deficits"). The reserves and related items accounts show how the surpluses are disposed of (often with additions to foreign convertible currency reserves), or how deficits are financed (usually by decreases in convertible currency held at the International Monetary Fund). Where deficits are large, "exceptional financing" packages are used, and often comprise IMF loans.

Table 4–4 shows the U.S. balance of payments for 1989–95. Note the following:

- The chronic crude trade balance (i.e., exports minus imports), which reached –$171.99 billion in 1995 (item 78 acd). The goals and services balance has been less negative (–$103.87 billion in 1995) and is the more frequently publicized of the two statistics.

- Direct investment abroad by U.S. companies since 1991 has consistently outpaced foreign direct investments in the U.S. (–$95.53 versus $60.23 inflows in 1995).

TABLE 4–3 ■ *Balance of Payments: Standard IMF Presentation*

A. Current Account	Debits	Credits
	Money outflows: Supply of currency leaving the country. U.S.: Conversions from $ into foreign currencies.	*Money Inflows*: Demand for currency. U.S.: Foreign currencies converted into dollars ("creating for demand").
1. Goods	Imports fob: 78 abd Paid for in home currency then converted to foreign currency	Exports fob: 78aad Paid for in foreign currency then converted into home currency
Trade balance (78acd)	Exports (78aad) - Imports (78abd) Exports > Imports: Balance of trade *surplus* Imports > Exports: balance of trade *deficit*	
2. Services	Freight, insurance, etc., paid out to foreigners (78aed)	Freight, insurance, etc., paid to residents (78add)
Balance on goods and services (78afd)	Money inflows from goods and services *minus* money outflows from goods and services	
3. Income	Repatriated earnings of individual's incomes and corporate profits *out of* country by foreigners/foreign corporations (78ahd)	Repatriated earnings of individual incomes and corporate profits *into* country by residents/companies abroad (78agd)
Balance of goods, services, and income (78aid)	Money inflows from goods, services, and income	*minus* money outflows from goods, services, and income
4. Government transfers (unrequited)	Paid by resident government to foreigners (78akd)	Made by foreign governments to resident country (78ajd)
Balance of Payments on Current Account: 1+2+3+4: 78 ald		

The reverse is true for portfolio transactions, where investments in the U.S. stock market were $192.38 billion, against $98.96 billion invested by Americans in foreign stocks and shares in 1995.

- As capital inflows into the U.S. have increased, foreign liabilities have reached new heights. Overseas influences on the American economy have positive overtones in that they contribute to the U.S. economy. They also have potential negative influences if downturns in economic confidence cause potentially destabilizing outflows of foreign funds out of the American economy.

Determination of Foreign Exchange Rates with Supply and Demand for Currencies

Exchange rates are determined by the interaction of supply and demand for two individual currencies. Hence, the exchange rate of yen

B. Capital Account	Debits	Credits
1. Capital account: Payments for fixed assets (machinery, equipment)	Paid by domestic residents for foreign operations (78bbd)	Payments by foreigners for equipment entering domestic market (78bad)
2. Direct investment (10% + shares/equity + green field operations)	Paid out by residents to enter foreign markets (78bdd)	Payments by foreigners to enter domestic market (78bed)
3. Portfolio investments	Investments by residents in foreign stocks, shares, stock markets (78bfd)	Investments by foreigners in domestic shares, stock markets (78bgd)
4. Other investments (currency transactions, deposits, loans, trade credits, debits, etc.)	By residents to nonresidents (78hld)	By nonresidents to residents (78bid)

C. Net Errors and Omissions (78cad)

A + B + C + Overall Balance of Payments

Net inflows = Balance of payments *surplus*

Net outflows = Balance of payments *deficit*

Reserves and related items

Reserve assets

Use of fund credit
Liabs. constit. for. auth. reserves   } How surpluses are disposed of
Exceptional financing   and how deficits are financed

for dollars is determined by the international transactions (recorded in the balance of payments) between the United States and Japan.

DOLLAR SUPPLY: YEN DEMAND ▪ When the United States imports goods from Japan, initial payments to the Japanese exporter are in U.S. dollars. This transaction represents an *outflow of dollars* and increases the world dollar supply. Usually, because Japanese exporters must pay their workers and cover other costs, these dollars are converted into yen, thereby *creating demand for yen*.

When U.S. residents travel in Japan or when Japanese companies based in the United States transfer profits home or repatriate management fees or royalties, there is an outflow of U.S. dollars, *an increase in supply*. Subsequently, these U.S. dollars are exchanged for yen and *demand for yen increases*.

Finally, increases in dollar supply and in yen demand occur when U.S. citizens or companies make direct or portfolio investments in Japan, and dollars are exchanged for yen.

TABLE 4-4 ▪ *U.S. Balance of Payments, 1989–95*

		1989	1990	1991	1992	1993	1994	1995	
Balance of payments									
Goods: Exports f.o.b.	78aad	362.16	389.31	416.91	440.35	458.73	504.55	577.82	
Goods: Imports f.o.b.	78abd	-477.30	-498.34	-490.98	-536.45	-590.10	-669.15	-749.81	
Trade balance	78acd	-115.14	-109.03	-74.07	-96.10	-131.37	-164.60	-171.99	
Services: Credit	78add	127.72	147.35	163.67	177.14	184.09	193.62	208.55	
Services: Debit	78aed	-102.54	-117.64	-118.46	-118.29	-123.62	-132.23	-140.43	
Balance on goods & services	78afd	-89.96	-79.32	-28.86	-37.26	-70.91	-103.21	-103.87	
Income: Credit	78agd	152.35	160.42	137.14	119.21	120.05	141.84	182.85	Current
Income: Debit	78ahd	-139.68	-140.54	-122.33	-109.04	-111.42	-147.87	-192.02	Account
Balance on goods, svc & inc.	78aid	-76.99	-59.44	-14.05	-27.09	-62.27	-108.51	-113.04	
Current transfers, n.i.e.: Credit	78ajd	4.09	8.79	46.84	6.50	5.20	5.22	5.65	
Current transfers: Debit	78akd	-31.737	-43.61	-42.05	-40.77	-42.65	-44.48	-40.84	
Current account	78ald	-104.26	-94.26	-9.26	-61.36	-99.72	-147.77	-148.23	
Capital account, n.i.e.: Credit	78bad	.24	.26	.28	.43	.47	.47	.53	
Capital account: Debit	78bbd	-	-	-	-	-.67	-1.08	-.43	
Capital account, n.i.e.	78bcd	.24	.26	.28	.43	-.20	-.61	.10	
Direct investment abroad	78bdd	-36.83	-29.95	-31.38	-42.66	-78.17	-54.47	-95.53	Capital
Dir. invest, in rep. econ, n.i.e.	78bed	67.73	47.92	22.01	17.58	43.01	49.76	60.23	Account
Portfolio investment assets	78bfd	-22.10	-28.80	-45.69	-49.17	-146.26	-60.29	-98.96	
Portfolio investment liab., n.i.e.	78bgd	65.60	-4.20	53.29	62.20	103.83	91.11	192.38	
Other investment assets	78bhd	-83.40	-13.73	13.81	17.79	31.18	-41.31	-103.63	
Other investment liab., n.i.e.	78bid	72.44	42.52	1.69	29.59	35.68	104.15	66.21	
Financial account, n.i.e.	78bjd	63.44	13.75	13.74	35.34	-10.73	88.96	20.70	
Net errors and omissions	78cad	55.83	46.54	-26.83	-23.11	43.55	13.71	31.54	
Overall balance	78cbd	15.25	-33.71	-22.07	-48.70	-67.11	-45.72	-95.89	
Reserves and related items	78dad	-15.25	33.71	22.07	48.70	67.11	45.72	95.89	
Reserve assets	79dbd	-25.27	-2.23	5.76	3.92	-1.38	5.34	-9.74	
Use of fund credit and loans	79dcd	-	-	-	-	-	-	-	
Liabs. constit. for auth. reserves	79ddd	10.02	35.94	16.31	44.77	68.49	40.38	105.63	
Exceptional financing	79ded								

These exchanges of dollars into yen constitute in total the dollar-supply side of the foreign exchange equation.

DOLLAR DEMAND: YEN SUPPLY ▪ The other side of the foreign exchange equation, dollar demand and yen supply, works in a similar fashion. When the United States exports products to Japan, American companies require payment in dollars. This requirement causes firms to exchange yen for dollars, increasing the yen supply in the foreign exchange market and creating dollar demand. Hence, the yen supply should equal the dollar demand.

Likewise, profits, royalties, and management fees repatriated from Japan to the United States, as well as Japanese tourist expenditures in the United States, all involve exchanging yen for dollars, thus increasing dollar demand. Similarly, increases in Japanese investments in the United States mean that yen are being converted into U.S. dollars. Thus, from a balance-of-payments viewpoints, U.S. exports to Japan and Japanese investments in the United States have similar effects on the supply and demand for currencies; they both increase dollar demand.

IMBALANCE OF SUPPLY AND DEMAND ▪ What happens when supply and demand of a currency are not perfectly balanced? The answer is that currencies appreciate or depreciate in value. If the dollar's value drops from 240 yen to 120 yen, it takes fewer yen to buy 1 dollar; thus, the yen's value has *risen* (or *appreciated*) and the dollar's value has *declined* (or *depreciated*). But if the number of yen per dollar goes from 120 to 140, the dollar is *appreciating*, because it takes more yen to buy 1 dollar; in this case, the yen is *depreciating*, because 120 yen only buys $0.86 when $1 equals 140 yen.

Knowledgeable international marketers understand why currency realignments occur, know what to look for as indicators of exchange-rate movements, and most importantly, appreciate the effects of currency realignments on marketing and corporate strategies. Figure 4–1 shows how supply and demand influence exchange-rate values. The dollar supply is made up of all the dollars being converted into yen (for example, from Japanese imports into the United States, Japanese profits being repatriated, and American investments in Japan). Similarly, dollar demand is made up of all the yen being exchanged into dollars (caused by U.S. exports to Japan, American profits being brought back from Japan, and Japanese investments in the United States). Let us say that the exchange rate is now at 180 yen to the dollar. For the exchange rate to remain stable at 180 yen, all transactions from dollars into yen (dollar supply, yen demand) must equal the transactions from yen into dollars (yen supply, dollar demand). For simplicity's sake, if we ignore the capital account and the services part of the current account and focus just on the trade part, stability means that the value of U.S. exports to Japan should equal the value of Japanese exports to the United States.

However, as has been true for many years, Japanese exports to the United States have substantially exceeded American exports to Japan. This fact means that dollar supply (representing Japanese imports into the United States) is significantly larger than dollar demand (representing U.S. exports to Japan). As Figure 4–1 shows, instead of there being a D_2 level of U.S. exports, there is only a D_1 level. Because there are so many dollars that need to be exchanged and relatively few yen to effect the exchange, the number of yen per dollar must decrease to accommodate all transactions for that period of time. Decreasing the number of yen per dollar from 180 to 140 represents a depreciation of the dollar and an appreciation of the yen.

FIGURE 4–1 ■ *Supply and Demand and Determination of Dollar-to-Yen Exchange Rates*

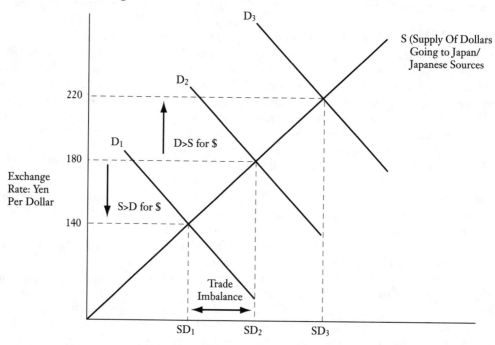

Supply and Demand of U.S. Dollars

Supply of dollars (= Demand for yen) comprising:	Demand for dollars (= Supply of yen) comprising:
* Japanese imports into U.S.	* U.S. exports to Japan
* American tourists in Japan	* Japanese tourists in U.S.
* U.S.-based Japanese companies repatriating profits to Japan	* Japan-based U.S. companies repatriating profits to U.S.
* American investments in Japan	* Japanese investments in U.S.

When the opposite situation occurs, and dollar demand exceeds dollar supply (as it would if the United States had a trade surplus with Japan), the price of U.S. dollars against the yen increases, and more yen per dollar results (from D_2 to D_3, or from 180 to 220 yen).

While trade is an important part of the current account component of the balance of payments, the analyst also considers capital movements, which are critical when capital inflows and outflows are extensive. Indeed, one explanation of why the dollar failed to depreciate against the yen during the 1996–97 period (when the United States had chronic trade deficits with Japan) is that even though Japan was exporting far more to the United States than it was importing, the shortfall in demand for dollars was effectively countered by inflows of Japanese capital investments in the United States. The combination of Japanese exports to the United States and U.S. investments in Japan was roughly equal to U.S. exports to Japan plus Japanese investments in the United States.

How and Why Exchange Rates Change: What Managers Should Watch For

There are fixed and floating components in all exchange-rate arrangements. Some Latin American currencies are fixed (pegged) to the U.S. dollar, but their values against other currencies vary with the weakening or strengthening of the dollar. Many corporations, especially banks, have econometric models to predict exchange rates, but many of the factors affecting exchange rates are not quantifiable; hence, careful monitoring of trends and managerial experience are useful additions to (but not substitutes for) more rigorous techniques. Effective managers distinguish between exchange-rate movements among floating currencies and pegged realignments of one currency against another.

CURRENCIES THAT FLOAT ■ Long-term

exchange-rate values are determined by supply and demand for the two currencies. But if market mechanisms do not produce the desired results (as they did not during the mid-1980s when U.S. trade deficits were accompanied by an appreciating dollar), then governments may act. Moving a currency in a desired direction, however, requires coordinated buying or selling by not one but several economically powerful countries. To this end, the Group of Seven (or G-7) was formed. Comprised of the United States, Japan, Germany, Britain, France, Canada, and Italy, this group coordinates the buying and selling of specific currencies in major

markets to push individual exchange rates up or down over the short to medium term. The G-7 countries do this to maintain competitive exchange rates among the major trading countries.

Short-term movements in floating exchange rates (that is, day-to-day rates) are influenced by publicized economic events, such as trade figures, interest-rate movements, or other economic indicators. Generally, good news (growth, trade surpluses, lower interest rates) causes a strengthening of the currency, as people buy more of it; bad news causes speculators and financial institutions to sell, causing currencies to then become weaker.

FIXED EXCHANGE RATES ■ Most developing

countries peg their currencies to those of advanced countries. However, the volatility associated with economic development and some inherent weaknesses of developing trade policies (for example, reliance on one or a few commodities for exports) make realignments, or re-pegging, advisable from time to time. It is difficult to predict the devaluations of currencies, but the following conditions are associated with currency realignments.

- *Balance of trade problems.* Many countries (not just developing ones) run trade deficits. When these are severe or occur over a number of years, then governments are likely to devalue their currencies. The hoped-for outcome is to make their imports more expensive and their exports cheaper.

- *Debt repayment problems.* Many countries have severe debt problems (e.g., Mexico, and Brazil). Debt puts considerable pressure on exporters to be internationally competitive, as they must earn enough hard currencies through exports to enable the country to make its payments. In these situations, a ratio of debt-servicing to exports is used to determine if the country is having, or is likely to have, problems repaying its debt. If problems are likely, one option is for the government to devalue the currency to increase export revenues, but this option also increases payments to creditor countries. Debt-service ratios in Latin America in 1994 varied from 34.4 percent of export revenues for Peru to 18.2 percent for Venezuela.[4]

- *Reliance on single commodity exports.* Many developing countries have exports based on commodities, such as oil, copper, and rubber. Their abilities to pay import bills depend on commodity prices being buoyant. When they are not, there are pressures to devalue currencies.

- *Convertible currency reserves.* A factor affecting both currency values and the ability to pay import bills is a country's convertible currency reserves—its store of convertible currencies, such as dollars, francs, and yen. The IMF is the major source of information on how many weeks of imports are covered by a country's currency reserves.

- *Inflation.* Inflation is probably the biggest cause of currency realignments, especially devaluations. Devaluations push export and domestic prices up and make imports relatively cheap and competitive compared to domestic goods. To counter this effect, governments periodically devalue their currencies to keep export prices down and import prices competitive. When inflation rates are high (hundreds or thousands of percent a year), monthly or weekly devaluations occur, based usually on movements in the consumer price index. When faced with these conditions, company managers prefer to exchange local currencies into

dollars or to exchange other stronger currencies into dollars or other stronger currencies as quickly as possible. Of course, with periodic devaluations, it is wise to convert money *immediately before* a devaluation in order to preserve its diminishing purchasing power.

In hyperinflationary environments where inflation rates are very high, managers can only monitor price increases and assume that currency devaluations will be proportionate to the inflation rate. That is, over a given period, if prices rise by 40 percent, the government is likely to devalue the currency by 40 percent.

EFFECTS OF CURRENCY REALIGNMENTS ON WORLD MARKETING PRACTICES AND GLOBAL BUSINESS STRATEGIES

Whenever currency realignments occur, there are appreciating and depreciating currencies, and potentials exist for financial gains and losses. For an overview of the effects of currency realignments on various international business activities, see Table 4–5, which shows their effects on balance-of-payments components—trade, services, royalties, and investments. Three currency examples (dollar, yen, and pound) are used to illustrate the effects of depreciation and appreciation on currencies. Basically, when a currency is strengthening (that is, when fewer units of it are needed to buy one unit of a foreign currency), exporting goods becomes more difficult as export prices rise. However, travel abroad becomes cheaper. Other effects include getting back fewer units of that currency from a fixed amount of royalties, management fees, and repatriated profits in foreign currency. Finally,

TABLE 4–5 ▪ *Effects of Currency Realignments on Balance of Payment Components*

Effects on	Japan–USA		USA–United Kingdom	
	From $1 = ¥240 to $1 = ¥120. Dollar weakening; yen strengthening.	From $1 = ¥120 to $1 = ¥140. Dollar strengthening; yen weakening	From £1 = $2.00 to £1 = $1.10. Pound weakening; dollar strengthening.	From £1 = $1.10 to £1 = $1.60. Pound strengthening; dollar weakening.
TRADE $1,000 export from U.S. to (a) Japan (b) U.K	Price in Japan falls from ¥240,000 to ¥120,000.	Price in Japan rises from ¥120,000 to ¥140,000.	Price in U.K. rises from $1,000/2 = £500 to £909.09 ($1,000/1.10).	Price in U.K. falls from £909.09 ($1,000/1.10) to £625.00 ($1,000/1.60)
¥10,000 Japanese export to U.S.	Price rises from $41.67 (¥10,000/240) to $83.33 (¥10,000/120).	Price falls from $83.33 (¥10,000/120) to $71.43 (¥10,000/140).	Price falls from $2,000 ($1,000 x 2.00) to $1,100 ($1,000 x 1.10).	Price rises from $1,100 ($1,000 x 1.10) to $1,600 ($1,000 x 1.60).
Overall Effects	Good for U.S. exporters to Japan. Unfavorable for Japanese exports to U.S.	Unfavorable for U.S. exporters to Japan. Good for Japanese exporters to U.S.	Unfavorable for U.S. exporters to U.K. Good for U.K. exporters to U.S.	Unfavorable for U.K. exporters to U.S. Good for U.S. exporters to U.K.
Trade/Tourism American traveling to Japan, $5,000 expenses	@¥240 = $1 gets ¥1,200,000. @¥120 = $1 gets ¥600,000.	@¥120 = $1 gets ¥600,000. @¥140 = $1 gets ¥700,000.		
Japanese traveling to U.S., ¥500,000 expenses.	@¥240 = $1 gets $2,083.33. @¥120 = $1 gets $4,166.67	@¥120 = $1 gets $4,166.67. @¥140 = $1 gets $3,571.43		
American traveling to U.K., $5,000 expenses.			@ £1 = $2.00 would get £2,500. @ £1 = $1.10 would get £4,545.45.	@ £1 = $1.10 would get £4,545.45. £1 = $1.60 would get £3,125.00
U.K. resident traveling to U.S., £2,000 expenses.			@ £1 = $2.00 would get $4,000. @ £1 = $1.10 would get $2,200.	@ £1 = $1.10 would get $2,200. @ £1 = $1.60 would get $3,200.
Overall Effects	Weaker dollar makes American travel to Japan expensive and Japanese travel to U.S. cheaper.	Stronger dollar makes U.S. travel to Japan less expensive and Japanese travel to U.S. more expensive.	Stronger dollar makes U.S. travel to U.K. cheaper and U.K. travel to U.S. more expensive.	Weaker dollar makes U.S. travel to U.K. more expensive and makes U.K. travel to U.S. cheaper.

TABLE 4–5 (continued) ■ *Effects of Currency Realignments on Balance of Payment Components*

Effects on	Japan–USA		USA–United Kingdom	
Repatriated Earnings Profits/Fees $5 million sales, 3% profits/royalties to Japan = $150,000.	@¥240 = $1 would receive ¥36 million.	@¥120 = $1 would receive ¥18 million.		
	@¥120 = $1 would receive ¥18 million.	@¥140 = $1 would receive ¥21 million.		
¥100 million sales 3% profits back to U.S. = ¥3,000,000.	@¥240 = $1 would receive $12,500.	@¥120 = $1 would receive $25,000.		
	@¥120 = $1 would receive $25,000.	@¥140 = $1 would receive $21,428.50.		
$5 million in sales in U.S., 3% profits/royalties/ fees repatriated to U.K. = $150,000.			@ £1 = $2.00 would receive £75,000.	@ £1 = $1.10 would receive £136,363.63.
			@ £1 = $1.10 would receive £136,363.63.	@ £1 = $1.60 would receive £93,750.
£10 million sales in U.K. @ 3% = £300,000 to U.S.			@ £1 = $2.00 would receive $600,000.	@ £1 = $1.10 would receive $330,000
			@ £1 = $1.10 would receive $330,000.	@ £1 = $1.60 would receive $480,000.
Overall Effects	Weaker dollar results in more revenues from U.S. interests in Japan and less revenues from Japanese interests in the U.S.	Stronger dollar means less revenue from U.S. interests in Japan and more revenues from Japanese interests in U.S.	Stronger dollar means less revenue from U.S. interests in U.K. and more revenues from U.K. interests in the U.S.	Weaker dollar means more revenues from U.S. interests in U.K. and less revenue from U.S. interests in U.K.
Investments in land, equipment, securities $1m U.S. investment in Japan	@$1 = ¥240 can by ¥240 million of Japanese investments.	@¥120 = $1 can buy ¥120 million of Japanese investments.		

TABLE 4–5 (continued) ▪ *Effects of Currency Realignments on Balance of Payment Components*

Effects on	Japan-USA		USA-United Kingdom	
	@$1 = ¥120 can obtain ¥120 million of Japanese investments.	@¥140 = $1 can buy ¥140 million of Japanese investments.		
¥900 million Japanese investment in the U.S.	@$1 = Y240 can buy $3,750,000 of U.S. investments.	@¥120 = $1 can buy $7,500,000 of U.S. investments.		
	@ $1 = ¥120 can buy $7,500,000 of U.S. investments	@¥140 = $1 can buy $6,428,571 of U.S. investments.		
$100 million U.S. investment in the U.K.			@ £1 = $200 can buy £50 million of U.K. investments	@ £1 = $1.10 can buy £90.91 million of U.K. investments.
			@£ 1 = $1.10 can buy £90.91 million of U.K. investments	@ £1 = $1.60 can buy £62.5 million of U.K. investments.
£300 million U.K. investment in the U.S.			@ £1 = $2.00 can buy $600 million of U.S. investments.	@ £1 = $1.10 can buy $330 million of U.S. investments
			@ £1 = $1.10 can buy $330 million of U.S. investments.	@ £1 = $1.60 can buy $280 million of U.S. investments.
Overall Effects	Weaker dollar makes investments in Japan more expensive and Japanese investments in the U.S. cheaper.	Stronger dollar buys more investments in Japan and makes Japanese investments in the U.S. more expensive.	Stronger dollar enables U.S. investors to buy more U.K. assets for a given dollar investment. It also makes U.K. investments in the U.S. assets more expensive.	Weaker dollar means American investors in the U.K. can buy fewer assets for a given dollar investment. It makes U.K. investments in U.S. assets cheaper.

while strong currencies are a hindrance to exporting, they encourage direct investments in countries with weak currencies, as more assets and investments are purchasable for a given capital outlay.

Effects on Trade and Marketing

Changes in exchange rates affect trade; hence, all companies that export and import goods are affected. For example, at any one moment, some currencies are appreciating against the dollar (that is, the dollar is depreciating against them), and some are depreciating against the dollar (that is, the dollar is appreciating against them).

EXPORTERS ■ Exporters monitor trends in exchange rates and reorient their marketing efforts in two ways. First, when the home-market currency falls, it becomes feasible to sell in markets where export prices had been too high, as depreciating currencies result in price advantages. Where the dollar rises (or appreciates) in value, U.S. exporters anticipate fall-offs in demand.

Second, exporters make in-market adjustments to foreign marketing mixes in order to stay competitive. Where export prices are falling, firms refocus their promotional efforts to emphasize their price competitiveness. Likewise, when an appreciating domestic exchange rate is forcing overseas prices upward, a switch in marketing emphasis from price to nonprice elements is appropriate. When the Japanese auto industry began to lose its price competitiveness under an appreciating yen, companies such as Toyota played down price and reoriented promotions toward superior product quality and service capabilities.

Companies faced with stiff import competition can also take advantage of currency realignments. When import competition loses price competitiveness with a depreciating currency (as in 1985–89, when the dollar depreciated and pushed import prices up), home-market competitors emphasize price elements in their marketing mixes. American auto manufacturers and consumer electronics companies (for example, Zenith) went to price-oriented strategies when the rising value of the yen put price pressures on their Japanese competitors.

IMPORTERS ■ Importers are also affected by currency realignments. For example, U.S. importers can find price-competitive imports in countries whose currencies are depreciating against the dollar (that is, the dollar is appreciating against that country's currency). Likewise, importers that monitor exchange rates know when to switch sources of supply.[5]

Effects on Manufacturing

All exporters experience gains or losses in price competitiveness when their currency depreciates against other currencies. However, multinational companies with overseas production facilities have a strategy option that purely domestic forms do not have—to obtain merchandise for the home market from foreign-based manufacturing affiliates. When currency realignments make manufactured exports from one country expensive, MNCs shift outputs among overseas production units to obtain goods at the lower cost.

The appreciation of the U.S. dollar in 1996 caused both companies and governments to rethink some of their strategies. Chile's peso had strong links with the dollar, and its export and economic growth was adversely affected by strong dollar movements. The American movie industry, with Warner Brothers and Paramount Communications leading the way, spearheaded moves to shift film production into cost-competitive Western Europe. The strong dollar situation also caused U.S. chemical companies to strengthen their manufacturing positions in Mexico.[6]

Likewise, when the yen appreciated against the dollar in the mid-1980s, Japanese companies found it hard to compete against Korean and Taiwanese products, whose currencies were tied to the dollar and whose labor rates were five times lower than Japan's. Their solution was to boost foreign production to maintain price competitiveness. As the yen went from 250 to the dollar to 180 and then to 150, overseas manufacturing, even for small and medium-size Japanese companies, became an economic necessity. Between February and June 1986 alone, Japanese companies established 89 new plants in Taiwan, South Korea, and Southeast Asia. While some of these were sources of components, in many cases, entire products were involved. Toshiba, for example, began obtaining its low-end television sets from Korea instead of Japan to serve the Latin American, Australian, and New Zealand markets.[7] Company executives, therefore, are always aware that their company's ability to be competitive in cost and price in international markets hinges on favorable (or at least not unfavorable) exchange rates and the capability of switching production among overseas sites.

Effects on Financial Activities

Many financial decisions either affect international marketing strategy or are affected by it. For example, where global financial resources are allocated depends on the locations of the company's major markets and manufacturing sites. Similarly, methods of financing overseas investments (debt-equity decisions, internal-external sources of capital, and local or international currencies) all affect local subsidiary operations. How unfavorable political and economic circumstances are factored into return-on-investment considerations affects the marketing and sales function, as do cash-management policies (for example, whether to centralize or decentralize international cash management).

Close coordination between marketing and financial functions is essential in the areas of accounts payable and accounts receivable. When there are currency realignments and payments to suppliers, and receipts from customers are made over time, opportunities exist to make or lose money. Likewise, the choice of currency and the decision of when to convert back into the home-market currency are also affected. The following are some general principles used by finance professionals in choosing credit policies.

Home-Market Currency Appreciation against Major World Currencies

Suppose a U.S. company has a Japanese creditor to whom it owes ¥21 million. If the dollar is strengthening (that is, more and more yen are required to buy each dollar), the company has two choices. It can exchange the ¥21 million now at, for example, 120 yen to the dollar, and pay $175,000 to the Japanese company, or it can wait until the exchange rate is at 140 yen to the dollar and pay only $150,000 to obtain the same ¥21 million. Hence, when the home-market currency is appreciating, it helps to delay paying accounts payable.

The opposite strategy holds where the company is owed money. For example, if a Japanese company buys $10 million of goods when the exchange rate is 120 yen to the dollar, if the American company does not insist on being paid in dollars (which most do), then the Japanese company would make a

¥1.2 billion payment. If the exchange takes place at 120 yen to the dollar, there are no problems. But if payment is delayed until the rate is 140 yen to the dollar, then the U.S. company receives only $8,571,428. This example illustrates a *foreign exchange transaction loss*. Most U.S. companies try to avoid such losses in one of three ways: (1) They request *immediate* payment, minimizing the possibility of getting less dollars in return; (2) they request payment in dollars, so that the debtor carries any exchange-rate risks (in this case, the Japanese company will also pay up quickly, as at 120 yen to the dollar it pays ¥1.2 billion; if it delays, the price of $10 million would be ¥1.4 billion, in effect a price increase of 16.6 percent); or (3) if there is a legitimate delay (such as installing equipment and ensuring it works) and the company thinks the home-country currency will appreciate, the U.S. company may avoid an exchange loss by using the forward rate (explained later).

Summarizing, when the currency of the home market is appreciating against other currencies, payment of accounts payable in those currencies is delayed as long as possible, and accounts receivable are collected as soon as possible.

HOME-MARKET CURRENCY DEPRECIATION AGAINST MAJOR WORLD CURRENCIES ▪ In

the opposite situation—when the home-market currency is depreciating—not surprisingly, the appropriate policies are the reverse of those outlined above. That is, when the home-market currency is depreciating, home-market companies pay their bills as quickly as possible. Alternatively, they delay collecting accounts receivable (what is owed to the company) as long as possible. Let us illustrate this situation by assuming that a dollar goes from 200 yen down to 150 yen.

With a $2 million U.S. export to Japan, if the Japanese pay up immediately at 200 yen to the dollar, it costs them Y400 million.

If they wait until a dollar equals 150 yen, obtaining $2 million in U.S. currency will cost them just ¥300 million—a substantial saving. But it would also be advantageous for the U.S. company to obtain immediate payment in yen (¥400 million) and delay the conversion back into U.S. dollars, as ¥400 million at 150-yen exchange rate would yield $2,666,667, a net gain on the original transaction. These figures illustrate a basic principle of financial management: To maximize the likelihood of making exchange gains and to minimize the possibility of losses, companies prefer to hold cash reserves in strong or strengthening currencies.

If a U.S company owes money to a Japanese creditor (for example ¥150 million for a Japanese import into the United States), then when the home-market currency is depreciating (that is, requiring few foreign currency units to purchase a single home-country unit), if the company pays ¥150 million at 200 yen per dollar, it expends $750,000. If the company waits and the exchange rate moves to 150 yen to the dollar, it must then pay $1 million to obtain the same number of yen. Hence, the American company is likely to pay off its debts as quickly as possible.

IN WHICH CURRENCIES SHOULD ONE DO BUSINESS? ▪ Effective financial managers

make foreign exchange gains by staying away from weakening currencies and keeping cash reserves in strengthening currencies. International corporations can choose the convertible currencies in which they wish to do business. To hedge against exchange-rate losses, most companies opt for currencies that are growing stronger. For example, holding dollars when the currency is appreciating (e.g., going from 100 yen to 120 yen) means that $1 million held during this period of dollar appreciation will buy ¥120 million instead of ¥100 million.

Likewise, when the home-market currency is depreciating, a company holds as much currency as it can in non-home-market currencies. For example, Fiat, an Italian automobile multinational with 421 affiliates in 55 countries, exercises tight financial control over its subsidiaries. Because the Italian lira was prone to devaluation, the company made it a policy to bill all exports in the buyer's currency and to do its international borrowing in local currencies. By pursuing this policy and maintaining close surveillance on cash holdings in various currencies, Fiat avoided significant exchange-rate losses.[8]

What happens when the exporter's currency is appreciating against the importer's currency (for example, a U.S. exporter with dollar values rising from 100 to 130 yen or the British pound going from $2.00 to $1.50)? If the transaction is in one of the major currencies, forward exchange rates are used to avoid exchange losses. Table 4–1 shows typical spot rates (for instantaneous exchanges of currencies) and forward rates for leading currencies. Forward rate quotations are for 30-, 90-, and 180-day periods. For example, the spot price for Canadian dollars is $0.7404. For a one-month forward rate, the U.S. company must pay $0.7417; for 90 days, $0.7448; and for 180 days, $0.7490. On average, it appears that the foreign-exchange traders expect the Canadian dollar to appreciate in value over the next six months (that is, it will take more U.S. dollars to buy one Canadian dollar) from $0.7404 to $0.7490 (a rise of 0.7490/0.7404, or 1.2 percent). If the Canadian dollar rises in value so that less than $0.7490 is needed to purchase one Canadian dollar, the foreign trader suffers a loss, but if the six-month price is between $0.7404 and $0.7490, the trader has a profit.

Traders have access to sophisticated econometric models that predict future exchange rates, so it is rare for them to experience foreign exchange losses, and while their margins are slim, the large sizes of transactions make their profits substantial.

Where there are no forward rates (as in situations involving developing countries) and there are fears that the developing country's currency is to be devalued, companies can request immediate payment or goods in payment of balances due.

Depreciating and appreciating exchange values primarily affect transactions between developed countries with readily convertible and easily traded currencies. However, where countries do not earn sufficient hard currencies through exports, they are forced to allocate foreign exchange through a system of controls.

Foreign Exchange Controls

Foreign exchange controls are imposed by governments to limit the availability of foreign exchange for particular transactions. Foreign exchange controls can affect the full range of international payments. Figure 4–2 shows typical control measures.

Restrictions on Profit/Dividend Remittance and Royalties

Where currencies are not freely convertible, governments often restrict outflows of hard, convertible currencies such as dollars, pounds sterling, yen, and so on. This means there are periods when outgoing payments (for imports, profit repatriations, etc.) are stopped or limited. Thailand and Romania frequently restricted profit/dividend outflows during the mid-1990s, as did Russia and China until their 1996 loosening of foreign exchange controls.[9]

* Restrictions or outright prohibition of certain remittance categories such as dividends or royalties.

* Import restrictions.

* Required surrender of hard-currency export receipts to central bank.

* Limitations on prepayment for imports.

* Requirements to deposit in interest-free accounts with the central bank, for a specified length of time, some percentage of the value of imports and/or remittances.

* Multiple exchange rates for buying and selling foreign currencies, depending on the specific category of goods or services into which each transaction falls.

Source: Adapted from Alan C. Shapiro, *Multinational Financial Management*, 2nd ed. (Boston, Mass.: Allyn and Bacon, 1986), 51.

FIGURE 4–2 *Typical Currency Control Measures*

Import Licenses

Many countries that typically have merchandise imports greater than their exports (developing countries, for example) require importers to obtain licenses granting them permission to import certain goods. Essential products (basic foods, machinery, and raw materials) rarely have import license problems, but nonessential, or luxury, items are likely to experience difficulties. Because local banks need valid import licenses before they can secure access to scarce hard currencies, import licenses, in effect, are foreign-exchange restrictions.

Multiple Exchange Rates

Countries not prohibiting imports of luxury goods but restricting demand for them apply different exchange rates for essential and luxury items. In the 1990s, the Ukraine, Iran, Egypt, and the Sudan have used multiple exchange rates to restrict flows of nonessential products. Low rates are used for essential items, and higher rates are used for luxury goods.

OTHER FINANCIAL FORCES AFFECTING INTERNATIONAL MARKETING OPERATIONS

Tariffs

There are two major types of tariffs. One type, the ad valorem tariff, is a fixed-percentage tax on the total value of a product. For example, a 10 percent tariff on a $25 leather pocketbook comes to $2.50. The other type of tariff, specific duty, is a fixed sum per imported unit; for example, $1 per barrel of oil. These duties would not distinguish between different versions of the same basic product (such as light versus heavy oils). Under some circumstances, compound duties, incorporating both ad valorem and specific tariffs, are applied.

Country Taxation Levels

Marketers in multinational corporations often interact with global strategists to minimize the taxes paid worldwide. During the 1950s and early 1960s, some U.S. corporations channeled their products through low-taxation countries, where markups were added. This practice was outlawed under the 1962 U.S. Revenue Act, but a 1977 ruling by the Internal Revenue Service (IRS) again made tax havens and reinvoicing popular. This ruling allows the allocation of parent-company expenses to foreign affiliates, increasing the foreign tax credits that affiliates can build up and apply to foreign-source income.[10] The overall affect is to make reinvoicing centers more popular among MNCs and encourage them to set up subsidiaries in Bermuda, Hong Kong, Europe's Channel Islands, and other low-tax countries. In some cases, goods are imported, assembled or modified and reshipped from free trade zones (FTZs), which are duty-free areas within ports or airports.[11]

While the United States forbids transfer pricing per se (section 482 of the IRS Code), foreign multinationals can and do underprice and overprice intracompany transfers of goods.[12]

Inflation

While many advanced countries panicked during the 1960s and 1970s, when inflation reached double digits, their situations were mild compared to what other countries experienced today. In Latin America, Brazilian, Argentinean, and Bolivian inflation rates have often been in the hundreds, sometimes thousands, of percents. Hyperinflationary conditions present challenges for marketers, especially for those trying to price products competitively and profitably. When a company underestimates the need for price increases, it experiences substantial cash-flow problems as sales revenues prove insufficient to pay for new raw materials and components. But underpriced goods are likely to capture increased market shares. If, however, the company overprices its goods, price-conscious customers switch to lower-priced, alternative products. Case 4–1 reviews Procter and Gamble's experiences with inflation in Latin America.

SUMMARY

Financial elements, especially exchange rates, are critical to successful international marketing. All international transactions require the conversion of money or money values from one country's currency to that of another country. In this chapter, we examined the 10 major exchange-rate arrangements and noted the key role of the dollar and the popularity of managed and freely floating foreign currencies. We also analyzed the effects of appreciating and depreciating currencies on international marketing transactions and global business strategies.

Few countries allow total freedom in currency exchanges. Many countries, because of balance-of-payments problems, earn insufficient hard currencies to cover their import bills. These countries are forced to control currency outflows through restricting profit or dividend remittances, requiring import licenses, and using multiple exchange rates.

We also examined the effects of certain financial forces on international marketing practices and identified the main types of tariffs and the impacts of taxation levels and inflationary conditions on marketing.

DISCUSSION QUESTIONS

1. For each of the following exchange rates, do the following:
   a) Name the exchange-rate arrangement under which the currency falls (see Table 4–2). How does the arrangement affect the currency's foreign exchange value?
   b) Determine whether the currency is appreciating or depreciating, and over which period.
   c) Describe the ways foreign exchange fluctuations affect (1) trade, (2) investments, and (3) tourism.

EXHIBIT 4–1

	1989	1990	1991	1992	1993	1994	1995	
France	5.7880	5.1290	5.1800	5.5065	5.8955	5.3460	4.9000	Ffr/$
Germany	1.6978	1.4940	1.5160	1.6140	1.7263	1.5488	1.4335	DM/$
Ecuador	648.40	878.20	1270.60	1844.30	2043.80	2269.00	2923.50	Sucre/$
Colombia	433.92	568.73	706.86	811.77	917.33	831.27	987.65	Pesos/$
Philippines	22.440	28.000	26.650	25.096	27.699	24.418	26.214	Pesos/$
Korea	679.60	716.40	760.80	788.40	808.10	788.10	774.70	Won/$
Iran	70.24	65.31	64.59	67.04	1758.56	1735.97	1747.50	Ryals/$

2. Review the following balance of payments statement for Japan. What do these statistics tell you about Japan's international situation?

EXHIBIT 4–2

Balance of Payments	Yen/$	1898	1990	1991	1992	1993	1994	1995	
		143.45	134.40	125.20	124.75	111.85	99.74	102.93	⎫
Goods: Exports f.o.b.	78aad	269.55	280.35	308.10	332.50	352.90	385.99	429.32	
Goods: Imports f.o.b.	78abd	-192.66	-216.77	-212.03	-207.80	-213.32	-241.55	-297.24	
Trade balance	78acd	76.89	63.58	96.07	124.70	139.58	144.44	132.07	
Services: Credit	78add	41.72	43.34	44.83	49.05	53.25	58.31	65.21	
Services: Debit	78aed	-80.33	-88.03	-86.61	-93.01	-96.34	-106.38	-122.70	
Balance on goods & services	78afd	38.28	18.89	54.29	80.74	96.50	96.37	74.59	⎬ Current Account
Income: Credit	78agd	102.19	122.64	140.89	142.69	148.23	155.37	192.61	
Income: Debit	78ahd	-79.20	-100.14	-114.98	-107.26	-107.63	-115.06	-148.20	
Balance on goods, svc & inc.	78aid	61.27	41.39	80.19	116.17	137.10	136.67	118.99	
Current transfers, n.i.e.: Credit	78ajd	1.01	1.00	1.42	1.67	1.58	1.83	1.98	
Current transfers: Debit	78akd	-5.29	-6.52	-13.24	-5.51	-6.70	-7.95	-9.73	
Current account, n.i.e.	78ald	56.99	35.87	68.37	112.33	131.98	130.56	111.25	⎭
Capital account, n.i.e.: Credit	bad	-	-					.01	⎫
Capital account: Debit	78bbd	-	-	-1.20	-1.29	-1.46	-1.86	-2.27	
Capital account, n.i.e.	78bcd	-	-	-1.20	-1.29	-1.46	-1.86	-2.26	
Direct investment abroad	78bdd	-44.16	-48.05	-31.49	-17.36	-13.83	-18.10	-22.66	
Dir. invest, in rep. econ, n.i.e.	78bed	-1.06	1.76	1.30	2.76	.13	.92	.06	⎬ Capital Account
Portfolio investment assets	78bfd	-113.24	-40.20	-81.72	-34.93	-64.03	-91.13	-88.07	
Portfolio investment liab., n.i.e.	78bgd	84.48	35.39	125.87	7.50	-6.68	64.46	51.96	
Other investment assets	78bhd	-171.54	-89.14	26.94	47.60	13.04	-35.88	-105.71	
Other investment liab., n.i.e.	78bid	197.59	118.70	-108.45	-105.51	-31.22	-5.80	100.04	
Financial account, n.i.e.	78bjd	-47.93	-21.54	-67.54	-99.93	-102.59	-85.53	-64.40	⎭
Net errors and omissions	78cad	-21.82	-20.92	-7.88	-10.44	-.28	-17.80	14.06	
Overall balance	78cbd	-12.76	-6.59	-8.26	.67	27.65	25.36	58.64	
Reserves and related items	78dad	12.76	6.59	8.26	-.67	-27.65	-25.36	-58.64	
Reserve assets	79dbd	12.76	6.59	8.26	-.67	-27.65	-25.36	-58.64	
Use of fund credit and loans	79dcd	-	-	-	-	-	-	-	
Liabs. constit. for auth. reserves	79ddd	-	-						
Exceptional financing	79ded								

Marketing in Adverse Economic Climates: Procter and Gamble in Latin America

Colombian-born, Stanford-educated Procter and Gamble manager Raphael Henao said it best: "When the waters are rough, the good fishermen get the best fish. When it's quiet, anyone can fish." The waters referred to were the economic waters in Latin America, which had been turbulent throughout the 1980s.

Henao, one of P&G's managers in Venezuela, knew what he was talking about. In the early 1980s, falling oil prices made Venezuela's debt-laden and oil-oriented economy falter and then slump. In a bid to boost exports and reduce imports, the bolivar was devalued. Up went inflation, and on went government controls over prices and imports. P&G found rising costs of raw materials and political reluctances to grant price increases. The subsidiary reported a loss in 1983.

Austere economic policies continued throughout much of the 1980s. In 1988, phosphate imports, essential for manufacturing detergents, were curtailed after the imports quota was reached. P&G informed consumers that its detergent plant would close until supplies resumed. Panic buying followed. The subsidiary was accused of hoarding the product to take advantage of spiraling prices. A warrant was issued for Henao's arrest. He fled to Colombia until company lawyers eventually sorted the problem out.

But then economic problems had always plagued the affiliate. In the late 1970s, the Venezuelan government had itself imported Pampers disposable diapers, in direct competition with the subsidiary, which also imported them. Unfortunately, under a multiple exchange-rate system, the government was able to bring the product in at more favorable exchange rates and effectively undercut the subsidiary. P&G ceased to be in the diaper business until the late 1980s, when the company entered a joint venture with Industries Mammi. Locally produced Mammis is now the market leader in Venezuela.

Peru has been described by Patrick Egan, head of Unilever's Latin American operations, as "a political economic mess." During the 1970s, a military regime had forced foreign businesses to give local workers control of operations. Once that law was rescinded, the economy slowly got further out of control. By 1988, inflation was at 2,000 percent, price controls were in effect, and the local currency, the inti, was devalued from 33 to 250 per U.S. dollar. By April 1989, it was 1,440 intis per dollar. Up went subsidies, and on went stiffer price controls and tiered exchange rates. Violence escalated. Leftist terrorists kidnapped or murdered local business leaders. Susana Elesperu de Freitas, P&G's manager in Peru, was given armed bodyguards.

Procter and Gamble made its biggest concession to Latin American economic conditions by moving its managerial team from Cincinnati to Caracas, Venezuela, in 1987. From the new location, marketing-strategy adjustments were easier to make. These included the following:

- The company repackaged its detergents in smaller, 100-gram plastic bags, which not only kept the product dry but fit into local consumption patterns better. The bag size was just sufficient for a single wash and suited women who wash and shop daily.

- Business costs went up horrendously, so P&G restricted the use of copiers and telephones and also business lunches and magazine subscriptions.

- It maintained product quality. Consumers stuck to P&G's major detergent, Ace Lemon, because of its superior whitening power. As a P&G researcher noted: "Here, a family evaluates a woman by how the clothes look. It's a very (male) chauvinistic culture." Loyalty remained even though detergent prices rose 20 to 30 percent every two or three weeks.

- To aid distributor cash flows, P&G put its delivery people into Volkswagens to allow small orders to be filled quickly.

- The company left price, a given in most markets, open to negotiation with large-scale customers such as wholesalers. It did, however, reduce its free-credit period from 60 to 30 or 15 days.

- To give greater value to soap buyers, P&G redesigned its Moncler soap into a kidney shape so that a smaller surface area is exposed on wet surfaces. The soap remains hard and lasts longer. Other local brands of bar soap are also used for cleaning clothes.

- Also to aid economy-conscious consumers, P&G introduced an economy detergent, Rindex, which sells for 30 to 40 percent below the market leaders. In most of its world markets, the company strenuously avoids low-cost brands.

As the 1990s began, P&G's Latin American division accounted for 15 percent of the international division's $1 billion in sales. The company was adding new lines and was being successful.

QUESTIONS

1. Review Proctor and Gamble's strategies. In which situations did the company amend existing policies to cope with adverse economic and financial conditions? When did it introduce completely new policies?

2. Which of those new policies do you think could have been initiated from Cincinnati, Ohio, rather than from Caracas, Venezuela?

Source: Case adapted from Alecia Swasy, "Foreign Formula: Procter and Gamble Fixes Aim on Tough Market: The Latin Americans," *The Wall Street Journal,* 15 June 1990, A1, A4.

Transfer Pricing Controversies

Foreign-owned multinationals in the United States were avoiding between $13 billion and $30 billion in U.S. taxes. This was the main conclusion of the U.S. House Ways and Means oversight subcommittee, which examined 10 years of tax returns from 11 European and 25 Asian distributors in the United States. Half of the companies surveyed paid "little or no" tax over the decade in question. As a consequence, the IRS had brought cases against Hitachi America, Mitsubishi Electric, Tokai Bank (all Japanese), and Daewoo (Korean). "Death and taxes" are the two things most difficult for Americans to avoid, so how did foreign firms manage it?

There are several ways for multinationals to use transfer pricing (which are methods used to determine prices among a multinational's subsidiaries to minimize their world tax liabilities). First, they can ship goods at cost from a high-tax location, such as Germany, Japan, or Canada, to a low-tax location, such as Puerto Rico, Singapore, or Malaysia, and make their profits in the low-tax country.

Second, they can ship products between two high-tax locations but via a low-tax reinvoicing center, where the markups (and profits) are added before products are moved to the final destination.

Third, multinationals can elect to keep their profits in the home market. This is how they do it: A product is made in Korea or Japan, for example, for $25. The home-based manufacturing affiliate elects to make its profits there and adds on a $100 margin. The product is shipped to its company-owned foreign distributor, where internal transportation and promotional costs are added (but no profit). The product reaches the retailer without the foreign multinational making a profit outside of its home market.

Some interesting facts:

1. Two-thirds of Sony's sales are outside Japan. But only one-third of its pretax profit is generated in overseas markets.

2. In the late 1980s, U.S.-controlled firms earned four times the return on assets as foreign-controlled companies.

3. To head off a direct legal confrontation on transfer pricing, the British called for a joint U.S.-British study of international taxation policies.

The IRS (under whose jurisdiction this study falls) is currently revamping its Section 482 rules dealing with transfer pricing. Most countries have laws or guidelines on transfer pricing, and their aims are the same: maximizing the amount of taxes collected within their borders.

The problem is that monitoring MNC activities is next to impossible. Tax audits are lengthy and costly. To be above suspicion, major exporters would have to make similar returns on investments in all of their markets.

Some companies have come up with their own policies. Hewlett-Packard's accounting and finance manual spells out how the company's tax department is responsible for allocating profits between H-P's functional areas (R & D, manufacturing, sales, subsidiaries). The split between the functions is based on a value-added tax at each stage of the process.

QUESTIONS

1. Transfer pricing is clearly very difficult to monitor. The British, Koreans, Japanese, and Americans all want to maximize in-country tax revenues. Do you think it is too hard on the multinationals to be pulled in many different directions?

2. Why not let multinationals earn profits where they wish?

3. If transfer pricing is to be controlled, how best might it be achieved?

Source: Adapted from "Can Uncle Sam Mend This Hole in His Pocket?" *Business Week*, 10 September 1990, 48–49; "Transfer Pricing: New Rules and a Flatter Playing Field in 1991," *Business International Money Report*, 7 January 1991, 6–7; and "Hewlett-Packard: Making Transfer Pricing Work," *Business International Money Report*, 12 November 1990, 433–434.

ENDNOTES

1 See the seventh exchange-rate arrangement, "Flexibility Limited in Terms of a Group of Currencies' Cooperative Arrangements: The 'European Snake'."

2 "Chile," *Crossborder Monitor,* 4 September 1996, 2.

3 Walter Enders and Harvey E. Lapan, *International Economics: Theory and Policy* (Englewood Cliffs, N.J.: Prentice-Hall, 1987), 293.

4 "Status Report on Foreign Debt," *Business Latin America,* 20 February 1995, 5.

5 This topic is addressed again in Chapter 14, "International Logistics."

6 "More Smooth Sailing in Santiago," *Business Week,* 15 January 1996, 24; Julia Flynn, "Tinseltown on the Thames," *Business Week,* 5 August 1996, 47–48; and Charles Thurston, "Peso's Fall Spurs Chemical Exports," *Chemical Marketing Reporter,* 19 February 1996, SR6.

7 "The Muscular Yen Is Shaving Investment Abroad," *Business Week,* 18 August 1986, 50–51.

8 "Clever Cash Management Revs Fiat's Finances," *Business Week,* 30 April 30 1984, 60.

9 "Hunting Kwachas," *Economist,* 20 July 1996, 61.

10 Alan C. Shapiro, *Multinational Financial Management,* 2nd ed. (Boston, Mass.: Allyn and Bacon, 1986).

11 FTZs are discussed more fully in Chapter 14.

12 Transfer pricing, as a strategy, is discussed in Chapter 17 and in Case 4–2.

2

Assessing the International Marketing Environment

This section starts out with the all-important first step in international marketing: self-assessment. It is maintained here that a firm, regardless of its size and existing international opportunities, must first and foremost evaluate its international capabilities. Chapter 5 deals with this general problem. If the self-assessment results are positive, then the firm starts exploring international market potentials.

A number of unique analysis techniques are presented in Chapter 6. These techniques can be used separately or jointly in studying international market potential. Of these, the multiple-factor technique (MFT) is particularly useful for approximating international market potentials when the available data are very sketchy and deal only in generalities. This technique will enable the marketer to extrapolate market potentials by using some of the known specific data.

Analyzing international market potentials is an important step, but it is not the only one; international markets must be divided into segments according to their similarities and dissimilarities. Chapter 7 explores different aspects of this second step.

Entering international markets is the third step. Chapters 8 and 9 deal with this topic. Because exporting is very important for the American economy, the authors put special emphasis on it by devoting a whole chapter to it. Chapter 8 discusses some of the key aspects of export management, which enables a firm to enter the international market quickly.

Entry strategies are further discussed in Chapter 9; this discussion puts additional emphasis on export management companies (EMCs), export trading companies (ETCs), and consortia. Export trading companies, also called *sogo shoshas*, are considered to be mainly responsible for the success of Japan and NICs (newly industrialized countries) in international marketing. These are unique middlemen arrangements through which international entry is made not only easy but also effective. The remainder of the chapter briefly discusses other modes of entry. Deciding on an entry mode that is most suitable for a firm is extremely critical to its success or failure in the international arena. A series of internal and external factors enter into the equation to make the correct entry

117

decision. These factors also are discussed in Chapter 9.

Thus, a firm must assess the international marketing environment if it wants to be successful internationally. It is maintained here that the more carefully a firm plans at this stage, the more likely it is to be successful in its international endeavors.

CHAPTER

5

Appraising a Company's International Capabilities

Chapter Outline

Learning Objectives

When you have mastered the contents of this chapter, you will be able to do the following:

1   Explain why management has to internationalize to be successful in international markets.

2   Discuss the reasons that firms go international.

3   Analyze the several factors influencing the international capabilities of the firm.

4   Explain why internationalization is an ongoing process in constant need of evaluation.

Many, if not most, companies have an aversion to entering international markets. There are two reasons for this aversion: (1) lack of international knowledge, which results in a fear of international markets and an uncertainty about how to enter them, and (2) lack of the human and financial resources needed to attain overall international competence.[1] Unless this aversion is overcome, however, a firm will not be able to take advantage of international market opportunities. In order for a firm to capitalize on international opportunities, it must first evaluate its own international capabilities. Foremost among these capabilities is management's ability to internationalize—the level to which management has made a commitment to become international and has the training and talent to function in international markets.[2]

THE INTERNATIONALIZATION PROCESS

Internationalization is a process whereby a domestic firm becomes international.

Basically, internationalization represents a change in the company's overall philosophy. Consider, for example, Inland Motors, a small firm located in the mountains of western Virginia that makes a wide variety of small motors with many applications. Recently, this company has received many requests to do export business, to enter into joint ventures, or to otherwise enter international markets. If Inland Motors decides to enter international markets, it must internationalize. It must begin to think internationally, reorienting itself into a polycentric mode. Polycentric orientation means learning to do business in different ways in order to cater to consumers in different cultures. In effect, Inland Motors will be moving from an ethnocentric (home country) to a polycentric (multicountry) orientation. The company will change its outlook from *unicultural* to *multicultural*.

Understanding the difference between ethnocentric and polycentric management attitudes is extremely critical to successful internationalization. Table 5–1 illustrates the differences between the two. The five conditions discussed all deal with two concepts, ethnocentricity (uniculturalism) and polycentricity (multiculturalism). Regardless of

TABLE 5–1 ■ *Ethnocentric versus Polycentric Management Attitudes*

Ethnocentric	Polycentric
Our way of doing business is the right way.	In many parts of the world, the ways of doing business vary.
Our way of doing business is applicable anywhere in the world.	There are other ways of doing business that are more suited to the needs of different world markets.
We know what consumers need. They are pretty much the same everywhere.	We must find out what consumers need. They are quite different in different world markets.
Our understanding of consumer behavior is very good and applicable anywhere in the world.	We must understand consumer behavior patterns in each and every separate world market.
Our way is the only way. Let us do it all over the world.	Let us find out what we must do in each and every market.

whether the firm is thinking about its way of doing business or thinking of consumer behavior, if it is ethnocentric, it thinks that the firm's way of doing business or treating the customer is appropriate and is applicable anywhere in the world. If the firm is polycentric, it thinks that "there are many different ways of doing business, any of which are as good as ours or even better," or "consumers are different in different world markets, and we must understand their needs and their behavior patterns to be successful."

Although the United States is domestically a "melting pot," American orientation toward international markets has been more ethnocentric. Japan, by contrast, domestically has almost a uniform culture, but its international orientation has been polycentric. Japanese polycentricity can be seen in the behavior of Shiseido, a giant cosmetics company. After comparing its products with the products that existed in the U.S. markets, the company tried to enter U.S. markets in the 1960s with the same products it sold in Japan. After selling its products in more than 800 U.S. stores, the company realized that American taste in cosmetics is very different from Japanese taste. Application of Shiseido's makeup required a time-consuming series of applications, which Japanese women did not mind but American women did not like. Instead of being discouraged, Shiseido designed a new line of products that met the needs of American women. These cosmetics are beautifully packaged, easy to use, and have the advantage of being graced with subtle scents. Shiseido, in order to push its products, developed effective advertising programs to put most of its promotional efforts into service designed for American consumers.[3] Thus, the company displayed its polycentric orientation. This change in management philosophy from ethnocentricity to polycentricity is very closely related to the firm's willingness to go international and, therefore, to its efforts to internationalize.

REASONS FOR INTERNATIONALIZATION

There are both internal and external reasons for internationalization.

Internal Reasons

Among the internal reasons that firms decide to internationalize are the following:

1. Attractive overseas markets

2. Perceptive management

3. Saturated or closed domestic markets

4. New management

5. International development

Let us examine each one.

ATTRACTIVE OVERSEAS MARKETS ■ From time to time, certain overseas markets grow spectacularly, providing tempting opportunities for expansion-minded firms. Many Hawaii-based, small U.S. companies find Japan an attractive market for expansion; cultural and ethnic ties as well as a growing two-way business and tourist trade have made available lots of information on the Japanese market and have stimulated interest on the part of Hawaiian companies in participating in the growing Hawaii-Japan trade. One maker of chocolate-covered macadamia nuts, for example, with the help of Japanese acquaintances, succeeded in entering the market.

Other markets that are presenting tempting opportunities include those in Southeast Asia (e.g., Thailand, Singapore, and Taiwan) and Eastern Europe (Russia and other former Soviet states, Poland, Hungary, the Czech and Slovakian Republics, Bulgaria, and Romania). The attraction of the Southeast Asian markets is based on their economic successes, while the attraction of the Eastern European markets is rooted in their newfound political freedoms and desires to develop trade and economic relationships with countries in Western Europe, North America, and Japan. Other countries that are likely to increase in market attractiveness as key changes occur include the People's Republic of China, the Republic of South Africa, and Cuba.

The company may be lured by one or more of these markets because it may have special connections, know-how, or personnel to help the company function in these markets. Thus, attractive growing international markets may be selected and acted upon because of certain internal capabilities, skills, and knowledge.

PERCEPTIVE MANAGEMENT ■ Perceptive

managements gain early awareness of developing opportunities in overseas markets, make it their business to become knowledgeable about these markets, and maintain a sense of open-mindedness about where and when their companies should expand overseas. Perceptive managements generally have many cosmopolites in their ranks (people who have lived abroad and traveled extensively, as well as those who have many contacts in potential overseas markets). Perceptive managements also keep abreast of current developments overseas, and their open-mindedness leads them to investigate evolving potential opportunities and to question past preconceptions.

SATURATED OR CLOSED DOMESTIC MARKETS

■ Many U.S. appliance manufacturers and automakers initially entered international markets because of what they viewed as near-saturated domestic markets. U.S. producers of asbestos products found the domestic market legally closed to them, but because

some overseas markets had more lenient consumer protection laws, they continued to produce for overseas markets.

Saturated domestic markets are accompanied by excess production capacity, and firms with unused production capacity often look overseas for new marketing opportunities. Sometimes, excess production capacity arises because of changing demand in the domestic market. As domestic markets switch to new and substitute products, companies making older product versions develop excess capacity and look for overseas market opportunities. In some cases, the domestic market may be completely closed but the company may be producing for international markets. For instance, whereas the old-fashioned manual-wringer washing machines are totally outdated in the U.S. markets, in many less-developed countries, they are very desirable because they are better than manual washboards or rocks to clean the laundry.

NEW MANAGEMENT ■ The arrival of new

management on the scene often provides the stimulus for the company to internationalize. Mergers, acquisitions, buyouts, and takeovers are all likely to be accomplished by the arrival of new key management personnel. Sometimes, the new management is internationally oriented, and as a result, the company internationalizes. Increasingly, however, foreign companies are involved in the takeovers, and internationalization occurs automatically.

INTERNAL DEVELOPMENTS ■ Certain inter-

nal developments may provide the stimulus for internationalization. For instance, a company's research activity may develop a by-product suitable for sale overseas, as happened with a food-processing firm that discovered a low-cost protein ideal for helping to alleviate food shortages in some parts of Africa. Many years ago, DuPont, during its multitudinous research projects, developed a material called Corfam. Corfam was used to produce very sturdy shoes, and DuPont sold the product to the Polish army.

External Reasons

Included among the external reasons for internationalization are the following:

1. Market factors

2. Product-generated inquiries

3. Outside experts

4. Government

Let us have a look at each one.

MARKET FACTORS ■ Growth in international markets per se causes the demand for the products of some companies to grow, pushing the makers of these products into internationalization. Many pharmaceutical companies entered international markets when growth in the international demand for their products was first getting underway. Squibb entered the Turkish market before that market was large enough to be profitable. But the market was growing rapidly, which encouraged Squibb to internationalize further. In addition to growth in demand, knowing that other firms, particularly competitors, are internationalizing provides a strong incentive to internationalize. Competitors are an important external factor stimulating internationalization. Coca-Cola became international much earlier than Pepsi did, but there is no doubt whatsoever that Coca-Cola's move into overseas markets influenced Pepsi to move in the same direction.

PRODUCT-GENERATED INQUIRIES ■ Many a small company has become international because its products generated inquiries from overseas. Sometimes the product is entirely new; at other times it is an existing product that appears suitable for some overseas markets. For instance, a trade journal article about a small company making tractors for use on small plots of land resulted in an inquiry from the Indonesian government, which was interested in adapting these tractors for rice cultivation. Similarly, there may be an obvious need for the products of the business even though inquiries are not quite generated as yet. The Trade Opportunities Program (TOP)[4] provides 50 to 70 leads every week indicating market opportunities all over the world. An obvious opportunity discovered this way can be a strong incentive to enter international markets.

OUTSIDE EXPERTS ■ Several outside experts encourage internationalization, including export agents, chambers of commerce, and banks.

1. *Export agents.* Export agents, as well as export trading companies and export management firms, generally qualify as experts in international markets. They are already dealing internationally in other products, have overseas contacts, and are set up to handle other exportable products. Many of those trade intermediaries approach prospective international marketers directly if they think that their products have potential markets overseas.

2. *Chambers of commerce.* Chambers of commerce and similar organizations are interested in stimulating international business, both exports and imports. These organizations seek to motivate individual companies to get involved in international marketing, and provide incentives for them to do so. These incentives include putting the prospective

exporter or importer in touch with overseas businesses, providing overseas market information, and referring the prospective exporter or importer to financial institutions capable of financing international marketing activity.

3. *Banks.* Banks and other financial institutions are often instrumental in getting companies to internationalize. They alert their domestic clients to international opportunities and help them to capitalize on these opportunities. Of course, they look forward to their services being used more extensively as domestic clients expand internationally.[5]

GOVERNMENT ▪ Government may also encourage internationalization. For many years, the U.S. government has worked to expand exports. The U.S. Department of Commerce and other governmental agencies engage in a variety of activities aimed to help American companies internationalize. Each U.S. Department of Commerce district office seeks to increase the international involvement of those companies in its district. The U.S. Department of Education has involved itself in providing an international education program for the personnel of U.S. firms. (For more details, see Chapter 8.)

Almost all of the states have offices of economic development that encourage local firms to go international. These offices provide information about overseas markets, and they display products at international trade fairs. Some even have offices in different parts of the world (such as Hong Kong, Singapore, or Brussels) to stimulate international marketing by establishing contacts with overseas businesses.

In nearly all countries, governments try to stimulate international business by providing international marketing expertise.

The Republic of Ireland and Northern Ireland jointly developed a European export marketing program, the purpose of which was to encourage and assist companies from both countries to enter European markets. Irish companies already cultivating these markets are helped to expand their involvement. The Hungarian government provides assistance, help, and guidance to Hungarian firms that want to become more international.

EVALUATING THE INTERNATIONAL CAPABILITIES OF A COMPANY

Evaluating a company's international capabilities begins with an assessment of its management's capabilities.

Evaluating Internationalization of Management

Assessment involves answering questions such as those in Figure 5–1. Question 1, which relates to management's understanding of polycentricity, is of key importance. Polycentricity is, in essence, orientation toward the host country (or host countries), in contrast to ethnocentricity, which is orientation toward the home country. For example, a polycentric management reasons, "If the Arabs don't like American-style catsup, then we must adjust the taste to their liking," while an ethnocentric management complains, "Why don't the Arabs like our catsup? What is wrong with them?"

Even if a management has a polycentric orientation, there still may be a need for international training or talent. International

1. Does management have a polycentric orientation?

2. Does management have any international talent—for example, middle management people who are multicultural—who have lived in different parts of the world, can speak foreign languages, and/or have studied some aspect of international business?

3. What are the key aspects of this talent?

4. What additional international talent is needed?

5. Should the company internationalize its existing talent?

6. Can other managerial personnel be trained in order to develop international talent?

7. What are the quickest and most effective means for training this international talent?

8. Where can the company get the best advice on internationalizing?

9. What additional information on internationalizing is needed?

FIGURE 5–1 *A Checklist for Assessing Internationalization in Management*

talent must fit the market a firm is planning to enter. If management is experienced in more developed industrial markets but the firm is planning to sell its product line in some less-developed countries, it has a need for different talent. It is important to determine the extent of whatever international talent management already has. Is there enough talent to carry through on the firm's first ventures into international markets? Should additional international talent be recruited? Sometimes, all that is needed is for existing international talent to secure additional training. Management needs to determine where it can go for such training and for other advice on internationalizing. Established business contacts and professional consultants may be in a position to provide additional information and advice.

Evaluating Products and Services

Another aspect of analyzing a company's international capabilities is an evaluation of its product. If a firm has products that are truly in demand in international markets, its potential for international marketing success is high. If a firm's technological capabilities are behind those of other competitors active in the same markets, the resultant higher costs and poor product designs may deter it from entering the markets.

Figure 5–2 details some key questions to ask when assessing the internationalization potentials of company products. Overall, of course, for each product, management attempts to answer several questions. How much, if any, demand will there need to be for the product in order to justify adapting it to international market needs? If adaptation

---

1. Which company products have a future in overseas markets?

2. Which of the existing product lines is most promising?

3. Is company technology competitive?

4. For selling company products overseas, are changes needed in any of the following areas?

   • design

   • content

   • brand and packaging

   • components

5. Is the company capable of providing the necessary services?

6. Is the company capable of product repairs, product installation, and related support services?

7. Is the company developing other products with international marketing potential?

FIGURE 5–2 *A Checklist for Assessing the Internationalization Potentials of Company Products*

is required, how extensive must it be? A company's international capability is enhanced to the extent that its products are ready for sale in the targeted overseas markets. However, except for certain global firms, such as IBM and Xerox, and a few product lines, such as pharmaceuticals and chemicals, product adaptation in preparation for overseas sale is common. Automobiles imported into the U.S. must be adjusted at least to the safety standards that are specified by the American government. A global company such as Coca-Cola even has slight differences in the tastes of its products to satisfy regional or local tastes in different parts of the world.

If an adaptation is likely, a company must ask if the adaptation will relate to the product design, its components, its contents, its brand and package, some combinations of these, or other factors. Can adaptations be made at home before the product is shipped abroad, or should they be made overseas? The more internationalized a firm and the more long term its international orientation, the greater the chances that the product will be shipped first and then adapted overseas. With the emergence of free trade zones and free trade areas throughout the world, manufacturing and assembling facilities are readily available in many overseas markets. These facilities, coupled with the availability of skilled labor and the attractiveness of tax-free status, provide real incentives for the marketer to adapt the product near the market rather than at the home plant.

Assurance of after-sales service is a big selling feature, particularly for exporters.[6] Therefore, a product's service components need careful consideration. Certain products, such as appliances and other technical items, have service components critical to their successful marketing. If a firm's products require minimum service, or if it is in a position to provide needed services, a firm's international readiness is high. The availability of repair services, spare parts, installation, and related support capabilities all require assessment. After-sales service is a critical consideration not only for exporters but for all types of international marketing. When marketing products that require after-sale service overseas, management must consider at least five options:

1. Disregard service altogether.

2. Find a local firm to service the products.

3. Train the distributor (if there is one) to provide repair and maintenance.

4. Establish service personnel in the country.

5. Be prepared to provide these services long distance.

All of these options have advantages and disadvantages that need to be evaluated. The first option is not viable unless the international marketer is not planning to stay in foreign markets for very long. The second option is problematic because it is quite difficult to estimate the cost of an overseas service organization and factor this cost into overseas prices. Perhaps this problem could partly be overcome by establishing such service on a short-term basis until the third option can be used; that is, until distributors can be properly trained. The company must consider the provision of service to overseas customers if it wants to remain in international markets. Because the cost and quality of service is questionable when it is given by others, the international company must consider the fifth option, servicing its products in overseas markets. Long-distance delivery

of services can be effected by dispatching service personnel when a product breaks down. Because of time lapse and irregularity, however, this solution may not be very satisfactory. In fact, even if the product is not prone to breakdowns, foreign customers feel happier if they know that the fourth option, service personnel stationed permanently in the country, is available to them.

Are other products with promising international possibilities on the drawing boards? If so, this helps to assure that the firm will enter international markets to stay longer.

Evaluating Distribution Capabilities

In evaluating international capability, the area of distribution is critical. If a company cannot find appropriate ways of distributing its products, it will proceed no further with internationalization. Figure 5–3 raises basic considerations in evaluating the distribution aspects of a company's international capabilities.

The simplest solution is that of a company whose existing distribution system can easily extend itself into overseas markets. But accomplishing this extension means having overseas contacts capable of performing needed functions.

Many, perhaps most, companies have the choice of whether or not to develop a distribution system for international markets—direct or indirect—from scratch. They must also consider how elaborate the distribution system must be. If a vertical (multilevel) distribution system, which is time consuming and demanding to build, is needed, so many extras and so much special talent may be required that a company will drop all consideration of internationalizing further.

1. Is the company's distribution system capable of internationalization?

2. Does the company have overseas contacts?

3. Are overseas contacts capable of distributing the products effectively?

4. Will it be necessary for the company to start a distribution system from scratch?

5. Can the distribution system perform effectively?

6. Will the company have to develop a vertical (multilevel) distribution system?

FIGURE 5–3 *A Checklist for Assessing the Distribution Aspects of a Company's Products*

Evaluating Promotion Capability and Financial Support

In analyzing international capabilities, managers must also consider product promotion. Many domestic firms are baffled when they think of promoting their products in international markets. If a company's products require minimum promotion, its internationalization can be accelerated. However, important questions need to be answered: How much international advertising should there be? Who is going to do it? How can promotional messages be localized? There may be other promotional needs that a company may not understand without professional advice. It all boils down to how committed the firm is to being a local competitor in the market and to whether, as Alan Zakon terms it, the firm can develop a presence in new markets. In other words, a company must be committed to entering a market and staying there for a long time and to competing there just like other companies in that market.

Consideration must also be given to needed financial and other types of support.

A company's banks may stand ready to extend credit for its internationalization activities.

Putting It Together

Figure 5–4 shows the internationalization process. The starting point is to raise management's awareness of international opportunities. Next, there is a self-evaluation by management of its international capabilities. Then comes an assessment of the potential of the products for internationalization. Distribution and promotion, essential components of the marketing mix, are appraised relative to existing products and product lines. Pricing, although a key component of the marketing mix, is considered only indirectly. But, of course, if a producer's price is beyond the financial capabilities of consumers in target overseas markets, there is no point in proceeding further with the product's internationalization.[7]

The next to last step in the internationalization process is to evaluate necessary external support, such as financing. The final

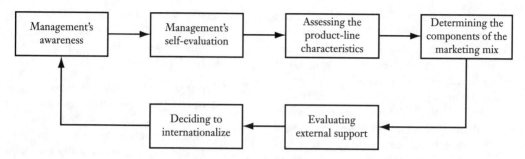

FIGURE 5-4 *The Internationalization Process*

step is to decide whether or not to internationalize. After following the process described in this chapter, the company will have evaluated its international strengths and weaknesses, and carefully assessed its international opportunities and threats (a process called SWOT analysis); now, the decision needs to be made regarding the internationalization of the firm in question. Note that Figure 5-4 shows the final step looping back to the first step, indicating that the internationalization process is flexible and self-adjusting. This latter feature is essential in internationalization, as changes in a firm's international operations occur continuously. Similarly, conditions in international markets may be changing. Therefore, the firm must continuously evaluate its international competencies. Remember, having international presence does not necessarily mean that a company is properly internationalized. Although Fiat, the automotive manufacturing company, has had a long-standing presence in international markets, it was not satisfied with its performance. An in-depth study of the company indicated that people at the company's headquarters were not quite international; they did not correspond to those abroad, and they did not quite understand what needed to be done so that the social, political, cultural, and technical differentiation of standards in different markets could be adequately managed.[8]

The internationalization process is complex, and the level of sophistication that is required to be successful in international markets is not easy to measure.[9] The self-adjustment activity in the overall internationalization process can be illustrated by Itokin, a Japanese company that makes and sells clothing for young working women. Itokin opened its first shop on Madison Avenue in 1984, carrying more than 20 designer labels. Although such a wide choice is quite common in Japanese retailing, it confused American customers. Sales languished. As a result, the company got rid of all but three key designer lines. Business improved to the point that Itokin built a 20-store chain across the United States and expects to expand further.[10]

A review of the American Business Conference's successful efforts may illustrate this overall internationalization process.[11] ABC is composed of 100 fast-growing companies with revenues between $10 million and $12 billion. ABC has been very successful in world markets. Although the member companies are not exactly similar, they followed a five-point success formula:

1. *Product excellence.* They have been dedicated to serve international markets with the best possible products. From Cray Supercomputers to Cross Pens to Stryker Medical Products, ABC companies offer what the world markets need.

2. *Marketing excellence.* Recognizing Japan's fascination with American popular culture, Brown-Forman managed to enter the Japanese market by presenting it with California Coolers and Jack Daniels bourbon as part of classic American culture. Loctite, a manufacturer of industrial and household adhesives, impressed the French market with an advertisement showing a beautiful young woman repairing a rip in her miniskirt with Super Glue. ABC's high-tech firms have been paying close attention to changing engineering standards in many foreign markets and have been modifying their products accordingly.

3. *Getting started early.* ABC companies recognized early that they wanted to enter global markets. Milipore, a manufacturer of advanced filter systems, started exporting when its total sales were less than $10 million. Analog Devices, which manufactures linear integrated circuits, was dealing with foreign customers before the company's sales reached $1 million.

4. *Incremental expansion.* ABC companies expanded their international activities incrementally. They started entering markets that were most similar to those where they were used to doing business, such as Canada and the United Kingdom. Eventually, they started entering more challenging markets. Similarly, they kept their investment modes and their international activities flexible.

5. *Organizational commitment.* Without exception, the chief executive officers of ABC firms led their companies into world markets. They all had the vision and desire to take advantage of global opportunities.

SUMMARY

The process of internationalization begins with a shift in managerial orientation from ethnocentricity to polycentricity. While ethnocentricity implies a narrow domestic orientation, polycentricity means understanding various world markets well and acting accordingly. It is the combined impact of a whole series of internal and external factors, however, that brings about a company's internationalization. At some point, management undertakes self-assessment. Management evaluates its own international capabilities, examines the products for their potential for internationalization, and determines if the required and appropriate components of the marketing mix can be brought together and if other necessary external support factors exist. Once internationalization commences, it expands and becomes more complex. Internationalization is an ever-changing and continuous process. Therefore, it requires a certain degree of self-adjustment as internal and external conditions change. A company must understand how it could internationalize and how it could maintain this internalization to achieve global success. It is clear that such a global success is the outcome of carefully conducted SWOT analysis (strengths, weaknesses, opportunities, and threats). SWOT analysis is referred to in this chapter and will be undertaken throughout this book.

DISCUSSION QUESTIONS

1. Why should a company internationalize?

2. What are the key internal reasons for internationalization? Can you prioritize these? How? Can you think of reasons other than those listed in this chapter? What are they?

3. What are the key external reasons for internationalization? Can you think of reasons other than those listed in this chapter? What are they?

4. "Assessing international capabilities of the firm begins with evaluating the management." What does this statement mean, and how is this to be accomplished?

5. How would you evaluate a firm's products? Refer to Chapters 10 and 20 and compare what is in this chapter. Can you develop a more exhaustive list to evaluate a firm's products?

6. Can you add more questions to Figure 5–3? Why do you want to add to these questions? Explain.

7. Refer to Figure 5–4 and describe the internationalization process and its management.

An Irish Dairy Marketing Firm

A firm marketing Irish dairy products has been thinking of entering European markets. It has targeted West Germany. Because Germans are not extremely fond of dairy products—milk, in particular—this is expected to be a rather difficult task. The company has been only domestic thus far; however, it has the capabilities of developing multiple new dairy products.

QUESTIONS

1. How should the company internationalize?
2. Analyze the process step by step.

Matsushita and the American Market

Matsushita has restructured its U.S. divisions to give them more autonomy so that the company can benefit from large-scale manufacturing and locally oriented marketing. Matsushita established two new U.S.-based divisions: (1) North American TV Division and (2) Business Development Groups. The company's goals were to bring more production into the U.S. markets and to localize both manufacturing and marketing efforts. Thus, Matsushita expects greater responsiveness to market conditions.

This restructuring is based on Matsushita's perception of the U.S. market today as being one in which it is extremely difficult to enter and succeed. The political and economic situations made exporting televisions and running the business from Japan totally impossible. This reorganization is expected to give Matsushita more direct feedback from the market.

QUESTIONS

1. Discuss the internationalization process of Matsushita as it relates to its American operations.

2. Do you foresee some problems?

CKD of Prague

CKD is the only manufacturer of streetcars in the old Eastern Europe. CKD was designed to provide streetcars for all of the U.S.S.R. After the Czech Republic was established, the steady business that the company enjoyed was no longer there. Of course, being part of the old communist system, the company never thought of the need for marketing. The company was designed to produce 1,000 streetcars a year. Currently, with the orders from Greece, Uzbekistan, and Germany, the actual capacity is around 100–150 streetcars a year. The company has put its meager research funds into improving the design of streetcars. Since the Soviets left, the company has not changed its production orientation. The company is well equipped to repair old streetcars, but it does not have much research and development activity. Its labor force is highly skilled, and the production process is quite labor intensive.

CKD's competition is not only individually owned streetcars but also fast trains, monorails, and underground transportation. All of these transportation methods use units that basically resemble streetcars. The company hopes that old streetcar nostalgia will return. However, in the process, CKD is almost totally privatized and not well financed, and the world streetcar demand is still rather limited.

QUESTION

1. Prepare a marketing plan for CKD.

ENDNOTES

1 S. E. Emunds and S. J. Khoury, "Exports: A Necessary Ingredient in the Growth of Small Business Firms," *Journal of Small Business Management*, Spring 1986, 54–65.

2 Kathryn Sullivan, Frederick Orr, and Dayr Reis, "Going International? Here's How," *Industrial Management*, January–February 1994, 22–25.

3 Brian Dumaine, "Japan's Next Push in U.S. Markets," *Fortune*, September 1988, 135–141.

4 Katherine Glover, "TOP Program Helps U.S. Firms Tap Foreign Markets," *Business America*, 27 February 1989, 12–13.

5 Michael R. Czinkota and Illka A. Ronkainen, *International Marketing*, 5th ed. (Fort Worth, TX: Dryden Press, 1996), 143–164.

6 "A Big Selling Feature for Exporters: The Assurance of After-Sales Service," *Business America*, 15 February 1988, 19–20.

7 Alan J. Zakon, "Globalization is More Than Imports and Exports," *Management Review*, July 1988, 56–57.

8 Vittorio Tesio, "Redefining the 'Foreign Legion' Internationalization of Fiat S.P.A.," Research Roundup: Global, *Across the Board*, April 1994, 47–48.

9 Peter Bukley, "The Limits of Explanation: Testing the Internationalization Theory of the Multinational Enterprise," *Journal of Business Studies*, Summer 1988, 181–193.

10 Dumaine, "Japan's Next Push in U.S. Markets." See endnote 3.

11 John Endean, "The ABCs of Export Success," *Business America*, 12 March 1988, 28.

CHAPTER 6

Assessing International Market Opportunities and Developing Market Potentials

Chapter Outline

Techniques for Estimating International Marketing Potentials

Evaluating Market Opportunities

A Look at Eastern European Market Potentials

Present versus Future

Case 6–1: The Chilean Market

Case 6–2: The Argentine Market

Learning Objectives

When you have mastered the contents of this chapter, you will be able to do the following:

1   Explain the importance of analyzing international market potentials and why it is more difficult than analyzing domestic market potentials.

2   Compare and contrast some techniques of market-potential analysis.

3   Explain how techniques of market-potential analysis are adjusted to fit special needs.

4   Demonstrate why the techniques for market-potential analysis are not equally useful in forecasting.

5   Calculate international market potentials using the techniques discussed in this chapter.

6   Discuss why projecting past trends is not the best means for predicting the future.

More than 15,000 U.S. firms are active in international marketing, and all need information about their target markets. Regardless of whether overseas markets are serviced through plants established overseas or through exporting, American management makes estimates of the amount of sales opportunity for its products in each overseas target market.

International marketers contemplating entry into new foreign markets need two kinds of information. First, for each country under consideration for entry, they need to know the size of current market demand and the market potential for their products. Second, international marketers need to know about trade patterns in order to determine the feasibility of exporting and to identify other means of servicing each prospective market. While statistics that marketers can use in making entry decisions are readily available for the United States and most European countries from secondary sources, there are only dated statistics for most other countries. The result is that international marketers use other methods for estimating current market demand and market potentials.

The discussion in this chapter focuses on some important techniques used for estimating international market potentials. This discussion begins with an analysis of the estimating techniques, and then it moves to various forecasting approaches. Next, basic problems met in international forecasting are explored, and an example of the multiple-factor technique is presented.

TECHNIQUES FOR ESTIMATING INTERNATIONAL MARKET POTENTIALS

Trend-Analysis and Regression Techniques

If past sales data are available for the market, it is possible to project future sales in the market through trend-analysis and regression techniques. The estimating equation used in trend analysis is

$$Y = a + bX$$

where

Y = Total sales
X = Year
$a = \Sigma Y/n$
$b = \Sigma XY/X$

Regression techniques are used in cross-section studies to estimate demand. For example, analyzing relationships between gross economic indicators in one country and the demand for a particular product in that country sets the stage for the analyst to apply these relationships to other countries. For example, if a regression equation is established for the relationship between gross national product (GNP) and auto sales in country A, and the GNP for country B is known, and similarities exist between country A and B, the same equation is usable for analyzing the auto market in country B.[1]

Assume that management wants to estimate the market potential for automobiles in South Korea and that it has several years of past data for the South Korean GNP and auto sales. The correlation coefficient between changes in South Korea GNP and auto sales is 0.8. If the South Korean GNP is

21 billion won, auto sales in South Korea are 200,000 units annually, and a 7 percent (147 million won) increase in GNP is forecast for next year, the expected percentage increase in auto sales in South Korea will be $0.7 \times 0.8 = 0.56$, or 5.6 percent, or 11,200 additional units, making total estimated auto sales in South Korea 211,200 units for next year. While this approach appears simplistic, it does provide an approximation extremely important not only to South Korean automakers but also to automakers elsewhere who are considering exporting to South Korea.

Annual Sales Formula

When actual sales data are not available, market potential is often estimated using the formula $Sa = Pa + (Ma - Xa) - Ia_1 - Ia_0$, where Sa is annual sales of the product in country A, Pa is annual production of the product in country A, Ma is country A's annual imports of the product, Xa is country A's exports of the product, and Ia_1 and Ia_0 are the ending and beginning inventories of the product in country A.[2] If inventory figures are not available, the formula reduces to $Sa = Pa + (Ma - Xa)$.

To illustrate use of this technique, consider a hypothetical study of the German dishwasher market. Assuming production imports and exports were as shown in

TABLE 6–1 ▪ *Dishwashers in Germany (hypothetical data)*

	Number of Units
Production	426,650
+ Imports	+55,090
	481,740
- Exports	-95,270
= Estimated consumption	386,470

Table 6–1, then estimated consumption in Germany was 386,470 units for the year.

Survey Data

Data gathered from primary sources through surveys and syndicated data obtained from international marketing research firms are sometimes used for estimating market potentials. Many problems are faced in gathering data from primary sources: There are chronic shortages of trained field workers, large numbers of prospective respondents who are unwilling to cooperate, and occasional falsification of responses by field workers.

Coefficients of Income Sensitivity

Coefficients of income sensitivity are useful for making rough estimates of market potentials. Such coefficients express relationships between income and consumption patterns and indicate the percentage of increases or decreases in consumption expected for each 1 percent increase in spendable income. A product with a coefficient of 1.0, for example, has a demand that increases exactly in proportion to income increases.

In Latin America, overall coefficients of income sensitivity of 0.5 and 0.6 exist for nonprocessed foods, of 0.8 and 1.2 for processed foods, and of 1.2 and 1.5 for manufactured goods. Hence, to obtain a demand estimate, these coefficients are applied to the product's present sales volume and are adjusted for the expected increase in volume. The formula used is

$$MP = (C \times I_e \times St) + St$$

where

MP = Market potential
C = Income sensitivity coefficient
I_e = Expected percentage increase in income
St = Total industrial or product sales at present

For example, if 1.5 is the coefficient of income sensitivity, a 3 percent income increase is expected, and there are $4 million total industry sales at present, then market potential is 1.5 × (0.03 × 4,000,000) + 4,000,000 = $4,180,000.

Multiple-Factor Technique

The multiple-factor technique is a more sophisticated approach than those discussed earlier. In this technique two major aspects of the foreign market are distinguished: size and quality. The usual indicator of market size is population. The indicator of market quality is derived from a study of the country's internal situation to determine its "economic level" and the "quality-of-life level." Seven variables are often used in determining market quality: (1) gross national product, (2) steel consumption, (3) kilowatt-hours of electricity produced, (4) telephones in use, (5) radios in use, (6) televisions in use, and (7) dwellings with electricity.

The first three variables (GNP, steel consumption, and kilowatt-hours of electricity produced) indicate the level of economic development, while the other variables reflect the quality-of-life level. Individual market analysts add and delete variables depending upon the country market being studied. If, for instance, one wants to determine market potentials for appliances in a Third World country, steel consumption is unimportant, but the proportion of houses with running water, electricity, and indoor plumbing is important. Also, variables are added or deleted as required within the context of the particular product whose market potential is under study.

For example, see Table 6–2 for a comparison of Mexico and the United States in 1995. The size of the Mexican market (based on population) is 35.6 percent that of the U.S. market. The quality of the Mexican market (based on the seven other variables in the table) is presented on a per capita basis and is also expressed as a percentage of the U.S. per capita figure. The average of these seven variables gives an approximation of what might be called the quality of this market by American standards. Mexico's market quality by 1995 was 18.6 percent of the market quality in the United States. To arrive at an overall figure for market potential, market quality is multiplied by market size. Thus, Mexico's 1995 market potential was 18.6 percent of the 35.6 percent, or 6.6 percent of the U.S. market potential (in other words, market quality times market size).

This market potential can be used by multiplying it by the product sales in the United States of the product for which a market-potential volume is to be derived. For instance, if 3 million refrigerators are sold in the United States, 3,000,000 × 6.6% = 198,000 is the estimated market potential for refrigerators in Mexico.

Input-Output Analysis

Input-output tables depict interrelationships between the economic sectors of an area (such as a city, region, or country). Input-output analysis makes it possible for the international market analyst to determine the market potential for either exports or domestic production and distribution. One important use of input-output tables is to predict future output levels for an international company's customers in a particular country or region.

TABLE 6–2 ▪ *Mexico and the United States in 1995*

Variables	Mexico	United States
Population 1995	94,000,000	264,000,000
GDP (1993)	$8,200 per capita 33.2% of U.S.	$24,700 per capita
Steel Production (1992)	83.5kg per capita 26.1% of U.S.	319.4kg per capita
Kilowatt-hours of electricity produced (1992)	120.7 billion kWh 1,284 per capita 10.5% of U.S.	3230 billion kWh 12,235 per capita
Telephones in use	12,368,421 0.13 per capita 16.9% of U.S.	203,076,920 0.77 per capita
Radios in use	17,108,000 0.182 per capita 9.1% of U.S.	528,000,000 2 per capita
Televisions in use	14,029,851 0.149 per capita 17.9% of U.S.	220,000,000 0.833 per capita
Motor vehicle registration	11,100,000 0.118 per capita 16.4% of U.S.	190,000,000 0.72 per capita

Source: George Thomas Kurion, *The New Book of World Rankings* (New York: Facts on File, 1995); and U.S. Commerce Department, Bureau of the Census, *1995 Statistical Abstract of the U.S.* (Washington, D.C.: U.S. Government Printing Office, 1995).

Input-output tables are divided into processing sectors and final-demand sectors. Processing sectors buy goods and services for resale purposes, while final-demand sectors buy for consumption or use. The final-demand sectors are autonomous; their demand creates the demand for processing sectors. Hence, processing sectors face a derived demand. While purchases by a sector from other sectors are inputs, the sector's sales to other sectors are outputs.

If demand for household appliances increases, demand also increases for such primary resources as iron and steel and nonferrous metals, screw machine products and bolts, business services, and the like. In addition, as a whole, there is an increase in the GNP that is directly attributable to increased demand in the household appliance industry. Thus, once interrelationships among the sectors are determined, it becomes possible to trace the impact of a change on one sector to other sectors.

Typically, input-output relationships for an area, a region, or a country are presented in an input coefficient matrix. The availability of such matrices enables exporters and other international marketers to estimate market potentials.

If, for instance, projections show that there will be a $750 million annual increase in U.S. auto sales by 1997, by looking at the

TABLE 6–3 ■ *Example of Direct Requirements per Dollar of Gross Output by Motor Vehicles Industry*

Industry	Requirements per Dollar Output
Primary iron and steel manufacturing	0.08543
Primary nonferrous metals	0.01113
Stamping, screw machines, products, and bolts	0.03019
Other fabricated metal products	0.03506
Engines and turbines	0.00369

Source: Adapted from U.S. Department of Commerce, *Measuring Markets* (Washington, D.C.: U.S. Government Printing Office, 1968), 77.

TABLE 6–4 ■ *Partial Picture of Total Requirements per Dollar of Gross Output by Motor Vehicles Industry*

Industry	Requirements per Dollar Output
Primary iron and steel manufacturing	0.20265
Primary nonferrous metals	0.05101
Stamping, screw machines, products, and bolts	0.05161
Other fabricated metal products	0.06236
Engines and turbines	0.00730

Source: Adapted from U.S. Department of Commerce, *Measuring Markets* (Washington, D.C.: U.S. Government Printing Office, 1968), 81–82.

"direct requirements per dollar of gross output" table indicating interindustry relationships in 1988, the world's chromium exporters can estimate their U.S. market potential for 1997. Table 6–3 shows the requirements of motor vehicles from other industries.

As Table 6–3 shows, for each dollar's worth of auto output, 1.1¢ worth of nonferrous metals are directly required. Table 6–4 shows total *direct* and *indirect* requirements by the motor vehicles industry, indicating that for each dollar's worth of auto output, 5.1¢ worth of nonferrous metals are utilized. Assuming that in both cases 40 percent of these requirements for nonferrous metals are for chromium, by 1997 the U.S. auto industry will directly require an increase of $18.6 million worth of chromium. Through using this approach, the Turkish chromium industry, for example, can establish its U.S. market potential. Unfortunately, input-output matrices are not available for every country or region.

The ISIC Method

The ISIC technique is used effectively in industrial marketing to determine market potentials.[3] It is based on the International Standard Industrial Classification (ISIC) system, and it requires knowledge of specific markets based on ISIC classifications.

The ISIC method is based on two key assumptions. The first is that the use of some

TABLE 6–5 ▪ *A Hypothetical Illustration of the ISIC Method*

ISIC (1)	Weight per Employee (lbs) (2)	No. of Employees in Romania (3)	Market Potential (2) × (3) (4)
Motor vehicles	250	100,000	25,000,000
Aircraft	300	50,000	15,000,000
Aircraft engines	400	30,000	12,000,000
Radios and related products	125	100,000	12,500,000
Finished metal products	400	150,000	60,000,000

TABLE 6–6 ▪ *Partial Growth Scale*

Steps	Named and Autonomous Locality Group	Discriminant Quotient
2	A church	1.00
3	A functional school	0.84
4	Access to electric power	0.76
5	Village public square; people from other villages shop at the village market	0.29
6	Telephones	0.16
7	Secondary school; 20 or more stores	0.08

Growth coefficient = 0.92

industrial products can be traced to the weight used per worker in different sectors. The weight per worker in each sector is a reflection of the technological know-how. The second assumption is that technological know-how diffuses rapidly (for example, the United States and most East European countries have about the same knowledge of basic industrial technology).

Table 6–5 displays a hypothetical illustration of using the ISIC method for a sector analysis for steel ingots. Five specific sectors (see column 1) are utilized. Column 2 is derived by dividing the total volume of steel ingots used in a particular year by the number of total employees in that industry. Column 3 is the key to the whole analysis, as we need employment figures by industry in the country (in this case, Romania) to do the analysis. Column 4 (which is column 2 multiplied by column 3) indicates market potentials for steel ingots in the different sectors. These figures represent upper limits for the market potentials. If an industry in Romania is not as efficient as it is worldwide, or if all of an industry's employees are not fully utilized, these estimates will exceed the real market potentials. Furthermore, those upper-limit estimates are reduced according to national growth plans and priority lists.

The Macro Survey Approach

The macro survey technique is based on the presence or absence of specialized types of institutions in a community.[4] As a community develops, it gains more specialized institutions, such as a church, a school building, a government organization, a clinic, or, perhaps, a radio station. The technique is not widely used, but it is particularly appropriate for use in situations where market information is either not available or inadequate. There are two steps in using the macro survey technique. The first step is to construct one scale indicating the stages of community growth and another scale indicating its stages of commercial advancement. The second step is to infer growth and market potential. Growth is indicated by the position on the community growth scale, and the position of the commercial scale reflects the extent of market opportunity. If the market is not adequately developed in terms of commercial activity, it cannot carry the load of distributing imported goods. The market potential is inferred by applying both scales to certain absolutes.

Table 6–6 illustrates a community growth scale. Discriminant quotients provide a measure of marginal contribution of each institution to the growth factor. If, as in this particular case, the community in question has all of these institutions, it has a growth scale of 0.92 out of a possible 1.00. If the community does not have all of these institutions, then only the relevant discriminant quotients are considered.

Table 6–7 illustrates the commercial development scale. Even though the community in this situation is 92 percent developed (see Table 6–6), it is only 84 percent developed commercially. It is quite possible for a community to be, say, 95 percent developed and less than 50 percent developed commercially.

Population dispersion and population density may also be considered in applying the macro survey approach. According to population dispersion and population density,

TABLE 6–7 ■ *Partial Commercial Development Scale*	
Quotient	Discriminant
Convenience grocery store	1.00
Gas station	0.72
Beauty shop	0.46
Hotel	0.40
Clothing store; movie theater	0.25
Cluster of stores	0.16
Commercialization coefficient = 0.84	

the country or the region may be classified into five groups, as shown in Table 6–8.

Assume, for instance, that a manufacturer of electronic products, such as radios and TVs, is interested in determining market potentials in Indonesia. Each region in Indonesia can be assessed using scales containing criteria similar to those in Tables 6–6 and 6–7. It is also possible to assess the market potentials of a whole country on an average basis if the growth and commercial development scales are regarded as applicable to national markets.

The criteria presented in Tables 6–6 and 6–7 are applicable for assessing either national or local markets. Market potentials are pegged on the development scales indicating that in small rural communities, instead of 100 radios per 1,000 population, there are 92 (growth coefficient of 0.92). The number of radios per 1,000 population is reduced further because of deficiencies in commercial development (commercialization coefficient of 84 percent). The expected market potential for radios per 1,000 population, therefore, is 77, which is the product of 92 percent and 84 percent ($0.92 \times 0.84 = 77.3$). If the community being studied has 3,000 people, the total market potential for radios is 231 ($77 \times 3 = 231$). If there are 1,000 such communities in the

TABLE 6–8 ▪ *Different Community Sizes*

Group	Community	Population Density (per square mile)	Hypothetical Market Saturation Levels		
			Radios	Stereos	TVs
1	Small rural	1,000–3,000	100/1000	75/1000	150/1000
2	Larger rural	3,000–10,000	150/1000	100/1000	175/1000
3	Semi-rural	10,000–25,000	200/1000	125/1000	200/1000
4	Small urban	25,000–50,000	235/1000	150/1000	220/1000
5	Metropolitan	50,000 and above	325/1000	180/1000	150/1000

TABLE 6–9 ▪ *Relative Merits of Market-Potential Analysis Techniques*

Technique Value	Complexity	Data Needs	Time Dimension	Forecasting Value
Trend analysis and regression analysis	Simple	Limited	Short- and long-run	Medium
Annual sales formula	Simple	Limited	Short-run	Medium–low
Survey data	Simple	Limited	Short-run	Low
Coefficient of income sensitivity	Simple	Extensive	Short- and long-run	Medium
Multiple-factor analysis	Complex	Extensive	Short- and long-run	High–medium
Input-output analysis	Complex	Extensive	Short-run	High
The macro survey	Complex	Limited	Short-run	High–medium
ISIC	Simple	Limited	Short- and long-run	Medium

country, the total market potential for the group is 231,000.

The data required for using this technique are secured in various ways. One way is to use aerial photographs showing specific features such as population dispersion, TV antennas (which imply TV ownership), shopping facilities, and the like. Another data-gathering approach is to use Yellow Pages or other available directories. Analysis of Yellow Pages reveals types of businesses, their proportion to total population, and the depth and breadth of the business population. A third data-gathering approach is to visit communities in order to assess the stage of development. For analyses of the national

market potential, a sample of different sized communities is analyzed and averaged.

Which of these techniques is the best choice? Table 6–9 shows a summary of the relative merits of each technique. While trends and regression analyses are simple and require a limited amount of data, their forecasting value is of only medium value. By contrast, multiple-factor and input-output analyses are rather complex and call for extensive data, but their forecasting value is high. However, only a small number of the world's nearly 200 countries provide adequate input-output data. For market analysts seeking techniques useful both in the short run and in the long run, the coefficient-of-income-sensitivity and ISIC techniques are excellent choices.

Any one of the eight techniques can be used to determine a country's market potentials. Each technique is also usable for clustering several countries and, hence, for segmenting international markets.

EVALUATING MARKET OPPORTUNITIES

Years ago, a St. Louis shoe manufacturer dispatched two representatives to West Africa with instructions to "check out the market there for shoes." The first representative cabled back, "Nobody here wears shoes. There is no market here for them." The second representative cabled back, "Nobody here wears shoes. There is a hell of a big market here for shoes!" What is the moral of this anecdote? Simply this: *Perception has a great deal to do with evaluating market opportunity.*

In analyzing opportunities in international markets, it is important to identify both existing and nonexisting market potentials. There are three basic categories of demand, implying three types of market opportunities: (1) existing demand, (2) latent demand, and (3) incipient demand.[5]

Existing demand is present when customers are already buying the product or service in question. They are being served by existing suppliers. Existing demand is easy to measure.

Latent demand is demand that would surface if the product were offered to customers at a price acceptable to them and if other components of the marketing mix were right. Latent demand is also demand that materializes almost immediately if a product previously unavailable in a market is made available. In many countries, latent demand for VCRs existed before they became available. Latent demand is difficult to measure precisely.

Incipient demand is demand that does not exist but that is indicated when there are good chances that needs for the product will emerge later on. At some point, incipient demand becomes latent demand. If products with incipient demands become available, the market does not respond immediately because it lacks *market readiness*. For instance, consumers in many parts of the world are not yet ready to use amniocentesis tests during an early stage of pregnancy to determine if unborn babies have genetic disorders; in time, however, the incipient demand for this product likely will evolve first into latent demand and then into existing demand. Where multiple-factor techniques for evaluating market opportunities are used and the reference country is a mature market (the United States, as in the examples used here), the results may combine both existing and latent demands and may even include some incipient demand. Thus, it is necessary for the analyst to estimate how much of the calculated market potential will materialize in the short run. It is unrealistic to assume that the results of using a multiple-factor technique will indicate how large existing demand really is— usually, existing demand is overstated.

A LOOK AT EASTERN EUROPEAN MARKET POTENTIALS

To illustrate use of the multiple-factor technique in determining market potentials, consider the problem posed in attempting to determine market potentials in the Eastern European countries. Detailed data about the Eastern European countries are in short supply, and even most of the experts are not

TABLE 6–10 ■ *The Seven Variables Expressed as a Percentage of the U.S. Rate, 1995*

Variables	Countries							
	Bulgaria	Czech	Croatia	Hungary	Poland	Romania	Slovenia	Slovakia
Income per capita	15.38	29.15	18.22	22.27	18.95	10.93	30.77	23.48
Steel production per capita	100.00	388.89	12.22	7.78	122.22	133.33	111.11	461.11
Kilowatt-hours of electricity produced	41.89	48.70	20.13	23.75	28.84	20.77	39.82	36.09
Motor vehicle registration per capita	23.61	37.50	20.83	30.56	26.39	9.72	40.27	25.00
Telephones in use per capita	42.91	40.64	30.25	26.01	19.70	18.31	38.24	33.34
Radios in use per capita	17.25	13.85	13.85	11.35	13.50	6.58	15.15	10.00
Televisions in use per capita	44.40	37.50	26.09	50.00	30.77	21.05	27.27	33.21

Sources: United Nations, Statistical Division, *1993 Statistical Yearbook* (New York: United Nations, 1995); and Robert Famighetti, ed., *The World Almanac and Book of Facts 1996* (Mahwah, N.J.: Funk & Wagnalls Corporation, 1995). © 1995 Funk & Wagnalls Corporation.

familiar with market conditions in these countries. Both these reasons favor use of the multiple-factor technique, and in fact, this technique may be the only one capable of providing a reasonable approximation of total market potentials.

In addition, the multiple-factor technique enables the analyst to compare the quality of a foreign market with the quality of the U.S. market. This comparison makes it possible for the analyst to utilize his or her familiarity with the U.S. market in evaluating a foreign market.

The multiple-factor technique, as described earlier, focuses upon two aspects of foreign markets: population size and market quality. The data needed for determining market quality were assembled from a variety of secondary sources. The most recent year for which most of the required data were available was 1995, so this analysis reflects conditions in Eastern Europe in that year. Table 6–10 shows data (expressed as a percentage of the U.S. rate) on seven variables for each of the eight Eastern European countries. In reading this table, notice that the data are expressed on a per capita basis; that is, production per capita in the United States is 100 percent, and steel production per capita in Croatia is 12 percent of the U.S. production rate.

Using the Multiple-Factor Quality Index.

The data on the variables reported in Table 6–10 were used to develop an index of market quality. This index serves as a joint measure

TABLE 6–11 ▪ *Market Quality Indices*

Country	Market Quality Index
Bulgaria	40.78
Croatia	20.23
Czech Republic	85.17
Hungary	24.53
Poland	37.20
Romania	31.53
Slovenia	43.23
Slovakia	88.89

of the economic development level and the quality-of-life level. Therefore, this index serves a measure of market quality, indicating relative overall market potential (for various kinds of products) rather than potential for a particular product.

The first step was to calculate the arithmetic means of the data in Table 6–10 (see Table 6–11).

As shown in Table 6–11, in terms of the quality index, the Czech Republic and Slovakia were the two most developed countries. Taking the American market as 100

percent, the Czech market, in terms of market quality but not market size, had an index of 85.17. The implication is that if the Czech market had a population equal to that of the United States, only 85.17 percent as much goods and services would be purchased. In Slovakia, only 88.89 percent as much goods and services would be purchased, and Croatia (with the lowest market quality index) would purchase only 20.23 percent as much of the goods and services.

In order to determine the total market potential, it is necessary to use some measure of market size and adjust it by applying a market quality index. Population figures, which were used here, are a readily available measure of market size. The population of each country expressed as a percentage of the U.S. population is shown in column 1 of Table 6–12. Poland's population, for example, is 14.70 percent as large as the U.S. population, while Bulgaria's population is 3.33 percent as large as the U.S. population.

By multiplying these relative population figures by the market quality indices, we determine the market potential. Because market sizes are adjusted by market quality

TABLE 6–12 ▪ *Market Potential of Eastern European Countries as Percentages of the U.S. Rate*

Country	Total Population as % of U.S. Rate (1)	×	Market Quality Index (2)	=	Market Potential (3)
Bulgaria	3.33	×	40.78	=	1.36
Croatia	1.77	×	20.23	=	0.36
Czech Republic	3.95	×	85.17	=	3.36
Hungary	3.91	×	24.53	=	0.96
Poland	14.70	×	27.20	=	5.47
Romania	8.80	×	31.53	=	2.52
Slovenia	0.78	×	43.23	=	0.34
Slovakia	2.06	×	88.89	=	1.83
Total					16.20

indices, both the U.S. and the Eastern European markets reflect the same common denominator of market quality.

Column 3 of Table 6–12 reports the resulting market potentials. Poland has the highest market potential; Bulgaria has the lowest. The total market potential of Eastern European countries in 1995 (expressed in terms of the total U.S. market potential) was 16.20 percent. The implication is that the market potential in Eastern Europe for any product is 16.20 percent as large as the market potential for that product in the U.S.

Three Examples of the Multiple-Factor Quality Index

To demonstrate the usefulness of this index for determining market potentials, consider three consumer products: soft drinks, juices, and bottled water. For all three products,

market information is difficult to obtain for the Eastern European countries, both individually and collectively. In 1994, U.S. consumption of soft drinks, juices, and bottled water was 13,206,000, 1,827,000,000, and 2,401,200,000 gallons, respectively. Table 6–13 shows the market potentials for these three product groups in Eastern Europe. These figures are computed by multiplying U.S. consumption figures by each country's respective market potential figure.

The availability of these data enables exporters of these three groups of products to decide whether the entire market of Eastern Europe, or only those of individual countries, are worth cultivating. American exporters, too, may use data similarly to determine the feasibility of selling a variety of products in Eastern Europe. The basic procedure is to look at the American market and its consumption patterns, and then make inferences for the target overseas market.

TABLE 6–13 ■ *Market Potentials for Selected Beverages*

1994 U.S. Consumption of Selected Beverages:

Soft drinks	13,206,600,000 gallons
Juices	1,827,000,000 gallons
Bottled water	2,401,200,000 gallons

Eastern European Market Potentials for Selected Beverages

Country	Soft Drinks	Juices	Bottled Water
Bulgaria	179,609,760	24,847,200	32,656,320
Croatia	47,543,760	6,577,200	8,644,320
Czech Republic	443,741,760	61,387,200	80,680,320
Hungary	126,783,360	17,539,200	23,051,520
Poland	722,401,020	99,936,900	131,345,640
Romania	332,806,320	46,040,400	60,510,240
Slovenia	44,902,440	6,211,800	8,164,080
Slovakia	241,680,780	33,434,100	43,941,960

Source: Consumption data from "And the 1994 per Cap Winners Are . . . ," *Beverage Industry*, April 1995, 10(2).

Only seven variables plus the population figures, each given equal weight, were used in determining these market potentials. Sometimes it is appropriate to use different variables and/or to employ a weighting technique. For instance, if the purpose is to determine a country's potential for X-ray equipment, the numbers of doctors or hospital beds per 1,000 population are more important than the numbers of television sets or radios in use. Different weights are developed through use of multiple-regression analysis or partial-regression coefficients to indicate the relative weights and importance of the variables in the equation.

PRESENT VERSUS FUTURE

Much international marketing activity is based on anticipating the future. Most companies enter world markets in the hope of increasing future returns. International market forecasting is a highly important matter, but it presents numerous problems.

Problems in International Market Forecasting

Establishing current market potentials, although helpful, is inadequate as a basis for planning future operations. Forecasting is necessary to planning. Of the eight techniques discussed in this chapter, trend and regression analyses, coefficient of income sensitivity, and multiple-factor analyses are usable both for obtaining present market potentials and for making future objections. The input-output analysis technique requires the existence of other forecasts in order to predict expected sales in different sectors.

There are certain problems unique to international market forecasting. These problems are of two general types: (1) problems in estimating industry demand, and (2) problems in estimating company demand.

ESTIMATING INDUSTRY DEMAND ■ Unlike his or her national counterpart, the forecaster on the international scene deals with many national markets and, depending on each market's uniqueness and the available data, may use a variety of forecasting tools and techniques. Five major problems are common in forecasting industry demand.

1. *Key factors vary among countries.* Market indicators differ from one market to another in terms of their use for predictions, their measurability, and their availability. These differences make it impossible to use a uniform forecasting formula for all of an industry's markets.

2. *Markets in different countries do not experience similar changes simultaneously.* Because market conditions and fluctuations are not the same in different countries, building realistic forecasting models is a major problem and may cause the forecaster to adopt different base periods and time limits for different countries. If, for instance, coefficients of income sensitivity are going to be used for forecasting market growth for food, but there are exaggerations of income estimates, using these exaggerated data will produce exaggerated forecasts.

3. *Relationships between indicators and markets are not uniform.* The fact that unique relationships exist between given indicators and given markets often causes the forecaster to use a different forecasting model for each market.

4. *The durability of forecasting models varies from country to country.* Because the rate

of economic development and change in the quality of life among countries is not homogeneous, a particular forecasting model is not appropriate for similar use in many countries simultaneously over some period of time. While a forecasting model may remain useful for many years in country A, it may become useless at any time for country B (perhaps because of dramatic changes in country B's economy). Selection and evaluation of demand indicators require regular reviews; otherwise, while yielding good results for one market, a forecasting model may become inappropriate for use in another market.

5. *Data needs are great and data availability is limited.* The international forecaster has a greater problem than the domestic forecaster in obtaining reliable data. Often the international forecaster must use much subjective judgment and resort to mechanical forecasting techniques, both of which may reduce the value of the forecast. As a prominent international marketing research firm president stated:

> I think there are real good reasons for the differences between countries which make it difficult for us to want to do the same kind of job everywhere. . . . Attempting to impose or otherwise force an umbrella methodology from headquarters may prove both organizationally and methodologically harmful.[6]

Clearly, it is futile to attempt a high degree of standardization in international market forecasting. It is necessary to develop country-specific forecasting techniques, which, consequently, have limited international comparability.

ESTIMATING COMPANY DEMAND ■

Determining a company's relative market share within an industry is more difficult for a foreign market than for a U.S. marketer. The main reason is that numerous special variables significantly affect the flow of exports. Variables such as internal supply capacity of foreign-based exporters, the structure and nature of international competition, and governmental export and import controls are unique to the international market. The international market forecaster must cope with these and similar variables.

While in domestic market forecasts a company's foreign competition often is either ignored or lumped together with other domestic competition, in international market forecasting, the roles of foreign (one country), multinational, and U.S. competitors are separated. Each of the three types of competitors is affected differently by socioeconomic and political changes, and even under similar conditions, they conduct themselves differently. A tariff increase in an importing country, for instance, generally strengthens the positions of multinational and other firms participating in the market.

After national competitors are accounted for, the rest of the estimates of market demand are translated into "market share available for U.S. sellers." Making these estimates requires some assumptions about how exporters from other countries will behave. Then, how rival U.S. firms are likely to behave must be determined.

Table 6–14 provides an example of the structure of export competition in the international market for motor vehicles. After slumping greatly in 1982, the U.S. share slowly started back up. Japan has been the largest player among the big seven; its share rose from 6.17 percent in 1962 to 45.70 percent in 1985. However, this number has been

TABLE 6–14 ■ *Vehicle Exports of the "Big Seven" in Percentage of Total Sales*

Year	1988	1989	1993	1994
Total number of units	14,811,000	14,982,000	13,458,059	13,518,521
British share	1.92%	2.52%	4.64%	5.31%
U.S. share	6.86	6.51	7.77	7.70
German share	18.07	19.34	16.17	17.83
French share	15.26	15.88	16.82	16.00
Italian share	5.58	5.66	5.18	5.00
Canadian share	11.09	11.24	12.14	15.27
Japanese share	41.21	38.86	37.30	33.00

Sources: 1988 and 1989 data from Motor Vehicles Manufacturers Association of the United States, *World Motor Vehicle Data*, 1991 edition (Detroit, Mich.: Motor Vehicle Manufacturers Association of the United States, 1991); 1993 data from Motor Vehicles Manufacturers Association of the United States, *World Motor Vehicle Data*, 1995 edition (Detroit, Mich.: Motor Vehicle Manufacturers Association of the United States, 1995); and 1994 data from Alan K. Blinder, ed., *Ward's 1996 Automotive Yearbook* (Southfield, Mich.: Ward's Communications, 1996). © 1996, Ward's Communications, a division of Intertec Publishing.

steadily on the decline. Estimating the total U.S. participation in the export motor vehicle market is not the same, of course, as forecasting a particular company's world market share. Just as in domestic markets, a company's market share depends upon such factors as product differentiation, promotion, efficiency in distribution, price, and other elements of the marketing mix. If the forecast is developed for the total industry, then the forecast for a company might be obtained by multiplying the industry forecast by (1) the company's average share over some period of years, (2) last year's percentage share, or (3) the desired percentage share of the market. In each case, a target volume is arrived at to use as the starting point in planning a marketing program. If, for instance, forecasts indicate $5 million total industry sales for the coming year, and the company's expected share is 5 percent, then the target volume is 5 percent of $5 million, or $250,000.

Can We Predict the Future from the Past?

One critical issue in international forecasting is the matter of projecting into the future on the basis of past experiences. As Table 6–14 shows, Japan has had a notable decrease in its share of the world's motor vehicle market. Along with increasing competition, changes in the international picture, such as a sudden upsurge of protectionism in world markets, an unexpected shortage of hard currency in world markets, or political upheavals, could alter the large Japanese share even further. Indeed, in the case of Japan, the share started declining because of the very keen competition that has emerged in recent years. While time-series analyses are used successfully by many firms in making forecasts for the U.S. market, such analyses must be used only with great care and caution in forecasting international markets.

The multiplicity of international factors greatly complicates the task of predicting the future from the past. So many extraneous factors that are neither controllable nor predictable enter into the picture that their combined impact is difficult to estimate. If an international company, for instance, had been planning to set up a plant to make clothing in Ethiopia, in estimating Ethiopia's economic growth, there would have been no way to predict the famine of 1983–1985 and the resulting total economic disruption. Therefore, in addition to taking an account of data availability and data accuracy, the possibility that unexpected data needs will arise must also be assessed and addressed.[7]

The international market forecaster must be familiar not only with the standard techniques of market potential analysis but also with the problems in applying them at the international level. He or she must understand the key problems in applying them and must choose among techniques according to their applicability and appropriateness.

SUMMARY

Assessing international market potentials is a necessary first step in planning international marketing. Several techniques for determining market potentials are available, but many of the more sophisticated techniques used in analyzing U.S. markets cannot be used internationally because of lack of data and the multitudinous variables that cannot be accounted for. Eight separate techniques used for determining market potential were explained in this chapter, some of them not well known or widely used. All of these techniques, however, are sound approaches and are practical in their application. This chapter also covered some of the problems met in international forecasting; included was a detailed discussion of the use of multiple-factor technique. The multiple-factor technique is most appropriate and adoptable in cases where statistical market information is lacking, a frequent situation encountered in international marketing.

DISCUSSION QUESTIONS

1. What are the reasons for determining international market potentials? Why can't many of the techniques used for determining domestic market potentials be used at the international level?

2. Name the eight techniques for determining international market potentials. Contrast and compare these techniques in terms of their relative advantages and weaknesses.

3. Why make a distinction between the techniques of market potential analysis and those of international forecasting? What problems are there in estimating industry and individual company demand in an international context?

4. Explain what perception has to do with evaluating market opportunity.

5. Distinguish among existing demand, latent demand, and incipient demand. How might the importance of each of these types of demand vary from country to country? Why?

6. Explain how to develop a multiple-factor quality index. Then, demonstrate how such an index can be used in determining potentials in prospective overseas markets.

7. In forecasting sales in international markets, to what extent can the past be used to predict the future? Does this hold for *all* overseas markets? Why or why not?

8. Outline the main differences between determining international market potentials and international market forecasts.

9. How are industry sales forecasts converted into company sales forecasts?

10. Contrast and compare how account is taken of foreign competition in making domestic and international market forecasts.

The Chilean Market

Foods International (FI) is interested in determining the potential for purchasing prepared foods in Chile. Information on this potential would help management decide whether FI should open a factory in Chile or serve the market through exporting. If the Chilean market potential is large enough, management is leaning toward setting up a plant to process and can foods. Management has learned that Chileans annually spend US$60 million on nonprocessed foods and US$100 million on processed foods. Analyses indicate that the coefficient of income sensitivity for nonprocessed foods is 0.6; for processed foods, it is 1.2. Over the next five years, income in Chile is expected to increase (after adjustments for inflation) as much as 40 percent. If expected total food sales exceed US$200 million, FI plans to set up a food processing plant.

QUESTIONS

1. Should FI open the plant?

2. What are the reasons for the opposite point of view?

The Argentine Market

A large U.S. retailer has been analyzing the quality and size of the Argentine market. If this market is promising enough, the retailer may decide to launch an operation there. Among the data collected by the retailer's research department is that shown in Exhibit 6–1.

In the United States, the retailer's annual sales exceed $1 billion, and management estimates that with a US$200 million base, it is worthwhile entering Argentina.

QUESTIONS

1. Can you establish the market potential in Argentina by considering the size and quality of that market?

2. What would you advise management as to whether it should open stores in Argentina?

EXHIBIT 6–1 ■ *Argentine Market Characteristics (hypothetical per capita figures)*

Factors	Percentage of the United States*
Income	52
Steel consumption	45
Kilowatt-hours of electrical power produced	75
Motor vehicle registration	43
Telephones in use	72
Radios in use	69

*U.S. population, 260 million; Argentina population, 37 million.

ENDNOTES

1 Reed Moyer, "International Market Analysis," *Journal of Marketing Research*, November 1968, 358–359; and A. Coskun Samli, "Market Potentials Can Be Determined at the International Level," *Australian Journal of Marketing Research*, August 1972, 85–94.

2 Franklin R. Root, *Entry Strategies for International Markets* (Lexington, Mass.: Lexington Books, 1987), 38–42.

3 A. Coskun Samli and Irene Lange, "Marketing Research Techniques for Assessing Markets of East European Economies," *Baylor Business Studies*, October 1977, 35–44.

4 Richard P. Carr, Jr., "Identifying Trade Areas for Consumer Goods in Foreign Markets, *Journal of Marketing*, October 1978, 75–80.

5 Warren J. Keegan, *Global Marketing Management* (Englewood Cliffs, N.J.: Prentice-Hall, 1989), 234–236.

6 John G. Keane, "Internationalizing Marketing Research: Factors and Futures," in *It Won't Work Here*, AMA/ESOMAR Proceedings (Chicago: Chicago American Marketing Association, 1979), 77.

7 Nicholas Papadopoulos and Jean-Emile Demis, "Inventory, Taxonomy, and Assessment of Methods for International Market Selection," *International Marketing Review* 3 (1988): 38–51.

CHAPTER **7**

International Market Segmentation

Chapter Outline

Learning Objectives

When you have mastered the contents of this chapter, you will be able to do the following:

1 Define international market segmentation and identify the problems managers face in achieving it.

2 Know how marketers screen potential targets using secondary data.

3 Realize the importance of segmentation in the formation of international marketing strategy.

4 Discuss the many criteria marketers use to segment world markets.

Market segmentation is the process by which marketing executives divide up markets into homogeneous groups of customers who respond in similar fashions to particular marketing mixes.[1] Market segments themselves must be identifiable (by geographic, demographic, or other criteria), reachable (through media), and have common responses to specific marketing approaches; they also must be sufficiently large to be profitable. Also, from a strategic viewpoint, companies should have a competitive advantage in serving a particular segment.

For international marketers, the task of dividing up world markets is fraught with difficulty. Linguistic, religious, educational, and economic differences complicate the process of locating customers with common characteristics. As noted earlier in Chapters 2 and 3, such differences occur not just among countries but also within them. Most notably, developing countries may be multilingual and have several religions. They also may have developmentally distinct urban and rural sectors. These characteristics, combined with low purchasing power, often make the tailoring of a marketing mix uneconomical for such customer groups. Thus, because of cultural diversities, developing countries may need even more tailoring of marketing mixes than developed countries.

As countries industrialize, customer tastes are shaped by the homogenizing force of technology. Similarities develop among consumer groups in different countries, and common products and services can be used (usually with adaptations) to meet their needs. Global companies concentrate on these commonalities to market across countries. Typical cross-cultural segments are babies, children, teenagers, business people, and senior citizens.

For international marketers, the segmentation process has three stages. In stage 1, likely markets are identified. In stage 2, they are grouped according to common national characteristics (such as language, geographic proximity, and state of development). At this point, some preliminary evaluations are made as to marketing strategies. These judgments depend on the company's level of experience in foreign markets as well as on its international goals. Then, in stage 3, depending on how far managers feel they are going to customize or standardize their offerings (or both), further segmentation tasks are performed. Customized strategies require in-depth examinations of individual countries, regions, or groups; standardized approaches entail evaluating cross-cultural segments over a number of markets.

STAGE 1: LOCATING LIKELY MARKETS

There are more than 200 national markets in the world. Management's first task, therefore, is to identify the best market prospects for the company's products and services. These preliminary screenings are objective and not too time consuming.

For this purpose, managers use secondary data; they are, of course, aware that secondary information has numerous disadvantages. The figures may not be current, and they can also be unreliable (especially if governments see merit in distorting them for political reasons). This information is inconsistent in that many developing countries do not collect detailed statistics. Finally, there are questions about comparability. For example, the rigor of literacy tests varies by country. In spite of these disadvantages, secondary data are commonly used in this first attempt to classify markets.

TABLE 7–1(a) ■ *Total Retail Sales of Consumer Electronics, 1993 (thousands of units)*

	Color TVs	Video Recorders	Video Cameras	Home Computers	Audio Separates	CD Players
EU						
Belgium	335.6	256.5	115.5	98.0	333.6	65.3
Denmark	300.0	205.0	30.0	34.0	500.0	41.0
France	3625.0	2153.0	490.0	900.0	1031.0	1185.7
Germany	5968.1	3150.0	1250.0	1330.0	7730.0	1799.3
Greece	177.7	175.7	12.9	22.4	68.8	10.4
Ireland	143.8	71.4	32.3	9.7	90.2	9.6
Italy	2900.0	1170.0	470.0	650.0	533.0	417.4
Luxembourg	14.4	11.0	5.0	4.2	14.3	6.5
Netherlands	647.6	610.2	314.7	144.2	915.4	136.0
Portugal	288.4	315.2	29.6	14.8	305.5	17.7
Spain	2038.0	807.0	300.0	275.0	367.0	64.1
UK	3450.0	2280.0	720.0	1000.0	1700.0	465.1
Subtotal	19888.5	11204.9	3770.1	4482.3	13588.8	4218.1
EFTA						
Austria	410.0	175.0	74.0	85.0	229.0	45.0
Finland	186.85	152.0	8.5	33.5	250.3	41.4
Iceland						
Liechtenstein						
Norway	91.8	95.0	37.0	28.0	390.3	10.4
Sweden	450.0	280.0	66.0	63.6	690.0	97.4
Switzerland	410.5	274.8	42.0	82.0	582.5	229.4
Subtotal	1548.7	976.8	227.5	292.1	2142.1	423.7

Source: European Marketing Data and Statistics (London: Euromonitor Publications, 1995), 369.

Preliminary Screening: Consumer Products

Unless companies are pioneering totally new products or technologies, most managers are first interested in countries where current demand exists for their products. Ascertaining such demand involves finding statistics on national patterns of consumption or sales. Such statistics are available. Sources such as *International Marketing Data and Statistics* (and its European version, *European Marketing Data and Statistics*)

supply product-specific and industry-specific data. Table 7–1(a) shows typical data for household durables, such as TVs and CDs in Europe; Table 7–1(b) shows the variety of figures available from this source.

Surrogate Indicators of Market Size

Often, however, executives lack detailed data for specific products and must rely on other

TABLE 7–1(b) ■ *Market Size Indicators: International Marketing Data and Statistics and European Marketing Data and Statistics*

Per Capita Consumption Measures	Total Retail Sales
Meat and fish	Disposable paper products
Fresh produce	OTC health care products
Dairy products and eggs	Clothing and footwear
Bakery products	Home furnishings and housewares
Convenience and miscellaneous foods	White goods
Drinks	Small electrical appliances
Tobacco products	Consumer electronics
Household cleaning products	Selected personal and leisure goods

Source: European Marketing Data and Statistics (London: Euromonitor Publications, 1995).

market-size indicators. Because demographic details, such as income, age, education, and gender, are part of target market descriptions in home markets, they are often used for foreign markets also.

Income is a most important indicator, as consumers must have financial resources to qualify as target markets. Gross national product per capita is a widely used and, in broad terms, reasonable indicator of market affluence. However, it has drawbacks. First, GNP per capita does not indicate how gross national products are divided among citizens, and this might lead to distorted views of some countries. For example, GNP per capita for oil-rich Middle Eastern states is high, but money is very unevenly distributed; most oil revenues accrue to a few individuals. Similarly, countries such as India and the People's Republic of China with low GNP per capita often hide substantial pockets of affluent consumers (who number over 100 million in India). Also, the GNP distribution in rural populations is not adequately recognized because many fall outside the monetarized economy. Thus, some rural populations appear to be poorer than they actually are. The second drawback is that GNPs include government expenditures. Where government spending accounts for large proportions of national budgets, as in Scandinavia and Eastern Europe, GNP per capita figures overestimate consumer affluence.

Education, age, and *sex* breakdowns are widely available through the United Nations and private sources. These demographics should only be used in conjunction with appropriate income data. For example, the existence of large numbers of babies and young children is not a good indicator of market potential for baby food or toys unless consumers have adequate discretionary income. This is often lacking in developing countries.

Preliminary Screening: Industrial Products

Because it is hard to obtain product-related statistics for industrial products, figures for related activities are used. Sellers of hospital equipment might use statistics on the number of hospitals; clinics; beds; or available doctors, dentists, pharmacists, or nursing personnel (all are to be found in United Nations sources or *International Marketing Data and*

TABLE 7–2 ▪ *Selected Statistics of Market Size Indicators for 115 Countries* *from* Crossborder Monitor

	Private Consumption Expenditures ($bn)	Passenger Automobiles (× 1,000)	Telephones (1993 × 1,000 units)	TVs (1995 × 1,000)	Steel Consumption (1994 KMT)	Electricity Consumption 1994 billion kWh
North America	4,690.0	159,792	164,555	234,400	129,300	3,679.9
South America	1,037.0	17,272	33,086	108,266	33,991	650.0
Central America	26.8	234	953	1,686	541	14.5
Asia	4,106.0	56,800	122,304	407,789	318,523	2,826.0
Australasia	229.6	9,511	10,133	9,100	6,680	195.0
Africa	227.0	7,593	7,647	16,278	10,672	276.0
Middle East	265.0	8,181	12,786	23,791	22,185	308.0
Eastern Europe	128.0	24,894	36,198	122,109	40,060	1,277.0
Western Europe (total)	4,546.0	163,029	189,307	155,852	134,110	2,439.0
Major Markets						
France	798.0	24,385	30,900	29,300	15,900	471.0
Germany	1,013.0	39,202	36,900	30,500	35,300	453.0
Italy	639.0	29,600	24,176	17,000	25,530	222.0
UK	655.0	23,402	28,681	20,000	14,070	331.0

Source: Adapted from "Marketplace Indicators for 115 Countries," *Crossborder Monitor,* 28 August 1996, 1–12.

Statistics). Similarly, vendors of educational equipment can screen markets according to the number of primary, secondary, and higher schools. Manufacturers of agricultural equipment can use production figures for cereal or other crops. The amount of construction activity can be detected from figures on cement or steel consumption. Table 7–2 shows one source of these types of statistics, *Crossborder Monitor*'s indicators of market size for 115 countries.

Surrogate Indicators of Market Size

When there are no specific statistical data, managers look for other indicators. For example, commercial activity in specific industry sectors helps marketers quantify market sizes for industrial products. Sources such as *Dunn and Bradstreet's Principal International Businesses, Marconi's International Register,* and other commercial directories show that foreign markets have companies in certain industries. Lists are also available from commercial attachés at embassies. Often included are company details such as sales turnovers, number of employees, and product lines carried.

Once executives have compiled preliminary lists of targeted countries, they must make initial decisions about marketing strategy, because marketing approaches to individual or multiple countries depend on how they further segment prospective markets.

STAGE 2: BASES FOR SEGMENTING MARKETS

Once prospective markets have been located, managers then seek to identify common elements that may enable them to use similar strategies across a number of countries. This splitting up of world markets into groups allows firms to manage trade-offs between local tastes and scale economies. Scale economies allow some standardization of products across markets. The need to tailor products to local customer preferences necessitates product differentiation.

International markets can be segmented according to various criteria. Table 7–3 illustrates some of them. One group of criteria, called macrosegmentation criteria, are traditional and stereotypic. They also are quite objective. With macrosegmentation criteria, international marketers can evaluate the big picture (which is identified in the table as "general") or a smaller picture (which is called "specific" in the table and is a component of the big picture).

A second group of criteria is called microsegmentation criteria. These are relatively nonstereotypic and are rather subjective. Here again, the international marketer has the option of evaluating the whole world market ("general" in the table) or a smaller section ("specific" in the table) based on certain microsegmentation criteria such as behavioral factors or more specific components of this general world market. It must be remembered that in segmenting international markets, marketing executives often use more than one variable. Furthermore, macro and micro criteria may be used together to segment the world markets. The key criteria used for macro segmentation are as follows:

1. *Language.* Countries that share common languages give marketers the chance to use similar brand names, instructions, promotions, and labeling for multiple markets (though all should be tested for acceptance in each marketplace). The English-speaking countries of the United States, United Kingdom, most of

TABLE 7–3 ■ *Basis for Segmenting International Markets*

Criteria	General	Specific
Macro Segmentations (Objective)		
Language	All French-speaking countries	People who prefer French cuisine
Religion	All Muslims	Sunnis
Geography	Asia	Taiwan
Economic bloc	European Union	Books written in German
Level of economic development	All industrialized countries	Countries with specific need for mainframe computers
Micro Segmentations (Subjective)		
Behavioral factors	Heavy cigarette smokers	Heavy smokers in Japan
Lifestyles	Food-consumption habits	Spicy-food eaters
Attitudes, tastes, or predispositions	Status symbols	Identifying with American Western heroes

TABLE 7–4 ▪ *Islamic Market Characteristics and Marketing Strategy Implications*

Some of the Key Elements of Islamic Societies	Meaning	Marketing Strategy Implications
Unity	Centrality; oneness of God; harmony in life.	Product standardization; mass media techniques; unity in advertising copy and layout; strong brand loyalties.
Legitimacy	Fair dealings; reasonable profit levels.	Less-formal product warranties; switch from profit maximization to reasonable profit levels.
Supremacy of human life	Supremacy of human life when compared to other life forms.	Symbols in advertising to reflect human values; pet foods and pet products are not very important.
Community	Achievement of universal brotherhood.	Formation of an Islamic economic community to develop Islamic-oriented products. Support for local small retailers.
Abstinence	Fasting without food or drink from sunup to sundown during the month of Ramadan.	Production of products that are nutritious, cool, and digested easily.
Obligation to family and traditions	Family elders respected; traditional values honored.	Because certain family members function as opinion leaders, advertisements to indicate parental approval and traditional behavior patterns.

Source: Adapted from Mustaq Luqmani, Zahir A. Quraeshi, and Linda Delene, "Marketing in Islamic Countries," *MSU Business Topics*, Summer 1980, 17–25.

Canada, Australia, and New Zealand; the French-speaking countries of North Africa; Arabic countries in the Middle East; and Spanish-speaking countries in Latin America are all examples of linguistic segmentation. Additionally, products created for one country can be more easily transferred and tested in markets with common languages.

2. *Religion.* Because religion is a strong influence on lifestyles, especially in developing countries, it is a basis for segmenting markets. Table 7–4 shows that firms can tailor marketing strategies to accommodate Islamic beliefs and behaviors.

It can be seen that such tailoring has definite effects on product, brand, warranty, advertising, public relations, pricing, and credit policies.

3. *Geography.* Countries are often grouped according to their position on the world map. North America, Central and South America, Western and Eastern Europe, the Middle East and Africa, and Asia are common geographic groupings. Companies often organize themselves geographically and establish regional headquarters to coordinate strategies for individual countries. Out of such structures come strategies for entire regions,

such as for all of Europe or all of Asia. These regional strategies become possible when there are sufficient cultural commonalities within a region (brought about through commerce, communications, and personal travel) for common marketing mixes to be successful.

4. *Economic bloc.* Economic and political similarities among countries sometimes result in the formation of multicountry blocs such as the European Union. While there are different sorts of economic and political unions, they all have similar objectives—to foster closer economic relations through trade and to move towards megamarket status. This trend allows firms within the union access to multiple-country markets. Over time, with the flows of products and technologies among bloc members, other cultural differences among member states tend to fade.

  Free movement of goods within country groupings encourages the adoption of similar marketing mixes. However, the less developed the group, the more likely it is that national cultures affect individual country strategies because modernization may not as yet have affected the group and homogenized its cultures. Also, as economic blocs progress, region-wide legislation comes into force, and labeling, product testing, safety, processing, and packaging laws are unified. As with the European Community's 1992 package, companies respond by standardizing their marketing efforts. In the EC's case, this response involves Europe-wide branding and promotional strategies.

5. *Level of economic development.* Managers often assume that countries at the same stage of economic development have similar needs. In part, the basis for this

assumption is to be found in the economics literature in the country similarities theory.[2] For marketers, this is a useful tool in grouping countries with specific needs. Firms catering to markets at one stage of development would like to identify countries at the same economic level so that they may use the same marketing strategies. But what criteria can managers use to evaluate market development levels? Two early attempts stand out.

The first, by Rostow, classifies countries according to economic development criteria.[3] There are five stages of industrialization:

1. *Traditional societies.* These countries comprise self-sufficient communities. They have little or no modem technology. Educational standards are low. Many are not monetarized. Their pressing needs are for investment of any kind (private or public) to expand the money economy and provide employment. Examples are Gabon, Ethiopia, and some other African states.

2. *Preconditions for take-off.* Countries at this level are developing infrastructures necessary for industrialization, including roads, ports, telecommunications, postal services, power grids, and energy sources. Agriculture becomes mechanized and expands to compensate for the rural-to-urban population shift. Malaysia, Thailand, People's Republic of China, and Indonesia are at this stage.

3. *Take-off.* At this stage, urban-based manufacturing becomes prominent and distribution systems develop. Country infrastructures are mainly in place, and emphasis is placed on upgrading national education and improving health

care systems. Some Latin American countries (Venezuela, Chile, Mexico, and Argentina) and Asian nations (Taiwan, South Korea, and India) are at this level.

4. *Drive to maturity.* Nations at this level have increasing international involvements, and emphasis is placed on technology-based products and entrepreneurial activities. Wide varieties of products start to become available, and service sectors develop. Ireland, Spain, and some Eastern European countries are at this stage of development.

5. *High mass consumption.* Countries at this level are heavily dependent on trade and have rapidly expanding service sectors. These countries have established middle-income groups with significant discretionary income. The United States, Canada, Japan, and many Western European countries fit this profile.

A second means of categorizing countries is according to GNP per capita. The assumption here is that if companies are selling consistently to markets in, for example, the $3,000 to $5,000 per capita GNP range, then other countries at this level of affluence should also be viable targets. This analysis is useful to companies with a wide assortment of products. Electric stoves vary enormously in sophistication. Stoves with basic options sell better in developing countries, whereas elaborate stoves with multiple options are more likely to appeal to customers in upscale markets. There are many other ways for marketers to classify countries, including the size and development of its middle class, political indicators, the nature of the economic system (capitalist, mixed, communist), and the type of industrial structure (raw-material-producing, industrializing, fully industrialized).[4] Classifications may vary according to industry. Arms manufac-

turers, for example, might choose to segment markets according to the degree of political turmoil. Such assessments are obtainable in commercial services such as *Business Risk Services* (see Figure 3–2 in Chapter 3).

STAGE 3: MARKET SEGMENTATION AND INTERNATIONAL MARKETING STRATEGY

The Importance of Segmentation

Once executives have initially grouped market prospects according to their common characteristics, they must make initial decisions about what strategies to use in which countries (or groups of countries). Here, the company's international experience plays an important role. Firms already established in foreign markets adjust previous strategies. Where a firm has little experience, extra preparation is necessary in order to find out what approaches work best in specific markets.

Companies either treat each country as a unique entity (a multinational or multilocal approach) or look at world markets as being essentially similar (a global approach). In the first case, companies prepare individual marketing mixes for each region or country. In the second, they adopt a "one size fits all" marketing mix for all foreign activities. Of course, many firms adopt mixtures of customized and standardized strategies, but from a segmentation perspective, the research emphases for each differ. Companies that use multinational and multilocal approaches are aiming to use market differences to their advantage by either adapting their products heavily to different segments or by creating new goods and services for them. Companies that use a global approach look for similarities among customers so that they can appeal to them with essentially similar offerings. These two opposing approaches require different segmentation procedures.

Looking for Differences: Segmentation Strategies for Multinational and Multilocal Marketers

Some companies seek to tailor their outputs extensively to specific market needs. They identify certain criteria to evaluate customer groups within targeted countries. A major factor affecting intramarket segmentation is the level of country development. Hence, we contrast intramarket segmentation practices for developed and developing countries.

Segmentation Criteria for Developed Countries

Developed countries are sufficiently culturally homogeneous for marketers to use traditional segmentation criteria. These include demographic and other factors.

DEMOGRAPHIC FACTORS ■ Demographic factors include age, sex, education, income, family size, and so on. For most developed countries, marketing data broken down in these categories are available for products and services. In some cases, U.S.-style information is available. A. C. Nielsen operates in 27 foreign markets, including 17 in Europe.[5] In other countries, there are country-specific

breakdowns, often incorporating multiple demographic characteristics. The United Kingdom's IPA system is typical. It encapsulates income, occupation, and social status into six consumer segments.

GEOGRAPHIC FACTORS ■ Geographic submarkets exist in most countries. The American market, for instance, can be split into nine regional submarkets.[6] Other countries are also divisible into geographic regions with distinctive tastes. In the United Kingdom, regional tastes in television are catered to by locally oriented companies including Granada, serving North England; London Weekend Television, serving the capital and its environs; and various companies serving Scotland and Wales. While much programming is shared, advertisers can target messages regionally. In France, geographic regions with their own dialects have distinctive tastes (for example, Provence, Brittany, Alsace, Catalonia, and the Basque areas). In Spain, the Basque and Catalan areas have different tastes from those of Castile. In Germany, there are differences between the more industrial north and the more agricultural, more conservative south, particularly Bavaria. Many of the other macrosegmentation criteria listed in Table 7-3 can also be used for evaluating markets, as can many microsegmentation criteria. In some cases, for specific products, the latter may be more critical than macrosegmentation criteria.

BEHAVIORAL FACTORS ■ Behavior patterns stem from certain personality traits and from socioeconomic and political conditions. If the causes of certain consumer behaviors are understood, then consumer groups can be segmented on that basis. This type of segmentation criteria includes usage rates (nonuser and light, moderate, and heavy users), group influences, consumer motivation, and consumer benefits. For example, RJR Nabisco would be concerned about world-wide cigarette-smoking habits. As a result, it would segment world markets according to numbers of heavy smokers, light smokers, and nonsmokers.

LIFESTYLES
■ Consumers' tastes are affected by their lifestyles and attitudes, which reflect their values. The fast-foods industry detected certain international patterns in lifestyles that enabled it to enter many world markets. The industry determined that its demand is not price elastic. In many areas of the world, family size was decreasing and smaller families ate out more often. The entry of more women into the workforce meant there was less available time to cook. The younger generations preferred eating in fast-food places. Increase in leisure time and travel also helped the popularity of fast foods.[7] Certainly, McDonald's or Kentucky Fried Chicken considered such lifestyle factors before expanding into many world markets.

ATTITUDES, TASTES, OR PREDISPOSITIONS
■ Using attitudes, a marketer can break down markets in terms of whether people are innovators, early adopters, early majority, late majority, or laggards in accepting new products or services. It has been maintained, for instance, that NICs are more prone to accept new products than traditional societies such as those in the Islamic world. Because such NICs have a relatively larger group of innovators, new products gain acceptance faster.

Another attitude to consider is people's choice of status symbols to enhance their image. For example, identifying with American Western heroes is important to young people in Japan. Levi Strauss, maker of blue jeans, has made good use of this aspect of the Japanese consumer market.

Segmentation Criteria for Developing Countries

Although the basic categories for segmentation presented in Table 7–3 remain the same, some criteria may be more suitable for developing countries than for developed countries. Developing markets lack the spending power of advanced countries. They are likely also to be culturally heterogeneous; to have a low rate of literacy, which limits choices of advertising media; and to be deficient in infrastructure, which makes some areas difficult to reach. These problems make it difficult for managers to define potentially profitable market segments. Nevertheless, developing countries are the markets of the future, and getting established early is a key to market success. In many respects, the segmentation criteria in these countries are not so different from those in advanced countries.

ETHNIC AND RACIAL SEGMENTS
■ In countries characterized by ethnic divisions, marketers must decide whether to sell products to all groups, using multilingual packages and promotional mixes, or to some groups, perhaps the most populous, such as the Shona and Matabele tribes in Zimbabwe, or the Zulu and Xhosa in South Africa. Or marketers may decide not to market their offerings at all. This last option is realistic for products requiring some degree of education, such as computers. Which strategy marketers choose depends in a large part on the size and composition of the various groups. For example, there may be many ethnic subdivisions, but only a few are good target markets; also, there may be a culturally dominant group, such as speakers of the Mandarin dialect in mainland China.

GEOGRAPHIC SEGMENTS
■ Geographic regions are closely allied to ethnic divisions; and insofar as particular ethnic groups inhabit certain parts of countries, these two segmentation criteria coincide. However,

there are other aspects to geographic segmentation. For example, in physically large, developing countries, not all regions are accessible. Some areas are remote, lacking roads, sources of power, and distribution capabilities. (Advanced countries such as Canada and northern Sweden also have such remote areas.) In such situations, marketers can only do pioneering work, such as giving out samples, until either infrastructures develop or firms build their own distribution and communications networks.

MODERN-TRADITIONAL SEGMENTS ■ A useful method of segmenting markets in countries is by their degree of development. As was noted in Chapter 3, as countries industrialize, inhabitants slowly shift from traditional to modern outlooks and lifestyles. In most cases, urbanization is the process by which individuals acquire new living standards. MNCs, in response, must adjust their marketing strategies to the level of development. At lower levels, they must adapt products more to cope with diverse rural tastes, and they must orient advertising toward broadcasting to counter illiteracy.[8] Segmenting markets into modern-traditional (or more conveniently, urban-rural sectors) also helps marketers distinguish innovators and early adopters from groups that are more resistant to new products and techniques. Operationally, MNCs can reach economically significant consumers more easily because they tend to live in towns.

Looking for Similarities: Global Marketing and Cross-Cultural Market Segmentation

Many companies serve similar customers in most or all of their international markets. Under these circumstances, they use identical or similar marketing mixes in at least some of them. It should be noted, however, that cross-cultural similarities do not always mean standardized mixes. Rather, they indicate that products and services are transferable between markets, although adaptations are usually advisable. For these firms, cross-cultural segments should be identified using demographic, geographic, and psychographic criteria.

Demographic Cross-Cultural Segmentation

AGE ■ Age is a primary variable in segmenting both domestic and international markets, because human development is a root cause of changes in consumption behavior. Marketers take advantage of cross-cultural similarities in a variety of ways. Companies make a variety of products for babies. Johnson and Johnson's baby powder and lotions are available in many countries, as are Gerber baby foods. Similarly, Procter and Gamble have made Pampers diapers a household word in many markets. Other companies make children's toys and clothes with a cross-cultural appeal. Mattel's Barbie doll, with suitable adaptations, has reached many countries, as have Pound Puppies. Video games by Atari and the Nintendo system have swept world markets. Mario Brothers products—from game cartridges to underwear, lunch boxes, and bed linen—are popular.[9]

Teenagers have sufficiently similar behaviors in many markets for the term "global teenager" to have meaning.[10] Records, cassettes, compact discs, fashion clothes, and magazines are often transferable between countries, and (for British and American performers) often in their original English-language formats. Elvis Presley, the Beach Boys, the Beatles, the Rolling Stones, The Who, Michael Jackson, Sting, and the

New Kids on the Block are all global performers appealing to similar segments worldwide. Likewise, Swatch, Pepsi, and MTV have taken advantage of common teenage interests in many major markets.

Senior citizens (or pensioners as they are known in Europe) are a global segment with similar cross-cultural needs. Marketers have responded with new financial products (such as retirement and health care plans), fitness services, cosmetics for "mature" women, and pharmaceuticals and ambulatory products oriented toward the elderly.[11]

OCCUPATION ▪ Job-related similarities are another way of segmenting the global market. In the professions, doctors, dentists, pharmacists, chemists, lawyers, accountants, nurses, computer programmers, engineers, and educators all have cross-cultural similarities and have contributed to the globalization of medical, legal, and technical services. While there are always some differences in professional outlooks (due to national variations in training programs and professional standards), there are sufficient similarities in training programs to enable doctors, for example, to practice in more than a single country, although a certificate for that country may be required. In the medical profession, many journals, including the *New England Journal of Medicine* and the *British Lancet*, are distributed worldwide. Many textbooks are routinely translated into many languages. Businesspeople are another global segment. *The Wall Street Journal, Business Week, Fortune,* and Europe's *Financial Times* all service similar needs in many markets. The *Economist* magazine is direct-marketed to over 160 countries.

GENDER ▪ Gender is still another way to divide global segments. For women, some cosmetics have global appeal (for example, Chanel No. 5 and Giorgio), as do some feminine-hygiene products. For men, the magazines *Penthouse* and *Playboy* have overcome cultural obstacles and achieved worldwide distribution. *Playboy* was even launched in Islamic Turkey, where it sold out its first 90,000 copies. Despite differences in national obscenity laws, these magazines have maintained their appeal to affluent males age 18 to 34 throughout the world.[12]

Lifestyle Segmentation

Within the area of lifestyle, various criteria allow cross-cultural consumer segments to be discerned. Consumer *sophistication* has been identified as an important criterion for cross-cultural segmentation.[13] Three levels of consumer sophistication have been posited. International *sophisticates* are middle-income and high-income consumers who have genuine interests in international products, fashion, and cross-cultural activities. Extensive travelers, they often speak many languages, and they are likely to have more in common with sophisticates from other countries than with their compatriots. *Semi-sophisticates* are middle-income and high-income consumers who know only a little about world affairs and foreign cultures. They are curious about international events but buy products from other countries mainly for status reasons. Provincial consumers may be poor or wealthy, more or less educated. They are nationalistic and have little interest in or appreciation for international products or services. Such consumers are often biased against foreign-made products, and labels indicating foreign origin tend to discourage purchase of the items that bear them.

In the 1980s, yuppies entered the marketing scene. In most countries, they promoted the demand for conspicuous-consumption products such as luxury cars, consumer electronics, specialty foods (especially health foods), sports equipment, and leisure activities. Designer clothes and accessories such as Gucci shoes and Louis Vuitton luggage cater to yuppies, as do international retail chains such as Häagen-Dazs ice cream. Sushi bars, health-and-fitness centers, home-exercise equipment, and fitness accessories have all surged with the yuppie movement. On an international scale, consumption similarities among the United States, Europe, and Japan have been recognized.[14]

Geographic Segmentation

To varying extents, marketers have always been interested in common regional characteristics among consumers. African, Latin American, European, and North American stereotypes can indeed be useful, but only after marketers have verified the presence of consumer similarities for their products or services within particular regions. Debates continue, however, about the efficacy of regional stereotyping.

Europe is a typical example, with cases being made for and against the "European consumer." There is evidence of trans-European similarities among teenagers and urbanites. Research suggests that for women, lifestyle indicators, such as whether they are stay-at-home wives, part-time working women, or career-minded women, are better predictors of international behavior than are national differences.[15]

Nevertheless, while many multinational companies are launching pan-European brands and promotions in Europe (including Kellogg's, Johnson and Johnson, Johnson Wax, and Colgate-Palmolive), there are still discernible geographic differences. One study found three distinct European consumer groups: Spain, Italy, and France; German-speaking Switzerland, Austria, and Germany; and the United Kingdom and Scandinavia.[16]

Developing Strategically Equivalent Segmentation

In developing global marketing strategies for cross-cultural market segments, the international marketer faces similar pockets of people in different parts of the world. These pockets of people can become a worldwide segment. In such cases, S. H. Kale and D. C. Sudharshan's concept of strategically equivalent segmentation (SES) can be used effectively.[17] The technique is composed of four steps:

1. *Criteria.* Criteria development involves determining common denominators in identifying the pockets of world segments, such as teenagers around the world who like American Western attire.

2. *Screening.* Screening means that once these pockets are identified, a decision needs to be made as to whether one, some, or all pockets should be included in the firm's target. This process identifies the viable and qualified candidates for inclusion in the target.

3. *Micro segmentation.* Micro segmentation is further identification of these particular pockets of groups in each qualified country.

4. *SES creation.* SES creation, the last step, entails two specific activities. First, the international marketer closely evaluates the similarities across segments in qualified countries. Second, the marketer clusters, or groups, highly similar pockets on the basis of cost-benefit analysis. In some cases, for instance, the pockets are so small and the distances are so great that it may not be cost effective to include these pockets in the target. This kind of creative segmentation is particularly important for cost-conscious international firms that have limited resources.

SUMMARY

International market segmentation requires three separate procedures. First, marketers should identify countries that produce or consume their type of products. This can usually be done by consulting secondary sources or by seeking countries with characteristics similar to those of known markets. Second, once target countries have been identified, they can be segmented according to such characteristics as language, level of development, and so on. Third, firms must make decisions about how they are going to tackle these markets. Multinational and multilocal marketers segment markets one at a time so that they may individualize their marketing strategies for each country. In developed countries, demographic, geographic, behavioral, or lifestyle segmentation criteria may be used. In developing countries, ethnic, geographic, and degree-of-development criteria are useful.

For global marketers, cross-cultural similarities among customers are important. Demographic, geographic, and lifestyle criteria help marketers identify suitable targets for competitive marketing mixes. In the final analysis, international firms with limited means need to be creative enough to use strategically equivalent segmentation.

DISCUSSION QUESTIONS

1. Discuss the notion that there is a feasible "North American" stereotypical consumer. How useful might such a stereotype be?

2. What sorts of segmentation criteria would you use to divide up the following markets:
   a) a CAT-scan machine
   b) a perfume
   c) a line of combined harvesters for agricultural use
   d) a new line of frozen yogurts

   For each, say whether you think an individual or global approach to markets might be best, and support your reasoning.

3. Discuss the statement that as markets develop, traditional segmentation criteria such as ethnic groups and level of development are replaceable by modern criteria such as age, gender, income, education, occupation, and lifestyle criteria. Why do you think this change occurs?

Emergence of Global Lifestyles: Teens and Yuppies

The Global Teen

It all began in the 1950s with Elvis. It gathered momentum in the 1960s and 1970s with the Beatles, the Beach Boys, and the Rolling Stones. Through commonalities in musical tastes, teenagers around the world became a global segment. From vinyl records to jeans to sneakers to PCs, marketers gradually became aware of their emerging global audience. "Teens go from teddy bears to condoms" as one company noted, and firms began to specialize in young consumers. The U.S. ad agency BSB videotaped teenage bedrooms in 25 countries. They found it hard to differentiate teens in Los Angeles, Mexico City, or Tokyo. Bedroom contents were remarkably similar: basketballs, soccer balls, Levi's, Diesel jeans, shoes from Timberland or Doc Martens, sneakers from Nike and Reebok, comic books, soft drinks, rap music, rollerblades, and PCs. In a rural Chinese school, Michael Jordan tied with Zhou En-Lai in a survey to identify "the world's greatest man."

The numbers are there. The U.S.'s 35 million teens combine with Mexico, Brazil, and Argentina's 57 million 10–19 year olds; Europe's 50 million teenagers; and Korea, Singapore, Vietnam, and Japan's 42 million strong group to comprise a formidable global segment. And, taking increasing advantage of those similarities are hordes of companies seeking to tap into the precocious, curious, impatient, thrill-seeking teenage mindset. Reebok introduced its Instapump sneaker line into 140 countries. Marvel comics sold 12 million copies a year in Britain, Spain, and Italy. MTV, a prime mover in determining and following teenage lifestyles, tripled its European audience to 59 million households in the first half of the 1990s. Its 200 commercial sponsors include Procter and Gamble, Johnson and Johnson, and Apple Computers. Pepsi introduced its sugarfree carbonated beverage Pepsi Max into 16 countries to do battle with the mighty leader, Coca-Cola.

Today's teens are a little different from their forebears. They are more worldly about global events, more environmentally conscious, and more computer literate. Marketers see opportunities to bond their brands onto young minds and to nurture loyalties that last into adulthood. As teens earn money, they have become the darlings of commercial marketers.

The Global Yuppie

The emergence of a global middle class has become a hallmark of 1990s marketing. Developing markets in Asia, Latin America, and Eastern Europe are expected to grow in real terms by at least 5 percent per year through the year 2005. The world's 10 largest emerging markets (China, Indonesia, India, South Korea, Turkey, South Africa, Poland, Argentina, Brazil, and Mexico) will account for over 20 percent of world GNP by 2010. Free trade, privatization, deregulation, working women, international corporations, and global media have contributed to world economic growth and, significantly, a new global middle class.

While definitions of middle class vary (in China, it is household incomes over $1,000 a year; in Poland, over $3,000; and in Indonesia, about $2,000), its major characteristic does not. Households with significant discretionary income comprise the global middle-class segment. At the upper levels, there are 83 million Chinese, 30 million Indians, 17 million Brazilians, and 15 million Indonesians earning between $10,000 and $40,000 annually. Of course, subsidized rent, transportation, health, and education increase household discretionary spending, as do multiple earners living in extended-family dwellings.

The net result has been huge upswings in demand for the "good things" in life: washing machines, dryers, TVs, microwaves, VCRs, cars, refrigerators, and the like. Associated products ranging from power stations to convenience foods get demand boosts as well. Companies such as Unilever, Gillette, Asea-Brown-Boveri, General Electric, Mercedes, BMW, GM, Whirlpool, Sony, Xerox, and Citibank have all taken advantage of these trends to globalize their supply and demand functions, and arguably, they have contributed to world economic development.

DISCUSSION QUESTIONS

1. What factors have contributed to the growth of the global teen and yuppie markets? Are they the same (or, in what ways have these segments developed differently)?

2. In what parts of the world would there be resistance to teen and yuppie trends? Why?

3. As world supply keeps up with customer needs, do you foresee any resource limitations in coping with global demand (for example, in the year 2000 or 2050)?

Source: Adapted from Sawn Tully, "Teens: The Most Global Market of All," *Fortune,* 16 May 1994, 90–98; and Rahul Jacob, "The Big Rise: Middle Classes Explode Around the Globe," *Fortune,* 30 May 1994, 74–90.

The European White-Goods Market

You are an executive of an American white-goods manufacturer. You have been asked to provide an overview of the European white-goods market at short notice. Your assistant provides you with the following statistics.

What would you say? What preliminary recommendations would you make and why? What other information would aid your decision-making process?

EXHIBIT 7–1 ■ *Total Retail Sales of White Goods, 1993 (thousands of units)*

	Refriger-ators	Refrig./Freezers	Freezers	Cookers	Microwave Ovens	Washing Machines	Tumble Dryers	Dish-washers
Austria	303.0	309.0	144.0	352.0	171.0	234.0	34.0	139.0
Belgium	230.0	24.0	121.0	116.0	230.0	243.0	150.0	102.0
Denmark	185.0	79.7	146.7	105.0	74.6	124.0	55.0	73.0
France	1386.0	513.0	740.0	2292.0	1163.0	1982.0	546.0	712.0
Finland	91.4	41.4	72.4	119.8	97.6	119.4	13.0	53.6
Germany	1489.9	722.6	1009.5	3052.9	1877.0	2614.5	656.9	1128.3
Greece	290.0			172.5	27.4	200.0	18.5	35.0
Ireland	54.4	27.5	12.1	75.6	42.1	142.6	17.1	11.5
Italy	1532.0	615.0	311.0	2042.0	665.0	1181.0	4.0	517.0
Luxembourg	9.9	1.0	5.2	4.5	9.9	9.5	5.9	4.4
Netherlands	352.0	74.1	144.0	334.0	385.4	440.0	240.0	79.0
Norway	68.3	71.3	68.0	80.0	78.0	116.0	35.0	61.0
Sweden	148.0	160.0	157.0	200.0	235.0	165.0	65.0	116.0
Switzerland	270.6		87.5	139.3	73.4	119.0	45.5	115.5
Portugal	497.1	475.4	105.1	356.0	51.8	244.2	14.8	87.8
Spain	915.0	204.0	238.0	1533.0	625.0	1220.0	125.0	301.0
UK	655.0	732.0	602.0	1559.0	1135.0	1470.0	520.0	299.0

Source: Adapted from *European Marketing Data and Statistics* (London: Euromonitor Publications, 1995), 367.

ENDNOTES

1 Definition adapted from E. Jerome McCarthy and William D. Perrault, Jr., *Basic Marketing*, 10th ed. (Homewood, Ill.: Richard D. Irwin, 1990).

2 For elaboration, see S.B. Linder, *An Essay on Trade and Transformation* (New York: John Wiley and Sons, 1961).

3 W.W. Rostow, *The Stages of Economic Growth* (London: Cambridge University Press, 1960).

4 For more details, see Ernest Dichter, "The World Customer," *Harvard Business Review*, July 1962, 119–21; Bertil Liander, Vern Terpstra, M.Y. Yoshino, and Aziz A. Sherbini, *Comparative Advantage for International Marketing* (Boston, Mass.: Allyn and Bacon, 1967); William Dymza, *Multinational Business Strategy* (New York: McGraw-Hill, 1972); and Philip Kotler, *Marketing Management* (Englewood Cliffs, Prentice-Hall, 1980).

5 Howard Schlossberg, "Nielsen Chairman Outlines Thrust into Europe," *Marketing News*, 12 November 1990, 27.

6 Joel Garreau, *The Nine Nations of North America* (Boston, Mass.: Houghton-Mifflin, Co., 1981).

7 V.H. Kirpalani, *International Marketing*, 2nd ed. (New York: Random House, 1982).

8 For further details, see John S. Hill and Richard R. Still, "Effects of Urbanization on Multinational Product Policies," *Columbia Journal of Business* 19 (Summer 1984): 62–67; and John S. Hill, "Targeting Media in Lesser-Developed Countries: A Study of Multinational Corporation Strategies," *Journal of Advertising* 13, no. 4 (1984): 39–48.

9 Jerry Adler, et al., "The Nintendo Kid," *Newsweek*, 6 March 1989, 64–68.

10 Andrew Feinberg, "The First Global Generation," *Adweek's Marketing Week*, 6 February 1989, 18–20, 26–28.

11 John Templeman, "Grappling with the Graying of Europe," *Business Week*, 13 March 1989, 54–56.

12 Sherrie Shamoon, "Men's Magazines in Foreign Markets," *International Advertiser*, December 1986, 14–15.

13 J.K. Ryans, Jr., "It Is Too Soon to Put a Tiger in Every Tank," *Columbia Journal of World Business* 4 (March 1969): 69–75.

14 Kenichi Ohmae, *The Triad Power: The Coming Shapes of Global Competition* (New York: The Free Press, 1985), 15.

15 Lyn S. Amine, "Targeting the 1992 Euro-Consumer," *Academy of Marketing Science News* 11, no. 1 (January 1990): 1, 18.

16 Janette Martin, "Beyond 1992: Lifestyle Is Key," *Advertising Age*, 11 July 1988, 57.

17 Sudhir H. Kale and D.C. Sudharshan, "A Strategic Approach to International Segmentation," *International Marketing Review*, Summer 1987, 60–71.

CHAPTER

Exporting

Chapter Outline

Learning Objectives

When you have mastered the contents of this chapter, you will be able to do the following:

1 Explain the nature of exporting and its importance in world business.

2 Discuss the major exporting systems, both indirect (through agents, export management, and export trading companies) and direct (from manufacturer to customer).

3 Know how to locate export markets through use of trade statistics.

4 Explain the major documents used in international trade and the role of intermediaries such as freight forwarders and bankers.

5 Describe how international payments systems work.

6 Discuss how to transform occasional exporters into professional traders.

The movement of goods among countries is a dominant form of international business, with more than $4 trillion worth of merchandise being traded annually. Countries trade with one another because none produces all the goods and resources it requires. From an economic standpoint, growth based on exports is less inflationary than growth based on domestic expansion. The "Four Tigers" (Singapore, Hong Kong, South Korea, and Taiwan), as well as Japan, have all modernized their economies by means of export trade.

From the company viewpoint, exporting is the usual way firms "go international."

Many begin exporting by responding to unsolicited inquiries from abroad. Then, realizing that shipping goods abroad is not that difficult, many become regular exporters. Table 8–1 shows top U.S. exporters as of 1995. Note that most are large multinationals. Just 100 companies account for almost two-thirds of U.S. exports.[1]

The emphasis here is on small-business exporting. Multinational export-import activities are examined later as part of international logistics (Chapter 14), where they are viewed in their corporate contexts as linkages between global manufacturing and marketing activities.

TABLE 8–1 ■ *Top U.S. Exporters, 1995*

Company	Location	Amount Exported	Product
Boeing Co.	Seattle, WA	$14,616,000,000	Aircraft
Goodyear Tire & Rubber Co.	Akron, OH	$12,000,000,000	Tires and inner tubes
Caterpillar, Inc.	Peoria, IL	$11,436,000,000	Construction and mining machinery
General Motors Corp.	Detroit, MI	$10,200,000,000	Automobiles and other motor vehicles
Akzo Nobel Chemicals, Inc.	Chicago, IL	$10,000,000,000	Chemicals and allied products
Digital Equipment Corp.	Maynard, MA	$7,000,000,000	Computer peripheral equipment
United Technologies Corp. Pratt & Whitney Div.	East Hartford, CT	$6,170,000,000	Aircraft engines and engine parts
CPC International, Inc., Best Foods Div.	Englewood Cliffs, NJ	$5,000,000,000	Food preparations
Cooper Industries, Inc.	Houston, TX	$4,900,000,000	Power-driven handtools
Abrasive Distributors Corp.	Hackensack, NJ	$4,500,000,000	Abrasive products
Navistar International Transportation Corp.	Chicago, IL	$4,000,000,000	Truck and bus bodies

Source: Adapted from "Directory of United States Exporters 1997." *The Journal of Commerce,* 1997.

INITIATING EXPORTS

Firms go after overseas markets either to capitalize upon unique products, technologies, or expertise, or in response to marketplace stimuli, such as unsolicited inquiries and competitive pressures. Those choosing the first option are *proactive exporters*. Those choosing the second are *reactive exporters*. Table 8–2 shows export-initiating motives classified into proactive and reactive categories.

Export studies suggest that most U.S. firms are reactive. One researcher found that, on average, 60 percent of companies begin exporting in response to the receipt of unsolicited inquiries.[2] Most businesses are apprehensive about sending goods abroad and perceive numerous obstacles to exporting. These include insufficient finances, foreign government restrictions, ignorance of overseas distribution, few foreign connections, and little awareness of international sales opportunities.[3]

How can executives (or outside consultants) generate interest in exporting where previously there has been none? To stimulate interest, top management needs to be convinced about the advantages of exporting. There are several persuasive arguments: First, exports can offset domestic sales fluctuations. Second, companies can reduce total manufacturing costs through exporting. Third, competitors may already be exporting. Fourth, export statistics and Department of Commerce reports show that export markets exist for the company's products.

Top management also needs to be reassured that it is possible to overcome the problems associated with exporting. For instance, the plethora of documents needed to export can be turned over to a competent freight forwarder; and payment for exports can be assured by using the correct payment methods (such as confirmed, irrevocable letters of credit). Furthermore, the language problem can be overcome initially by either focusing on English-speaking markets or by using competent translators. Such reassurances encourage companies to look for export markets and give them confidence in their ability to cope with overseas inquiries and export quotations. However, underconfident or resource-poor companies can get "their feet wet" using others' export expertise. This is indirect exporting.

TABLE 8–2 ▪ *Reasons to Export: Major Motivations to Internationalize Small and Medium-Sized Firms*

Proactive	Reactive
Profit advantages	Competitive pressures
Unique products	Overproduction
Technological advantage	Declining domestic sales
Exclusive information	Excess capacity
Managerial urge	Saturated domestic markets
Tax benefit	Proximity to customers and ports
Economies of scale	Unsolicited inquiries

Source: Adapted with permission from Michael R. Czinkota, *Export Development Strategies* (New York, N.Y.: Praeger Publishers, 1982), 53.

INDIRECT EXPORTING

Indirect exporting occurs when a third party handles the exporting for one or more manufacturers. These third-party intermediaries take many forms. There are small independent operations such as export management and export trading companies, industry-wide exporters such as Webb-Pomerence Associations, and specialized trading units that represent large corporations (as buying offices) or even entire countries (as buying offices).

Export Management Companies

Export management companies (EMCs) are typically small, with three or fewer employees and annual turnovers of under $10 million. Most handle four or fewer industries and build up expertise and contacts for particular product lines. Their strength lies in representing several manufacturers and offering overseas customers complete product assortments.

EMCs provide clients with instant market knowledge and contacts for little or no commitment of resources. They determine where the markets are for a company's products and arrange sales without the manufacturer having to know anything about exporting—documentation, receiving payment, and the physical moving of goods. More complex tasks, such as political risk analysis, foreign sales force management, obtaining financial information about prospects, and providing repair services, are among the more difficult activities that EMCs perform.[4]

Export Trading Companies

Export trading companies (ETCs) were established under the 1982 Export Trading Company Act. There are two types of ETCs. The first consists of small independent entities (similar to EMCs) that are able to consort with, or are partially owned by, banks. The second are trading appendages of banks and major corporations (among these are affiliates of Citicorps, Bank of America, Sears, General Electric, and General Motors). ETCs aim to develop international marketing expertise, enabling companies to conduct transactions globally.

American ETCs got off to a slow start, with only 108 being formed between 1982–1989. Together with EMCs, though, they totaled over 3,100 in 1996. One reason for the lack of success is rooted in the founding philosophy that inadequate financing prevents EMCs and ETCs from succeeding abroad. Japanese and Korean trading companies (after whom the American ETCs were modeled) succeeded mainly because of their size, market contacts, and marketing information.

Industry-Oriented Export Operations: Webb-Pomerene Associations

Webb-Pomerene Associations (WPAs) permit U.S. companies to join together in export-related activities without violating U.S. antitrust laws. WPAs are organized along industry and regional lines. Examples are WPAs in cotton (American Cotton Exporters Association), peanuts, poultry, movies, woodchips, avocados, tobacco, pulp and paper, onions, citrus fruits, dried fruits, and chemicals. About 25 WPAs were registered at the beginning of the 1990s, down from their peak years in the 1950s, when over 50 were in operation.[5]

WPAs consolidate individual exporting efforts into unified industrywide strategies.

They collect information on world markets and pass on trade leads to member companies that are bidding on or filling orders. They represent their client industries at trade shows and act as organized lobbies in legislative matters. They establish product standards for exporters and undertake industrywide promotions targeted to specific markets. For example, there have been such promotions on behalf of American peanuts, peanut butter products, and pecans in the European market.

Other Indirect Exporters

COMPANY BUYING OFFICES ▪ Regular merchandise importers, such as retailers, have purchasing offices in major buying centers abroad. U.S. fashion houses have Paris and London offices, and many U.S. retailers have buying offices in Hong Kong or Taiwan. Foreign purchasing facilities allow U.S. companies to special-order goods, maintain on-site quality control, and arrange their own shipping of orders.

Foreign buying offices situated in the United States are also indirect exporters. The Japanese trading companies account not only for about 30 percent of all U.S. imports but also for about 15 percent of all U.S. exports. They are particularly large buyers of American agricultural produce for shipment back to Japan.

COUNTRY BUYING OFFICES ▪ Up until the late 1980s, many countries (particularly in Eastern Europe) maintained buying offices abroad. However, as perestroika has progressed, state trading organizations have become privatized, and their missions have broadened to include the generating of exports. These new activities have included initiating direct contacts with Western companies and negotiating their own deals.[6] More

recently, foreign trade organizations have been used to bolster commercial relations among former communist bloc countries.[7]

THE GENERAL TRADING COMPANY: JAPANESE AND SOUTH KOREAN MODELS ▪ Foreign market expertise and contacts are keys to successful international trading. For a small company or one just getting started internationally, this expertise is difficult to acquire and expensive to maintain. For this reason, some countries allow general trading companies (GTCs) to handle their export-market-development activities. In Japan, the GTCs (or *sogo shoshas*) include Mitsui, Mitsubishi, C. Itoh, Marubeni-Ida, and Sumitomo. In Korea, the major GTCs are Daewoo, Gold Star, and Samsung.

Japanese General Trading Companies. Japan has thousands of trading companies, but about 9 or 10 dominate. They account for nearly one-third of the Japanese gross national product, 50 percent of Japanese exports, 60 percent of imports, and 10 percent of world trade.[8]

The *sogo shoshas'* international trade successes are mainly due to their extensive international marketing network. Mitsubishi is typical. Its trading arm consists of a 225-office worldwide network with more than 15,000 employees. Its Tokyo headquarters processes upward of 60,000 fax and telex messages daily, and its daily transactions cover up to 25,000 different products ranging from raw materials to satellite systems. Collectively, the *sogo shoshas* have more than 1,000 offices worldwide and approximately 25,000 local employees.[9]

These trading companies have been so successful that other countries—including the United States (through its ETC Act 1982), Brazil, and Korea—have tried to emulate them. Of these, Korea's effort has been the most successful.

Korean General Trading Companies.
During the 1970s, Korea adopted the trading company concept to stimulate export-oriented economic growth. Using trading companies as export springboards, Korea's trading performance improved sharply, with exports growing from $55 million in 1962 to $1 billion in 1971 and $100 billion in 1977.

Much of Korea's success may be traced to the trading structure the Korean government decreed for the GTCs. To enjoy tax privileges as a GTC, a company must have some minimum export value ($50 million originally in 1975 to 2 percent of total Korean exports in 1981) and a minimum capital requirement (2 billion won in 1977). Other stipulations include a minimum number of product lines with sales over $1 million, and a market diversity requirement. By the mid-1980s, nine GTCs had met these criteria, and trading companies transacted almost 50 percent of Korean exports.[10] A decade later, however, their export trading mission completed, and in line with governmental efforts to establish more competitive trading conditions, the eight major general trading companies were demanding deregulation of GTC exports, imports, and overseas investments.[11]

DIRECT EXPORTING

Most companies in North America and Western Europe opt to do their own exporting. Direct exporting requires time, patience, attention to detail, and an organizational commitment. One difficulty is knowing whether company products are exportable, and another is identifying the best markets. Export market research, however, is straightforward, given access to the right sources of information.

International Market Research: Export Market Analyses

What information does a company need in order to evaluate exporting opportunities? Here are some of the questions that need answering:

1. What are export prospects like for particular U.S. products? Are overseas markets for these products increasing, decreasing, or fairly stable?

2. Is the United States a major competitor in world markets for particular product categories? If yes, and if the company is competitive within the United States, the firm should do well abroad.

3. Which countries are major competitors in this industry?

4. In which parts of the world is the United States most competitive?

5. Which individual markets represent the best prospects?

The questions are answerable using two sets of statistics: the U.S. Bureau of the Census National Trade Data Bank (now available on CD-Rom); and the *United Nations Trade Data Yearbook*. The seven-step process shown in Figure 8–1 outlines how to use these data. The steps are described in detail as follows.

The Seven-Step Process

Let us use as our example the process for an insecticide manufacture:

STEP 1: ASSEMBLE EXPORT STATISTICS SOURCES ■
For U.S. exports, the Department of Commerce has its National Trade Data Bank, a giant information source bringing together data from more than 50

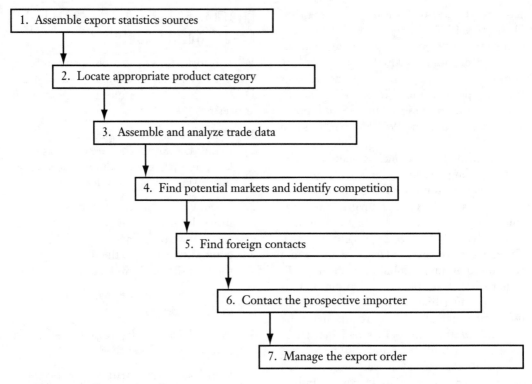

1. Assemble export statistics sources

2. Locate appropriate product category

3. Assemble and analyze trade data

4. Find potential markets and identify competition

5. Find foreign contacts

6. Contact the prospective importer

7. Manage the export order

FIGURE 8–1 *Exporting Steps*

federal sources. It is available on the World Wide Web at: http://www.stat-usa.gov; or on CD-Rom from Department of Commerce offices. The appropriate category to search is Merchandise Trade: U.S. Exports by Commodity.

STEP 2: LOCATE APPROPRIATE PRODUCT CATEGORY

■ Product categories are located either by the Harmonized System (HS) number (which is 3808 for insecticides, rodenticides, and fungicides for retail) or by product description. HS codes are available on the World Wide Web at: http://www.trading.wmw.com/codes.htm. Note that product categories in official sources rarely coincide exactly with those of the exporter, but they still serve as excellent indicators of market opportunities.

Basic product categories leading to the insecticides classification are shown in Figure 8–2.

STEP 3: ASSEMBLE AND ANALYZE DATA

■ Table 8–3 shows the top 30 export markets for insecticides HS 380810. Note that a complete table would show exports to over 140 markets over the 1993–95 period. A starting point for the analysis is aggregate trends. In Table 8–3, total U.S. exports rose from $334 million in 1993 to $351 million in 1995, with a dip in 1994 sales. This shows a growing market for this type of product. Declining sales would be a cause for concern to beginning exporters.

The strategies exporters follow depend largely on the types of analyses they do. The simplest strategy would be to target the top

FIGURE 8–2 ▪ *Deriving Harmonized System Product Codes: Insecticides*

	Section	Product Categories
1	Live animals; Animal products	15
2	Vegetable products	6–14
3	Animal or vegetable fats and oils	15
4	Prepared foodstuffs: Beverages, spirits, tobacco and manufactured tobacco substitutes	16–24
5	Mineral products: Salt, sulphur, ores, minerals, fuels, oil	25–27
6	Chemical or allied industries products	28–38
7	Plastics and rubbers and articles thereof	39–40
8	Raw hides, skins, leather, saddlery, travel goods, handbags	41–43
9	Wood and wooden articles; cork, manufacturers of straw	44–46
10	Woodpulp, paperboard	47–49
11	Textiles, textile products	50–63
12	Footwear, headgear, umbrellas	64–67
13	Articles of stone, plaster, ceramic products, glassware	68–70
14	Pearls, precious stones, metals	71
15	Base metals and articles	72–83
16	Machinery, appliances, electrical equipment	84–85
17	Vehicles, aircraft, transportation equipment	86–89
18	Optical, photographic equipment; surgical/medical instruments; clocks, watches	90–92
19	Arms and ammunition	93
20	Miscellaneous manufactured articles (bedding, furniture, prefab buildings)	
21	Works of art, antiques	97
22	Special classifications	98–99
	380810 Insecticides, rodenticides and fungicides	

markets (Canada, Brazil, and Japan in this case), but other analyses suggest different approaches. A regional analysis breaks down exports to specific parts of the world (North America, Central America, South America, Asia, and so on). Individual market analyses yield classifications by size (small, medium, large) and by market condition (increasing, stable, decreasing). From Table 8–3, large markets might be those over $10 million a year; medium would be those between $4 million and $10 million, and small would be

TABLE 8–3 ■ *U.S. Exports of Insecticides, Retail: HS 380810, 1993–95 ($ millions)*

	Rank Partner Country	1993	1994	1995	Condition
	World	334.385	303.325	351.479	
Large Markets	Canada	37.231	46.665	54.760	Expanding
	Brazil	15.703	24.790	36.485	Expanding
	Japan	19.062	19.950	33.873	Expanding
	France	17.054	24.670	20.301	Constant
	Belgium	10.063	9.203	19.986	Exp.
	Australia	14.413	14.917	17.032	Constant
	Mexico	12.259	18.002	15.509	Constant
	Argentina	6.873	7.609	15.308	Med/Large Expanding
	United Kingdom	17.959	7.792	11.891	Constant
Medium Markets	Costa Rica	9.209	8.803	8.415	Constant
	Indonesia	5.139	7.217	7.945	Constant
	South Africa, Rep. of	6.577	6.170	7.605	Constant
	Ecuador	8.578	7.228	7.128	Constant
	Netherlands	17.579	11.493	6.193	Declining
	Thailand	15.053	6.446	5.133	Declining
	Spain	2.169	5.741	5.011	Constant
	Taiwan	9.192	6.371	4.615	Declining
	Colombia	7.391	6.567	4.515	Declining
	Philippines	5.223	4.164	4.352	Constant
	Switzerland	1.928	0.156	4.315	Expanding
	Israel	0.863	1.071	4.000	Expanding
Small Markets	Italy	2.600	2.902	3.954	Expanding
	Chile	6.469	3.495	3.940	Constant
	Singapore	7.453	8.003	3.894	Declining
	Honduras	4.215	4.149	3.842	Constant
	Guatemala	7.925	4.303	3.188	Declining
	Pakistan	0.862	2.300	3.179	Expanding
	Korean Republic	1.495	4.387	3.126	Constant
	Egypt	8.506	0.788	2.756	Declining
	Venezuela	3.358	0.945	2.402	Constant

those below $4 million. Table 8–4 shows regional and individual market analyses for the top 30 markets.

The regional analyses show increasing dollar values for North and South America, with Central America in a small decline. Both Asia and Western Europe are important regions for insecticide exporters, though both show minor relative declines (from 24.6 percent to 22.1 percent for Western Europe and from 22.5 percent to 20.4 percent for Asia). Exporters opting for regional strategies out

TABLE 8–4 ▪ *Regional and Individual Market Analyses: U.S. Exports of HS 380810 ($ millions)*

	1993	1994	1995
North America (Canada, Mexico)	49.49	64.667	70.269
	17.5%	23.4%	21.6%
Central America	21.349	17.255	15.445
	7.6%	6.3%	4.8%
South America	48.372	50.634	69.778
	17.1%	18.3%	21.5%
Western Europe	69.352	61.957	71.651
	24.6%	22.4%	22.1%
Eastern Europe	—	—	—
Middle East (Israel)	0.863	1.071	4.000
	0.3%	0.4%	1.2%
Africa	15.083	6.958	10.361
	5.3%	2.5%	3.2%
Asia	63.479	58.838	66.117
	22.5%	21.3%	20.4%
Oceania (Australia, NZ)	14.413	14.917	17.032
	5.1%	5.4%	5.2%
Total (top 30 markets)	282.401	276.297	324.653
Top 30 markets: % total	84.5%	91.1%	92.4%

TABLE 8–4 *(cont'd)* ▪ *Individual Market Analysis: Classifications*

Market Size/Condition	Expanding	Constant	Declining
Large	Canada	France	
	Brazil	Australia	
	Japan	Mexico	
	Belgium	UK	
	Argentina		
Medium	Switzerland	Costa Rica	Netherlands
	Israel	Indonesia	Thailand
		Ecuador	Taiwan
		Spain	Colombia
		Philippines	
Small	Italy	Chile	Singapore
	Pakistan	Honduras	Guatemala
		Korea	Egypt
		Venezuela	

of the U.S. would probably look first and hardest at South American markets.

The individual market analyses in Table 8–4 show Canada, Brazil, Japan, Belgium, and Argentina to be large, expanding export markets, with France, Australia, Mexico, and the UK as large, fairly constant markets. Firms that are industry leaders through technical skills, cost advantages, or competitive product mixes have maximum freedom in choosing export markets. Less-cost-competitive firms or those not having great product variety generally focus on medium and small export markets.

However, U.S. companies may not export to all available markets. That is, there may be countries that import insecticides from other countries but not from the United States. To identify these countries, the *United Nations Trade Data Yearbook* is used.

STEP 4: FINDING POTENTIAL MARKETS AND IDENTIFYING COMPETITION ▪ U.N. trade

data are categorized according to the Standard International Trade Classification (SITC) typology. SITC classifications differ from Harmonized System (HS) classification. Using SITC data requires caution because, first, these data are classified into broader product categories than those in the Harmonized System, and second, the data are usually two years late in appearing. A sample of SITC data is shown in Table 8–5. From a complete table, we get three types of information:

1. *Competitive position of U.S.-based exporters.* Export statistics show that the United States is the world's third-leading exporter of pesticides, disinfectants, insecticides, fungicides, and herbicides. Germany leads, with France in close attendance as the second-leading export base. In this case, it is good to know that U.S.-based companies are among the world leaders.

2. *Regional comparisons of U.S. export markets versus world import markets.* Comparing the regional U.S. analysis with percentages values of imports to various parts of the world turns up some interesting contrasts. First, the U.S. does relatively well in South America, with between 17–22 percent of export directed there, but this amount only accounts for between 6–9 percent of world imports. Similarly, Central America accounts for about 2 percent of world imports but takes up 5–7 percent of U.S. exports. But perhaps where the U.S. misses out is in Western Europe, which accounts for about one-half of world imports but only about one-fourth of U.S. exports. Closer inspection of Table 8-5, however, shows three out of the top four exporters to be European (Germany, France, and the UK). This would make the European market very competitive for outsiders.

3. *Individual market comparisons: U.S. exports and major import markets.* Some countries are large importers of insecticides and similar products but do little business with U.S. exporters. Germany is the second-largest importer, but it does not break the American top 30 listing. Netherlands is the sixth-largest importer, but it is a medium declining market. Iran also does not appear in the top U.S. export listings. Although they are not shown in our partial listing of importers, China, Denmark, Russia, and Saudi Arabia are prolific buyers of insecticide-type products on world markets, but they do not feature in the top 30 American markets. It is possible that there are problems, such as tariff barriers, in breaking into certain markets, but it is also possible that U.S. companies have given little effort to cultivating those markets.

TABLE 8–5 ■ *United Nations Trade Data Analysis ($ thousands)*

Imports (Regional)

	1992	1993	1994
Total	7,594,868	7,169,496	7,935,004
Africa	497,641	460,071	505,298
	6.6%	6.4%	6.4%
Americas	1,362,591	1,448,137	1,701,808
	17.9%	20.2%	21.5%
South America	46,798	522,833	694,944
	6.1%	7.3%	8.8%
Central America	169,235	154,190	162,596
	2.2%	2.2%	2.0%
Asia	1,385,218	1,417,479	1,434,265
	18.2%	19.8%	18.0%
Middle East	359,290	454,546	346,470
	4.7%	6.3%	4.4%
Europe	3,982,921	3,395,371	3,780,672
	52.4%	47.4%	47.6%
Oceania	110,214	118,400	143,607
	1.5%	1.6%	1.8%

Top Four Exporters of Insecticides

Leading Exporters	1992	1993	1994
Germany	1,451,712	1,279,344	1,567,244
France	1,094,294	1,074,134	1,336,325
USA	1,069,838	1,093,736	1,162,816
UK	919,786	953,385	970,338

Top Ten Importers of Insecticides

Leading Importers	1992	1993	1994
France	1,220,365	940,249	1,132,733
Germany	645,253	376,386	391,544
UK	324,955	370,855	366,432
Italy	318,206	334,335	378,920
Canada	300,686	325,434	420,257
Netherlands	311,504	256,361	270,523
USA	262,794	294,948	274,899
Belgium	210,986	248,299	288,307
Iran	112,935	212,370	116,993
Spain	200,606	180,096	220,340

Source: Adapted from *United Nations Trade Data Yearbook*, Vol. 2 (Washington, D.C.: United Nations, 1996, 106.

A. **Multimarket Sources**

The International Directory of Importers (Healdsburg, Calif.: Blytmann International). 7 volumes covering Europe (2 volumes), Middle East, North America, South Central America, Asia Pacific, and Africa.

Stores of the World Directory (London: Newman Books).

Bottin International (Paris: International Business Register). 2 volumes: Europe and Rest of World.

Principal International Businesses ([city], N.J.: Dun and Bradstreet).

Marconi's International Register (Larchmont, N.Y.: Telegraphic Cable & Radio Registrations).

The Export Guide to Europe (London: Graham and Trotman). 3 volumes.

Major Companies of Argentina, Brazil, Mexico and Venezuela (London: Graham and Trotman).

European Directory of Retailers and Wholesalers (London: Euromonitor Publications Ltd.)

Owens Commerce and International Register (London: Finchley).

B. **Country-Specific Sources**

Directory of Japanese Importers by Products, U.S. ed. (Tokyo: Business Intercommunications).

Japan Trade Directory (Tokyo: Japan External Trade Organization).

The China Directory of Industry and Commerce (New York: Van Nostrand Reinhold Co.).

Business Directory of Hong Kong ([place of publication: (Hong Kong: Current Publications Ltd.).

Major Companies of the Arab World (London: Graham and Trotman).

Taiwan Buyers Guide (Taipei: China Productivity Center).

C. **World Wide Web Sites: Directories**

Europages (search engine for European companies)	www.europages.com
European Yellow Pages	www.euroyellowpages.com
Contacts for the Gulf region	www.he.tdl.com/nishad/index.html
World Trade Center (search engine for trade centers worldwide)	tanuki.twics.com/PICOTYO/wtc.html
Worldwide Yellow Pages (search engine for international and domestic companies	www.yellow.com
Global Yellow Pages	www.globalyp.com/world.htm
National & International Yellow Pages	home.netscape.com/escapes/yellowpages/index.htm

FIGURE 8–3 *Directories for Locating Market Contacts*

STEP 5: FINDING MARKET CONTACTS ▪

Once companies have decided where to focus export marketing efforts, the next step is to locate prospective buyers. Directories are the best sources; a partial listing of them appears in Figure 8–3. Also listed are some Internet addresses.

STEP 6: REACHING THE PROSPECTIVE IMPORTER ▪

Direct mail is the easiest way to reach prospective importers overseas. Introductory letters along with enclosed company and product information should be in the local language. A company should not be disappointed if orders do not materialize quickly. In the domestic market, salespersons often make three or more calls on prospects before getting orders. Internationally, exporters routinely use several mailings per year. Even those importers who fail to respond to the first few mailings should be retained on the mailing list.

Response rates rise when both the letters and the sale literature are in the local language and when high-quality brochures are used. When product updates are frequent, translations costs rise. Many exporters keep costs down by using multilingual sales literature (see Figure 8–4 for an example). English is used in correspondence to countries where it is a major commercial language, such as in India or Hong Kong.

STEP 7: MANAGING THE EXPORT ORDER ▪

The next step is to negotiate the order and make shipment. This procedure involves clarifying the order, confirming it, arranging the payment methods, and then packing and transporting it to the customer.

The Export Quotation. Importers want to know whether it is cost effective to have goods shipped from the United States. Hence, before committing themselves to a particular supplier, they ask for export quotations on an international pro-forma invoice. The importer's order is then confirmed with an international purchase order. Together, these documents (the "negotiating documents") establish what is to be shipped, where, when, and the means of payment.

There are many forms of export quotations, depending on the costs included. The following explanations mainly relate to "who pays the freight."

- *FOB plant*: Free on board at the (manufacturing) plant is the factory price of the goods, without inland freight, port charges, ocean freight, and insurance, but usually including export crating (a charge passed on to customers).

- *FOB port*: Free on board to the port includes export crating and inland freight charges to the port of departure.

- *FAS (name of ship)*: Free alongside vessel includes delivery to pier of departure, the freight forwarder's fee, and wharfage charges.

- *C and F port of destination*: Cost and freight takes in all the above charges and adds on ocean freight and any ship-associated tolls such as bunker surcharges and container rentals.

- *CIF port of destination*: Cost, insurance, and freight is the most widely used form of export quotation. It tells importers the approximate landed price of the goods at the port of destination. Other types of quotations exist; for example, a CIF ex-dock quotation includes not only cost, insurance, and freight but also any tariffs, taxes, or other charges at the port of destination.

Order Confirmation: The International Purchase Order. Once the importer receives the quotation, the decision to buy (or not to

1. Specialized Paint for Marking Trees
2. Chemicals for Export Market
3. Chemical Preparation
4. Loading Liquid Chemicals into Tank Trailers

١ — دهان خاص لتعليم الشجر
٢ — مواد كيماوية للتصدير
٣ — تحضير المواد الكيماوية
٤ — تعبئة الشاحنات بالمواد الكيماوية

The abundance of natural resources gives Alabama chemical firms a reliable source for a broad spectrum of products including feedstock chemicals, organic and inorganic industrial chemicals, agricultural chemicals, plastics, pharmaceuticals, polymeric chemicals, paints, cleaners and other consumer items. Large deposits of salt, limestone, and coal found throughout the state are complemented by regional supplies of natural gas and petroleum.

Alabama currently exports various industrial organic and inorganic chemicals as well as agricultural chemicals that make up fertilizers, herbicides, and insecticides. Alabama is the home of both the International Fertilizer Development center (IFDC), an international non-profit corporation whose objectives are to develop new and improved fertilizer techniques for food-producing farmers around the world; and the National Fertilizer Development Center (NFDC), under the direction of the Tennessee Valley Authority in norther Alabama and one of the world's leading fertilizer development centers.

Other chemical products exported include rocket propellants, explosives, synthetic fibers, plastics, paints, food preservatives, adhesive materials, hair preparations, soaps and detergents.

Of the $2,685.8 million in shipments in 1980, 25.2% ($679.5 million) were from exports, a substantial increase from 1976 when exports were only 7.7% of total shipments ($134.0 million out of $1,739.5 million). Export related employment as a percentage of total chemical industry employment has also increased dramatically, from 7.6% in 1972 to 23.5% in 1980. In order to insure the continued growth of this industry, Alabama is committed to further development of international trade.

ان توفر الثروات الطبيعية بكثرة في آلاباما يؤمن لشركات المواد الكيماوية مواد أولية لكثير من منتجاتها كعلف الحيوانات ، المواد الكيماوية العضوية وغير العضوية المستعملة في الصناعة ، المواد الكيماوية الزراعية ، البلاستيك ، المواد الصيدلانية ، الدهانات بانواعها ، مستحضرات التنظيف وعدد كثير من المواد المستهلكة منزليا . يوجد كميات كبيرة من الملح والحجر الكلسي والفحم في جميع انحاء الولاية بالاضافة الى كميات كبيرة محلية من الغاز الطبيعي والنفط .

تصدر حاليا آلاباما كثر من المواد الكيماوية الصناعية العضوية وغير العضوية كالمواد الكيماوية الزراعية التي ينتج منها السماد الكيماوي ، مبيدات الحشرات ومبيدات المزروعات الضارة . يوجد في آلاباما مركزان عالميان للابحاث في مجال الأسمدة الأول مركز ابحاث السماد وهو مركز عالمي غير تجاري لاجراء ابحاث لايجاد احدث الطرق للتسميد وذلك لتمكين الفلاح الذي ينتج المحصولات التي تستعمل في انتاج الاطعمة من تحسين انتاج وتحسين انواع السماد التي يستعملها . المركز الثاني هو مركز تنمية السماد وهذا المركز تابع لهيئة وادي تينيسي في شمال آلاباما وهومن اكبر المراكز الدولية لاجراء ابحاث السماد .

تتضمن المواد الكيماوية المصدرة الى الخارج وقود الصواريخ ، المتفجرات ، الخيوط الصناعية ، البلاستيك ، الدهانات بانواعها ، المواد الكيماوية لحفظ الأطعمة ، المواد اللاصقة ، المواد التجميلية للشعر ، الصابون العادي وصابون الغسيل .

صدرت آلاباما في عام ١٩٨٠ ما قيمته ٦٧٩٫٥ مليون دولار اي ٢٥٫٢ بالمئة من مجموع ما شحن والذي قيمته ٢٦٨٥٫٨ مليون دولار وهذا زيادة كبيرة عن ما صدر عام ١٩٧٦ حيث بلغت نسبة الصادرات ٧٫٧ بالمئة من مجموع ما شحن (١٣٤ مليون دولار من مجموع ١٧٣٩٫٥ مليون دولار) . بلغت نسبة العاملين بصناعة المواد الكيماوية المصدرة ٢٣٫٥ بالمئة من مجموع العاملين في هذه الصناعة عام ١٩٨٠ وهذا زيادة كبيرة عن نسبة ال ٧٫٦ بالمئة في عام ١٩٧٢ .

لتأمين التوسع في هذه الصناعة تقدم آلاباما جهودها لتوسيع سوق الاستهلاك للمواد المنتجة محليا وعالميا .

Source: Alabama International Trade Center, Tuscaloosa, Alabama. Reproduced with permission.

FIGURE 8–4 *A Multilingual Brochure in English and Arabic*

buy) is made. If prices are reasonable and tariffs and other duties (which the importer usually pays) are not excessive, then the buyer arranges importation. In most advanced markets, importation presents few problems, but in countries that have trade deficits, there are often shortages of hard currency (for example, dollars, yen, and pounds). Importers in these countries often need to obtain *import licenses*, which contain government permission to buy foreign products and enable overseas banks to allocate hard currency reserves to that order. Not surprisingly, some requests for import licenses are refused, often because goods are not essential. Some import licenses are secured only after importers make significant deposits with their governments. Once the import license is obtained, the importer returns an international purchase order to the exporter along with information on the proposed means of payment.

Controlling the Order. Every export order is subject to controls. In the United States, general licenses for most exports and destinations are obtainable from and granted by local Department of Commerce offices. Special licenses are granted by the U.S. Department of Commerce in conjunction with the U.S. State Department; these licenses apply to technical exports such as computers or to shipments to "unfriendly" countries. Permission to export certain technical goods to these countries takes considerable time to obtain (if granted at all).

Most countries keep track of outgoing exports. In the United States, the document used for this purpose is the *export declaration*, which is filled out by either the shipper or the freight forwarder.

In some cases, importing countries have particular documentation requirements. Some countries require *consular invoices*, which document the shipment in local languages as well as in English. Exporters obtain these from country consulates in the United States.

Many countries require *certificates of origin*, which testify as to the national origin of the goods. Obtainable from local chambers of commerce, these certificates document the nationalities of shipments and are used by customs officials in assessing tariffs and taxes.

Responsibility for Correct Documentation and Transportation: The International Freight Forwarder. New exporters are often discouraged when they learn about the many documentation requirements. In most cases, however, international freight forwarders are the ones who collect and arrange the necessary export documents. All the exporter has to do is tell the forwarder what the cargo is, where it needs to go, and when it has to be there, and the forwarder does the rest. The freight forwarder's usual duties include the following: helping with export quotations (FOB, C and F, CIF), booking space on carriers, assembling and typing appropriate documents, arranging inland freight and insurance, and facilitating the payment process, if necessary. Freight forwarders perform all of these duties at relatively low cost because their revenues come from the carriers, who pay commissions on steamship or airplane space leased.

Getting Paid: Major Payment Methods and the Role of the International Banker. New exporters sometimes are nervous about being paid by foreign customers. Inevitably, of course, as with domestic transactions, there is a risk of nonpayment. Such risks are minimized by using the proper payment instruments (letter of credit and sight and time drafts) and through credit checks.

There are four major means of payments for exports. The first is *cash in advance*, which is always a preferred means but is seldom used because importers are usually unwilling to disburse payment until they know the goods received are exactly as ordered and have not suffered damage in transit. However, for orders of specialty products (for example, specialized machine tools or computer programs), some up-front money may be required.

The second major means of payment is *goods on consignment*. When goods are sold on consignment, the importer pays the exporter only after reselling the products ordered. Generally, this means of payment occurs in one or more of the following situations. First, the exporters and importers belong to the same corporate entity (for example, both are subsidiaries of a multinational corporation). Second, the exporter and importer have an established relationship. Or third, the goods are part of a barter transaction in which the goods must be sold before the exchange products are shipped.

The third major means of payment is *bills of exchange* or *sight and time drafts*. A bill of exchange is a demand for payment, or "reverse check." The exporter (or exporter's representative or bank) sends or presents the draft to the importer's bank, normally along with the title documents. When the importer goes to the bank to collect the title documents (the commercial invoice, bill of lading, and perhaps other items), he or she either must pay the bank immediately (as with a sight draft) or must sign for the goods and pay within a previously specified period. For example, a 90-day time draft means the importer must pay the bank within 90 days following release of the documents.

Time drafts and sight drafts are customary when exporters and importers have established relationships. Where there is any doubt about either an importer's (for example, a new customer) or a country's ability to pay, a letter of credit is used.

The fourth major means of payment is *letters of credit*, documents that confirm that payment will be made. There are three types currently used in international trade. The first is a *revocable letter of credit*, which is used rather infrequently because its terms do not legally bind either the importer or the exporter. Its terms and conditions can be changed by either party without notifying the other.

The second and third types are both *irrevocable letters of credit*, the terms of which cannot be changed without the consent of both parties. There are two types, unconfirmed and confirmed. An unconfirmed letter of credit is opened by the importer's bank in favor of the exporter's. It states that the importer has the money to pay (has good credit) and that the importer's bank guarantees payment. For many types of transactions (such as exporting to the United States or to other developed countries), unconfirmed letters of credit are sufficient, as payments in dollars, pounds sterling, yen, or Swiss francs are both acceptable and automatic.

But developing countries often have hard currency shortages owing to balance-of-trade problems. Even where import licenses are granted, problems can occur. For example, there may be payment delays. For this and other reasons, many exporters ask their banks to confirm the letter of credit. Confirmation involves checking the importer's bank and the currency flow in and out of the country in question. The exporter's bank charges a fee for this service, but the result, a *confirmed irrevocable letter of credit*, is a guarantee of payment by both the importer's bank and the exporter's bank. This makes it the safest means of international payment.

The payment procedures for letters of credit and time and sight drafts consist of six steps.

1. After the export order has been negotiated and prices and payment methods have been agreed upon, the exporter and the freight forwarder assemble the needed

documents, which include commercial invoices, originals and multiple copies, packing lists, insurance certificates, certificates of origin, and the like. The cargo is then transported to the port and placed on the vessel, and the steamship line issues a "clean, on-board bill of lading."

2. The clean, on-board bill of lading and other documents are sent to the importer's bank.

3. The importer is notified when the goods arrive at the port (often by a customs house broker). The importer then goes to the bank, pays for the goods (as with a sight draft) or signs for them (as with a time draft), and receives the title documents to use in claiming the goods.

4. The importer goes to the port, claims the goods, pays the relevant duties and taxes, and arranges transportation to the importer's business premises.

5. The importer's bank pays the exporter's bank (immediately in most cases, or before the time draft expires).

6. The exporter's bank pays the exporter.

Banks then, along with freight forwarders, are facilitators in the exporting process. But other institutions provide services that lubricate and facilitate export trade. Many are government sponsored, and although the emphasis in this text is on the United States, many governments, especially those in Europe, have similar services.

GOVERNMENT ASSISTANCE ▪ The government provides a number of aids to help marketers perform their business. Among them are the following:

Help in Finding Markets. Besides the National Trade Data Bank and UN trade data analyses, the U.S. Department of Commerce's International Trade Administration provides additional sources of information. *Global Market Surveys* are reports on market potentials for particular industries or products that have known market potentials. Examples of product-sector reports include ones for building products; biomedical equipment; water purification and pollution-control equipment; pumps, valves, and compressors; and many others. Trade Opportunities Program (TOP) bulletins collect and publish government contracts and tenders and large private contracts by U.S. embassies worldwide. They are updated biweekly. In addition, help is given in preparing tenders. Subscribers to this service also can be matched to overseas parties seeking companies to represent.

General-Background Publications. Exporters require background information on markets. To serve this need, the Department of Commerce puts out two series. The first, the *Overseas Business Report* (OBR), furnishes updates on political and economic conditions in major world markets, along with information on prices, wages, distribution, and other trade-related matters. The second series, *Foreign Economic Trends and Their Implications for the United States* (FET), provides in-depth data on trade patterns, exports to and from the United States, and news on the economic progress of various countries (such as growth of GNP, analyses by industry sectors, and so on).

Help in Financing and Insuring Exports. The major governmental agency dealing with financing is EximBank (the Export-Import Bank). EximBank has made loans of about $200 billion to U.S. exporters since its inception in 1934.[12] The bank protects exporters against political and commercial risks, including nonpayment of importers, civil or political disruptions, and simple non-availability of hard currency.

EximBank's financial services to exporters are mainly long term (up to 5 years) and medium term (up to 18 months). EximBank's short-term efforts are administered by the Foreign Credit Insurance Association (FCIA). Formed in 1961, the FCIA is made up of major insurance companies that, together, provide a financial underwriting of commercial risks. The FCIA has numerous programs ranging from six months to over five years, but its most popular programs are short term, with export credit insurance and loan guarantees.[13]

There are numerous other government or government-backed services that give financial help to international businesspeople. Among them are the following:

- The EximBank-backed Private Export Funding Corporation (PEFCO), a private corporation owned by banks and major exports (such as Boeing and GE), provides foreign importers with financing to purchase U.S. exports.

- The Overseas Private Development Corporation (OPIC) give investment guarantees to U.S. businesses investing abroad and stands ready to reimburse companies whose subsidiaries have been confiscated (that is, taken over without compensation) or which have received inadequate remuneration for expropriated property.

- The Agency of International Development (AID) provides linkages between government-administered funds given as assistance to foreign countries and American companies that can supply needed goods and services bought with these AID funds.

Contact Lists in Overseas Markets. The government sponsors the *Foreign Traders Index*, a 143,000-name listing of foreign importers, distributors, wholesalers, and retailers. In addition, the International Trade Administration's (ITA) Agent Distributor Service matches foreign distributors with U.S. companies exporting to particular industries or geographic areas.

Promotion of American Products and Services Abroad. One of the most efficient means of promoting products and services overseas is through trade fairs and commercial exhibitions. Forty-six ITA-sponsored exhibitions were scheduled in major markets worldwide in 1997.[14]

The United States is a market where "novelty" products thrive. The ITA sponsors a New Product Information Service, which details new American products and promotes them through U.S. embassies overseas.

Information Checks on Foreign Companies and Distributors. U.S. companies, like all others, always want to know something about their customers, especially if they are dealing with them for the first time. Credit and general business checks can be made through the commercial staffs of U.S. embassies abroad. Known as *World Traders Data Reports*, these reports detail company histories and commercial reliability.

PRIVATE SOURCES OF COMMERCIAL INFORMATION

In the private sector, there are numerous companies specializing in providing international business information. *Dun and Bradstreet's Exporter's Encyclopedia* gives updates on trading conditions worldwide and outlines documentation requirements for most markets. Dun and Bradstreet also runs credit checks on overseas businesses.

The most comprehensive source of world business information is Business International (BI). Apart from its basic weekly world business update, BI provides geographic news information, including *Business Europe*, *Business Asia*, *Business China*, *Business Eastern Europe*, and *Business Latin America*.

In addition, there are specialized publications. *Investing, Trading and Licensing (ITL)* provides details on foreign commercial environments, including attitudes toward private investment, economic outlooks, and laws governing commercial practices. *Financing Foreign Operations (FFO)* outlines local money markets and prevailing financial conditions.

Other publications include *The Wall Street Journal*, the British *Financial Times*, and the daily *Journal of Commerce*. There are also numerous trade and government publications, including the U.S. Department of Commerce's *Business America*.

BECOMING A PROFESSIONAL EXPORTER

There are several steps firms can take to consolidate and upgrade the importance of their exporting activities.

1. *Form an international department.* Make managers responsible for various parts of the world, such as Europe and Asia. They should have appropriate language skills for their areas.

2. *Represent international interests in top management.* Give recognition to overseas business at the highest corporate management level, with a vice president or director overseeing foreign business activities. Without such representation,

international activities remain subordinate to domestic operations.

3. *Separate overseas and domestic planning, budgets, and procedures.* While extremely large corporations integrate domestic and foreign interests, when companies are first starting export operations, it is useful to separate the two so that the international department is recognized as being "different" and, where appropriate, separate sets of operating procedures can be identified.

4. *Use foreign-language promotional brochures and product markings and labeling.* As companies become involved internationally, they arrange for translating and adapting promotional literature to fit foreign tastes. They develop multilingual labeling and custom-designed sales brochures. As Europe has become integrated, many products, regardless of their country of origin, are marked in English, French, German, Spanish, Portuguese, and other languages. This practice gives these products easy access to other English, French, and Spanish markets worldwide (e.g, Australia, New Zealand, French-speaking countries in North and West Africa, and Spanish- and Portuguese-speaking countries in Latin America).

5. *Adapt products to overseas needs and develop new products.* Keeping in touch with distributors and monitoring foreign market trends opens up ideas for modifying present product lines to make them more competitive. Such contacts also stimulate new-product development as ideas from foreign markets flow back to the United States.

6. *Extend company influence into foreign markets.* Exporting is one way for firms to penetrate overseas markets. To

consolidate and further company interests, especially in stable or expanding
markets, some firms establish a corporate presence overseas. They do so by
acquiring stakes in foreign distributors
or establishing company-owned sales
forces and networks. Company representation in foreign markets gives overseas buyers confidence that a firm is serious about market development, and out
of such confidence, growth occurs. The
many different ways to extend corporate
commitments overseas—licensing, joint
venture, subcontracting, wholly owned
subsidiary, and so on—are explored in
the next chapter.

SUMMARY

Exporting is an important way to serve foreign
markets. Experienced multinationals and Japanese
trading companies are all extensive exporters.
Companies without export knowledge, experience, and resources can export indirectly through
intermediaries such as Webb-Pomerene associations, export trading companies, and export management companies.

The export process is straightforward. First,
suitable export markets are identified using U.S.
government and United Nations trade statistics.
Second, export management procedures and key
export documents fall into four categories: negotiation, travel, control, and payments.

Becoming a professional exporter is largely a
matter of organization. Having separate domestic
and international departments is desirable, as is
having distinct planning and organizational functions. Adapting product offerings and promotional efforts to fit overseas markets also
contributes to corporate success internationally.

DISCUSSION QUESTIONS

1. Table 8–2 lays out proactive and reactive reasons for exporting. Categorize each of the following situations into one of the two
   classifications.
   a) Company learns that its major competitor
      is exporting.
   b) Firm has a unique technological process.
   c) Industry association distributes details of
      recent trade leads and contacts.
   d) Domestic sales are down.
   e) Domestic sales are cyclical.
   f) Company responds to an unsolicited
      inquiry.

2. In what ways do knowledgeable international
   bankers and freight forwarders make life easier
   for the exporter?

3. Under what sets of circumstances would
   exporters use the following methods of payment:
   a) Revocable letter of credit
   b) Unconfirmed irrevocable letter of credit
   c) Confirmed letter of credit
   d) Time draft (i.e., bill of exchange)

4. What functions do the documents listed in
   Question 3 perform?

Hard Candy Incorporated— The Case of the Inexperienced Exporter

Hard Candy Inc. was a manufacturer of boiled candies in Alabama. For many years the firm had exported its products through an export management company in California. Then, management decided that the firm should become a direct exporter. You are an international trade specialist at the William R. Bennett Alabama International Trade Center, and you have been assigned to this company.

QUESTIONS

1. What would you advise?

2. Specifically, how should Hard Candy Inc. organize itself?

3. What sorts of information should it seek?

Toys and Sports Inc.: Looking for Export Markets

You are a toys and sports manufacturer looking for your first export sales. You obtain the following list of prime U.S. export markets.

What would you recommend and why? What would be your next steps?

EXHIBIT 8–1 ■ *U.S. Export Sales, Select Countries*
(U.S.$ millions)

Rank	Partner Country	1993	1994	1995
	World	2,950	3,376	3,858
1	Canada	677	781	822
2	Japan	479	502	729
3	United Kingdom	196	230	237
4	Mexico	232	359	220
5	Korean Republic	154	157	199
6	Germany	155	162	175
7	Taiwan	128	180	154
8	Hong Kong	72	84	148
9	Brazil	36	59	108
10	Australia	69	80	89
11	France	88	77	74
12	China	12	17	70
13	Singapore	61	65	68
14	Netherlands	48	54	65
15	Italy	51	48	56
16	Paraguay	26	32	46
17	Argentina	42	38	40
18	Colombia	20	25	32
19	Belgium	31	28	30
20	Spain	28	22	29
21	Chile	20	19	27
22	Switzerland	24	20	26
23	Venezuela	25	18	26
24	Sweden	20	20	26
25	Peru	5	7	21
26	Austria	17	20	20
27	South Africa, Rep. of	10	14	19
28	Malaysia	8	12	18
29	Saudi Arabia	14	14	15
30	Thailand	8	11	14
31	Philippines	13	10	13
32	New Zealand	8	10	13
33	Panama	10	11	13
34	Greece	4	5	12
35	Ecuador	7	9	12
36	Ireland	7	9	11

ENDNOTES

1 Ronald H. Brown, "U.S. Exports: Room for Everybody," *The Wall Street Journal*, 15 June 1995, A15.

2 Warren J. Bilkey, "Integration of Literature on Export Behavior," *Journal of International Business Studies* 9 (Spring/Summer 1978): 33.

3 Ibid.

4 Don G. Howard, "The Role of Export Management Companies in Global Marketing," *Journal of Global Marketing* 8, no.1 (1994): 95–110; and Robert W. Haigh, "Thinking of Exporting? Export Management Companies Could Be the Answer," *Columbia Journal of World Business*, Winter 1994, 66–81.

5 James D. Witney, "Causes and Consequences of WPAs: A Reappraisal," *Antitrust Bulletin*, Summer 1993, 395–418.

6 "Hungarian FTO Competition Can Mean Manager Headaches," *Business Eastern Europe*, 25 August 1985, p. 253; and "Hungary Converts FTOS into Trading Houses," *Business Eastern Europe*, 20 September 1985, 297–98.

7 "Bulgaria Looks at Russia Again," *East European Markets*, 16 April 1995, 5.

8 Heiwa-Keizai-Keikaku-Kaige, *Sogoshosha* Oohanomiza-Shibo (December 1984), 9.

9 H. Kohiyama, "Japanese Sogo Shosha—An Insider's View," in *Advances in Applied Business Strategy*, 4th edition, Robert Lamb, ed. (Greenwich, Conn.: JAI Press, 1984), 154.

10 Dong Sung Cho, *The General Trading Company: Concepts and Strategy*. (Lexington, Mass.: Lexington Books, 1987).

11 "GTCs Meet MOTIE Minister to Improve Conditions of Exports," *Business Korea*, February 1996, 66.

12 Michael R. Czinkota and Ilkka A.ds Ronkainen, *International Marketing*, 2nd ed. (Chicago, Ill.: Dryden Press, 1990).

13 Ibid.

14 *Business America*, "International Trade Fairs: Calendar 1997," December 1996, 32–34.

9

Entry Strategies

Chapter Outline

Learning Objectives

When you have mastered the contents of this chapter, you will be able to do the following:

1 Explain the problems involved in being casual when entering a foreign market.

2 Identify and describe 13 different modes of entry.

3 Name the factors to consider when choosing an entry strategy.

4 Discuss how to make proper entry choices.

Consider the following examples:

- A button manufacturer in Mexico has been trying to enter the U.S. market but knows very little about it.

- U.S. cigarette manufacturers want to enter the Japanese market but find many barriers.

- A textile manufacturer in Turkey wants to enter the European Common Market but does not know how to go about it.

- Sony wanted to enter the U.S. market and was successful.

- IBM learned that it had to use different entry strategies in different markets in order to succeed.

- Singer used a uniform strategy to successfully enter all of its world markets.

How should these or other businesses go about entering international markets? Should they commit themselves at the outset to enter and stay, or should they proceed very cautiously and make only tentative entries? These are only some of the important questions for both large and small businesses contemplating entry into foreign markets.

Entering international markets is a critical step. Once entry into a market is made, it becomes difficult to retreat without incurring additional costs. A company desiring to enter international markets has numerous alternatives. Its management must know these alternative entry strategies well and know what each represents in terms of benefits and costs.

Many factors should be considered when deciding on the appropriate entry strategy. The factors and the relative importance of each vary with the situation. This chapter includes a discussion of some of these factors. Some research indicates that it is rather common for companies to use naive approaches in making entry decisions.[1]

ENTERING FOREIGN MARKETS

Once a company assesses its international capabilities and evaluates international market potentials, the next step is to make plans for capitalizing on perceived marketing opportunities. The general tendency for most companies is to enter international markets tentatively, slowly, and through exporting (either directly or indirectly through a third party). The third party, for example, may be an export management company (EMC) or an export trading company (ETC).

As companies learn through experience and become more successful, they become more committed to long-term involvement in international marketing, and work toward bringing it under tighter control. As they adopt long-term perspectives, they tend to move away from exporting and toward other entry strategies that provide more permanence, more competitive power, more control, and greater long-run profits. The discussion in this chapter covers 13 entry strategies. In order of their discussion, they require progressively higher investment in plant, equipment, and service personnel, and increasing commitment to developing a competitive edge through marketing. But they also provide increasing potential to compete and more direct control.

The decision on market entry strategy deserves to be made objectively, carefully, and with conviction. Choosing the wrong entry strategy often proves costly, as the following three examples illustrate.

1. Caterpillar's name became known overseas during World War II when its earth-moving equipment accompanied Allied troops in operation after operation. Much Caterpillar equipment was left behind and used in these countries for years afterward. During this period,

parts "specifically for use in" Caterpillar products (but not supplied by Caterpillar) appeared in these countries. At the time, the company had little overseas visibility and was not in a position to prevent distribution of the parts. Had Caterpillar set up overseas sales offices, licensed foreign representatives, or even established joint ventures with foreign partners soon after the war, this situation could have been avoided.

2. A U.S. pharmaceutical company licensed some production methods to an Asian concern, which then used them to make extremely high profits. The U.S. company missed a golden opportunity, probably because it lacked needed information that might have led it to become more involved (for example, through joint venturing with the Asian company).

3. When H.J. Heinz wanted to enter the Japanese market quickly, it bought an interest in Nichero Fisheries. Unfortunately, Nichero had neither the resources nor the proper channels to distribute Heinz's products. Further, the Japanese company's fish-based reputation detracted from Heinz's desired image in Japan.[2]

Some companies are so anxious to enter particular markets that they overcommit resources. Pepsico International, in order to enter the Indian market, agreed that for every $1.00 of imports that Pepsi brings into India, $5.00 of Pepsi-generated exports will materialize. Furthermore, Pepsi promised to help the Indian government start a second "green revolution" to enable farmers to shift from growing wheat and rice to growing more lucrative crops such as fruits and vegetables. Pepsi established a research center to improve the quality of fruits and agreed to take on Indian partners.[3]

WHAT ARE THE ENTRY ALTERNATIVES?

Basically, there are 13 entry strategies for foreign markets (Figure 9–1). Other strategies exist, but they are either combinations or slight variations of these 13. The strategies presented in Figure 9–1 are arranged along two dimensions—risk and control. Horizontally, as the firm moves from entry strategy number 1 to entry strategy number 13, the degree of risk it assumes increases.

International risk is reviewed in three categories: (1) general environmental, including variables such as political risks and government policies; (2) industry, including variables such as input markets and material and labor supplies; and (3) firm-specific risks, including variables such as operating uncertainties and credit uncertainties.[4]

Because of the increasing degree of risk, the firm takes steps to increase its control (the vertical dimension). The implicit assumption is that adequate control will counterbalance or at least reduce the impact of risk. Consequently, as shown in Figure 9–1, as entry alternatives represent increasing risk from left to right, they also indicate increasing importance attached to control. Compared with export trade (strategy number 1), where a foreign company brings in the products and markets them as it pleases, a fully owned subsidiary with home-country management (strategy number 13) indicates greatly increased control.

Risk and control interact. The greater the risk, the greater is the attempt to control. Conversely, the greater the attempt to control, the greater the risk. A major development in the past few years has been the Internet and the ability to export with it. Although it is still an aspect of export–import trade, this development is discussed briefly in

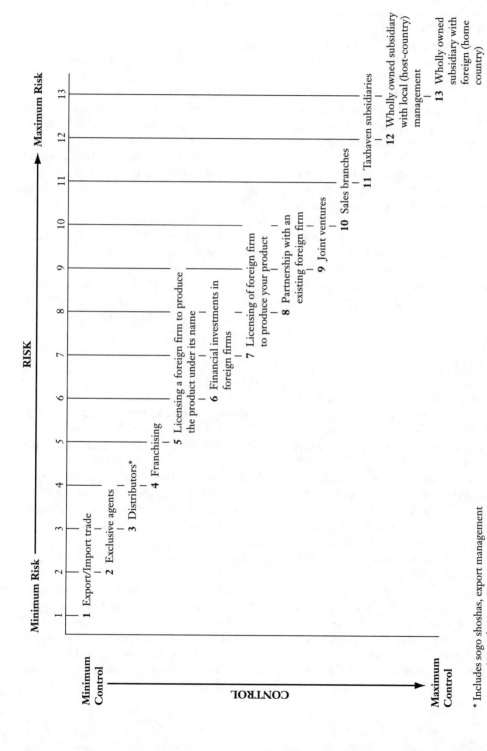

FIGURE 9-1 *Entry Options into International Markets*

* Includes sogo shoshas, export management companies, and consortia.

RISK

Minimum Risk ——▶ Maximum Risk

1 Export/Import trade

2 Exclusive agents

3 Distributors*

4 Franchising

5 Licensing a foreign firm to produce the product under its name

6 Financial investments in foreign firms

7 Licensing of foreign firm to produce your product

8 Partnership with an existing foreign firm

9 Joint ventures

10 Sales branches

11 Taxhaven subsidiaries

12 Wholly owned subsidiary with local (host-country) management

13 Wholly owned subsidiary with foreign (home country) management

Minimum Control

Maximum Control

CONTROL

this chapter. The Internet is a worldwide computer network that is sometimes called the World Wide Web. It has its roots in a network developed by the U.S. Department of Defense in the early 1970s. Its popularity has been growing at an unbelievable rate as its commercial uses have been expanded. Because of individuals' and groups' direct access to the Internet, a prospective exporter (or importer) can enter the world market almost immediately. The Internet gives an opportunity to smaller firms to enter international markets and compete on the basis of cost, communication, logistics, sales, and the like.[5]

The first three entry strategies were discussed in detail in Chapter 8, and the reader may wish to review that discussion. In this chapter, the export entry strategies are contrasted and compared to other entry options.

Commissioners

Perhaps the simplest way of entering international markets is through export commissioners, middlemen who bring suppliers and overseas customers together. Another type of middlemen are foreign-based importing wholesalers and retailers, who also provide a simple way to transact overseas business. For their services, export commissioners receive commissions of from 5 to 7 percent. Export commissioners represent the manufacturer or the internationalizing company, while the importing wholesalers and retailers simply represent themselves. Typically, neither of these types of middlemen has much power in setting the terms of the exchange conditions. At the same time, the exporter using these middlemen has virtually no voice in how the product is marketed in the overseas market.

Exclusive Agents

Another way to enter international markets is through exclusive agents, who represent an exporting company and sell to wholesalers and retailers in the importing country. The exporter ships the merchandise directly to the customers, and all arrangements on financing, credit, promotion, and the like are made between the exporter and the buyers. Exclusive agents are widely used for entering international markets. They cover large geographic areas and have subagents assisting them. Agents and subagents share commissions (paid by the exporter) on a preagreed basis. Some agents furnish financial and market information, and a few also guarantee the payment of customers' accounts. The commissions that agents receive vary substantially, depending upon services performed, the market's size and importance, and competition among exporters and agents.

Distributors

Exporting companies may work through distributors, who are the exclusive representatives of the company and generally are the sole importers of the company's product in their markets. As independent merchants, distributors buy on their own accounts and have substantial freedom to choose their own customers and to set the conditions of sale. For each country, exporters deal with one distributor, take one credit risk, and ship to one destination. In many cases, distributors own and operate wholesale and retail establishments, warehouses, and repair and service facilities. Once distributors have negotiated with their exporters on the price, service, distribution, and the like, their efforts focus on working their own suboperations and dealers.

TABLE 9–1 ▪ *Comparative Analysis of ETCs, EMCs, and Consortia*

Characteristics	Export Trading Companies (Sogo Shoshas)	Export Management Companies	Consortia
Size Orientation	Gigantic Readily available	Average Can be obtained	Average Already has been obtained
Specialized information	Active	Passive	Active
Ability to market any product	High degree	Low degree	Low degree
Ability to generate new products	High degree	None	High degree
Ability to bring small manufacturers together	High degree	None	High degree
General description	All-around international marketers	Specialized middlemen	Specialized international marketers

Source: Harold Berkman and A. Coskun Samli, "The Consortia Approach," in *Proceedings of Second World Marketing Congress*, Vol. II, ed. Shaw, et al. (Stirling, Scotland: Academy of Marketing Science, 1985), 503.

The distributor category is broad and includes three variations, which have come into prominence in the 1980s. These variations are important entry options, particularly for small enterprises. Each of these variations provides small businesses with the strength and know-how that generally only large businesses possess. The three variations are (1) export trading companies, (2) export management companies, and (3) consortia. All three are sole exporters for their principals. See Table 9–1 for a comparison of these three types of distributors.

EXPORT TRADING COMPANIES ▪ ETCs
(called *sogo shosha* in Japan and in countries emulating Japan, such as Singapore, Hong Kong, South Korea, and Taiwan) have been outstandingly successful. They are gigantic umbrella organizations representing thousands of manufacturers and suppliers. They often take the initiative in generating export trade, and they handle all necessary production, distribution, and communications activities as they take advantage of evolving market opportunities around the world. Export trading companies thrive on their access to special information sources that provide early notice of unfolding international market opportunities. Most ETCs are prepared to handle almost any product at any time. They also have special skills and abilities in developing new products, chiefly for small markets. They are capable of bringing the talents of hundreds of thousands of small manufacturers to bear on a particular export opportunity; most of them are flexible and not overburdened with fixed costs. Thus, ETCs are often instrumental in facilitating the development of special products for small markets.

ETCs are complete international marketers. In addition to generating the product, they handle the entire business process from production to completing sales transactions in overseas markets.[6] They have been instrumental in the international success Japan and newly industrialized countries have enjoyed in international markets. Because of their success, the U.S. government decided to pass *sogo sosha* legislation in 1982. The aim of this legislation was to make it easier to develop *sogo shosha*–like American organizations. However, this legislation failed to generate such organizations.

EXPORT MANAGEMENT COMPANIES ▪ EMCs

are expert middlemen who have expertise in a particular product (for example, only railroad maintenance supplies) and concentrate in a particular geographic area (for example, Central America). They provide marketing expertise and manage the required financing for American companies desiring to enter international markets without lasting commitment. These companies vary in size, but they are typically just large enough to handle their clients' requirements. Unlike *sogo shosha*, EMCs are rather passive in soliciting clients. They expect small and medium-size companies seeking international markets to come to them. Thus, many companies seeking to enter international markets via exports approach EMCs; after they are approached, the EMCs search out needed specialized information.

EMCs are not equipped to go to manufacturers and ask them to develop specific products with given specifications designed especially for the idiosyncrasies of some overseas market. Instead, they take existing products and try to market them in their chosen geographic areas. They do not bring sellers and buyers together or solicit business from firms with export potentials. EMCs are best described as export middle managers: They handle the exporting function for certain products destined for sale in their chosen geographic areas. They export products

varying from jams and jellies to electrical generating equipment, and they specialize in territories from the far Western Pacific to Muslim North Africa.

CONSORTIA ▪ Consortia are made up of

groups and companies, often domestic competitors, who join for international marketing purposes and develop, jointly, new products to satisfy unanswered market needs at the international level. They then plan and implement marketing programs for these new products. Although there are a few large industrial consortia, most are no larger than is needed to carry out the project that caused the consortium to be formed in the first place.

Consortia are organized specifically to transact international business. Restricting themselves to one or a few especially developed product categories, they generate special versions of product for exporting and they follow through with their marketing. Consortia, then, like *sogo shosha*, are *proactive* organizations, in contract to the EMCs, which are passive, or *reactive*, organizations. Consortia, also like *sogo shosha*, thrive on having access to flows or special information that provide indicators of international market opportunities. Consortia are organized especially to generate new products for world markets. Like the *sogo shosha*, the consortia have special abilities to develop and market new products. They organize groups of small manufacturers who have the capability to customize products for international markets. Typically, this product differs from those of member companies.

On Prince Edward Island, a Canadian province, 17 registered fish-processing plants got together in 1978 and organized a consortium to tackle problems they could not handle individually. They modified a traditional product, hot-pack and cold-pack lobster, into a new product, lobster in brine. In the product-development stages, they discovered several ways to reduce processing costs and effect other savings. After the international market potentials have been evaluated, they developed a three-year business plan to guide their operations. A few months later, the consortium packed and shipped the first lobster-in-brine product to its export markets using the name North Cumberland Seafoods.

Franchising

Franchising provides exporters with a closer and tighter relationship to international markets than does the use of distributors. Franchising grants to the franchisee the right to carry on a certain manufacturing process and to use the brand name. Franchise arrangements generally are of longer duration than are relationships with agents and distributors. Conditions under which franchising is appropriate include the following:

1. A widely known and advertised product, brand, or trademark.

2. Marketing needs overseas similar to marketing need in the United States.

3. Limited capital required for producing the product.

4. Insignificant amounts of imported materials required to produce the product.

5. Large proportion of the materials required to produce the product available locally.

6. High transportation costs for moving the finished product from the United States to the overseas market.

7. Economic manufacture or small quantities.

8. Sales that are highly sensitive to intensive local promotion.

From McDonald's to Kentucky Fried Chicken to international hotel chains such as Hilton and Holiday Inns and soft drinks such as Pepsi-Cola and Coca-Cola, a wide variety of products and services are marketed internationally through franchising. The franchisee generally has a small but exclusive territory and is bound by the terms of the franchise contract. The contract provides for close supervision by the American franchiser, to assure adherence to standards and specified marketing practices. The franchiser also acts as the supplier of necessary imported ingredients, such as for the syrup used by Coca-Cola bottlers.

McDonald's uses a network of local suppliers in its overseas markets, each of whom has an operation that conforms to McDonald's standards. The company has had difficulty, however, in the complete cloning of its franchises. Menus are modified to appeal to local tastes. In West Germany, for example, McDonald's stores sell beer, and in Brazil, they sell a soft drink flavored with guarana, an Amazon berry. In Thailand, Malaysia, and Singapore, McDonald's stores feature a popular milkshake flavor called durian, an Asian fruit local people consider an aphrodisiac.[7]

Licensing

Note that licensing (also called subcontracting) is listed twice in Figure 9–1; this is because licensing a foreign company to make a product under its own name differs from licensing a foreign company to make a product under the international company's name. From the licensor's standpoint, making a product under the licensee's name is less risky and requires less control. Inasmuch as the advantages and shortcomings of licensing are basically the same under either arrangement, the two licensing situations are discussed together here.

Licensing is one step beyond franchising in terms of providing tighter control of a market. Licensors, in general, grant permission to the foreign producer to manufacture a product that is unique and patented. A secret process or a highly specialized technical procedure is almost always involved in licensing situations. Among the many reasons for licensing are the following:

1. Licensing is the fastest way to enter a market that is largely reserved for domestic manufacturers and difficult for outsiders to enter on their own.

2. It requires minimum investment because the licensee is an already established manufacturing firm producing similar and related products.

3. The licensee already has sales and distribution organizations.

4. The licensee has experience in dealing with local government.

5. No danger is present of being expropriated or nationalized.

Licensing agreements, however, also have potential shortcomings, including the following:

• Quality control may deteriorate as foreign manufacturers vary in their quality-control practices.

• Competition can develop if the licensee decides to make its own products independent of the licensing agreement.

• There may be problems in securing patent protection. Through patenting, the licensor receives protection varying from 5 to 20 years. Because a patent makes a trade secret public knowledge, the owner has to have rights for exclusive use. As long as the company holds a valid patent, it has these rights.

However, some countries are more lax in enforcing patent rights than others. In some cases, technical details may cause some difficulties for the patent holder. For instance, the Minnesota Mining and Manufacturing Company failed to pay a fee to keeps its patents in force in the United Kingdom and went through a complicated and lengthy legal process to establish its patents again.[8] It is much more difficult to obtain patent rights in Japan than in the United States (six years versus two years).

Licensing negotiations often become complex because of the diverse issues involved. Four basic areas are typically covered: (1) technology package, (2) use conditions, (3) compensation, and (4) other provisions. The technology package includes the definition and description of the licensed procedures. Use conditions specify how the licensee is to use the technology and in which markets; they specify safeguards for the trade secrets and other use-related issues. The compensation section covers the payment of licensing fees, specifies the currency of payment, and so on. The other-provisions section includes the license's duration, the renewal processes, and rules for dispute settlement.

Financial Investment

Some companies enter foreign markets by affiliating with foreign companies or by buying financial interests in them. The strategic objective is to penetrate a target market from a production base inside that market. Thus, an international firm may become a silent partner of a domestic firm in a foreign country. A financial arrangement of this sort may evolve into a marketing arrangement if the investor decides to penetrate and capture more of the market. Marketplace pressure often forces financial investments as an aid to marketing effectiveness.

Partnership

Partnership with an existing foreign firm is a significant step beyond either licensing, or financial investment in, a foreign firm. Partnership provides more room for cooperation and for joint participation in marketing.

Acquisition of a foreign firm, of course, is the ultimate financial investment. Among the reasons for acquiring a foreign company are (1) product diversification (for example, American Motors' acquisition of Renault's North American division), (2) geographical diversification (for example, Japanese automakers bought U.S. plants to produce Japanese cars), and (3) acquisition of "unique" assets such as technology, distribution channels, or skilled workers. Entering a foreign market by acquiring a local firm that has a good distribution system is a frequent occurrence, as happened when Merck and Company bought Bany Pharmaceutical Company in order to enter the Japanese market.[9]

The key advantage of the acquisition is speedy entry into a foreign market. The acquiring company buys a going business that already is selling established products in that market.[10] Finding the right company to purchase and working through complex legal and political barriers to purchase are the major shortcomings of this strategy.

Joint Ventures

Joint ventures are developed primarily for new undertakings, such as a new chain of hotels, a new store group, or a new product line. A joint venture, simply put, is an equity and management partnership between an international company and a local concern in a foreign market. Joint ventures are developed according to the international marketer's needs. Many foreign countries encourage the formation of joint ventures as a way to build international cooperation and to secure technology transfer. For some markets, the joint venture may be the only entry strategy available. The Indian government, for instance, over the years has insisted on the formation of joint ventures with majority ownership by Indian partners. Similarly, joint ventures have long been regarded as the only feasible entry strategy for many Eastern European and Middle Eastern markets.

Each partner agrees to a joint venture to gain access to the other partner's skills and resources. Typically, the international partner contributes financial resources, technology, or products. The local partner provides the skills and knowledge required for managing a business in its country.[11]

In 1984, 741 joint ventures were started in China. Joint ventures typically get off to a slow start in China, and the international partners have to wait a long time before they receive profits.[12] However, joint ventures are still attractive for those firms wishing to tap the huge Chinese market. Joint ventures are encouraged and, for the most part, adequately supported by the Chinese government.

In the industrial equipment field, joint ventures have become popular. Caterpillar has a joint venture with a South Korean company to produce Caterpillar's forklift trucks for Asian markets. Caterpillar also has a joint venture in Japan with Mitsubishi enabling it to attack Komatsu, a major competitor, in the Japanese home market; and John Deere and Hitachi have a joint venture that assembles small-size and medium-size hydraulic excavators in Great Britain.[13]

In analyzing Sino-American joint ventures, Richard Holton identified the 10 following problems.[14] These same types of problems occur not only in China but also in joint-venture situations elsewhere.

1. Fundamental differences exist in objectives. While the American firm, for instance, is trying to enter the Chinese market, the Chinese partner wants to maximize exports in order to earn foreign exchange.

2. The Chinese are under pressure from their government to strike a deal that is unquestionably better for the Chinese than for the Americans.

3. Major contrasts exist between the American enterprise and its Chinese counterpart as decision-making units. The American manager needs to recognize that the Chinese enterprise is a semiautonomous governmental unit linked to the government through group agencies and that it is a part of the overall bureaucracy.

4. Managing the labor force is rather different. U.S. managers are accustomed to viewing labor as a variable cost and assume that they are free to adjust labor costs to variations of demand and to dismiss unsatisfactory workers. But in China, as part of the overall welfare system, labor, in effect, is a fixed cost and remains so regardless of fluctuations in demand.

5. Valuations placed on the technology provided by the American firm and the land or building or both contributed by the Chinese partner differ considerably. In particular, the American partner has difficulty in establishing a fair value for the technology, and the Chinese partner has difficulty in conceptualizing and accepting that value.

6. An enforceable contractual agreement is almost impossible to reach. Although some Chinese partners abide by their joint-venture agreements fully, others ask that agreements be modified whenever some parts become inconvenient for them.

7. Infrastructure problems frustrate American managers in Sino-American joint ventures. The telephone system, trains, and other aspects of the infrastructure do not come anywhere near American standards. Transportation uncertainties have been particularly serious. Because railroads refuse to accept shipments of less than a certain tonnage, operating costs increase.

8. Supplies are unreliable. Because it is impossible to obtain supplies locally, joint ventures maintain high inventories. This fact increases operating expenses. While the Japanese use efficient, "just-in-time" inventory management systems, the Chinese joint ventures appear to use high-level, "just-in-case" inventories.

9. Reliability of suppliers and supply quality is a problem. Until recently, Chinese managers have not been full-scale managers. They are slower and less assertive than their Western counterparts in making decisions and understanding the importance of providing materials of certain quality standards on time. They are also used to operating within the *guanxi* ("old friend") system.[15] This custom makes it difficult for them to work with people (outsiders) they have not worked with before. In the *guanxi* system, everyone is an insider and negotiations or dealings proceed smoothly.

10. Finally, because of shortages of hard currencies, repatriation of joint-venture profits has not been allowed. Chinese

authorities need to maintain certain foreign exchange reserves, and as imports and capital purchases increase, they are increasingly reluctant to allow profits to leave the country.

Sales Branches

An international firm can enter foreign markets by establishing sales branches to put needed emphasis on the sale and service of its products. Sales branches are extensions of the company's American business complex. If the company has certain products that require selling and servicing the "American way," then sales branches are an appropriate choice. If the product is highly technical and requires support services in terms of teaching buyers how to use, maintain, and repair it, sales branches are effective in delivering these services.

Tax-Haven Subsidiaries

Some companies enter certain markets in order to shelter income from high taxation. These tax-haven countries include Switzerland (for a long time the only one), Hong Kong, the Cayman Islands, the Netherlands Antilles, the Bahamas, Indonesia, the Philippines, and Singapore. For the most part, these are markets in which there are few sales but that offer inordinate tax advantages, such as the following:

- Easy and simply corporation chartering.

- Low corporate and business taxes.

- Many stable and efficient financial institutions.

- Few or no restrictions on ownership and operations of businesses.

- An adequate supply of skilled local staff and other personnel.

Tax-haven countries are typically anxious to bring in foreign investments, so they make it easy and attractive for international companies to enter their markets.

Wholly Owned Subsidiaries with Local Management

When companies establish production or assembly operations in foreign markets, they commit substantial financial as well as human resources. There are two basic ways to make foreign direct investments: (1) custom-build foreign affiliates or (2) acquire local companies. Both approaches have advantages and disadvantages.

Custom-made subsidiaries follow company specifications and are staffed and operated the way the parent firm wishes. But subsidiaries also must start from scratch in building up contacts, suppliers, and distributors, making for a slow start in the foreign market.

Firms wishing to make an immediate impact on a local market often acquire a local company. This acquisition gives the firm almost instant access to local distribution channels and suppliers, but as happens in joint ventures, it creates problems as the international firm seeks to mesh its products, technologies, and management methods with those of the acquired firm. Historically, one U.S. acquisition in three has failed.[16]

If the product needs total attention from start to finish in its production and distribution and if the international firm wants to do it properly, the way to go may be a full-scale foreign subsidiary or affiliate. This branch provides the same manufacturing and distribution flexibility that the company enjoys in its home country. Using local personnel in management position is politically astute, but problems can occur in their training and motivation, as Union Carbide learned in its operations in Bhopal, India. Although the Bhopal plant was almost an exact replica of the plants Union Carbide had in the United States, local Indian personnel were inadequately trained in safety procedures, leading to one of the worst industrial accidents in the twentieth century.

Wholly Owned Subsidiaries with Home-Country Management

The alternative to employing local help is to use American expatriates. This is the most risky alternative, but it provides the most control. Directly investing in a foreign plant that is an exact replica of the company's U.S. plants provides the best production facility; often, these are known as turnkey operations. Although this entry alternative provides the most control, it is rarely used, because in many parts of the world, it is almost impossible to maintain a management composed solely of expatriates. Companies with foreign management in time become targets of local politicians and often find themselves subject to expropriation.

SHOULD ENTRY STRATEGIES BE UNIFORM?

An international company does not necessarily use the same entry strategy in all of its world markets. IKEA, the world's largest furniture retailer, has used different entry strategies in its different markets. Before IKEA enters a large market, it chooses a similar small market, enters it first, and gains experience. German-speaking Switzerland was its small test market before IKEA

entered West Germany, and French-speaking Switzerland was its small test market before it entered France. To keep the expansion under control and to avoid overtaxing the company's resources, IKEA franchises its retail concept in many countries and has its own stores elsewhere.[17]

Anheuser-Busch, the largest U.S. brewer (with 34 percent of the market), decided to enter the overseas beer market, which is roughly three times as large as the U.S. beer market. Anheuser-Busch entered overseas markets using multiple entry strategies. It licensed foreign brewers in the United Kingdom, Japan, and Israel to produce, market, and distribute its Budweiser beer (but not Bud Light). The company also exports U.S.-brewed beer to 10 foreign countries, and it plans to enter certain overseas markets through acquisition of foreign breweries.[18]

Choosing the Entry Strategy

Several criteria are to be considered when deciding which entry strategy to choose (see Table 9–2). These criteria are categorized into external and internal types.

EXTERNAL CRITERIA ■ The following eight external criteria from time to time play a critical role in deciding entry strategy. They are as follows.

Risk. Risk varies from market to market. The greater the risk inherent in a market is, generally, the smaller and shorter-term is the company's commitment. Consequently, markets perceived as high risk are generally entered using low-risk strategies—commissioners, exclusive agents, or distributors. However, if other considerations push the company toward making a larger and longer-term commitment, higher-risk entry

TABLE 9–2 ▪ *Criteria Used in Choosing Entry Strategies*

External Criteria	Internal Criteria
Market risk factor	Time orientation
Competition in the market	Need for control
Political conditions	Degree of internationalization
Market conditions	Urgency of going international
Future market potential	Ability to handle international risk
Availability of desired distribution outlets	
Availability of venture capital	
Availability of know-how	

strategies (which provide greater control) such as licensing or joint ventures may be chosen.

Competition. Competition differs in intensity from one market to another. If there is keen competition in a market and the company simply wants to "try out" the market, it will likely choose a low-risk strategy—commissioners, exclusive agents, or distributors. Note, however, that these three strategies all are low key, competitively speaking. So if the aim is to make more than a mere dent in a highly competitive market, the choice of entry strategy will be from among the higher-risk options, such as licensing, joint ventures, or even setting up a sales branch, which are more suited for keenly competitive environments.

Political Conditions. Political conditions in the target country often influence the choice of an entry strategy. Where political conditions are unstable, management generally prefers the so-called noncommittal options—exporting, exclusive agents, or distributors. In countries with stable political conditions, management is willing to make greater commitments, such as through joint ventures, sales branches, or subsidiaries.

Market Conditions. Market conditions exert a strong influence on choice of entry strategy. If market conditions imply an excellent marketing opportunity, management leans toward making a long-term commitment and choosing strategies ranging from franchising to opening a subsidiary (see Figure 9–1).

Future Market Potential. Future market potential is an even stronger consideration than current market conditions. If reason exists for believing that market potential is expanding rapidly, long-term commitment is likely and strategies may range from franchising to subsidiary operation. Conversely, if it seems that market potential is declining, short-term commitment and a desire to minimize risk move management to choose exporting, exclusive agencies, or distributors.

Availability of Desired Distribution Outlets. The availability of desired distribution outlets pushes management toward long-term commitment and higher-risk entry strategies (licensing through subsidiaries as shown on Figure 9–1). If the desired type of distribution outlets are not available in the target market, management faces the decision of whether to develop them (perhaps through direct investment) or not. For example, if the product requires distribution through specialized retailers (for example, those providing repair and installation services) and there are none available, other considerations enter in, such as management's willingness to invest for the long term and to commit itself to developing either its own distribution organization in the country or recruiting and training others to build an independently owned distribution system.

Availability of Venture Capital. The availability of venture capital in the target market is another external consideration. If there is adequate venture capital in the market, franchise investments, for example, become more viable.

Availability of Know-How. The availability of know-how in the target country concerning the product, its manufacturing, and its distribution is important. Availability of local know-how makes it attractive to enter with a long-term commitment (franchising or more). This situation, too, facilitates eventually turning over management of the operation to local personnel.

The relative importance of these external criteria varies from business to business and situation to situation. A soft drink company looks first for the availability of desired distribution outlets and know-how as well as the presence of many small retail outlets. A computer maker is most concerned about labor and service, competition, and future market potential. To a greater or lesser degree, all of these criteria relate to expected future profits and their likelihood of repatriation.

INTERNAL CRITERIA ▪ Table 9–2 lists five internal criteria, each occasionally playing a deciding role in determining entry strategy.

Time Orientation. Time orientation strongly influences choice of entry strategy. A company with a short-term orientation

concerning its international involvement generally chooses from among commissioners, exclusive agents, and distributors, and shies away from making direct investments in overseas manufacturing, assembling, and distribution facilities. By contrast, a company with a long-term orientation does not consider commissioners, exclusive agents, or distributors, but evaluates alternatives ranging from franchising and licensing to such direct investments as joint ventures and wholly owned subsidiaries.

Need for Control. The need for control over the product's manufacturing and/or distribution is sometimes an important factor in choosing entry strategy. If the need for this kind of control is substantial, the company considers only strategies involving direct investment—partnership with an existing firm in the market, a joint venture, a sales branch, or a wholly owned subsidiary. If the need for control is minor or nonexistent, entry may be through exclusive agents or distributors.

Degree of Internationalization. The degree of internationalization influences choice of entry strategy. A company firmly committed to internationalization generally already has developed marketing and distribution systems in its existing overseas markets, and it enters new markets using strategies ranging from licensing to wholly owned subsidiaries, thus also indicating its long-run orientation and willingness to assume risk. A company with a lower degree of internationalization leans toward exporting agents or distributors, but it may stretch itself in some instances and use licensing. Using commissioners, agents, or distributors means that the company turns over the details to intermediaries, while licensing means turning them over to a foreign licensee.

Urgency of Going International. The urgency of going international sometimes influences the choice of entry strategy. Urgency arises from such situations as dwindling sales in domestic markets, growing overseas demand for the product type, general growth in selected international markets, and excess manufacturing and/or distribution capacity. Companies confronted with these types of situations often are those with low degrees of internationalization and little international marketing experience. Thus, the tendency is to play safe and be noncommittal and to turn the details over to the export middlemen, agents, or distributors.

Ability to Handle International Risk. The ability to handle international risk is a factor in choosing entry strategy. International risk arises from changing political conditions, shifts in diplomatic postures and alignments, wars and civil disturbances, and the like. A company not equipped to deal with these and other unanticipated risks usually shifts them to outsiders such as agents and distributors. A company that has the requisite expertise and experience to handle international risks selects entry strategies ranging from a relatively small direct investment in a foreign firm to a relatively large direct investment in a wholly owned subsidiary.

Gray Marketing

Gray marketing is an "involuntary" entry mode for products whose prices vary significantly from one market to another. Consider, for example, certain higher-quality Seiko watches, such as those commonly sold in the United States through better jewelry and department stores. Such watches retail at fairly high prices and carry a good warranty from the manufacturer. Suppose that a buyer for Kmart scanning the world for bargains learns that the same watches are retailing for much lower prices in stores in Kenya. Quickly, he buys up all of these Seikos available in Kenya, ships them to the United States, and Kmart promotes them at prices substantially under those asked by conventional outlets, the only difference being that the Kmart Seikos do not carry the manufacturer's warranty. Gray marketing, then, is entry of a product into a market not planned by the product's manufacturer. Many manufacturers and, of course, their conventional outlets frown upon gray marketing and, at least on the surface, try to discourage the practice.

The size of the U.S. gray market is estimated at around 25 percent of total U.S. imports. Although conventional outlets and many manufacturers complain about gray marketing, the practice is still growing. Substantial volumes of cameras and other photographic equipment, small appliances, watches and clocks, and other items move through gray marketing. Defenders of the practice point to the fact that this is one way to eliminate dramatic price discrepancies among different markets.

Free Trade Zones

A free trade zone (FTZ) is an isolated, enclosed, and policed area located in or adjacent to a port of entry. It is run as a public utility and typically has facilities for loading, unloading, handling, sorting, manipulating, manufacturing, assembling, storing, and displaying. Any foreign or domestic merchandise may be brought into an FTZ without becoming subject to the customs laws of the country in which the FTZ is located. Merchandise may be brought into an FTZ for reshipment to another country; reshipments do not make the merchandise subject to customs duties in the country in which the FTZ is located.

From the perspective of entry strategy, FTZs may be an intermediate step in entering a particular market. For instance, using an FTZ located on the southwestern coast of Turkey may facilitate entry into markets throughout the whole Middle East. Or using an FTZ in Miami, Florida, is an attractive for European manufacturers seeking entry to markets throughout Latin America and the Caribbean.

FTZs provide numerous benefits. They have available needed facilities, including energy and telecommunications utilities, and they are attractive from the standpoint of taxes and transportation. For the region and country in which they are located, FTZs provide opportunities for expanded involvement in international trade and expanded employment and income. They also facilitate technology transfer through their manufacturing and assembling operations.

Summary

Entering international markets is a critical step. Basically, there are 13 entry strategies, varying in the degree of risk assumed by the company and in the amount of control it desires over its international operations. Three distributors—export trading companies, export management companies, and consortia—are given particular attention. Of these, ETCs, or *sogo shosha*, have been very instrumental in Japan's extraordinary success in international markets. Companies use both external and internal criteria in choosing particular entry strategies; the significance of particular criteria vary both with the company and its situation. It is not uncommon for companies to use more than one entry strategy to enter different world markets. Gray marketing, involving "involuntary" entry of some of all of a manufacturer's products into a particular market, is growing in importance. Also rising in importance are the growing number of free trade zones throughout the world, providing international marketers with an intermediate step prior to moving their products into particular markets.

Discussion Questions

1. What are the common causes of poor market-entry decisions? How can bad entry decisions be avoided?

2. Under what circumstances should franchising be considered? How do these circumstances vary from those leading to licensing?

3. Contrast and compare EMCs, consortias, and ETCs. Under what conditions is each appropriate?

4. Name two internal criteria affecting entry decisions. Discuss how these affect the choice of an entry strategy.

5. Name two external criteria used in making entry decisions. Discuss how these affect the choice of an entry strategy.

6. Should international firms use only a single entry strategy? Why? Why not?

7. What is gray marketing? Do you favor or oppose it? Why?

8. What are the benefits of FTZs to international marketers? To developing countries?

Pepsi and the Indian Market

In the soft drink business, the company that enters a foreign market first usually dominates that market. Pepsi had high hopes for India and its 850 million potential consumers. In 1977, however, Pepsi was forced to withdraw from the Indian market. Its departure left a void in the soft drinks field. India's two current soft drink bottlers are protected from foreign competition. Soft drink prices are relatively high, and distribution is limited mainly to urban areas.

Soft drink consumption in India is about three bottles per person per year. This market may expand. In neighboring Pakistan, consumers drink about 13 bottles per person per year.

In order to enter China, Pepsi offered to export $1 of locally made products for every $1 of materials it imported. The company was contemplating a similar strategy in India. Knowing that the Indian government is very protective of local industries and does not allow foreign companies to have majority ownership, Pepsi knew it had to do something. Furthermore, the company managers were of the opinion that there needed to be some legitimate favor to the Indian government in order to establish goodwill.

QUESTION

1. If you were a consultant to Pepsi, what would you recommend?

Source: Adapted from *Forbes*, 17 November 1989, 43–44.

Toys R Us in Japan

With more than $6 billion annual sales, Japan is the world's number two toy market after the United States. Japanese toys are sold in small traditional toy stores. The relationship between these small stores and toy makers has been traditionally strong. This factor makes it difficult for Toys R Us to buy some of its products domestically in Japan because Japanese toy manufacturers and wholesalers are loyal to their existing clientele. Furthermore, in addition to its size, the Japanese toy market is attractive because Toys R Us can easily introduce 10 to 15 percent discounts.

MITI (Japan's Ministry of International Trade and Industry) has had a practice of delaying the development of large retailers so that strong, traditional small retailers can be protected. In addition, Japanese consumers do prefer buying Japanese-made toys.

Toys R Us, therefore, will have to rely on local supplies for 50 to 60 percent of its inventories. Among the products Toys R Us is planning to import are Huffy bikes, Mattel's Barbie dolls, and Tonka trucks. Because the typical small Japanese toy store stocks between 1,000 and 2,000 different items, Toys R Us is planning to attract consumers with a starting stock level of 8,000, which will rise to about 15,000 products.

QUESTIONS

Assume that you are in charge of Toys R Us in Japan.

1. How will you enter this market?

2. How will you overcome the market's problems?

Source: Adapted from *Business Week*, 9 December 1991, 72–76.

Sara Lee's L'Eggs— What Entry Strategy?

Sara Lee Corporation, whose products range from the L'Eggs and Hanes hosiery lines to a vast array of food lines, has been concerned recently with some key decisions. It views the emerging (1992) single European marketplace as a tremendous marketing opportunity.

In Sarah Lee's experience, many of the same products, particularly the same brand names, don't appeal to all European markets. Brand names such as Sara Lee, Hanes, and L'Eggs, which are well known in the United States, have little meaning in Europe. Hundreds of European companies make, import, or ship knitwear and hosiery-related products.

What is the future in Europe for L'Eggs? Company executives are concerned about the cultural and language differences. They view Europe as a heterogeneous rather than homogeneous market, and they believe it is ludicrous to think that Europe can be blanketed with a single brand name. In Europe, Sara Lee is planning to use Dim, a hot hosiery brand in France, to sell throughout Europe, but the company does not have substantial hosiery production capacity in Europe.

QUESTIONS

1. Discuss how (if at all) Sara Lee should enter the European market with L'Eggs.

2. Which entry strategy would be most appropriate and why? Discuss in detail and state your assumptions clearly.

Global Esthetics, Inc. [GEI]

Global Esthetics, Inc. (GEI), is a small distributor of medical/cosmetic equipment located in a small town in the southeast. The company had a hunch that there is a good market potential for the equipment the company distributes in South America, but it did not have specific information to use in formulating a marketing strategy. After contacting the commercial service office in Charleston, West Virginia, GEI received an industry sector analysis report for Brazil that gave specific market information and contacts to be pursued. The report included some analysis of market potentials. This enabled GEI to identify its best markets.

QUESTION

1. Prepare an export marketing plan for GEI. (*Note:* Use Figure 8–1 in Chapter 8 as a guide for your plan.)

ENDNOTES

1. Hans Schollhammer, *Locational Strategies of Multinational Firms* (Los Angeles: Pepperdine University, Center for International Business, 1974); and James D. Goodnow, "Developments in International Mode of Entry Analyses," *International Marketing Review*, Autumn 1985, 17–32.

2. David A. Ricks, *Big Business Blunders* (Homewood, Ill.: Dow Jones-Irwin, 1983), 104–107.

3. Subrata N. Chakravarty, "How Pepsi Broke into India," *Forbes*, 27 November 1989, 43–44.

4. Keith D. Brouters, "The Influence of International Risk on Entry Mode Strategy in Computer Software Industry," *Management International Review*, January 1995, 241–265.

5. A. Coskun Samli, Michael J. Charest, and Souad Jawhar, "Developing a Better Software Marketing Strategy by Using the Internet: The Case of Mexico," in *Proceedings of International Management Development Association* (IMDA), ed E. Kaynak, D. N. Lascu, and K. Becker, (1996), 546–550.

6. Harold Berkman and A. Coskun Samli, "The Consortia Approach," in *Proceedings of the World Marketing Congress*, ed. Susan Shaw, et al. (Stirling, Scotland: Academy of Marketing Science, 1985), 500–510.

7. "International Marketing Strategies of U.S. Fast Food Franchises," in *Developments in Marketing Science*, ed. J. J. Hawes and J. Thanapoulos (Miami: Miami Academy of Marketing Science, 1989), 123–127.

8. Franklin R. Root, *Entry Strategies for International Markets* (Lexington, Mass.: Lexington Books, 1982), 185–188.

9. "Want to Buy a Japanese Company?" *Fortune*, 27 June 1983, 106–109.

10. Franklin Root, *Entry Strategies for International Markets*. See endnote 8.

11. Ibid.

12. "Firm Finds There Aren't Any Shortcuts in China," *The Wall Street Journal*, 25 April 1985.

13. Kathryn Rudie Harrigan, *Strategies for Joint Ventures* (Lexington, Mass.: D. C. Heath, 1985), 288–289.

14. Richard Holton, "Foreign Investments and Joint Ventures: An American Perspective," in *U.S.-China Economic Relations—Present and Future*, ed. R. H. Holton and Wang Xi (Berkeley, Calif.: University of California at Berkeley, Institute of East Asian Studies), 224–225.

15. James A. Brunner, Jiwei Chen, Chao Sun, and Nanping Zhou, "The Role of Guanxi in Negotiations in the Pacific Basin," *Journal of Global Marketing* 3, no. 2 (1989): 7–23.

16. William H. Davidson, *Global Strategic Management* (New York: John Wiley and Sons, 1982), 63.

17. Rita Mastenson, "Is Standardization of Marketing Feasible in Culture-Bound Industries? A European Case Study," *International Marketing Review*, Autumn 1987, 7–28.

18. "Bud is Making a Splash in the Overseas Beer Market," *Business Week*, 22 October 1984, 52–53.

3

Implementing International Marketing Strategies

Part 3 deals with the specifics of international marketing strategy development and implementation.

Different strategic alternatives are discussed in Chapter 10. In general, two opposing generic strategies are identified: global and multilocal. Global strategy treats the whole world as one market and develops similar strategies everywhere. Multilocal strategy treats every market separately according to its specific characteristics. Between these two extremes is a hybrid, multinational strategy. Following this orientation, Chapters 11, 12, 15, and 17 follow the strategy implementations for consumer products, industrial goods, advertising, and pricing, using the global-multilocal dichotomy.

Because of its importance in everyday business, the international marketing of industrial products is a separate chapter (Chapter 12). Also, because of the unique conditions surrounding industrial buying and selling, a complete treatment of accompanying marketing mixes is described.

Chapter 14 deals with international logistics. This area is important in considering the movement of unfinished, semi-finished, and finished products in international markets. International sourcing is discussed as a means of gaining competitive cost advantages internationally. Finally, there is a chapter on sales management and personal selling. Proper management of foreign sales forces is an imperative for effective international strategy implementations. This chapter (Chapter 16) presents specific ways of managing this important area.

In all chapters dealing with the four Ps (product, place, price, and promotion), the decision-making process is directly related to an intricate interaction between a company's internal and environmental (external) situations. The importance of these variables and their nature are discussed particularly in Chapters 11, 12, 13, 15, and 17.

CHAPTER **10**

International Marketing Strategy

Chapter Outline

Learning Objectives

When you have mastered the contents of this chapter, you will be able to do the following:

1 Distinguish between global, multinational, and multilocal marketing.

2 Know how global firms customize their offerings and how multinational companies gain international synergies.

3 Discuss company, market, political, and competitive aspects of market expansion.

4 See how firms gain and exploit competitive advantages.

5 Understand why the Japanese have been successful in the United States.

International marketing strategies are the overall game plans firms use in foreign markets to satisfy customer needs and to compete with rivals. The keys to marketing success are similar for domestic and international executives: Survival and good profits come from supplying tailor-made products and services to customers at low prices. Unfortunately, these two objectives are rarely achievable at the same time. One reason is that custom-made products are expensive to produce. Another is that internationally marketed products and services face such variable market conditions and customer needs worldwide that it is often impossible to secure sufficiently large-scale economies to make low-cost production feasible.

Nevertheless, all international firms know that they must achieve one of these two basic objectives to be competitive. That is, they must produce quality products more cheaply than competitors, or they must satisfy individual customer tastes better.

GLOBAL, MULTINATIONAL, AND MULTILOCAL MARKETING

International marketing strategies occupy a range between two extremes that are associated with these two marketing objectives. At one extreme is *global marketing*, which focuses on customer similarities and uses large-scale manufacturing and superior quality to standardize products and services worldwide. For this strategy to succeed, a firm's customers should have similar needs wherever they are. Industries that produce such goods as aircraft, automobiles, copiers, watches, and TV sets use global marketing.

At the other extreme is *multilocal marketing*, which focuses on customer differences. This strategy treats each market as unique and invents products to fit it. Insurance and consumer financing are marketed multilocally.

TABLE 10–1 ■ *International Marketing Strategy Comparison: Global versus Multinational Strategies*

	Global Strategies	**Multinational Strategies**
Market-entry method	Often export	Often local production
Manufacturing emphasis	Large-scale manufacturing to maintain cost competitiveness and to defray large R&D expenses. Either "world scale" single-site or offshore production	Large-scale manufacturing not important
Target market	Usually aimed at same segment in all markets	Products suited to many segments within individual national markets
Product strategy	Globally recognized products (Mercedes, Kodak, IBM, Sony) with mandatory adaptations as necessary	Some globally renowned products (Coca-Cola, Pepsi) with mandatory adaptations; many heavily adapted product transfers; some locally conceived and produced goods
Other marketing	Localized services (warranties, service, distribution, "local" promotions)	Brand images maintained for international products; prices, promotions, and distribution strategies customized for all products.

In between is *multinational marketing*, a strategy that adapts existing products to greater or lesser degrees to suit particular markets.[1] Food products, soap products, and cosmetics are usually marketed according to multinational philosophies.

It should be noted that neither global marketers nor multinational marketers follow their respective strategies exclusively. Global marketing companies do localize some of their products and marketing mixes, and multinational marketers gain scale economies by transferring products and services between nations. The characteristics of these two strategies are illustrated in Table 10–1. All three strategies are shown in Table 10–2.

Global Marketing: Strategy Options

When international marketers transfer products and services among nations, they often encounter different market conditions from country to country (for example, variations in legal systems, climatic conditions, levels of economic development, and so on). Customer characteristics and needs also vary.

In response, managers either standardize or adapt various parts of their marketing mixes.

GLOBAL MARKETERS WHO STANDARDIZE ■

Some global marketers maintain their products in their original, standard form across many or all markets. Foreign market conditions are either similar to those in the home market or are not dissimilar enough to warrant adaptations. Commodities such as agricultural produce are standardized global products, as are consumer products such as French champagne, Italian Chianti, Russian caviar, Scotch whiskey, and Scandinavian furniture.

GLOBAL MARKETERS WHO THINK LOCALLY ■

Other global marketers adapt to market conditions and customer characteristics in two ways. One way is to make mandatory changes to otherwise standardized products. Changing from left-wheel to right-wheel drive is necessary for autos; changing from 110 volts to 220 volts is necessary in consumer electronics products, as is putting numbers on watch dials in the number system of the country.

TABLE 10–2 ■ *Degrees of Globalization and Localization in Global, Multinational, and Multilocal Strategies*

Global Orientation	Global Strategies	Multinational Strategies	Multilocal Strategies	Local Orientation
Total	Global standardization	International products (locally produced with mandatory adaptations)		None
	Mandatory product changes and/or local tailoring of promotions, prices, and distribution	Heavily adapted product transfers		
			Totally locally created lines and marketing mixes	
None		Locally conceived and built products		Total

The second way to adapt is to make changes in nonproduct areas of the marketing mix. Translations are necessary for product names, labels, and instructions; warranties may be changed, different forms of promotion may be used, heavier emphasis may be put on after-sales service, and so on. Through these efforts, marketers give local appeal to largely or completely standardized products.

How Multinational Marketers Capture International-Scale Economies

If companies blindly followed consumer-oriented marketing philosophies, they would custom-build all of their foreign products according to the desires of each separate market. In doing so, they would incur heavy research and development costs and would have few advantages over local competitors. Custom-building products is often not feasible because of the size or the composition of local markets. Companies have three product strategy options within the multinational context. First, they can identify products and services they think (or know through experience) have some universal appeal. International products such as Coca-Cola, Pepsi-Cola, Canada Dry mixers, Colgate toothpaste, Lever Brothers' products, and Pond's Cold Cream are used in similar ways by most consumers in different parts of the world. They also give their manufacturers product-line commonalities from country to country and some semblance of global identity.

Many of these products are produced locally. Thus, local touches such as labels, pack sizes, and the like may be added. While such products may be marketed somewhat differently than in their home country, they retain their original brand identities.

A second option is to make adaptations to meet local needs. In such a case, these products may lose their original brand identities. New package colors, sales features, and brand names are often used.

A third option is to design custom-made products to meet consumers' needs. A six-industry study determined that multinational marketers produced custom-made products that accounted for one-fifth of their product lines. Food and drink and other general consumer goods companies customized fully one-fourth to one-third of their foreign lines.[2] Colgate-Palmolive reformulates its periodontal toothpastes in many markets. Likewise, Canada Dry reconstitutes its orange nonmixer drinks in different markets; and Gillette invented a tube-packaged shaving cream, Prestobarba ("Quick-Shave"), when the company realized that its U.S. product, an aerosol, would be too expensive for Mexican consumers.[3]

Multilocal Marketing Orientations

In some industries (such as insurance and consumer financing) there are few or no carry-overs of products or services between markets. In such cases, everything is localized. In these industries, the only competitive advantage foreign firms enjoy is a one-time transfer of technology from the home markets to set up administrative procedures and organization. Otherwise, they operate as local companies.

Combining Global, Multinational, and Multilocal Strategies

Marketing strategy would be easy to implement if all companies had to do was to select a strategy and then implement it. In practice, of course, firms use whatever strategy is prudent for particular markets. Some industries use predominantly one strategy. Makers of autos, steel, consumer electronics, and high-profile consumer goods (such as Scotch whiskey or Japanese sake) mainly use global marketing methods. However, this practice does not stop NCR or IBM affiliates from custom-building products when they see suitable opportunities.

Similarly, companies making consumer-packaged goods can service many countries from a single manufacturing location, using exporting rather than on-site production. Procter and Gamble's operation coordinates manufacturing and marketing activities for its European operations. Colgate-Palmolive has more than 40 manufacturing plants worldwide, yet services well over 100 markets. Clearly, where country demand does not justify local manufacturing, export-oriented global marketing is the answer.

Finally, both global and multinational marketers acquire multilocal dimensions when they locate profitable business opportunities outside of their major corporate domains. Japanese businesses, for example, had invested more than $9 billion in U.S. real estate through 1995, and Sony had entered both the restaurant and construction businesses. Similarly, Coca-Cola's Japanese operation entered the local market for juice and potato chips where the company discovered plentiful supplies of local oranges and potatoes.[4]

GLOBAL ALLOCATION OF COMPANY RESOURCES: STRATEGIC MARKET EXPANSION

A key decision that international marketers must make is selecting the right markets. Initially, countries are chosen on the basis of market size and market potential, and marketers employ a variety of techniques to evaluate them (see Chapter 6 on market analysis and Chapter 8 on exporting). However, once they have ascertained where to focus their marketing efforts, given finite resources, they must then make decisions about specific markets. Here, other factors affecting market selection come into play.

Factors Affecting Foreign Market Expansion

COMPANY PERSONNEL AND RESOURCES ■

Companies without international experience often lack personnel with the managerial or language skills to approach some foreign markets. Consequently, they are reluctant to tackle some parts of the world (see Chapter 5). For example, smaller companies may not seriously go after the Russian or mainland Chinese markets. This reluctance leads firms to expand first into countries that are psychologically and culturally similar to the home market. U.S. companies often enter Canada, the United Kingdom, Australia, and New Zealand first.[5] German companies first evaluate opportunities in the German-speaking countries of Austria and parts of Switzerland. Similarly, French firms have close connections (from colonial days) and linguistic ties with the countries of North Africa.

MARKET BARRIERS ■ Market barriers hinder a company's abilities to service markets in particular countries. These barriers take many forms.

Tariffs. One form of market barrier is tariffs, which are duties applied to goods entering a country for consumption. These may be *ad valorem duties*, which are fixed percentages of invoice values. For example, alcohol-free perfumes entering the United States pay a tariff of 7.5 percent of their value; that is, a $100 import becomes $107.50 after duties. *Specific duties* are evaluated by the physical unit. For example, ground ginger is taxed coming into the United States at 1.7¢ per kilogram. Finally, compound duties are specific and ad valorem duties. For example, tuning pins for pianos are assessed at 10¢ per 1,000 and 3.5 percent of total value.

Tariff rates vary according to national economic priorities. Japan during the 1950s and 1960s had substantial tariff barriers. Today, the average Japanese tariff rate, at 3 percent, is the lowest in the industrialized world. However, critical industries (such as manufacturing and agriculture) average tariffs of more than 20 percent.[6]

Tariffs have varying effects on strategy. In most cases, they are minor irritants that boost the price of imported goods. In some cases, they may be severe enough for companies to take countermeasures. These vary from taking a fall in profits to maintain competitive prices to, in extreme cases, prompting alternative market-entry methods such as in-market production. Fear of a "fortress Europe" after 1992 (the notion that non-European traders would be shut out after economic unification) caused many firms to establish manufacturing or assembly within the European Union.

Quotas and "Voluntary" Constraints. Another market barrier is quotas. Countries can limit the physical quantities of specific products being imported. Quotas are imposed by the importing country. Throughout most of the 1980s, the U.S. government limited specialty-steel imports. Because quotas are frowned upon by the World Trade Organization (WTO), countries encourage foreign exporters to "voluntarily" restrict their sales. The Japanese auto industry restricted its sales throughout most of the 1980s. To compensate, it traded up from compact cars to medium- and large-sized autos, which netted more sales and profits. Eventually, the quota restriction and rising prices (due to the appreciating yen) forced Honda, Nissan, and Toyota to either assemble or produce cars in the United States.

Regulatory Barriers. Product standards and safety regulations, while not originally intended to be restrictive to trade, often are. American companies have long complained about Japan's industry-set product and technical-design standards. Trade associations typically set regulatory barriers without foreign input, and because they are design oriented rather than performance oriented, they favor local producers.[7]

National Procurement Policies. Most countries favor domestic companies when awarding government contracts. While the GATT and its successor, the WTO, attempted to make governmental purchasing procedures more open to non-nationals through the Tokyo and Uruguay rounds of trade liberalization talks, foreign firms rarely obtain government contracts. Restrictions occur most frequently in military, national security contracts and in infrastructure industries such as airlines, telecommunications, and energy.

Strategic Barriers. Strategic barriers occur when governments and business collaborate to protect certain industries from foreign influence. Some sectors are protected to nurture infant industries that need time to build large-scale markets to make them cost competitive. For example, automobile production in Japan, Brazil, Argentina, and Australia was protected to allow domestic industries to grow.[8]

Some industries are designated as "nationally strategic" by governments, and foreign ownership and competition are forbidden or limited. For example, the United States restricts ownership in radio communications, domestic air transportation, hydroelectric power companies, and atomic energy. Oil concessions in Norway are difficult for foreign firms to obtain. And in Nigeria, foreign ownership is prohibited for nearly 40 industries and professions, including advertising, cinemas, transportation, and poultry farming,

POLITICAL FACTORS ■ Governments can help or hinder international marketing strategies in a variety of ways.

Political Hindrances. One form of political hindrance is *political boycotts*, which are extensions of government foreign policies. They include trade and investment embargoes such as those imposed on South Africa to pressure the white-dominated government to end its policies of separate racial development. Ongoing tensions in the Middle East between Israel and its Arab neighbors have effectively meant that outsiders could only trade with one or the other.

Another form of hindrance is *political restrictions*, which are less severe than boycotts but do limit trade and investment options. U.S.-Soviet tensions made trade between the two countries difficult until the late 1980s. The United States required special export licenses to trade with Eastern bloc countries. High-tech products were heavily scrutinized to ensure they would not contribute to any communist military buildup. In the U.S. case, most favored nation (MFN) status denial to a country made its exports to the United States subject to prohibitively high tariffs. The United States used this to pressure China into improving its human rights record until 1994 when the two issues were delinked.

China's emergence onto the world trading scene has caused problems for the United States and for international companies intent on doing business in the PRC. Its mid-1994 imposition of 100 percent tariffs on imported cars angered a number of foreign governments. Likewise, its demands on incoming foreign firms are high. Companies entering the PRC must bow to government needs to export over 70 percent of production and have active programs to transfer skills and technologies to local personnel.[9]

International companies can become targets for governmental takeovers of property (expropriation). Companies in extractive industries (such as minerals or oil), banking, utilities, or other sensitive sectors are likely candidates for government takeovers, especially in developing countries. The wave of government takeovers of industries in the 1970s died down in the 1980s and 1990s, as governments have recognized the value of international firms in national economic development programs. In the 1990s, only in Africa have the dangers of government takeovers persisted.[10]

MNCs nevertheless must monitor foreign political environments carefully and avoid being identified as "exploitative foreign corporations." If companies are vulnerable, they try to reduce their political exposure. Reduction can be achieved by building up local political connections, contributing to local community developments, and pursuing positive public relations policies. If these options are unavailable, U.S. MNCs insure their foreign assets with the Overseas Private Investment Corporation (OPIC), a government agency specializing in international investment insurance.[11]

Political Aids. There are several political aids to marketing strategies. One is *government export promotion programs* covering market analyses, trade leads, promotions, and financing packages. These programs help both beginning and established exporters gain entry into foreign markets (see Chapter 8 for details).

Tax breaks for exporters is another political aid. In the United States, one or more companies can form foreign sales corporations (FSCs). These are offshore sales organizations that allow companies to exempt a portion of their export income from U.S. corporate income tax. FSCs may be operated by 25 or fewer unrelated exporters or by trade associations, banks, or export management or export trading companies.[12] In Europe, exporters are exempt from the value-add taxes (VAT), which must be paid on domestically consumed production.

Tax breaks for investments is an aid that most governments offer. They include tax holidays (i.e., no taxes for a period of time), accelerated depreciation allowances, low-interest loans, and construction of support-

ing infrastructures (roads or rail facilities) to service new investments. State governments in the United States compete in using such incentives for investments, and the European Union offers financial help to companies locating in less advanced parts of the EU (such as Ireland, Northern England, Spain, Portugal, and southern Italy).

Less common is *government aid in strategy formulation and execution*. While most governments have incentive programs for trade and investment, politicians usually leave international strategy formulation to individual companies. Japan's invasion of world markets since the 1960s is the exception. The close relationship between Japanese business and government (known as "Japan Inc.") has resulted in Japanese industries "moving as one" in world markets.[13] Two government ministries, the Ministry of Finance and the powerful Ministry of International Trade and Industry (MITI),

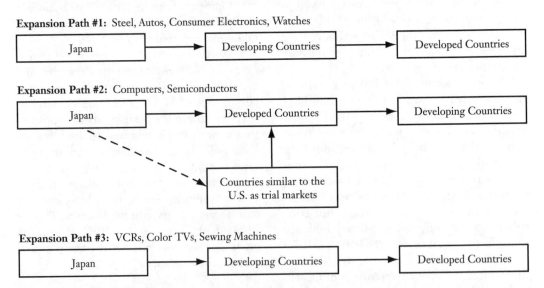

Expansion Path #1: Steel, Autos, Consumer Electronics, Watches

Expansion Path #2: Computers, Semiconductors

Expansion Path #3: VCRs, Color TVs, Sewing Machines

Source: Adapted from Somkid Jatusripitak, Liam Fahey, and Philip Kotler, "Strategic Global Marketing: Lessons from the Japanese," *Columbia Journal of World Business* 20, no. 1 (Spring 1985): 47–55.

FIGURE 10-1 *The Three Key Japanese Global Expansion Paths*

have played active roles in formulating national economic priorities and deciding how industrial resources should be allocated both inside and outside of Japan.

Japanese expansion into the world marketplace was orchestrated to the point where individual industries followed one of three paths (see Figure 10–1).[14] The first and most popular path was from Japan to developing markets and then into developed markets. This path was used in the consumer electronics, home appliance, watch, camera, steel, auto, and petrochemical industries. After securing their home market, the Japanese targeted emergent markets in Southeast Asia and Latin America. There, they honed their manufacturing processes and marketing techniques to the point where they could compete in the advanced markets of North America and Western Europe. Over time, Japanese products replaced their western counterparts. Their quartz technology overtook the more traditional Swiss watch; and Canon and Pentax created cameras superior to those produced by West Germany, at that time the market leader.

For high-tech products such as semiconductors and computers, the Japanese used a different path. After securing state-of-the-art technology from IBM (in return for entry into the Japanese market), NEC, Fujitsu, Hitachi, Toshiba, Mitsubishi Electric, and Oki Electric set about first establishing themselves against "Big Blue" in the home market. Using vigorous price competition and "buy Japan" policies, they secured the home market. Then, realizing there could be no long gestation periods to gear up for the major markets in Europe and the United States, the Japanese test-marketed their products in markets that resembled the United States and Europe: Canada and Australia. After that, they moved swiftly into developed markets, using competitive pricing and local distributors to gain market share. Finally, these Japanese computer firms went after the developing world, with each company targeting a different market— Hitachi and NEC went to Singapore and Hong Kong, Fujitsu went into the Philippines, and NEC went into Thailand.

Finally, there were some products and technologies that needed large initial sales to recoup heavy research-and-development expenses. Hence, color television sets, electric sewing machines, and video tape recorders (VTRs) were marketed first in the United States. After some initial success (which took four to five years), the Japanese took these products back to Japan and then into developing countries.

Competitive Aspects of Foreign Market Expansion

Industry competitors are important benchmarks by which companies evaluate their marketing effectiveness. Market expansion is a key area in which monitoring competitors assists the formulation of strategy. Such monitoring affects two types of decisions: how many markets to enter and which markets to enter.

COMPETITOR MARKET COVERAGE ■ Few companies have the resources to maintain assets in all of the world's 200-plus national markets. In some countries, MNCs invest heavily in both manufacturing and marketing. In others, they may only have a distributor. Companies gain competitive edges by having significant presences in a market. Procter & Gamble employs more than 73,000 people in 25 markets. A competitor, Colgate-Palmolive, has 53,000 employees, but they are spread over 46 countries. Similarly, Young and Rubican advertising agency is in 21 markets, while archrival

A Geographic Scope/Competitor Strength Profile for Competitor X

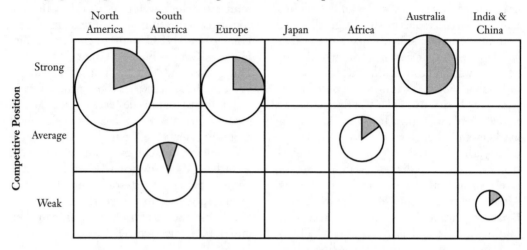

Note: The areas of the circles represent the relative size of the markets, and the pie-shaped wedges indicate the relative share of each of these markets held by Competitor X.

A Geographic Scope/Resource Deployment Matrix for Competitor X

	North America	South America	Europe	Japan	Africa	Australia	India & China
R&D Laboratories							
Raw Materials Sourcing							
Component Sourcing & Manufacture							
Assembly Operations							
Distribution Facilities							
Source of Financing							
Marketing & Sales							
Management							

Source: Charles W. Hofer and Terry P. Haller, "Globescan: A Way to Better International Assessment," *Journal of Business Strategy* 2 (Fall 1980): 53. Reproduced with permission.

FIGURE 10–2 *Geographic Evaluation of Competitors*

McCann-Erickson is in 58 countries.[15] Clearly, it is useful to know where competitors are located geographically.

When companies attack competitors, they must know not only where the competitors are located but also how strong they are. Figure 10–2 shows how firms chart competitive positions geographically.

COMPETITORS AND MARKET SELECTION ▪

Competitors also affect market selection.[16] One way to choose a market is a *follow-the-leader* pattern, in which a dominant industry member leads other companies abroad. Citicorp was the front-runner in foreign markets in the U.S. banking industry during the 1950s. It was followed by J. P. Morgan, Chase Manhattan, and Banker's Trust. Similarly, Firestone and Goodrich followed Goodyear's global expansion path.

Undermining a global competitor is another motive in market selection. When a dominant international company is being globally challenged, one way to counterattack is to mount an assault in the competitor's home market. Caterpillar did that when challenged by Komatsu; it entered a joint venture with Mitsubishi in Japan to pose a significant threat to Komatsu's bread-and-butter market.

A company can use a *market-avoidance strategy*; that is, it can avoid meeting a competitor head-on in some markets. For example, both John Deere and International Harvester have been internationally active for over 70 years, but mainly in different foreign markets. By the mid-1960s, out of 13 major agricultural markets around the world, both companies appeared in only 6.

Control Data competes in the highly competitive high-tech office equipment industry. To avoid seasoned competitors such as IBM and NCR, the first foreign markets Control Data entered were Israel and Hong Kong. The company then focused its foreign efforts on other secondary markets such as Yugoslavia and other Eastern European countries. Chrysler similarly avoided General Motors and Ford in its initial foreign market entries, preferring instead to develop secondary markets such as Greece, Algeria, Venezuela, Peru, Morocco, Iran, and Turkey. Today, however, as global competitors establish beachheads in both major and minor world markets, market-avoidance strategies are difficult to implement.

GAINING THE COMPETITIVE ADVANTAGE

Generic Strategies

Once management has decided where to allocate its global marketing efforts, it must then decide how to out-compete its rivals in those markets. Beating the competition involves first, ascertaining why competitors are being successful, and second, devising a means to differentiate the company's own efforts. Key success factors include the following:

1. *Technical superiority* in products and services; for example, supercomputers and multifeatured dishwashers.

2. *Low prices*, which give products broad appeal and a competitive advantage.

3. *Distribution and service availability:* Some products (such as autos, earth-moving equipment, and durable consumer goods) reap competitive advantages abroad by having on-site maintenance and offices. These require capital but are viewed as worthwhile investments.

4. *Broad product mixes:* Making available multiple sizes, colors, and other features for different customer segments.

5. A *reputation* for "goodwill," which is built up over time and maintained through quality products, promotions, consistently superior strategies, and satisfied customers (achieved, for example, by IBM, NCR, Panasonic, Toyota, Sony, and Shell).

Few companies achieve excellence in all aspects of marketing strategy, because research and development (which determine technology levels), distribution, service, broad product mixes, and customer goodwill all require significant resources. If all are achieved, company price levels are pushed up toward the premium end. Similarly, low prices and margins make superior technologies, distribution, service, and so on difficult to maintain. Price then becomes a key factor in differentiating between competitive company offerings. U.S. companies with established reputations (such as IBM, Hewlett-Packard, Harley-Davidson, and Xerox) have gained significant competitive advantages through combinations of superior technologies, product quality, service, and reputation. Realizing this fact, the Japanese won marketplace attention with low price strategies.

Where markets are price competitive with adequate (but not outstanding) technologies, then service, product quality, distribution, and product variety offer opportunities for competitors to establish reputations based on these attributes. Sony, Toyota, and Canon cameras decided on such an approach. These strategic alternatives are illustrated in Table 10–3.

Of course, one characteristic of Japanese strategies in the United States has been not only the quality and assortment of their products but also their low prices. Part of Japanese success can be attributed to their undervalued currency, which until its appreciation between 1985 and 1988, maintained Japan's price competitiveness (see Chapter 4 on exchange rates). Since that time, Japan has used off-shore manufacturing to maintain price advantages. Japanese competitive successes, especially in the United States, have been significant enough to warrant further evaluation.

Competitive Strategy: Japanese Style

The Japanese have been phenomenally successful in the global marketplace over the past 20 to 30 years. Some of this success has been attributed to internal factors (a protected

TABLE 10–3 ■ *Competitive Postures: Two Extreme Situations*

	Company	
Competitive Advantage	**Sony, IBM, Caterpillar, Toyota**	**U.S. Auto Industry, Consumer Electronics**
Level of technology	Superior	Adequate
Distribution/Service	Superior	Adequate
Product mix width	Broad	Narrow
Company-product reputation	Established	Not established
Product quality	Good/Superior	Adequate/good
Price orientation	Premium prices	Competitive low prices

home market, close government-business relations, a high rate of savings, low-cost capital, a strong work ethic, and so on). But international marketing success occurs when companies consistently satisfy customer needs and out-compete their rivals. The Japanese have done so in a number of industries—automobiles, motorcycles, cameras, watches, televisions, consumer electronics, optical instruments, and others. Their recipe for success has been remarkably similar in these industries. First, they research dealers, distributors, and retailers to find what current needs are likely to be.[17] Then, through combinations of computer-aided design (CAD), computer-aided manufacturing (CAM), robotics, and off-shore sources of supplies, they produce goods at low cost. Finally, they evaluate competitive offerings and select a strategy to differentiate their output in the marketplace.

A Typology of Competitive Strategies

There are five basic competitive strategies: frontal attack, outflanking, encirclement, bypass attack, and "guerrilla warfare."[18]

FRONTAL ATTACK
■ Frontal attack, or meeting competitors head on, is the strategy favored by American companies (for example, Coca-Cola versus Pepsi, Avis versus Hertz, MacDonald's versus Burger King, and Ford versus General Motors versus Chrysler). Such strategies require resources and staying power. The Japanese have never favored head-on attacks, preferring instead to compete in more subtle ways. For example, throughout the 1980s, advertisements for Japanese autos stressed quality (partially because a strong yen ruled out low-price appeal). However, they never sought the maximum competitive advantage by openly comparing their superior quality levels to those of U.S. cars. American manufacturers have not been as reticent. When Chrysler found it had a competitive advantage over the Japanese, it went ahead with direct U.S.-Japanese comparisons.

OUTFLANKING
■ Outflanking the competition involves locating competitor weaknesses, attacking them, and building a commercial base. This strategy is implemented either on a market basis (geographic outflanking) or on a product basis. Geographic outflanking involves attacking markets where competitors are not strong *before* entering their major markets. Japanese auto, motorcycle, pharmaceutical, copier, and home-appliance industries geographically outflanked U.S. and European rivals by focusing first and most on developing markets such as Asia and South America, where competitive retaliation was less likely.

Product outflanking occurs when attacks are made on market segments not being served by domestic producers. The Japanese executed outflanking attacks on the automobile, motorcycle, copier, and television industries. They did so also to benefit from some natural advantages of their home market. Japan is a crowded country with small amounts of living space. Consequently, Japanese manufacturers automatically designed physically small products for the home market. American companies, by contrast, faced no such physical constraints in the United States and built large products in the auto, motorcycle, and copier industries. In reviewing the American market, Japanese manufacturers sensed that smaller versions of these products had been neglected. Toyota, Honda, and Nissan all took advantage of this neglect and built their markets by catering to wanted small cars. Only when they were asked "voluntarily" to limit their exports to the United States did they move up to medium-size and full-size autos. Similarly, Canon and Sharp attacked Xerox at the small end of the copier market; and Honda and Yamaha went after Harley-Davidson in the smaller bike ranges (250cc and 500cc sizes). Finally, in the television sector, the Japanese focused initially on portable sets, but eventually, they sensed opportunities in large screen televisions and went on to establish themselves in the large TV segment (40- to 60-inch screens) for the American market.

ENCIRCLEMENT ■ The strategy of encirclement involves producing more types, sizes, colors, and styles of products than the competition, often at similar or lower prices. Seiko used this strategy to strangle traditional, nonquartz competition in the watch industry. Casio tried a similar strategy for calculators but had less success against the tough and responsive Texas Instruments Corporation. Encirclement is difficult to combat because rivals must not only match low-cost manufacturing technologies but also compete with greater varieties of competitor products. Inflated costs are a problem, and often consumers end up switching between different brands produced by the same manufacturer ("cannibalism").

BYPASS ■ A bypass strategy ignores competitors' present markets or technologies and does something completely different. In the consumer-electronics field, the Japanese commercialized quartz technology for watches and bypassed traditional record and tape markets with their compact disc and digital-audio technologies (DAT). In the camera industry, the Japanese were the first to popularize 35mm technology with the Canon AE1. They maintained their innovativeness with auto-focusing technology (in Pentax cameras) and by using cassette technology to make camera slides viewable through televisions.

GUERRILLA WARFARE ■ In guerrilla warfare, companies use local dealers and distributors to attack specific products, product lines, or channels. Guerrilla tactics include matching competitors' auto discounts, having special event promotions to keep rivals off-balance, or devising other means to maintain revenues during slow sales periods.

SUMMARY

International marketing strategy is concerned with satisfying customers and out-competing rivals in the world marketplace. To satisfy customers, marketers use global strategies where price, technology, and large-scale markets make product standardization necessary except for mandatory adaptations. Marketing differentiation is achieved by localizing prices, promotion, and distribution.

Multinational strategies are effective where products and elements of the marketing mix need to be localized to have customer appeal. Often, on-site manufacturing enables products and marketing to be custom designed for specific areas. Multinational marketers use international product transfers to reduce local new product developmental costs and to obtain synergies from their international marketing operations.

In some cases, MNCs use multilocal strategies when there are few marketing or business advantages from transferring technologies between countries. In these situations, they perform just as local businesses. Often, companies simultaneously use global, multinational, and multilocal strategies according to marketplace needs.

Market expansion is an integral part of international marketing strategy. While market size and potential are important indicators of where companies should go, corporate personnel, market barriers, political factors, and competitive aspects actively intervene to dictate where firms eventually go.

Finally, successful international marketing strategies require companies to have different advantages over competitors. Typically, technology, price, distribution, service, product mix, and reputation are areas in which competitive advantages can be gained. Once obtained, different advantages can be exercised competitively using frontal-attack, outflanking, encirclement, bypass, or guerrilla-warfare strategies. Japanese companies have been prime exponents of such strategies in the United States.

DISCUSSION QUESTIONS

1. Define the following terms: international marketing strategy; global, multinational, and multilocal strategies; quotas; strategic (market) barriers; political boycotts; "Japan Inc."; and competitive strategy.

2. Kodak recently made significant investment in Japan to attack Fuji. What sort of strategy is this? Why is attacking Japanese companies in their home markets likely to be successful?

3. Do you think Americans could organize themselves as "U.S. Inc." the way the Japanese have? Why or why not?

4. Why do Americans prefer "frontal attacks" in formulating their competitive strategies while the Japanese do not? (Think in terms of their culture and review relevant materials in Chapter 2 if necessary.)

Meeting the Japanese Challenge— The Case of Motorola

In 1979, during a strategy meeting in a Chicago hotel, Motorola top executives were warned that if the company continued its present course, its position as a world leader in semiconductors and in high-tech telecommunications would be inexorably jeopardized by Japanese competitors with technically advanced, low-cost products.

The company responded with a top-to-bottom examination of its operations and a rethinking of its goals. By 1989, Motorola had made itself competitive in semiconductors (ranking fourth behind three Japanese companies) and was the world leader in cellular telephones, having just introduced the MicroTac, a pocket-sized phone. It became a leader in two-way mobile radios, and it had become the only American company in the pager market.

How was such a turnaround achieved? Motorola followed a multipronged strategy:

1. The company launched a company-wide education program to update and teach new skills to its entire 96,000-employee workforce. Its aim was to transform its corporate culture to focus on "total" customer satisfaction. Its employee-education program cost close to $50 million, or nearly 2.5 percent of its payroll.

2. The company initiated a massive push for quality production. It achieved a tenfold reduction in defects by 1986. By 1991, CEO Bob Galvin was aiming for a "Six Sigma" performance, or 99.997 percent error-free production—a hundredfold improvement over 1987.

3. Motorola made an extensive study of Asian competition, with 150 of its top officers taking intensive courses on Asian culture, economy, and politics.

4. The company formed a joint venture with Toshiba, the number two world producer of semiconductors behind Japan's NEC. This step was the final twist in a change of attitude toward Japanese competition, which was described as "first ignore 'em, then sue 'em, and finally learn from 'em." During the 1980s, Motorola had successfully lobbied a 106 percent duty on Japanese exporters of pagers and cellular phones to the United States.

5. The company shifted more of its production and assembly facilities to Japan, South Korea, Malaysia, Singapore, and Taiwan. In 1991, Motorola had 3 percent of its manufacturing abroad. It expected to have 50 percent by the year 2000.

6. Motorola also managed to decentralize operations where there was a promise of market potential. The company invested $200 million in a state-of-the-art manufacturing plant in Hong Kong. Nicknamed "Silicon Harbor," the 300,000-square-foot facility was designed to service increasing numbers of assembly operations in mainland China.

In 1991, 13 European countries officially standardized cellular radio specifications (as part of the 1992 European economic unification package). European-based producers were gearing up to tackle Motorola and NEC's expected onslaught. The market was expected to have more than 3 million users of cellular telephones by the mid-1990s. NEC was making new investments in the United Kingdom in preparation, and Motorola's plans included doubling its British subsidiary's size before 1992.

QUESTIONS

1. To what extent do you think Motorola's success has been due to manufacturing innovations rather than marketing innovations?

2. How far do you think Motorola's strategy can be copied by other firms with broader rather than narrower product lines?

3. You are advising Motorola's CEO Bob Galvin. How would you recommend he deal with his major rivals, the Japanese? Would you advise him to (a) go it alone, (b) form more alliances with the Japanese (for example, with NEC or Hitachi), or (c) try to establish closer relationships with European manufacturers? Why?

Source: Case based on Jack Gee, "Motorola and NEC Gear Up for Car Phone Clash in Europe," *Electronic Business*, 15 April 1988, 86, 88; Lois Therrien, "Motorola Sends Its Work Force Back to School," *Business Week*, 6 June 1988, 80–81; Thomas J. Murray, "How Motorola Builds in Speed and Quality," *Business Month*, July 1989, 36–7; Euan Barty, 'Motorola Stalks the Hong Kong ASIC Market," *Electronic Business*, 1 May 1988, 60, 62; and Ronald Henkoff, "What Motorola Learns from Japan," *Fortune*, 24 April 1989, 157, 160, 164, 168.

Jollibee versus the Giant: How Local Firms Can Compete against Global Franchises

At first, most people would have thought it a mismatch. The $30 billion McDonald's going up against the $250 million Philippine food company Jollibee in the hamburger restaurant market. But then Pulse Research Group (an affiliate of A.C. Nielsen) checked the numbers: Jollibee had 46 percent of the Philippine hamburger restaurant market against 16 percent for McDonald's. Now Jollibee has 177 outlets versus 90 for McDonalds (and the Philippine chain plans to open another 36 in 1996).

Jollibee's recipe was to take a few leafs out of McDonald's play book—target children with ads and play activities; surround McDonald's at prime locations (and give consumers local options everywhere); fast service; cleanliness—and to add local touches. The Philippine restaurant chain cashes in on local tastes, favoring spicy, sweet, and sour flavors, which it puts in its hamburgers and fried chicken. Rice is also offered as a side order. While McDonald's has introduced its own Filipino spicy hamburgers, the fast-food king still finds it tough to compete against Jollibee's signature characters (a spaghetti-haired female called Hetty and a hamburger-headed boxer named Champ). Another reason is Jollibee's prices, which are 5 to 10 percent lower than McDonald's.

McDonald's, however, was not always the underdog. The two rivals competed restaurant-for-restaurant in the 1980s. Then, a military coup in 1989 caused McDonald's to rethink. Jollibee's added 30 more outlets in 1990 and has never looked back. But restrictions prohibiting foreign companies from owning Filipino retail chains will be lifted by 1998, permitting McDonald's to operate its own stores.

But Jollibee has McDonald's-like plans itself. The family-owned chain has 15 restaurants in the Middle East and Southeast Asia and plans to double that number. Jollibee is also targeting the Filipino, Asian, and Hispanic populations in the U.S.

DISCUSSION QUESTIONS

1. Distinguish between the key success factors that have contributed to Jollibee's success and the competitive advantages they perceive they have over McDonald's. What was the role of the Philippines' foreign ownership restrictions?

2. If you were Jollibee, would you focus additional resources in 1996–98 in the Philippines or overseas? Why?

3. What do you think of Jollibee's global aspirations? Is there a global segment for their wares, or must they adapt to every country's taste in spiciness?

Source: Adapted from: Hugh Filman, "Happy Meals for McDonald's Rival," *Business Week*, 29 July 1996, 77.

ENDNOTES

1 The concepts of global and multinational marketing are adapted from Theodore Levitt, "The Globalization of World Markets," *Harvard Business Review* 61 (May–June 1983): 92–102; and Michael E. Porter, "Competition in Global Industries: A Conceptual Framework," in *Competition in Global Industries*, ed. Michael E. Porter (Boston, Mass.: Harvard Business School Press, 1986), 15–16. The concept of multilocal marketing is noted in Kenichi Ohmae, *The Mind of the Strategist* (New York: Penguin Books, 1983).

2 John S. Hill, "Origins of MNC Products Lines: Structural and Environmental Determinants," working paper, University of Alabama, 1989.

3 Nancy Giges, "C-P Shifts Favor Regional Approach," *Advertising Age*, 9 December 1985, 1; John S. Hill and Richard R. Still, "Adapting Products to LDC Tastes," *Harvard Business Review* 62 (March–April 1984): 92–102; and David Wessel, "Gillette Keys Sales to Third World Tastes," *The Wall Street Journal*, 23 January 1986, 35.

4 See U.S. Department of Commerce, *Survey of Current Business* 76, no. 6 (July 1996): 50; Philip Kotler, Liam Fahey, and S. Jatusripatak, *The New Competition* (Englewood Cliffs, N.J.: Prentice-Hall, 1985), 135; and Ian R. Wilson, "American Success Story: Coca-Cola in Japan," in *International Marketing: Managerial Perspectives*, ed. Subhash Jain and Lewis R. Tucker, Jr. (Boston, Mass.: Kent Publishing, 1986), 184–92.

5 For amplification, see William H. Davidson, "Market Similarity and Market Selection: Implications for International Marketing Strategy," *Journal of Business Research* 11, no. 4 (December 1983): 439–56.

6 William H. Cooper, *Japan-U.S. Economic Relations: Cooperation or Confrontation?* (Washington, D.C.: U.S. Library of Congress, 1989), vii.

7 *Market Access in Japan: The U.S. Experience*, CRS Report 85-37 (Washington D.C.: U.S. Library of Congress, 1985).

8 John D. Daniels and Lee Radebaugh, *International Business: Environment and Operations*, 4th ed. (Reading, Mass.: Addison-Wesley, 1986), 167.

9 Pete Engardio, "Global Tremors from an Unruly Giant," *Business Week*, 4 March 1996, 59–64.

10 Charles R. Kennedy, Jr., "Multinational Corporations and Expropriation Risk," *Multinational Business Review* 1, no. 1 (Spring 1993): 44–55.

11 For more on this topic, see Thomas W. Shreeve, "Be Prepared for Political Changes Abroad," *Harvard Business Review* 62 (July 1984): 111–18.

12 John J. Korbel and Charles M. Bruce, "Shared FSCs: An Innovative, New Benefit for Small and Medium-Sized Exporters," *Business America*, 20 January 1986, 11–14.

13 The Term "Japan Inc." has been attributed to Eugene J. Kaplan, *Japan: The Government-Business Relationship* (Washington, D.C.: U.S. Department of Commerce, 1972), 56–72.

14 The following discussion is based on Somkid Jatusripitak, Liam Fahey, and Philip Kotler, "Strategic Global Marketing: Lessons from the Japanese," *Columbia Journal of World Business* 20 (Spring 1985): 47–53.

15 Taken from *Directory of American Firms Operating in Foreign Countries*, 14th ed. (New York: Uni-World Business Publications, 1995).

16 This typology and examples are taken mainly from William H. Davidson, *Global Strategic Management* (New York: John Wiley & Sons, 1982), 85–96.

17 Johnny K. Johansson and Ikujiro Nonaka, "Market Research the Japanese Way," *Harvard Business Review* 65 (May–June 1987): 16–18, 22.

18 Based on Kotler, Fahey, and Jatusripitak, *The New Competition*, 123-49.

CHAPTER **11**

Marketing Consumer Products Internationally

Chapter Outline

Learning Objectives

When you have mastered the contents of this chapter, you will be able to do the following:

1 Explain the international product concept and describe the components of consumer products marketed internationally.

2 Distinguish between and explain consumer product strategies as they relate to the global, multinational, and multilocal categories.

3 Discuss and analyze the determinants of product-mix decisions at the international level.

4 Analyze the process of product transfer and adaptation, especially as they relate to developing countries.

5 Describe the nature of product cycles and explain their significance.

6 Explain the portfolio analysis of products sold internationally and evaluate its usefulness for international marketers.

7 Discuss the concept and process of positioning products in the international market.

When you travel around the world, time and again you encounter familiar consumer products. You see Coca-Cola signs just about everywhere, and IBM, Xerox, and Volkswagen are household words on every continent. Aspirin, Frigidaire, and Levis are not only household words but generic names. These are global products. Some products are not available worldwide. Russian balalaikas are a local Russian product. Some local products become global; others remain local or reach only a few countries. In this chapter, we examine the decisions managers make on the international marketing of consumer products. Some companies specialize in global products; others develop local products. Still others transfer products from home or foreign markets and adapt them to local country needs.

INTERNATIONAL PRODUCT CONCEPTS

Consumer products are sold to individuals for their own personal use. They can be physical entities, services, or some combination of the two. Because international marketing mostly concerns physical products, the emphasis here is on physical products. A physical product, considered internationally, has five parts: (1) physical component, (2) brand name, (3) packaging, (4) auxiliary services, and (5) country-of-origin identification (Figure 11–1).

Physical Components

The "same" physical product often is "different" from one country to another. Take household appliances such as household washers and dryers. In North America, such

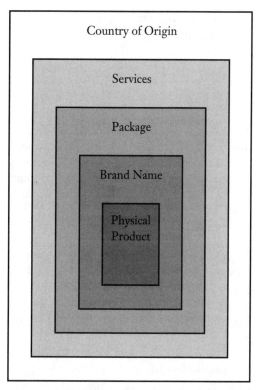

FIGURE 11–1 *Components of Consumer Products for the International Market*

appliances are large, each taking up 20–30 cubic feet, and they are not particularly designed to conserve either water or energy. By contrast, in Turkey, washers and dryers are not only small but also water and energy efficient—highly important factors in this country's heavily populated urban areas. In fact, all home appliances in Eastern Europe, as well as in most other parts of Europe, are limited, chiefly because of the small size of most living units. Many European families live in small apartments, in sharp contrast to North America, where single-family homes and spacious condominiums and apartments are common and small "efficiency" apartments are almost entirely confined to the largest cities. Because of this availability of space, almost all home appliances are larger in North American than in Europe or in Japan.

Brand Name

Names such as Rolls-Royce, IBM, Xerox, and Coca-Cola are known everywhere around the world. Such brand familiarity can be, and most often is, an additional product feature. Because of this additional feature, some products can enter world markets very easily. Justifiably, consumers in these markets may think that it is a lesser risk to buy such a well-known brand, particularly because they are familiar with it. Additionally, the ownership of some of these brands in many parts of the world is a status symbol. It may give the consumer additional satisfaction through pride of ownership. [1]

Compared to the U.S., Europeans clearly distinguish between brands, have strongly expressed brand preferences, and are more loyal to brands. These patterns are particularly detectable in the U.K. While German and French consumers are more open to buying foreign-made goods, Italian and British consumers are more likely to choose their country's national brands.[2]

Packaging

The packaging of a product is substantially more important in international marketing than in domestic U.S. marketing. There are three reasons for this. First, products that travel great distances must be specially packaged for protection. Second, the package is often the company's first opportunity to communicate with prospective buyers, and it can be internationally effective through pictures or logos on the package. Third, in many parts of the world, packaging is

recycled because of heightened awareness of preserving the environment.

Auxiliary Services

Besides repairing the product and providing needed parts, the service component is instrumental in teaching the customer how to use and maintain the product. As the product becomes more complex, the service component grows in importance. It is difficult, if not impossible, for Japanese or European companies to sell electronic products such as VCRs, TVs, and video cameras in consumer markets such as in Turkey or Pakistan, without having adequate service support systems in place. When Nissan entered the U.S. market with its Datsun autos in the mid-1960s, it confined its operations to California, because that was the only state in which it had an effective dealer network to provide service. As Nissan built up its dealer network, its U.S. operations expanded over the entire country.

Country-of-Origin Effects

Identification of a product's country of origin affects the international sale of consumer products unequally. Identification influences the reputations of products because consumers respond at an emotional level to where they were made. Some countries have good reputations and others have bad reputations for certain products. For example, Japan and Germany have good reputations for producing quality engineering-based products. Interestingly, until the 1960s, Japan had a reputation for producing low-quality products, just as Hong Kong did during the 1960s. One analysis of numerous country-of-origin studies concluded that country-of-origin identification plays a key role in terms of perceived importance or quality of products.[3] Such studies have shown the following facts:

- Calculators or computers made in Hong Kong present a lesser risk than those made in less-developed countries.

- If a country is a well-known exporter of a particular raw material, its reputation carries over to the processed products from the raw material, as with freeze-dried coffee from Brazil.

- Romanians have no confidence in Russian-made products.

- Guatemalan students gave lower evaluations to products from El Salvador and Costa Rica than to domestic and Mexican products.

- Higher-income students in Taiwan and India indicated that they preferred products made in countries that were more developed than their own. Similarly, better-educated students rated products made in more-developed countries more highly than their national products.[4]

The positive effect of country-of-origin identification is not only country specific, it is also product specific. For certain consumer goods, such as apparel, cars, and cameras, the country of origin is critical. Quality cameras are made in Japan and Germany, quality automobiles in Japan and Germany, and quality apparel in France.[5] Because of the importance of country-of-origin identification, sometimes a country develops a nation-wide strategy of product design. In Japan, such strategy is *kei-haku-tan-sho* ("light-thin-short-small"). Japan's good reputation for some products spills over to many other Japanese-made products.

INTERNATIONAL PRODUCT MANAGEMENT

When management does not match products with target markets effectively, a product blunder occurs. Two common problems are (1) when management markets the wrong product in a particular market and (2) when it markets the right product but does not adapt the product properly to fit the target market. Here are some examples:

- Campbell's soups have had some unfortunate experiences in world markets. In Brazil, women did not want to serve a soup that they had not prepared. In England, because people preferred ready-made soup, they did not like condensed versions. In France, Campbell used the word *soup*, but the French preferred *potage*.[6]

- Jell-O failed in England because the British are not accustomed to powdered gelatin.

- American firms making copiers did not adapt to one country's paper standards, and that country's paper products were not usable in their copiers.

- American soft drinks were not popular in Australia because Australians did not like the taste.

- Ford Werke was at first very successful in Germany. The sales declined because of Detroit-style face-lifts; the cars became wider, longer, heavier, and more expensive, making them undesirable in the German market.

These blunders demonstrate that managers have at least two major tasks to perform when they formulate product strategies for overseas markets. The first task is to take care in deciding what product to market. Should the company extend U.S. products abroad, custom-build products, or transfer products from other foreign locations? The second task is to decide whether the company should standardize its brands or make the adaptations necessary to compete effectively.

Product-Mix Decisions

Deciding on the product mix, the first task of forming product strategies, requires considering the composition and development of the product mix.

COMPOSITION OF THE PRODUCT MIX ■

Deciding on appropriate product assortments for overseas markets depends partly on how similar foreign markets are to the home market and partly on the relation of the product to the foreign culture. When similarities exist among countries, overlaps occur in product mixes between company markets. International companies encounter different industry conditions and variable environmental settings, so they develop expertise in diagnosing needs in new markets and draw on their experiences elsewhere in building product mixes that satisfy customers.

All markets have cultural idiosyncrasies, especially at the lower socioeconomic level.

When a multi-national corporation finds groups of potential customers with unmet needs in a particular product category, it scans its product portfolio to determine whether it has an appropriate product. If it has no such product and if the target market has a large enough potential, the MNC may custom-make a product for that market.

Industry patterns dominate other factors in determining foreign product mixes. Table 11–1 shows the mixes for four types of nondurable consumer goods: food and drink, pharmaceuticals, cosmetics, and general consumer goods. Note the high proportions (between 42 and 75 percent) of the U.S.-made products sold abroad by American MNCs. MNCs can and do exploit the basic similarities that exist between U.S. and overseas consumers.

Other product mixes are characteristic of individual industries. In Table 11–1, both food and drink and general consumer goods have higher proportions of localized products than do either cosmetics or pharmaceuticals. This difference reflects cultural sensitivity; food and drink products are closely associated with national lifestyles, and the use of general consumer goods (such as household cleansers and washing powders) varies among cultures, reflecting different domestic situations and attitudes toward cleanliness. Hence, compa-

TABLE 11–1 ■ *Consumer Product Mix Compositions*

Industry	% Product Lines of U.S. Origin	% Product Lines from Non-U.S. Markets	% Product Lines Locally Created
Food and drink	52.5	14.8	32.7
Pharmaceuticals	42.2	48.6	9.2
Cosmetics	74.1	14.3	11.6
General consumer goods	61.4	12.3	26.3

Source: John Hill, "MNC Product Origins: Structural and Environmental Determinants," working paper, University of Alabama, Tuscaloosa, 1989.

nies such as General Foods and Quaker Oats obtain only limited advantages from their products originating in the United States.

Pharmaceutical MNCs such as Sterling Drug and Pfizer are worldwide marketers, with nearly half of their subsidiaries' product mixes coming from non-U.S. markets, and with few products created for single-market use. Pharmaceutical research-and-development facilities are globally spread throughout their MNCs' many world markets. Admittedly, some of this global spread can be traced to strict U.S. Food and Drug Administration testing procedures which, while thorough, raise the development costs of new products. The key to pharmaceutical marketing is a worldwide marketing network that enables the rapid diffusion of new products into numerous foreign markets.

Cosmetics manufacturers have the highest proportions of U.S.-originated products among their overseas lines. Companies such as Helena Rubenstein, Revlon, and Max Factor capitalize on the adoption of U.S. beauty standards elsewhere around the world. These standards are transmitted through the media, often through American syndicated television series such as "Dallas," "Dynasty," and "Miami Vice." Of course, different groups of cosmetics are more popular in different places. European women, for example, place more emphasis on skin-care products than do Americans.

DEVELOPING THE PRODUCT MIX: EFFECTS OF MARKET-ENTRY METHOD ▪ Overseas product mixes do not remain constant over time. How they change depends very much on market-entry methods. Figure 11–2, the

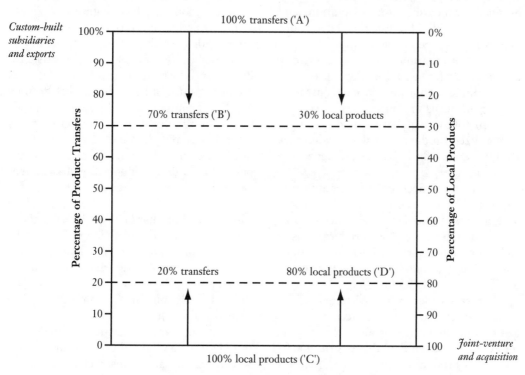

FIGURE 11–2 *Product Origins Box Showing Effects of Market Entry Method on Subsidiary Product Mixes and Probable Changes over Time*

TABLE 11–2 ■ *International Product Strategy Options*

Conditions	Product Strategy
Internal factors and strengths outstrip external barriers	Globally standardized products by global firms
Internal factors and strengths are much stronger than external factors and barriers	Product adaptation by multinational firms
Internal factors and strengths are less strong than external factors and barriers	International product innovation by multilocal firms

Product Origins Box, portrays various product-mix options for major market-entry methods.

Companies servicing foreign markets through exports begin by transferring products from home-markets. These three strategies—global, multinational, and multilocal—are associated with three options for treating products: standardization, adaptation, and innovation. Table 11–2 lists the general conditions appropriate for each option.

Some international firms enjoy strong customer preferences for their products. When these conditions occur, customer adaptation needs are minimal, and companies can follow a global strategy, selling a standardized product on a worldwide basis. IBM, Xerox, and Mercedes-Benz are examples.

Other firms need internal manufacturing economies to be cost competitive but still have to cater to market-specific needs to be successful. These firms use product transfer and adaptation strategies. Levi, for example, sells its blue jeans internationally but adjusts to different body types in different countries.

For still other firms, certain international markets have strong external barriers and product innovation is necessary. Nissan, for example, first entered the American market with a product specifically designed for U.S. conditions (the Datsun, later renamed Nissan).

DEVELOPING STANDARDIZED CONSUMER PRODUCTS ■ Many products initially catered to local needs and appealed to local culture. At the outset, ethnic music, restaurants, and crafts are specialized, local products. But in time, some become global. Singer sewing machines and Levi blue jeans are examples. What causes a local product to become a global product? Figure 11–3 shows a three-tier hierarchy of need in terms of international settings. The bottom tier is composed of basic needs related to existence itself. A product catering to basic needs has the best chance of becoming global in time. Aspirin, for instance, was not a global product at the time of its introduction, nor was Coca-Cola, but because they met basic needs, they have become global. Microwave popped corn does not appeal to basic needs and probably will not evolve into a global product. The top tier is the other place where global products evolve. Every country has upper-class consumers interested in self-actualization relating to meta needs; they give rise to global markets for some high-priced and high-quality products. Mercedes-Benz, Ferrari, and BMW automobiles are such global products.

Companies that want to globalize their products first appraise them in terms of their worldwide appeal to consumer needs, either basic or meta needs. After this appraisal, they formulate strategy.

PRODUCT: FUNCTIONS IN:

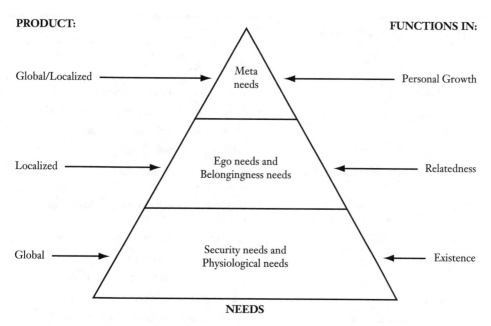

FIGURE 11-3 *A Global Hierarchy of Needs*

Many consumer durable goods (such as automobiles, televisions, radios, videocassette recorders, and so on) appeal to similar basic needs in all markets. Generally, their promotional features emphasize reliability and quality (for example, Mercedes-Benz and Volvo), superior performance (Porsche and Sony) or price-quality combinations (Japanese automobiles). For these companies, the same formulas for market success work in most or all markets. They pursue global strategies, which entail marketing essentially the same product everywhere and making only mandatory adaptations to secure market acceptance. Mercedes-Benz cars are slightly different only because of local government safety requirements. Corning Ware products are also very similar almost everywhere. These items are not only well known for their physical characteristics and corporate images; they are also unique in the eyes of buyers everywhere, without close substitutes.

MULTINATIONAL ADAPTATION STRATEGIES ■

As companies extend their marketing operations overseas, most find market segments with sets of needs that cannot be satisfied by global standards. If these market segments have large enough sales potentials, then MNCs adapt products to fit these localized needs.

Adaptation of Global Consumer Product Lines. Most markets possess some unique characteristics that have the potential of rendering a global product unmarketable unless appropriate adaptations are made. For instance, because roads and streets in many old European cities are narrow and twisting, large American cars (such as the Cadillac and Lincoln Continental) are difficult to maneuver and sometimes impossible to use. Many Europeans live in such small housing units that an average-size, U.S.-made refrigerator or washer and dryer are too large even to bring in through their small doors. Thus,

TABLE 11–3 ■ *Thirteen Factors Affecting Product Adaptation*

Critical Factors Prevailing in the Target Market	Impact of the Factor in Product Adaptation Process
1. Technical skill level	Developing a simplified version of product
2. Labor cost levels	Manualization or automation of the product
3. Level of illiteracy	Simplification of the product and instructions
4. Income level	Adjustment in quality and price
5. Availability and level of consumer credit	Adjustment in quality and price (investment in low quality may not be financially desirable)
6. Isolation of the target country (heavy repair difficult and expensive)	Product simplification and improvement in product reliability
7. Emphasis on and quality of maintenance	Change in product tolerance and durability
8. Climatic conditions	Adjusting product design
9. Product size	Resizing the product and recalibration
10. Energy supply	Resizing the product
11. Availability of other products	Consideration for product integration
12. Availability of raw materials	Changing product structure and design
13. Unique market conditions	Product redesign or innovation

large American cars cannot be marketed in Europe unless they are made to satisfy the specific needs of different markets, and appliances destined for markets in these countries must be scaled down to fit the environment. The argument for localized products is particularly strong in developing markets. Table 11–3 shows 13 factors affecting product adaptations, each of which is discussed below.

1. *Technical-skill level.* If the target country's level of technical skill is low and the product is highly sophisticated or technical, the marketer may develop a simplified version. In many developing countries, for example, TV-set manufacturers market single-station, black-and-white televisions; and Ford, as well as other automakers, sells simplified automobiles.

2. *Labor cost.* If the target country's labor costs are low (as in Third World countries), manufacturers may develop a product that is less mechanized and more manual, cutting both manufacturing and operating costs. For example, to build a market for its detergents in Third World countries, Colgate-Palmolive developed a hand-cranked washing machine. Conversely, for markets in highly industrialized countries with high labor costs, manufacturers make products that are more highly automated.

3. *Level of illiteracy.* Illiteracy is widespread in many parts of the world. In such areas, products must be simplified and carry clear and easy instructions. In some cases, as in Central Africa, instructions are in the form of stick-figure drawings rather than in writing.

4. *Income level.* Average personal income is low in Third World markets, and consumers equate product quality with durability. By contrast, in highly industrialized markets, consumers associate quality with how recent the model is. Thus, in low-income markets, manufacturers build more durability into the product, and in higher-income markets, manufacturers aim for future sales of repair parts and service.

5. *Consumer credit.* Availability of consumer credit has a direct impact on adaptation in terms of product prices. If consumer credit is plentiful, the marketer sets the product's price higher than if credit is nonexistent or difficult to obtain. Furthermore, the decision between offering expensive or cheaper models often largely depends on the availability of consumer credit.

6. *Isolation.* Geographically isolated markets are a real challenge because they typically discourage major repairs by making them difficult and expensive. These situations call for simplifying the product and making it more reliable in order to reduce the likelihood of major repairs.

7. *Maintenance.* In some countries, consumers consider the need for product maintenance as a key factor in making buying decisions. In other countries, they regard the need for maintenance as important but not a key factor. In both situations, adapting to market needs requires adjustments in product tolerance and durability.

8. *Climate.* Some countries' climates are so demanding that certain products require adjusting in order to function properly. Sensitive mechanical items, chemical-based products, food items (such as chocolate bars), and other products must be redesigned or reformulated.

9. *Product size.* In certain markets, cultural and other differences require that product size be altered from what it is in the home market. In addition, product sizes must conform to the country's measurement system. Furthermore, while the customary system of weights and measures has wide acceptance in the United States, the international metric system is more accepted abroad. A company attempting to sell products that do not conform to the local market's system of weights and measures ensures its own failure. The product, then, frequently must be both resized and recalibrated.

10. *Energy supply.* Energy availability may influence the product's size and power specifications. In countries with limited energy production, energy efficiency in products is highly important. In addition, in many countries, the energy specifications used for appliances and home electronics are not those used in the United States, and unless products have certain attachments or adjustments, they do not function properly.

11. *Availability of other products.* An international marketer attempting to sell products not suitable to a foreign market's local needs is destined for failure. Simply put, if the maker of Lean Cuisine wants to sell its frozen foods in Israel, it needs to offer *kosher* quality. Similarly, if the target country has a paper industry, to sell there, Xerox or Mita copiers must work with locally made paper.

12. *Raw materials.* The availability of raw materials and the way they are used force an international firm to adjust its products to local conditions. The Fiat Dachia is made in Romania and the Fiat

Polonaise is made in Poland, with from 40 to 50 percent of their content coming from materials produced in these two countries. If fuel is in scarce supply, cars, trucks, and tractors are fitted out with fuel-efficient engines. In Argentina, for example, many makes of autos are adapted to run on alcohol, because the country has scant petroleum resources.

13. *Unique market conditions.* Unique market conditions dictate product adaptation. As mentioned earlier, food products destined for Israel must be kosher. Rice and seaweed (among other foods) need special preparation in processing ready-made foods for the Japanese market. The British have certain barriers on imports of woolen content in their products.

Product Transfer and Adaptation by Mandatory and Nonmandatory Changes. The chances of transferring a product into a market with no adaptations whatsoever are slim. Only 1 product in 10 is transferred totally unchanged from a developed market into a developing one. This proportion is somewhat higher for goods transferred from a partly developed market to a developing one.

In considering transfer, MNCs have two options. The first option is to make only mandatory product changes, an appropriate strategy for international or flagship products (such as Coca-Cola, Ajax, Colgate Toothpaste, Pond's Cold Cream, and Canada Dry mixers), which give their marketers global identities. The second option involves thorough screening and, if necessary, making nonmandatory changes to reshape the product into a form that enhances its consumer appeal.

Up to 70 percent of product changes are not made to meet legal requirements but to strengthen the product's market appeal.

Aesthetic changes in packaging improve the product's appeal at the point of purchase. Package color is assessed with a view toward conveying favorable impressions. Colors denote different things in different parts of the world. The mourning color in the United States and Western Europe is black, but in Asia it is white, and in Latin America, it is purple. Patriotic colors such as red, white, and blue are effective in the United States, as are red and white in Japan. Green is associated with sickness in parts of Asia, and red is not well received in parts of Africa. When management assesses packaging requirements for a market, it seeks to substitute colors denoting joy, pleasure, or personal well-being for "unhappy" colors.

Product ingredients change for various reasons. Local ingredients may be superior, as Cheeseborough-Pond's discovered when it came upon an excellent oil for its nail-polish remover in Central Africa. Lever Brothers uses whatever oils are available in local markets for its margarine—cottonseed, fish, or other oils.

Sometimes, there are mandatory product changes in constituents. Candy manufacturers conform to a variety of laws on artificial sweeteners such as cyclamates, saccharine, and aspartame (G.D. Searle's Nutrasweeet). Searle in France found the use of aspartame blocked by a nineteenth-century law making sugar the only permissible sweetener. Because of religious restrictions against pork, Pillsbury in the Middle East substitutes vegetable shortening for animal fats in its cake mixes.

Protective packaging sometimes requires modification. For less affluent Mexican consumers, detergents in smaller quantities are put up in plastic packaging, at low prices. In tropical markets, Quaker Oats uses vacuum-sealed cans for its cereals. Such changes depend somewhat upon distributors' expertise and facilities. In most urban areas worldwide, there are few problems. Elsewhere, wholesaler-retailer expertise and facilities drop off dramatically, and stronger packaging to prolong shelf life is needed.

Product feature adaptations usually mean repositioning a brand. Repositioning to reflect a different appeal occurs for different reasons. Central African consumers handwash clothes, making the appeal of a low-suds detergent ineffective. Detergent marketers substitute a high-suds feature, which denotes superior washing power. Kellogg's Rice Krispies cereal has snack appeal in Mexico, so the product was advertised as a snack there. "Personal" product features are avoided in the high-context cultures of Asia and the Middle East—deodorants become "body sprays" and suntan products become "skin conditioners." Managers pretest products in markets looking for alternative sales features, but often, additional uses turn up only after a product is launched. Post-launch monitoring is important. For example, sanitary napkin marketers in Latin America discovered that their products were being used as dust masks for crop spraying.

Instructions are rarely changed in developing countries (only about one product in four or five). Some products require additional explanations of sales features. Cheeseborough-Ponds had a difficult time explaining to rural Africans that Vaseline Intensive Care lotion is "absorbed" into the skin (local buyers assumed it evaporated or was blown away). Eventually, the company settled on the term "soaks into" and used the analogy of water soaking into clothes.

A complex product needs explaining to buyers whether in developing markets or advanced ones. Even in the United States, 7 out of 10 owners of VCRs do not know how to take full technical advantage of them. Introducing toothpastes into societies where previously there were none requires special promotional effort. Companies such as Lever Brothers and Colgate-Palmolive use company-owned media (COM) and traveling entertainment shows to promote dental care and demonstrate proper usage. Film shows are interrupted with educational commercials demonstrating, for example, the way to use a toothpaste, the benefits of using laundry detergents, or the way to use a particular brand of self-rising flour in family cooking.

In multilingual markets (such as in Indonesia, Zaire, and Zimbabwe), instructions appear in several languages. This approach has also been widely adopted for European markets, where product instructions are in several languages (English, French, German, Dutch, Spanish, and Italian). In the United States, manufacturers selling in California, Texas, New Mexico, and Florida include instructions in Spanish for Hispanic market segments.

Brand names are rarely changed (other than translations) if an MNC wants to maintain some marketing uniformity worldwide. Schweppes found in the 1940s that U.S. consumers of their soft drinks had trouble pronouncing their British name. Subsequently, the company used an advertising campaign to teach American consumers the proper pronunciation.

PRODUCT INNOVATION TO MEET LOCAL NEEDS ■

Product innovation is almost an absolute necessity for firms pursuing multilocal marketing strategies. These firms develop products from scratch for particular markets.

Seven key factors must be taken into account in planning product innovations for local markets abroad: (1) target market, (2) environment, (3) government, (4) competition, (5) product characteristics, (6) packaging, and (7) service. In innovating a product for a specific international market, planners study the external factors prevailing in that market (see Table 11–4 items 1 through 4). These areas dictate the features that a product

TABLE 11–4 ■ *Planning for International Product Innovation*

External Factors	Internal Factors
1. The Target Market Who is likely to buy the product? Who is likely to use the product? How is the product likely to be used? Where is the product likely to be bought? How is the product likely to be bought? Why is the product likely to be bought?	**1. Characteristics of the Proposed Product** Size and physical characteristics Overall design materials used Weight and color
2. Environmental Conditions Geographic uniqueness Climatic characteristics Economic conditions Social differences Political profile	**2. Product Packaging** Product protection features Color and design Promotional aspects of the package Brand name and materials used
3. Government's Role Protective legislation Labeling requirements Patent and trademark rules Licensing requirements Condition for joint ventures Taxes and other influencing factors	**3. Product's Service Component** What kind of installation is needed? Repair and maintenance provisions Warranties and after-purchase service (e.g., adjustment) Availability of parts and components
4. Competition Prices of primary and secondary substitutes Performance of competitor's products Design and style of competing products Uniqueness and patent protection of competing products Brand name package and service for competing products	

needs for successful marketing in a particular market. However, there are also three internal factors that planners must take into account (see the internal factors listed in Table 11–4).

1. *Target market.* In designing a new product, the manufacturer must consider who is likely to buy the product, for what purpose, and how. For instance, a unique time-piece with a compass was designed especially for religious Muslims to remind them of daily prayer times and to help them locate the direction of Mecca. It is purchased by religious Muslims away from home or traveling or as a gift.

2. *Environment.* Some target markets are isolated and relatively inaccessible, making product repairs or parts procurement difficult and costly. These factors influence product design and manufacture. Special climatic conditions also influence product design, while economic conditions dictate whether the product is made by machine (requiring capital) or by hand (requiring cheap labor) and how it is priced. Furthermore, social characteristics of the target market affect product design and are reflected in products ranging all the way from pre-prepared foodstuffs to apparel and appliances.

3. *Government.* Through their protective legislation, governments decide what products and what repair and replacement parts are imported. Some countries have domestic laws protecting consumers that specify the pretesting and research standards that certain products must meet before being allowed in the country. Different governments require products to carry different amounts of consumer information, so there are varying requirements as to labels, product care, and use information. Patent and trademark rules also vary, facilitating or blocking the choice of local partners.

4. *Competition.* It is important to assess actual and potential competition in terms of primary and secondary substitutes for the product. In appraising competing products vis-à-vis a proposed product, their performance characteristics as well as their designs and styles are considered. If products already available in the target market are close substitutes to the projected product, the wisdom of market entry needs weighing. Decisions are needed on how to establish a competitive

edge in the product, its performance characteristics, and its design features.

5. *Product characteristics.* Specific characteristics of the proposed product are spelled out as to size, weight, color, and other features. Major determinants in deciding these characteristics are the needs of the target market and competitors' offerings.

6. *Packaging.* Packaging details are planned carefully. Different markets require different types of packaging.

7. *Service.* Developing a product from scratch necessitates planning the service needs. Without provisions for service needs all the way from installing to repairs, it is almost impossible to gain market acceptance.

Factors 5, 6, and 7 are primarily internal factors. Planners must decide which of these two groups of factors—internal or external—plays a more important role in the overall product innovation process.

INTERNATIONAL PRODUCT LIFE CYCLES

Product life-cycle analyses in domestic marketing detail the introduction, growth, maturity, and decline of individual products and brands. Internationally, life-cycle analyses enable marketers to track consumption and production trends in domestic and foreign markets.

Figure 11–4 shows two macro product cycles. The first is the cycle in the product's parent country. Production accelerates faster than consumption; before domestic consumption peaks, the product is being

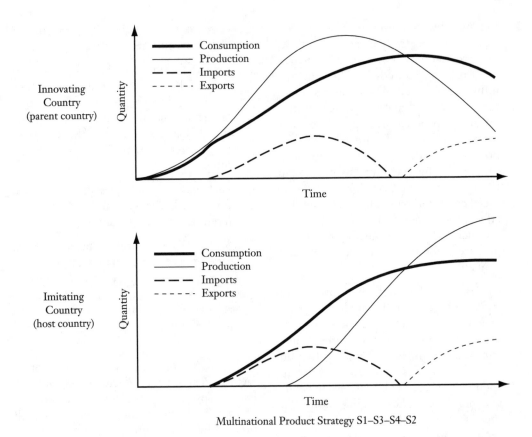

Multinational Product Strategy S1–S3–S4–S2

Source: Georges Leroy, *Multinational Product Strategy: A Typology for Analysis of Worldwide Product Innovation and Diffusion* (New York: Praeger Publishers, 1976).

FIGURE 11-4 *The International Product Cycle Theory*

exported and the country becomes a net exporter. Then, surpluses develop and production is cut, even while consumption is still rising. Finally, the parent country becomes a net importer.

The second cycle is the cycle in the host country where the innovating country's product is either imitated or received as a technology transfer. The consumption curve in the host country develops later than in the parent country. It takes time for a product to be accepted in its home country, and it takes even longer for a product to be accepted in foreign markets. When the product first gains acceptance in the host country, none of it is made there—the host country is a net importer. Later, the host country begins manufacturing the product, and productive facilities expand faster than the country's ability to absorb the output. At that point, the host country becomes a net exporter to other markets and even exports to the parent country. This is how many newly industrialized countries develop an active role in international markets. They learn from industrialized countries how to make the product, make it cheaper, and, sometimes, make it better, and thus become exporters.

INTERNATIONAL PRODUCT PORTFOLIO ANALYSIS

The Boston Consulting Group (BCG) originated an early version of product portfolio analysis. The BCG version classifies a company's products into four categories: stars, cash cows, problem children, and dogs (see Figure 11–5). The classification is based on market share and market growth rate.[8] The optimum product portfolio for one market is different from that for another. Product A, for example, may be a star in country X, a cash cow in country Y, and a dog in country Z.

The international marketer individualizes the use of the portfolio technique. Different portfolios are appropriate for different markets. Figure 11–6 shows how a company might decide to allocate its cash resources among different markets. This version of portfolio analysis is based on the attractiveness of the national market and the firm's ability to compete. If a market is attractive and the firm has high ability to compete, then the product is a star—this is a prime site and worthy of future cultivation. But if a market has low attractiveness and the company's ability to compete is low, then the product is a dog, indicating avoidance or divestiture. If a market is attractive but the company has low ability to compete, the product is a problem child, and the company needs to rethink its aspirations in that market. Relevant costs and benefits must be weighed before the firm can decide if a problem child can be transformed into a cash cow or a star. If a company in an unattractive market has a high ability to compete, the product is a cash cow. But a cash cow may be

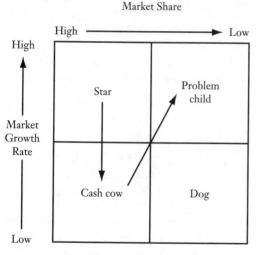

Market Share

Note: Arrows indicate preferred allocation of cash resources.

Source: Adapted with permission from Barry Hedley, "Strategy and the Business Portfolio," *Long Range Planning*, vol. 10, February 1977, Pergamon Press Ltd.

FIGURE 11–5 *International Product Portfolio Analysis*

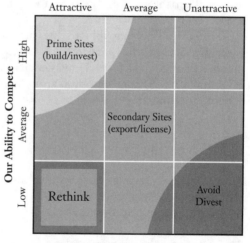

Source: Adapted with permission from S. J. Q. Robinson and D. P. Wade. "The Directional Policy Matrix–Tool Strategic Planning," *Long Range Planning*, vol. 11, June 1978, Pergamon Press, Ltd.

FIGURE 11–6 *Further International Considerations*

short lived unless market attractiveness improves. This version of product portfolio analysis provides numerous possible product states and product decision options.

Portfolio analysis of products for international sale is relatively new. The advanced version presented in Figure 11–6 is not yet in wide usage. Methods for determining market attractiveness are still being developed. While determining market potential is easy, determining market attractiveness is difficult. An attractiveness scale for a country would incorporate four variables: (1) aggregate market size, (2) rate of market growth, (3) government regulation, and (4) economic and political stability. The government regulation variable encompasses price control, monologation requirements (nontariff barriers such as local safety and product regulations), and local content and compensatory export requirements. The economic and political stability variable includes the degree of inflation and the trade balance. A rating system combining these four groups of variables makes it possible to calculate a country's attractiveness.[9]

Similarly, it is possible to measure a competitive strength by means of a system incorporating four factors: (1) market share, (2) product fit, (3) contribution margin, and (4) market support.

An Illustration

Assume XYZ Company wants to determine the attractiveness of countries A and B as markets for a low-priced washer that is both energy efficient and water efficient. Table 11–5 illustrates the components of an attractiveness scale and the weights assigned to its various components. Based on these scales, the attractiveness scores are presented in Table 11–6 as follows:

Country B is significantly more attractive than Country A. But let us also develop an absolute attractiveness rate from the standpoint of the XYZ Company. Assume that XYZ's past experience has been that any country scoring less than 40 points does not represent a good potential market for XYZ's product. That means Country B is attractive, but just barely so. The weights used in this illustration as well as the categories included only exemplify the suggested procedure. The weights and the categories require changing to suit the needs, experience, and skills of the company using the technique.

Table 11–7 is an illustration of the weights that might be used to determine a company's competitive strength. Based on these scales, competitive strength in Countries A and B is calculated (Table 11–8) as follows:

In Country B, the company's competitive strength is spectacular. In these examples, country attractiveness and competitive strength work in the same direction. But if the country attractiveness is positive and company competitive strength is negative, things become complicated. Management then must decide whether to increase the company's competitiveness or concentrate on the market with the highest attractiveness score.

INTERNATIONAL PRODUCT POSITIONING

Positioning a product for marketing begins with a set of possible specific products, describable as different bundles of attributes (each capable of generating a flow of benefits to buyers and users). The international marketing planner puts together these attributes into bundles so that the benefits created match the special needs of specific market segments. This product designing goes beyond deciding the four essential product components (physical, package, service, and

TABLE 11–5 ■ *The Components of an Attractiveness Scale*

COUNTRY ATTRACTIVENESS

Market Size		Market Growth	
Units	**Rating**	**Growth %**	**Rating**
25,000	10	5+	10
20,000–24,999	8	4–4.9	8
15,000–19,999	6	3–3.9	6
10,000–14,999	4	2–2.9	4
5,000–9,999	2	1–1.9	2
0–4,999	0	Below 1	0

GOVERNMENT REGULATION

Price Control		Homologation		Local Content	
Type	**Rating**	**Type**	**Rating**	**Type**	**Rating**
None	10	None	10	None	10
Easy to comply	6	Easy	6	Easy to comply	6
Moderately easy	4	Moderate	4	Moderately easy	4
Rigid controls	2	Heavy	2	Heavy	2

ECONOMIC AND POLITICAL STABILITY

Inflation		Trade Balance		Political Stability	
%/year	**Rating**	**%/year**	**Rating**	**Type**	**Rating**
10 and under	10	+5 and over	10	Stable	10
11–25	8	1–4.9	8	Moderate	5
26–40	6	0 to –5	6	Unstable	1
41–75	5	–5.9 to –10	4		
76–100	2	–11 to –20	2		
over 100	0	–20 and over	0		

Source: Adapted and revised from Gilbert D. Harrell and Richard O. Kiefer, "Multinational Strategic Market Portfolios," in *International Marketing*, 5th ed., ed. Philip R. Cateora (Homewood, Ill.: Richard D. Irwin, 1983).

country-of-origin) and encompasses the brand name, styling, and similar features.

Product positioning is viewed in a multidimensional space, commonly referred to as the "perceptual space" or "product space."[10] In terms of perceptual space, a particular version of a product is graphically represented as a point specified by its attributes. Competitors and other products are similarly located. If points representing other products are close to the point representing the prototype product, then these are products similar to the prototype.

TABLE 11-6 ▪ *Market Attractiveness of Countries A and B*

	Attractiveness of Country A	Attractiveness of Country B
Market size	4	6
Market growth	4	6
Price control	2	4
Homologation	6	4
Local content	6	4
Inflation	2	6
Trade balance	2	6
Political stability	1	5
Total	27	41

TABLE 11-7 ▪ *Competitive Strength of a Company*

MARKET SHARE

Percentage of Market		Position	
Share	Rating	Rank	Rating
30+	10	1	10
21–28	8	2	8
15–19	6	3	6
10–14	4	4	4
5–9	2	5	2
1–5	0		

PRODUCT FIT

The company's competitiveness based on 10 point subjective index to match product characteristics with key local product needs.

CONTRIBUTION MARGIN

Profit Per Unit		Profit Percentage of Net Dealer Cost	
Amount $	Rating	Amount %	Rating
$5,000	10	40+	10
3,000	7	30+	7
1,000	5	20+	4
500	3	10+	1
100	0		

TABLE 11–7 ■ *Competitive Strength of a Company (Continued)*

MARKET SUPPORT			
Market Representation No. and Quality of Distributors		**Advertising and Promotion of Company's Products**	
Evaluation	**Rating**	**Evaluation**	**Rating**
Excellent	10	Excellent	10
Average	6	Average	6
Weak	2	Weak	2
Poor	0	Poor	0

Source: Adapted and revised from Gilbert D. Harrell and Richard O. Kiefer, "Multinational Strategic Market Portfolios," in *International Marketing*, 5th ed., ed. Philip R. Cateora (Homewood, Ill.: Richard D. Irwin, 1983).

TABLE 11-8 ■ *Competitive Strength of ABC in Countries A and B*

	Competitive Strength of Country A	**Competitive Strength of Country B**
Percentage of market	6	8
Position	8	8
Product fit	5	7
Profit per unit	3	7
Profit percentage net dealer cost	1	7
Market representation	2	6
Market support	2	6
Total	27	49

If the prototype is positioned away from its closest competitors in the world markets and its positioning implies positive features, then it is likely to have a significant competitive edge. Figure 11–7 is a positioning map showing a product space map for automobiles in the U.S. The same type of mapping is possible for other countries and markets. This figure is based on American respondents' perceptions of 10 car makers, and the mapping is based on two features—performance and economy. This figure also shows the overall rating vector for automobiles—the direction in which the desirability of a car increases regardless of price. The vector was derived from the respondents'

answers to all overall rating questions for each car. By projecting each car's position on the vector through a perpendicular line (such as the one from Audi), the market segment's most popular choices are identified.[11] Similar analyses are made for different world markets and for other products such as TVs, VCRs, and compact disc players.

Summary

This chapter explained the concept of the consumer product for international markets and analyzed its four key components: the physical product, the package, service, and country-of-

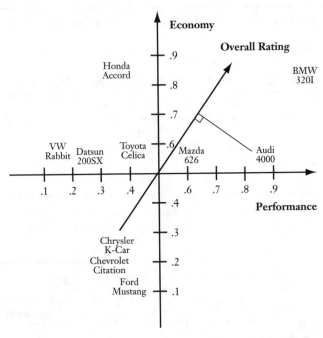

Source: "International Product Positioning," by John K. Johannson and Hans B. Thorelli, *Journal of International Business Studies*, Fall 1985.

FIGURE 11–7 *Automobile Space Map with Preference Vector (United States)*

origin identification. Strategic options for managing products were analyzed in terms of standardizing global products, adapting existing products, or developing new products from scratch for specific markets. Product cycles indicate that in the country from which the product originates (the parent country), productive facilities develop faster than consumption and the country exports the surplus to become a net importer. Similarly, the initiating or host country that imports the technology to make the product starts out as a net importer but evolves over time into a net exporter. Portfolio analysis of products for international markets, a technique developed originally by the Boston Consulting Group, suggests an advanced, two-dimensional mode, with the dimensions being international market attractiveness and the firm's ability to compete. Product positioning is an analytical technique for determining a product's positions in different international markets and for assessing the need for changes in positioning.

DISCUSSION QUESTIONS

1. If there are four components of consumer products for international markets, are there differences in the relative importance of these components on the basis of products or on the basis of the economic development stage of the target markets?

2. How can a firm avoid blunders in marketing products internationally?

3. How would you partially avoid such blunders by considering country of origin information?

4. Under what conditions should a company standardize, adapt, or localize its products?

5. Distinguish between localizing and adapting products. Is this difference realistic?

6. Are there other factors that directly influence product adaptation? What are they?

Casio Company

Casio Company makes watches and pocket calculators. Most of its competitors are organized around the traditional functions of engineering, manufacturing, and marketing. Furthermore, the competition has gone heavily into vertical integration. For example, many competitors own integrated-circuitry production facilities.

Casio remains basically an engineering, marketing, and assembly company with little investment in production facilities and sales channels. Its strength is flexibility. The company's functional strategy is to integrate design and development into marketing in such a way that consumers' desires are analyzed by those closest to the market and quickly converted into engineering blueprints. Because Casio has developed this function so well, it can afford to make its new products obsolete quickly.

Casio has two recent developments: First, a 2mm-thick, card-size calculator. Second, a model that emits musical notes as the numerical keys are touched.

QUESTIONS:

1. Describe and discuss the market-by-market entry strategy that Casio should follow. Give reasons why.

2. Do you foresee problems for Casio in the short run? In the long run? What kinds? Why?

Source: Adapted from Kenichi Ohmae, *The Mind of the Strategist* (New York: Penguin Books, 1982).

Pepsi-Cola in Romania

In Romania, Pepsi-Cola is a status symbol. While the local soft drinks, especially delicious fruit nectars, are sold for small sums, Pepsi is very expensive there. Young men, when they want to treat their favorite girl-friends "properly," buy Pepsi for them. Although this snob appeal is not objectionable to Pepsi, the company is not interested in setting precedents in such a way that only a group of privileged Romanians will drink Pepsi, nor does the company want the Romanian practice to occur in other Eastern European countries.

QUESTIONS

1. Why should Pepsi be objecting to this marketing practice in Romania? Explain.

2. What could Pepsi do (if anything) if it wanted to change the Romanian practice?

ASKO's New Product

ASKO washers and dryers, which were designed in Sweden, are both environmentally friendly and economical. They provide superior performance, durability, and convenience.

ASKO washers use as little as 11 gallons of water per load, while a conventional top-load washer uses from 40 to more than 60 gallons. This difference is based on the principle that agitator machines depend on submerging clothes, while tumble-action washers clean by lifting and dropping laundry in and out of the water hundreds of times during a cycle. Additionally, only half as much detergent is needed for a load of laundry washed in an ASKO unit. This is particularly important for septic systems.

An internal heater generates hotter water at a lower cost than a washer that is dependent on a home's hot-water heater. This also increases the effectiveness of laundry detergent, so no bleach is required. The savings in water and electricity bills, detergent, and bleach can total more than $200 a year, the company claims.

The ASKO wash cycle includes up to five rinses to remove soil and residual detergent, which otherwise would irritate sensitive skin. The ASKO washer spins the laundry at significantly higher speeds, removing more water, so clothes need less time and lower temperatures in the dryer.

ASKO washer and dryer tanks are made of surgical-quality stainless steel to last longer and resist rust and corrosion. Because of the availability of many of their parts, these products can be easily recycled.

Finally, ASKO washers and dryers do a better job with less noise and challenge to the environment than a conventional washer and dryer set.

QUESTION

1. Comment on the global marketability of this product. What features may be emphasized in which markets?

ENDNOTES

1 A. Coskun Samli, *International Consumer Behavior* (Westport, Conn.: Quorum Books, 1995).

2 Elaine Gross, "Commitment, Patience Key to Exporting," *Textile World*, October 1996, 74–77.

3 Warren J. Bilkey and Erik Nes, "Country-of-Origin Effects on Product Evaluations," *Journal of International Business Studies*, Spring–Summer 1982, 89–99.

4 Ibid.

5 A. Coskun Samli, "Importance of Product Information Cues to Global Marketing," in *Global Marketing*, ed. S.S. Hassan and R.D. Blackwell (Fort Worth, Tex.: The Dryden Press, 1994).

6 *Business Week*, 1 March 1967; and *Business Week*, 12 October 1981.

7 *Sales Management*, 1 March 1967, 31–38.

8 See James C. Leontiades, *Multinational Corporate Strategy* (Lexington, Mass.: Lexington Books, 1985); Gilbert D. Harrell and Richard O. Kiefer, "Multinational Strategic Market Portfolios" in *International Marketing*, 5th ed., ed. Philip R. Cateora (Homewood, Ill.: Richard D. Irwin, 1983), 397–406; and George S. Day, "Diagnosing the Product Portfolio," *Journal of Marketing*, April 1977, 29–30.

9 John T. Mentzer and A. Coskun Samli, "A Model for Marketing and Economic Development," *Columbia Journal of World Business*, Fall 1981, XV.

10 Johnny K. Johanson and Hans B. Thorelli, "International Product Positioning," *Journal of International Business Studies*, Fall 1985, 57–75.

11 Ibid.

CHAPTER **12**

Marketing Industrial Products Internationally

Chapter Outline

Learning Objectives

When you have mastered the contents of this
chapter, you will be able to do the following:

1 Explain what industrial products are,
   and why most of them require "think
   globally, act locally" strategies.

2 Discuss how manufacturers of industrial
   goods respond to worldwide competition by "thinking globally"; and why
   they emphasize technology, low-cost
   manufacturing sites, and intercompany
   coalitions.

3 Assess "act-locally" strategies in terms of
   target marketing, product, pricing, promotion, and distribution strategies.

4 Describe the nature of competition in
   industrial services and explain why
   industries such as banking and advertising utilize combinations of global and
   local strategies.

Industrial products and services are purchased for commercial use and are usually inputs into other firms' business processes. Machine tools, telecommunications, aircraft, computers, earth-moving equipment, chemicals, iron and steel, advertising, financial services, and accounting services are all part of the industrial sector.

In contrast to consumer products, industrial products require larger investments for their manufacture. They are purchased by skilled buying professionals, usually after considerable planning. Frequently, industrial products are critical to the manufacture of other products, and they often have derived demands that fluctuate with changes in demand for the consumer products they help to make. Because of these differences and the importance of integrated marketing mixes in industrial selling, managers pay extra attention to the nonproduct parts of marketing strategies.

There are some key differences in selling industrial products in domestic and international markets. One study, for instance, reported the following:[1]

- Buyers are more service oriented in some countries than in others in terms of the importance given to reliability, promptness of delivery, convenience in order placement, and flexibility in payment terms.

- Management styles or organizational structures that are workable in some countries do not work in others.

- International buyers exhibit considerable differences as to efficiency levels, motivation, leadership styles, pragmatism, intellectual caliber, and management effectiveness.

- Buying processes vary from country to country in terms of information processing and the utilization and participation of individuals.

- The product's country of origin affects buyers' evaluations.

- Industry by industry, the behavior of organizational buyers is similar in Australia, Canada, the United Kingdom, and the United States.

- International buying involves the interactions of four "exchange" elements (product/service, information, financial elements, and social elements). These interactions vary from country to country.

For marketers of industrial products and services to survive internationally, they must be technologically conscious, globally cost competitive, and responsive to individual markets. Ideologically, the general philosophy of these companies is "think globally, act locally." Most of this chapter will deal with the marketing of industrial products. It will conclude with a section on marketing industrial services.

GLOBAL COMPETITION AND INDUSTRIAL MARKETERS

The 1980s and 1990s have been traumatic for international marketers of industrial products. Four factors have made global industrial markets more competitive than ever before: free trade policies, political considerations, financial elements, and the increasing use of worldwide product standards.

The Free Trade Era

Since the 1947 General Agreement on Tariffs and Trade (GATT), the world has gradually become more oriented toward free trade. The Kennedy round of trade agreements in 1962 and the Tokyo trade agreements in 1979 encouraged world trade and made it easier for international companies to move products and components among markets. Companies in the computer equipment, software, medical equipment, automotive parts, and information services in particular have been propelled into the turbulent global markets for industrial products, as firms search international markets for top-quality components and services.[2] The formation of trade blocs such as NAFTA have similarly stimulated U.S. industrial suppliers to expand their export efforts into Canada and Mexico.[3]

Political Factors

Industrial companies are highly susceptible to political pressures. This susceptibility stems largely from the fact that in some countries, many large industrial companies were or still are government owned. In the mid-1980s, significant proportions of the postal, telecommunication, electricity, gas, railways, airlines, and steel industries in major world markets were government controlled.[4] The Tokyo agreements of 1979 made some progress in requiring governments not to favor domestic companies for local tenders. Yet, for political reasons, contracts for improvements in national infrastructure and government procurement are most often awarded to domestic companies. Two trends, however, have forced these industries to become more competitive: privatization and deregulation. Both of these trends are government efforts to stimulate competition.

THE PRIVATIZATION TREND ▪ Throughout the 1980s and 1990s, many publicly controlled industries passed into private hands. These included airlines, telecommunications, container terminals, electricity and energy suppliers, data processing, banks, mass transit systems, aerospace, steel, and airports.[5]

One major by-product of privatization was that companies became free to choose suppliers. For example, in the mid-1980s, the Japanese government opened up its $32 billion telecommunications industry to foreign suppliers. Soon after, Northern Telecom (a Canadian company) became Nippon Telephone and Telegraph's first foreign supplier with a seven-year, $250 million contract for large digital switches for use in public telephone networks. Northern Telecom's success in winning this contract was attributed to three factors. First, commitment of resources: The company expected to double its Japanese presence to 130 people as soon as the contract was obtained. Second, patience: Northern Telecom had courted NTT for five years before landing the contract, and it made no profits on it until 1989. Third, the company took pains to "Japanesize" its subsidiary, joining the appropriate trade and standards associations to keep abreast of industry developments.[6]

THE DEREGULATION TREND ▪ Deregulation has contributed to increased competition in many industries, most notably in banking, telecommunications, and airlines. Deregulation of banking and other financial institutions in the United States, Japan, and Europe resulted in fierce competition in world financial markets. Japanese banks, fueled by a domestic base of consumers with a high rate of savings (averaging 17 percent of incomes) and by companies earning more than $50 billion a year in trade surpluses, have accumulated $1.2 trillion worth of overseas banking assets (or double that of U.S. banks).[7]

In response to deregulation, British banks in the late 1980s began competing with building societies (similar to American savings and loan institutions) and with retailers (such as Marks and Spencer), who not only issued their own credit cards but also established themselves in stockbroking and selling mutual funds; British banks also had to compete with non-Japanese foreign banks such as Citicorp and Chase Manhattan and with American Express.[8]

In the international telephone business, deregulation transformed a "gentlemen's club into a business." The arrival in Europe of MCI and GTE Sprint resulted in competition for the $1.5 billion transatlantic telecommunications market. In response, deregulated British and Belgian telephone industries cut their rates to attract MNCs wishing to establish European communication hubs.[9]

Deregulation has caused major readjustments in many industries and markets.

- In the U.S., utilities such as gas, electricity, and water have moved from strategies stressing supply to those emphasizing new products and services dictated by market demand.[10]

- In Japan, the setting up of a no-frills airline to cut regular fares by as much as 50 percent.[11]

- The World Trade Organization was putting together a global agreement to facilitate international competition in telecommunications services.[12]

- A ten-step global program to reform education in the 21st century through deregulation and the introduction of competition into education. The program involves redefining learning with team-based concepts, eliminating credit hours and degrees, and emphasizing interactive critical thinking.[13]

Financial Elements

Exchange-rate realignments are critical elements in marketing industrial products because they affect the prices of goods and components moved between markets. Strong currencies in Switzerland and Germany over the period 1995–1996 caused downturns in export demands for machinery and auto exports;[14] while Mexico's peso devaluation caused surges in exports, particularly in chemicals.[15]

Establishment of World Standards

One by-product of the increasingly competitive world industrial markets has been the trend toward world standards in specific industries. Although American industry dominates many sectors, U.S. standards are not always adopted. For example, in telecommunications, the Japanese have been pushing for a worldwide X75 standard (already approved by the United Nations International Telecommunications Union and widely used in Europe and Japan). Most U.S. suppliers, including General Electric, do not comply with this standard, preferring to lock customers into their own systems.[16] In cellular phone telecommunications equipment, a Swedish company's (Ericsson) design for digital mobile radio transmission was adopted as the U.S. standard by the Cellular Telecommunications Industry Association, in spite of opposition from AT&T and Motorola.[17] The international trade picture has become complicated by the simultaneous existence of national, regional, and world standards in some industries. Efforts by regional bodies have been increasingly directed toward the adoption of international product standards.[18]

RESPONDING TO WORLDWIDE COMPETITION

Manufacturers of industrial products respond to worldwide competition by "thinking globally and acting locally."

Thinking Globally

One way that companies are meeting the upsurge in competition is by overhauling their research and development (R&D) capabilities to meet global technological standards. They are also reviewing their global manufacturing systems to minimize worldwide costs. And through crossborder coalitions, they are both spreading R&D costs over two or more companies and taking advantage of established distribution and sales networks.

MAINTAINING AND UPGRADING R&D CAPABILITIES

■ For many makers of industrial products, international marketplace success depends on product innovations (for example, electronics, telecommunications, and computers) and skill in diffusing new technologies throughout world markets. One major problem faced by high-tech industries is maintaining healthy R&D expenditures when global competition puts pressure on prices and profits. This pressure makes decisions on R&D organization critical. To get the most out of research resources, firms must first decide whether to centralize R&D capabilities, and second, whether to share development expenses with other companies or go it alone.

Arguments in favor of centralizing R&D include gaining the advantage of research on a large scale, easier communication and coordination of activities, better protection of expertise, and leverage with foreign governments on transferring or withholding technology.

A number of strategic factors impact the decision of where to locate R&D activities. For example, some countries take the lead in innovations in specific industries (U.S. for computer software, Japan for consumer electronics, Western Europe for high fashion). Being outside of the lead market deprives firms of the competitive stimulus that drives innovation. International firms also look for highly skilled R&D workers (e.g., Eastern Europe for engineers); or skilled, low-cost researchers (e.g., India for software development). Finally, R&D capabilities should be maintained in markets with highly demanding customers (e.g., U.S. auto buyers) and in countries with unique problems (e.g., pharmaceutical firms in nations with specific medical problems).[19]

One survey of Canadian marketing executives showed that 86 percent found foreign products valuable sources of new ideas. Many U.S. industrial companies subscribe to international new-product newsletters from Europe and Japan. In recent years, aseptic beverage cartons and pump dispensers for toothpaste have come from Europe.[20] In bioengineering and super-computer engineering, Japan is a major source of innovations. The European company Philips recognizes the importance of foreign R&D talent and maintains 4,000 people abroad in 8 major laboratories: Eindhoven (the Netherlands), Redhill (England), Hamburg and Aach (Germany), Paris (France), Brussells (Belgium), Briarcliff Manor (New York), and Sunnyvale (California). Philips's main concern had been to convert pure research into actual products and services; consequently, each research laboratory was associated with one of Philips's corporate businesses.[21]

A second major problem of high-tech industries is deciding whether to go solo on specific research projects or join forces with other companies. Philips has traditionally had as many as 60 joint research projects with other companies.[22] The trend towards intercompany coalitions not only spreads R&D risks and resources but also provides companies with access to distribution in other countries. The vast sums required to develop new jet aircraft and engines, for example, resulted in numerous joint projects, among them the French-German, British-Spanish development of the European

Airbus, Boeing's coalition with Japan and Italy on the Boeing 767 aircraft, and General Electric's work with Britain's Rolls-Royce on jet engines.[23]

GLOBAL MANUFACTURING STRATEGIES ■

Many makers of industrial products have streamlined their worldwide production systems. Caterpillar, after coming under fierce price competition from Komatsu in Japan and Fiatallis Europe in Italy, invested $1 billion in modernizing its 30 factories worldwide, combining just-in-time inventories, robotics, and computer-orchestrated material

---

China[a]

- Motorola USA and China Cellular Infrastructure Division (subscriber capacity: 60,000) signed a digital cellular telephone contract.

- Orga of Germany and several Shenzhen-based companies joined forces to produce 80 million smart cards by 1998.

- A joint venture was formed between SKF of Sweden and Wafandian Bearing in which Wafandian is to develop spherical roller bearings using SKF technology.

Others

- Solvay (Belgium) buys 60% of Bulgarian soda producer Sodi Devnya.[b]

- Deutsche Telecom and France Telecom acquire 30 percent of Sprint to form the world's largest packet data network, known as Atlas.

- Concert, a telecommunications joint venture has been formed between BT and MCI.

- AT&T formed an alliance with Unisource, a group of national telecommunications operators from Sweden, Switzerland, Netherlands, and Spain.[c]

- M.W. Kellogg (U.S.) and Chiyoda (Japan) join forces to design and build ethylene plants worldwide.[d]

[a] From "Industry Monitor," *Business China*, 3 March 1997, 10.

[b] From "What's New in Your Industry?" *Business Eastern Europe*, 24 February 1997, 8–9.

[c] Mary E. Thyfault, "Sprint's Global Alliance," *Information Week*, 10 July 1995, 74; and "Giants from Global Alliances," *Banking World*, March 1995, 31–33.

[d] J. Robert Warren, "Kellogg, Chiyoda in Ethylene," *Chemical Marketing Reporter*, 30 September 1996, 8.

FIGURE 12–1 *Global Alliance, Joint Ventures, Coalitions, and Consortia in Industrial Products*

supply and delivery systems. The company also moved into offsourcing (sourcing from overseas suppliers) of components and products.[24]

Many other makers of industrial products are following similar strategies. During the 1970s and early 1980s, high-tech companies went to Taiwan, Hong Kong, Singapore, and South Korea to take advantage of low labor costs. In the 1990s, these firms have moved to mainland China, Indonesia, and Malaysia to take advantage of low labor costs to assemble products.

BUILDING INTERCOMPANY COALITIONS AND CONSORTIA

■ While some industries, such as aircraft manufacturing, enter into coalition arrangements to spread financial risks and combine R&D expertise, others join consortia, which have other advantages. One is gaining access to foreign markets through other companies' distribution systems. For example, Italy's Olivetti established liaisons with the United State's AT&T to sell Olivetti personal computers in the United States. Olivetti also gained access to the British and continental European markets by buying a controlling interest in Acorn Computers in the United Kingdom and by purchasing Exxon's office-systems business and dealer network on the continent. In another deal, AT&T gave Italian semiconductor maker SGS the European marketing rights to its computer chips, and it contracted with Toshiba to sell AT&T office automation equipment in Japan.[25]

These examples and those in Figure 12–1 indicate that technology, low-cost production, and marketing strength are the key ingredients for global success of companies marketing industrial products. Within individual countries, though, it is localized marketing and support systems that clinch the sale. These aspects of marketing industrial products are now examined.

Acting Locally

CHARTING THE BEHAVIOR OF INTERNATIONAL INDUSTRIAL BUYERS

■ In order to act locally, marketers must understand how industrial buyers behave in different parts of the world. Motivation to buy is either a group or an individual phenomenon. In countries where individuals defer to group desires, motivation to buy commonly requires a consensus decision. In some authoritarian countries, motivation to buy is ordained from industry officials or government hierarchies.[26]

One general model (Figure 12–2) has been proposed that helps industrial marketers to localize international marketing efforts.[27] Much company buying in international situations is done by industrial buying units within customers' organizations. Six factors affect the buying unit's behavior: individual, environmental, organizational, societal, uncertainty, and governmental factors.

Individual. In some societies, individuals are more important than groups in buying situations. In traditional societies, for example, department heads make decisions for entire buying units, with subordinates playing minor roles. In Saudi Arabia and Middle Eastern countries, family power and connections predominate. In other countries, especially in Latin America and Africa, politicians are the keys to unlocking markets. In Japan, many individuals both inside and outside of buying units must be met and influenced. Marketers of industrial goods know that they must investigate the backgrounds of purchasing managers to identify optimal buying approaches.

Environmental. Company performance and buying-unit activities are affected by such environmental factors as inflation and economic cycles. Marketers must study these

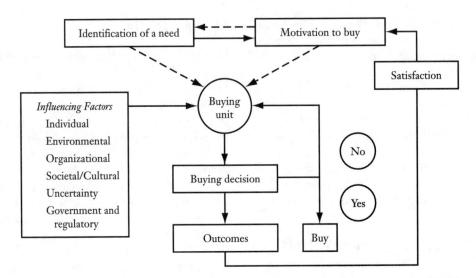

Source: A.C. Samli, P. Grewal, and S. Mathur, "International Industrial Buyer Behavior," *Journal of the Academy of Marketing Science*, Summer 1988, 21. Reproduced with permission.

FIGURE 12–2 *Influences on Industrial Buying Unit Behavior: A General Model*

factors and also evaluate the client company's customers.

Organizational. In evaluating organizational factors, sellers must ask several key questions: What are the organization's goals and objectives? How centralized is the organization and its buying activities? How well is the company doing? What are its competitive advantages? How does the buying unit operate within the total organization?

Societal. Societal factors are especially important. Japan, in particular, has attracted much attention because of its traditional culture and high-performance economy (see Chapter 16 on personal selling and negotiation). Beliefs, attitudes, family patterns, and business practices are all critical societal factors.

Uncertainty. Dealing with the uncertainty factor determines whether transactions take place smoothly and whether repeat business

is likely in the future. Important questions must be asked: Under what time pressures is the buying unit working? What sorts of risks are considered by members of the buying unit? What kind of purchasing agreements are they likely to request?

Governmental. All industrial transactions are affected to a greater or lesser extent by government regulation. Marketers should ask these questions: Are there special government goals or controls that may influence the buying unit? What, if any, are the legal constraints influencing this transaction (for example, special contractual provisions)? Are there trade restrictions that might affect the transaction (such as special licenses needed for export)? Does government bureaucracy need to be dealt with? Are bribes necessary to get action and are they legal? How stable is the present government? If changes in the government occur, will they interfere with future transactions?

In addition to regulation, governments influence industrial transactions by their great purchasing power. All governments are large purchasers of products and services. They begin by developing "shopping lists," which contribute to their own economic plans. Marketers must identify what needs are on these lists.

EFFECTIVE LOCAL MARKETING STRATEGIES
▪ After charting buyer behavior, companies must develop local marketing strategies.

Locating Target Markets. Industrial marketing is business-to-business marketing, so locating potential customers for industrial goods is easier than it is for consumer products. Business directories, company specifics compiled by commercial attachés at overseas embassies, government lists, trade associations, and chambers of commerce are all good sources for identifying potential clients.

Mandatory Adaptations. A successful market strategy usually includes mandatory adaptations, which are essential before products can enter foreign markets. Examples are adjusting electrical voltages from U.S. 110-volt to European 220-volt standards and left-hand to right-hand drives for cars. When Eastman Kodak entered the European photocopier market, it did not redesign its product line to suit European tastes; instead, it made only necessary changes, including: (1) altering keys on control panels to conform to local language requirements, (2) incorporating an optical system that could reduce images to any reasonable size (a feature it later built into the entire Eastman North American line), (3) conforming to the specifications of European electrical systems in wiring and voltage, and (4) adding safety doors to meet European product safety standards.[27]

Nonmandatory Adaptations for Product Differentiation. Many companies, such as makers of computers, medical equipment, and telecommunications equipment, rely on a strategy of superior technological design and competitive pricing to be effective in the local marketplace. Yet to meet competition, other companies find they must do something to differentiate their products. Redesigning products for individual customers is prohibitively expensive; therefore, these companies make minor changes, such as cosmetic adjustments and individualized service-related components.

Some companies go further, as Komatsu did to challenge Caterpillar in the global earthmoving-equipment market. In the early 1980s, Caterpillar was the undisputed leader in the field, with more than 50 percent of the world market. The problem for competitors was that "Cat" was well respected by the industry it served, and it was difficult for competitors to get and maintain customer attention over anything but short time periods. Komatsu examined Caterpillar's product line and its customers; then it initiated a product differentiation strategy.

First, it built machines that were slightly heavier or had more horsepower than equivalent Caterpillar machines. For example, Komatsu built a 720-horsepower hydraulic excavator to compete with Cat's 700-horsepower D-I0. Second, Komatsu opted for continuous differentiations of its product lines. For example, it produced an amphibious bulldozer; a remote-controlled bulldozer for deep-mine work; a quiet, electric-powered, fume-free bulldozer; and instrument panels with automatic warnings about overheating and product abuse warnings. These warnings were spoken in sexy female voices and came in any one of a dozen different languages.[29]

Service Differentiation. When products break down, disruption occurs in some part of the user's entire operation. This provides industrial marketers with opportunities to use a strategy of distinguishing products on the basis of the firm's superior servicing ability. During Komatsu's worldwide onslaught against Caterpillar, the one aspect of Caterpillar's corporate strategy that Komatsu was unable to match was its marketing network, which featured more than 200 dealerships worldwide. These dealers provided backup services through a comprehensive communications network. To counter this advantage, Komatsu produced low-maintenance machines.

In some industries, service has superseded product sales as the major revenue earner. As computer hardware became increasingly standardized, European computer companies staked out positions as service suppliers rather than equipment sellers. Nixdorf, Europe's fifth largest computer company, reorganized itself to act as a consulting service, integrating other companies' systems and custom-building softwares. IBM also recognized this trend and established Finesse, a data communications network, to serve the European financial-services industry, especially firms in the insurance and brokerage fields.[30]

DISTRIBUTION, PROMOTION, AND PRICING OF INDUSTRIAL PRODUCTS

Distribution

There are two basic ways to distribute most industrial products: direct sales through a sales force, direct marketing through other media, and indirect sales through dealer-distributor networks. The trend has been away from costly sales forces toward direct marketing (which relies heavily on mail, telephone, and fax) and indirect sales.

DIRECT SALES: SALES FORCES ■ Sales of large or complex products (such as computer systems, telecommunications networks, and specialty medical equipment) and sales to original equipment manufacturers (OEMS) are usually handled directly through salespersons or, more frequently today, sales teams. The costs of fielding and maintaining sales forces are on the rise, so industrial marketers look for ways to use their salespersons more cost effectively. Three methods that are gaining popularity are salesperson pooling, telephone marketing, and global sales information systems.

Salesperson Pooling. Salesperson pooling occurs when companies with noncompeting lines agree to share a joint sales force. This sales force makes a contracted number of sales calls in a specific region for a given price, with each salesperson working for a maximum of four clients. Breckhill Ltd., a British company, initiated this method in the construction and light manufacturing sectors.[31]

Telephone Marketing. Telephone marketing by salespersons is aimed at making face-to-face selling time more efficient by cutting down on unnecessary calls. In the 1980s, Lever Ltd., a British company, reduced its direct sales force from 165 persons to 100. Instead of personally visiting 9,000 stores, they called on only 1,300 stores and telephoned the remainder.[32]

Global Communications Systems. Minebea, a Japanese manufacturer of high-precision mechanical and electromechanical components, coordinates its sales and promotional efforts for more than 50 manufacturing and 200 sales and service centers through its

Lotus Notes communications program. This coordinates corporate, regional, and remote users for sales and marketing teams in Asia and Europe via a worldwide mail system.[33]

DIRECT SALES: INTERNATIONAL DIRECT MARKETING

▪ As tariffs and other trade barriers fall, direct sales abroad increase. One of the ways manufacturers of industrial products have tried to cut sales costs is to reduce sales forces and concentrate their efforts on international direct marketing (IDM). This form of direct sales, which U.S. and European firms use to tap foreign markets, is especially popular because of advances in international communications. Airmail reaches every part of the world. AT&T and other companies now offer toll-free international numbers, enabling customers to place orders directly to manufacturers.[34] Fax machines have made communications easier not only between firms but also between marketers and their customers.

Advantages of International Direct Marketing. Direct marketing has many uses, including preselling customers and identifying sales prospects. For example, Bristol Sidderley, a British company, set out to sell small aircraft in the United States. To ascertain the degree of interest in its product, this firm obtained a list of likely American customers, who were mailed sales brochures along with offers of historic aircraft prints. A 45 percent response rate enabled the company's sales team to locate and zero in on prospects, making their U.S. sales trip very productive, with about $50 million worth of sales obtained.[35]

International direct marketing has advantages over other forms of market entry. It requires relatively little investment (compared to a joint venture or wholly owned subsidiary, for example). Also, it is flexible in that many markets can be approached simul-

taneously, the only limitation being availability of foreign mailing lists. Feedback from customers is obtained quickly, and as a result, marketing mixes are adjustable to market conditions.

International Direct Marketing Strategies. International direct marketing strategies generally involve combining suitable mailing lists (in the case of direct mail) with appropriate messages to consumers. In the United States, marketers obtain lists at prices between 8 and 15 cents per name. In Europe, appropriate lists are likely to cost between 25 cents and $1.00 per name, with European-wide lists being more expensive. Some companies develop their own lists from commercial registers, directories, overseas embassies, trade associations, and international chambers of commerce. Some foreign lists are obtainable from U.S. sources. Lists of Asian subscribers to *Newsweek* are obtainable for a few hundred dollars per thousand names; *Business Week Asian, The Wall Street Journal,* and *Fortune* offer similar services. However, there are problems in executing IDM strategies. These include variable qualities of foreign lists, additional expenses in translating direct-mail pieces where English cannot be used (for example, in Japan), and variable perceptions of direct mail's usefulness (positive in Sweden and Germany but negative in France). Finally, in some European countries, regulations blunt the effectiveness of direct marketing. In Europe, direct mailers often avoid personalizing commercial pieces because of restrictions prohibiting anyone other than the addressee from opening mail. Also in Germany, it is forbidden to offer free gifts to prospects.[36]

Many large companies are relying more and more on direct marketing in their international sales efforts. IBM's direct sales went from nothing in 1992 to $10 billion in 1996, with $2.3 billion generated from telesales (catalog, mail, etc.) and $7.7 billion coming from phone sales. Europe accounted for $3.2 billion; next came Asia at $1.2 billion, followed by Latin America at $600 million.[37]

INDIRECT SALES: DEALER-DISTRIBUTOR NETWORKS

■ The other way manufacturers of industrial products cut sales costs is by reducing sales forces and building networks of dealers and distributors. This trend has been encouraged by two factors. First, this approach cuts marketing costs for manufacturers because dealers are allowed to stock products from numerous OEMs. Second, it is convenient for manufacturers to have dealers arrange and coordinate service arrangements.

Some companies work through intercompany coalitions and consortia to build marketing networks abroad. Rank-Xerox, the British-based joint venture subsidiary of the U.S. Xerox Company, sells office-systems equipment (particularly electronic printers) from different OEMs. At the same time, Xerox's printers are also being marketed by Siemens, a German company, which integrates them into its computer mainframe systems. Xerox's printers are also sold by the U.S.-based Digital Equipment Company in its European marketing operations.

Other companies, including many Japanese firms, are building their own exclusive networks. This process is part of a long-term strategy that makes initial use of local distributors to "test" their products. Then, after fine-tuning their marketing mixes, these firms put resources into their own networks.[38] Canon and Ricoh are implementing this type of strategy in Europe, with Canon's British dealers handling only Canon products.[39]

Promotion

Industrial products are generally promoted differently from consumer goods. Technical and scientific magazines are used to solicit inquiries, and follow-ups via personal selling are common. Trade fairs, exhibitions, and technical seminars are used to identify prospects and make sales pitches.

Companies must also decide how global their promotions must be. IBM conducts global, regional, and local campaigns for their products. The company uses global standardized campaigns for their 19 core software products, because their use is identical worldwide and they are sold the same way everywhere. Other campaigns might be regional. One campaign devised for a banking terminal unique to Europe was centrally produced and then customized for local European partners who provided the service, terms, and conditions in individual country markets. Finally, local campaigns are necessary in some parts of the world. Call centers were opened in Beijing and Shanghai to promote sales in China.[40]

NEW DEVELOPMENTS IN INDUSTRIAL ADVERTISING

■ **Corporate Image Advertising.** The increased use of dealer-distributor networks has made many companies users of showrooms. Mass-market advertising has become a popular means of attracting buyers to these showrooms. In Europe's fast-growing microcomputer market, companies such as Apple and Compaq focus major efforts on building dealerships, but they use Europe-wide corporate-image advertising to build reputations among a broad range of potential customers.[41]

Globalization of Industrial Goods Messages. Promotional trends in industrial goods are toward balancing inputs from headquarters with degrees of local control over advertising content and execution of strategy. For example, in Western Europe, satellite transmissions across countries were making unified messages feasible. European broadcasters expanded the European Business Channel (EBC) to offer breakfast-time world business briefings in a two-language format (English and German); they added briefings in French, Italian, and Spanish. EBC's primary target audiences are business people, financiers, civil servants, and politicians; it numbers among its advertisers IBM, Nixdorf Computer, British Petroleum, and Exxon.[42]

Advertising agencies have responded to these trends by setting up special Europe-wide networks to aid industrial marketers. BBDO Worldwide was the first to establish an affiliate, BBDO Business Communications, to coordinate an eight-country networking operation. A major competitor is Dialogue International, a 22-country network of independent agencies coordinated by Anderson and Lembke, a Swedish firm. These networks enable their organizers to pitch for international accounts and multinational advertising campaigns.[43]

Exhibitions and Trade Shows. Other opportunities for companies to showcase their products and technologies are exhibitions and trade shows. Euroshop '96—the International Trade Fair for shop-fitting, display, and merchandising—attracted over 900 exhibitors, and Softbank Comdex's software show in the U.K. attracted 250 exhibitors and over 30,000 prospective buyers.[44]

Many large companies, however, especially those with specialized technologies, are convinced that large trade shows dilute the impact of their offering. Many have turned to smaller, specialized shows or their own company exhibitions. For example, the International Chilled Food Festival held in Germany was a spin-off from the larger food exhibitions. IBM's British subsidiary put on a single-company, 11-day exhibit. In Scandinavia, the trend has been toward traveling exhibitions.[45]

Seminar Selling. Whenever new technologies are introduced, seminar selling is valuable. It is an efficient means to educate potential users and line up sales prospects. MetCoils Systems Corporation, a Cedar Rapids, Iowa, machine-tool maker, held a one-day seminar on its sheet-metal-shaping machines at the former Soviet Union's world trade center. More than 90 people attended the seminar, which cost about $30,000 to present, but company representatives estimated that sales tracing to the seminar could run as much as $1.5 million. The company followed up with visits to Soviet firms, hosting a Soviet delegation at the Cedar Rapids headquarters, and with the presentation of an exhibit at Metaloobrabodka, the Soviet machine-tool show.[46] Seminar selling also keeps selling costs down. Software specialist Lotus Development Canada uses a variety of seminars, each designed to reach particular customer segments. Getting customers to come to the company allows Lotus to economize on maintaining large sales forces.[47]

Pricing

Price-setting decisions for industrial products vary according to whether the item is a new or existing product. For a new product, a tentative price is determined by considering production costs, market conditions, and competitive activities. If test marketing is warranted (which depends on how new or innovative the product is), then different pricing strategies can be evaluated.

For existing product lines, price reviews occur when there are changes in costs or market conditions (for example, inflation or actions by competitors). If price increases are contemplated, effects on demand are balanced against the advantages of not increasing prices. For example, if a company looks upon itself as a market leader and offers superior products or services, or has extremely loyal customers (as IBM does), then it may feel confident in passing on cost increases to customers or in not retaliating against price-cutting competitors. Pricing decisions are then passed along to foreign sales offices, which factor in exchange-rate realignments with in-market adjustments (discount rebates, cash discounts, and the like). Final price adjustments are made depending on whether the product is "exclusive" (which provides some price-setting latitude) or "common" (price is dictated by the market).

Industrial products such as telecommunications, construction equipment, and heavy machinery are often part of the economic plan of developing countries. Because these are big-ticket items and developing countries are usually unable to free up sufficient dollars, pounds, francs, or yen, barter is often the way to obtain industrial goods. The International Reciprocal Trade Association noted that barter transactions accounted for over $8 billion of trade in 1994. The American Countertrade Association similarly estimated that barter accounted for 25 percent of world exports.[48] Companies such as General Cable Corp., Witco Corp., and Pam and Frank Industrial Co., have used corporate barter (whereby business services and products are exchanged among firms) to do business particularly in Eastern Europe.[49]

Schiess AG, a German machine-tool manufacturer, had problems selling in Eastern Europe because of hard-currency shortages. The company solved the problem by importing Soviet machine tools from Stanko import, the Soviet state trading organization, and upgrading them to meet Western needs by adding hydraulic options, electronic controls, and measuring systems. Using hard currency freed up by this operation, Venbore Sedin, one of the Russian

machine-tool makers, imported tools and parts for sale in the Russian market.[50] Examples of similar deals are shown in Figure 12–3.

MARKETING INDUSTRIAL SERVICES

Industrial services include banking, advertising, accounting services, construction, consulting, and similar industries. Where industrial products are tangible objects, industrial services are intangible—the performance of deeds. Where many services are linked to a product (as discussed earlier), many industrial services are on a "stand alone" basis (that is, they are pure services).

Adjusting to Local Circumstances

Companies that provide industrial services take into foreign markets sets of skills and processes developed in the home market (such as advertising and construction), but their applications abroad are heavily influenced by local factors. For example:

- *Construction and architectural services* must conform to local building codes, and the end product must not clash with local building aesthetics. However, foreign construction materials and architectural methods are often usable.

- *Advertising agencies* must operate within local advertising standards. They must also work around obstacles such as undeveloped media, noncommercial media, and shortages of skilled advertising personnel. Nevertheless, more than 75 percent of U.S. agency affiliates abroad work on multicountry campaigns.[51]

- *Accounting firms* such as Arthur Young, Ernst and Whinney, and Klynveld Main and Goerdeler typically earn between one-third and three-quarters of their revenues outside their home markets.[52] Their foreign offices must conform to local accounting and taxation principles; yet in the case of MNCs, they must be flexible enough to incorporate local accounts into MNC accounting systems.

Competing in the World Services Market

BANKING ▪ Global banking was long dominated by U.S. concerns such as Citicorp, Chase Manhattan, and Bank of America, but by 1989, the top 5 banks and 14 of the top 20 were Japanese.[53] Fueled by huge trade surpluses and a protected domestic financial market, which accumulates about $1 billion daily in savings,[54] the Japanese now heavily influence world banking. In stock trading, Japan's Nomura Securities is 10 times bigger than the largest U.S. securities broker, Merrill Lynch, and the Eurobonds market denominates one-fifth of its bonds in yen.

By the mid-1990s, the global banking industry had again changed. The top 10 banks worldwide included National Westminster (UK), the Netherland's ING Bank, Swiss Bank Corp., France's Credit Lyonnais, Deutsch Bank, Mitsubishi Trust and Banking, and National Australia Bank. Deregulation had forced some banks to retreat back into their national markets. Others, including the world's top global

---

1. Turner Broadcasting set up an office in London to trade airtime on CNN and TNT/Cartoon Network in exchange for the advertisers' product.[a]

2. After the lifting of the UN trade embargo, Serbia was looking to set up barter deals to rebuild international trade channels with the outside world. Serbia has an acute foreign exchange shortage.[b]

3. The bread crisis in Bulgaria forced the government to lift a ban on sunflower seed and oil exports so that they could barter oil for wheat. The country has a serious foreign currency exchange shortage.[c]

4. China's Inner Mongolia autonomous region bartered coal in return for the construction of new power plants.[d]

[a] Alasdair Reid, "Will Turner's Proposed Barter System Meet with Approval?" *Campaign London*, 5 April 1996, 22.

[b] "Serbia Tries to Rebuild Trade," *Project and Trade Finance*, February 1996, 29.

[c] "Bread Crisis in Bulgaria," *Eastern European Markets*, 30 August 1996, 2–3.

[d] "Inner Mongolia's Ambitious Power Generation/Export Plans," *East Asian Executive Reports*, 15 May 1996, 10–11.

FIGURE 12–3 *Examples of Barter Deals Facilitating the Trading of Industrial Goods and Services*

banks, went on corporate buying sprees and extended their influences into major world markets. Some specialization occurred as banks realized the need to segment their markets and focus on particular niches (industrial financing, home mortgages, consumer credit, etc.).[55] Increasingly, international banks have globalized their investment functions and localized the consumer sides of their businesses to counter fierce competition from insurance companies, finance companies, and the financial arms of industrial companies.[56]

Local presences are essential in world banking, so international banks, like international manufacturers of industrial goods, position themselves as local entities in their major markets. But many are starting to tighten controls over their worldwide branch networks. Deutsche Bank, a top 20 global bank, is forging its 41-country operations into a strong international network and is

---

To help U.S. risk managers become *au courant* about pollution liability coverage in Europe, we have prepared the following analysis.

Belgium. The policy type is general liability, on either an occurrence or claims-made basis. Damages covered include sudden and accidental property damage and bodily injury liability, pure financial losses, and, sometimes, gradual property damage liability.

The policy wording is pollution occasioned by "an unforeseen, abnormal and unintentional event."

France. The policy type is general liability on a claims-made basis, plus N.E.S.P., a separate policy for cleanup expenses. Damages covered include property damage and bodily injury for an "unforeseeable event." Some gradual coverage is available (not excluded) if the policyholder acts in accordance with laws and regulations.

The policy wording contains no "sudden" requirement but specifies that it must be an "unforeseeable event." Pollution of "soil, atmosphere or water" is included in the general liability policy wording. Coverage is also available for "pollution from noise, temperature, smell, vibrations and natural radiation."

Germany. The policy type is general liability on an occurrence basis, plus a separate water pollution liability policy. Damages covered include sudden property damage and bodily injury liability, pure financial losses, and cleanup if the latter prevents imminent third-party damage.

Germany's comprehensive environmental impairment policy wording covers only "damage to water, air and soil that results from the breakdown of normal operations."

FIGURE 12–4 *Pollution Liability: Business Insurance Guidelines for European Countries*

positioning itself as the Europe-wide investment bank, specializing in asset management for institutional investors.[57]

Japanese banks are setting up financial beachheads in the major centers and establishing strong local presences. There are 40 Japanese banks in Switzerland. In London, there are 29 Japanese banks, 22 Japanese insurance companies, and 52 Japanese securities companies; while New York has 50 Japanese financial concerns.[58] Thus, the "think globally, act locally" strategy also applies to financial services.

ADVERTISING ▪ Advertising became a global industry in the 1980s, with Saatchi and Saatchi leading the acquisition-oriented rush into international markets. More recently, rapid growth of the advertising industry outside the United States (which accounts for about one-half of the world's advertising) and the increasing popularity of global advertising

---

It is expected that bodily injury and property damage arising from water pollution hazards will be subject to these restrictions in the near future. Other expected changes include pure financial/cleanup losses that are substantially reduced by a sublimit, as well as an exclusion for owned property.

Italy. The policy type is general liability on a claims-made basis. Sudden and gradual pollution coverage is excluded.

ANIA, the Italian pollution coverage pool, provides sudden and accidental as well as gradual pollution coverage on a claims-made basis. Pure financial losses and cleanup expenses to prevent third-party damage are also available.

Netherlands. The policy type is general liability on an occurrence basis. Damages covered include sudden and accidental damage and bodily injury liability.

The policy wording excludes liability for damages as a result of environmental pollution as defined within the policy "unless the environmental pollution concerns a sudden and accidental occurrence that is not the direct result of a slowly acting process."

Spain. The policy type is general liability on either an occurrence or claims-made basis. Damages covered include sudden and accidental property damage and bodily injury liability, plus salvage or cleanup costs when sudden and accidental is available.

Under the policy wording, no liability coverage "unless such seepage, pollution or contamination is caused by a sudden, unintended, unexpected happening during the period of the insurance policy."

campaigns have made overseas presences essential for many U.S. agencies.

Then, too, as their industries have globalized, companies have also internationalized their advertising campaigns. Bankers Trust unveiled a 56-market global print campaign to emphasize their global resources, innovation, and performance; and Electronic Data System Corp. and Amnesty International initiated their first global campaigns in 1996.[59]

Again, paralleling the trend among international marketers of industrial products, merger-and-acquisition strategies are part of agencies' strategies to broaden their global influence. Leading the way have been large agencies such as Saatchi and Saatchi Advertising Worldwide, McCann-Erickson Worldwide, J. Walter Thompson, and Grey Advertising. This has put considerable pressure on smaller players, who are forced to play "catch-up." The American agency TBMA (part of the Omnicom Group) bought majority stakes in agencies in Brazil, Hong Kong, and Singapore to boost its international exposure.[60]

INDUSTRIAL INSURANCE AND BROKERAGE ▪

In the 1980s, the insurance industry went global to offer its domestic clients worldwide coverage. International companies have many special uses for foreign insurance. They need it to insure against risks not only of fire but also of confiscation and damage from war, revolution, or insurrection. They need to secure protection against legal damages for worker injury and involvement in environmental and pollution accidents. U.S. insurance brokers offer global programs to American clients featuring worldwide insurance rates, common worldwide standards for asset conservation, and good citizen status as to local insurance laws.[61]

But regulatory and legal requirements make for substantial differences among countries. For example, Europeans are sensitive to environmental pollution, with each country having its own laws. In handling these risks, insurers use separate sets of guidelines for each country (see Figure 12–4). Notice that, in most cases, coverage is only for "unforeseen, abnormal or unintentional events" (see Belgium). Some countries require insurance policies with clean-up provisions (for example, France, Germany, Italy, and Spain). In line with the 1992 European unification scheme, efforts have been made to consolidate individual country laws and the more than 100 European Community legislative measures into a cohesive set of comprehensive insurance laws.

SUMMARY

Global industrial products and service markets are becoming increasingly competitive. Free trade movements have contributed to unified product standards. Privatization and deregulation of formerly protected markets such as telecommunications and airlines are causing firms to become more competitive and to emphasize product innovations and cost-competitive global manufacturing strategies.

To maintain competitiveness in individual markets, international firms use acquisitions of, and coalitions with, local firms to acquire technologies and to gain access to local distribution systems. To complete the "act locally" part of the "think globally, act locally" strategy, companies invest heavily in dealer-distributor networks and promote their offerings through diverse advertising media, exhibitions, trade shows, and educational seminars. Barter and buy-back strategies are often part of the pricing package for big-ticket industrial products.

Industrial services (such as advertising, accounting, and insurance) originally go overseas to serve home-market clients in their international expansion. Though these service providers take certain skills and proven knowledge overseas with them, often they must tailor their services to meet local market needs and to conform to local regulatory environments.

DISCUSSION QUESTIONS

1. Define the following terms and give industry and product examples where possible: privatization, deregulation, intercompany coalitions and consortia, mandatory product adaptations, service-differentiation strategies, international direct marketing.

2. You are part of a telecommunications company industrial buying unit. Map out a tentative strategy for buying cellular phones from Asia, using Figure 12–3 as your guide.

3. What are the advantages and disadvantages of using direct marketing to exploit foreign markets? What sorts of products do you think can be direct-marketed internationally? Why?

4. You are about to sell $3 billion of telecommunications equipment to an Eastern European country. Finally, the government of that country approaches you to say that it is short of hard currencies to pay you over the five-year contract. What options do you have and which would you select? Why?

5. For what sorts of products or services would you use seminar selling? How might you set up such a seminar?

The Race to Semiconductor Leadership

- A street map of the world etched on a thumbnail sliver of silicon.

- Desktop computers that do the same jobs as mainframes.

- Computer graphics that are 20 times sharper than premium-printed pictures.

How can these things become possible? The answer is with the development of a 64-megabit, dynamic random-access memory chip (DRAM). The race is on to develop and market a chip that has 16 times the capacity of 4-megabit chips. The costs are high: $600 million to $1 billion to develop the chips, and an additional $600 million to $750 million to build a plant to manufacture them. The payoffs are equally impressive: leadership in an industry where technology is king and a possible 10 percent of the world chip market. The race pits IBM against the cream of Japan's high-tech firms—Toshiba, Hitachi, NEC, Mitsubishi Electric, and Fujitsu—with about a dozen firms in total competing. By the late 1990s, it is expected that sales of products with these chips, including computers, laser printers, and fax machines, will top $2 trillion, with chip sales forecast at $25 billion by the year 2000.

The Japanese are favorites to win the race. Toshiba has largest market shares in both 1-megabit and 4-megabit chips. Five Japanese manufacturers were expected to be shipping 64-megabit samples by the mid-1990s. All are putting millions of dollars into design and manufacturing alternatives that will produce circuits less than 0.35 micron wide (about 4/1,000 the diameter of a human hair).

But what of non-Japanese companies? IBM, still bruised from its competitive struggle with Japan in the 1980s, opted during that time to develop this critical technology internally. Yet even "Big Blue" feels pressure. With the stakes so high, IBM joined forces with Germany's Siemens to speed up development of the chip. To spread their risks, IBM was also contemplating teaming up with Motorola. Texas Instruments, however, developed a relationship with Hitachi with the same end in mind. Finally, a U.S. research association, Sematech, was also making progress. That 14-company consortium had already produced circuits better than 0.5 micron wide, or just twice the required width for 64-DRAM chips. The group was looking forward to the future, past its last $100 million federal subsidy in 1992, to developing technologies with 0.1 micron lines. This would make 150-megabit chips possible—or the ability to put a supercomputer on a chip.

QUESTIONS

1. Evaluate the three approaches to technology development—the Japanese, IBM-Siemens and Sematech methods. Are they that different?

2. Suppose someone develops a 150-megabit DRAM. What might the commercial ramifications be (in general)? Is it possible to overdevelop technology to the point that it surpasses the market's ability to use it? Explain.

3. What do you think of the U.S. government's subsidy of Sematech?

4. Evaluate Texas Instrument's commercial liaison with Hitachi. Is it a case of "working with the enemy"?

Source: Adapted from "The Costly Race Chipmakers Can't Afford to Lose," *Business Week*, 10 December 1990, 185–186; and "Sematech May Give America's Middleweights a Fighting Chance," *Business Week*, 10 December 1990, 188.

▪

CASE **12-2**

Privatization and Deregulation in Telecoms: A Global Free-for-All

The global telecommunications industry is booming in the 1990s. Within 5 years, international phone traffic doubled to 47 billion minutes in 1993, and it was scheduled to hit 100 billion minutes by the year 2000. And at about U.S. $1.00 for each minute, this was truly big money in a global growth industry.

Market opportunities were opening up so quickly that newly privatized telecommunications giants were hard-pressed to know on which markets they should lavish their attentions. Competition in telecoms was occurring from Canada, through the U.S., and down to the significant South American markets of Mexico, Chile, and Argentina. In Western Europe, the U.K. market had been privatized since 1984. Deutsch Telecom was to be sold off at the end of 1996. Eight telecommunications giants were sold off

between 1993 and 1996. The European Union had mandated deregulation of regular voice services by 1998. Tele Danmark paid out $7.8 million for a stake in two Hungarian phone companies, and AT&T was helping to run a phone system in the Ukraine. Europe had some catching up to do. French, German, and Spanish telephone bills were 15 to 50 percent higher than in the low-cost U.S. Some businesses found it economical to route international calls via the U.S., allowing them to cut costs by as much as 70 percent.

But it was in the developing world that market potential was highest. Over 70 percent of the world's telephone lines were located in countries housing 15 percent of its population. In the U.S., 56 percent of the population has access to a phone; in Latin

America, 7 percent; and in Asia and Africa, about 1 percent.

The speed of privatization and deregulation took the industry's breath away. Most telecom companies were languishing monopolies a decade ago. Now it is a global free-for-all. To take advantage of the new markets, companies have formed alliances, partnerships, and mergers. Four supergroups have emerged. AT&T joined Japan's KDD, Singapore Telecom, Telecom New Zealand, Australia and Hong Kong Telecoms, and Unisource, an alliance of Scandinavian firms, to form World Partners Association; British Telecom linked up with MCI; France Telecom, Deutsch Telecom, and U.S.'s Sprint got together; and last (but not least)

Japan's Nippon Telegraph and Telephone is to be broken up into separate divisions to compete globally. The aim of each group is to give the best around-the-globe service.

QUESTIONS

1. You are a newly privatized national telecom company. What would be your first priorities in assessing the global marketplace?

2. How would you defend your home market against foreign competition?

Source: Adapted from Catherine Arnst, "The Global Free-for-All," *Business Week*, 26 September 1994, 118–126.

ENDNOTES

1 A. C. Samli, P. Grewal, and S. Mathur, "International Industrial Buyer Behavior: An Exploration and a Proposed Model," *Journal of the Academy of Marketing Science*, Summer 1988, 19–29.

2 M. Ray Perryman, "The Outlook for 1996 United States Corporate Earnings," *Journal of Business Forecasting Methods and Systems*, Summer 1996, 38–40.

3 "The Prospects for Central and South America," *Industrial Distribution*, May 1996, NA11.

4 "Public Enterprise and Privatization of State-Owned Assets," *Economist*, 21 December 1985, 72–73.

5 Ibid.

6 "Hello, Tokyo . . . What? Your Market is Open," *Business Week*, 24 November 1986, 102, 104.

7 Compiled from Barbara Buell, et al., "The Tidal Wave That's Sweeping International Finance," *Business Week*, 13 July 1987, 56–57; Edward Mervosh, "When Japan Speaks, the World Listens," *U.S. News and World Report*, 19 May 1986, 65–66; and William Glasgall, "The World's Top 50 Banks: It's Official—Japan Is Way Out Front," *Business Week*, 27 June 1988, 76, 77.

8 David Manasian, "British Banks Abandon Standoffish Ways," *The Wall Street Journal*, 28 February 1989, A18.

9 Joy Heard, "The Invasion of the Phone Discounters," *Business Week*, 26 November 1984, 72.

10 Matthew Oja and Christopher Molloy, "Beyond AMR," *Electrical Perspectives*, November–December 1996, 26–41.

11 "A Beardless Branson for Japan," *Economist*, 2 November 1996, 65.

12 Elizabeth de Bony, "Worldwide Telecom Agreement Sought," *Computer World*, 4 November 1996, 64.

13 Joseph N. Pelton, "Cyber Learning versus the University: An Irresistible Force Meets an Immovable Object," *Futurist*, November–December 1996, 17–20.

14 Adolph Haason, "Opel Eisenach Gmbh—Creating a High Productivity Workplace," *Organizational Dynamics*, Spring 1996, 80–85; and "National Financial Markets: Switzerland," *Financial Market Trends*, February 1996, 125–127.

15 Charles W. Thurston, "Peso's Fall Spurs Chemical Exports," *Chemical Marketing Reporter*, 19 February 1996, SR6.

16 Frances Seghers, "Memo to U.S. Computer Makers: Standardize or Else," *Business Week*, 3 October 1988, 34.

17 Jonathan Kapstein, "Ericsson's True Calling," *Business Week*, 6 March 1989, 42, 44.

18 "Standards," *Business America*, September 1996, 126–137; and Karen E. Lee, "Cooperative Standard-Setting: The Road to Compatibility or Deadlock?" *Federal Communications Law Journal*, June 1996, 487–509.

19 From George S. Yip, *Total Global Strategy* (Englewood Cliffs, N.J.: Prentice-Hall, Inc., 1995), 96–97.

20 Ronald Alsop, "U.S. Concerns Seek Inspiration from Overseas," *The Wall Street Journal*, 3 January 1985, 13.

21 Jonathan Kapstein, "Enough with the Theory—Where's the Thingamajig?" *Business Week*, 21 March 1988, 154–158.

22 Ibid., 158.

23 Richard W. Moxon and J. Michael Geringer, "Multinational Ventures in the Commercial Aircraft Industry," *Columbia Journal of World Business* 20, no. 3 (Summer 1985): 55–62.

24 "A Shaken Caterpillar Retools to Take on a More Competitive World," *Business Week*, 5 November 1986, 91–96; Constance Mitchell, "Komatsu Threatens Caterpillar Recovery," *USA Today*, 8 March 1985, B1; and Kathleen J. Deveny, "For Caterpillar, the Metamorphosis Isn't Over," *Business Week*, 31 August 1987, 72–74.

25 Thane Peterson, et al., "AT&T's European Invasion Finally Hits the High Ground," *Business Week*, 10 March 1986, 44–45.

26 Samli, Grewal, and Mathur, "International Industrial Buyer Behavior." See endnote 1.

27 Ibid.

28 Joseph A. Lawton, "Kodak Penetrates the European Copier Market with Customized Marketing Strategy and Product Changes," *Marketing News*, 3 August 1984, 1–6.

29 Bernard Krisher, "Komatsu on the Track of the Cat," *Fortune*, 20 April 1981, 164–174.

30 Sean Milmo, "Computer Companies in European Accent Service Market Position," *Business Marketing*, January 1989, 26.

31 "Pooling Salesmen," *Business International* UK, 21 June 1985, 200.

32. Dominique Xardel, "The Changing Role of the Sales Force in France," *Interfaces* 13, no. 6 (December 1983): 105–191.

33 Pat Speer, "Flipping the Switch without a Hitch," *System Management 3X/400*, September 1996, 40–42.

34 Elaine Santoro, "Telemarketing Globalized, " *Business Marketing* 49, no. 2 (1987): 102.

35 Sean Milmo, "European Telemarketers Go International," *Business Marketing*, June 1986, 25.

36 Tom Eisenhart, "Savvy Mailers Tap Foreign Markets," *Business Marketing*, September 1988, 55–57, 60, 62, 64.

37 Thomas Weyr, "IBM Sees DM as Secret Weapon to Spur Global Growth, Sales Boom," *DM News International*, 10 March 1997, 1, 4.

38 Philip Kotler, Liam Fahey, and Somkid Jatusripitak, "Strategic Global Marketing: Lessons from the Japanese," *Columbia Journal of World Business* 20, no. 1 (Spring 1985): 47–53.

39 Sean Milmo, "Dealer Networks Surge for European Office Machines," *Business Marketing*, July 1987, 35.

40 Thomas Weyr, "IBM Sees DM as Secret Weapon." See endnote 37.

41 "World Industrial Ad Meeting Focuses on Unified Messages," *Business Marketing*, June 1988, 18–20.

42 Sean Milmo, "European Business Gains New TV Ad Medium," *Business Marketing*, January 1989, 31–32.

43 Sean Milmo, "Ad Agencies Set Up Networks for European 'Single Market'," *Business Marketing*, January 1988, 36.

44 Emily McAuliffe, "Many Europshop Exhibitors Scale Back," *Advertising Age's Business Marketing*, April 1996, 12; and Charles Siler, "Comdex/UK Pulls 'Corporate'," *Advertising Age's Business Marketing*, May 1996, 3, 29.

45 Sean Milmo, "European Trade Show Boom Features One Company Trend," *Business Marketing*, October 1987, 20–24; and Sean Milmo, "Europe's Exhibitors Turning to Smaller Shows," *Business Marketing*, March 1988, 22.

46 Tom Eisenhart, "Soviet Seminar Draws Business for Toolmakers," *Business Marketing*, January 1989, 22.

47 "Tell 'Em, Don't Sell 'Em," *Canadian Business*, January 1994, 34.

48 Nigel M. Healey, "Why is Corporate Barter?" *Business Economics*, April 1996, 36–41.

49 Angela Briggins, "Why Barter is Better," *Management Review*, February 1996, 58–60.

50 Sean Milmo, "Europeans Use Two-Way Deals to Succeed in Soviet Market," *Business Meeting*, April 1989, 32.

51 Alan T. Shao, "An Empirical Study of the Structures, Strategies and Environments of U.S. Multinational Advertising Agencies," Ph.D. diss., University of Alabama, 1989.

52 Gerhard G. Mueller, Helen Gernon, and Gary Meek, *Accounting: An International Perspective* (Homewood, Ill.: Richard D. Irwin, 1987), 3.

53 Nora E. Field, "Japan Is Still No. 1," *Fortune*, 30 July 1990, 324–25.

54 Daniel Burstein, *Yen: Japan's Financial Empire and Its Threat to the United States* (New York: Simon and Schuster, 1988); and Richard W. Wright and Gunter A. Paul, *The Second Wave: Japan's Global Assault on Financial Services* (New York: St. Martin's Press, 1987).

55 David Conner, "Home and Away," *Banker*, February 1996, 44–47.

56 David B. Dyche, "Now We Have Global Banking," *Bankers Magazine*, November–December 1996, 3–4.

57 Evert Clark, "Deutsche Bank Makes a Bid for Global Powers," *Business Week*, 28 March 1988, 78–79.

58 Edward Mervosh, "When Japan Speaks the World Listens," *US News and World Report*, 19 May 1986, 65–66.

59 Rebecca A. Fannin, "Change Puts Focus Back on Bankers," *Advertising Age*, September 1996, 142; Bradley Johnson, "EDS May Pour $80 million into First Global Campaign," *Advertising Age*, 30 September 1996, 4; "Bates Takes Global Task to Coordinate Amnesty Campaign," *Campaign London*, 6 September 1996, 3.

60 Rebecca Fannin, "TBWA Focuses International Moves on Asia, Latin America," *Advertising Age*, 14 October 1996, 28.

61 Jermone Karter, "Global Approach," *Business Insurance*, 6 February 1989, 21.

CHAPTER **13**

International Marketing Channels

Chapter Outline

Learning Objectives

When you have mastered the contents of this chapter, you will be able to do the following:

1 Explain how international marketing channels differ from one another.

2 Discuss the key points in putting together and managing international marketing channels.

3 Describe channel functions, composition, structure, and number of intermediaries.

4 Explain how an international marketing channel is motivated so that its performance will improve.

As you walk the streets of Honolulu, Hong Kong, or Singapore, you see local people wearing Banana Republic and Benetton sportswear; you see tourists from all over the world carrying Canon and Nikon cameras, and many local people as well as tourists wearing Nikes or Reeboks. These and other products with well-known brand names are sold not only in these countries but also in lots of others. To penetrate these markets, managers must decide not only how to get the product to the foreign country (through exports, licensing, or local production—see Chapter 9), they must also get their products through foreign distribution channels. Marketers used to competitive, price-oriented American channels get rude shocks as they encounter foreign wholesaling and retailing systems for the first time. The following discussion explores some of the key differences between international marketing channels and those in the United States.

DIFFERENCES BETWEEN U.S. DOMESTIC AND INTERNATIONAL CHANNELS

International and U.S. domestic marketing channels differ along one or more of four dimensions: (1) function, (2) composition, (3) power structure, and (4) number of intermediaries.

Function

It is a mistake to assume that a foreign wholesaler is purely a wholesaler and that a foreign retailer is just a retailer, as is generally true in the United States. Functional specialization of this sort is not a reality in many countries. A Turkish wholesaler is quite different from a U.S. wholesaler. In Turkey, Kenya, Jamaica, and other developing countries, the typical retailer simultaneously engages in wholesaling and the typical wholesaler is also a retailer. Moreover, wholesalers in these countries generally perform more tasks than their counterparts in developed countries.

It is revealing to contrast the functions of U.S. and Turkish wholesalers (see Table 13–1). Turkish wholesalers are geographically concentrated and stationary, while American wholesalers generally can move wherever there is a feasible location. Turkish wholesalers are supply oriented and play a key role in overseeing the production of the items they handle. Only a few American wholesalers follow this practice; they focus more on understanding and satisfying their customers' demands. All Turkish wholesalers provide partial or substantial financing (by serving as factors for the producers and providing capital to the retailers), but only a few American wholesalers do such financing. Most Turkish wholesalers are partially or fully vertically integrated with manufacturing enterprises, making them not only supply oriented but also directly involved in manufacturing; only a few American wholesalers have any involvement in production. Almost all Turkish wholesalers engage in export-import activities, while American wholesalers are hardly ever involved in international trade. Turkish wholesalers are never involved in advising their retail customers, but for most American wholesalers, giving advice is a normal activity. No Turkish wholesaler engages in joint or cooperative promotional activity, but almost all American wholesalers are involved in some promotion with their retailer customers or on their own account, or both. These characteristics of Turkish wholesalers resemble those of wholesalers in developing countries elsewhere.

TABLE 13-1 ■ *Contrast in Turkish and American Wholesaling*

Characteristics	Turkish Wholesalers	American Wholesalers
Geographically stationary and concentrated	All	Some
Supply oriented	All	Some
Involved in partial financing of retailers	All	Some
Vertically integrated and involved in production	Most	Some
Involved in exporting and importing	Most	Almost none
Involved in consulting and other customer services	None	Most
Involved in sales promotion	None	Almost all

Source: Adapted from A. Coskun Samli, "Wholesaling in an Economy of Scarcity: Turkey," *Journal of Marketing*, July 1964, and updated by the author in November–December 1985.

Composition

The components of marketing channels are manufacturers, intermediaries (including middlemen, wholesalers, and retailers), and consumers. In developing countries, channels are likely to have more middlemen, and they do not have clear-cut, multiple functions. For instance, middlemen unspecialized by commodity or function predominate in serving West African markets.[1] Long distances between market centers, antiquated and inefficient communication facilities, and shortages of capital in many (if not most) less-developed economies deter the expansion of markets. The small shops and stalls that comprise the bulk of the retail establishment in West Africa engage in "scrambled" merchandising, and their sources consist of a host of unspecialized middlemen.

Figure 13-1 illustrates some alternatives regarding international marketing channels. As can be seen, these channels vary in length and complexity.

Some international marketing channels are highly complex, with complicated networks of intermediaries. Japan's existing marketing channels are complex, reflecting a strong and intricate network among intermediaries. The complexity and intricacies of the Japanese distribution system have made it difficult for American exporters to penetrate the Japanese market.[2]

Japan has more retail shops and wholesalers per capita than does any other developed country. Typically, Japanese retail outlets employ no more than two people, and almost half of the wholesalers employ no more than four people. Resistance by small shopkeepers (who collectively are politically powerful) has hampered the development and expansion of larger and more efficient retail institutions. As late as the early 1980s, Japanese goods were going through an average of four intermediaries, compared with 1.8 in the United States and West Germany and 1.2 in France.[3]

Power Structure

All marketing channels have a channel captain who exercises channel leadership. The

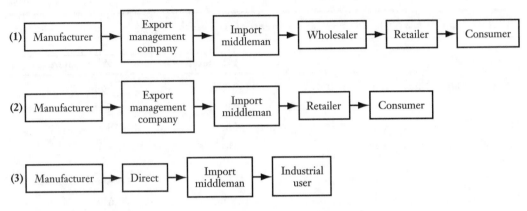

FIGURE 13-1 *Illustration of Some International Channels*

channel captain influences the composition of the channel, the specific tasks of various middlemen, the performance criteria, the way channel members are rewarded, and the way communication is maintained among them. In North America and Western Europe, most channel captains are manufacturers. Although some retailing giants such as Sears Roebuck occasionally challenge the manufacturer's leadership and sometimes even take the captainship away, the more usual arrangement is that the manufacturer is the channel captain.

By contrast, in many developing countries, the channel captain is the wholesaler. Consider, for example, the channel captainship held by a typical dry goods wholesaler in Turkey. The wholesaler imports the raw wool and sends it to a small manufacturer to make yarn; the yarn then goes to a small processor for dyeing. The dyed yarn is distributed among numerous cottage manufacturers, small-scale makers of garments who work out of their homes. The cottage manufacturers produce sweaters, blouses, and the like. Finally, the wholesaler sells the finished products to rural retailers and extends 90 to 120 days of credit to them. Note that this wholesaler takes the lead both in production

and distribution. Other middlemen, both retailers and jobbers, are decided upon based on the channel captain's (the wholesaler's) needs. Identifying channel leadership is highly important in international marketing. This identification is necessary to assure that proper negotiations take place with the right intermediaries.

Length

Most marketing channels in overseas markets, particularly in developing countries, have a longer string of intermediaries than do American channels. The reason for this is that individual intermediaries are generally small enterprises, have ill-defined functions, and perform a small number of tasks rather than a broad spectrum of tasks.

POWER AND CONFLICT IN INTERNATIONAL CHANNELS

A channel's power and the amount of conflict between members of a marketing channel are critical not only in terms of evaluating a channel's performance level but also in terms of managing the channel.[4]

Power

Power is the ability of one channel member to influence or control the decisions of another member. Power can derive from some attribute of the powerful member, such as the ability to reward or punish another member for behaving in certain ways or (if the member is a middleman) for good reputation or great expertise. One middleman, say, the wholesaler, may strongly influence a retailer to take a full line of products rather than just those required. Such uses and abuses of channel power occur in both advanced and developing countries.

Power can also accrue to one channel member from the dependence of another member. For example, the more dependent the retailer, the more powerful the wholesaler. Dependency is the usual source of power in most developing countries. If no member of a channel has enough power to influence others, the channel may not function very well. Thus, the international marketer needs to examine dependency levels among channel members before deciding whether to enter a channel agreement.

Conflict

Conflict is likely to arise in a channel when the members consider themselves too independent of one another. For instance, a retailer may take on himself an independence that a wholesaler is unwilling to allow. Food retailers in Jordan willingly cooperate with wholesalers who provide them with quality assistance, but they resist wholesalers whom they think are likely to punish them. That situation creates conflict.[5] If there is too much conflict in a channel, its performance can be undesirable.

In competitive market places, marketing channels tend to have many conflicts among competing members. In Japan, marketing channels are characterized by cooperation among members because they are interdependent. In many developing countries, market channels tend to have less conflict among members because the members are interdependent and the channel captain, who occupies a strong position, will not allow it. These channels are effective but substantially passive.

ALTERNATIVE INTERNATIONAL MARKETING CHANNELS

The structure of a country's marketing channel is affected by that country's economic development, its consumers' disposable income, and the physical-distribution infrastructure. Marketing channel structures are also shaped by other factors, such as tradition, geography, and legal and political systems. In Japan, for instance, even with advanced economic development and high disposable income, the distribution system for the most part remains bound by tradition. The typical Japanese retailer knows all or most of the store's customers because the owners' ancestors have dealt with customers' ancestors for generations. Similarly, networks of intermediaries have been doing business together for decades, if not for generations. The outcome is a complex distribution system difficult for outsiders to penetrate. Under the Japanese system, soap, for instance, may move through three layers of wholesalers and a distributor before it reaches the retailer. A cotton dress made overseas travels from the foreign textile factory to a Japanese trading company, which has its network of distributors or other intermediaries charged with getting the dress to the retail store. Experienced international traders say that it is next to impossible for foreigners to understand the Japanese distribution channels unless they have Japanese partners.

Figure 13–2 shows international marketing channel alternatives. International marketing channels have both home-country channel members and foreign-country channel members. The number of possible combinations of channel members—and the number of possible channels—is very large. For instance, the diagram below shows just three of the possible combinations. All of them are common.

As Figure 13–2 indicates, international marketing channels range from short to long, simple to complex. (The key international intermediaries are discussed in Chapter 9.) It is important for the international marketer to know not only who the intermediaries are but also what they do.

In the People's Republic of China (PRC), for instance, most manufacturers sell to, but do not deliver to, retailers. But this

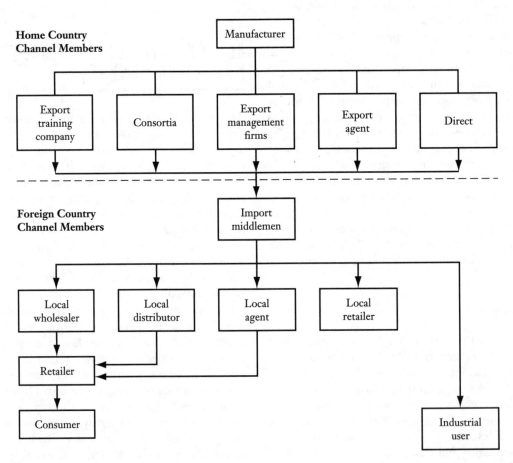

FIGURE 13-2 *Alternative International Marketing Channels*

practice is changing. Coke and Pepsi have been competing in a distribution duel; both have moved from a situation where retailers bicycled to bottling plants to pick up cases of soda to one in which orders are delivered from the plants direct to retailers. Both companies have invested heavily in fleets of retail delivery vehicles and refrigeration equipment for use by their retail dealers.[6]

CHANNEL ORIENTATION

There are still other differences between U.S. domestic channels and international marketing channels. These differences relate to channel orientation. There are three contrasting channel orientations: (1) active versus passive, (2) dynamic versus static, and (3) market-oriented versus channel-oriented product decisions.

Active versus Passive Orientation

The basis of the active-passive distinction is whether or not the channel generates further marketing activity on its own and reflects synergetic unity among its members. Many American channels have an active orientation and function synergetically. Individual channel members take the initiative in making changes in the channel's overall performance.

Elsewhere in the world, many marketing channels have passive orientations. These channels perform the tasks they have always performed, but they do not exercise any additional initiative. They are traditional channels whose members have performed their accustomed functions the same way for generations. Most of the small Japanese retailers and their suppliers fall into this mold.

Dynamic versus Static Orientation

Marketing channels in the United States are dynamic—they change. New channel patterns and new types of marketing intermediaries emerge from time to time. Some of these new intermediaries play new and different roles in the distribution process.

In most developing and less-developed countries, however, channels are static; they remain the same way they have been for centuries. These countries are just the places where the process of economic development could be accelerated by dynamic channels, but unfortunately, these channels simply don't change.

Campbell Japan, Inc. (CJI), had been having a bad time with its local distributors in distributing its Pepperidge Farm cookies. Products were not pushed, new outlets were not sought, and markups were inflated. CJI decided to bypass the traditional channels and negotiate a deal with 7-Eleven Japan to stock Pepperidge Farm cookies in its 3,300-store chain. By doing its own importing and delivering directly to one of 7-Eleven's wholesale suppliers, CJI placed its cookies quickly within reach of more Japanese consumers than was possible before.[7] Interestingly, this type of distribution development occurs so frequently in North America that it rarely makes the headline news!

Market-Oriented versus Channel-Oriented Product Decisions

Whether product decisions result from a market or a channel orientation provides yet another contrast between American channels and those in the tradition-bound developing countries, and even some in the more traditional industrialized countries, such as Japan.

American marketing channels are relatively united and are sensitive to market changes and trends in market needs, providing all channel members with new opportunities. By contrast, most of the traditional marketing channels are composed of intermediaries headed by people who have strong positions in a more traditional society; these intermediaries decide what products are to be distributed and why.

Thus, the market itself is the main determinant in American marketing channels as to what is distributed and how this distribution should be made. The marketing channel determines these details in the traditional-industrial and developing countries. This kind of market orientation on the part of distribution channels can open up products to new markets and thus prepare the ground for economic growth. This kind of market orientation on the part of distribution channels can open up products to new markets and thus prepare the ground for economic growth.[8]

CHANNEL SELECTION

In much of the world, channel relationships are long lasting. Generally, once the decision on an international marketing channel is made, it is difficult to change. Selecting a marketing channel that will serve the international firm well results from thorough appraisals of both internal and external factors.

Internal Factors

Although diverse internal factors influence specific channel selection situations, the most important are (1) company size, (2) the need for distribution control, (3) required special functions, (4) product characteristics, (5) desired entry speed, and (6) desired penetration.

COMPANY SIZE ▪ International companies of different sizes require different marketing channels. Companies the size of Sears or IBM do not enter foreign markets little by little. Companies this large generally need channels capable of delivering substantial volumes of business. Some large companies opt for *direct distribution channels* (that is, for partial or full ownership of the channel). Smaller concerns are much more likely to utilize *indirect distribution channels* through long chains of existing marketing intermediaries.

NEED FOR DISTRIBUTION CONTROL ▪ A company's need for distribution control stems from different circumstances. Companies with worldwide images related to distribution performance generally desire considerable control. Godiva chocolates, for instance, requires sufficient distribution control in order for its product quality to remain intact and its product line to receive desired promotion at the various distribution levels. Godiva also needs assurance that distribution points within markets are strategically located and are performing according to prescribed procedures. Similarly, IBM needs assurance that intermediaries in its marketing channels are handling and selling its products according to established procedures.

Developing and maintaining an international reputation necessitates some degree of control over the distribution channel. Inadequacies in Fiat's distribution in the United States, stemming from Fiat's lack of control, were responsible for this popular European car not making much progress in, and ultimately withdrawing from, American auto markets.

REQUIRED SPECIAL FUNCTIONS ▪ An international company may require the performance of special distribution functions in order to perform well in certain world markets. Automakers opening up markets overseas absolutely require special and adequate services from their distributor-dealer networks. That is why Japanese automakers entered the U.S. market one region at a time, starting with the West Coast. High-tech companies such as IBM and Xerox can only function effectively in world markets when their distribution channels provide competent repair and maintenance facilities and stock adequate supplies of spare parts.

PRODUCT CHARACTERISTICS ■ Some products have special characteristics that influence marketing channel selection. Certain products require a speedy introduction to a market. Fashion items have to be in dealers' salesrooms at the start of new seasons. Other products (for example, fruits and vegetables and seafood) are perishable and require special handling (even refrigeration) as well as speedy distribution to points of sale. Moreover, certain chemical products, dairy products, and items such as fresh-cut flowers require special characteristics in the distribution channels.

DESIRED ENTRY SPEED ■ Sometimes, international firms have special reasons for wanting to enter certain markets quickly. Companies taking advantage of Western Europe's economic unification in 1992 (for example, Whirlpool) invested early and spent much time and effort putting together pan-European distribution channels swiftly. If entry speed is a prime concern, this may affect the channel that is chosen; for example, a channel "available now" may be selected over a more desirable channel that is "tied up for the foreseeable future."

DESIRED PENETRATION ■ Some companies enter international markets only to skim the high end of these markets; others enter

from the low end and seek deeper market penetration. The desired degree of penetration affects the channel structure that is sought. In some parts of the world, certain dealers or distributors are associated with subdealers or subdistributors. It is common for such dealers or distributors to have specific regions within their countries as their exclusive territories. At one extreme, the multinational firm desiring a high degree of penetration in a particular market needs to incorporate a large number of dealers and distributors in its channels. At the other extreme, multinationals who simply want to skim the cream of the market may establish, or even own, their own direct distribution systems.

External Factors

Certain external factors also influence the choice of an international marketing channel. Four of these external factors are (1) competition, (2) market characteristics, (3) legal barriers, and (4) availability.

COMPETITION ■ The intensity of competition varies not only in different world markets but also among different components of marketing channels. If there is keen competition in certain markets, it is highly desirable to have marketing channels capable of being strong competitors. The multinational firm entering a new market seeks to choose a marketing channel that can compete on an equal basis with local channels. When Japanese car makers entered the U.S. market, they set up networks of distributors and dealers fully capable of competing head on with the U.S. automakers' channels.

In choosing a marketing channel, a company must also assess the degrees of competition that exists among wholesalers, other marketing intermediaries, and distributors as well as retailers. A company has to decide where to focus the competitive edge. Should it aim at having competitive edges at all channel levels, or should it concentrate on one or more specific distribution levels?

MARKET CHARACTERISTICS ▪ Unique market characteristics play a critical role in shaping marketing channels in some countries. If the market is geographically widespread rather than concentrated, for instance, a channel must be capable of serving this kind of market. It must have both the type of marketing intermediaries and the number of intermediaries that a dispersed market requires. Other market characteristics also need to be considered. The Japanese market, for example, is controlled by an intricate and complex network of wholesale distributors and subdistributors. Most multinationals entering the Japanese market find it necessary to work with this existing network.[9]

Non-Muslims, such as the Japanese, have experienced difficulties in entering Arab markets. Turkey (a non-Arab but Muslim country) and Japan have been working on a deal in which Japan enters Arab markets through Turkey, which acts as mediator. Turkey has long-established business relationships with the Japanese and is anxious to help.

LEGAL BARRIERS ▪ In some countries, there are legal and ownership requirements that force multinationals to use indirect marketing systems made up of local institutions.

AVAILABILITY ▪ Whether certain types of distribution institutions exist or are available also makes a difference. In many overseas markets, both IBM and Xerox were unable to find the types of marketing institutions they desired for their marketing channels. Therefore, market by market, these companies built their own marketing channels from scratch. But if local institutions that are capable of functioning effectively in the international marketer's proposed distribution channel exist, the marketer is likely to utilize them.

CHANNEL STRUCTURE

Channel structures are either direct or indirect.

Direct Channels

A direct international marketing channel is one that is owned and managed by the international firm, which owns and operates all of its intermediary institutions and other facilities. Figure 13–3 shows that direct marketing channels can be either vertical or horizontal. A vertical direct marketing channel is one in which the international firm owns all manufacturing, wholesaling, retailing, and other intermediary institutions. Examples include the worldwide distribution systems of IBM and Xerox.

A horizontal direct marketing channel is one in which an international retailer both owns and operates multiple retail outlets in a market. Sears and Benetton provide examples of this type of distribution structure.

	Vertical	**Horizontal**
Direct	IBM, Xerox	Sears, Benetton
Indirect	Squibb, Merck	Indonesian textiles

FIGURE 13-3 *Different Channel Structures*

These retailers partially or fully own their outlets in foreign markets and run them according to corporate guidelines.

Indirect Channels

Indirect marketing channels are distribution systems that are owned not by international marketers but by others, particularly by local people. Vertical indirect marketing channels, for instance, are commonly used by international pharmaceutical companies, all of which typically work closely with local wholesalers and retailers. Among these companies are such well-known firms as Squibb and Merck.

Horizontal indirect marketing channels are used by international marketers desiring access to large numbers of retail establishments scattered throughout the target markets. Indonesian textiles utilize this type of channel structure in their international distribution. Pakistani, Korean, and Turkish textiles are also distributed this way.

The presence of a specific internal or external factor may determine the choice between a direct and indirect structure. Sometimes, an internal factor, such as the company's large size or a strong need for distribution control, causes an international firm to opt for direct marketing channels. At other times, an external factor, such as a legal barrier or a high level of competition, causes an international form to utilize indirect channels.

CHANNEL MANAGEMENT

Four key aspects of channel management are (1) locating and selecting members, (2) coordinating, (3) communicating, and (4) optimizing performance.

Locating and Selecting Members

It is important to find the right channel members. Although locating prospective marketing intermediaries is a problem in itself, selecting the ones most appropriate for the international marketer's purposes is an even greater problem. The international marketer is well advised to identify specific criteria to use in choosing marketing intermediaries as channel members. These criteria are based on the internal and external factors discussed earlier. A list of possible candidates for channel membership can be compiled from information provided by a number of sources: the U.S. Department of Commerce, commercial directories, foreign consulates and commercial attachés, foreign chambers of commerce, manufacturers of noncompeting products, other middlemen associates, business publications, management consultants, and international carriers such as the airlines.[10] In the 1980s, U.S.-based firms have found that exhibiting their products at foreign trade fairs is helpful in identifying local agents and in conducting serious negotiations.[11]

Screening potential candidates for channel members is a four-step process.[12] The first step is to send the candidate firm a letter with detailed product information and representation requirements. This letter must be in the prospective distributor's native tongue. The second step is to direct follow-up correspondence to the most promising respondents requesting detailed information regarding enterprise size, experience, familiarity with the territory, other product lines, and references. The third step is to check the candidate's references for character, credit, and reliability. The fourth step is by far the most important. A representative of the international firm should visit the foreign country and interview key prospective channel members in person.

The firm must consider the fact that the Japanese and most other Asians, as well as Turks and Arabs, refuse to do business with those they consider "strangers." Many exporters learn, sometimes the hard way, that one must know not only the prospective middleman in person but also his family or close associates. Often, exporters suggest that prospective overseas representatives and their families spend significant time together before signing any agreement. A signed agreement should spell out the responsibilities of both parties, and it will usually specify a minimum annual sales volume; failure to meet these responsibilities can be used to terminate the agreement.[13] Local laws should be consulted before the agreement is drafted. In most cases, local laws interfere substantially and are binding in terms of superseding other laws.[14] Some experts suggest that the initial contract should be for no longer than a year, but this short period may lead to misunderstanding and an unsatisfactory relationship.

Coordinating

For effective performance, the plans and activities of channel members require coordination. The international marketer must ensure that its plans, promotional activities, strategic decisions, and product changes include all members of the channel team. Similarly, each of the marketing intermediaries in the channel must keep its activities congruent with those of others in the channel. Individual intermediaries must not take actions that offset the actions of others. A particular retailer, for instance, unlike other retailers carrying the same product line, may decide to start a different kind of promotion. Unless skillfully coordinated, such a campaign might offset the efforts by other retailers on the marketer's behalf.

Communicating

Communication is essential to coordination; indeed, coordination and communication go hand in hand. If the marketing channel's performance is to conform to company standards, its members must be kept abreast of progress and problems. The international marketer communicates its plans as to its promotion, strategic objectives, and product and service adjustments to all channel members. Information flow among the marketing intermediaries is also important. The intermediaries must keep other channel members informed about market changes and their marketing moves that proved profitable. It is the channel captain's responsibility to take the lead in maintaining communications and coordination among all channel members.

Optimizing Performance

The most critical aspect of managing an international marketing channel is optimizing its overall performance. To optimize total channel performance, four areas need attention: training, motivating, compensating, and evaluating.

TRAINING ▪ Proper training of all dealers, distributors, and other channel members is the responsibility of the international marketer. Appropriate training in service matters, product maintenance and repair, and related activities pays dividends in enriching the channel's overall performance.

MOTIVATING ▪ The motivation level of channel members has a direct impact on total channel performance. Effective leadership by the channel captain helps in motivating the members. Channel leadership takes such forms as designing and implementing cooperative advertising campaigns, coordinating the efforts of all channel members, and communicating with all distribution levels effectively.[15] Psychologically rewarding intermediaries means recognizing good marketing performance. Stimulating a sense of belonging in channel members requires, first, strengthening the brand and corporate image and, second, promoting directly to the intermediaries.

Promoting directly to channel members is more critical in world markets than in the United States. There are three main reasons: (1) The marketing intermediaries have substantial power in "pushing" the product through the channel; (2) consumer advertising may have limited effectiveness as product availability fluctuates; and (3) consumer loyalty to the product or brand is often questionable, so channel promotion is critical.

COMPENSATING ■ Offering adequate financial rewards to channel members makes it reasonable to expect high performance levels from them.[16] Margins and commissions need to be set at levels sufficiently high to motivate marketing intermediaries to motivate middlemen to turn in good performances and to provide all necessary services. If the international firm does not provide adequate financial rewards to its channel members, they are unlikely to give the product line their full support. In addition, the enlightened international marketer supports its channel members by providing reasonable credit terms, sufficient product information, technical assistance, and product service.

EVALUATING ■ In order to evaluate channel members' performances effectively, the firm must establish certain performance criteria. Sales quotas in terms of units of product or market share, actual sales figures, and some measure of customer satisfaction are all needed for this evaluation. The evaluation of channel members abroad, largely because of

cultural considerations, is generally more flexible than is common in the United States. Often, therefore, there exists a greater need for positive reinforcement of personnel overseas than in the domestic U.S. market. Many societies abroad are based more on cooperation than on competition; thus, positive rewards are more appropriate than negative appraisals and corrective actions.

IMPROVING INTERNATIONAL DISTRIBUTION MANAGEMENT

International marketing channels are strategic assets critical to success in overseas markets. Effective channels provide cost-effective and responsive market coverage and serve as pipelines for launching new products. Kodak, for instance, introduced its lithium battery line quickly through its established international channels.

Two experts suggest a 10-point system for improving channel management.[17]

1. *Set definite marketing objectives and communicate them to all channel members.* To gain the full support of channel members, the international firm must communicate its marketing vision clearly and consistently both in words and in its own performance. IBM decided to develop an indirect distribution system for its PCs, so IBM executives carefully selected its resellers in order to aim at different end users. Throughout this operation, IBM communicated with and closely monitored the performance of these resellers.

2. *Base channel arrangements and policies on a thorough market analysis.* This analysis may indicate where the key tradeoffs are in the distribution system. For instance,

Coca-Cola decided to emphasize coverage in Turkey because it wanted intensive distribution in that market. Coca-Cola considers cost as the most important factor in India, because the distribution system there is to be selective at the outset. In most markets, there are tradeoffs between coverage and cost.

3. *Determine the division of tasks among channel intermediaries and the channel captains.* A manufacturer should separate its own distributive tasks from those it wants to share or must share with the channel members. Thus, the distribution task of each channel member is clearly defined. Benetton's success in the United States stems largely from the fact that its retail outlets communicate their inventory needs quickly to Benetton's distribution center. Informed estimates are that Benetton stores receive their orders about two weeks faster than their major competitors, such as The Limited and The Gap.

4. *Understand channel members' view of the world.* Firms such as Levi Strauss, Haggar Apparel, and Arrow Shirt work very closely with their retailers and distributors. They aim to understand clearly channel members' needs so as to develop computerized and sophisticated order-processing and inventory-management systems that link retailers to the manufacturers.

5. *Examine the balance of power among channel members.* The balance of power within the channel often shifts. The manufacturer may regret allowing too much power to move into the hands of some channel members at the expense of others. The outcome of this situation often is an inefficient channel with complex morale problems.

6. *Ensure that margins and other supports provided are equitable for all of the channel members.* If, for instance, a reseller's cost of carrying a producer's inventory, displaying it, promoting it, assorting it, selling it, delivering it, and handling accounts receivable amounts to 25 percent of the selling price, then giving that reseller a 20 percent margin is simply not enough. Resellers given inadequate margins cut service quality, make unauthorized increases in prices, and make other moves that are not in the manufacturer's best interests.

7. *Predict conflicts within channels.* Conflicts are likely to arise within channels, particularly when there are numerous retail outlets and distributors. Conflicts occur, for instance, if resellers in one market are treated differently from resellers in another, or if some resellers in the same channel try for and receive additional support from the manufacturer.

There are a variety of ways to mitigate conflict. These include developing new plans for overall distribution, using multiple brands or nearly identical items so that resellers will not be in direct competition, partitioning markets among resellers, describing sales policies clearly, negotiating larger territorial issues, and openly recognizing and rewarding certain resellers as master distributors.

8. *Help sales representatives develop skills in working with channel members.* Sales representatives calling on resellers must know how to communicate. This knowledge is especially important when sales reps are American expatriates who call on resellers and distributors overseas. These individuals need to know the product lines fully, and they require a high degree of acculturation. In other

words, they must understand the resellers' culture in order to understand their attitudes and behavior.

9. *Monitor channels to make sure that they are viable.* Pepsi-Cola, for example, could not rely entirely on traditional marketing channels even in the United States. The company found that instead of relying upon grocery and convenience stores as its main outlets, a better strategy was to emphasize distribution through fast-food stores such as Taco Bell, Pizza Hut, and Kentucky Fried Chicken. Pepsico is planning to use a similar approach as it expands its presence in international markets. Carefully monitored activity within channels is necessary to the adjustment of strategy.

10. *Treat marketing channels as strategic assets.* Marketing channels require management as total systems in order to optimize profitability. Such management is particularly important in international marketing channels, where the functions, problems, capabilities, attitudes, and values of resellers are all so different than are those of U.S. resellers.

INTERNATIONAL STRATEGIC ALLIANCES

Strategic alliances involve the participation of two or more entities to achieve a specific business objective. These alliances can take a variety of forms and do not require new legal entities or new organizational structures.[18] A strategic alliance emerges to provide long-term competitive advantage for a company or a number of companies as part of a global game plan. There are at least three typical factors leading to the creation of strategic alliances: (1) market entry, (2) internationalization, and (3) financial risk.

Market Entry

The increasing difficulties in entering and competing in many world markets necessitate the development of strategic alliances. Sometimes such entry-related international strategic alliances are necessary to counteract existing strategic alliances that may be strong hurdles to the international firm's entry into that market. For instance, if an American auto-part manufacturer were to try to enter the Japanese market, it would have to counteract informal domestic Japanese strategic alliances, which are called *keiretsu*. Keiretsus are systems of alliances composed of multiple dealers, suppliers, and manufacturers that have been in existence for a long time. Thus, an American firm must enter into an international strategic alliance by developing a partnership with another group of suppliers, dealers, and, perhaps, manufacturers.

In the People's Republic of China, such domestic alliances are called *quanxi*. Quanxis, unlike keiretsus, are more social alliances, which include groups, families, and certain fraternal organizations, as well as businesses. Again, in order to counteract quanxis, an American firm will be forced to develop a strategic alliance with a group of Chinese businesses in order to enter and succeed in that market.

Internationalization

Internationalization was discussed in Chapter 5. An American company may lack international knowledge and skills. However, it may have certain products that may be very desirable in many international markets. In such cases, the company may enter international strategic alliances with different partners in different world markets. AT&T created an alliance with Olivetti of Italy to exchange technology and gain market access. A similar alliance was developed between AT&T and Philips of the Netherlands. Two other European partners, Telefonica of Spain and Stet of Italy, also joined this venture. By joining an alliance through the formation of a joint venture, AT&T gained immediate market access. Other partners in the alliance gained access to certain technologies that would have been very costly for them to develop.[19] The company entered these markets easily and performs well, particularly because of strategic alliances.

Financial Risk

The extensive financial requirements and high risks of international ventures lead to the formation of strategic alliances. These alliances allow for negotiated, contracted distribution of all of the various risks (financial, technological, and political) among the members.[20]

Although strategic alliances can be related to technology, production, and finance, perhaps the most critical strategic alliances are in the areas of entry and distribution channels. Small American firms can develop strategic alliances with overseas distributors, export trading companies, or importers. Similarly, developing certain types of licensing or partnership agreements can be considered as parts of strategic alliances.

However, all international corporate alliances are not quite strategic; much of the time, they are based on convenience and, perhaps, on one party trying to take advantage of the other party. In such cases, the alliance does not last long. For successful strategic alliance formation, both parties must benefit equally and both must learn from this experience.[21]

International marketing channel alternatives are illustrated in Figure 13–2. When a manufacturer makes an arrangement with home-country and foreign-country channel members and develops a functional and enduring marketing channel, that manufacturer actually has entered an international strategic alliance. Such an alliance is essential to gaining and maintaining an international competitive edge.

SUMMARY

This chapter has covered international marketing channels and their organization, selection, and management. International channels differ from U.S. domestic channels in terms of functions, composition, power structure, and number of intermediaries. International marketing channels have different orientations from most U.S. channels in that they are typically passive and static. But marketing channels in most overseas markets carry a lot of power because they have major voices in deciding which products are carried and distributed in those markets.

Power in American channels can be traced to an intermediary's ability to reward or punish, or to their reputation and expertise. Power in international channels is more readily attributed to dependence on other intermediaries. While American channels show more conflict, many international channels show more cooperation.

Selection of a particular international marketing channel results from the evaluation of internal and external factors. The international marketer decides whether it needs a direct-vertical, direct-horizontal, indirect-vertical, or indirect-horizontal marketing channel. The marketer then locates and selects the desired channel members. Effective and efficient management of the international marketing channel is also important. Proper management of international channels depends on skillful selection of members, coordination, communication, and optimization of performance.

Strategic alliances such as joint ventures are essential in establishing an international competitive edge.

DISCUSSION QUESTIONS

1. Why are international marketing channels generally different from U.S. domestic channels?

2. How do the roles and responsibilities of channel captains differ in international markets?

3. Besides those detailed in this chapter, what additional internal or external factors might influence or affect international channel selection?

4. Which of the internal and external channel selection factors are the most important? What does their relative importance depend upon?

5. If Kmart enters additional international markets, what type of international channel structure would best fit its needs? Why?

6. In managing international marketing channels, what is the difference and interrelationship between coordination and communication?

7. In attempting to optimize international marketing channel performance, which of the following should a U.S. firm emphasize: training, motivating, or compensating? Why?

8. Explain why an American export firm must involve itself in managing the international market channel. Why not let the channel manage itself?

GM Goes to Asia

In Bangkok, Thailand, sitting for hours in traffic jams, one sees bumper-to-bumper Nissan, Toyota, and Mitsubishi cars, and an occasional Mercedes or BMW. The probability of seeing an American car is less than 1 in 250. But in other parts of Asia, American firms are doing better. Despite the Japanese competition and poor odds, Ford Motor Company has captured well over 25 percent of the market in Taiwan. In Malaysia, Ford sales are growing fast; they went from 0 to 4.4 percent of the market within a year or two.

Ford's modest success has encouraged GM also. GM recently set up a regional office in Hong Kong and established sales offices in Thailand, Malaysia, and Indonesia. The company realized that Buick is very popular in Taiwan. GM has had a joint manufacturing venture in South Korea, but it has been unsuccessful so far. GM executives have not been getting along with their Korean partners.

GM has started making modest inroads in Japan. It has expanded its dealer network by finally using the Japanese affiliates in which it invested more than 10 years ago. Aiding GM's effort are its lower prices. For instance, in 1989, a well-equipped Grand Am sold for about $20,000, about half the U.S. price. GM also started advertising on TV, in subways, and in magazines. Racy cars such as Camaro are popular.

GM executives were surprised to find that the same methods that work in the United States are also working in Japan. In 1989, GM hoped to sell about 3,000 cars, as compared to 300 in 1986.

Ford has been moving faster, too; it is automating its partners in Malaysia and Taiwan. In its Taiwan plant, the company is building up a core of Chinese managers who may help the company enter the mainland Chinese market. First, the company planned to assemble subcompacts in Taiwan (a low-wage, low-cost operation) and export from there. This idea did not work well, but the company kept its struggling joint-venture operations on Taiwan and Malaysia. The Malaysian partner decided to become a "volume player," and today, the highest-quality cars in Malaysia are produced at the jointly owned plant. Many Ford cars coming from factories in Malaysia and Taiwan are stamped out in Mazda's Japanese factories. Ford also moved its Asian headquarters to Tokyo in order to monitor the rivals better.

QUESTIONS

You are in charge of GM Asian operations.

1. What do you think you must do to enter Far Eastern auto markets?

2. What must you do to develop a functional distribution system in this region?

Source: Case adapted from *The Wall Street Journal,* 21 March 1991, A1, A9.

Digital Commerce, E-Shopping, E-Tailing, Cybershopping, Virtual Retailing (or Any Other Name)

Whatever we may call it, the emerging computer technology takes from the existing pool of products and services that are traded and offers a unique service by making it available through a new distribution channel.

Many companies are entering the world of electronic and digital home shopping for the first time. Direct marketers will be designing web sites. There will be 60 to 70 new home-shopping channels spread throughout the world within the next 12 months. Interactive TV, CD-ROM, and the Internet are all adding to the growth of global electronic retailing.

Electronic retailing provides a great deal of product information and the ability to demonstrate product features, advantages, and benefits. It is quite likely that in the near future, smart agents and product finders will provide customers with time-saving and cost-cutting services. This form of trade will shift power in international markets toward consumers.

QUESTIONS

1. If you were giving advice to, say, Sears or Kmart, what kind of advice would you give regarding electronic retailing? Why?

Source: Adapted and condensed from Budd Margolis, "Digital Commerce: The Future of Retailing," *Direct Marketing,* January 1996, 41–47.

ENDNOTES

1 Raymond Bauer and Reed Moyer, "The Structure of Markets in Developing Economies," *MSU Business Topics*, Autumn 1964, 43–80.

2 Shimaguchi Mitsuaki and William Lazer, "Japanese Distribution Channels: Invisible Barriers to Market Entry," *MSU Business Topics*, Winter 1979, 49–62; and William Lazer, Joji Murato, and Hiroshi Kosaka, "Japanese Marketing: Towards a Better Understanding," *Journal of Marketing*, Spring 1985, 69–81.

3 "Japan: A Nation of Wholesalers," *The Economist*, 19 September 1981, 88–89.

4 Robart A. Robicheaux and Raef T. Hussein, "Power and Conflict in Jordanian Food Distribution Channels," *Journal of International Food and Agribusiness Marketing*, 4 March 1989, 69–91.

5 Ibid.

6 "Laying the Foundation for the Great Mall of China," *Business Week*, 25 January 1988, 68–69.

7 "Campbell's Taste of the Japanese Market Is MM-MM Good," *Business Week*, 28 March 1988, 1–12.

8 Bruce Mallen, "Marketing Channels and Economic Development," *International Journal of Physical Distribution and Logistics*, May 1996, 42–49.

9 Mitsuaki and Lazer, "Japanese Distribution Channels."

10 *Business International*, 8 March 1985, 27–29.

11 J. Schafer, "Using Overseas Trade Fairs to Locate Agents and Distributors," *Business Week*, 18 July 1988, 3–4.

12 Phillip Cateora, *International Marketing* (Homewood, Ill.: Richard D. Irwin, 1987).

13 *Business International*, 8 March 1985, 27–29.

14 Ibid.

15 Robert D. Shipley, "Selection and Motivation of Distribution Intermediaries," *Industrial Marketing Management*, October 1984, 149–56.

16 Ibid.

17 Kenneth L. G. Hardy and Allan J. Magrath, "Ten Ways for Manufacturers to Improve Distribution Management," *Business Horizons*, November–December 1988, 65–69.

18 Riad A. Ajami and Dara Khambara, "Global Strategic Alliances," *Journal of Global Marketing* 5, nos. 1, 2 (1991): 55–69.

19 Jean-Pierre Jeannet and Hubert D. Hennessey, *Global Marketing Strategies* (Boston: Houghton Mifflin, 1992), 309–13.

20 Ajami and Khambara, "Global Strategic Alliances."

21 A. Coskun Samli, Erdener Kaynak, and Haroon Sharif, "Developing Strong International Corporate Alliances: Strategic Implications," *Journal of Euromarketing*, 1996 4, no. 3, 23–36.

14

International Logistics

Chapter Outline

Learning Objectives

When you have mastered the contents of this chapter, you will be able to do the following:

1 Define international logistics and explain its contribution to global corporate effectiveness.

2 Outline the importance of raw-material, component, and final-product sourcing in the corporate and multinational manufacturing systems.

3 Discuss the key aspects of moving products from manufacturing to distribution sites, including new developments in freight transportation and alternatives in warehousing systems.

4 Analyze how and why the Japanese integrated raw-material and component outsourcing into comprehensive logistics systems.

Logistics management is a total systems approach to maintaining and managing the distribution process, including all of those activities involved in physically moving raw materials, in-process goods, and finished goods from point of origin to point of use, or consumption.[1]

In order to compete effectively, whether domestically or internationally, companies must do two things well. One is to manufacture (or procure) goods at competitive costs. To do this, manufacturers must procure raw materials and components, and wholesalers and retailers must obtain finished goods, from the most cost-effective sources, domestic or overseas. The second is that the manufacturers, wholesalers, and retailers must move finished products rapidly and cost effectively to needed locations.

THE IMPORTANCE OF LOGISTICS: SOME ILLUSTRATIONS

1. Footlocker, the U.S. sports footwear retailer, had been expanding from 4 to 20 stores in Mexico's Golden Triangle (the region bounded by Mexico City, Guadalajara, and Monterrey, where half of the country's 85 million citizens live). Until 1994, Footlocker had supplied the Mexican stores directly from its U.S. distribution center. But as outlets and sales grew, its Mexican carrier, TNL, was unable to service the extra stores efficiently. Border crossings were slow, and store managers spent most of their time performing traffic functions.

    Footlocker's solution was to open a local warehouse in Mexico City and have a U.S. company, GATX Logistics, run it, headed by Bob Simcoe, a 30-year Mexican logistics veteran. He devised a system to link Footlocker's warehousing and transportation system with a state-of-the-art information system. Footlocker's Mexican operations have been running smoothly ever since.[2]

2. Caprock, a New Jersey-based company, regularly shipped printing screens to Ontario, Canada. The nature of the industry demanded speed in delivery. Surface transportation took a week, and air shipments carried a $40 minimum charge. Overland shipment was relatively inexpensive, but final prices were unacceptably high because of the added fees of customs brokers (who expedited the movement of goods through customs for, in this case, $25 or $30 per shipment). Eventually, Caprock settled on using United Parcel Service, which shipped from New Jersey to Ontario in three days for just $15 total per shipment, a significant savings.[3]

3. View-Master Ideal, a Portland, Oregon, toy manufacturer, imported its Big Bird Story Magic, an animated talking toy, from Hong Kong and South Korea. As Christmas approached (its customers' main selling season), View-Master arranged to reroute merchandise directly to specific customers from its Portland port of entry. Rather than warehousing the goods first and then routing them to buyers, View-Master, working with Portland port authorities, intercepted the goods after entry through customs and rerouted half of its 500,000-unit shipment directly to customers.[4]

4. Global logistics and transportation services have become intensely competitive worldwide as transportation companies compete to take advantage of increased trading opportunities. In Asia, the

Pacific Rim countries accounted for 44 percent of world trade in 1991. This is expected to increase to 52 percent by the year 2005. Because of the geography, goods go by air rather than by sea; and because of intense competition, express service eclipses deferred service by a 7 to 1 margin for most carriers.

Belgian carrier DHL Express Worldwide is the market leader and has been in the Orient the longest—some 22 years. Its 30 percent market share grosses the firm $650 million in sales. The company was diversifying down into heavier freight assignments. They contain costs by using commercial flights, rather than leasing planes, whenever possible.

TNT Express Worldwide is the number two transportation company in Asia with a 20 percent market share. Both TNT and DHL were being pressured by the U.S. companies Federal Express and United Parcel Service. Fedex, still smarting from its enforced withdrawal from the European market, planned to take over part of the former U.S. military base in Subic Bay, Philippines. UPS has also been aggressive and, like Fedex, has been undercutting DHL prices by 20–30 percent. But while gaining market share, both have lost money in the process.[5]

5. Foreign sources of supply are often cheaper than domestic sources. From a logistics viewpoint, "foreign made" means manufactured outside of the country where it is sold. For many large companies, such as Caterpillar and IBM, imports into the United States often are from their foreign subsidiaries. This offshore capability gives companies with foreign manufacturing locations significant flexibility and cost advantages.

Offshore sourcing can be an integral part of a cost-effective manufacturing or retailing strategy. For companies facing low-cost competition, foreign sources are a necessity. For firms capable of processing, repackaging, or effectively marketing imports, foreign sources provide attractive opportunities for profits.

OVERSEAS SOURCING OF RAW MATERIALS, COMPONENTS, AND PRODUCTS

For many companies (retailers, importers, and some manufacturers), the decision to produce goods and materials overseas is easy. Simply stated, if the landed cost (with all tariffs, taxes, and duties added) of a quality product, raw material, or component from a foreign source is significantly less than the cost of its domestic equivalent, then foreign sources are feasible. Conditions favoring offshore procurement can be divided into two groups: marketing-related conditions and manufacturing-related conditions.

Marketing-Related Conditions

Conditions affected by marketing include low degrees of product differentiation (that is, standardized items) and high customer sensitivity to price. These conditions are likely to occur during the maturity stage of a product's life cycle when competition is intense and margins are low.

Items with little or no product differentiation are prime candidates for international sourcing. Regardless of whether it is a raw material, semifinished item, or finished item, if product differentiation is minimal, international procurement is attractive. An overseas source is often the only way to cut procurement costs significantly and improve the seller's competitive edge.

For products in the maturity stage, overseas procurement is often profitable. In maturity-stage items such as men's underwear, there is standardization both at the raw-material end and the ultimate-market end. International firms competing in this product market, such as Haines and Fruit of the Loom, continually search out and evaluate foreign sources of supply.

Manufacturing-Related Conditions

Where companies must invest substantial sums in a new plant or equipment to turn out new components or products in-house, they are likely to source those products or components outside the firm. Another such situation is where manufacturing costs are high relative to price (as they are in competitive markets) and when production costs differ substantially from country to country, usually because of

differences in labor costs. Still another situation is that in which companies have major operations in overseas markets. In all of these situations, foreign procurement is attractive.

Global Sourcing within Multinational Corporations

International firms continually search for ways to lower production costs, either to stay competitive or to increase operating margins. When they decide to manufacture overseas, they must decide on sources of components and raw materials. They can procure materials from within each market (decentralized sourcing) or from offshore sources. Other alternatives are to obtain materials from a single facility (centralized sourcing) either domestic or offshore, or from multiple offshore locations (distributed sourcing). Table 14–1 lists the advantages and disadvantages of centralized and decentralized sourcing.

TABLE 14–1 ▪ *Cost and Benefits of Two Sourcing Strategies*

	Decentralized Sourcing	**Centralized Sourcing**
Benefits	Responsiveness to local needs Multiple sourcing flexibility	Factory economies of scale Quality control
Costs and risks	High unit factory costs High management requirements Lower product consistency	Tariffs Transport Foreign exchange risk Import restriction risk Labor strike risk

Favorable conditions	Avoiding high tariff charges
	Host country preference for
	    local sourcing
	Taking advantage of import
	    restrictions and labor-
	    intensive production
		High value/bulk ratio
		Declining cost structure
		Continuous-process manufacturing
		Host-country export incentives

Source: Based on William H. Davidson, *Global Strategic Management*, New York: John Wiley & Sons, 1982, 191. Reproduced with permission.

Centralized Offshore Sourcing Strategies

Centralized offshore sourcing is appropriate where manufacturing is on a sufficiently large scale to make it economical. Where labor costs make up a large part of the total costs, the international company often centralizes production offshore in perhaps Asia or Mexico. The textile industry in particular has suffered significant job losses due to offshore production. Textiles employed 2.3 million workers in 1970 but experienced a 33 percent job loss down to 1.6 million by 1996.[6]

Centralized sourcing, however, has some unattractive features. One is the susceptibility to any form of disruption in manufacturing (such as shortages or strikes). Another is that distant markets can be difficult to penetrate if transportation costs are high. Perhaps most important, exports from a single facility suffer when the manufacturing base's currency appreciates, making prices less competitive.

Many companies equate offshore sourcing with developing countries such as Mexico, Taiwan, and Hong Kong, but substantial amounts of offshore manufacturing occur in developed countries as well. The Harvard Multinational Enterprise Project showed that only 22 percent of 362 pure export plants were in countries commonly identified as "low cost."[7] One-third were in five developed countries (Canada, Belgium, Netherlands, United Kingdom, and Italy). Clearly then, low labor costs are not the only reason to go off-shore. Availability of trained personnel, suitable economic infrastructures, and highly developed transportation systems also are key factors.

Decentralized and Distributed Sourcing

At the other end of the sourcing spectrum is decentralized purchasing, with local procurement of all components and materials. Decentralized sourcing is the usual choice where ultimate consumers prefer localized offerings (as with food, drink, and general consumer products); where countries have balance-of-payment problems and impose tariffs on imported components or supplies; and where there are local laws requiring high percentages of indigenous parts in products, for example, EU provisions that European-made foreign products must contain at least 40 percent European parts.[8]

A compromise between centralized off-shore sourcing and decentralized in-market sourcing is *distributed sourcing*. This occurs when multiple sources are used for particular products or components. That is, when multinational companies use several supply sources to serve their worldwide markets, thus giving them options in choosing the best vendors for particular sourcing assignments. Distributed sources, in common use among U.S.-based automakers, have disadvantages. Intracompany transactions are vulnerable to exchange-rate fluctuations and are subject to disruptions from labor strikes or transportation problems. Some companies set up "twin factories" to ensure continuous supplies of components.

Distributed sourcing does yield, however, the sorts of world-class-scale economies that MNCs seek when introducing offshore manufacturing. In addition, when properly managed, distributed sourcing combines impressively low costs with some ability to switch component sources among affiliates. This advantage gives MNCs needed operational flexibility in competitive markets.

The decision to foreign-source a particular product or component generally is based on economic criteria. Because of low labor costs, advantageous exchange rates, manufacturing and technical superiority, or some combination of these factors, many companies find importing products and components worthwhile.

TABLE 14–2 ■ *Import Profile: USA*

General Merchandise Imports (Customs Value, $ billions)
Principal End-Use Category

Year	Total	Foods, Feeds & Beverages	Industrial Supplies & Materials	Capital Goods Except Automobiles	Automotive Vehicle Parts and Engines	Consumer Goods (nonfood) Except Automotive
1990	495.3	26.6	143.2	116.4	87.3	105.7
1991	488.5	26.5	131.6	120.7	85.7	108.0
1992	532.7	27.6	138.6	134.3	91.8	122.7
1993	580.7	27.9	145.6	152.4	102.4	134.0
1994	66.33	31.0	162.0	184.4	188.3	146.3
1995	743.4	33.2	180.7	221.4	124.8	160.0

Source: Economic Indicators (Washington, D.C.: U.S. Printing Office, January–February 1997), 35.

INTERNATIONAL SOURCING

United States imports in 1995 came to $743 billion. Thus, imports accounted for nearly 10 percent of nongovernment expenditures. Table 14–2 is an import profile of the U.S. Note the over $400 billion of imported industrial supplies, materials, and capital goods. This is the extent of American manufacturing dependence on foreign supply sources.

Locating Foreign Sources

How does a manager find products to import? A preliminary step is to visit one or more merchandise marts in New York, Atlanta, Dallas, Los Angeles, and elsewhere. These "import emporia" show, at least for consumer goods, what is available from established sources. However, the merchandise mart assortments are selective. To identify a larger selection of products from overseas sources, it is necessary to examine country import statistics. In the United

States, the Department of Commerce's National Trade Data Bank identifies the sources from which the U.S. imported specific products. Similar to the export listings in Chapter 8, this data source starts with the largest country importers into the U.S. and works its way down to smaller suppliers. Table 14–3 shows 1994–96 U.S. import statistics for men's and boy's shirts HS# 61051; dollar values and unit quantities (numbers of dozens in this case) are shown. From these statistics, the third row (cost per dozen) can be calculated.

WHICH COUNTRIES EXPORT THE MOST TO THE UNITED STATES? ■ This question is a good barometer of which country markets have consistently met American tastes over, in this case, the period 1994–96. As with the export statistics in Chapter 8, totals are given, followed by import listings in descending order of importance. As can be seen, U.S. importers get their shirts from Asia and, increasingly, Latin America. Pakistan, India, Thailand, and the Philippines are major suppliers, followed by Honduras, Hong Kong, China, Guatemala, Turkey, and Indonesia.

TABLE 14–3 ■ *Imports of Men's and Boy's Shirts (HS# 61051) into the U.S., 1994–96*

	1996	1995	1994
World × $1,000	$1,362,260	$1,209,565	$882,574
No. dozen	7,390,817	15,155,613	10,508,621
Cost/doz. $	78.33	79.81	83.98
Pakistan × $1,000	$204,534	$196,670	$103,352
No. dozen	3,162,786	3,248,254	1,806,713
Cost/doz. $	64.68	60.55	57.22
India × $1,000	122,179	$73,119	$39,099
No. dozen	1,809,208	1,182,359	686,632
Cost/doz. $	67.53	61.60	56.99
Thailand × $1,000	$96,651	$94,401	$89,869
No. dozen	971,841	1,046,057	1,014,185
Cost/doz. $	99.84	90.24	88.62
Philippines × $1,000	$82,201	$97,795	$63,880
No. dozen	816,814	1,030,435	674,926
Cost/doz. $	100.73	94.94	94.77
Honduras × $1,000	$72,931	$43,585	$25,703
No. dozen	1,295,746	715,856	419,468
Cost/doz. $	56.31	60.95	61.34
Hong Kong × $1,000	$65,031	$93,856	$109,274
No. dozen	491,509	722,197	$909,457
Cost/doz. $	132.44	129.99	120.21
China × $1,000	$64,167	$69,800	$57,421
No. dozen	554,905	685,090	563,958
Cost/doz. $	115.82	101.89	101.99
Guatemala × $1,000	$52,805	$29,893	$20,271
No. dozen	852,679	449,892	280,629
Cost/doz. $	61.97	66.57	72.39
Turkey × $1,000	$46,312	$40,923	$27,149
No. dozen	652,114	546,506	345,707
Cost/doz. $	71.03	74.95	78.69
Indonesia × $1,000	$44,081	$52,198	$45,317
No. dozen	445,791	558,468	502,131
Cost/doz. $	99.05	93.54	90.27

Note: 1996 costs per dozen for selected countries at lower import levels: Dominican Republic, $66.12; Egypt, $57.87; Mexico, $62.91; and Haiti, $48.24.

Source: Adapted from: *National Trade Data Base* statistics (Washington, D.C.: International Trade Administration).

Note that well over 100 countries export shirts to the U.S. Only primary suppliers are shown in Table 14–3.

WHICH COUNTRIES ARE CONSISTENTLY THE MOST COST-EFFECTIVE SUPPLIERS? ■

Table 14–3 shows that the average landed price was around $80 over 1994–96 but that the lowest-cost Asian and Latin American suppliers are about 25 percent cheaper (about $60–$65 a dozen, or $5 a shirt). Overall, Haiti, at $48 a dozen, is the lowest-cost producer, with Honduras second in 1996 with a landed price of about $56. Note, though, that marketers should be wary of accepting landed prices at face value. There are three primary reasons for this. (1) There are variations within the product category. This listing includes both men's and boy's shirts. While most producers would manufacture both, where countries specialize in (for example) boys' shirts, some distortions can occur. (2) Prices say nothing of product quality and materials. (3) Exchange-rate fluctuations affect landed prices. The U.S. dollar is rarely consistently strong or weak against all currencies. Consistent devaluations of foreign currencies result in competitive export prices in the U.S. market.

Free Trade Zones

Free trade zones (FTZs), also called foreign trade zones and special economic zones, are legally secure areas, usually close to ports or international airports, that are free of normal customs regulations. Many importers have set up warehouses or assembly operations within the sanctuary of an FTZ.

FTZs have the following advantages:

1. Processing or assembly within FTZs reduces import tariffs or duties. Volkswagen pays only 2.9 percent duty on VW Rabbits assembled in its New Stanton, Pennsylvania, FTZ, which compares to 6 percent that it would pay on imported disassembled parts for assembly outside FTZs.[9] Similarly, Smith-Corona obtained FTZ status for its U.S. typewriter-assembly operation and was exempted from the 7 percent duty on parts.[10]

2. Components can be imported into FTZs in the United States, assembled, and reexported completely free of U.S. customs fees and tariffs.

3. Warehouses in FTZs are used to store goods. For example, retailers leave seasonal merchandise in FTZ storage facilities until it is needed. Duties are not payable until goods leave the FTZ, so storage delays customs charges and aids retailer cash flows. Retailers also use FTZs to process goods—for example, adding their own private labels to fashion merchandise.

4. Domestically produced goods can "officially" leave the country of manufacture and be stored in FTZs. In countries where exports are exempt from value-added taxes (as in Europe), FTZs speed up governmental tax rebates.

5. Showrooms and storage facilities within FTZs enable importers to bring in products, show them, and ship them to customers.

6. Companies establish assembly or production facilities within FTZs in developing countries to take advantage of low labor costs. U.S. medical supplier Becton-Dickinson uses its FTZ in Montevideo, Uruguay, to reach growth markets in Argentina and Chile. The new trade agreements in Latin America (MERCOSUR, Andean Pact, and NAFTA) have

spawned many new FTZs. The island state of the Dominican Republic has 42 FTZs. MERCOSUR members plan to add 57 new ones before the year 2000 in Argentina, Brazil, Paraguay, and Uruguay; and Panama's Colon FTZ has annual trade flows of $10 billion. The cumulative throughputs of Latin FTZs are estimated at over $60 billion a year.[11]

FTZs are common in the United States, where there are 145 active zones and 120 subzones (especially designated areas for duty-free operations at a company's manufacturing plant). FTZs are seeing increasing use, with the value of merchandise moving through them estimated at $40 billion in 1986, or 60 times more than in 1975.[12]

INTEGRATING PROCUREMENT INTO THE MANUFACTURING PROCESS: THE JAPANESE JUST-IN-TIME [JIT] SYSTEM

Raw materials and components feed into company production processes and add to company inventory. In the Japanese *kanban* (just-in-time, or JIT) system, subassemblies, fabricated parts, and other materials and components arrive at the manufacturing site "just in time" for inclusion in the production process. Finished goods are also manufactured and delivered to retailers "just in-time" for selling.[13]

Advantages of the JIT System

The advantages of a JIT system are as follows:

1. JIT methods enable Japanese automakers to keep on hand materials and parts worth only $150 per car, compared to $775 for U.S. car producers. JIT thus contributes to saving space needed for manufacturing as well as to reducing costs for inventory. One former Chrysler executive estimated that U.S. assembly plants needed on average 2 million square feet to make 1,000 cars per day, whereas Japanese plants needed only 1.5 million square feet.[14]

2. Because inventories are minimized, suppliers must continually ship components and materials. The entire manufacturing system is driven by market demand, so production schedules often are interrupted as model changeovers are made to reflect current market demand. This arrangement has made Japanese producers very efficient in minimizing manufacturing set-up times. It takes U.S. auto manufacturers about six hours to change auto process and dies, but in Japan, it takes only a few minutes.[15]

3. There are three main reasons that JIT works in Japan. First, the Japanese are fanatical about not letting the ordering company down and are meticulous in responding to changing manufacturing needs. Second, in many cases, the suppliers are owned by the manufacturer. Third, Japanese suppliers are usually geographically concentrated around the main production plant and are rarely more than four hours away. Both Toyota and Nissan structure their components and supply system around their primary manufacturing facilities. General Motors is one of many U.S. companies (others are GE and Westinghouse) that have implemented JIT systems. GM's facility in Buick City saves the company more than $3 billion per year in freight, inventory, and storage costs.[16]

It is possible to engineer just-in-time systems domestically. It can also be done internationally, but it requires excellent organization.

The GM-Toyota Joint Venture

General Motors entered a joint venture with Toyota to produce Novas using the JIT system.

THE CHALLENGE ■ "Customers determine what type of vehicle is made, how many, the model mix, the speed of the assembly line," said Ed Mirhead, manager of New United Motor Manufacturing, Inc. (NUMMI), the GM-Toyota joint venture.[17] Wanted: Eight Nova models for customers 10,000 miles away.

THE SYSTEM ■ GM and Toyota devised the following JIT system to meet this challenge.

1. NUMMI places daily orders with Toyota via satellite.

2. Orders are received in Toyota's factories in Aichi Prefecture, central Japan. The 1,600 Nova components are split between Toyota in-house sources and 70 smaller companies.

3. About 900 car sets (unassembled cars) are shipped daily to the Kamigo Vanning Center (KVC), which consolidates them into 30 containers each holding 30 car sets. Engines are shipped to KVC from Toyota's Shimoyama plant—16 truckloads of 56 engines each make the 20-minute trip per day. They are tightly packed into containers using 59.9 of the available 63 cubic meters of space.

4. Between 30 and 35 containers of car sets and engines are shipped daily to the port of Nagoya.

5. The containers make a 14-day steamship journey from Nagoya to Oakland, California; 10 percent of weekly shipments arrive on Fridays, 50 percent on Saturdays, and 40 percent the following Wednesday.

6. In Oakland, off-loading is streamlined. The in-out times for road haulers is 10 minutes per container. The containers are transported 31 miles to the FTZ at NUMMI, where they may be inspected, especially in the unlikely event that a container seal is broken. Because duties are only paid when the finished car leaves the plant, an estimated $56 per vehicle is saved (that is, the difference between duty costs of importing the entire auto against only bringing in components).

7. NUMMI informs its U.S. suppliers what to ship daily, although approximate and constantly updated forecasts up to seven weeks ahead are supplied to components producers. Twenty trailers of components per day are delivered to NUMMI. Generally, shipments are three days in transit from U.S. suppliers.

8. NUMMI, from these Japanese and U.S. supplies, builds 490 cars per day. NUMMI unloads 16 containers per work shift, an average of one container every 28 minutes.

THE RESULT ■ These combined GM-Toyota efforts resulted in a quality car very unlike its predecessor, the old Chevy Nova. NUMMI management believed the new car was as well made as the Toyota Cressida. The only problem was the product image, which had to be slowly overcome by special financing packages and word-of-mouth endorsements from satisfied owners.

MOVING THE PRODUCT TO THE CUSTOMER

Up to this point, this chapter has focused on identifying and moving materials and components from their sources to manufacturing sites. But that is only part of logistics management. The other part consists of moving finished products to customers. Two major concerns are particularly critical at this stage: transportation and warehousing.

Trends in Transportation

Ocean freight transportation still carries the lion's share of the world's shipments, but air freight has been slowly increasing in importance. Many trends have contributed to more efficient uses of the many transportation modes.

The development that had the greatest impact on U.S. ocean freight was the 1984 Shipping Act, which effectively deregulated ocean shipping lines and allowed them to adjust rates, auction off surplus space near sailing times, and offer discounts to smooth out their peak demand periods. This act also made it legal for international shippers to set up joint ventures with, for example, trucking companies, thus reaping the economic benefits of intermodal transportation (using different transportation modes for individual shipments). Figure 14–1 shows some options for intermodal international distribution.

LANDBRIDGES ▪ Landbridges are cross-country connections, often by rail, from port to port, usually for retransportation, (for example, goods from Japan destined for Europe via the United States). *Mini-land-bridges* are partial cross-country transportation connections, often from a port to an

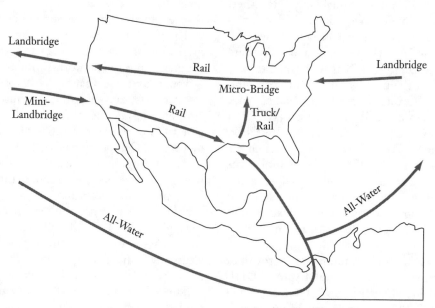

Source: David L. Anderson, "International Logistics Strategies for the 1980s," *International Journal of Physical Distribution and Materials Management* 15, no. 4 (1985): 10. Reproduced with permission.

FIGURE 14–1 *Options for Intermodal International Distribution*

in-country destination. Finally, *micro-land-bridges* are within-country transportation connections that are still parts of an international shipment system.

There have been other offshoots of increased intermodal transportation. Because containers play important roles in intermodal transportation, demand is increasing for larger container ships. American President Lines increased its use of C-10 vessels, each capable of carrying 4,300 containers, compared to 4,000, which was previously the largest container load. These wide vessels are fuel efficient and easy to load and unload. Sea-Land purchased 12 jumbo "Atlantic-class" ships, each with the capacity to hold 4,400 containers. It is anticipated that these larger vessels will significantly lower operating costs.[18]

Another important consequence of intermodal transportation and the 1984 Shipping Act is the movement toward the merging of international shipping lines. Royal Dutch Nedlloyd Lines joined with two U.S. companies, Trans Freight Lines and Sea-Land, to consolidate and eliminate excess capacity on North Atlantic crossings.[19] Britain's Ocean Transport and Trading Group formed an alliance with Dutch Royal Nedlloyd in which (1) Ocean Transport acquired Nedlloyd's New York, Singapore, West German, and French air cargo operations; (2) Nedlloyd took over Ocean's United Kingdom–based trucking operation; and (3) Ocean and Nedlloyd formed a joint venture to handle air freight in the Netherlands, Belgium, and Spain.[20]

AIR FREIGHT ■ The international growth of companies such as Federal Express, DHL Worldwide Express, and United Parcel Service (UPS) is symptomatic of the growth in air freight volume, but these companies and others like them account for only a small part of the international air freight business.

Most airline companies, including those that provide mainly passenger services, derive substantial revenues from their cargo services. In fact, most airlines are expanding and, in some cases, reorganizing their international cargo routes. In the Canadian air cargo industry for example, Air Canada operates four DC8 freighter services across the Atlantic to its hub in Brussels, with through-services to Singapore, Bangkok, and Hong Kong. Canadian Airlines has been assigned most of the Pacific routes east of Burma, including those to Australia and Japan.[21]

Federal Express and UPS coordinate air-ground transportation systems in the United States and abroad, and the European airlines also have built up their trucking capabilities. British Airways has trucking hubs for road-based feeder operations in Maastricht (Netherlands) and Helsingborg (Sweden). The Helsingborg hub, linking Scandinavia with London, enabled BA to improve delivery times by one day each way. Similarly, Air France regards its trucking services as an integral part of its total transport system. Air France management estimated that a European air cargo network—without trucks—would cost triple what the truck costs.[22]

Airport managements and authorities have entered the global arena as they compete to offer the best facilities for air cargo movement. Competition is particularly fierce among Europe's airports, all of which are trying to become the premier European air cargo transportation center. While Frankfurt, Germany's leading airport, led throughout the 1980s, London's Heathrow Airport has reshaped itself to become a viable alternative. In cooperation with British Airways, Heathrow brought in a new freight-handling system as well as a computer-controlled freight-movement system, which greatly increased both the efficiency and capacity of Heathrow's world cargo center. Other innovations include new 20-foot containers for intermodal transportation and a winged pallet (portable platform) that not only holds one-fourth more cargo than traditional pallets but also has enough efficient storage area to give British Airways the largest hold capacities in the business. At Heathrow, there are also new multilevel, friction-driven storage and retrieval racks with three elevating transfer vehicles (ETVs), which transport cargoes and containers between trailers and within the facility. These single-person-operated ETVs allowed British Airways to triple its storage capacity and speed up loading and unloading. BA also linked its new computer to its inventory control system and introduced bar and laser codings, voice recognition, and automatic guidance systems.[23]

Air freight has never lived up to its potential to dominate international transportation, but its contribution has been notable. With the advent of just-in-time supply systems, air freight will contribute more significantly, particularly as air transportation of components and merchandise becomes economically more feasible.[24]

HIGH-SPEED TRAINS ■ While most people think of air transportation as the quickest means of transportation between two points, in Europe, Japan, and, increasingly, in the United States, high-speed trains are emerging as an attractive alternative.

In Europe, 190-mile-per-hour trains are cutting travel times between major European cities such as Paris, Brussels, and Cologne, with eventual extensions via sea travel to Oslo (Norway), Madrid (Spain), Edinburgh (Scotland), and Vienna (Austria). The network was due to become operational in the mid-1990s. At present, individual countries have their own systems. The French, pioneers in this field, have had their *train a grande vitesse* (TGV) since 1981; it makes a 300-plus-mile journey in just two hours (compared to more

than six hours formerly). The Germans have the Intercity Experimental program (ICE); in 1988, ICE set a record of 254 miles per hour. The German government is also testing a magnetic levitation train, the Transrapid, which has speed potential of well over 300 miles per hour. The Italians have their Pendelino trains. The European Union expects these trains to replace shorter air trips (up to 300 miles) and longer car journeys.[25]

Other trends in transportation and distribution include the following:

- Global standards of electronic data interchange will be developed that erase distinctions between carriers; this will enable the computers of shippers and carriers to "talk" with each other.

- The transportation industry will polarize into an elite group of megacarriers and small niche carriers that cater to specific markets.

- Transportation and logistics services will be fully integrated into company supply chains, and transportation logistics technologies will be used to gain competitive advantages over rivals.

- Warehouse use in logistics systems will fall as JIT systems become the norm. Where warehousing is used, orders will be received, mechanically sorted, and retrieved by computer.

- Shipper-carrier partnerships will become long term—using perhaps 20-year contracts.

- Logistics will become the last frontier of cost reduction, with speed, responsiveness, and flexibility characterizing the best systems.

- Carriers and companies will continue trends toward leasing rather than owning transportation/logistics assets.

- There are increasing numbers of alliances, partnerships, and creative relationships among carriers.[26]

International Storage and Retrieval Systems

Storage and warehousing facilities can provide decided advantages in distribution of the final product and in customer service. Where multinationals have on-site manufacturing, local arrangements are possible for management of inventories, storage, and warehousing. Problems arise, however, when the international marketer must speedily and cost-effectively coordinate international storage and delivery to customers. Depending on the product's nature (its bulk and value), the level of customer service required, transportation costs, and market requirements, multinationals generally use one or more of four basic storage and retrieval systems: (1) classical, (2) transit, (3) direct, and (4) multicountry warehouse (see Figure 14–2).[27]

THE CLASSICAL SYSTEM ▪ In the classical system, bulk shipments are to subsidiary warehouses, where goods are stored until customers order. The advantages of this system include low transportation costs because of the use of ocean freight and the consolidation of cargoes. Bulk shipments also lessen documentation requirements. Buffer stocks built into the system minimize stockout probabilities. The classical system is costly to maintain. Nevertheless, it is an appropriate choice for companies with broad product assortments, where customer demand is stable and predictable and where customers want merchandise "from stock" immediately.

THE TRANSIT SYSTEM ▪ In the transit system, there are rapid movements of small

Classical Model's Physical Flow of Merchandise

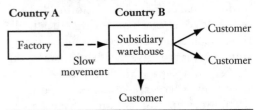

Transit Model's Physical Flow of Merchandise

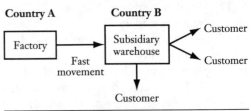

Direct System

Multicountry Warehouse

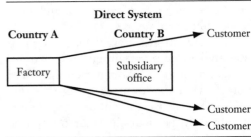

Source: Jacques Picard, "Typology of Physical Distribution Systems in Multinational Corporations," *International Journal of Physical Distribution and Materials Management* 12, no. 6 (1982): 30–33. Reproduced with permission.

FIGURE 14-2 *Multinational Warehousing Systems*

shipments of goods between manufacturing locations and warehouses, which serve only as distribution centers. Storage costs are low because only safety stocks are kept, but transportation costs are often high because speedy forms of transport are used (such as air freight); also, administration and documentation costs are high because of small shipment sizes. The transit system is used with shipments that have high value in proportion to their weight (such as computers, scientific equipment, and medical instruments) and where last-minute inspection is necessary before shipping the product to the customer.

THE DIRECT SYSTEM ■
The direct system involves shipping merchandise either directly from the production site to the customer or directly into a subsidiary's distribution channel. This system centralizes storage in the home market and makes possible large-scale marketing from large inventory sizes. Furthermore, it eliminates subsidiary handling, storage, or shipping expenses. Direct systems work best with high-value goods (such as computers and electronic equipment); perishable or seasonal goods (such as foods); where customer demand is erratic or fragmented; and where the products are custom made.

Direct systems have numerous disadvantages. Transportation costs are high, because frequent shipments are necessary, and it is rarely possible to economize by consolidating freight. Quality control, labeling, and packaging must be performed at the central manufacturing site, often making multilingual labeling necessary. Finally, customers (or their authorized representatives) must personally clear the goods through customs and pay the duties, which is often inconvenient for the buyers.

THE MULTICOUNTRY WAREHOUSE SYSTEM ■
The muticountry warehouse system is used by companies that have numerous subsidiaries in the same geographic area and by companies where affiliates produce different components that need consolidation before final shipments to customers. Costs are lower than maintaining several national warehouse locations, but they are largely offset by higher transportation costs to and from the warehouse. Other problems arise if multicountry warehouses fall under a particular market's jurisdiction or if disputes arise over the allocation of warehouse costs among participating affiliates.[28] The multicountry warehouse system is appropriate when product demand is erratic and the products have low turnover rates; where there are numerous small country markets in close proximity (for example, in continental Europe and Central America); and where there is much intracompany shipping of products and components.

Logistics in a Unified Europe. European unification has caused many companies to rethink their European logistics systems. The opening up of borders in the EU and the harmonization of product and industry technical standards have made country-based logistics and warehousing systems inefficient means of serving continental Europe. Hewlett-Packard brings its keyboard, components, and product literature together in Luxembourg, where they are consolidated and shipped to assembly and manufacturing sites in Germany, the Netherlands, and France. From there, they are shipped to resellers at 24 to 48 hours' notice (or even 4–5 hours in urgent cases). GE similarly rethought its region-wide logistics strategy. A computer analysis was used to determine that just five warehouses should be used in the new united Europe, with Metz as the primary location to serve the important markets of France, Germany, Austria, Switzerland, and the Benelux countries.[29]

Global Logistics in Footwear and Apparel: Timberland's Worldwide Supply Chain. Timberland's first international sale was in 1979. By the mid-1990s, one-half of its $419 million annual sales were outside its native U.S. market in any one of 50 countries worldwide. The company sourced its brand-name footwear and apparel from countries in Asia, Europe, and the Americas, but its average footwear shipment was just 12 pairs of shoes. Accordingly, the company consolidated its warehousing from a dozen centers in Asia down to just two; and it established single continental distribution centers in both North America and Europe. To integrate its information and transportation systems, Timberland worked with San Francisco–based freight-forwarder ACS and with software specialists Rockport to develop a comprehensive product tracking system.[30]

IMPROVEMENTS IN COMMUNICATION

Significant improvements in communication have made possible increased efficiencies in national and international logistics systems. Communications involve flows of information, whereas transportation and warehousing involve flows of materials and products. Traditionally, telephone services have provided nearly instantaneous oral communications between countries. Now, developments in communications technologies have provided visual communication and improved written communications. Among these developments are the following:

1. Telex systems, which enable companies to exchange printed messages.

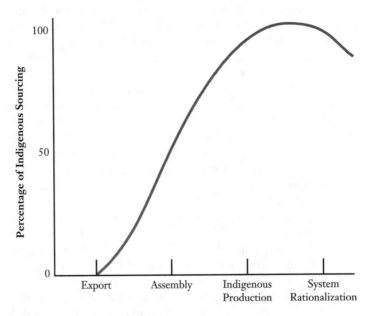

Source: William H. Davidson, *Global Strategic Management* (New York: John Wiley & Sons, 1982), 203. Reproduced with permission.

FIGURE 14–3 *Stages in the Sourcing Cycle*

2. Computerized networking systems, which enable companies to communicate quickly and to coordinate global activities.

3. Facsimile (fax) machines, which are high-speed electronic mail systems.

4. Video conferencing, which involves televised satellite transmissions, enabling the linking up of international executives for purposes of visual and oral communications.

5. International express mail services, which are based on state-of-the-art mailing technologies. Companies such as Federal Express, United Parcel Services, DHL Worldwide Express, Australia's TNT, and Japan's Nippon Cargo Airlines have made package delivery easy and quick almost everywhere.

THE FULLY INTEGRATED LOGISTICS SYSTEM: THE JAPANESE GLOBAL MARKETING NETWORK

Global logistics systems have the potential for maintaining company competitiveness in world markets in spite of changing circumstances in individual markets. By switching resources among plants in various countries, a company can offset adverse exchange rates, labor disruptions, political unrest, or rising costs.

The Four Stages of Procurement

MNCs go through four major stages in the sourcing cycle (see Figure 14–3). The four stages are classified according to the approximate percentages of indigenous (local) production. In stage one (no local production), firms service markets through exports. In stage two, because of growing competition, tariffs, or preferences for localized products, companies move to assembly-type operations (using locally made parts assembled in the firm's home country). In stage three, they move to indigenous production. Finally, in stage four, as the MNCs' global manufacturing experience accumulates, they establish affiliates that specialize in one aspect of production, taking advantage of large-scale markets, and the movement of materials and components between company affiliates becomes regular.[31]

The Japanese Approach to Global Sourcing and Logistics

While some U.S. companies have sophisticated global manufacturing operations (for example, Caterpillar, Ford, and IBM), the Japanese, perhaps because of their late arrival as a world economic force (the late 1960s, compared to the 1950s for U.S. firms), have put together a global logistics network combining the global efficiencies of integrated sourcing with the advantage of producing individual items at the most cost-competitive locations. Figure 14–4 shows a conceptualization of this system. It has four primary features: (1) Labor-intensive components are produced in developing countries; (2) high-tech parts are manufactured in developed countries; (3) proprietary or higher-tech features are put together in Japan; and (4) the system is integrated with assembly operations at each production facility that put all of the components together into the final product.[32]

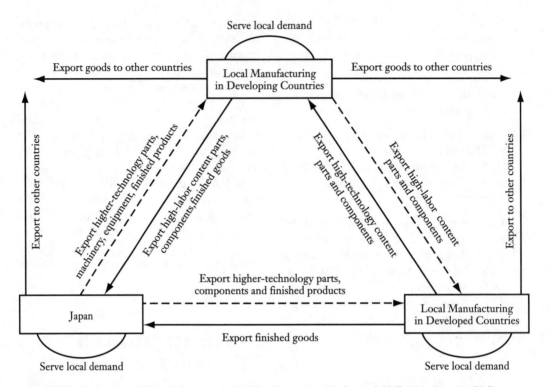

Source: Philip Kotler, Liam Fahey, S. Jaturipitak, *The New Competition* (Englewood Cliffs, N.J.: Prentice-Hall, 1985), 188.

FIGURE 14-4 *The Japanese Fully Integrated Global Logistics and Marketing System*

SUMMARY

Global logistics comprises two separate but interrelated areas—overseas sourcing of raw material and components, and physical distribution of finished products to overseas markets. Foreign sources, whether from a single or multiple locations, provide companies with low-cost materials and competitive selling prices. A simple process, using National Trade Data Base import trade statistics, is helpful in locating low-cost, quality suppliers.

Physical distribution to overseas customers can be either slow but cheap (by ocean) or quick but expensive (by air freight). Linkages between company affiliates worldwide, through computer networks, fax machines, and video conferences, are contributing to more tightly coordinated corporate global activities. Complementing these developments in communications are improvements in transportation, especially in air freight. Four warehousing systems are identified—classical, transit, multicountry, and direct. Each has its own advantages and disadvantages. A fully integrated logistics system, the Japanese global marketing network, vividly illustrates how sources can be integrated into a global manufacturing and assembly system.

DISCUSSION QUESTIONS

1. Define the following terms: international logistics; centralized, decentralized, and distributed offshore sources; foreign trade zones; just-in-time (JIT) systems; and fully integrated logistics systems.

2. Discuss the relative importance of advances in communication, transportation, and storage and delivery systems. Which parts of the corporate logistics system do they affect most? How will advances affect company logistical operations?

3. "Offshore sourcing results in unemployment in the home market." Discuss this statement. Who would make these sorts of generalizations? Why?

Managing the Fully Integrated Global Logistics System: Benetton

How can a company cater to a global fashion market that demands the latest styles and where product mixes change up to 10 times a year? The answer is to have a world-class logistics system linking demand directly to the manufacturing and procurement processes. This is the essence of Benetton's global logistics system. Here's how it works.

Demand is monitored daily through the company's Electronic Data Interchange (EDI) system, which transmits orders from Benetton's agents in over 100 countries. Each agent consolidates sales data from the company's 7,000 stores worldwide. Garments are cut using sophisticated computer-aided design (CAD) technology. They are then sent away to be assembled in any one of Benetton's 450 subcontractors and are brought back to be dyed in the latest fashion colors. This "cut first, dye later" process gives the company a major competitive advantage in the marketplace. Garments are then shipped to the $50 million robotic distribution center, where they are packaged for shipment to retailers. The distribution system handles 12,000 boxes a day (or 6,000 shipments) and 60 million garments yearly. Benetton's freight-forwarding function is managed by Worldwide Integrated Distribution Enterprise (WIDE), which air freights half of the $2 billion of garments to retailers. This enables the company to maintain an eight-day order-to-fulfillment cycle worldwide, keeps output abreast of fashion tastes, and permits low inventories. At the other end of the supply chain, Benetton's purchasing power enables it to get the best terms from its 180 raw-material buyers.

QUESTIONS

1. What are the key elements of Benetton's global logistics system? Which do you think is the most important and why?

2. Do you think that Benetton's logistical system could be used in other industries? Why or why not?

Source: Adapted from Peter Dapiran, "Benetton—Global Logistics in Action," *International Journal of Physical Distribution* 22, no. 6 (1992): 7–11; and Thomas A. Foster, "Global Logistics Benetton-Style," *Distribution,* October 1993, 62–66.

Waterford Crystal: To Outsource or Not to Outsource—That Is the Question

Is Waterford Crystal—"the ambassador of a nation" whose brilliance advertisements attribute to "deep prismatic cutting that must be done entirely by skilled hands rather than by machines"—produced by machines in Germany?

Very likely! At Christmas 1990, Waterford test-marketed four German machine-made crystal gift items in the United States, where 70 percent of Waterford crystal is sold. Market research showed that American consumers felt that the Waterford label was the primary sales feature, not the fact that it was handmade in Ireland. Were the test market successful, Waterford planned to obtain a substantial amount of its glassware from outside Ireland. The company had identified other candidates for manufacturing Waterford in Czechoslovakia.

Many were apprehensive about the company's plans. George Watts, owner of the Milwaukee China and Crystal store, noted: "People are willing to pay three times as much because it's made in Ireland." "Outsourcing," he further stated, "puts a stake through the heart of Waterford."

Competitors were not unhappy about the situation. Patrick Baboin, sales director of the French company Cristalleries Baccarat, had similar reservations. Baccarat and Waterford are towns with reputations built on crystal. Said Baboin, "We've been working with the same families for 250 years. It would make no sense to produce crystal in another country and call it Baccarat."

Another rival, Tipperary Crystal (which was started by a former Waterford employee), was ecstatic. Its U.S. sales agent noted, "Waterford is really making our job easier."

So why do it? Because the company was in dire financial straits. Waterford, which had been taken over by Wedgwood in 1986, had experienced a $26 million accounting error in 1989 and lost $26 million during the first half of 1990 on sales of $76 million. The Irish punt had risen 83 percent against the dollar since 1985, and Waterford had not even been able to make money in the U.S. market, where 70 percent of sales occurred. Despite a $140 million equity injection, the company believed that cost cutting was the answer. A 14-week fight with company unions won a longer workweek and other minor concessions. Waterford management, however, was convinced that further cost reductions were in order, and it looked to foreign sources to secure cheaper output.

QUESTIONS

1. Do you think Waterford should outsource its crystal from Germany or Czechoslovakia? Why?

2. What do you think are Waterford's real problems? Will the outsourcing solution address them?

3. Identify other solutions to Waterford's problems.

Source: Adapted from Mark Maremont, Mark Landier, and Stewart Toy, "Has Waterford Set Loose a Bull in Its Shop?" *Business Week*, 5 November 1990, 58.

ENDNOTES

1 David L. Anderson, "International Logistics Strategies for the 1980s," *International Journal of Physical Distribution and Materials Management* 15, no. 4 (1985): 5–19.

2 Peter Buxbaum, "Mexican Logistics: A Golden Opportunity," *Distribution*, October 1994, 28–36.

3 Bruce Heydt, "International Middlemen: Caprock," *Distribution*, October 1986, 50.

4 E. J. Muller and Gordon Jay, "Global Logistics: View-Master Ideal," *Distribution*, March 1987, 46–47.

5 Andrew Tausz, "Pacific Rim Carriers Fly High," *Distribution*, July 1994, 55–58.

6 Mark Mittelhauser, "Job Loss and Survival Strategies in the Textile and Apparel Industries," *Occupational Outlook Quarterly*, Fall 1996, 18–27.

7 J.P. Curham, W.H. Davidson, and Rajan Suri, *Tracing the Multinationals* (Cambridge, Mass.: Ballinger Publishers, 1977), 398–399.

8 "When 'Made in Europe' Isn't," *Economist*, 8 October 1988, 63–64.

9 Donald A. Ball and Wendell H. McCulloch, *International Business*, 3rd ed. (Plano, Tex.: Business Publications, 1988), 605.

10 Ken Slocum, "Smith-Corona Uses FTZ Status to Contain Costs," *The Wall Street Journal*, 17 November 1987, B1.

11 Charles W. Thurston, "FTZs: Gateways to Latin America," *Distribution*, December 1996, 44–46.

12 K. Slocum, "Import Battle," *The Wall Street Journal*, 30 September 1987, p. A1.

13 Richard J. Schoenberger, *Japanese Manufacturing Techniques* (New York: Free Press, 1982), 16.

14 Ball and McCulloch, *International Business*, 708.

15 Schoenberger, *Japanese Manufacturing Techniques*, 20–21.

16 Otis Port, "High Tech to the Rescue," *Business Week*, 16 June 1988, 100–108.

17 Adapted from E.J. Muller and Roger Schreffler, "NUMMI—How Toyota-GM Makes Cars by Crossing the Pacific, Just in Time," *Distribution*, October 1986, 53–60.

18 Dan Kelly, "Water...Bigger Containership Forecast as Intermodalism Expands," *Traffic World*, 24 April 1989, 36–37.

19 Ibid., 36.

20 Leigh Stoner, "British Ocean Trading Group Poised for North American Buy," *Traffic World*, 1 May 1989, 36–37.

21 Philip Hastings, "Competition and Capacity Grow in Battle to Fill Space," *Transport*, February 1988, 77–80.

22 Ibid., 79.

23 "Keeping Ahead in the Airport Race," *Transport*, February 1988, 82.

24 Stanley A. Faucett and Stanley E. Faucett, "The Role of Air Freight in Multinational Just-in-Time Systems," *Logistics Spectrum*, Fall 1987, 32–38.

25 Sabine Krueger, "Europe Prepares for High Speed Train Network," *Europe*, July–August 1988, 26–28.

26 Jodie E. Melbin and Robert J. Bowman, "Distribution 2010," *Distribution*, January 1996, 24–30.

27 Based on Jacques Picard, "Typology of Physical Distribution Systems in Multinational Corporations," *International Journal of Physical Distribution and Materials Management* 12, no. 6 (1982): 26–39.

28 Ibid., 32–33.

29 Jodie E. Melbin, "Vive La Logistique," *Distribution*, April 1996, 46–49.

30 Peter Buxbaum, "Timberland's New Spin on Global Logistics," *Distribution*, May 1994, 32–36.

31 W.H. Davidson, *Global Strategic Management* (New York: John Wiley & Sons, 1982), 202–204.

32 Philip Kotler, Liam Fahey, and S. Jatusripitak, *The New Competition* (Englewood Cliffs, N.J.: Prentice-Hall, 1985), 188.

15

Advertising and Cross-Cultural Communication

Chapter Outline

Learning Objectives

When you have mastered the contents of this chapter, you will be able to do the following:

1 Explain how the international advertising environment differs from that in the United States.

2 Discuss the importance and complexities of cross-cultural communication.

3 Describe the three stages of international advertising evolution.

4 Discuss how standardizing advertising globally has both benefits and drawbacks.

5 Explain how international advertising campaigns are managed.

Communication within a given culture is complicated enough, but when communication is cross-cultural, the process is even more complex. Cross-cultural communication is the essence of international advertising. The problematic nature of international promotion is highlighted by the following facts. American consumers tend to be well informed about the differentiating aspects of products and brands as compared to their foreign counterparts. In many respects, non-Americans view shopping as a means to an end; to Americans, consumption is an end in itself. Products are at different stages of their life cycles in different markets. Consumer values and behavior patterns vary from one market to another. Finally, communicating with overseas markets is complicated by differences in media and their availability. Discussion in this chapter focuses on advertising as cross-cultural communication.

THE INTERNATIONAL ADVERTISING ENVIRONMENT

While many types of mass media exist all over the world, not all of them are available everywhere to marketers. Even where media are commercially available, governments restrict the products that marketers can promote and the advertising messages that can be transmitted. Consider the following:

- In Saudi Arabia, radio is 100 percent government controlled.

- In Australia, all television commercials must be filmed locally.

- In Italy, a child's bare bottom in an ad is considered "licentious," but it is acceptable to display bare female breasts.

- In Spain, alcohol and cigarette TV advertisements are restricted.

- Illiteracy is widespread in many areas in Africa and Latin America, making print media of limited use in reaching the masses.

These and similar situations reflect the numerous difficulties encountered in planning and managing international advertising. Being knowledgeable about international advertising means knowing a great deal about market environments in many countries.

COMMUNICATION— EVERY SOCIETY'S BUSINESS

Advertising and promotion are prominent aspects of U.S. society. About two-thirds of the world's advertising occurs in the U.S. market. American companies entering foreign markets find differing arrays of media and different amounts of freedom of advertising expression. In many countries, especially less-developed markets, these differences are sufficient to warrant a company's using totally different messages and media. Other countries are sufficiently Westernized to make using modern advertising messages feasible. To illustrate the diversity in international advertising, consider advertising practices in Eastern Europe, the industrialized West, newly industrialized countries (NICs) and Japan, and less-developed countries.

Advertising in Eastern Europe

Early recognition that the economies of Eastern Europe had a need for advertising surfaced in the former U.S.S.R. in the 1950s.[1] At the time, many of the Soviet Union's government-owned and government-operated factories were turning out consumer goods, such as shoes and clothing, that were not selling well, so the government sanctioned the use of advertising. Since that time, advertising has spread throughout Eastern Europe, but it is not advertising as we know it in Western Europe and North America. Most advertisements are informative rather than persuasive. They provide only the most basic information about products or services. Most consumer goods and services are still in scarce supply in these countries, so there is little need for persuasion. Consumers buy once they know that a product is available, assuming its quality is reasonable. East European governments also use advertising for public service and propaganda purposes. For instance, when a surplus of milk products developed in Bulgaria, the government used advertising to encourage increased consumption of milk and milk products.

Advertising in the United States and Western Europe

The United States, United Kingdom, France, Germany, and Switzerland are affluent. These economies emphasize consumer goods, their retailing, and their advertising through mass media. Does heavy advertising cause economic development, or vice-versa? It doesn't matter, because the two go hand in hand. There are some restrictions on advertising in North America and Europe. In Europe, many major broadcast media are government owned (for example, British Broadcasting Corporation television and radio). In Scandinavia, television and radio commercials are prohibited. In Germany, commercial advertising on TV and radio is permitted, but only at certain times of day. There are also many restrictions on advertising content. Some European governments (for example, France and the United Kingdom) restrict advertising content aimed at audiences of children, and in Germany, there are sufficient content regulations to make legal advice advisable.

Advertising in Newly Industrialized Countries and Japan

In terms of overall influence, NICs are between advanced and developing markets. Japan and many NICs (such as Korea, Taiwan, Hong Kong, and Brazil) are high-context markets, so advertisers place heavy emphasis on visual media, and their messages are toned down and softened. For instance, the Japanese are turned off by crisp messages and direct and hard-sell approaches, so phrases such as "Drink Coke," or "Fly Pan Am," are softened and collectivized to become "Let's Drink Coke," or "Let's Fly Pan Am." Audiences in these countries are strongly impressed by expert testimonies and referrals, so advertising testimonials by well-known figures are common, more so than in the West. Japanese advertising features testimonials by both Japanese and American celebrities.

Advertising in Less-Developed Countries

Advertising in less-developed countries (LDCs) is not as advanced as in other parts of the world for a number of reasons.

1. LDCs are poor and do not have many resources to allocate for advertising. In addition, most LDCs do not have the large-scale industries that are the major users of mass media elsewhere. Additionally, many LDC governments

are unaware of advertising's power as a stimulant of economic growth.

2. Many LDC markets are sellers' markets. Because of prevailing scarcities across a broad spectrum of goods, whatever is produced is easily sold. Consequently, managers of businesses in LDCs very often regard advertising as a needless expenditure.

3. Many product markets in LDCs are geographically limited and are often easily served through personal selling alone. Because of the prevalence of scarcities, few marketers need to advertise their brands. Furthermore, many businesses in LDCs are not ambitious to grow and therefore see no reason for using advertising to expand primary demand.

4. Media in LDCs are not highly developed. Broadcast media are limited. Print media are limited partly because of high illiteracy and partly because newsprint is a costly import.

In developing countries, then, advertising plays a minor role. This situation is ironic inasmuch as they could benefit from advertising's ability to (1) provide information to consumers, (2) sharpen competition among manufacturers, thereby improving product and service quality, and (3) help adjust supply-and-demand levels through improving market efficiency. In other words, these countries are depriving themselves of a strong force that could help significantly to develop their economies.

THE INTERNATIONAL ADVERTISING PROCESS

To understand the task faced by managers of international advertising, it is helpful to view advertising as a form of communication. International advertising, in this view, has six components: (1) message, (2) sender, (3) receiver, (4) channel, (5) feedback, and (6) noise, plus the cultures of sender and receiver (see Figure 15–1).

The Message

Putting together any advertising message requires consideration of two sets of factors. The first set includes the factors influencing customer demographics (for example, income, size of family, education, and age), shopping patterns and preferences, and buying and rebuying patterns with respect to the

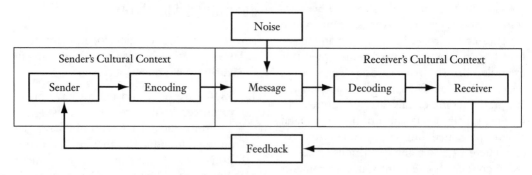

FIGURE 15-1 *Cross-Cultural Communication Process*

particular product, product class, or brand. The second set concerns customers' attitudes toward products, including particular products and brands, imported and local products, and the countries of origin of the advertisers' and competitors' products. An effective advertising message communicates with targeted consumers within the context of their behavior patterns and attitudes toward products. Some years ago, for instance, a manufacturer of dishwashers advertised to Swiss housewives using the theme "This is the efficient way to do your dishes so you will have more time for yourself." This same theme had been successful in the United States, but it was totally unacceptable to the Swiss. Swiss housewives were very serious about their homemaking activities, and shortcuts were not acceptable. Subsequently, the manufacturer changed the advertising theme to, "It is more sanitary to use dishwashers," and experienced great success.

FACTORS INFLUENCING CONSUMERS' BEHAVIOR PATTERNS
■ Those constructing an international advertising message must know the important distinguishing characteristics of consumers in the target country. Answers are needed for questions such as: Are the people in this market different from those in other markets? How? Do these differences affect message form, content, and theme?

Consider this example. When Coca-Cola first entered the Afghanistan market, initial consumer reaction was unexpectedly negative. Managers searched for the reasons behind this negative attitude. They found that Afghans did not object to Coca-Cola itself so much as to the container's red color (used worldwide on Coca-Cola containers, cans, and bottles). The Soviets had invaded Afghanistan, and the color red stood for the Soviet Union and communism; thus, Afghans rejected Coca-Cola because it was in red containers. Coca-Cola changed the color from red to green (the color of Islam), and the Afghan market accepted the product. Keen understanding of consumer values and reactions leads to message effectiveness.

Confronted with a multitude of scarcities in consumer goods, many people in developing countries believe that only defective, hard-to-sell products are advertised. Advertising, in general, is perceived with suspicion. Erasing this suspicion generally means incorporating testimonials by national heroes or local celebrities in the advertising message. It is vital that consumer beliefs are taken into account in developing the advertising message.

Particularly in high-context cultures, it is important to keep in mind that mass-media communication competes with interpersonal communication, which is preferred. A message appearing in the mass media must emulate interpersonal communication, perhaps by utilizing local conversations and settings. In high-context countries such as Indonesia and Turkey, special attention is given to "localizing" the advertising message. Local settings are used, the language and conversations are localized, and the characters in the advertising are local people.

Knowing the shopping patterns of consumers in the target country has an impact on both the content and the form of the advertising message. Most Americans do their grocery shopping at one stop once a week. Almost everywhere else in the world, most homemakers shop daily in different stores, buying just enough groceries to meet daily needs. In the process, they socialize with neighbors and storekeepers. Socializing is an important part of shopping, and in many parts of the world, it is the most important part. Similarly, in developing countries, bargaining over prices is a national pastime. Haggling is particularly evident in the Mediterranean countries such as Turkey or Greece, where it is part of the buying game. In these circumstances, an advertising message, particularly one that emphasizes prices, is redundant. Those constructing the advertising message need answers to such questions as: Do shoppers socialize? Do they bargain? How much shopping around do they do? How important is brand to shoppers? How important is the product? How important is the retailer's reputation?

Those constructing the advertising message also need to know a great deal about the purchasing patterns of consumers in the target market.[2] They need to ask a number of questions:

1. Is the product purchased by groups with similar incomes from country to country?

2. Who are the family members motivating purchase? Are they the same from country to country?

3. Who dictates the brand choice? Are these the same people in all countries?

4. Do most consumers expect a product to have the same appearance?

5. Is the purchase rate (the amount purchased) the same regardless of country?

6. Are most purchases made at the same kind of retail outlet?

7. Do most consumers spend about the same time making the purchase?

Consider, for instance, the fact that East Europeans spend much money and time in buying books from bookstores. These buyers are influenced in their selection of books by family members, friends, and, most important, their teachers. In the United States, by contrast, people buy books in supermarkets and drugstores as well as bookstores. They spend little time in shopping. Friends, advertising, and, most of all, the impulse power of point-of-purchase displays influence their choices.

Advertisers also need to know usage patterns in order to construct an effective advertising message. Some products are used differently in some parts of the world. Carnation has a dried milk product that was used chiefly as a fruit topping in the United Kingdom, as a coffee creamer in West Germany, as the base for homemade ice cream in Australia, and as baby food in Mexico. In addition, the quantity of the product used may vary, or its preparation may differ from market to market. In comparing usage patterns among countries, four key questions are asked:

1. Is the product used for the same purpose?

2. Does the quantity used vary?

3. Is this product's method of preparation the same?

4. Is the product used all by itself or along with other things?

Consumption patterns also influence advertising messages. Consumers spend their incomes in different ways around the world. In developing countries, greater proportions of income are spent on food and other necessities. In Nigeria, over 70 percent of income is spent on food, and less than 3 percent is spent on household items. In Greece, over 28 percent of income is spent on food, and 7.4 percent is spent on household items. In the United States, consumers spend less than 9 percent of their incomes on food and more than 5 percent on household items. Table 15–1 depicts the consumption patterns of six countries. Note particularly the country-by-country variations in food, transportation, and health.

FACTORS INFLUENCING CONSUMERS' ATTITUDES

■ Certain attitudinal and behavioral factors influence international advertising messages.

TABLE 15–1 ■ *Percentage of Total Personal Expenditures, 1993*

	United States	United Kingdom	Japan
Food	8.1	10.9	18.9[1]
Non-alcoholic beverages	0.9	0.9	*
Alcoholic beverages	1.1	6.2	*
Tobacco	1.2	2.7	*
Clothing and footwear	5.9	5.9	6.0
Rent	15.1	15.8	21.2[2]
Fuel and power	3.0	3.7	*
Household	5.8	6.6	5.4
Medical care	17.8	1.7	10.1
Transportation and communication	14.0	17.1	11.4
Recreation	10.3	10.2	13.0
Other	16.5	18.3	14.8
Total	100.0	100.0	100.0

	Greece	Netherlands	Denmark
Food	28.3	11.2	14.6
Non-alcoholic beverages	1.2	0.6	0.7
Alcoholic beverages	2.9	1.5	2.7
Tobacco	3.7	1.6	2.8
Clothing and footwear	7.7	6.8	5.2
Rent	11.1	19.0	22.8
Fuel and power	2.4	2.9	6.1
Household	7.4	6.9	6.1
Medical care	4.2	13.1	2.2
Transportation and communication	14.7	12.6	15.4
Recreation	5.3	10.2	10.4
Other	10.9	16.6	11.1
Total	100.0	100.0	100.0

[1]Includes food, non-alcoholic beverages, alcoholic beverages, and tobacco.
[2]Includes fuel and power.

Source: National Accounts Statistics: Main Aggregates and Detailed Tables, 1993 (New York: United Nations Publications, 1996).

Figure 15–2 shows three of these attitudinal factors and the five behavioral factors that influence the construction of messages in international advertising.

International Product Image. An international product image is a composite of the specific attitudes that consumers and prospective consumers hold toward a given product. Four important influences on an international product image are as follows:[3]

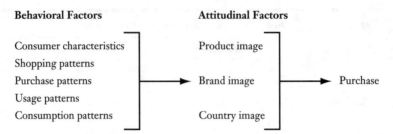

FIGURE 15–2 *Message-Building Factors*

1. Factors motivating the purchase of a product often differ from country to country. Small-scale, low-power, low-priced pieces of agricultural equipment are purchased in the United States mostly for leisure-time gardening. In many developing countries, these products are used for small-scale commercial farming.

2. Products convey different messages in different countries. In Western Europe, where female make-up is special-occasion oriented, cosmetic manufacturers change advertising pitches from those used in the United States, where cosmetic messages contain long-lasting appeals to working women.

3. The psychology of purchasing or using the product changes from one country to another. For example, the psychology of using water in the United States is different than in the Arab countries, where water is scarce.

4. The appeal of a product or a service varies among countries. An American type of freezer used for large amounts of frozen foods has little appeal in areas of the world where living quarters are scarce and crowded. There is no room for such a product, and in many countries, food is prepared daily and only a few essentials are kept in a small refrigerator.

International Brand Image. Some brands are internationally known, and the MNCs who market them use the same brands in all major markets. Examples of "international brands" include Bayer aspirin and Singer sewing machines. Similarly, IBM, Mercedes Benz, and Coca-Cola are all international brands. International brand images, which are composites of consumers' attitudes toward brands, vary from one country to the next. Variations in international brand image occur largely because these brands are not equally well known or equally well liked everywhere. Coca-Cola, for example, is popular everywhere but in Romania, whose people strongly prefer Pepsi-Cola.

Country Image. Country-of-origin studies show that countries project different images, and these images influence customer buying decisions. Country images also vary over time. After World War II (in the late 1940s and early 1950s), all Japanese products were thought of as being cheap and of low quality by consumers in many countries. Today, largely through a strong and persistent upgrading of quality, the Japanese image has changed; for many products, "made in Japan" stands for high quality. However, the country-of-origin studies also report that a particular country's image varies according to the nationality of the buyer. American-made apparel, for instance, is considered of high quality, well made, and attractive by

Japanese consumers, but it is often looked upon as awkward and gaudy by the Italians and French. Almost any U.S.-made product is considered of high quality in Poland, while any Russian-made product is considered of low quality in Romania.

The Sender

The second component in the communication process is the sender. In communications theory, the sender is the originator of the message. It is important, as has been noted, that the sender be familiar with the receiver's characteristics and situation. The sender or the professional working for the sender (the advertising agency working for, say, Pepsico International) encodes the message (see Figure 15–1). Encoding involves using symbols, pictures, words, color, and other creative elements to put the message into a conveyable form. Among many other considerations, as discussed earlier, the sender needs to take full advantage of the country-of-origin image. Japanese marketers, for example, take full advantage of the image that Japanese-made products have for high quality.

The Receiver

For the message to reach the receiver (as Figure 15–1 shows), it must be in a form understandable to the receiver. Mutual understanding occurs to the extent that messages reflect overlaps in the sender's and receiver's cultural backgrounds. If a message contains idiomatic phrases (which have meaning only in the sender's culture), then the receiver in a different culture will not be able to understand (that is, decode) the message. Consider these three advertising messages:[4]

- "Be a good egg"—an illustration of a present in an Easter basket.

- "Sweet Nothings by Maidenform"—an illustration of lingerie.

- "The Difference Will Floor You"—an illustration of floor wax.

These messages mean nothing if they are translated literally into another language. Even when idiomatic meanings are not a factor, translations go awry. "Body by Fisher" was translated as "Corpse by Fisher." "Schweppe's Tonic Water," "Aqua Tonica," became "bathroom water." In Puerto Rico, "Chevy Nova" translated into "a car that does not go."[5] When translated into Spanish, Chrysler's U.S. advertising theme of "Dart Is Power" translated into Spanish implied that the buyers lacked and were looking for sexual vigor. Ford named its low-cost truck Fiera, which in Spanish means "ugly old woman."

In international advertising, identifying the sender and the receiver as separate entities is particularly important. In cross-cultural communication, the sender and the receiver are far removed from each other not only in geographical distance but in terms of values, attitudes, and behavior patterns. Because accurate encoding and decoding of international advertising messages are so important, international advertising agencies have emerged.

INTERNATIONAL ADVERTISING AGENCIES ▪

As companies ventured abroad to service foreign markets, advertising agencies (especially U.S.-based agencies) followed. J. Walter Thompson was the first agency to go overseas, entering the British market in 1899. But up until 1945, only J. Walter Thompson, McCann-Erickson, and, to a lesser extent, Young and Rubicam had significant presences abroad.

In the post-1945 era, increasing numbers of agencies realized the benefits of going international—not only could they serve their U.S. clients abroad, they could also profit from the growth occurring in foreign markets. By 1987 most major American advertising agencies had affiliates in other countries, and 17 out of the top 20 agencies were American. These top 20 agencies accounted for about 29 percent of the world total advertising expenditures.[6]

In the 1980s, the rush abroad accelerated as global campaigns (that is, promoting a product similarly in several markets) became popular. MNCs preferred using agencies with international networks to implement these campaigns. BBDO lost the Polaroid account because it had insufficient foreign connections to execute the global campaign Polaroid wanted. Texas Instruments dropped 26 different agencies worldwide to go with McCann-Erickson and its international network.

This process of promoting a product similarly in several markets has become more noticeable in the 1990s. There are at least four different reasons for this:

1. *The cost factor.* Savings on production of creating on film rather than producing separate films for several markets can save the client vast amounts of money. Lintas, for instance, developed an advertising campaign for IBM that was used in 26 markets. It cost about £150,000 to make. A separate film for each market would have cost almost £4 million.

2. *Harmonized marketing plans.* In many categories, the clients rely on commonalities rather than differences that exist in consumers. This is made more possible by emphasizing fewer and better known brands.

3. *The emergence of cross-border media.* Satellite TV and the Internet and other similar media facilitate global advertising strategies.

4. *The world is getting smaller.* People are moving around more; therefore, advertising messages need to be somewhat harmonized so that consumers will not be confused.

However, the negative aspects of the global campaigns being favored by international advertising agencies are many. Numerous ethnic, religious, cultural, and legal restrictions occur from country to country. Furthermore, different world markets are at different stages of development (or maturity) regarding the products in question. Finally, as stated earlier, customs and behavior vary widely from one market to another (see Chapters 2 and 3).[7]

Message Channels: Media Considerations

Media such as television, radio, cinema, posters, newspapers, and magazines are the channels that carry the messages of international advertisers. Nowhere are the differences between domestic and international advertising more apparent than in the area of media.[8] Not only are there unique international media, but some international media function very differently from their domestic counterparts in the United States.

UNIQUE FOREIGN MEDIA ▪ There are some international media that are not known or are not now used in the United States. Three are particularly important: information towers, three-dimensional displays, and cinema advertising.

Information towers are kiosk-like structures that carry a number of posters. They are situated in areas of high pedestrian traffic in major cities where space is at a premium and there is extensive exposure to the general populace. Some towers cater to the literate population, carrying posters with long blocks of text. Other towers cater to the less literate population, using posters that are chiefly illustrations.

Three-dimensional displays are common in Eastern European countries. Located in crowded city areas, they are used for showing samples (behind glass) of consumer goods. Along with the product sample is some copy on the product's features. Generally, colorful posters provide the background for the samples.

Cinema advertising is widespread where television ownership is low (for example, in India and Afghanistan). In some countries, such as Zambia, cinema ads subsidize the movies. The ads either precede or follow the main feature. Cinema advertising has four advantages:

1. Time and space limits (common in other media) do not exist, and ads can be long or short, slide presentations, or flicks.

2. The ad gets the audience's undivided attention.

3. In many sections of developing countries, movie theaters have distinctive images and clientele. An Istanbul theater, for instance, shows only Arab movies (mostly sad love stories) and attracts older ladies who like to cry. Segmenting the market by clientele enables the advertiser to reach audiences with distinct characteristics.

4. Cinema ads are received by both literate and illiterate people. Low literacy levels, common in developing markets, makes cinema advertising very attractive. India holds the record for the country with the highest per capita movie attendance, and

India (not Hollywood) is the world's largest movie maker.

SOME WORLDWIDE DIFFERENCES IN MEDIA ▪

Television. Television advertising first emerged in the wealthier countries and rapidly spread to other countries. But even in wealthier overseas markets where TV ownership is widespread, the use of TV as an advertising medium varies considerably. In the United Kingdom and New Zealand, for instance, only a small number of TV channels exist, broadcasting typically ends at midnight or shortly after, and only a few commercials are aired. Most British and New Zealand TV is state supported, and advertising revenues are only part of their financing. Similar situations exist in some East European and developing countries. In Yugoslavia, all TV commercials are concentrated in one half-hour period of the broadcast day. On Turkish government-managed TV, only a few select products can be advertised in the few time spots available. The growing importance of satellites is expected to increase international television programming and expand and improve international TV advertising.

Radio. Radio, with its extensive outreach, is a good medium for international advertisers. In many places where illiteracy is high, radio is more effective than print media. In many countries, however, radio is government supported and there are restrictions on radio advertising; time allotted to advertising is limited, and the media managers allow only carefully selected commercials to be broadcast. This is the situation in Turkey, Egypt, and all Eastern European countries.

Newspapers. Many world markets are small enough geographically to have several national newspapers. The national (rather than local) coverage provides opportunities to target advertisements to specific audiences.

For example, in the United Kingdom, although evening newspapers are local, morning papers are nationally syndicated. Well-educated Britons read the *Guardian* (if they are of a liberal persuasion), the *Daily Telegraph* (if they hold conservative views), and the *Times* (if their politics are middle-of-the-road). At the lower end of the scale, the *Daily Mirror* and the *Sun* are blue-collar oriented; and in between are newspapers such as the moderately conservative *Daily Express*.

Turkish newspapers function like organs of political parties, favoring a particular party. Because party affiliations are different and identifiable, an opportunity exists for market segmentation via media selection.

Magazines. Many countries have numerous consumer magazines, but using them requires caution, because their circulation figures are not reliable. Some magazines have limited space available for advertising, while others have more ads than editorial content. But almost every country has numerous technical magazines and fashion magazines, appropriate media choices for exporters of high-tech items and apparel. In addition, some U.S. publishers have overseas editions: More than 20 countries have their own editions of *Reader's Digest*, *Time*, *Playboy*, and *Scientific American*, and others also have foreign editions. These U.S. magazines provide access to well-defined overseas markets and provide another media alternative for international and domestic advertisers. Recently, *Penthouse* added overseas editions, and it is building worldwide circulation among college-educated men age 18 to 34. The German *Penthouse* has been attracting numerous automobile advertisers, while the Hong Kong *Penthouse* has many advertisers of watches and jewelry.[9]

Direct Mail. Where only a few media alternatives exist, as in Scandinavia, direct mail is a viable choice. Where there are good postal services and suitable data bases (such as mailing lists), mail is targeted to a limited list of real prospects. This form of direct mail consists of letters to manufacturers, wholesalers, or retailers (all known genuine prospects). Direct mail advertising targeted to consumers is becoming popular in Western Europe. In Southeast Asia, where there are limited print media alternatives, there is much direct mail advertising of industrial products.

Table 15–2 illustrates a comparative analysis of some mass media in three groups of countries. Telephones and cellular phones are included in the table because they can be used for direct sale and for other promotional purposes.

The table indicates significant differences among these countries. The United States is by far the highest in terms of the number of TVs and radios per 1,000 population, but it is not even in the top seven for daily newspapers. This situation may have arisen because most Americans have access to the news from TVs and don't feel the need to buy a newspaper. Although Japan is number three in TVs, it is also number one in newspapers, which somewhat contradicts this theory. Sweden, the U.S., and Canada are the top three in telephones. The same pattern prevails for cellular phones as well.

The Necessity of Feedback

Because significant differences can exist between the message sent and the message received, a feedback mechanism is essential. Feedback mechanisms include pre- and posttesting of advertisements, agency and executive opinions, and, ultimately, sales levels in foreign markets. What companies want to avoid are the sorts of blunders described on page 341. Of course, an effective feedback mechanism and competent marketing

TABLE 15–2 ▪ *Conventional Mass Media and Telephones in Select Countries*

	1994 Telephones per 100	1992 Cellulars per 100,000	1990 Newspapers per 1,000	1991 TVs per 1,000	1991 Radios per 1,000
Highest					
United States	59	4,326	249	814	2,118
Japan	48	1,260	587	613	907
United Kingdom	47	2,595	394	434	1,143
Canada	58	3,727	228	639	1,029
Australia	50	2,510	246	480	1,268
Finland	55	7,028	558	501	997
Sweden	68	7,558	525	468	877
Medium					
Bulgaria	37	—	452	252	442
Romania	12	—	158	196	199
Poland	13	7	128	295	433
Russia	16	4	—	—	—
Germany	48	958	593	556	876
France	55	568	208	407	888
Lowest					
Cuba	3	2	172	163	345
Pakistan	1	12	15	18	90
Indonesia	1	19	28	59	146
Paraguay	3	33	39	50	171
Morocco	4	12	13	74	210

Source: 1995 Statistical Abstract of the U.S., Table 1381.

research go hand in hand. Some experts contend that international advertising research is best if it is centralized in the home office. Centralization makes it possible for the international advertising manager to receive reasonably comparable information in similar formats on all international markets. Comparable information enables the home office to detect important differences emerging in individual markets on such matters as image and awareness of the company name and/or its brands.[10]

The Noise Factor

A multinational company competes with other advertisers for attention in each of its markets. The appropriate amount of advertising for each market depends somewhat upon the noise levels in that market. Noise consists of unwanted signals, disturbances, or distractions interfering with the message's reception. If competitors are advertising heavily in a market, then the noise level is raised. The more noise, the more advertising that is required to penetrate the noise level and deliver the message to the receiver.

Noise-level variation in international markets occurs for different reasons. In some countries, advertising opportunities are limited. Private television stations in Italy, for instance, thrive on running commercials, but television stations in Germany, the Netherlands, and Switzerland are tightly controlled by governmental authorities and strictly limit commercial time. Therefore, not only is available TV commercial time limited, it is also expensive. In this situation, the "effective noise level is high unless the advertiser has equal access with the competition to television advertising time."[11]

Another reason for noise-level variations is outreach of commercial messages across national borders using transmissions in multiple languages. Luxembourg TV, for example, televises in three languages (French, German, and English). It has effective coverage over a large portion of Germany, parts of France and Belgium, and even the British Isles. Similarly, Yugoslavian television used to penetrate northern Italy.

National attitude on the social acceptability of advertising is another noise factor. Some Latin American and East Asian markets are "noisy" in that hard-sell advertising is not socially acceptable. Therefore, companies go to great efforts to produce subtle, "friendly," soft-sell commercials.

The amount of consumer sophistication in a particular market influences noise level. Consumer attitudes range from great admiration for heavy advertisers who present informative, tasteful advertisements to outright contempt for those who advertise their products "excessively."[12]

Adverse reactions to the advertiser's country of origin is still another type of noise. If, for instance, the United States is unpopular in a particular country, a U.S.-based advertiser requires additional advertising effort to penetrate the higher noise level.

MULTICOUNTRY ADVERTISING CAMPAIGNS

Some products are global products. From Coca-Cola to Tide to Singer to Volkswagen, many products are globally known and accepted. Implementing a global marketing strategy requires international marketers to treat the whole world as a single market and to ignore superficial regional and national differences.[13] Global marketing strategies call for globalization of advertising programs across markets. Procter and Gamble's advertising theme of "Trust Tide to get your clothes clean" experiences success all over Europe. Kellogg's "Tony the Tiger," "Coca-Cola adds life," and the Marlboro cowboy have had universal success.

International advertisers contemplating global advertising campaigns need answers to two questions: (1) How significant is local or regional culture for effective communication? and (2) How susceptible is the advertising message to cultural differences?

Using or Losing the Culture

Overlap in the sender's and the receiver's cultures, as noted earlier, is necessary for successful cross-cultural communications. Just because the sender "understands" the receiver's culture does not guarantee success. But it is possible to use knowledge of that culture to reinforce the message and increase communication effectiveness. For instance, in a high-context target market, an emphasis on human interaction and local details increases the message's impact. Similarly, known cultural preferences such as those of the Irish for green, of Europeans for sex appeal, or of the Japanese for tradition, are useful as message reinforcers. To understand how multinationals have viewed the impact of culture historically, a three-stage perspective must be discussed.

The Three Stages of Evolution

International advertising has evolved from centralization through decentralization to guided decentralization. Many well-known "blunders" have occurred in the process, most of them during the first stage.

Centralized International Advertising

Until the early 1960s, most international advertising consisted primarily of verbatim translations of advertisements planned for the American market. This was the era when "Come alive, you're in the Pepsi Generation" was translated as "Come alive out of the grave," and "Body by Fisher" was translated as "Corpse by Fisher."

Centralization was considered appropriate by American companies because they were the major players in world markets and their products had little competition in most markets. European and Japanese companies were still recovering from the aftermath of World War II and had not yet launched heavy drives for overseas trade. But competition from Europe and Japan intensified during the late 1960s and early 1970s, and in market after market, local orientation became synonymous with marketing success. Consequently, U.S. companies moved to the second stage.

DECENTRALIZED INTERNATIONAL ADVERTISING
▪ U.S.-based international companies began tailoring their advertising specifically to fit particular markets, utilizing local orientations, local values, and local motives. International advertisers set out to take full advantage of local cultures in communicating the merits of their products and brands, but the drawback was that this approach dissipated the natural strengths of companies that had products with global appeal. Pepsico International, Levi Strauss, IBM, and others benefit from the market power that their names have. If such companies totally decentralize their advertising, their market power shrinks. Recognizing this fact but also knowing that, in most cases, they could not simply translate their American ads, these companies moved toward the third stage.

GUIDED DECENTRALIZED INTERNATIONAL ADVERTISING
▪ International advertisers used guided decentralization to give local orientations to basic global messages. For example, Parker fountain pens are in demand in individual markets around the world, but Parker uses the common theme "Parker means a pen," in all markets. Similarly, Seven-up maintains certain advertising elements in all countries—the logotype, the basic Seven-Up color combination, Seven-Up bottle caps, and point-of-purchase promotional aids—but allows variations in the specific details of advertisements according to local market situations.

Certain factors enable international firms to standardize advertising appeals. Among these are (1) the existence of global market segments, (2) potential synergies from standardization, (3) the availability of a communications infrastructure capable of delivering the sender's message to the target markets, and (4) centralization of the company itself. Let us look at each in turn.

Global market segments exist for such luxury products are Omega and Rolex watches, DeBeers diamonds, and Ferrari and Mercedes Benz automobiles. Some consumer electronics such as stereo equipment, VCRs, and compact discs also have global market segments. Such products have little need for different advertising appeals. Global market segments are product conscious and brand conscious and expect globally standardized messages.[14] Other sizable global market segments exist for diapers, baby foods, toys, and other products for babies; fashions, records, and compact discs for teenagers; conspicuous-consumption products for yuppies; and sports and athletic equipment for sports enthusiasts.

Potential synergies from standardization include intercountry transfers. Thus, global images such as the Exxon tiger and the Marlboro cowboy are freely transferable from one market to another.

Availability of a suitable communication infrastructure is essential for advertising standardization. This infrastructure includes global advertising agencies such as London's Saatchi and Saatchi and New York's McCann-Erickson and Young and Rubicam, all of which have extensive international networks. Other parts of this infrastructure include linkages by communications satellite, international computers, telex, and fax systems—all facilitators that help in the delivery of international advertising messages.

The more centralized the company is the greater is its tendency to standardize advertising messages globally.[15] Soft drink and cosmetics firms are typically highly centralized organizations, and they rely heavily on standardized advertising. Chanel No. 5 and

---

TABLE 15–3 ▪ *Examples of Advertising Appeals with Potential for Global Usage*

Appeals	Description
Product characteristics described	Focus on product and its characteristics; product features
Individual and independence	Individual standing out from the crowd; self-confidence, originality, uniqueness
Hard-sell	Stress on brand name; comparative advertising; emphasis on "leader" or "number one"
Soft-sell	Mood and atmosphere conveyed through beautiful scene or emotional story
Youth, being lively and modern	Contemporary, younger models; stress on youthful benefits of products
Veneration of elderly and tradition	Older persons asked for advice and opinions; traditions stressed
Status appeals	Product said to enhance user's image in the eyes of others; includes foreign status appeals—foreign models, words, phrases
Group consensus	Individual depicted as part of a group; pressure on consensus and conformity to will of the group
Oneness with nature	Affinity of persons with nature; back-to-nature themes, including health and natural products
Manipulation of nature	Humans triumphing over the elements of nature; emphasis on technological achievements
Emphasizing the country of origin	Special emphasis on the country and its well-known characteristics and know-how, which make the product unique

Source: Adapted and revised from Barbara Mueller, "Reflections of Culture: An Analysis of Japanese and American Advertising Appeals," *Journal of Advertising Research* 27 (June/July 1987): 52–53.

Helena Rubinstein products in cosmetics and Coca-Cola and PepsiCo International in soft drinks represent outstanding success in implementing global advertising strategies.

Table 15–3 displays some advertising appeals with potential for global usage, or at least for standardization over several markets.

Barriers to Standardization

Not all companies can use standardized, worldwide appeals, however, because barriers such as culture, consumer response patterns, media availability, and other restrictions stand in the way.

Cultural preferences with respect to consumer behavior and lifestyles vary.[16] They may cause misunderstanding or improper decoding of a standardized message.

Consumer response patterns are not homogeneous among different markets. Some markets have horizontal or vertical homogeneity. Horizontal homogeneity exists when common market segments are present across national boundaries. Thus, consumer response patterns in northern Italy and southern France are homogeneous for many products. Vertical homogeneity exists when there is similarity among income groups or social classes within a particular country.[17] The Netherlands, the Scandinavian countries, and Germany exhibit vertical homogeneity. Some markets have no homogeneity at all. If homogeneity does not exist, advertising response is heterogeneous and success in advertising standardization is unlikely.

If the desired media are not available in a market, a standardized message is not transmittable. Governments in some countries, such as the Arab countries, limit the available advertising media or limit advertising time and space to only certain products or services. In other countries, certain kinds of mass media simply do not exist; for example, television does not exist in Guyana.

Other restrictions to advertising standardization relate to nationalistic tendencies and laws.[18] Many countries desire to create new national identities to resist foreign influence; therefore, they pass laws restricting the appearance of advertising prepared abroad. Some countries screen all aspects of advertising and have legal constraints outlining permissible and nonpermissible uses of advertising. For example, most West European countries and many developing countries forbid the advertising of prescription drugs and infant formulas through the mass media.[19]

Standardized global advertising often is not only impractical but sometimes impossible because of barriers to standardization. Companies facing these conditions generally turn to either guided decentralization or decentralization.

A guided decentralization strategy is used by Levi Strauss in its advertising. It recognized the waste involved in developing totally different campaigns for markets with substantial similarities. But Levis were sold in more than 70 countries, and sufficient similarities existed for some advertising standardization. Therefore, the company specifies the broad outlines of advertising campaigns but allows the use of different appeals in individual markets. For example:

- In Australia, the emphasis is on brand awareness and superior product; for instance, "A legend doesn't come apart at the seams."

- In Europe, TV commercials have super-sexy appeals.

- In Brazil (where European fashions are influential), the models in commercials wear Levis in European settings.

The three stages in the evolution of international advertising parallel the three strategic alternatives: global, which means standardizing advertising throughout the world markets; multilocal; and multinational. Centralized advertising is a global approach. Decentralized advertising is a multilocal approach. Guided decentralized advertising is a multinational approach.

Managing Multinational Advertising

Whether the decision is to centralize, decentralize, or partially decentralize advertising messages, implementing any multicountry advertising requires skilled management. There must be coordination and control of campaign objectives, image building, general advertising theme, standardized general features, local details, budgets, creative aspects, media mixes, agency relationships, and adherence to governmental regulations.

For example, Goodyear International Corporation uses a controlled decentralization pattern. The company developed a two-way communication system connecting the head office, the network head advertising agency, advertising agencies in the host countries, and Goodyear's local subsidiary representatives. Figure 15–3 is a schematic diagram of the Goodyear intercommunications framework. Note that the six steps in the process emphasize home office review throughout, formalizing the concerns of headquarters about the overall international advertising plan and investment.[20]

Two-way communication processes, such as Goodyear's, also can accommodate either centralized or decentralized advertising campaigns. The process has sufficient flexibility to incorporate varying conditions existing in different markets. Functioning properly, the system produces the right campaign approaches and appropriate set of

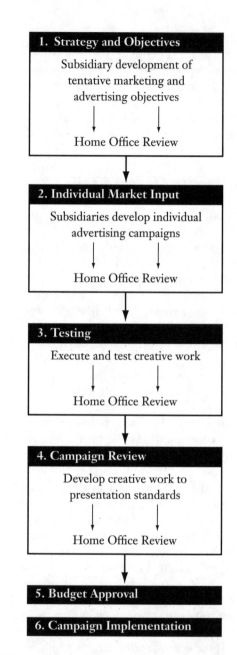

Source: Dean M. Peebles, John Ryans, Jr., and Ivan R. Vernon, "Coordinating International Advertising," *Journal of Marketing,* January 1978, 30. Reprinted by permission.

FIGURE 15–3 *Goodyear Intercommunications Network*

advertising appeals. Furthermore, the system provides a control mechanism to assure that local markets will not veer too far away from the corporation's general orientation.

ADVERTISING REGULATIONS AROUND THE WORLD

Almost every country has some regulation imposed on advertising. These regulations usually have a threefold purpose: (1) to protect consumers against misinformation and misleading advertising, (2) to protect smaller businesses against large corporations, and (3) to maintain traditional values and customs. Advertising activity is more carefully regulated in developed economies than in less-developed parts of the world, primarily because the advertising industry is still in its infancy in developing countries. They have not yet formulated the necessary regulations and enforcement mechanisms.

Some countries, such as Mexico and France, resist the use of foreign languages. In Muslim countries, the use of foreign themes and illustrations are regulated. However, in general, advertising regulation is focused on certain specific areas, including the following:[21]

- Certain product and service categories, including alcoholic beverages, tobacco, certain pharmaceuticals.

- Mail-order distribution.

- Advertisements targeted toward children.

- Comparative advertising.

- Product "puffery," or unfounded claims such as "the best in the world."

- Use of foreign language, foreign words, foreign backgrounds, and foreign illustrations.

- Media, such as the time limits for advertising.

- Sexism and racism.

Advertising is not only more tightly regulated in industrialized countries, it also attempts to regulate itself more readily. In addition, many consumer, business, religious, and educational groups try to influence advertising practice. Self-regulation is typically intended not only to forestall undesirable government regulations but also to shield the industry from unfair internal and perhaps international competition. The degrees of self-regulation and outside influence on advertising regulation vary from country to country according to each country's social values and level of economic development.

The amount of advertising in absolute terms, as a percent of GNP, and the degrees of regulation are shown in Table 15–4. U.S. advertising both in absolute and in relative terms is greater than anywhere else in the world. It is not possible to determine exactly which countries have the most rigorous controls; however, advertising regulations are quite stiff in North America and Europe, particularly in Scandinavian countries. It is obvious that the international marketer must become familiar with these countries' advertising rules and regulations.

TABLE 15–4 ■ *Advertising Volumes and Regulation around the World*

Region or Country	Advertising Regulation	Advertising as Percent of GNP	Advertising Expenditures
United States	Rigorous control by federal regulators, commissions, and effective self-regulation	2.4%	$110 billion
Europe	Strong community and national regulations	0.9	49 billion
Other developed countries[1]	Moderate to strict; heavy reliance on self-regulation	1.4	9.4 billion
Scandinavia	Strict ombudsman system; no TV advertising	1.0	2.7 billion
Japan	Moderate government control; established cultural traditions	1.4	27.3 billion
Eastern Europe	Significant dispersed government controls; foreign advertising permitted through state advertising enterprise	(na)	0.3 billion (estimated)
China and Socialist Asia	Significant government control; foreign advertising permitted	Insignificant	310 million
Arab Middle East	Culture bound; strong moral and religious codes, particularly in conservative countries under traditional rules	Less than 0.20	Less than 100 million
Latin America and the Caribbean	Significant regulation	Approximately 0.8`	2.5 billion
Third World Asia	Moderate regulation modeled on British system	0.3	About 900 million
Upper-income Asia[2]	Moderate	0.8–1.0	2.9 billion
Low- to middle-income Anglophone Africa	Developing mainly product specific; partly modeled on British system	0.4%	$21 million[3]
Low- to middle-income Francophone Africa	Developing mainly product specific; modeled on French laws	(na)	(na)

[1] Australia, Canada, New Zealand, and South Africa
[2] Hong Kong, Singapore, South Korea, and Taiwan
[3] Zimbabwe. Others not available.

Source: Developed from Barbara Sundberg Baudot, *International Advertising Handbook*, Lexington, MA: Lexington Books, 1990.

SUMMARY

Cross-cultural communication is the essence of international advertising. Overseas consumers generally are less informed about products than domestic consumers. Products are in different stages of development in different markets. Consumer values and buying patterns vary with the market, and advertisement placement and scheduling are complicated by differences in types and availability of media. Viewed as cross-cultural communication, the elements of international advertising are message, sender, receiver, channel, cultures of sender and receiver, feedback, and noise. There are three stages in the evolution of international advertising: centralization, decentralization, and guided decentralization. Each stage is influenced by the extent to which the product is global and by the barriers that exist to standardizing its promotion.

Strategically, centralization is a global approach, decentralization is a multilocal approach, and guided decentralization is a multinational approach. Management of all international advertising involves coordination and control of campaign objectives, images, promotional themes, budgets, creative work, media mixes, and advertising agency relations; conformance to different countries' government regulations; and other matters.

There are varying degrees of advertising regulations throughout the world. More industrialized countries typically have more stringent regulations.

DISCUSSION QUESTIONS

1. Discuss the international advertising process. How does it differ from the domestic advertising process in the United States?

2. How did international advertising evolve? Discuss the three stages of international advertising evolution.

3. What is the culture's impact on international advertising?

4. What is meant by the statement that advertising regulations vary around the world?

5. Why do more companies not standardize advertising messages worldwide?

6. Why do some countries have larger expenditures than others?

General Foods' Nondairy Dessert Topping in Germany

General Foods' German subsidiary has decided to market a German version of American Cool Whip. The product is a nondairy dessert topping that tastes and feels like fresh whipped cream. Traditionally, Germans love rich desserts served with whipped cream. Although the sales of a variety of packaged desserts and instant dessert creams have been growing, all of these products have been based on dairy products. The whipped cream market has been very large. Whipped cream is mostly purchased as fresh liquid cream at a grocery or a dairy store; it is whipped at home prior to use.

Cool Whip was introduced in the United States in 1967. It has an acceptable taste and eliminates preparation before serving. The product has been successful and popular. Although all Germans love fresh whipped cream, some Germans have realized that it is relatively expensive, perishable, and fattening. Test markets in Germany indicated that the proposed product had an acceptable taste.

An increasing trend in sales of low-calorie products is considered to be a factor to lure consumers away from the traditional whipped cream. However, German culture is rather routine oriented, and it is a low-context culture, meaning that the written word and legal and contractual relations are more critical than personal interaction. Consumer interest in new products is not widespread.

QUESTIONS

1. As the marketing manager of General Foods Germany, what are your promotional plans?

2. How specifically, would you deal with the overall promotional theme? The media mix? Needed educational or informational efforts?

Tea in Taiwan

Chin Chee tea is produced in Taiwan. Bottled in very attractive traditional bottles, Chin Chee tea is pre-brewed tea, similar to the Snapple product in the U.S. For years, the company tried to find a way to change the Taiwanese from brewing their own tea and drinking it hot to buying pre-brewed tea and drinking it cold. Finally, the company came up with a series of commercials that emphasized traditional settings; the importance of drinking tea with friends, relatives, and associates; and within the constraints of tradition, the importance of change. The company's production facility is now working full time, and sales have gone up by some 900 percent in about two years.

QUESTION

1. How might you further promote Chin Chee tea in Taiwan?

ENDNOTES

1 A. Coskun Samli, *Marketing and Distribution Systems in Eastern Europe* (New York: Praeger, 1978), 87.

2 Steward Henderson Britt, "Standardizing for the International Market," *Columbia Journal of World Business* (Winter 1974), 39-45.

3 Ibid.

4 Edward Cundiff and Marye Tharp Hilger, *Marketing in the International Environment*, 2nd ed. (Englewood Cliffs, N.J.: Prentice Hall, 1988).

5 David Ricks, *International Business Blunders* (New York: Dow Jones, 1983).

6 Barbara Sundberg Baudot, *International Advertising Handbook* (Lexington, Mass.: Lexington Books, 1987), 18–19.

7 Belinda Archer, "Euro Ads—Why Bother?" *Campaign*, 20 January 1995, 28–30.

8 Dean M. Peebles and John K. Ryans, Jr., *Management of International Advertising* (Boston: Allyn and Bacon, 1984), 163–94.

9 *International Advertiser* (December 1986), 14–15.

10 Peebles and Ryans, *Management of International Advertising*.

11 Baudot, *International Advertising Handbook*. See endnote 6.

12 Peebles and Ryans, *Management of International Advertising*.

13 Theodore Levitt, "The Globalization of Markets," *Harvard Business Review* (May-June 1983), 34–41.

14 Alan J. Greco, "International Advertising: The Search for the Universal Appeal," in *Proceedings of World Marketing Congress*, ed. W. Laser, et al. (Miami, Fla.: Academy of Marketing Science, 1989), 71–76.

15 Yoram Wind and Susan Douglas, "The Myth of Globalization," *Columbia Journal of World Business* 22 (Winter 1987): 19–29.

16 Barbara Mueller, "Reflections of Culture: An Analysis of Japanese and American Advertising Appeals," *Journal of Advertising Research* 27 (June/July 1987): 49–55.

17 Sak Onkvisit and John J. Shaw, "Standardized International Advertising: A Review of the Theoretical and Empirical Evidence," *Columbia Journal of World Business* 22 (Fall 1987): 43–55.

18 J. J. Boddewyn, "The One and Many Worlds of Advertising: Regulatory Obstacles and Opportunities," *International Journal of Advertising* 7 (Winter): 11–16.

19 Baudot, *International Advertising Handbook*. See endnote 6.

20 Peebles and Ryans, *Management of International Advertising*.

21 Subhash C. Jain, *International Marketing Management*, 2nd ed. (Boston: Kent Publishing Co., 1987), 558.

CHAPTER **16**

International Personal Selling and Sales Force Management

Chapter Outline

Learning Objectives

When you have mastered the contents of this
chapter, you will be able to do the following:

1   Explain how important sales force management and personal selling are in the
international marketplace.

2   Discuss why intercultural selling through
negotiation is one of the greatest challenges in international business.

3   Outline how far American sales-management methods can be used abroad
and identify the environmental impediments that stand in the way of standardizing sales practices.

4   Illustrate how industry practices influence foreign sales strategies.

Companies that succeed overseas always have personal representation. For exporters, the major promoters of products abroad are foreign importers and distributors. Many companies, especially those in the computer and industrial-equipment industries, set up their own overseas marketing subsidiaries. Other multinational corporations (MNC) maintain overseas on-site manufacturing and marketing operations. Because many MNCs, especially U.S.-based ones, sell many of their home-market products abroad, questions arise about the overseas usability of home-market sales techniques. Subsidiaries should not need to "reinvent the sales-management wheel" as MNCs move from market to market. Knowing which sales elements to retain and which to discard, and why, is the key to efficient, well-ordered foreign selling operations.

INTERNATIONAL PERSONAL SELLING AND NEGOTIATING

Personal selling is the process of informing customers and persuading them to purchase products or services through personal communication in an exchange situation. Most international business transactions require some personal selling or negotiation to set up the terms and conditions of the transaction. In the international context, the face-to-face exchange of ideas and viewpoints is best achieved when both parties understand each other. Because negotiations are prerequisites for most international business transactions, whether they be exporters seeking distributor agreements, joint ventures, licensing, or other technology transfer arrangements, skillful international personal selling and persuasive intercultural negotiating are crucial.

In all selling situations, but particularly in international ones, cultural differences are most evident in face-to-face negotiations. Although both parties share common goals in negotiation—to reach mutually acceptable agreements—how they achieve them often differs, and the tactics they use also vary. Let us examine the cultural characteristics Americans bring to the negotiations process and contrast them with the characteristics of other cultures. The emphasis here will be on *what* is different and *why*. Empathy, the ability to put oneself in another's shoes, is one mark of an effective intercultural negotiator.

Successful negotiating requires that participants know themselves, their own strengths and weaknesses, and also know as much as possible about the other side. It is interesting to note that Japanese negotiators routinely request background information on American companies and key negotiators. In-depth knowledge of the matter being negotiated, key elements, less-essential elements (where concessions might be possible), and—perhaps most important—the other company's likely position on key points is also required. Finally, successful negotiators know in advance the likely negotiating strategies and tactics of the other side.

Characteristics of American Personal Selling and Negotiating

U.S. businesspeople belong to low-context cultures in which they are used to business dealings being conducted objectively, efficiently, and competitively. To maintain this sort of negotiating posture, Americans prefer informality (to minimize time-wasting formalities) and rationality (to keep personal opinions from playing critical roles in decisions). However, Americans also come from an economy driven by market forces, so they are competitive and generally use persuasive tactics and power overtly. Their decision making is individualized, and subordinates provide key information (such as figures on sales, costs, and competitive analyses). Much of the rest of the world sees and does things differently.

Negotiating with the Japanese

Combined, Japan and the United States account for more than one-third of the free world's economic activity.[1] Opportunities abound for commercial interaction. Yet for most Americans, the Japanese are culturally the most different of all peoples. Most of these differences stem from the fact that the Japanese prefer personal trust rather than legal contracts as the basis for business relationships. In order to trust prospective partners, the Japanese want to know all about them—not just the product line, prices, and terms of sale and delivery, but the total U.S. company, including its history and its personnel. This position contrasts sharply with the American stance. Americans' knowledge of new clients often does not go further than a credit check through Dun and Bradstreet or a *World Traders' Data Report*.

The Japanese, however, want to know if Western companies and their personnel have "integrity," or "inner worth." In short, are they worth doing business with? Is it worth spending the time to establish relationships with this firm? This is only one of the many contrasts that can lead to embarrassment (which is avoided at all cost in Japan) or misunderstandings. Other contrasts concern sociability, use of lawyers and contracts, patience, business orientations, and negotiating habits.

SOCIABILITY ■ In American eyes, sociability helps move negotiations along. Hence, when

negotiating, U.S. businesspeople often try to create a relaxed atmosphere so as to avoid "red tape" formalities. Early on in the negotiations, Americans attempt to get on a first-name basis with their counterparts. This effort can cause initial problems in Japan (and in many parts of Europe), where preliminary meetings are formal. Business cards are exchanged (a ritual in Japan), titles are made known, and procedures are established for the negotiations.

The situation changes once the day's negotiations are ended. Most Americans go back to their hotels, dine, and prepare for the next day's negotiations. But at this point, their Japanese counterparts are ready to socialize. After-hours drinking (largely subsidized by lavish entertainment budgets) is part of Japanese business etiquette. This stage is where the Japanese establish social rapport and put business relationships on a firm footing. The practice often makes Americans uncomfortable because they are not used to mixing business with pleasure. In the United States, preferred business relationships are at arm's length, so that if competitive pressures arise, there is no personal discomfort in severing the relationship. The Japanese objective is just the opposite: The Japanese build up personal elements in order to buffer the commercial relationship against harsh competition.

USE OF LAWYERS ■ In the competitive, market-driven U.S. society, laws are the major constraints on personal or company behavior. In Japan and many other parts of the world (Europe, the Middle East, and Latin America), social codes take precedence over laws as the major arbiters of societal behavior. These codes govern and spell out "acceptable" behavior. The Japanese accept and conform to these behavioral codes, and lawyers and litigation are looked upon as "last resorts" (not, as in the United States, as the first resort). There are 13,000 lawyers in all of Japan, while the United States has more than 777,000, with more than 30,000 in Washington, D.C., alone.

Lawyers, then, are not key players in Japanese companies as they are in the United States. Hence, during negotiations with the Japanese, the roles of lawyers are usually limited until the end, when, generally at American insistence, they are brought in to summarize the proceedings and draw up an agreement. So strong is the Japanese dislike of litigation that just having a lawyer present during the negotiation makes the Japanese nervous and, in some cases, makes them view their American counterparts as "untrustworthy."

PATIENCE ■ Patience is a sign of strength in the Orient (and in many other parts of the world), but in the United States, it is viewed as a weakness. The efficiency orientation of American business causes U.S. executives to have low tolerances for what they consider a waste of time. They want to fly in, negotiate, sign a contract or agreement, and then move on to the next piece of business. Experienced international executives know that this scenario is generally not possible. The preliminary "getting to know you and your company" sessions take time. Presentations of the business proposals, too, are best paced to Japanese needs, slow, with many handouts and deviations from the plan. The usual, fast-paced, brass-tacks presentations common in the United States often come across to the Japanese as "insincere"—something untrustworthy people might do.

Patience is also required after the presentations, as the Japanese debate details of the U.S. proposal among themselves. Much time is taken up building consensus among the Japanese decision makers. In U.S. companies, important decisions are made by top management and are made quickly.

Implementation in the United States, however, takes a long time. In Japan, it may take two or three years to make an important decision, but once made, it is implemented in a few months or even a few weeks.

BUSINESS ORIENTATION ■ Differences in business orientation are another possible source of misunderstanding. American businesspeople have one primary motive—profits or profit maximization. They believe that low profits cause stock prices to fall and precipitate either a takeover or a shake-up in top management. Japanese managers have no such concerns; their corporate financial structures are largely based on debt rather than equity, and their major obligations are to banks, not to shareholders. Once Japanese managers have satisfied the banks' interest, they pursue whatever objectives suit them. The primary concern of Japanese management is to provide employment. Hence their business focus is primarily on market share. This view often confuses American companies that do not understand nonprofit orientations.

Another business contrast relates to planning perspective. The Japanese, because they have few short-term-profit pressures, focus more easily on medium-term and long-term planning than do most U.S. companies. Thus, during negotiations it is common to find U.S. executives focusing on short-term objectives with profits as the primary benchmarks, while the Japanese are planning sales over 3-, 5-, or 10-year periods.

NEGOTIATING INITIATIVES ■ Negotiating habits and tactics vary according to where the negotiations occur. American-Japanese discussions occurring in U.S. settings generally give the "cultural initiative" to the home team, and the Japanese try to operate and do things according to "American rules." When the meeting occurs in Japan, U.S. negotiators do things the Japanese way.

SEQUENCING NEGOTIATING POINTS ▪

American negotiating styles are generally oriented toward efficiency. U.S. negotiators take up one point at a time, negotiate it, finish it, and go on to the next item. Minor points often are discussed first to "warm up" the negotiators. While some Japanese, especially those with U.S. experience, go along with this order, many Japanese prefer to initiate general discussions on a number of points and talk around and through topics, continuing conversations for some time. Toward the end of the session or the day, participants from both sides summarize the major points on which they believe there is some agreement. These points may be formalized into "letters of understanding."

REACHING AN IMPASSE ▪

There comes a time in most negotiations when both parties are seemingly in total disagreement. During these times there is potential for conflict if one side presses for immediate solutions. Americans generally believe in discussing disagreements, talking them through, and reconciling them. In contrast, the Japanese avoid open conflicts *at all costs*. Alert negotiators know that when an impasse occurs, the Japanese become evasive and less communicative. At this point, a respected third party, or go-between, arbitrates between the two groups. Such people, often bankers or financiers, move between the two parties, comparing and modifying each group's position until a compromise is reached.

USE OF POWER ▪

In most negotiations, one company is clearly bigger and more powerful than the other. In the United States, power is recognized overtly and is often used to force concessions. In Japan and in many European countries, power is a more subtle thing—it is there but needs no display. Hence, in international marketing it is wise to avoid power plays. If Japanese (or European) companies perceive that they are being bullied, they grow wary and view the tactic as a bad omen.

SILENCE ▪

Moments of silence frequently occur in negotiations with the Japanese, who are, by nature, patient people. Americans generally are embarrassed by and have low tolerance for silence. Consequently, they often fill the void by overelaborating on details, volunteering additional information, or making concessions. Silence, then, is a valuable tool in negotiating with Americans. What makes the Japanese silence unnerving for Americans is that it is often interrupted with frenzied conversations. Experienced U.S. negotiators learn to ignore "silences" and even initiate their own periods of noncommunication.

RENEGOTIATING ▪

Japanese often like to renegotiate points. This preference tends to annoy time-conscious Americans, but they tolerate it to demonstrate good faith. Often, renegotiations result in little or no change.

Not all negotiations between Japanese and Americans are as we have just described them. As the Japanese accustom themselves to dealing with U.S. executives, they adopt Western negotiating habits. Similarly, Americans who are experienced negotiators know how to prepare for and react to unusual situations.

However, the Japanese are but one nation. Americans also have to consider Latin America, Europe, the Far East, and the Middle East, paying particular attention to the do's and don'ts of negotiating.

Negotiating with Latin Americans

Latin Americans are generally more outgoing and more emotional than most other peoples. As Table 16–1 shows, Americans try to keep emotions out of business, while the Japanese suppress them in formal situations.

TABLE 16–1 ■ *Japanese, North American, and Latin American Negotiation Styles*

Japanese	North American	Latin American
Emotional sensitivity highly valued.	Emotional sensitivity not highly valued.	Emotional sensitivity valued.
Hiding of emotions.	Dealing straightforwardly or impersonally.	Emotionally passionate.
Subtle power plays; conciliation.	Litigation not as much as conciliation.	Great power plays; use of weakness.
Loyalty to employer. Employer takes care of its employees.	Lack of commitment to employer. Breaking of ties by either if necessary.	Loyalty to employer (who is often family).
Group decision-making consensus.	Teamwork provides input to a decision maker.	Decisions come down from one individual.
Face-saving crucial. Decisions often made on basis of saving someone from embarrassment.	Decisions made on a cost benefit basis. Face-saving does not always matter.	Face-saving crucial in decision making to preserve honor, dignity.
Decision makers openly influenced by special interests.	Decision makers influenced by special interests but often not considered ethical.	Execution of special interests of decision maker expected, condoned.
Not argumentative. Quiet when right.	Argumentative when right or wrong, but impersonal.	Argumentative when right or wrong; passionate.
What is down in writing must be accurate and valid.	Great importance given to documentation as evidential proof.	Impatient with documentation as obstacle to understanding general principles.
Step-by-step approach to decision making.	Methodically organized decision making.	Impulsive, spontaneous decision making.
Good of group is the ultimate aim.	Profit motive or good of individual ultimate aim.	What is good for the group is good for the individual.
Cultivate a good emotional social setting for decision making. Get to know decision makers.	Decision making impersonal. Avoid involvements, conflict of interest.	Personalism necessary for good decision making.

Source: Reprinted from Pierre Casse, *Training for the Multicultural Manager: A Practical and Cross-Cultural Approach to the Management of People* (Washington, D.C.: Society for Intercultural Education, Training, and Research, 1982). Used with permission.

But in Central and South America, emotions permeate everyday life and are part of business and negotiation. Overt disagreements are not avoided as with the Japanese, and "sociable" disagreements occur during negotiations, such as when inconsequential items are "overnegotiated." Insight and experience are needed to distinguish "sociable" debates from serious disagreements. On the surface, both can be similar.

Other negotiating tips to remember when in Latin America include the following:

NO MIXING OF BUSINESS WITH PLEASURE ▪

Americans like "business breakfasts" and "working lunches," and often when abroad, they are "never off duty." Latin Americans make sharp distinctions between work and play. Hence, for example, it is often difficult, even impossible, to talk business over lunch. Eating occasions in Latin settings are usually strictly social times, and conversations about family, history, current affairs, and most other topics are expected. That is, one may talk about anything but business!

THE RELATIVE UNIMPORTANCE OF WORK ▪

In Japan, work is the focal point of an individual's life, and in the United States, work is a major part. But in Latin America, "one works to live, one does not live to work." Work is subordinate to family and other social pleasures, and nepotism (hiring relatives and friends) is more acceptable than in the United States. Social bonds also play an important role in getting and keeping business. In common with the Japanese, Latin Americans like to know with whom they are dealing, and personal friendship, confidence, and mutual trust may make the difference between doing and not doing business.

RECOGNIZING SOCIAL AND ETHNIC DISTINCTIONS, THE "PATRONE." ▪

Latin Americans, in general, recognize social distinctions more than Americans do (though this is slowly changing). Lighter-skinned groups are, for better or for worse, thought of as "socially superior" to their darker-skinned compatriots. "Respect" is accorded to those in positions of power. This *patrone* is "in charge" and makes the major decisions, usually unilaterally, often without subordinates' help.

Negotiating with Western Europeans

Culturally, Western Europeans tend to fall into a medium- or low-context category. The British, French, Spanish, Italians, Portuguese, Dutch, and Belgians are medium context, and the Germans, Swiss, and Scandinavians are low context. Low-context Europeans emphasize objectivity in business dealings, focusing on contracts, "plain talking," and efficiency. Medium-context Europeans (especially the French, Spanish, Italians, and Portuguese, and to a lesser extent, the British and Dutch) place more emphasis on personal relationships and trust, shying away from harsh competition. Because executives from low-context countries are similar to those in the United States, the focus in the following discussion is on the medium-context countries.

PROCEDURES ▪

Europeans are fond of procedures and guidelines, but unlike Americans, they observe them not for efficiency's sake but to give structure to business dealings. Agendas and protocols are established early on to ensure smooth negotiations and to confirm the meeting's purposes.

TITLES ▪

The formal exchanges of titles, positions, and functions is a business practice all Europeans observe (though it is less obtrusive in Scandinavia). Introductions, with titles, establish initial pecking orders within negotiating teams. Generally, formal barriers are broken down quickly (although more slowly among the Germans and Swiss), and sociability is substituted.

NEGOTIATING SEQUENCE ▪

Like the Japanese, Europeans generally recognize the interrelatedness of problems and the difficulty of dealing with individual items. Thus, several points are often negotiated simultaneously. Negotiations in Europe are shorter than in Japan but longer than in the United States.

LEGAL CONTRACTS ▪

Europeans use legal contracts to summarize major areas of agreement. "Water-tight" contracts, often favored by competitive Americans, are viewed with suspicion, and trust is a major element in agreements.

NEGOTIATING POSTURES ■ Americans view medium-context Europeans as elusive in meetings. E. R. Eggers notes the following French-American contrasts, many of which apply to other Europeans as well.[2]

1. Americans think in a straight line; the French think in a circle. Americans mistrust complicated things and try to oversimplify; the French mistrust simple things and overcomplicate. A French person spends much time trying to define the question; an American spends time trying to answer it.

2. The French mistrust items in which Americans have the most confidence—income statements (because in France the purpose is not to show how much money has been made but to demonstrate to the government how little has been made); the telephone (the French believe important business should not be conducted by telephone but face to face, so that the person making a proposal can be evaluated along with the proposal); the law; and the press (Americans believe in the formality of the written word, whereas Europeans often are at best skeptical).

3. American executives tend to forget what they wrote in a letter; French executives remember what they left out. In correspondence, Americans include lots of details, and the French purposely leave them out.

4. Small is beautiful. The French and Europeans generally believe that small companies can be as efficient as large ones; mass-production goods are inferior to custom-made products, and planning consists of countless small plans and details.

5. Life's pleasures to the French are non-durable pleasures such as eating and vacations. To Americans, they are tangible items, such as houses and automobiles.

Overall, medium-context Europeans are probably closer to the Japanese in negotiating style and technique than they are to the Americans. They have confidence in people rather than in "cold" facts and figures; they are less profit conscious, because European institutional investors are more conservative than their American counterparts and less concerned with maximizing profits (though this is changing). They negotiate with more flair and are hard to pin down on crucial points. For a typical profile, see Figure 16–1, "Portrait of an Italian Negotiator."

Negotiating with Asians

While it is difficult to generalize over all of the eastern and southern Asian countries (largely because of differences among the Islamic, Buddhist, and Hindu religions), there are some similarities among these countries. Most are high-context societies, which are largely tradition-based and emphasize personal relationships over the written word. As a result, there are some common elements in their general business practices and attitudes.

RESPECT FOR THE PAST ■ Old practices are not discarded just because new practices are superior. This respect for tradition makes change difficult.

IMPORTANCE OF THE FAMILY ■ Family-run businesses dominate in developing countries, and their commercial motives often differ from those of large Western organizations. Hiring preference is routinely given to family, relatives, and friends, and the profit motive, while present, often is tempered by other motives, such as religious duties.

PATIENCE AND HUMILITY ▪ As Figure 16–2, "Portrait of an Indian Negotiator," shows, Asian societies generally stress personal qualities that are somewhat different from those admired in the West. Eastern peoples value stoicism (not showing outward signs of emotion, especially anger) and the religious virtues of patience and humility. These are combined with a commercial pragmatism that at all times, even under adverse conditions, includes respect for the other side.

Negotiating with Middle Easterners

Middle Eastern countries, such as Saudi Arabia, Kuwait, Qatar, United Arab Emirates, Iran, and Iraq, share many characteristics. The people are predominantly Arabic; many

---

Italians define a successful negotiator as someone who:

1. Has a sense of drama (acting is a main part of the culture).

2. Does not hide his or her emotions (which are partly sincere and partly feigned).

3. Reads facial expressions and gestures very well.

4. Has a feeling for history.

5. Does not trust anybody.

6. Is concerned about the *"bella figura,"* or the good impression he or she can create among those who watch his or her behavior.

7. Believes in the individual's initiatives, not so much in teamwork.

8. Is good at being obliging and *"simpatico"* at all times.

9. Is always on the *"qui vive."*

10. Never embraces definite opinions.

11. Is able to come up with new ways to immobilize and eventually destroy his or her opponents.

12. Handles confrontations of power with subtlety and tact.

13. Has flair for intrigue.

14. Knows how to use flattery.

15. Can involve other negotiators in complex combinations.

Source: Excerpt from Luigi Barzini, *The Italians* (New York: Atheneum, 1964). Copyright © 1964 by Luigi Barzini.

FIGURE 16–1 *Portrait of an Italian Negotiator*

of these countries are kingdoms and largely Muslim. These last two elements affect business transactions. Figure 16–3, "Portrait of an Arab Negotiator," shows similarities to the high-context Asian nations. The Arab mediator resembles the Japanese go-between; both perform similar functions in their negotiating environments. Characteristics of Middle Eastern negotiating patterns are religiously, socially, and personally based.

Conflict situations are avoided at all costs (as in Japan), and much store is set on

---

Gandhi called his approach to negotiation *satyagrah*, which means "firmness in a good cause" and combines strength with the love of truth. A successful negotiator is someone who:

1. Looks for and says the truth.

2. Is not afraid of speaking up and has no fears.

3. Exercises self-control ("the weapons of the satyagrah are within him").

4. Seeks solutions that will please all the parties involved ("satyagrah aims to exalt both sides").

5. Respects the other party ("the opponent must be weaned from error by patience and sympathy. Weaned, not crushed; converted, not annihilated").

6. Does not use violence or insults.

7. Is ready to change his/her mind and differ with himself or herself at the risk of being seen as inconsistent and unpredictable.

8. Puts things into perspective and switches easily from the small picture to the big one

9. Is humble and trusts the opponent.

10. Is able to withdraw, use silence, and learn from within.

11. Relies on himself or herself, his/her own resources and strengths.

12. Appeals to the other party's spiritual identity ("to communicate, the West moves or talks. The East sits, contemplates, suffers").

13. Is tenacious, patient, and persistent.

14. Learns from the opponent and avoids the use of secrets.

15. Goes beyond logical reasoning and trusts his/her instinct as well as faith.

Source: Adapted from L. Fischer, "Satyagrah," in *The Life of Mahatma Gandhi* (New York: Harper, 1950); and L. Fischer, ed., *The Essential Gandhi* (New York: Random House, Inc., 1962).

FIGURE 16–2 *Portrait of an Indian Negotiator*

Those Arabs who are Muslim and are involved in negotiation believe in using the traditional way to settle disputes—namely, to use mediators. A successful mediator is someone who:

1. Protects all the parties' honor, self-respect, and dignity.

2. Avoids direct confrontations between opponents.

3. Is respected and trusted by all.

4. Does not put the parties involved in a situation where they have to show weakness or admit defeat.

5. Has the necessary prestige to be listened to.

6. Is creative enough to come up with honorable solutions for all parties.

7. Is impartial and can understand the positions of the various parties without leaning toward one or the other.

8. Is able to resist any kind of pressure that the opponents could try to exercise on him ("In sum, the ideal mediator is a man who is in a position, because of his personality, status, respect, wealth, influence, and so on to create in the litigants the desire to conform with his wishes").

9. Uses references to people who are highly respected by the opponents to persuade them to change their minds on some issues ("do it for the sake of your father").

10. Can keep secrets and in so doing gains the confidence of the negotiating parties.

11. Controls his temper and emotions (or loses it when and where necessary).

12. Can use conferences as mediating devices.

13. Knows that the opponents will have problems in carrying out the decisions made during the negotiation.

14. Is able to cope with the Arab disregard for time.

15. Understands the impact of Islam on the opponents who believe that they possess the truth, follow the Right Path and are going to "win" because their cause is just.

Source: Excerpt from Raphael Patai, *The Arab Mind* (New York: Scribner, 1983). Copyright 1973, 1976, and 1983 by Raphael Patai. Reprinted with permission of Charles Scribner's Sons.

FIGURE 16-3 *Portrait of an Arab Negotiator*

eloquent and (to Americans) overly elaborate modes of speech. Respect for both individuals (however menial) and institutions (the family) is extremely important. In contrast to Americans, who tend to think they can control their own destiny, Muslims believe that human beings only incidentally determine the future and that no one is to blame when things do not work out. Accountability, therefore, is difficult to pin down. (It may be considered God's will.)

Social formalities and courtesies based on a hereditary aristocracy are important in most Arabic countries. Many of them are monarchies, and most have cliques of powerful families that control many commercial interests. These families, who are often royally appointed (as in Saudi Arabia), command much respect. They are not "just businessmen." The family is important in business, with relatives having preference over friends. Profit, while desirable, does not come at the expense of employees—not, for example, if it means laying off workers.

Like Latin Americans, Arab businessmen are not time-conscious because efficiency does not equal money or status. As in Japan, negotiations take lots of time, with many formalities (tea and coffee drinking, especially) occurring before business is discussed. Westerners need to adjust to these ways if they are to succeed in the Middle East.

Negotiating with Eastern Europeans: The Former Soviet Bloc

Business negotiations in Eastern Europe are very different from those in other areas. Although communist ideals were softening in the 1980s, there were some notable differences at the negotiating table. Table 16–2 contrasts the negotiating styles of North Americans, Arabs, and Russians. The Russians drove hard bargains, often seeking to play off Western companies against one another. Because the Soviet bloc was insulated by the Iron Curtain for more than 70 years, only recently have Russian negotiators felt any empathy for their Western counterparts. In the Cold War days, empathy was viewed as a weakness that compromised state goals and commercial objectives for the sake of personal emotions.

The Russians were tough negotiators, suspicious about Western profit objectives. But their toughness varied with the product or service (for example, technical versus nontechnical goods) and with the experience of both negotiating teams. As East-West tensions ease, negotiating stances have softened. There is much Eastern European interest in transfers of technological and managerial expertise. Western negotiating concerns center around profit repatriation and technology protection issues, and around the adequacy of financial, legal, and physical infrastructures.

Organizing International Negotiations

All negotiations have increased chances of success when they are properly organized and the participants are both well prepared and experienced. The following discussion provides some perspective on the importance of physical arrangements, participants, and preplanning of negotiations.

PHYSICAL ARRANGEMENTS ▪ The adversarial relationships involved in many American negotiating situations (especially labor-management negotiations) make direct confrontation—two teams sitting directly across from each other—the natural seating arrangement. Experienced international negotiators avoid the "our team versus your

TABLE 16–2 ▪ *Negotiating Style Contrasts: North Americans, Arabs, and Russians*

	North Americans	Arabs	Russians
Primary negotiating style and process	Factual: Appeals made to logic	Affective: Appeals made to emotions	Axiomatic: Appeals made to ideals
Conflict: Opponent's arguments countered with	Objective facts	Subjective feelings	Asserted ideals
Making concessions	Small concessions made early to establish a relationship	Concessions made throughout as a part of the bargaining process	Few, if any, small concessions made
Response to opponent's concessions	Usually reciprocate opponent's concessions	Almost always reciprocate opponent's concessions	Opponent's concessions viewed as weakness and almost never reciprocated
Relationship	Short term	Long term	No continuing relationship
Authority	Broad	Broad	Limited
Initial position	Moderate	Extreme	Extreme
Deadline	Very important	Casual	Ignored

Source: E.S. Glenn, D. Witmeyer, and K.A. Stevenson, "Cultural Styles of Persuasion," *International Journal of Intercultural Relations* 1 (1984). Copyright © 1984 Pergamon Press, Ltd. Reproduced with permission.

team" competitive situation by using creative seating arrangements. For example, seating teams physically at right angles to each other psychologically makes the empty "upfront" space a focal point for compromises. Another arrangement seats advisory and junior executives at right angles to each other, but opposite them, senior executives alternating from each side are strategically positioned—Japanese, American, Japanese, and so on.

NUMBERS OF PARTICIPANTS ▪ The Japanese
believe in large-group negotiating. Numbers enable them to use consensus decision making and make division of labor possible, with some members being primary negotiators while others focus on the opposite side's reactions or on support functions. North Americans generally prefer small-group negotiation.

PLANNING THE NEGOTIATION ▪ What distinguishes the planning habits of successful negotiators from those of average negotiators? Neil Rackham's study of British negotiators offers some insights.[3]

- Both average and successful negotiators spend the same amount of time planning. The difference is in *what* is planned.

- Good negotiators develop twice as many options as less-effective negotiators. This abundance leaves them more prepared when negotiations deviate into uncharted waters.

- While the main objective of negotiations is to reduce and reconcile different interests, experienced negotiators spend much more time on areas where there is common ground and agreements are possible, rather than devoting inordinate amounts of time to topics where obvious differences exist. Experienced negotiators also "nibble away" at differences rather than tackling them head on.

- Skilled negotiators spend more time exploring long-term issues and their effects than do average negotiators. This practice puts Americans, who tend to be more short-term oriented, at a disadvantage.

- Good negotiators are flexible in setting goals. They define goals within ranges (for example, a return on investment of 10 to 20 percent) rather than as definite targets ("we must get a minimum 14 percent return").

- Unskilled negotiators have definite sequences of points to cover, ranked usually by their order of importance. Skilled negotiators go into meetings with a series of issues to tackle but do not have a predetermined sequence. The second method makes it more difficult for the other side to determine what the opposing negotiating team considers as the critical issues. This method also maintains a balance among the issues, thereby minimizing the chances that either side will hurt the negotiations by applying pressure on sensitive issues.

Successful negotiations generally go through four phases: (1) building up rapport; (2) learning about the proposed agreement, including its technical, legal, and business aspects; (3) bridging differences through reason, persuasion, and, occasionally, argument; and (4) making concessions and drawing up agreements.

INTERNATIONAL SALES MANAGEMENT

Companies selling internationally have a choice between using expatriate sellers (either sent out from the home market or their nationals based abroad) and organizing the overseas sales function from scratch.

Expatriates in Sales and Sales Management

After making commitments to serve a foreign market, companies must make several important sales-related decisions. One is whether to use expatriate or local salespeople. In countries where multinationals have sales subsidiaries or marketing and manufacturing facilities, they use mainly local sellers. But there are three situations in which using expatriates is both necessary and efficacious.

SMALL AND MEDIUM-SIZED COMPANIES ■

Companies with fewer than 500 employees typically cannot afford their own foreign sales forces. Instead, they build up extensive distributor networks overseas and service them through one or more home-country-based international sales managers and sellers. Commonly, but not always, these people know the overseas distributors' languages (for example, Spanish for Latin America, French and German for continental Europe). But because English is the world's foremost commercial language and because of language diversity in Europe and Asia, many transactions are in English. In addition, overseas agents and distributors often have English-language skills, especially those regularly doing business with companies from the U.S., UK, or other English-speaking countries. Several times a year, these sellers make "grand tours" of the overseas distributors that last from a few days to a few weeks.

COMPANIES WITH TECHNICALLY COMPLEX PRODUCTS ▪ Makers of technically complex products such as airplanes, specialized computer equipment, and high-tech medical products often use overseas selling teams. These teams generally are composed of technical experts backed up with a support staff of interpreters and others.

TOURS OF DUTY ▪ Another reason for sending expatriates abroad is to train local managers or technicians or to prepare junior executives for promotions. Ford, Coca-Cola, and Dow Chemical, for example, all look at foreign tours as essential preparation for senior management positions.[4] However, often between 20 and 30 percent of overseas tours are outright failures in that expatriates return without finishing the assignment.[5] The major reason for failure is the inability of expatriates or their families to adjust to new environments. In other cases, work-related problems (incompetence, personality shortcomings, or emotional immaturity) are to blame. Given the high costs of maintaining expatriates abroad, these are costly failures.

Some American companies have training and orientation programs for expatriates and their families. One study reported, however, that nearly 60 percent of these programs lasted only a week or less.[6] European and Japanese firms give their expatriates more comprehensive and longer training programs, incorporating formal instruction in language and cultural awareness.[7] European

and Japanese firms also give their expatriates time to adjust, and they are tolerant of failures by executives to achieve the same level of efficiency abroad as at home.

Managing the Overseas Sales Forces

When multinational companies venture overseas often their first commitment is to establish a sales force.[8] A sales force gives MNCs an overseas presence and opportunities to control their marketing destiny. Other advantages include enhanced feedback from customers and first-hand knowledge of market conditions. But questions arise when sales force commitments are made in foreign countries. For U.S. corporations, these questions traditionally have been: How far can we take American-style sales-management practices abroad? How much influence can local subsidiaries tolerate from the home office? What impediments are there to using U.S.-style sales management methods overseas?

HOW MUCH HEAD-OFFICE INFLUENCE? ▪ One problem in managing a multinational sales force is the wide variety of decisions required. There are three levels of sales decisions:

1. *International-level strategic decisions*
   (a) Deciding to have a company sales force or an independent sales organization (or both).
   (b) Setting subsidiary sales targets.

2. *National-level strategic planning decisions*
   (a) Sales force structure within a country (by territory, by product, by customer, and so forth).
   (b) Sales force compensation package (salary, commission, benefits).

3. *Country-level sales management activities*
   (a) Sales training.
       (1) Training methods (lecture, discussion, on-the-job experience).
       (2) Training content (product knowledge, company history, selling techniques, such as approaching the customer, making the presentation, following up).
   (b) Sales administration.
       (1) Sales job descriptions (delivery, order taker, order getter, goodwill, technical salesperson).
       (2) Sales duties and responsibilities (train distributors, check stocks, arrange displays, solve customer problems).
       (3) Salesperson selection criteria (education, appearance, experience, psychological tests).
   (c) Sales management control.
       (1) (Perceived) influence on an individual's sales target.
       (2) Routine methods for evaluating salespersons (sales against quotas, calls made).
       (3) Administrative procedures (call reports, expense reports, new business reports).

A study of 135 subsidiaries of 14 MNCs showed that MNC offices were selective in the subsidiary sales policies they influence. Figure 16–4 shows that headquarters of MNCs give more attention to international sales planning and sales training and less attention to subsidiary-level sales planning, administration, and control. This difference reflects the fact that these decisions are made on different levels.

At the international level, decisions are strategic and affect the entire MNC. The decision on the type of sales organization (sales force, independent distributors, or both) means a commitment of resources that will affect sales returns from markets over long periods. Large markets or those with high potentials warrant not only their own sales forces but also independent sales organizations. Strategic diversifications of product lines call for adjustments in the selling organization. When the computer industry put major marketing emphasis on computers for home use, NCR and IBM had to build new sales and distribution channels for them. Small markets or troubled countries (like Iran) usually draw small commitments, perhaps just a minimal sales organization.

Another strategic decision of top management is the setting of subsidiary sales targets. Today's multinationals often integrate their manufacturing systems worldwide, with individual subsidiaries having global responsibility for certain components or subassemblies. In these industries, including autos, computers, industrial goods, and electronics, sales goals are key inputs into global plans for coordinating group manufacturing efforts and markets. Accordingly, head-office influence on sales goals is substantial.

At the subsidiary level, local sales management makes most planning, training, administration, and control decisions. This practice reflects beliefs that local direction of selling operations is important. When subsidiaries are first set up, for example, they often distribute many home-market products. As time passes, they create more localized product lines, reflecting increasing knowledge of the market. Amway's experience in Japan is typical; it began with a one-year market test of selected U.S. home-care and detergent items. As the Asian market developed, the company stopped importing from the United States and subcontracted production to Japan (to meet cosmetics testing standards) and to New Zealand (to comply with that country's investment regulations.[9]

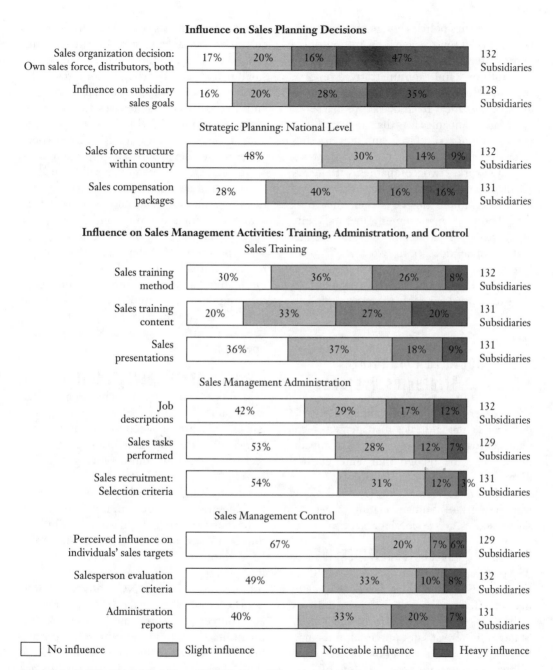

Influence on Sales Planning Decisions

Sales organization decision:
Own sales force, distributors, both — 17% | 20% | 16% | 47% — 132 Subsidiaries

Influence on subsidiary
sales goals — 16% | 20% | 28% | 35% — 128 Subsidiaries

Strategic Planning: National Level

Sales force structure
within country — 48% | 30% | 14% | 9% — 132 Subsidiaries

Sales compensation
packages — 28% | 40% | 16% | 16% — 131 Subsidiaries

Influence on Sales Management Activities: Training, Administration, and Control

Sales Training

Sales training
method — 30% | 36% | 26% | 8% — 132 Subsidiaries

Sales training
content — 20% | 33% | 27% | 20% — 131 Subsidiaries

Sales
presentations — 36% | 37% | 18% | 9% — 131 Subsidiaries

Sales Management Administration

Job
descriptions — 42% | 29% | 17% | 12% — 132 Subsidiaries

Sales tasks
performed — 53% | 28% | 12% | 7% — 129 Subsidiaries

Sales recruitment:
Selection criteria — 54% | 31% | 12% | 3% — 131 Subsidiaries

Sales Management Control

Perceived influence on
individuals' sales targets — 67% | 20% | 7% | 6% — 129 Subsidiaries

Salesperson evaluation
criteria — 49% | 33% | 10% | 8% — 132 Subsidiaries

Administration
reports — 40% | 33% | 20% | 7% — 131 Subsidiaries

☐ No influence   ▨ Slight influence   ▨ Noticeable influence   ▪ Heavy influence

Source: John S. Hill, Richard R. Still, and Unal O. Boya, "Managing the Multinational Salesforce," *International Marketing Review* 8, no. 1 (1991): 19–31. Reproduced with permission.

FIGURE 16–4 *Headquarter Influence on Subsidiary Sales Management Policies and Decisions*

When sales policies and guidelines are in writing, they tend to have an international impact. Items such as training manuals, job descriptions, and administrative reports, appropriately translated, facilitate the movement of sales ideas from market to market.

Many companies fear that American sales methods do not travel well, and they are slow to take them abroad, but in some countries, they do work. Two companies with heavy reliance on personal selling, Amway and Electrolux, found this out when they took their "hoopla" management methods into Hong Kong and Malaysia. Despite the fact that hoopla does not work well with Europeans and Japanese, both companies found that Hong Kong and Malaysian distributors responded favorably to these methods.[10]

Impediments to Extending U.S. Sales Strategies Overseas

What deters MNCs from taking U.S.-style personal selling and sales management techniques abroad? There are five types of impediments: (1) the geographic and cultural dimensions of individual countries, (2) the level of market development, (3) political and legal systems, (4) human-relations aspects of sales practices, and (5) local market conditions.

GEOGRAPHIC AND CULTURAL DIMENSIONS ■
The geography of countries affects MNCs as they structure their sales forces market by market, causing changes in representatives' selling tasks. The large size of the United States and the vast sales potential of its market results in specialization of sales responsibilities, encouraging the division of sales tasks by territory, product, and customer, and by what salespersons actually do. The considerably smaller markets of many overseas countries often make it uneconomical to

have sales specialists (especially product and customer specialists). In the electronic data processing (EDP) industry, for example, for smaller markets, Burroughs compresses its product structures into geographic designs and directs its representatives to sell broad ranges of products. With such realignments come changes in responsibilities. In Sweden, for example, Electrolux sales representatives service refrigerators as well as sell them.[11]

Cultural elements also affect sales structures. Belgium is often split in two; sales personnel in French-speaking southern Belgium are assigned to the French sales force, while sales personnel in the Flemish-speaking north are attached to the Dutch sales force. Germany and Austria, both German-speaking countries, are often treated as a single sales entity, and the Spanish-speaking countries of Central America become one sales operation.

LEVEL OF MARKET DEVELOPMENT ■ The
degree of market development has a marked effect on multinational selling, because inadequate educational, economic, and social infrastructures and amenities complicate recruiting, training, and deploying salespersons in developing markets.

Recruiting suitable sellers is always problematic in developing countries. University-educated applicants, hardly ever numerous, are difficult to attract into sales because of the competition from high-paying, prestigious jobs in government and the professions. Most MNCs, given limited pools of applicants, make the best of available sources. In Central and Southern Africa, the military is a good source of sales recruits, because the will to succeed, administrative skills, discipline, and steady work habits are desirable character traits in both military and sales careers.

Even when large pools of possible recruits exist, selection is difficult when

MNCs go after top-caliber candidates. Electrolux interviewed 400 applicants to fill just 10 sales positions in Hong Kong.[12] Other MNCs, including Procter & Gamble and Johnson and Johnson, recruit some foreign nationals in U.S. business schools. Not only is this a way to hire foreign salespeople with U.S. management training, it is a way to recruit without direct competition from more prestigious employment alternatives in their home countries.

MNCs first entering developing markets soon learn that these markets lack well-developed infrastructures and distribution channels. This lack may cause readjustments in selling operations. In its European markets, for example, Electrolux sells 85 percent of its vacuums through retail dealers. In developing markets, such as those in Southeast Asia, there was a dearth of suitable outlets, especially in rural areas, so Electrolux reverted to its traditional direct-selling approach. In India, reps sold by making door-to-door demonstrations. The strategy was successful, and Electrolux sold more machines than ever in these markets. Unfortunately, direct selling also stimulated demand for competing brands, and Electrolux saw its market share fall from 90 to 30 percent.[13]

One attractive feature of developing markets is low labor cost, a fact that encourages MNCs to use additional personal selling in promotion efforts. In Peru, it was economical for Sunbeam to hire one sales force to sell its private brands and another to sell its manufacturer brands; this tactic greatly expanded market penetration.

POLITICAL AND LEGAL SYSTEMS ▪

Differences in political and legal environments make it difficult to standardize compensation packages multinationally. A country's political orientation for the most part dictates the fringe benefits that subsidiaries offer employees. Europe's mixed economies legislate generous benefits by U.S. standards, including profit sharing, year-end bonuses, coverage of medical and dental expenses, high severance pay, and bountiful maternity and vacation allowances. Fringe benefits, which average about 35 percent of wages in the United States, rise to 45 percent in Germany, 55 percent in Belgium, 70 percent in France, and 92 percent in Italy.

While these benefits programs are financed jointly by governments and companies, the costs place added burdens on public finances, and European personal taxation levels are high. In many European countries, personal income taxes in the highest brackets range over 50 percent. This limits the effectiveness of sales commissions as incentives, because high performers view extra efforts as financially futile. Consequently, many companies, as in Germany and Switzerland, level down the incentive side of compensation systems from 70 percent salary/30 percent commission splits to 90/10 divisions.[14]

Government-sponsored benefit programs fall short in some countries, causing many MNCs to supplement benefits. In developing countries, for example, companies provide the "extras." Swedish Match's Southeast Asian sales forces receive clothing allowances to bolster morale and foster pride in being part of the company "family."[15] Japanese companies are famed for providing fringe benefits over and above legal minima, often providing commuting expenses and vacation resort houses for all employees. Clearly, MNCs need to set compensation packages at national norms and to build *esprit de corps* by going beyond what is expected or legislated.

Political climates affect sales force recruitment and training indirectly as well. Graduates with liberal arts backgrounds, especially in Europe and the developing countries, have business philosophies shaped by prevailing political doctrines, which are often socialistic. In countries such as Ethiopia and Pakistan, therefore, some MNCs provide initial business training for sales recruits to explain and justify company objectives such as profit and investment recovery, which many, if not most, Ethiopians and Pakistanis think are less important than the goals of employee security and welfare.

HUMAN RELATIONS ASPECTS

▪ It is in the human-relations aspects of personal selling and sales management that MNCs make their greatest adjustments. Differences from country to country in class systems, individual-group orientations, occupational hierarchies, ethnic divisions, and business practices make deviations from U.S. practices necessary and desirable.

Class. Class is a factor in U.S. society, but its importance there is dwarfed compared to its importance elsewhere. The United States is an advanced economic society, fast-paced and change oriented, and social rankings are strongly influenced by objective economic criteria such as income and education. Indeed, the phrase "time is money, money is power" is more characteristic of American values than is respect for class distinctions based on birth.

More traditional societies, including part of Europe and most of the developing world, regard criteria such as family background and seniority as prime determinants of social position. Such differences in the ways countries rank individuals socially cause MNCs to adjust the compensation systems, recruitment practices, and evaluation methods of their sales representatives.

In Thailand, a traditional society, family background determines social position. Because money confers only limited status, straight salaries are more "respectable" and desirable than larger incomes with a substantial but variable component made up of commissions.[16]

Group Versus Individual Orientations. Tradition also is an important determinant of Japanese compensation plans. Japanese respect for heredity and seniority and the strong Japanese group orientation discourage the use of individual financial rewards to stimulate productivity. Raises, even for sales forces, are based on longevity with the company. Similarly, commission systems are tied to the combined efforts of the entire sales force, fostering the team ethic and downplaying the economic aspirations of the individual.

Occupational Hierarchies. In Europe and developing countries, people traditionally attach little prestige to selling as a profession, a situation that makes selling relatively unattractive to university graduates. Governmental-supported education systems ensure that only small proportions of the populations go on to universities. Thus, university graduates occupy privileged positions and are not likely to be recruited into sales jobs. NCR has worked in the Japanese market for more than 70 years but has succeeded in recruiting university graduates only in the past 20.[17]

Ethnic Divisions. MNCs face special recruitment and selection problems in culturally diverse markets. In the United States, matching salespersons to territories is relatively simple, although there are occasional problems in matching up minority personnel with territories that have high African American or Hispanic concentrations. In developing markets, over 80 percent of which are culturally heterogeneous, most MNCs do as Swedish Match does in India. Faced with between 300 and 1,000 dialects, including more than 50 with a million or more speakers, the company completely decentralizes salesperson recruiting, ensuring that recruits speak the correct dialect(s) for the area and that they are respected in their communities and can capitalize upon personal contacts.[18]

Local Business Practices. Traditional Eastern cultures require total indigenization of sales practices. Written job descriptions, a key feature of American sales management, are scarcely used in Japan, where salespersons are oriented by on-the-job practice. This emphasis also requires special handling. Interpersonal contacts between instructors and trainees, featuring appraisals, feedback, and coaching, are conducted with ritualistic decorum so that even constructive criticism does not cause trainees to lose face.

Salesperson-client relationships are critical to successful selling. In the United States, Australia, Scandinavia, and other parts of Western Europe, nurturing relationships with clients is generally subordinated to sales tactics emphasizing product features and competitive pricing. Elsewhere, notably in Latin America and Southeast Asia, the personal side of business dominates transactions, and client-salesperson relationships are cultivated to build trust and respect. These relationships are vital elements in determining who gets the contracts. Often, after-hours socializing is the key to cementing relationships with clients. The effects of client entertainment are so marked that in Germany, big-ticket salespersons are said to average only 12 years of peak sales productivity before experiencing social burnout.

LOCAL MARKET CONDITIONS ▪
Local market conditions often impede MNC transfers of U.S. sales techniques. In some markets for example, import restrictions or boycotts cause product shortages, especially in industrial and high-tech items, with the result that

MNC salespersons become order takers rather than order getters. Under these circumstances, there is little need for U.S.-style competitive selling techniques.

Special market conditions provide opportunities to capitalize upon preferences in sales presentation. In the Middle East, the great pride people take in owning fine rugs enables Electrolux salespersons to emphasize the merits of their vacuum cleaners in maintaining rugs in peak condition. In China, the sales emphasis is on floor polishers to cater to Chinese preferences for stone floors.[19]

Industry Influences on Overseas Sales Strategies

While numerous local circumstances discourage multinationals from taking their U.S. sales methods abroad, certain industries habitually transfer U.S. products to overseas subsidiaries, providing opportunities for using U.S. sales methods abroad. However, industries differ in their abilities to take home-market methods and materials into foreign markets. In two industries in particular—general consumer goods and electronic data processing—industry practices dominate, as the following discussion shows.

SELLING GENERAL CONSUMER GOODS ▪
Why do MNC home offices pay so little attention to sales policies and practices in subsidiaries making general consumer goods? (See Figure 16–5.) The answer lies in the industry's needs for locally formulated marketing strategies.

It is natural to standardize sales practices when the product lines of subsidiaries vary little from country to country, but consumer goods are culturally sensitive products. The foreign product lines of MNCs that make

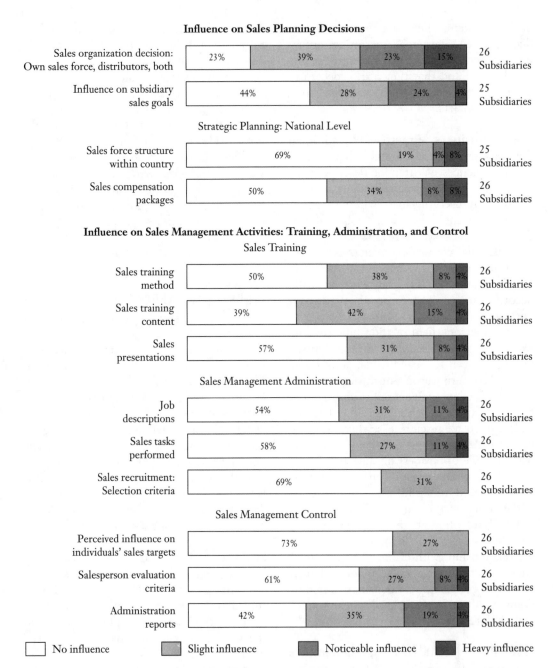

Influence on Sales Planning Decisions

Sales organization decision: Own sales force, distributors, both — 23% | 39% | 23% | 15% — 26 Subsidiaries

Influence on subsidiary sales goals — 44% | 28% | 24% | 4% — 25 Subsidiaries

Strategic Planning: National Level

Sales force structure within country — 69% | 19% | 4% | 8% — 25 Subsidiaries

Sales compensation packages — 50% | 34% | 8% | 8% — 26 Subsidiaries

Influence on Sales Management Activities: Training, Administration, and Control

Sales Training

Sales training method — 50% | 38% | 8% | 4% — 26 Subsidiaries

Sales training content — 39% | 42% | 15% | 4% — 26 Subsidiaries

Sales presentations — 57% | 31% | 8% | 4% — 26 Subsidiaries

Sales Management Administration

Job descriptions — 54% | 31% | 11% | 4% — 26 Subsidiaries

Sales tasks performed — 58% | 27% | 11% | 4% — 26 Subsidiaries

Sales recruitment: Selection criteria — 69% | 31% — 26 Subsidiaries

Sales Management Control

Perceived influence on individuals' sales targets — 73% | 27% — 26 Subsidiaries

Salesperson evaluation criteria — 61% | 27% | 8% | 4% — 26 Subsidiaries

Administration reports — 42% | 35% | 19% | 4% — 26 Subsidiaries

☐ No influence   ▨ Slight influence   ▨ Noticeable influence   ■ Heavy influence

Source: John S. Hill, Richard R. Still, and Unal O. Boya, "Managing the Multinational Salesforce," *International Marketing Review* 8, no. 1 (1991): 19–31. Reproduced with permission.

FIGURE 16–5
Headquarter Influence on Consumer-Goods Sales, Management Policies, and Decisions

consumer goods include high percentages of locally created goods and/or heavily adapted product transfers. Localized offerings encourage on-site manufacturing, which, coupled with the need for localized strategies, causes the subsidiaries to have considerable managerial autonomy. Demand for products is generated mainly through mass-media promotions, not by personal selling, and while head offices transfer some promotional material, local management determines the country advertising budget, the copy, and the media.

Consequently, sales practices for consumer goods are locally oriented. Sales compensation packages, for example, reflect country norms and motivation patterns. Swedish Match's Indian subsidiary uses straight salaries and bonuses based on sales volumes of the entire sales force, not on individual efforts. However, some traditional U.S. motivation methods work, with sales contests and special recognitions maintaining sales force morale even in such traditional countries as Burma, Sri Lanka, Pakistan, and Thailand.[20]

The relative inexpensiveness of personal selling in some overseas countries occasionally causes MNCs to rethink promotional mixes. Philip Morris hired an extra 200 assistants to work with its regular 100-person sales force in Venezuela. They acted as support salespersons, delivering products and helping with local promotions, thus allowing the regular sales force to concentrate on selling.[21]

Most head offices do not dictate salespersons' presentations, but situations exist where standardized presentations are useful. In direct selling, for example, Avon uses its door-to-door and party-plan selling overseas, although with some modifications. Avon toned down sales presentations in the British market, because sociability bonds among British neighbors caused them to refrain from pressuring friends to buy. In the Far East and Southeast Asia, direct-selling contacts come mainly from extended family kinship patterns, and "cold calls" are made only through go-betweens such as business acquaintances or mutual friends.

Controlling salespersons is important in the consumer-goods industry. Because demand is largely determined by mass media, compensation is not linked to sales performance. Intricate controls ensure sales performance, especially in developing countries where embezzlement is common. Electrolux controls its Latin American direct-selling operation through an elaborate matching up of six sales receipts in four separate departments.[22] Other companies use simpler controls. Swedish Match, for instance, uses daily reports, total sales, sales to quota, sales expenses, appearance, and improvements in distributor relations as performance yardsticks for its Southeast Asian sales forces.[23]

SELLING ELECTRONIC DATA PROCESSING EQUIPMENT
■ Strong head-office influence on overseas selling is characteristic of the EDP industry (see Figure 16–6). Global competitiveness for these high-tech firms depends, first, on technological breakthroughs and, second, on worldwide diffusion of technology. Consequently, many EDP companies—including NCR, Honeywell, and CDC—concentrate most global R&D and manufacturing facilities in their primary market, the United States, and do much overseas selling through exports and marketing subsidiaries. Hence, the industry's competitive position abroad depends on the effectiveness of its overseas sales organizations—how quickly they can get new products and technologies in front of customers.

To facilitate the flow of products and technology overseas, high-tech MNCs take their U.S. product-type sales structures abroad. Many high-tech sales structures are cloned on the parent company's model, a

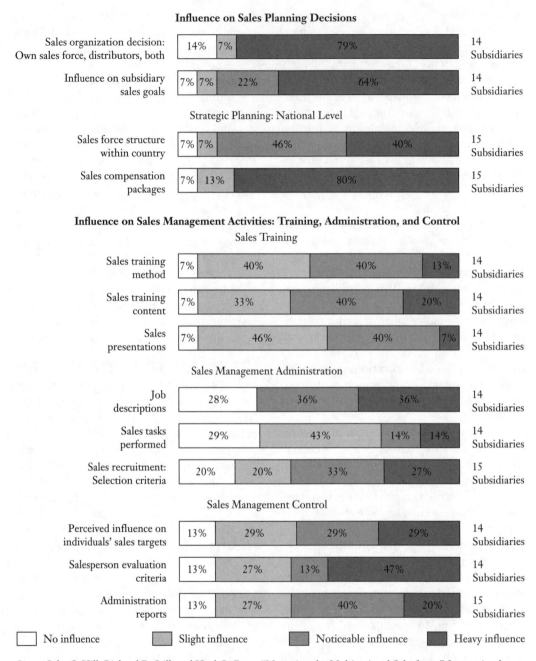

FIGURE 16-6 *Headquarter Influence on Subsidiary Sales Management Policies and Decisions in Electronic Data Processing*

practice that safeguards the orderly flow overseas of products and technologies.

Occasionally, market considerations dictate changes in sales structures. Hewlett-Packard modified its European product structure by combining its dozen product groups into three. This structure gave its salespersons greater flexibility in working with customers, facilitating the use of total-systems approaches.[24]

The EDP industry's global approach makes standardization of compensation packages and fringe benefits easy, even where cultural barriers exist. Commissioned sales, the staple EDP compensation plan, was introduced successfully by NCR into Japan, which formerly had been the deathbed of commission-driven compensation plans.

Heavy emphasis on sales training has long been the hallmark of high-tech companies. Knowledgeable, skilled sales personnel are essential in high-tech marketing. IBM invests up to 15 percent of its annual budget in training (roughly twice the industry norm). Sales recruits average from 6 to 18 months in initial training, and continuing sales training keeps experienced sellers abreast of the rapid diffusion of new products. This emphasis continues overseas. IBM's European training center processes up to 5,000 people a day, and NCR's 300 training specialists in Europe are backed up by traveling product experts who aid global product launches.

Not all EDP training, however, is head-office influenced. While hardware mainframes are mainly U.S.-made and exported, software items are developed locally. Thus, for high effectiveness, EDP sales training calls for both substantial head-office and local inputs.

With constant updating of products and systems, salesperson activities are reviewed constantly. The EDP industry does this by updating job descriptions and providing continuing training and retraining. Product divisions adjust job descriptions when technology shifts or market conditions change.

The highly competitive nature of the EDP industry makes sales control critical. The long lead times associated with complex systems, and sales negotiation processes covering many management echelons in clients' organizations, make most traditional ratios, like calls per day or sales per call, meaningless or misleading. Other performance measures are used, with the focus on expenses-to-sales ratios and on numbers and sizes of new customers and lost accounts.

The EDP industry has pioneered the computerization of sales procedures and administration. This trend, most noticeable in the United States and Europe, has spread to non-EDP companies using computers to control country-level sales operations. One purpose of computerization is to economize on salesperson calls, often by substituting telephone solicitations. Computerized prospecting systems are also being used not only by high-tech firms like Digital Equipment but also by less-technical organizations like Otis and Johnson and Johnson.[25] MNCs computerize sales management procedures not only to stretch selling time but to provide constant streams of sales information for control purposes.

SUMMARY

Personal selling and sales force management are both important in selling company products in foreign markets. Personal selling occurs at the field sales force level and during formal negotiation processes. Cultural factors are critical to understanding the negotiating styles of foreigners.

Generally, American and low-context European negotiation styles are relatively pragmatic, less lengthy, and more "efficient." High-context Japanese negotiators place more emphasis on getting to know the other company and its executives and on establishing an atmosphere of trust, a process that makes for elaborate and time-consuming negotiations.

The home office can direct sales management abroad by having domestic executives travel or put in tours of duty in foreign markets. More common for many large companies is foreign sales forces, which are managed with advice from the head office and from local management. In applying home-country sales methods abroad, all sales forces face geographic, market-development, political, legal, and attitudinal problems. Generally, industry requirements determine the relative degrees of local and head-office influence over foreign sales forces. Subsidiaries making general consumer goods receive relatively little attention from headquarters, because marketing success depends chiefly on local factors. By contrast, high-tech operations rely heavily on personal selling methods, and home-market-developed technologies minimize the need for sales adaptations to local conditions.

DISCUSSION QUESTIONS

1. You are an American preparing to negotiate with the Japanese for the first time. How would you prepare for the assignment if it is taking place (a) in Japan? (b) in the U.S.?

2. Compare and contrast the negotiating styles of Latin Americans and Asians. What are the similarities? The differences?

3. Review the planning habits of successful and average negotiators discussed on pp. 369–70. Given these characteristics, who do you think make better negotiators: Americans, Japanese, or Europeans? Why?

4. You are the CEO of a medium-sized company that exports to over 100 countries. In your export department, you have one person who speaks Spanish, one who speaks French, one who speaks German, one who speaks Russian, and yourself (who speaks just English). How would you divide the world up, and why?

5. Compare and contrast the sales practices for EDP equipment and general consumer goods. How are they different, and why?

Americans Doing Business in Europe

An American executive arrives at a potential business partner's headquarters in France. Entering his host's office, he pumps the French manager's hand and says: "I've heard a great deal about you; please call me Bill." Opening his briefcase, he suggests they get right down to business.

Seems quite normal, doesn't it? Except this is La Belle France. Things are done differently here. Had the U.S. executive done his homework, he would know that he should be more formal, giving only the customary brief handshake and not getting too familiar too quickly. Certainly, first names should be used only at the host's bidding—if at all. The comment, "I've heard a great deal about you," might also be embarrassing. Finally, the French executive would not be thrilled at "getting down to business" before getting acquainted.

To get to know each other, they might go out to dinner. The French executive again would be uncomfortable watching the American switch the knife and fork back and forth between hands. In France, only peasants and vagrants eat that way. When they finally get down to negotiations the next day, it is the American's turn to be nonplussed as the French executive starts a debate about the merits and disadvantages of the American's products and services.

Welcome to business negotiations European-style!

While there is no one European negotiating style, there are some commonalities among EU members, and Americans need to get used to them. Cultivating the personal aspects of business is important. For Americans, time is money; for Europeans, especially in Spain, Italy, and Greece, trust and long-term commitment, not contracts and short-term profits, are the keys to successful business relationships. Says Charles Valentine, director of international advisory services at Ernst and Young: "A European purchaser may sacrifice a few dollars by sticking with a familiar supplier, but these executives are more interested in linking up with companies that will make concessions over the long haul—for instance, to make a design change, or to hold the line on price increases in the event of a financial crunch."

Here are some contrasts worth noting:

Dutch and German businesspeople are competitive negotiators. German executives in particular are technically oriented, disciplined, and orderly. Americans can be direct and factual without giving offense. Similarly, Dutch and Germans do not emphasize the personal side of business relationships, unlike southern Europeans; commerce and social aspects are kept strictly separate. They are not keen, however, on the United State's emphasis on the "fast buck."

The British conduct business in an orderly and proper manner. They are polite but usually reserved, especially at first. They are uncomfortable when faced with openly ambitious or aggressive counterparts.

Similarly, the British rarely boast about their finances or position. They consistently understate things and have a subtle and indirect mode of speech that demands attention and sensitivity from listeners.

Doing business with Spaniards requires patience. Friendship is an important part of business relationships, which are assiduously cultivated over all-afternoon lunches, often three to six courses long, with little or no business being discussed.

Negotiating with Greeks is, in many ways, similar to negotiating with the French. Personal relationships are very important, whether at the family, business, or political level. Much commerce directly or indirectly concerns the government, which accounts for over 60 percent of the country's gross national product. Candor is appreciated, though it is best wrapped in silvery tongued oratory. Finally, Greeks regard contracts as evolutionary, not limited to written contractual specifications. Circumstances may force noncompliance to the strict letter of the contract.

Italians like style, even in their business dealings. Presentations should be elegant, organized, clear, and exact. Italians assume (until proved otherwise) that Americans are only interested in money and profits. Their decision-making styles are more autocratic, and top managers often make decisions without outside help from subordinates, consultants, or other specialists. Appearances are important to Italians, especially when combined with substance and integrity.

QUESTIONS

1. Review Chapter 2 materials as well as this chapter's discussions on negotiating. Examine each country's characteristics and try to explain why its negotiators behave as they do.

2. Do you think there is a single European negotiating style, a style for each country, or something between these two extremes?

Source: Adapted from David Altany, "Culture Clash: Negotiating a European Joint Venture Agreement Takes More Than Money. . . It Takes Savvy," *Industry Week*, 2 October 1989, 13–14, 16, 18, 20.

To Centralize or Decentralize Foreign Sales Forces—The Tale of Two Companies

Whether companies should centralize their selling activities and maintain a tight hold over them, or decentralize them to give more autonomy at the grass-roots level has always been a controversial topic. What works for some companies does not work for others.

Ellesse

Ellesse is a world leader in sportswear and is especially prominent in the upscale tennis-, jogging-, and ski-apparel markets throughout most of Europe. It maintains its own sales forces in most countries.

An Italian company, Ellesse's success is mainly due to its manufacturing and sales policy. The firm only produces items for which firm orders have been received. The advantage of this system, of course, is that inventory holding costs are minimal. The downside is that due to the seasonal nature of its product line, an order delivered late or delayed is a lost order. This places a premium on getting field orders to the Perugia factory promptly. Unfortunately, the order-taking process is lengthy. It includes (1) a salesperson manually filling out orders for any of the firm's 1,500 items; (2) mailing the order to the subsidiary office, where it is checked for errors and placed on computer diskettes; and (3) rushing the diskettes to Italy by courier.

The entire order process takes between a week and two weeks; only then can the order be started at the factory. How can Ellesse tighten up its sales cycle and get sales data to Perugia more quickly, free up seller time by reducing pen-and-ink order filling, and eliminate keyboard errors?

Hewlett Packard

Hewlett Packard had always prided itself on having a decentralized management style, which enabled it to respond quickly to marketplace changes in the computer and electronic-instrument industries. Then came the 1970s, and fierce competition from Europe and Japan forced HP and other high-tech companies to promote global manufacturing efficiency by reorganizing under mainly product-based groupings. By 1984, there had been three such realignments. The result was 11 separate product groupings, including electronic instruments, microwave and communications equipment, computer-aided design and engineering tools, electronic components, business computers, personal computers, and the like. Each group had its own marketing and sales team and had considerable autonomy to craft its own strategies.

Unfortunately, there were problems. New-product introductions were occurring at a frantic rate. The lack of interfacing between divisions caused R&D duplications and incompatibilities between company products.

At the market end, customers had moved toward broader, multiproduct systems that cut across HP's 11 product groupings. The company was not able to offer complete product and service packages to customers. As a result, HP was thought of as a supplier of individual high-tech pieces rather than as a "full-service problem solver."

To solve the problem, Hewlett Packard reorganized the 11 groupings into 3 business sectors, each serving a particular group of customers. These were (1) Market Systems and Networks (formerly five groups), including business computers, personal computational products, computer peripherals, and networks; (2) Components, Measurement, and Design Systems (formerly four groups), comprising electronic instruments, communications equipment, computer-aided design, and electronic components; and (3) the Manufacturing, Medical, and Analytic Systems Group.

QUESTIONS

1. What are the advantages and disadvantages of centralized and decentralized sales functions (that is, under what circumstances does each work)?

2. Compare and contrast the situations of Ellesse and Hewlett Packard.

3. Trace the string of organizational changes that Hewlett Packard has made since 1970 and examine the environmental changes causing them. Do you think the latest organizational shift will finally do it?

Source: Adapted from "Real Time Reporting: How Ellesse Does It," *Sales Management in Europe*, 1986, 27–27; and "Hewlett Packard Reorganizes for Sales Success," *Sales Management in Europe*, 1986, 122.

ENDNOTES

1 This section is drawn from Nancy Adler, *International Dimensions of Organizational Behavior* (Boston: Kent Publishing Co., 1986); and Mitchell F. Deutsch, *Doing Business with the Japanese* (New York: New American Library, 1983).

2 E. Russell Eggers, "How to Do Business with a Frenchman," in *Culture and Management*, ed. Theodore D. Weinshall (New York: Penguin Books, 1977), 136–139.

3 Neil Rackham, *The Behavior of Successful Negotiators* (Reston, Va.: Huthwaite Research Group, 1976), as reported in Nancy J. Adler, *International Dimensions of Organization Behavior* (Boston: Kent Publishing Co., 1986), 166–167.

4 Walter Kiechel III, "Our Person in Pomparippu," *Fortune*, 17 October 1983, 213.

5 R. L. Tung, "Selection and Training Procedures of U.S., European, and Japanese Multinationals," *California Management Review* 25, no. 1 (1982): 57–71.

6 M. E. Mendenhall, E. Dunbar, and G. R. Oddou, "Expatriate Selection, Training and Career Pathing: A Review and Critique," *Human Resource Management* 26, no. 3 (1987): 331–345.

7 Daniel Ondrack, "International Transfers of Managers in North American and European MNCs," *Journal of International Business Studies*, Fall 1985, 1–19; and Rosalie Tung, "Expatriate Assignments: Enhancing Success and Minimizing Failure," *Academy of Management Executive* 1, no. 2 (1987): 117–126.

8 Much of this discussion is from John S. Hill, Richard R. Still, and Unal O. Boya, "Managing the Multinational Salesforce," *International Marketing Review* 8, no. 1 (1991): 19–31.

9 "Amway Translates Its U.S.-Style Hoopla into Asian Consumer Sales," *Business International*, 1 November 1985, 346–347.

10 "Selling Asian Consumers Mixes Hoopla with Tight Controls," *Business International*, 28 June 1985, 204–205; and "Amway Translates Its U.S.-Style Hoopla."

11 Vern Terpstra, *International Marketing*, 3rd ed. (New York: Dryden Press, 1983), 462.

12 Vern Terpstra, *International Marketing*, 4th ed. (New York: Dryden Press, 1987), 483.

13 "Selling Asian Consumers." See endnote 10.

14 "Sales Management in Europe," *Business International*, 1986, 20–21.

15 V. H. Kirpalani, *International Marketing* (New York: Random House, 1985).

16 Richard R. Still, "Cross-Cultural Aspects of Sales Force Management," *Journal of Personal Selling and Sales Force Management* 1, no. 2 (Spring–Summer 1981): 6–9.

17 Terpstra, *International Marketing*, 4th ed., 483. See endnote 12.

18 Kirpalani, *International Marketing*, 428. See endnote 15.

19 "Selling Asian Consumers." See endnote 10.

20 Kirpalani, *International Marketing*, 428. See endnote 15.

21 Terpstra, *International Marketing*, 4th ed., 481. See endnote 12.

22 Kirpalani, *International Marketing*, 428. See endnote 15.

23 "Selling Asian Consumers." See endnote 10.

24 "The Marketing Challenge: How One MNC Reorganized to Meet Customer Needs," *Business International*, 22 February 1985, 57, 63.

25 "Sales Management in Europe." See endnote 14.

CHAPTER **17**

International Pricing

Chapter Outline

Learning Objectives

When you have mastered the contents of this chapter, you will be able to do the following:

1   Explain how internal and external variables influence international pricing decisions.

2   Discuss the strategic options in international pricing decisions.

3   Describe the key role played by transfer pricing in international marketing management.

4   Explain the major considerations in formulating international pricing strategy.

5   Outline the pricing implications of countertrading and the conditions giving rise to the need for it.

International pricing is an important component of the international marketing mix. While Pepsico International sells its products for less in Romania, ultimately these sales results are translated into U.S. dollars. Similarly, Rank Xerox (a joint venture of Britain's Rank Organization and Xerox) sells its products in India, but the final results of the Indian operation are expressed in dollars in the United States and in pounds in Great Britain. U.S. companies price their international products in the domestic currencies of the different countries; then, they evaluate their overseas operating results by converting these profits and losses into dollars.

Many multinationals try to refrain from engaging in price competition. Others compete strictly on the basis of price. Thus, pricing can be either an active or passive ingredient in the marketing mix. Discussions in this chapter focus on (1) factors influencing international pricing decisions, (2) determination of international prices, (3) international transfer pricing, (4) formulating international pricing strategy, and (5) countertrading.

THE IMPORTANCE OF PRICING IN THE INTERNATIONAL SETTING

As world trade grows, competition intensifies, and increasingly, price becomes either the main basis or an important basis of competition. Enterprises based in many newly industrializing countries use price as their main competitive weapon. Taiwan and South Korea, for instance, became major competitors in world textile markets because their enterprises sought business mainly through the use of lower-than-average prices. Many NICs and developing countries, such as Pakistan and Bangladesh, compete effectively in the world textile market by using lower-end pricing.

Price directly affects total revenues and ultimately determines profitability. Differences in world commodity and product prices, exchange-rate factors (strong or weak currencies), and variable wage rates contribute to cost and price differentials in the international marketplace. International companies have unique opportunities to capitalize on high-price–low-cost market situations. Prices directly relate to a company's growth rate and market share. For example, Zenith entered the computer market internationally by appealing to certain markets with offers of low prices, and its international growth rate and market share grew dramatically.

Development of mass markets anywhere, to a large extent, depends on bringing down prices. Although potential demand always exists, actualizing it requires some level of disposable income, which, of course, is directly related to the asking prices placed on products. If prices rise, real income declines and the market shrinks. Only if prices fall and stay that way do mass markets emerge.

In many industries, prices reflect the expected future, and contracts are made for future deliveries. In the construction, mining, and heavy-industrial-equipment industries, competitive bidding for future delivery is the usual operating model. Poor pricing of a competitive bid threatens the bidding firm's survival. When, for example, a Japanese engineering firm bids low on an American bridge-construction project and cannot complete the job at the agreed price, that firm is in a difficult position financially.

In both domestic and international marketing, there is a price-quality relationship. In some countries there is a relationship between price and perceived quality; that is, if a product's price is high, its perceived quality is also high, and vice versa. Customers around the world who know and

FIGURE 17–1 *Pricing Practices: Internal Parameters*

buy high-fashion items by Christian Dior or Charles of France expect and are willing to pay high prices. If buyers believe IBM products are higher in quality than those of competitors, quality-minded buyers expect to pay more than the prices IBM's competitors ask.

Throughout this book, international marketing-strategy options have been considered in terms of a spectrum. On one end of the spectrum there is the global marketing strategy; on the other end is the multilocal strategy. Strategic pricing options parallel these two extremes. The global firm is more rigid in its pricing practices throughout the world. The multilocal firm, by contrast, varies its prices from market to market. In order to decide which of these two strategies should be used we must consider the internal (company-related) and external (environmental) factors that influence pricing decisions.

FACTORS INFLUENCING INTERNATIONAL PRICES

Internal Factors

Each company establishes internal (corporate) parameters for its international pricing practices, based upon its worldwide corporate style and objectives. Four key internal parameters are (1) corporate goals, (2) centralized control, (3) long-range commitment, and (4) degree of internationalization (see Figure 17–1).

CORPORATE GOALS ■ In most companies, corporate goals govern pricing behavior. Because of stockholder pressure, for example, most U.S. companies seek to maximize short-run profits. U.S. companies doing business in international markets almost all require their international branches and subsidiaries to charge those profit-maximizing, standardized prices.

Some companies have service-oriented goals. The top managements of some multinational corporations expect their organizations to play an economic development role in some countries. Venezuela, for example, for years expected Creole Petroleum Company to provide economic growth and stability for the country. Corporate profit goals were intertwined with Creole's social responsibility to Venezuela. Similarly, Singer made its sewing machines available in developing companies at affordable prices so that an improved quality of life would foster growth in demand.

The corporate goals of multinationals often reflect global aspirations. Toyota, for example, aims to become the world leader in the auto industry. This goal makes Toyota responsive to both local competitive pressures and to local market conditions. Because Toyota exports from Japan, exchange rates affect Toyota's local prices. In general, global corporate goals create pressures within a multinational corporate entity to globalize its prices.

DEGREE OF CENTRALIZED CONTROL ▪
Companies vary in the control they exercise over their subsidiaries. Nestle is a centralized company, while Unilever is a decentralized company. Pricing decisions tend toward standardization in centralized companies and are more flexible in decentralized companies. Nestle's prices are determined at the home office, and local variations are minimized by the fact that the company responds only to those local conditions that are perceived as important by the central administration. Unilever prices are determined locally and vary substantially in different parts of the world. Thus, the more centralized the multinational firm, the stronger its tendency to use fixed prices.[1]

LONG-RANGE COMMITMENT ▪ A firm may be
internationalized temporarily or permanently, and this decision affects its pricing behavior. Some enter international markets on a short-term basis because they have surpluses that can be sold or excess capacities that can be utilized by expanding into these international markets. These firms generally price low in order to "sell the maximum in minimum time." Once the surplus is depleted or domestic markets recover or expand sufficiently to absorb the excess capacity, the company withdraws from international markets.

Other firms, including the movie and television programming producers, have long-term internationalization commitments

and continuously introduce new films and TV programs. These companies, whenever possible, set their international prices globally and at high levels. Of course, as their products "age" (move through the product life cycle), their international prices are scaled down gradually.

Still other companies, such as Sony and Nissan, have definite long-term commitments to internationalization that are reflected, as elsewhere, in their pricing. These companies set prices to maximize long-term rather than short-term returns on investment. The firm commitment to long-term internationalization also prompts them to price competitively around the world, varying their prices to meet or beat competition and to sell at prices that their target market segments can afford to pay.

DEGREE OF INTERNATIONALIZATION ▪ Some
scholars maintain that as the firm becomes more international, it establishes more stringent controls, but others say that controls become less restrictive and more indirect. In either case, as an enterprise becomes increasingly internationalized, some control over the pricing practices of its subsidiaries is needed. The more internationalized the firm, the greater the temptation to set global prices (uniform prices throughout the world). Even though it seems an attractive policy, complications inevitably arise from the incidence of local taxes, custom duties, and the like.[2]

In spite of these and other problems, some companies, among them Nestle and IBM, strive to price their products at approximately the same levels throughout the world. Other companies establish local manufacturing units and are more likely to allow local costs and demand conditions to dictate market prices. Consumer-goods corporations generally follow this pricing philosophy.

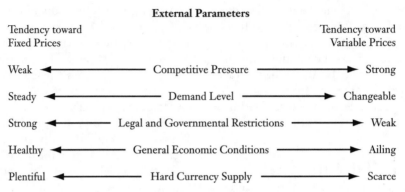

FIGURE 17–2 *Pricing Practices: External Parameters*

External Factors

External environmental factors also influence the establishment of international prices. The external factors, which are largely market related, include (1) competitive pressures, (2) demand level, (3) legal and governmental restrictions, (4) general economic conditions, and (5) currency supply (see Figure 17–2).

COMPETITIVE PRESSURES ■ Competitive pressures on international pricing decisions come from diverse sources and assume different forms. They result from direct and indirect price competition, nonprice competition, or some combination of these factors. An American auto manufacturer entering a developing country meets direct price competition from Nissan, Mitsubishi, and other foreign competitors who are entering the same market or are already there. Local automakers, if any, also compete, using a combination of lower-price and local-pride appeals.

Some price competition is indirect, meaning that price competition occurs between the product and its close substitutes. For instance, in many overseas markets, American automakers compete indirectly with public transport systems as providers of transportation. The countries of Western Europe have excellent public transport systems (rail and local and national bus), and the incidence of auto ownership is low.

Nonprice competition occurs in many markets. In developed countries, nonprice competition takes on a promotional orientation with emphases on better advertising, improved design, and good service more than on price. In developing countries, nonprice competition frequently takes the form of appeals to local pride and patriotism.

Some products are more pricing sensitive than others, thus inducing their marketers to use price rather than nonprice competition. Numerous factors stimulate price sensitivity:

1. General knowledge of a product's price level both within and outside its home country affects the product's price sensitivity. This knowledge causes automakers such as Hyundai and Yugo to compete chiefly on the basis of price. Prospective buyers everywhere are more acquainted with the approximate prices of Hyundais or Yugos than they are with the likely prices of Ferraris and BMWs.

2. Price sensitivity is influenced by directly and indirectly competing products. Headache remedies, for instance, compete not only with other headache remedies but also with other flu remedies, diarrhea remedies, and the like. In many developing countries, these products also compete with soups and folk medicines. Thus, in many countries, the price sensitivity of headache remedies is very high.

3. Either close or not-so-close substitutes of a product may be aggressively pushed through their distribution channels, intensifying the product's price sensitivity. High-quality and high-priced American-made and Swiss-made watches, for instance, have been subjected to strong price competition from Japanese-made watches. Japanese-made watches also were pushed through unconventional (non–jewelry store) channels such as supermarkets, drug stores, variety stores, and the like. The result has been a general heightening of price sensitivity for watches in general.

4. Existence of price instability in a country sometimes causes its population to have a high level of price awareness. If, for instance, there is runaway inflation in a country and the product is vital for human existence, the product's price sensitivity rises with the inflation rate. Food products in certain Latin American countries, plagued with high rates of inflation, are extremely price sensitive.

5. The likely reactions of competitors to price changes from inflation or deflation also contribute to a product's price sensitivity. In industrialized countries, price competition is emphasized less and non-price competition is emphasized more.

This situation causes slow responses by competitors to price changes. In some countries in particular, competing marketers' reactions to inflation are slow and modest. In Japan, for instance, manufacturers often absorb cost increases through increasing operating efficiency rather than by raising prices.

6. Conditions in different countries vary dramatically. All five conditions described earlier are present in some countries some of the time. Only a few or even none of these conditions are present in other countries. Highly competitive situations create a tendency for marketers to decentralize decisions on pricing and to charge different pricing in different markets[3] (see Figure 17–3).

DEMAND LEVEL ▪ The structure of demand in target markets influences pricing decisions. The total potential demand in each market and the demand elasticities both play critical roles.[4] If potential demand is high and only a few companies compete in the market, then high prices are likely. But if the level of demand is readily changeable, no competitor can afford the luxury of charging high prices. If the demand for Merck pharmaceuticals products in Turkey is strong and there is only token competition, it is feasible for Merck to charge high prices. But if Merck charges these same prices in Costa Rica, only a few people can afford to buy the product; as a result, Merck loses money and market share.

Elasticities are another aspect of demand. There are four forms of demand elasticity: price, cross, complementary, and promotional.[5] *Price elasticity* indicates the amount of incremental change in the quantity demanded as incremental price changes occur. Price elasticity often is more pronounced in international markets than in the

General Tendency of Factors: External

	Tendency toward Fixed Prices	Tendency toward Variable Prices
Tendency toward Fixed Prices	**A** Fixed global prices	**B** Possible general tendency to use fixed global prices
Tendency toward Variable Prices	**C** Possible tendency to use variable prices (multilocal)	**D** Variable prices (multilocal)

General Tendency of Factors: Internal

Note: For A and B, internal parameters dictate a global marketing strategy management. If external parameters instead of internal parameters were to dictate the pricing strategy, then C would have fixed global pricing and B would have variable (multilocal) pricing.

FIGURE 17–3 *Interaction among Internal and External Parameters*

domestic U.S. market, and it also varies from one market to another. Price elasticity is most pronounced in low-income countries, where people pay close attention to prices. If prices are high, they buy less, and if prices are low, they buy more.

Prices of competing or substitute products create *cross elasticities*. If many local substitutes compete with a product of an international company and their prices vary, then their prices influence demand for it.

Prices of complementary products create *complementary elasticities*. If, for example, the prices of auto tires and gasoline are high in a particular country, a price cut by a multinational automaker may not result in the expected levels of sales increases. A cut in the price of tires, gasoline, or both, however, would have beneficial effects on automobile sales.

Promotional elasticity measures the effect of promotion on sales; it varies from country to country. In country A, for instance, advertising may be a more effective sales stimulant than cutting the price. But in country B, a price cut may be more effective than advertising in stimulating sales.

If demand is strong and constant, and there are few marketplace limitations, the firm can do what it needs to do. In this situation, most multinationals tend to fix prices at high levels (see Figure 17–2). This is particularly true if the demand is also inelastic.

LEGAL AND GOVERNMENTAL RESTRICTIONS

▪ Legal and governmental influences affect price setting at the multinational firm's subsidiary level. These influences can take the form of import tariffs, import quotas, subsidies to local industries, and other governmental policies and practices favoring local industries. Some countries, particularly those in South America, have prohibitively high tariffs protecting certain of their domestic industries. The United States and most other developed nations are signatories to the Multi-Fibres Agreement, which sets quotas on textile imports into the United States and Western Europe. In addition, a country that uses subsidies and otherwise has practices and policies favoring local industry places external competition at a disadvantage; for example, Japan has traditionally favored Japanese suppliers over foreign suppliers in buying for governmental purposes. Furthermore, some nations permit horizontal price fixing (pricing agreements among competitors) and the setting of maximum or minimum price levels on some items (for example, the price of bread in the former U.S.S.R. did not change from the 1940s until the mid-1970s). Many countries restrict the use of price discrimination among buyers and limit the use of price advertising. Because governmental regulations differ from country to country, it is normal for multinational firms to vary their prices accordingly (see Figure 17–2).[6]

GENERAL ECONOMIC CONDITIONS ■ The
health of the target country's economy affects pricing decisions. One indication of economic health is the general price level. Some countries (for example, Bolivia, Brazil, and Argentina) often experience annual inflation rates in the hundreds of thousands of percent. Others (such as Germany and Switzerland) are disturbed when the inflation rate is more than 2 or 3 percent a year.

Is the target country experiencing inflation, stability, or deflation? Does the country have pronounced business cycles or not? What is the country's general buying mood? The answers to these questions provide key directions to those making pricing decisions. The more economically unstable and unpredictable a market, the more latitude subsidiaries must have in price-setting matters (see Figure 17–2).

CURRENCY SUPPLY ■ MNCs exporting to
developing countries and to Eastern Europe often find that their buyers lack hard (universally acceptable) currency. Some countries have shortages of hard currencies because their imports exceed the value of their hard-currency-earning exports. MNCs dealing with customers in countries with hard-currency shortages typically have three options: (1) accept payment in the local soft currency; (2) accept delayed payment in dollars or other hard currencies; or (3) accept goods in exchange. Countertrading, the name given to the option of accepting goods in exchange, has become popular in trading with developing countries. Roughly 90 countries have countertrade requirements for specific trading situations (for example, the importing of nonessential goods). Countertrade is a major means used by international companies to enter and do business with countries that have currency shortages. Commensurate with their degree of readiness to countertrade, multinational firms tend to vary their prices (see Figure 17–2).

Interaction between Internal and External Factors

Figure 17–3 shows that various combinations of internal and external factors (or parameters) represent separate strategic options. One extreme, A, is to use fixed global prices, while the opposite extreme, D, is to use variable prices throughout the world. In other words, A is a situation in which fixed global prices are used in conjunction with an overall global marketing strategy, and D is a situation in which variable prices are used in conjunction with an overall multilocal marketing strategy. In these two cases, both external and internal factors push the pricing decisions in the same direction.

Differential pressures from internal and external factors, however, may push the firm in opposing directions. For instance, situation B occurs when pressures emanating from internal factors push the firm toward a global marketing strategy but pressures from external factors cause it to use variable prices throughout the world. Similarly, situation C arises when pressures emanating from internal factors push the firm toward a multilocal marketing strategy but pressures from external factors cause it to use mixed global prices.

Differences exist among companies as to the relative emphasis placed upon internal and external factors. In general, North American and Western European businesses emphasize the internal corporate factors, whereas Japanese and other Far Eastern companies emphasize the external factors. Based upon the relative emphasis management gives to the internal (corporate) versus the external (environmental) factors, there could be four alternative scenarios (as shown in Figure 17–3):

Situation A: External and internal parameters both dictate fixed global prices.

Situation B: External parameters indicate variable prices but internal factors indicate fixed global prices.

Situation C: External parameters indicate fixed global prices but internal parameters indicate variable prices.

Situation D: External and internal parameters both dictate variable prices.

In situations A and D, the organization follows the dictates of both the internal and external factors. Clearly, these are situations where following the indicated scenario optimizes the pricing decision.

Situations B and C are more complicated, because in both, the assumption is that internal factors outweigh external factors (as they appear to do in most North American and Western European companies). In B, external factors indicate variable prices but internal factors indicate fixed global prices, and emphasizing the internal factors, the firm chooses fixed global prices. In C, external factors indicate fixed global prices but internal factors indicate variable prices, and again emphasizing the internal parameters, the firm chooses variable prices. However, firms emphasizing external factors more than internal factors (as most Japanese and other Far Eastern firms appear to do) make precisely the opposite choices (in B they choose variable prices, and in C, they opt for fixed global prices).

What explains these differences in perspective? Most large North American and Western European organizations perceive internal factors as more important than external factors because they typically have large amounts of sunk costs and other operational inflexibilities. Small North American and Western European firms and the more dynamic Japanese, South Korean, Taiwanese, and Hong Kong firms emphasize the external more than the internal factors, seeking first to satisfy market conditions even though this may mean lower operating profits in the short run.

In situations B and C, then, the decision depends upon whether the company is oriented ethnocentrically or polycentrically. The ethnocentrically oriented company pays the most attention to internal factors when making pricing decisions, while the polycentrically oriented company pays the most attention to external factors. While the former is using a global marketing strategy, the later uses a multilocal strategy.

ESTABLISHING INTERNATIONAL PRICES

The basic international pricing decision, then, is between using fixed global prices and variable prices. Implementing the decision to use fixed global prices, however, generally means allowing small price variations from country to country based on differences in the values of local currencies and in transportation costs. Implementing the decision to use variable prices takes into account not only differences in local currency values and transportation costs but also differences in demand and market conditions.

One study reported that many companies use fixed global prices and that these companies have high growth rates.[7] Companies that achieve a high degree of price standardization throughout the world generally also enjoy a certain degree of monopoly power. IBM, for instance, charges virtually identical prices in all of its world markets. Ethnocentric pricing of this sort is also practiced in situations where there is some dominant international economic force

(a cartel, a combine, or a strong trade association). Although American antitrust laws make it illegal to conspire to control prices, international cartels operate legally in world markets, generally controlling the prices of their commodities. Petroleum, diamonds, and tin are examples of commodities controlled by near-monopoly cartels, which also set fixed global prices.

Implementing the decision to use variable prices worldwide involves making choices among several different options (see Figure 17–4).[8] This decision tree indicates that the firm chooses first between demand-oriented and cost-oriented pricing. If a multinational firm chooses to vary its prices based on varying demand conditions, it has two alternatives: (1) use prestige prices or (2) price competitively.

When prevailing demand in a market is strong and likely to stay that way indefinitely, the multinational firm may use prestige pricing. Prestige pricing involves giving a product a high price to connote high prestige to those who buy it. Certain automobile makers, such as the Italian-made Ferrari and the German-made Mercedes-Benz, carry

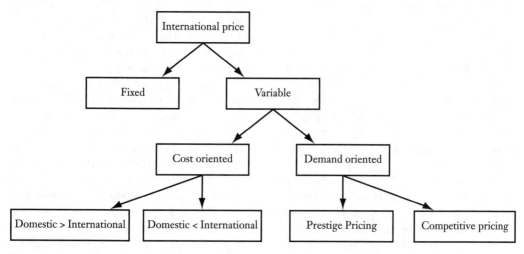

FIGURE 17–4 *International Pricing Options*

prestige prices. Wherever in the world they are purchased, buyers of these makes buy more than simply a means of transport—they also buy the prestige of owning a fine luxury car, a true status symbol. Similarly, high-fashion houses such as Christian Dior and Charles of France put prestige (high) prices on their offerings.

Actually, competitive pricing is more widespread than prestige pricing in world markets. Because the intensity of competition varies, the international company using competitive pricing varies its prices from market to market. In markets where competitors are large and strong, it sets its prices "competitively" (at prevailing prices). In markets where competitors are small and weak, the firm may set its prices higher than the competition to skim the cream, or lower than the competition to capture market share.

As Figure 17–4 shows, some international firms choose to relate their variable prices to costs. Cost functions in the operations of an international company may vary quite dramatically from market to market. When this occurs, an international firm may either (1) price higher in its home market than in its international markets or (2) price lower in its home market than in its international markets.

Prices Higher in the Home Market

Different conditions can result in home-market prices being higher than the international prices. First, the product may be manufactured in the home market, say in the United States, and shipped to or assembled in different overseas markets. If significantly large-scale economies exist, it is common to base prices upon "incremental manufacturing costs" plus the costs of transporting the product to market. Because many companies still consider international business as incremental business, this causes costs of the products going overseas to be lower than costs in the home market, thus making international prices lower than those in the home market.

Second, there are situations in which products sold internationally are manufactured overseas, where raw materials are more plentiful and labor costs are lower than in the home market, again causing international prices to be lower than those in the home market.

Third, situations exist in which individual international markets have strong domestic or other foreign competitors vying for the business; some countries discourage higher-priced imports by encouraging lower-priced local products or by persuading foreign competitors to enter with low-priced products. To forestall the development of situations such as this, managements of many international firms price their products lower overseas than at home.[9]

Fourth, management may use lower prices in foreign markets than in the home market simply to encourage growth in market share; many overseas markets are small but fast growing, so low-price "penetration pricing" is used to build market share quickly.

Fifth, an international market may have large potential but low buying power, which is the reason that Seiko watches are priced lower in certain African countries than in Japan or the United States.

Sixth, governments in some home markets may offer special incentives in order to obtain hard currency, encouraging their manufacturers to price lower overseas than at home. Many Japanese companies, early on, were suspected of charging prices in the United States that were not only below their domestic prices in Japan but even below their costs. This practice is called *dumping*. Many foreign companies dump in American markets for the purpose of gaining much-needed hard currency.

Prices Lower in the Home Market

Prices are lower in the home market than internationally when the six conditions just discussed are reversed. This means using price *skimming* in international markets. The six reverse conditions making for this situation are as follows:

1. No significantly large-scale economies exist.

2. There are no overseas cost advantages to justify lower international prices.

3. Competition in international markets is weak.

4. International market potentials are unattractive.

5. International markets are rich and buyers can afford to pay high prices.

6. It is possible to gain hard foreign currency by charging high prices.

In addition to these six conditions, higher prices internationally than in the home market may reflect the higher costs that result from lower sales volumes in particular markets. In some cases, the company may charge higher international prices because it is not committed to remaining in an international market; or if the company's international markets are high-political-risk areas, it might keep its international prices high in order to skim the cream.

TRANSFER PRICING

Increasingly, however, products are assembled from materials and parts brought in from several different countries. Many General Electric products, for instance, are assembled from parts made by affiliates in Taiwan, South Korea, China, and Mexico. Multinational corporations scan their affiliates and other contacts throughout the world seeking the best materials and parts; this scanning and the associated buying is known as *sourcing*. When materials and parts are secured from affiliates in different countries, their prices are transferred to the assembly site. This pricing process, which has many variations, is called *transfer pricing*.

As multinational corporations decentralize and expand their activities worldwide, their divisions and affiliates interchange more and more products and services among themselves. Divisions and affiliates serving as sources have some latitude in pricing to the buying division or affiliate. This latitude has led many multinationals to formulate transfer-pricing policies governing these transactions. Formally defined, a transfer price is the price that is attached, for the purpose of management control, to the goods and services moving from one profit or cost-responsibility center to another.[10]

Market-Based Transfer Pricing

In pricing raw materials and parts moving between multinational subsidiaries, one option the international firm has is to use market prices. These are the prices currently charged in those markets from which the raw materials, parts, or components originate.

If it is possible to choose the country in which to earn profits, then economic and political conditions as well as the country's strategic importance are all-important considerations. As shown in Figure 17–5, taxation, liquidity, inflation, and expropriation are important factors to consider when choosing this country. Consider, for instance, a U.S.-based manufacturer who buys large quantities of semifinished components from its subsidiary in Indonesia.

Scenarios

1. Choose a country to → Decide if profit or → Decide if there is → Use market-based
   disclose key profit   liquidity is preferred   strong competition   price plus additional
   considerations: in this country   for the intermediate   charges
   - taxation   product in this market
   - liquidity
   - inflation
   - expropriation

2. Choose a market → Use market-based
   where there is   price plus additional
   strong competition   charges
   for the intermediate
   product

3. Choose a market → Decide if there is a → Use managed price:
   where there is a   large volume of   full cost + mark up
   high product inter-   intergroup sales   + marginal costs (if
   dependence   available) or negotiate

4. Choose a market → Use managed price:
   where there is a   full cost + profit
   large volume of   + marginal costs
   intergroup product   (if available) or
   sales   negotiate

FIGURE 17-5 *Considerations for International Transfer Prices*

Because of Indonesia's low taxes and friendly government, the manufacturer may use Indonesia to disclose profits and for transfer-pricing calculations. If the Indonesian market for the intermediate product is strongly competitive, then the transfer price would include the market price plus disclosed profits.

However, the manufacturer's need for liquidity may cause it to choose a country whose currency is readily convertible into hard currency and whose tax situation and banking conditions may also be attractive. In these circumstances, as Figure 17–5 shows, the transfer price will be the market price plus the disclosed charges.

Similarly, Singapore may be chosen for profit disclosure purposes because its inflation rate is low, also a desirable condition for pricing the end product. Using Singapore as the base for pricing the end product may be attractive because of that country's stable economic conditions and the low risk of expropriation.

Thus, the international company chooses the country in which to disclose some or all of its profits. Transfer prices are set on the basis of conditions in the chosen country. If there is a strong market for the intermediate product, the transfer price is the market price plus the disclosed profit component.

If the product is unique with no external sales (sales outside the company) or if significant geographical differences exist among markets, it is difficult to use market-based transfer-pricing techniques. But other pricing techniques are available, including the following:

- Using the market price of a similar product.

- Deducting cost savings from the prevailing market price.

- Sharing the profit contribution margin between the supplier and the receiver of the product.

- Negotiating the price between the supplier and the receiver of the product.

Non-market-based pricing techniques, most of them primarily cost oriented, are also available.

Cost-Based Transfer Pricing

Unlike the market-based and profit-based techniques, establishing transfer prices through cost-based techniques is simple. There are two groups of cost-based techniques: actual cost and standard cost.[11] The actual cost sets the transfer price on the basis of the "actual" variable, or full cost of the transferred product. One difficulty is that it is only possible to determine actual costs at the end of the production process. However, many transferred products are finished and reenter the production process after transfer. Furthermore, where multiple components enter the same assembly operation, it is difficult to use the actual-cost approach; MNCs with this situation often use the standard-

cost approach, basing the transferred product's price on its standard variable cost, or its full cost. It is easier to determine standard costs than actual costs. Even so, standard costs are somewhat subjective and lend themselves to manipulations.

Among the cost-based transfer-pricing techniques are the following:

- Using the opportunity cost (the profit foregone by the supplier when he sells the product).

- Using the marginal cost (the cost difference resulting from manufacturing or processing the quantity of the product now being transferred).

- Using cost plus (cost of the product plus an arbitrary markup).

It has been claimed that proper transfer pricing practices would ensure goal congruence, efficient allocation of resources, and proper evaluation of performance among multinational firms. It helps these companies to coordinate their operations internationally in a socially responsible manner. [12]

THREE INTERNATIONAL PRICING STRATEGIES

International pricing strategy is part of an overall international marketing strategy. As discussed earlier, there are three international marketing strategies: global, multilocal, and multinational.

Under certain conditions, multinational firms charge the same (or very similar) prices throughout the world. This *global pricing* can occur where companies enjoy strong market positions and their products do not encounter heavy price competition. (Dow Chemicals, Xerox, and IBM use global pricing.) There are also circumstances where either market conditions favor global pricing or cartels exist (for example, OPEC for oil).

MNCs with multinational policies use combinations of global pricing and *multilocal pricing*. For instance, they may charge the same standardized price in all of the Common Market countries and charge different prices in each African country. *Multinational pricing* is, therefore, a blend of global and multilocal pricing. Philips, for example, a large European manufacturer of TVs and other home electronics, appears to use similar pricing for its markets in North America and Japan but multilocal (variable) prices in other world markets.

COUNTERTRADING

One aspect of international pricing is critical in dealing with formerly communist and developing markets. These countries rarely earn sufficient quantities of hard currencies to cover their import bills, so countertrading (exchanging goods for goods) develops. Countertrading was estimated to account for 28 percent of world trade in 1984.[13] Since the beginning of time, traders have exchanged goods. Countries using countertrading do so either to generate hard currency (by selling the exchanged product to a third party) or to save hard currency for other purposes. Countertrade basically means any commercial arrangement whereby purchases are made to offset sales as a means to reduce or restrict the flow of hard currency across national boundaries.[14]

Why Countertrade?

Four reasons that countries engage in countertrading are (1) to offset currency problems,

(2) to open up world markets, (3) to involve the country in trade at all, and (4) to aid balance-of-payments problems.

Currency problems are the most critical factor pushing countries to engage in countertrading. Developing countries and even many countries in the industrialized world do not have hard currencies. In order to buy goods they need or want, they are forced to exchange their products; exchanging "apples for ammonia" becomes necessary.

Opening up world markets may call for countertrading. When Coca-Cola entered the Bulgarian market, it exchanged Coca-Cola for Bulgarian calculators. In Hungary, Coca-Cola exchanged its products for Hungarian wine. Countertrading made it possible for Coca-Cola to open up these and other markets.

Developing countries improve their economies through trade. Without countertrading most of them cannot participate in international trade. But almost every country has something that some other country does not have. Exchanging these products paves the way for these countries to participate in international trade.

Balance-of-payments problems may necessitate countertrading. When a country has a negative balance of payments, increasing its debt hinders the country's chances of borrowing from major world banks. Thus, the country may agree to engage in countertrading with other countries. Balance of payments, therefore, become manageable, at least partially, through countertrading.

Types of Countertrade

There are many types of countertrade, including barter, clearing agreements, switch trading, compensation agreement, counterpurchase, offset, buy-back, and corporate bartering.

BARTER ▪ Barter is the oldest and the least used form of countertrade. Barter means trading one type of good or service for another without making use of any currency. Exchange rates or prices are expressed as so many units of good A for so many units of good B. Cash prices are not quoted but do exist as "shadow prices," and they are considered in establishing the countertrade exchange rates.

Simple barter takes place between two countries, but more complex forms sometimes involve as many as three or four countries. A typical example of simple barter is Occidental Petroleum Corporation's 20-year agreement to ship annually 1 million tons of phosphate rock to Poland, in exchange for an annual shipment of 500,000 tons of Polish molten sulfur.

An example of barter involving more than two parties occurred when Israel sent potash to Poland, Poland shipped a quantity of sugar with an equal value to Brazil, and finally, Brazil sent a shipment of coffee with an equal value to Israel.

CLEARING AGREEMENT ▪ Clearing agreements provide greater flexibility than straight barter for all parties involved. In clearing agreements, countries agree to trade one another's products up to a set value within an established time span. When imbalances occur in these countries' accounts with one another, the imbalances are known as "swing credits." Imbalances are cleared periodically using a specified "clearing currency." The clearing currency is either some mutually acceptable currency or a value stated in "clearing account units" or, occasionally, in gold. Clearing agreements are common in South America, Central America, Eastern Europe, and the Middle East.

An example of a firm using a clearing agreement was Britain's Rank Xerox, which produced copiers for India for sale in the U.S.S.R. through the clearing agreement between India and the U.S.S.R.[16]

SWITCH TRADING ▪ If bilateral trading contracts are already in place, the contract completion responsibility can be transferred to a third party. This process is called switch trading. Switching a certain portion of a trade agreement to a third party is a movement away from bilateral trade and toward multilateral trade, providing greater flexibility and increasing trade efficiency. One example of switching involved the sale of industrial adhesives by 3M to Brazil through Hungary. Because Brazil and Hungary have a bilateral trade agreement, 3M shipped the adhesives to Hungary, where the product was repacked and sent to Brazil as Hungarian exports. 3M benefited because it was able to work within Brazil's import restrictions, Hungary benefited by a commission on the sale, and both Brazil and Hungary fulfilled their bilateral trade agreement.

COMPENSATION AGREEMENT ▪ A compensation agreement is a type of long-term countertrade and is usually limited to one industry. A company in one country sells machinery, equipment, technology, or a complete plant to a buyer in another country and receives payment, partially or fully, in the form of products produced by that plant. Levi Strauss's agreement with Hungary is an example. Levi Strauss sold a turnkey plant and the right to use its blue-jean design to Hungary; in return, it received payment in goods from the Hungarian plant.[17]

COUNTERPURCHASE ▪ A counterpurchase is an agreement that obligates a seller to buy or market goods from the buyer's country. It involves two separate but related transactions. The originating transaction and the subsequent counterpurchase are usually covered in separate cash contracts that ultimately offset the effects on the balance-of-payments accounts of the buyer's country. Typically, counterpurchases are short-term agreements. Colombia and Spain, for instance, agreed that Colombia would sell coffee to Spain and that Spain would sell buses to Colombia. Colombia's sale of coffee to Spain was the originating transaction, and Spain's sale of buses to Colombia was the counterpurchase (that is, the agreement that the supplier agreed to purchase and market products from the buyer).[18]

OFFSET ■ An offset is a form of counter-trade that is mainly used in selling defense-related aircraft or other items to foreign governments. The supplier agrees to market items produced in the buying country to "offset" all or a portion of the contract price.

Offsets are different from counterpurchases. The seller in an offset transaction does not take title to the items accepted as the offset but assists in their marketing. In the 1960s, for instance, McDonnell Douglas sold Yugoslavia $250 million worth of aircraft and agreed to market (as an offset) $70 million worth of Yugoslavian goods.

BUY-BACK ■ A buy-back is a form of countertrade that resembles a compensation agreement, except payment in the buy-back takes one of many forms. When the selling firm in a buy-back sells machinery, technology, or a plant, it receives payment either in cash or in goods as part of a barter transaction, but the selling firm also agrees to buy a portion of the production resulting from the original transaction. The resulting production is not the compensation to the seller in the original transaction but a separate transaction.

A buy-back example is China's contract with an Italian firm, Technotrade, to improve Chinese railroads and expand Chinese coal mines. Technotrade received $500 million for supplying the needed technology, and in addition, it agreed to purchase coal from China.

CORPORATE BARTERING ■ When companies have excess inventory, vacant office space, or limited distribution, they have been opting for corporate barter as a flexible solution. For instance, Atwood Richards, a New York–based barter firm, will buy the product from the cosmetic company, textile company, shoe manufacturer, sporting goods company, or electric appliance company, and as part of the condition of sale, will agree to take that product and move it into a market where that product is not being distributed or sold. Thus, the barter firms help the client companies penetrate new markets without disturbing the client companies' normal distribution systems and regular markets.[19]

The pricing implications of countertrading are important. An international company doing countertrading must know not only the market value of its own product but also the value of the customer's product taken in payment. Besides knowing the comparative product values, the international marketer must be extremely market sensitive as to market potentials and existing competition in the different product categories.

SUMMARY

Five key aspects of international pricing were discussed in this chapter: (1) factors influencing international pricing decisions, (2) establishing international prices, (3) international transfer pricing, (4) international pricing strategy, and (5) countertrading.

Both internal and external factors influence international pricing. The internal factors include corporate goals, centralization of control, long-range commitment, and degree of internationalization. The external factors include competitive pressure, demand level, legal and governmental restrictions, general economic conditions, and currency supply. In establishing international prices, the two key alternatives are standardized global prices or variable local prices. Variable prices vary on the basis of cost or market situation. If prices vary according to cost they may be above or below domestic prices. Pricing according to the market situation may take the form of either prestige pricing or competitive pricing.

Multinational firms use transfer prices in moving products among subsidiaries scattered throughout the world. Transfer prices are based either on profit or on cost.

International pricing strategy options parallel the general strategic options: global, multilocal, and multinational.

Countertrading is related to international pricing because it requires the identification and comparison of relative values.

DISCUSSION QUESTIONS

1. In establishing international prices, are internal or external factors more important? Discuss.

2. How do the internal and external factors influencing international prices interact?

3. Explain the strategic options in establishing international prices.

4. What is transfer pricing? What are the two key components on which transfer prices are based?

5. Why is countertrading so popular when trading with developing countries?

6. If its domestic prices are higher than international prices, a company may be accused of doing something illegal. What is this, and why do companies still follow this practice?

7. How is countertrading related to pricing?

Nissan's Penetration of the European Market

Nissan's European market penetration began with exports to Finland in 1959. The company historically has first moved into a limited market representing a larger one. After entering Finland, the company concentrated on the northern European countries. Nissan did not enter the European Common Market until the late 1960s.

To manufacture passenger cars in Europe, Nissan founded Nissan Motor Manufacturing U.K. Ltd. in 1984. Nissan produced an upper-medium-sized car, the Bluebird. The car was produced with 80 percent local content and materials.

The integration of the European Common Market will have a major impact on Nissan's operations. With the expected growth of the European market, Nissan planned to increase its market share, improve its brand image, and decentralize further its operations, product design, production, marketing, and sales. Nissan plans to accomplish these European goals through its British operations.

To coordinate European operations, the company established a European technical center. Through the joint efforts of both the Japanese and European staffs, this center will produce new cars designed to meet European consumer needs.

The European car market is growing. In 1988, Nissan had 2.8 percent of total market share. The Fiat and VW groups, with 15.3 and 14.4 percent, respectively, were the strongest competitors. Utility cars and super-mini cars combined amounted to about 43 percent of the market in Spain, 14.5 percent in West Germany, 44.3 percent in France, 27.8 percent in the United Kingdom, and 57.4 percent in Italy. Executive-type cars accounted for only 6.0 percent of the market in Spain, 24.7 percent in West Germany, 10.3 percent in France, 12.3 percent in the United Kingdom, and 9.1 percent in Italy. In all these markets, the share accounted for by lower-medium-sized cars was high (35.6 percent in West Germany, 23.0 percent in France, 34.4 percent in the United Kingdom, 25.4 percent in Italy, and 37.1 percent in Spain).

Studies indicated that with the exception of Germany, the importance of price was relatively high.

Nissan planned to introduce a new car, the Micra, by 1990. The Micra was planned as a smaller car than the Nissan Bluebird. The Bluebird had already been profitable and had high unit profit margins. Micra entered the market from the lower end; it was a relatively lower-priced car. In Europe, Nissan, so far, has the image of being an average Japanese car maker, probably because the company has focused on low-priced cars.

QUESTIONS

1. Considering the development of the European economic union, what kind of pricing strategy should Nissan use in Europe?

2. What (if any) should Nissan's emphasis be—Micra-type or Bluebird-type pricing? Discuss in detail.

3. What additional information would you need to make a better pricing decision for Nissan?

ENDNOTES

1. Penelope J. Yunker, "A Survey Study of Autonomy, Performance Evaluation and Transfer Pricing in Multinational Corporations," *Columbia Journal of World Business* 18 (Fall 1983): 51–64.

2. Simon Majaro, *International Marketing: A Strategic Approach to World Markets*, rev. ed. (London: Unwin Hyman, 1982), 109.

3. George Norman and Nancy K. Nichols, "Dynamic Market Strategy under Threat of Competitive Entry: Analysis of the Pricing and Production Policies Open to the Multinational Company," *Journal of Industrial Economics* 31 (September–December 1982): 153–174.

4. Nathaniel H. Leff, "Multinational Pricing Policies in Developing Countries," *Journal of International Business Studies* 6 (Fall 1975): 55–64.

5. Kent B. Monroe, "Buyers' Selective Perceptions of Price," *Journal of Marketing Research* 15 (February 1973): 70–80.

6. Homi Katrale, "Pricing Policies of Multinational Enterprises: Host Country Regulations and Welfare," *International Journal of Industrial Organization* 2 (December 1984): 327–340.

7. A. Coskun Samli, "International Marketing Strategy Decisions," *European Journal of Marketing*, Summer 1974, 108–119.

8. A. Coskun Samli and Laurence Jacobs, "Pricing Practices of American Multinational Firms: Standardization versus Localization Dichotomy," *Journal of Global Marketing* 8, no. 2 (1994): 51–73.

9. John V. Farley, James M. Hulbert, and David Weinstein, "Price Setting and Volume Planning by Two European Industrial Companies: A Study of Comparison of Decision Process," *Journal of Marketing* 44 (Winter 1980): 46–54.

10. Y. Tsurumi, *Multinational Management* (Cambridge, Mass.: Balinger Publishing Co., 1985).

11. R. L. Benke and J. D. Edwards, "Transfer Pricing: Techniques and Uses," *Management Accounting*, June 1980, 75–83; and L. L. Knowles and R. Mathur, "International Transfer Pricing Objectives," *Management Finance* 4 (Spring 1985).

12. Albert Y. Lew, "Multinational Transfer Pricing: Implications for North American Firms (Advance Pricing Agreement)," *The National Public Accountant*, August 1996, 37–42.

13. Sandra M. Huszagh and Frederick W. Huszagh, "International Barter and Countertrade," *International Marketing Review*, Summer 1982, 7–19.

14. Leo G. B. Welt, "Barter and Countertrade," *American Import Export Bulletin*, May 1980, 34–39; and Leo G. B. Welt, "Straight Cash-for-Goods? No Longer a Sure Bet!" *American Import Export Management*, October 1983, 36–37, 44.

15. Welt, "Straight Cash-for-Goods?"

16. Ibid.

17. Ibid.

18. Huszagh and Huszagh, "International Barter and Countertrade."

19. Angela Briggins, "When Barter is Better: Corporate Bartering," *Management Review*, February 1996, 58–61.

4

Coordinating and Controlling Marketing Programs

Implementing international strategy is based on developing specific marketing programs. The success of the overall activity is related to the international firm's ability to coordinate the overall marketing activity and control the implementation process. This section of the book dwells upon these coordination and control processes.

Although international market research is a necessary component of coordination and control processes, in this book, the authors attempt to go beyond the *scope* of typical international market research. We introduce a concept that we call international strategic intelligence systems (ISIS). Part of international market research *must* revolve around generating and using information for strategy development. Chapter 18 deals with this topic.

Regardless of the adequacy of international strategy, unless the firm has the structure to facilitate such a strategy, success is not forthcoming. Thus, there must be a balance between the strategy and the structure. Organizing a structure appropriate for international marketing is extremely critical and is discussed in Chapter 19.

Much of the time, feedback and resultant control functions are triggered by financial indicators. However, in this book, we maintain that there are nonfinancial indicators of performance as well. We also maintain that, in some cases, by the time the financial indicators of international performance are being noticed, it may be too late. Thus, the international firm should be able to use both monetary and nonmonetary indicators equally well. We present a number of nonmonetary indicators and discuss how they may be used in the coordination and control of international marketing operations. Chapter 20 presents this information.

Finally, Chapter 21 deals with the attitude and behavior of CEOs in regard to international marketing. In a sense, this chapter is a summary of the managerial part of this book. The chapter focuses on the fact that, in general terms, the overall orientation of the CEO to international marketing is perhaps the most important determinant of the firm's success in the international arena.

CHAPTER 18

International Market Research and Information Systems

Chapter Outline

Learning Objectives

When you have mastered the contents of this chapter, you will be able to do the following:

1 Illustrate the complexities of international market research by discussing different research approaches, data sources, and data types.

3 Explain procedures for obtaining desired international information.

3 Discuss the various key problems faced when gathering and using international information.

4 Describe the importance of having a carefully designed international information system.

Many years ago, an international business scholar commented that "management is management whether you are in Tokyo or Toledo."[1] Similarly, marketing research is marketing research wherever you are.

International marketing research and marketing research are synonymous because the research process is basically the same whether applied in Hoboken, New Jersey, or Sri Lanka.

Generally, the tools and techniques for research remain the same in foreign and domestic marketing, but the environments within which they are applied are different, thus creating difficulty.[2]

DIFFERENCES BETWEEN INTERNATIONAL AND DOMESTIC MARKET RESEARCH

International and domestic market research differ in degree rather than in kind. Environment is a key factor because research efforts are applied within an environment and information is collected from it. From market to market, environmental differences cause researchers to emphasize and search for different items of information or to use different techniques to collect similar items of information. Information about the management of Western households is collected primarily from women, but it is impossible to collect similar information from women in Middle Eastern countries because in Islamic cultures, women do not talk to strangers.

Compared to their domestic counterparts, international marketing researchers face additional, as well as different, problems. Frequently, the nature of an international marketing research project calls for individual creativity on the part of field workers. Key decisions often must be made

while the project is underway. However, the traditional orientation of the particular country may cause local field workers to look for guidance as to what tradition dictates, to previous instructions, or to past practice. The result is that field workers do not use their own initiative nearly as much as do their counterparts in the United States.

There are also differences in developing international and domestic information systems. In the international arena, competition forces each company to develop unique strategies in order to shape a competitive edge. This may mean negotiating directly with a host government for special treatment, cooperating with other companies in the same industry in some markets and competing head on with them in other markets, and working with numerous joint-venture partners.[3]

In developing and monitoring appropriate competitive strategies, international companies require data sources at multiple levels—local, national, regional, and global. Researchers develop analytical tools to process the data into information useful for strategic planning and its implementation. Merely undertaking market research projects is not enough. Ciba Geigy, the giant Swiss multinational, has more than a one-time need for data on medicinal-drug-consumption patterns worldwide; it requires functioning databases or information systems. These are used as needed in formulating and adjusting marketing strategies to fit changing situations. Consider the following vignettes.

Parker Pen Company, a long-time leader in the writing instrument market, failed to detect worldwide deterioration in its leadership. It did not have the information to spotlight those countries where its positions were strong, weakening, and weak, nor did management have data available with which to evaluate the market performance of newly introduced product models. There was no way of knowing which markets had reacted positively to new products and models and which had reacted negatively. Because of the lack of market information, Parker used the same advertising theme and the same product positioning in all markets worldwide.[4] It had no way to detect the impact of the advertising theme in individual country markets. Similarly, the company's many overseas manufacturing plants lacked the guidance that comes from marketing research data, resulting in needless inefficiencies and inventory imbalances.

Procter & Gamble was beaten at its own game in the Japanese disposable-diaper market, when the American firm's market share nose-dived from 90 percent to 15 percent. Complacency over more than three years had caused the company to ignore moves by a Japanese competitor aimed at eroding P&G's market share. P&G not only lost the lead in technological development of this product but also lagged in its marketing research. Meanwhile, the Japanese competitor was studying consumer buying habits in Europe, the United States, and Japan. P&G's information system did not detect the news that competition was getting keener. Before long, P&G's market share was dropping fast. In Japan, the Japanese company was marketing a new disposable diaper—a highly absorbent one providing a better body fit for Japanese babies! P&G's product was not at all adapted to the needs and desire of Japanese consumers.[5]

This chapter focuses particularly on those aspects of international marketing that cause differences in international market research and information systems compared to domestic counterparts. Different approaches to the analysis of comparative marketing systems are presented, and market research needs at the international level are explored. There are three types of international data: (1) secondary, (2) primary, and (3) syndicated. The discussion of these types of data centers on their usefulness, their availability, their applicability, and problems encountered in their utilization.

APPROACHES TO COMPARATIVE MARKET RESEARCH

Multinational firms do considerable comparative market research. One reason for this is to determine how much of their experience in one market is applicable to another. For instance, Pepsico learned that the general promotional appeal of its advertising was transferable everywhere around the world, while Carnation, studying markets for its evaporated milk products, found just the opposite. Carnation milk products were used in different countries in different ways; in some countries, the primary use of the product was in coffee; in others, for feeding babies; and in still others, as cake topping. If primary use varies from one market to another, management individualizes strategies to fit different markets. When company X plans to enter the country B market, after succeeding in the country A market, it has two options: (1) use the same approach in B as in A or (2) use a different approach. Comparative market research assists management in determining the degree of market similarity.

There are seven different approaches to comparative market research. Each is geared to answer a different question. Table 18–1 lists the seven approaches and the questions they seek to answer. These approaches are described below.

1. *Marketing instructions.* In appraising possible new markets and comparing them with the company's present markets, the

TABLE 18–1 ■ *Approaches to Comparative Market Research*

Approach	Question
Marketing institutions	Who are the marketers?
The functional relationship	What do marketers do?
Competition and cooperation	How are the marketers related to each other?
Role of government	What is the government's role in the marketplace?
Quality and quantity relationship	What are the dimensions of the prevailing markets?
Marketing performance	What do marketers contribute?
Ecological analyses	How are markets affected by their environment?

Source: Adapted and revised from Jean Boddewyn, "A Construct for Comparative Marketing Research," *Journal of Marketing Research*, May 1966, 141.

international market researcher for each prospective market determines just who the marketers are. Which institutions do the marketing job in each new market?

2. *Marketing functions.* Marketing practices vary from country to country, so the international market researcher determines who does what for each prospective market. Which institutions perform which functions? How does the performance of these functions in this country compare with their performance in countries where the company already has markets?

3. *Competition and cooperation.* All markets feature competitive and cooperative relationships. The researcher determines how the degrees of competition and cooperation vary in market A as compared to market B. In Eastern Europe, for instance, competition has been less intense and cooperation more evident than in Western Europe. Ascertaining how a country's marketers relate to each other competitively and cooperatively is basic information required for the formulation of marketing strategy.

4. *Role of government.* The government's role in marketing, particularly in socialist countries, is extremely important for strategy formulation. Socialist governments shape the nature of competition and name the participants in the marketing process.

5. *Quality and quantity relationships.* The international market researcher assesses specific qualitative and quantitative characteristics of individual country markets. How large is the market and its segments? What are the demographics and attitudes?

6. *Marketing performance.* The quality of marketing performance within a given country is valuable information. How effectively and efficiently do marketers perform? What and how do marketers contribute to the country's economic and social well-being?

7. *Ecological analyses.* Ecological considerations—the relationships of markets and marketers to the environment—are critical aspects of international comparative market research. Not only the nature of existing environmental constraints but

also the relative importance that the country's government and citizenry place upon environmental protection are key inputs to marketing strategy formulation.

Most comparative market research projects use several approaches. Working with the researchers, management specifies the questions to which it needs answers, and in turn, this information, dictates the approaches that are chosen. The choices reflect the background and sophistication both of marketing management and of the international market researcher.

PHASES AND KINDS OF INTERNATIONAL MARKET RESEARCH

Market knowledge is essential to planning a successful international marketing operation. The task of the international market researcher is to identify the critical items of information concerning target markets before a company launches marketing operations there.[6]

There is a certain uniqueness about international market research. Especially in analyzing markets in the developing countries, the researcher must cope with a general disdain for statistics and statistical information. In some countries, an influential citizen's opinion is considered more important by local decision makers than results obtained through research and statistical analysis. The international researcher also considers economic problems much more closely than is usual for the domestic marketing researcher. For instance, appraisals of a target country's balance-of-payments and foreign-exchange situations necessarily

precede market and marketing analyses. Thus, the first phase of international market research is to gather all *pertinent* information about international markets. The specific information gathered depends upon the purpose of the study, but the study begins with a broad review. If the purpose is to ascertain whether country X has an attractive potential as a market for the products of company A, either for investments or for exports, the broad review often is aimed at determining the following:[7]

1. A 5- to 10-year forecast of total industry sales in country X for each product under consideration.

2. Characteristics of products now on the market in country X.

3. Characteristics of the country X market.

4. Number and relative strength of competitors in country X and the intensity of competition.

5. Design features, performance characteristics, and price levels that A's products must have to compete successfully in country X.

6. Methods of distribution available in country X.

7. Expenditures necessary to distribute, sell, and promote successfully A's products in country X.

8. Share of industry sales company A can reasonably expect in country X and the amount of income it can obtain in that market.

The broad review often is mainly derived from secondary data obtained from international banks, business and government publications, and other sources of published data. If the situation as presented in the broad review seems encouraging, then

TABLE 18–2 ▪ *Broad Reviews of International Markets*

Information Items		Information Sources
1. A 5 to 10-year forecast of total industry sales for each product under consideration	Sales volume of products; sales volume or growth of cohort variables; surrogate variables	Secondary sources; syndicated data sources
2. Characteristics of products now on the market	Existing products and their in-depth analyses and comparative basis	Primary data through observation; syndicated data sources
3. Characteristics of market	Size; growth; distribution; location; degree of sophistication	Secondary sources; some primary data through surveys
4. Numbered strength of competitors and degree of competition	Number of present and future competitors and their relative sizes and particular strengths	Secondary and territory sources; primary data through observation
5 Standards of design, performance, and price that the company's products must meet to compete successfully	Information for No. 2 as well as in-depth analyses of market needs and sophistication	Internal analyses of data from external sources; some primary data through research
6. Methods of distribution required	Availability of different modes of distribution; efficiency of infrastructure	Secondary sources
7. Estimated cost of distribution, promotion, and selling force	Projected market; sales prices; and promotion elasticity and effectiveness	Secondary sources; internal analyses; sales
8. Share of industry the company can expect and projected income	Effective projections based on market performance of competitor's items No. 1 and No. 2 above	Internal analyses; secondary sources

the researcher may decide either to collect additional and more detailed secondary data or to obtain primary data, or both. Thus, the broad review leads to a second phase, which focuses upon gathering more specific information on (1) the economy, (2) industry data, (3) product data, (4) competitive structure, (5) channels of distribution, (6) competitors' marketing practices, and (7) other critical variables. In gathering this additional information, international market research makes increasing use of syndicated data.

Phase 1: Exploratory Research and Use of Secondary Data

Table 18–2 shows the eight information items that broad reviews seek to provide, the information needs, and the sources of information. Of these eight items, six are either partially or fully obtainable from secondary data. During the exploratory phase of international market research, secondary data sources are particularly important. Much can be learned about marketing conditions,

I. Internal Sources of the Country under Analysis
   A. Official government statistics
         production reports
         foreign trade (imports and exports)
         statistical abstract
   B. Industry associations
         production, consumption, in use, saturation
         industry directory (list of member firms, products)
         Industry magazines
   C. Periodicals
         magazines directed to wholesale and retail trade

II. Official External Sources
   A. United Nations
   B. International Monetary Fund
   C. World Bank
   D. Regional organizations
         Organization for Economic Cooperation and Development
         (OECD)

III. Worldwide Industry Sources
   A. Complementary or served industry publications
         frozen foods, coffee, steel, shipbuilding
   B. International press and newsletters
         "Business International"
   C. Research organizations
         Ford Foundation
   D. International banking publications

IV. U.S. Industry Sources
   A. U.S. industry associations' international publications
         E.I.A. "International News"

V. U.S. Department of Commerce
   A. U.S. import and export statistics
   B. Overseas business reports
   C. Short market surveys and trade reports
   D. Foreign Service Dispatch Loan Service
   E. "International Commerce"

VI. Competition
   A. Annual reports of major competitors, U.S. and foreign

FIGURE 18–1 *Types of Key Sources of Secondary Data*

opportunities, problems, and successful marketing methods from the experiences of others. There are difficulties in precise identification of the information sources. Because of the burgeoning amount and varying availability of information, selective bibliographies identifying data and information sources are of increasing interest to international market analysts. The European Productivity Agency, the United Kingdom's Market Research Society, and the U.S. government are among the many organizations publishing selective bibliographies.

Secondary data sources for international market research are varied and reasonably plentiful. Six key types of sources are listed in Figure 18–1 and are described in the following discussion.

INTERNAL SOURCES OF THE COUNTRY UNDER ANALYSIS ■

Of internal information sources, the statistical abstracts collected by the government generally are the most helpful, and almost all countries publish them. Most are compact, available in English, and feature a considerable amount of general information about the country. The abstracts and other official government publications usually include a large variety of data covering population, employment, income and the like.

Industry associations within the country may provide data on production, consumption, products in use, and saturation for individual products and industries. This information is valuable for determining market potentials. Industry directories, or sometimes industry listings, and industry magazines are used to identify possible business contacts and other needed connections in the country.

OFFICIAL EXTERNAL SOURCES ■

Official sources of information outside the country, such as the publications and information sources of the United Nations, International Monetary Fund (IMF), and the World Bank are important providers of secondary data. Though much of this data is financial, some of it is economic and commercial.

WORLDWIDE INDUSTRY SOURCES ■

Many industries provide worldwide information through their international industry associations. Furthermore, several research organizations and international banking and other business publications disseminate published industry information worldwide.

U.S. INDUSTRY SOURCES ■

Nearly every major industry in the United States has a national association that accumulates and disseminates international industry information.

U.S. DEPARTMENT OF COMMERCE ■

The largest single compiler and disseminator of international data and information is the U.S. Department of Commerce. It collects and publishes a wide variety of statistical data series on international trade, business, and economics. One basic reference item, the *U.S. Statistical Abstract*, includes a tremendous amount of international and domestic data.

COMPETITION ■

A company's competitors are sources of international business information. Most multinational companies issue annual reports, which provide a wealth of usable information.

Phase 2: Obtaining and Processing Additional Secondary Data and Primary Data

Once target markets are identified and their potentials are estimated, the next task is to obtain and process additional market information. This information is needed for use in developing marketing programs for the target

The National Trade Data Bank (NTDB). The NTDB is a major source of international trade data collected by federal agencies.

The Economic Bulletinboard (EBB). The EBB provides online trade leads and time-sensitive market information.

Country Commercial Guides (CCGs). CCGs are comprehensive reports focused on single countries. They cover a variety of topics important, particularly, to exporters.

Best Markets Reports (BMRs). BMRs are country- and industry-specific reports. They describe the best prospects for U.S. sales abroad.

Industry Sector Analyses (ISAs). ISAs are structured market research reports produced on location in leading overseas markets. They include such things as market size, market characteristics, and competitive and end-use analysis.

International Market Insights (IMIs). IMIs are short profiles of specific foreign market conditions or opportunities. They are prepared at embassies and consulates abroad.

The Customized Market Analysis (CMA). A CMA is market research made-to-order. It is designed for a specific company that needs to develop or refine a marketing strategy for a specific product or service in a target country.

The Trade Opportunity Program (TOP). The TOP program provides timely sales leads from international firms seeking to buy or represent U.S. products or services.

The Agent/Distributor Service (ADS). ADS is designed for companies seeking a customized search for qualified agents, distributors, or representatives abroad.

International Company Profiles (ICPs). ICPs provide information and portray the reliability of prospective trading partners.

Commercial Service International Contacts (CSIC). CSIC gives contact and product information on more than 46,000 firms abroad that are interested in U.S. products. It also includes country directories of international contacts.

FIGURE 18–2 *Department of Commerce Market Research Programs*

markets. The second phase of international market research then consists of gathering, analyzing, and interpreting additional market information about the target countries. While the data collected during the first phase come entirely from secondary sources, data obtained during the second phase come from both secondary and primary sources.

ECONOMY OF THE COUNTRY ▪ Many items of information are considered in sizing up a country's economy. Most of this information is obtainable from official statistics published by the country's government and from those issued by such official outside sources as the United Nations and the IMF (see Figure 18–2).

Data are needed on the country's population, its distribution, and changes in it; generally, this is the most readily available information. Information is required on the national income, historical changes in it, its rate of change, and its sources. In estimating the market potential, especially for consumer durables and household items, data are needed on per capita or per family income, or both. Average wage levels and retail sales figures are indicators of economic fluctuations. Electrical output, value added by manufacturing, and transportation statistics reflect the level of economic activity. The state of current business conditions is indicated by data on the country's foreign trade and the value of its currency on world financial markets. More often than not, the international market analyst breaks down countrywide data into geographic and socioeconomic segments; frequently, individual segments have unique characteristics, making them substantially different from other segments.

INDUSTRY DATA ▪ The international market analyst is interested in industry data because of their use in determining the country's stage

of development vis-à-vis the company's product. For the particular industry involved, data are needed on the value of the country's total imports, production, and exports. Similar data are needed for individual products of that industry. Data are collected for use in making estimates of the market saturation point in terms of product ownership and use. Data are required, too, for assessing the availability and nature of facilitating factors; for example, in the case of electrical appliances, it is necessary to have data on the percentage of homes wired and on the characteristics of the country's electrical system. Most of this information is readily available from secondary sources, such as statistics from official government agencies, outside official sources (the UN and others), and from industry information bureaus (see Figure 18–1).

PRODUCT DATA ▪ More specific information is needed on the country as a market for the product. Getting this information requires either the tapping of primary information sources or using syndicated data. Among the product information items needed are consumption rates, proportion of product owners in the population, product-buying intentions of nonowners, product-buying decision-making process, and identification of who influences or contributes to the buying decision. The international market analyst also needs to know how to locate the normal prospective buyers for the product, where they are, and how many there are. These are all items of information needed for planning the product's distribution, promotion, and pricing.

In Switzerland, for instance, in order to appeal to upper-middle-class housewives, an American maker of dishwashers was thinking of using a time-economy appeal. The same appeal had been used successfully by marketers of instant coffee and cake mixes. However, a market study indicated that Swiss housewives were still bound by a social code that required devotion to their home and domestic duties. This circumstance caused the manufacturer to use a promotional approach emphasizing the extra sanitation made possible by the high temperatures in dishwashers. This approach was successful.[8]

In another situation, a preliminary study reported a healthy increase in sales for vacuum cleaners in a European country. One vacuum cleaner manufacturer, in evaluating this country as a market, decided that further research was necessary. The second study confirmed the healthy pattern of increase but revealed that market demand was mainly for a light, inexpensive vacuums, not at all like the items in the manufacturer's line. Consequently, the manufacturer decided not to enter this market.

COMPETITIVE SITUATION ■

For realistic marketing planning and ease in implementing the marketing program, management needs a clear picture of the competitive situation in the country. Thus, data are gathered and processed on companies in the targeted country that are making or importing products similar or identical to those of the would-be manufacturer. These data include such things as numbers, sizes, product lines, brands, market shares, and the like. Similarly, the planners must have data necessary for the evaluation of the strengths and weaknesses of individual competitors and their products, the alternative distribution channels, and price structures. Some of these information items are obtainable through such secondary sources as industry publications, business news journals, publications of the U.S. Department of Commerce, and competitors' annual reports (see Figure 18–1). However, the international market researchers will almost certainly need to tap primary data sources and utilize syndicated data.

Analysis of the competitive situation helps prevent international marketing blunders. Foreign marketing research rather often indicates that particular countries are not ready for or not appropriate for popular American products. And foreign-made products that, on the surface, appear to offer little or no competitive threat actually turn out to be more suitable to a particular foreign market than the product that the manufacturer finds the American market accepts enthusiastically. For instance, while large, expensive, and complex U.S.-made washing machines are widely accepted by American buyers, in many overseas markets, they cannot compete at all with simple, basic, compact, and inexpensive machines that do not require plumbing attachments of any sort.

CHANNELS OF DISTRIBUTION ■

The international market analyst needs answers to numerous questions about channels of distribution for the product in the target country: What are the normal channels for this product? What other channels are available? Which types of wholesalers and retailers are active in its distribution? How many are there, what arrangements do they have with other marketers of the product, and what are their operating methods and philosophies? What are the characteristics of the country's transport systems, and what warehousing facilities are available?

Channels differ considerably from country to country. In many developed markets, channels are typically simple and short (have a minimum of distribution levels). But in many countries, channels are underdeveloped in the sense that they are long (have many distribution levels) and there is much confusion about the functions performed by channel intermediaries.

Knowledge of the prevailing distribution situation in a prospective market is essential for planning marketing strategy. Such information is needed for making plans to distribute the product effectively and efficiently, providing the company with an opportunity to develop a differential advantage. The planners must know not only what channels are available but also the kind of performance that can be expected of each and how to go about making arrangements for the product's distribution in the country. Most, if not all, of this information is gathered from primary sources—by observing, by running marketing surveys, by consulting with experts, and by talking directly with prospective channel members.

COMPETITORS' SALES ORGANIZATIONS ■

The international market analyst needs to know certain things about the sales organizations of competitors in the target market. The aim is not only to know how competitors are organized for selling but also to evaluate their effectiveness, which requires identifying both strengths and weaknesses. Basic, of course, is the knowledge as to whether competitors are using their own sales forces or manufacturers' agents. If they are using their own sales forces, details are needed concerning the usual caliber of sales personnel, rates of sales-force turnover, recruitment and selection systems, training, compensation methods, territories, quotas, and other matters. If they are using manufacturers' agents, detail about relationships with the principals, commission schedules, territories, quotas, and the like must be determined. Details such as these nearly always are obtainable only from primary sources—local marketing experts, field surveys, and on-the-spot observations.

OTHER CRITICAL VARIABLES ■

Industry factors often dictate what other data need to be collected. For consumer nondurable products (food, cosmetics, and the like), competitor advertising and promotional outlays are necessary information. For big-ticket consumer goods (appliances and so on) information is needed on competitors' repair and maintenance services and policies, availability and role of credit in the society, and attitudes toward foreign products. Identifying the other critical variables and gathering information on them means tapping primary sources—consulting with experts, observing what goes on in the market (a source much used by Japanese firms), and doing field investigations and surveys.

RECENT DEVELOPMENTS ■

With the development of modern information systems (IS) and the emergence of the Internet, research for secondary data has become significantly easier and proficient. In fact, it is possible to research foreign markets without ever leaving one's office chair, let alone the country. In some circles, this is coined as "armchair global commerce."[9] In particular, the U.S. government has developed an extensive repository of international trade information. The website for the International Trade Administration (http://www.ita.doc.gov/), which is a division of the Department of Commerce, stores information by region, country, or industry.

International market research programs by the Department of Commerce are briefly described in Figure 18–2. Almost all of these are available in different forms: hard copy, CD-ROM, or the Internet. The Commercial Service of the Department of Commerce plans to make the National Trade Data Bank (NTDB) available to all of its trade specialists through the Internet.[10] (Additional information regarding this topic is also available in Chapter 8.)

Methods of Collecting Primary Data

Survey, observation, and, sometimes, experimentation are the methods used for gathering international primary data. The survey is the method that is most often used. But its use, especially in developing markets, is complicated by the simultaneous existence of advanced and primitive market sectors. These are known as dual economies.

The fact that dualism exists influences the collection of primary data and the interpretation of the findings. Researchers must take into account the target country's business, economic, and political environments (which give rise to the dualism) in setting research objectives. Analysts must recognize possible limitations present in the research design and the findings because they lack full knowledge of the country's socioeconomic dualism. Finally, analysts must formulate their interpretations of research findings in terms of the known dualism.

If the primary research is being done in a developing country and the researcher has the job of determining the market potential for product X, depending upon the product, it may be more realistic to determine the product's market potential either in the country's advanced sector or in the more primitive sector, but not necessarily both.

Finally, findings from primary-data analysis must be interpreted in light of the dualism. It has been suggested that there is an inherent tendency for members of the advanced sector to be over-represented in any general survey. Furthermore, interpretations, articulations, and beliefs are all subject to the impact of the dualism. Hence, analyses must take it into account in interpretations of research results.

Primary data are obtained either internally (from within the organization itself) or externally (from outside sources). If the company is heavily engaged in international marketing, it generally has its own in-house research operation, enabling it to satisfy its periodic research requirements as well as to work on unanticipated projects as they arise. But if the company is only now considering international marketing, does only a limited

amount of international business, or faces unusual and unrelated information needs, the choice often is to use outside research organizations. Companies whose situations lie between these two extremes use some blend of internal and external researchers, the exact blend depending upon the relative costs and benefits.

Companies that make consumer products use outside sources as suppliers for data that are all but impossible to obtain as cheaply on a direct basis. A. C. Nielsen Company, for example, provides for its subscribers (client data users) a variety of store-audit data gathered from outlets in many countries. The Nielsen Retail Index Services provide information on the movements of products through retail channels, usually for both the subscriber's and competitor's products. Neilsen conducts detailed audits of invoices and inventories every 60 days in more than 12,000 chain and independent retail stores around the world. Subscribers utilize these data for many purposes, including the following:

- Deciding on the introduction of new brands in a monopoly market.

- As historical data for making decisions on market entry.

- Analyzing test market results.

- Deciding on introducing new package sizes.

- Evaluating price-quality relationships.

- Monitoring in-store support by retailers.

SYNDICATED INFORMATION SYSTEMS

During the 1980s, there was a major movement from data to information. Operators of syndicated information systems have learned not only how to gather large amounts of data but also how to master the art of transforming data into information useful for making decisions. Syndicated information systems, which gather, organize, and disseminate data, have mushroomed, especially throughout Europe and in Japan (see Figure 18–3). Syndicated data, (that is, various forms of the raw data or of the information based on the data) are available for purchase on a fee basis. Subscribers to computerized syndicated

---

Express. This advanced, interactive analysis system developed by management decision systems (MDS) is designed to overcome the constraints of fixed reports to improve the quality and speed of analysis required for confident decision making.

Denjon International Limited. Their services cover areas such as international market research, European market research, data preparation and tabulation, and software and systems development.

Quantime. This system is organized to provide three major groups of services: *Quantum,* which is a tabulation package for data analyses; *Quanvert,* which is an interactive tabulation package to create tables easily and quickly; and *Quancept,* which is a system for questionnaire design and interactive entry of market research data.

Sisdata. This system is an interactive statistical information system. It is available online through an international time-sharing network.

Seigos. This system is part of an information and research organization, and it provides data on marketing, consumption patterns, and the like.

Xcaliber. This unique interactive data-analysis and cross-tabulation system is designed to analyze and report tabular data. Customer surveys, product-use records, and warranty and repair data are the typical data sources.

F & S Index. This system provides information needed to make investment decisions, to develop market strategies, and to analyze competitors' behavior. It organizes article summaries by industry, country, and company from 350 newspapers, trade journals, bank reviews, and government reports.

Source: Information gathered from ESOMAR Seminar on Information Systems in Action, Amsterdam, March 1980, and Wiesbaden, Germany, August 1985.

FIGURE 18–3 *Some Examples of Syndicated Information Systems*

information systems have access to data banks, allowing them to manipulate and analyze the data.

Many of the syndicated databases are worldwide. Available systems can be grouped into two major categories, static and dynamic. Static systems are passive systems, and dynamic systems are interactive systems. Static and dynamic systems are further categorized into micro or macro systems. Micro systems are typically management information systems (MIS) dealing primarily with a particular firm and its immediate problems. Macro systems provide national or international broad-based economic, trade, population, and other data. Micro systems are mostly for interactive use.

Databases of syndicated information systems are expanded, updated, and revised according to changes in time series data, panel data, and survey data. *Time series data* derive from longitudinal studies (similar studies made at different times) either of panel or of national and international economic statistics. *Panel data* (gathered from a relatively stable group of respondents) provide periodic or ad hoc reports on a wide variety of topics. *Survey data*, reported on a more intermittent basis than either time series or panel data, are supplied by diverse organizations.

SOME PROBLEMS OF INTERNATIONAL MARKET RESEARCH

There are some problems in doing international market research, problems that are exacerbated if the research is being done in a developing country. Within many developing countries, there is a prevailing negative attitude toward marketing, let alone market research. Such countries have production-oriented economies, as are the majority of their business executives, so most companies are headed by people who are unaware that marketing "problems" exist. They believe that the problem is to produce and that getting products to users is not a problem at all. Imagine trying to do market research in this kind of atmosphere!

Going hand in hand with the negative attitude toward marketing is the pervasive scarcity of goods so characteristic of developing countries. Demand is normally in excess of supply, resulting in minimum pressures to market products aggressively. These conditions are not conducive to persuading decision makers of the need for marketing research.

In addition, the indigenous firms of developing countries generally exhibit a lack of interest and little ambition to grow larger (either in sales or in profits). Most firms are family owned and small, and their managements are mostly interested in maintaining the status quo. They see little reason to undertake research, as they can see no way that the findings could be utilized and still maintain the status quo.

Finally, there is no "felt need" for doing market research to guide research and development efforts. Many, if not most, of the products made in the developing countries are copies of those made in the Western world. That fact, coupled with the weakness or nonexistence of competition, means there is little incentive to undertake market research.

Table 18–3 contrasts conditions surrounding international marketing research in developed and developing countries. In doing marketing research in the developing countries, each of these conditions has the potential for creating problems for marketing research.

TABLE 18–3 ■ *Domestic versus International Market Research*

Developed Country	Developing Country
Single language and nationality	Multilingual, multinational, and multicultural factors
Relatively homogeneous population	Fragmented and diverse markets
Data available, usually accurate, and collection easy	Data collection a formidable task, requiring significantly higher budgets and personnel allocation
Political factors relatively unimportant and the system is stable	Political factors frequently vital and the system is generally unstable
Relative freedom from government interference	Government involvement and influence in business decisions
Relatively stable business environment	Multiple environments, many of them unstable
Legal and regulatory constraints	Same
Availability of research infrastructure and technological advancement	Lack of research infrastructure and technological advancement
Market research stresses operational issues	Market research stresses strategic issues
Cultural homogeneity	Cultural taboos and differences
Media availabilities and mix satisfactory	Unsatisfactory media
Adequate telephone and postal systems	Inadequate telephone and postal systems

Source: Adapted from Erdener Kaynak, "Marketing Research Needs of Less-Developed Countries: Standardization versus Localization," in *Developments in Marketing Science vii*, ed. Jay D. Lindquist (Kalamazoo, Mich.: Academy of Marketing Science, 1984), 161.

Problems with Using Secondary Data

Using data from foreign markets also presents problems, regardless of whether the data are secondary or primary. Four problems in working with foreign-market secondary data are as follows:

1. Breakdowns of detailed data are often lacking. Until the United Nations began rather extensive data collecting, little in the way of internationally comparable data was available. Even today, the UN's data, especially for developing countries, are sparse and inadequate.

2. The reliability of some data is questionable. Because of the techniques used or the personnel who gathered the data, many data lack statistical accuracy.

3. The noncomparability of data and the unavailability of past data are further limitations. National definitions of statistical phenomena differ from one country to another, and there are different emphases placed on gathering specific items of economic data. Most available data concern the recent past, and the lack of series of past data makes time series analyses impossible.

4. Differences exist in the time it takes to collect data for a project. For instance, while it may take a month and a half to complete a desk-research project (using secondary data) in the United States, the

same project would take three to five months in Western Europe. The ready availability of references, data sources, and the skills and experience of analysts account for the differences. Needless to say, doing the same project in a developing country verges on the impossible!

What are the implications for the users of secondary data? Research analysts using secondary data generally desire reasonable reliability in the data and the data sources. Using secondary international market data makes it imperative that the analysts know whether or not data sources have reasons for purposeful misinterpretation of the facts. Analysts need to know who gathered the data, why the data were gathered, and the collection methods. Ideally, analysts are in positions to evaluate particular secondary data in terms of their consistency with other know data and market facts.

Problems with Using Primary Data

Problems in using primary data on international markets fall into three areas: sampling data-collecting methods, and response error in field research.[11]

SAMPLING ■ Probability sampling is not feasible in most developing countries. Information about the characteristics of the universe from which the sample is drawn are generally unavailable or of doubtful validity. Detailed maps, especially city block data, are difficult to obtain. Inadequate transportation facilities make using dispersed samples out of the question. The absence of numbering systems for identifying dwelling units and the existence of multiple families in single dwelling units further complicate the sampling task. The existence of multiple families in single dwelling units leads to problems in

determining which family to interview. Furthermore, city directories, telephone directories, and reliable publications providing detailed demographic characteristics are rarities.

However, probability sampling is feasible in some foreign markets. In most West European countries and Japan, it is possible to obtain voter lists. Sweden, in particular, has especially detailed tax records, which are utilized by researchers. Each year, the Swedish government publishes a blue book listing the income of every person above a certain income level.

DATA-COLLECTING METHODS ■ Numerous limitations constrain the methods used for collecting data. In many countries, only limited numbers of people have telephones, so telephone surveys (if used) create limited and biased samples. The lack of good mailing lists and postal system inefficiencies, coupled with widespread illiteracy, reduce the effectiveness of mail surveys. Cultural barriers—such as not believing in giving written responses that will be read by unknown persons, or the custom that the male head of the family will answer the questionnaire, regardless of the addressees—also hamper data collecting and introduce biases into survey results.

RESPONSE ERROR IN FIELD RESEARCH ■ Accuracy of primary data also is diminished by response errors and field researchers' inadequacies. While the not-at-home problem is not great in many cities in developing countries, that problem is substantial in the countryside, where wives often work alongside their spouses in the fields. Also, evening call-backs generally not feasible because of poor lighting, high crime rates, and the like.

The custom of not talking to strangers is prevalent in many parts of the world (the Middle East, much of the Mediterranean area, throughout most of Southeast Asia, and, in fact, wherever strong, traditional societies persist). Imagine how this custom interferes with field surveys! In doing a personal survey of business executives, for example, it means that interviews cannot be conducted on a spur-of-the-moment, drop-in basis. Unless arrangements are made for introducing the interviewer to the right "contacts," there is practically no chance that the designated interviewee will consent to the interview, let alone that he or she will provide accurate information.

Conducting consumer surveys is complicated both by the "don't talk to strangers" custom and by widespread fear of government officials, especially tax collectors. Consider the following situation: The director of a household budget study for a Middle Eastern government expected that less than 50 percent of the households contacted would be willing to cooperate, due primarily to mistrust of strangers in general and of the government in particular.[12]

Cultural traits and traditional orientations in some societies result in certain "taboo" topics, which naturally, are totally or partially ignored in survey research. Furthermore, it is traditional throughout the Middle East that the male has the dominant role in managing the family's shopping. While certain shopper surveys done during daylight hours obtain fairly good participation by housewives, the resulting findings are often misleading if they report on items mainly purchased by husbands.[13]

Lack of well-trained and trustworthy field interviewers in the developing countries is an important source of research error. Throughout Latin America, for example, organizations doing studies put much verbal emphasis on their use of the latest and most scientific market research methods, their perceptive analysis of findings, and the like. Yet in reality, the market research done in Latin America is of questionable quality. The same is true in many other countries but mostly in the developing world. There simply are not enough well-trained and effectively supervised people to assure high-quality results from survey research. In addition, partly because of cultural restraints and partly because of training deficiencies, supervisors and project directors, as well as field interviewers, exercise little autonomy and operate rigidly (rather than flexibly). Everyone operates "according to the book"—taking orders and adhering to them inflexibly. This approach all but precludes survey designs that call for on-the-spot decisions by field research personnel.

Problems of Data Analysis and Interpretation

There also are problems in data analysis and interpretation. In spite of data deficiencies, the analyst needs skill in combining data from secondary and primary sources into meaningful and useful reports. Because of environmental circumstances and cultural restraints, both data quantity and quality vary importantly from one situation to the next. Rarely is it safe for the analyst to take the data at face value. Data must be considered in light of their source.

Consider what happened in a seven-country study of the giving and receiving habits of husbands and wives with respect to diamonds and diamond jewelry. While in six of the countries, husbands were the buyers and wives were the receivers, in Japan it was found that husbands customarily do not buy presents for their wives (though husbands are generous in giving their wives cash). While husbands were the ones interviewed as the gift buyers in six of the countries, preliminary results caused the sample design for

Japan to be changed so that wives rather than husbands were interviewed as jewelry buyers. Interpreting diamond jewelry buying as "gift buying and gift receiving" would make no sense whatever for Japan!

Another study focused on hotel selection criteria used by European businessmen. One-third of the German and Dutch respondents and 85 percent of the British respondents took their wives with them on business trips, while nearly all of the French respondents left their wives at home. Not surprisingly, the Germans and Dutch used different criteria in appraising hotels than either the British or French. In situations where the selection criteria for products or services differ considerably from country to country, not only are meaningful multinational comparative studies difficult to design but their findings are difficult to interpret.

The findings of multinational studies of product usage are also difficult to evaluate when the product is used in different ways and for different purposes from one country to the next. Consider, for instance, a study made of the use of chocolate bars for cooking or in sandwiches. German housewives regarded the study as frivolous, because in Germany, chocolate bars are not used for either purpose. But French housewives reported chocolate bars as important for cooking, while Italian housewives said they often gave chocolate bars between slices of bread to their children to eat at school during breaks.

Analyzing and interpreting data from multinational studies calls for substantial creativity as well as skepticism. Not only are data often limited, but frequently, results are significantly influenced by cultural differences. This suggests that in analyzing and interpreting these data, there is need for properly trained local personnel to function as research specialists; alternatively, the researchers require substantial advice from knowledgeable local inhabitants.

INTERNATIONAL STRATEGIC INTELLIGENCE SYSTEMS

There has been an increasing awareness of needs for more international data and different kinds of information. This awareness has led to the development of specialized data-gathering organizations, many of them subsidiaries of U.S. market research firms. Meanwhile, multinational corporations have become more established, and their data needs have shifted from the basic information used to evaluate entry into individual markets to data useful for managing their continuing operations in active markets. Thus, there is continuously accelerating demand for usable, operating-level information by MNC managements at the country level, as well as at the world headquarters.

The key purpose in both international and domestic market research is to obtain sufficient usable data. *There is no shortcut from data to usable information.* During earlier stages in international marketing, many firms gathered too much data and either did not use them or found them useless. Data were poorly organized and analyzed and were generally of little use to decision makers. These firms suffered from both *data overload* and *information underload.* Clearly, that situation called for systematic methods for generating information from data. That requires systematic and intelligent data analysis and interpretation.[14]

As company information needs intensify, management information systems (MIS) develop. Their mission is to generate, store, manipulate, and analyze information from both external and internal sources. For effective use for worldwide and country-specific decision making, the MIS must become a multinational management information system (MMIS). As visualized by leading scholars, an MMIS is an interacting complex of persons, machines, and procedures designed to generate an orderly flow of relevant information.[15]

The MIS concept has been refined and further developed by other scholars. Management decision support systems (MDSS) have been proposed as an "umbrella-type" replacement for management information systems.[16] The claim is that an MIS is a subset of an MDSS. Compared to the MIS, the MDSS concept appears to be more specific with regard to decisions and seems to have less emphasis on "just making relevant information available." The strategic intelligence system (SIS) has

also been proposed.[17] The argument for SIS is that a strategic plan can be no better than the information on which it is based. Thus, the SIS aims to identify strategic opportunity and provides "offensive intelligence." SIS appears broader than DSS and more specific than MIS, so both DSS and MIS seem to be subsets of SIS.

The authors propose still a different concept: the international strategic intelligence system (ISIS). ISIS has all of the characteristics of MIS, but it is designed to support decision making, especially strategic decision making. Figure 18–4 shows the ISIS model.

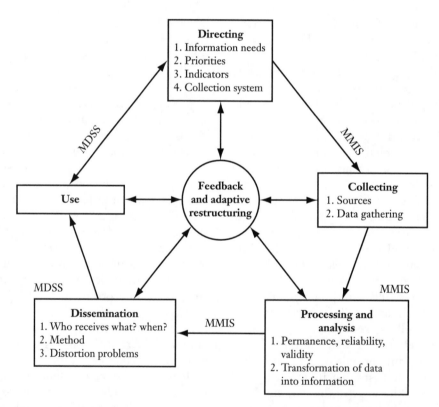

Source: David B. Montgomery and Charles B. Weinberg, "Toward Strategic Intelligence System," *Journal of Marketing,* Fall 1979, 43.

FIGURE 18–4 *International Strategic Intelligence System (ISIS)*

Components of an International Strategic Intelligence System

The diagram's circular arrangement implies the ongoing nature of the international strategic intelligence system (ISIS). ISIS has five functional phases: (1) directing, (2) collecting, (3) processing and analyzing, (4) disseminating, and (5) using.

1. *Directing*. The directing phase poses the questions. It establishes information needs and priorities, determines the indicators to monitor, and decides on the information-collection system.

2. *Collecting*. The collecting phase is where the multinational management information system (MMIS) enters into the picture. International and national data sources are tapped continuously.

3. *Processing and analyzing*. MMIS continues its contribution in processing and analyzing the data to prevent both data overload and information underload.

4. *Disseminating*. MMIS further continues its contribution by disseminating the information whenever and wherever it is needed.

5. *Using*. Where MMIS leaves off, MDSS takes over for using the information. MDSS pinpoints the specific information needed for making the strategic decisions.

MMIS and MDSS function together in developing feedback and redirection at each and every stage of the total system. Ideally, an ISIS exists before the firm goes international, but the existence of an ISIS is essential to the survival of multinational firms in multiple world markets.

Key Characteristics of an International Strategic Intelligence System

An effective ISIS has five basic characteristics: (1) flexibility, (2) retrievability, (3) recency, (4) regenerativeness, and (5) generality as well as specificity.[18]

1. *Flexibility*. ISIS requires sufficient flexibility not only to collect and interpret the data but also to manipulate the data into forms that facilitate strategic decisions. As ISIS collects sales data in world markets, for instance, it needs the capability of providing the information on the degrees of market penetration and market saturation that facilitates strategic planning.

2. *Retrievability*. For ISIS's broad database to be effective, it must have retrievability; that is, users must be able to call up any and all bits of information in the database whenever and wherever they are needed. Retrievable information allows ISIS to facilitate strategic planning.

3. *Recency*. The recency of data is important because strategic plans are based on fresh data. An effective ISIS has built-in facilities to update and purge its database according to recency, reliability, and usefulness.

4. *Regenerativeness*. An ISIS must have regenerativeness, which means creating new data from old data by inferential reasoning, simulation, forecasting, and other approaches. ISIS, for instance, may simulate market potentials in country A on the basis of data from country B and estimate data reliability on the basis of comparability of the two markets.

5. *Generality and specificity*. An ISIS must provide generality in international data

as well as specificity in company and industry data. Strategic planners need both types of information for making comprehensive plans.

One last point about an ISIS is its location. Should an ISIS be located at the international headquarters or at national home offices? An ISIS must respond to corporate needs and decision-making styles. If the company decision making is centralized, the ISIS should be situated at the international headquarters. If company decision making is decentralized, the ISIS should also be decentralized at multiple locations. Ideally, an ISIS provides access to all decision centers for all strategic planning matters.

SUMMARY

International market research, like domestic market research, is concerned with data and information. Data are transformable into information useful for decision making. With such information, making decisions means taking calculated risks. Without that information, making decisions is assuming unknown risks. Comparative international market research is done mainly to determine whether experience gained in one country is transferable to another country.

There are two phases of international market research. The first phase consists of exploratory research and utilization of data chiefly from secondary sources. The second phase deals with identifying specific information needs and with collecting data from secondary and primary sources. Supplementing secondary and primary data sources is another type of international information source—syndicated data.

The trend is toward improved organization and systematization of international market research. The future will see the development of more international strategic intelligence systems. ISIS has five functional phases: (1) direction, (2) collecting, (3) processing and analyzing, (4) disseminating, and (5) using. Many MNCs are developing or are on the verge of developing ISISs or similar marketing research systems.

DISCUSSION QUESTIONS

1. The difference between international market research and domestic market research is one of degree rather than kind. Discuss.

2. There are at least seven approaches to comparative international market research. If you were to consider exporting computers to Bulgaria, which approach(es) would you use? Why?

3. If you were in charge of marketing research at Pepsico International and the opportunity arose for a joint venture with the Romanian government to develop Romanian Pepsi, what information would you need in order to help management make this decision? What kind of problems with secondary data would you anticipate?

4. If you had a contract to do marketing research in Iran, what would you expect in the way of primary-data problems in that country?

5. The exploratory phase of international market research includes eight specific activities. What are they? Describe each. What other information categories not listed in this group of eight might there be?

6. If you had been with the management of Volvo International prior to the company's entry into the U.S. market, what bits of market information would you have sought? Why?

7. Distinguish among and describe MMIS, MDSS, and ISIS. Assume that you have been asked to develop an ISIS for a major global company, say Eastman Kodak. What components would you include in the ISIS? How would you fit in MMIS and MDSS? Construct a diagram to show how the whole system functions.

CASE **18-1**

A Classic Case: Beetle versus Pinto—
Should VW International Be Concerned?

In 1970, the VW Beetle was a very popular compact, low-priced car. The company naturally did not want to lose its market position. Management did not know the extent to which the Ford Pinto would become a substitute for the VW Beetle. Assume that the year is 1970 and that you are a consultant to VW International. There are a few samples of Ford Pinto in the United States, and the car is scheduled to go into mass production in the coming year.

QUESTIONS

1. What kind of marketing research would you conduct? Discuss this situation in detail. (Imagine that the Hyundai Excel is entering the American market and the makers of the Honda Accord are concerned.)

2. What specific bits of information would you need? Why?

Disposable Nappies in Western Europe

Colgate-Palmolive developed Nappies, a disposable diaper, for marketing in Western Europe. The company decided to develop an MMIS to analyze the effects of its marketing efforts. It needed to collect, process, and evaluate market information. The MMIS achieved the system after it had accomplished the following risks:

1. Identification of the variables that significantly influenced the market.

2. Exact description of the market under investigation and the requirements for optimizing the marketing mix.

3. Continuous audit of the company's performance and its competitors' reactions and counteractive policies.

4. Early warning of sales changes needed to avoid dramatic short-term adjustments in marketing plans.

The MMIS was based on six subsystems linking a series of key variables that provided specific information for decision makers. The subsystems dealt with the following areas:

1. Economic and demographic conditions affecting the market.

2. The changing unemployment picture and its impact on the demand for Nappies.

3. The effectiveness of the company's distribution system and varying degrees of market penetration.

4. Comparative pricing and the impact of price changes on demand as well as on competition.

5. The effects of sales promotion campaigns on product sales.

6. Statistical analyses used to determine the real growth or decline in the company's sales after the seasonal and inflationary variations were taken out of sales data.

The company has done quite well in a growth market, and the MMIS is considered more than just partially responsible for Nappies' positive performance in the West European markets.

QUESTIONS

1. If you were developing the MMIS for this company, list specifically the bits of information you would need for each of the subsystems. Explain why.

2. Which one of the specific bits of information that you listed above would be difficult to obtain and how would you go about obtaining it?

3. If you were to develop an ISIS instead of an MMIS for this company, how would your system vary? Construct two diagrams to show the differences. Explain the differences between the two systems.

ENDNOTES

1 John Fayerweather, *International Marketing* (Englewood Cliffs, N.J.: Prentice-Hall, 1965).

2 Philip Cateora, *International Marketing* (Homewood, Ill.: Richard D. Irwin, 1981), 331.

3 C. K. Prahalad and Yves L. Doz, *The Multinational Mission* (New York: Free Press, 1987), 67–100.

4 *Advertising Age*, 2 June 1986, 1–3.

5 "How P&G Was Brought to a Crawl in Japan's Diaper Market," *Business Week*, 13 October 1987, 71–74.

6 Charles S. Mayer, "The Lessons of Multinational Marketing Research," *Business Horizons*, December 1978, 7–13.

7 A. C. Samli, "Critical Problems and Data Needs in International Marketing Research," *Business and Economic Dimensions*, January 1968, 9–15.

8 Fayerweather, *International Marketing*. See endnote 1.

9 Jenny C. McCune, "Armchair Global Commerce," *Management Review*, August 1996, 6–7.

10 Karen Holderman, "Improved Research Programs Help U.S. Exports Find Opportunities Abroad," *Business America*, October 1996, 7–11.

11 Warren J. Keegen, *Global Marketing Management*, 4th ed. (Englewood Cliffs, N.J.: Prentice-Hall, 1989), 228–241.

12 Fayerweather, *International Marketing*, 90–94.

13 Samli, "Critical Problems and Data Areas." See endnote 7.

14 E.D. Jaffe, "Multinational Marketing Intelligence: An Information Requirement Model," *Management International Review* 19, no. 2 (1979): 53–60.

15 Steven L. Alter, *Decision Support Systems* (Menlo Park, Calif.: Addison-Wesley Publishing Co., 1980).

16 David B. Montgomery and Charles B. Weinberg, "Toward Strategic Intelligence System," *Journal of Marketing*, Fall 1979, 41–52.

17 Ibid.

18 A. C. Samli, "International Strategic Information Systems: ISIS" in *Proceedings of Second World Marketing Congress*, ed. Susan Shaw, et al. (Stirling, Scotland: Academy of Marketing Science, 1986).

Organizational Structure for International Marketing

Chapter Outline

Learning Objectives

When you have mastered the contents of this chapter, you will be able to do the following:

1 Discuss the importance of having an organizational structure to implement marketing strategies.

2 Articulate the differences between a domestic and an international organizational structure.

3 Discuss the internal and external factors influencing international organizational structure.

4 Identify and evaluate functional, geographic, product, and matrix organizations as the key international structural alternatives.

5 Explain what is meant by the structural evolution of multinational firms.

6 Show how congruence between strategy and structure optimizes the firm's international efforts.

All firms, both domestic and international, need structures to facilitate their operations. Market opportunities; degrees of competition; and domestic economic, social, and political conditions vary in different parts of the world. These variations cause international marketers to choose among (1) formulating diverse strategies to fit different markets, (2) organizing a global strategy and implementing it in different markets, or (3) using some combination of the first two options. Regardless of the option chosen, implementing it requires an organizational structure. Unless the strategy fits the structure and, conversely, the structure fits the strategy, the firm cannot function at its best. In other words, the firm will reduce its overall effectiveness, fail to capitalize on attractive market opportunities, and accrue unnecessarily high marketing costs.

In theory, the structure of an organization should be commensurate with its strategy, functions, technology, and environment. But in reality, a proper structure is difficult to achieve, because international firms face not only diverse external environments but also numerous internal constraints—restrictions that are economic, technological, or are related to the firm's long-range objectives. These conditions make it difficult to develop an appropriate international structure.

THE STRUCTURE OF THE INTERNATIONAL FIRM

Consider the following:

- An American soft-drink company has bottling facilities in each of the Latin American countries. Bottles are manufactured in regional centers, and bottling and other machinery are imported from West Germany. Local manufacturers in each country hold franchises on the process, and they make the local pricing, production, and advertising decisions.

- Several nationalities are represented on the board of directors in the highly mobile staffs of a European drug manufacturer. Research and development on new products is going on in several countries, and raw materials are procured locally, but home-office personnel make the pricing, production, and advertising decisions.

- A retail company with outlets in many Latin American countries buys from local suppliers and manufacturers whenever possible. However, several products are exported from facilities in the United States to the company's foreign outlets. Regional headquarters coordinate area operations and determine most policies for stores in each country.

These situations are typical of international marketing today. What kinds of international structure should these companies have in order to facilitate their operations? These particular companies developed their own unique organizational structures to serve the purposes of the enterprises efficiently and effectively.

How does a company develop an international marketing organization that will provide the structure needed to reach the company's international marketing objectives? Only comparatively recently have U.S. firms focused specifically on organizing for international operations. Many companies have had little or no international experience, and most of them have been preoccupied with serving the enormous domestic American market.

Problems in Internationalization

As overseas markets gained in importance for American firms, and their international sales volumes increased greatly, internationalization of the organization became critical. By the early 1970s, most large companies transacting international sales had reorganized themselves to acknowledge the growing importance of foreign operations. Most of such companies abolished international divisions and set up multiple international product divisions. As a result, the overseas subsidiaries of U.S. companies totaled in the thousands, carrying about 1 million employees on their payrolls and accounting for a substantial proportion of corporate profits for their American parent companies.[1] Among these companies were ITT, Xerox, and IBM.

These structural changes, however, fell somewhat short of the ideal. For the most part, these structures provided for only one-way management—the central headquarters issued commands, and the subsidiaries obeyed. The structure did not provide for the transmission of unsolicited data from the subsidiaries back to the central headquarters. As a result, central headquarters did not receive the information they needed to readjust their products and perhaps redirect their marketing efforts. Subsidiaries were forced to push products generated at the command center onto local markets. The subsidiaries had to try to convince the local populace that these products were appropriate to fulfill their needs. These companies, in other words, were following a global strategy of rigidly standardizing marketing activities.[2]

Developing rigid centralized structures did not help American firms. Their structures did not allow for sensitivity to local needs, nor did structural adjustments allow them to take advantage of local opportunities. They were not geared up to develop local marketing strategies to fit local market situations.

Eventually, a two-layer problem emerged. The multinational firms developed significant structural differences as compared to their domestically oriented competitors; hence, a "structural gap" appeared. Because of the gap, international companies lagged behind their domestically oriented competitors in effective strategy implementation—an imbalance showed up between strategy and structure. This two-layer problem (the structural gap and the imbalance in strategy-structure relationships) blocked firms from gaining the full advantages of international synergism. In other words, different efforts exerted by multinational firms in diverse world markets along with the operations of their many subsidiaries did not generate overall results greater than the sum total of the powers and efforts of all of the subsidiaries.

A Structural Contrast

Many companies just getting started internationally simply used their domestic organizational structure to handle international business. Out of this situation, international divisions emerged and became part of the existing organizational structure. As Figure 19–1 shows, the "core" structure was domestically oriented. The international division was far removed organizationally from staff functions, all of which tended to focus on domestic matters. Typically, the international division did not receive treatment equivalent to that given to domestic divisions, and it experienced difficulties in getting help and guidance from the staff.

An international division, by its very nature, is an *ethnocentric* organization. All of its activities are dominated by the core organization, which specializes in catering to the

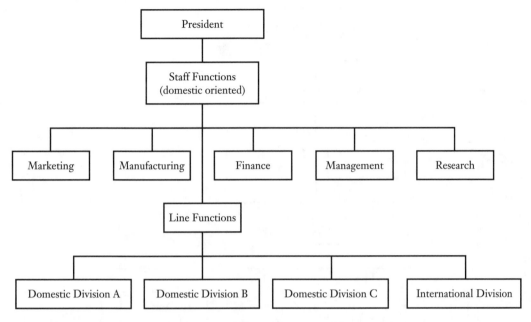

FIGURE 19–1 *Domestically Oriented Organization Chart*

U.S. domestic market. But in some companies, as international activity gained momentum, changes again occurred in the organizational structure. Figure 19–2 shows a globally oriented organizational structure, the type of structure that became more common as companies became more international. Note that all of the divisions have equal access to the company's resources and staff talent. Certainly, each division, focusing on a geographical region, has an organizational structure appropriate to its operations and objectives, and at least in theory, all of these divisions are coequals. This type of structure is a *polycentric* organization; that is, people throughout the entire firm think that the purpose of the organization is to cater to different international markets according to their needs.

FACTORS AFFECTING INTERNATIONAL MARKETING ORGANIZATIONS

Organizational structures reflect the influence of certain factors, both internal and external.[3]

Internal Factors

Several factors within the firm influence its organizational structure. Among these internal factors are (1) magnitude of international-business volume, (2) diversity of international markets where the firm has interests, (3) commitment to international operations, (4) availability of human resources, (5) flexibility desired by the company, (6) management style, and (7) corporate goals.

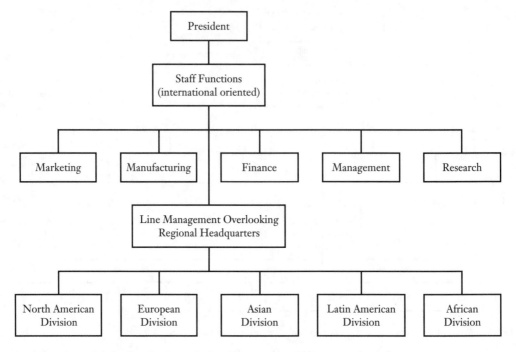

FIGURE 19–2 *Globally Oriented Organization Chart*

MAGNITUDE OF INTERNATIONAL BUSINESS VOLUME
■ If international business volume is small (both in dollar terms and as a percentage of the firm's total sales), the tendency is to develop a simple organizational unit—an international division or an export department—to handle it. As international sales increase, the organizational structure evolves into something more complex, often taking the form of an international or a worldwide structure.

DIVERSITY OF INTERNATIONAL MARKETS
■ If the firm is involved in a wide diversity of international markets, the organizational structure needed for managing the marketing activity becomes more complex. The firm needs more people with greater expertise to handle transactions with all of these markets effectively.

COMMITMENT TO INTERNATIONAL OPERATIONS
■ If the firm is only casually involved internationally, chances are that it will not have a recognizable and well-balanced organizational structure for handling its international business. As the firm strengthens its commitment to international operations, it develops the organizational structure to facilitate its marketing actions.

AVAILABILITY OF HUMAN RESOURCES
■ An organization is as good as the people in it. If the firm does not have sufficient people with the needed qualifications, it cannot develop the appropriate organizational structure. American "expats" who are sent overseas—at least those lacking the needed qualifications—often fail to do well in these different environments.[4] There are many reasons for these failures, among them, psychological barriers and insufficient or misdirected training.

DESIRED FLEXIBILITY ▪ Because changes continually occur in international markets, the organizational structure must have high flexibility, even though it reduces the strong management control characteristic of more rigid structures. The need to manage continuous change and uncertainty cannot tolerate a rigid structure.[5]

MANAGEMENT STYLE ▪ What makes managers comfortable in their dealings with others in the overall organization? How do they interpret the organization chart? What is the power base? How do managers see the world? Answers to these and related questions indicate the company's management style. An effective organizational structure is in alignment with management style. Three key factors reflecting management style are: (1) concentration of power, (2) agreement on the firm's competitiveness, and (3) the mind set of managers.[6]

Concentration of power. The locus of power relates to the ability to allocate resources. The individual who makes product decisions and allocates the firm's resources accordingly, and how these decisions work against local managers' predispositions and decisions, reflect the level of complexity in the organizational structure. For instance, consider a worldwide manager who makes blanket decisions that are difficult for country managers to follow because markets have different needs and different degrees of competition. Generally, this disparity causes a buildup in organizational complexity, because each country manager requires a full-fledged organization, while the worldwide manger focuses more on coordinating and controlling the overall organization.

Agreement on the firm's competitiveness. If managers at all levels are concerned about and oriented to global competition, then it is possible to simplify the organizational structure somewhat. The reason is that there is then no longer a need to cater to multilocal strategies. When each country organization is primarily geared toward implementing local strategies, complexities are built into the organizational structure.

The mind set of managers. The mind sets of managers are conditioned by the information at their disposal. The total array of information may cause managers to think globally. Their mind sets may become global because they are in position to track profitability data worldwide, to install and monitor uniform costing and accounting systems, and to scan markets and competition in all world markets. Moreover, managers eventually grow accustomed to managing people, products, and resources across country borders.[7] By contrast, if the main function of the organizational structure is to facilitate a multilocal strategy, managers are likely to have local mind sets.

CORPORATE GOALS ▪ Development of an international organizational structure occurs after the firm has established its goals. If, for example, the company is planning to grow or decentralize and let regional managers take over, it requires an appropriate organizational structure. Eastman Kodak, for instance, consolidated its worldwide product managers at corporate headquarters, and it made marketing directors in some countries regionally responsible for a line of business as well as for sales of all Kodak products in their own countries. The result was a decentralized organizational structure aimed at facilitating a multilocal marketing strategy.[8]

A common failing is not being able to communicate the corporate goals carefully to different line operations around the world. Another is to "freeze" the structure in the form needed to take care of business at the time the structure was designed, therefore not allowing changes to take place as needs arise.

External Factors

Four important external factors that influence the international firm's organizational structure are: (1) geographic distance, (2) levels of economic development in the firm's markets, (3) type of consumers, and (4) government regulations.

GEOGRAPHIC DISTANCE ▪ Geographic distance causes communication barriers, which, in turn, generate ineffective management, supervision, and control. For companies operating in developing countries, the barrier of distance is magnified because fax machines, teleconferencing facilities, and rapid and dependable transportation may not exist in these countries.

Furthermore, time differences are functions of geographic distances. When it is daytime in most of the United States, it is late evening or early morning in Western Europe. Time differences sometimes cause delays in recognizing problems and making decisions, thus accentuating the problem.

LEVEL OF ECONOMIC DEVELOPMENT ▪ The level of economic development in the firm's markets has a direct impact on organizational structure. Highly developed economies are natural hosts to the more complex and more sophisticated international companies. As an international firm accustoms itself to functioning in highly developed economies, it has a need to develop the required skills and the ability to compete with highly sophisticated competition.

TYPE OF CONSUMERS ▪ As companies gain understanding of their consumers and the ways their products are used, they are in position to design their organizational structures more appropriately. Consider, for example, the manufacturer of small vehicles who discovers that its vehicles are being used by golfers and retirees in North American markets, by municipal-services personnel and police forces in India, and by local governments for public transportation in the Middle East. These conditions will motivate the company to develop the organizational structure needed to market its products appropriately in each of these different markets.

GOVERNMENT REGULATIONS ▪ How different countries encourage or discourage foreign business operations in their jurisdictions affects the company's organizational structure. For instance, while it may be easier for a company to export to certain countries, these same countries may insist that foreign companies open local plants to hire and train indigenous labor, to transfer all or part of its unique technology to the host country, and to invest in the host country's future. Unlike the organizational structure needed for direct exporting, these demands call for a structure perhaps manned with Americans living abroad and *paralleled* by a decision-making group composed of local citizens. In other words, all administrative positions filled by Americans would have local understudies.

Organizational Structure Alternatives

In order to take advantage of ongoing market opportunities, organizational structures take many forms. Congruency is needed between the organizational structure and the strategy. The Italian automaker Fiat, for instance, entered the U.S. market too early and too

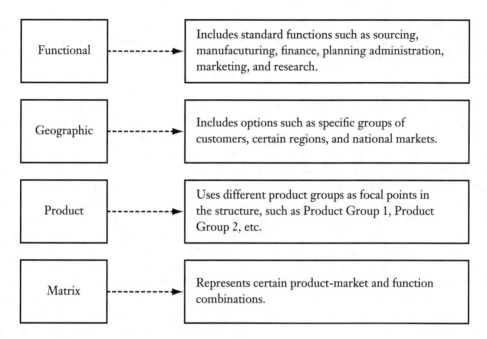

| Functional | - - - - - - - - → | Includes standard functions such as sourcing, manufacuturing, finance, planning administration, marketing, and research. |

| Geographic | - - - - - - - - → | Includes options such as specific groups of customers, certain regions, and national markets. |

| Product | - - - - - - - - → | Uses different product groups as focal points in the structure, such as Product Group 1, Product Group 2, etc. |

| Matrix | - - - - - - - - → | Represents certain product-market and function combinations. |

FIGURE 19–3 *Bases for Organizational Structures*

fast and did not develop the organizational structure it needed to deliver service and provide maintenance for its products. The structure did not support the strategy, and eventually Fiat withdrew from the market. Figure 19–3 shows the bases for four organizational structures: (1) functional, (2) geographic, (3) product, and (4) matrix.

FUNCTIONAL STRUCTURE ■ Many companies begin their international business activities as a result of having received buying inquiries from abroad. These prospects may have seen the company's products in a catalog, at a trade show, or in an advertisement. The company, being new to international business, has no international specialists, and typically has few products and few markets. But as its international involvement intensifies, the company designates someone as its part-time international specialist and tools up for exporting. Eventually, an export department or international department becomes part of its organizational structure. Typically, the export department in what is basically a domestically oriented organization is somewhat isolated from the general organizational structure. It is an appendage, added to handle activities not provided for in the already existing organizational structure.

As the volume of international sales grows, at some point, an international division emerges. This division becomes directly reponsible for the development and implementation of overall international strategy, embracing the functions of marketing, production, finance, sourcing, management, and the like. As the company develops into a truly multinational entity, the international division gives way to a global functional organization, such as the one shown in Figure 19–2. In this organization, those in charge of major functions have worldwide responsibilities. If the product lines are narrow or homogeneous and the company's geographic markets bear marked similarities, the global functional type of organizational structure is appropriate.

GEOGRAPHIC STRUCTURE ■
MNCs using geographic structures typically have few products, but they market them in many countries. Manufactures of consumer goods, such as Unilever, CPC International, and Colgate-Palmolive, favor geographic organizational structures. The reason is their need to know each market intimately and to cater especially to its requirements. Geographic structures allow companies to become intimately acquainted with the individual markets served. There are two types of geographic organizational structures: (1) regional management centers and (2) country-based organizations.[9]

Regional management centers. Regional management centers (RMCs) serve a particular region, such as Western Europe, Latin America, or the Middle East. There are two main reasons for the existence of RMCs. One is that as sales volume in a particular region becomes substantial, needs develop for a specialized staff to focus on this region, because it is this focus that will allow the company to realize more fully its market potentials in an already growing market. The second reason is that homogeneity within regions and heterogeneity among them necessitate treating each important region separately. However, since markets for the firm's products within given regions show little variation, a regional management center becomes an appropriate organizational feature. Procter & Gamble has three European RMCs, each responsible for a country grouping.[10] These groupings were based on similar histories, climates, resources, and languages and life styles. RMCs, although requiring added organizational expenditures, make it more feasible to take advantage of market opportunities and to supervise production logistically and appropriately for regional requirements.

Country-based organizations. Country-based organizations feature a separate organizational unit for each country. The general structure resembles the regional management center. Instead of having a regional center, for example, in Paris, each European country has its own organizational unit. The same two reasons underlying the emergence of RMCs also support the formation of country-based organizations. As sales in particular countries become substantial, the need arises for a specialized staff to focus on individual countries in order to realize more of the market potentials. Individual countries are internally homogeneous but externally heterogeneous. Country-based organizations are highly sensitive to local market characteristics.

Country-based organizations pose some difficulties. First, they are costly. Second, because they are numerous, their coordination with headquarters is an involved process; if there are, say, 35 country-based organizations, and if each reports to world headquarters, there are complications in maintaining two-way communication and control. Third, the existence of country-based organizations may interfere with taking advantage of possible synergies from regional groupings. For instance, there may be opportunities for synergistic savings through coordinating activities in the European Community, but the existence of a country-based organization may make it impossible to take advantage of these opportunities. Each country-based organization develops its own unique activities and its own autonomy. Thus, some companies feel compelled to have both RMCs and country-based structures.

PRODUCT-BASED STRUCTURE ▪ The third type of organizational structure focuses on the product line. This type is used mainly by high-tech companies with wide product lines and relatively few markets. The aim of the structure is to diffuse technologically complex products quickly and efficiently through world markets to gain competitive advantages. This goal is possible because the end users of a product group are highly homogeneous. The products involved undergo few or no changes to fit country or regional needs (except, of course, for such changes as voltage in electrical items).

A product-based organizational structure concentrates basically on managing the individual product line. This specialized focus is particularly important if the product line is changing continuously due to technological advances. This focus also provides the organization with substantial flexibility.

Products may be controlled based on their respective stages in the product life cycles in different world markets; they may be eliminated or given added support, depending upon their contributions to the profit picture.

Figure 19–4 illustrates a product-based organizational structure. Line responsibilities are based on the management of different product groups. The vice president of marketing and other high executives at the corporate home office have indirect input into all of the product groups. Bold dotted lines indicate this point. Note that each product group has access to any of the staff functions.

The product-based organizational structure gives rise to some problems. The existence of organizations based on multiple products may cause duplications of effort and organizational activity. If the composition of

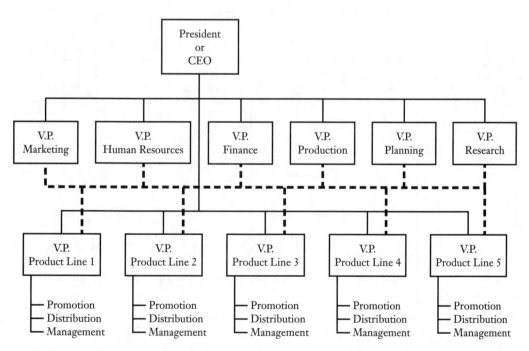

FIGURE 19-4 *Product-Based Organizational Structure*

the product groups is not clearly identified, somewhat similar products may be managed by different product organizational groups, possibly a needless expense. Somewhat similarly, the existence of product-based structures may detract from recognizing the needs for developing in-depth market knowledge of specific countries and regions. Because local organizations for each product group generally are out of the question because of cost, evolving market opportunities may go unrecognized or, if recognized, may not be capitalized upon fully. Furthermore, because each product group has its own management and focus, it is difficult for the entire company to build and enjoy worldwide synergism, thus detracting

from its competitive strength and special position in world markets.

MATRIX-BASED STRUCTURE ■ As companies expand, their organizational forms change. As product-based, high-tech MNCs enter more markets, strains are placed on their organizational structures to maintain control over marketing activities. Similarly, when manufacturers of consumer goods broaden their product lines, they find that commonalities among country product lines make a greater coordination of product strategies desirable. For these and other reasons (often growth related), MNCs find that matrix structures are the most appropriate ways to manage product lines over many different markets.

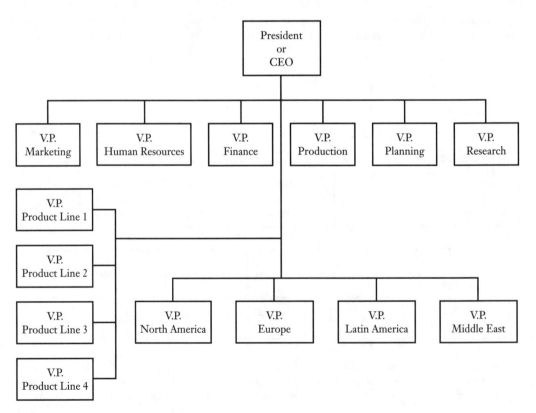

FIGURE 19-5 *Matrix Organizational Structure*

While the product-based element in the organizational structure has responsibilities for managing specific product lines worldwide, the geographic-based organizational element has responsibilities for all product lines in specific geographic areas. By contrast, the aims of the matrix-based organizational structure are twofold. The first aim is to take advantage of product-line similarities among subsidiaries and, perhaps, some centralizing of production or marketing activities. The second aim (achieved through the geographic feature) is to localize specific aspects of the marketing strategy (for example, promotion). Thus, the overall aim is to have the best of both worlds—cheaper products with locally oriented appeals.

A simplified matrix-based organizational structure is illustrated in Figure 19–5. Under each regional vice president, there is a complete functional organization responsible for all of the products. At the same time, under each product-line vice president, there are product members who are in direct contact with regional marketing directors. Thus, it is possible for each product to receive special attention in each market.

Proctor & Gamble has a matrix organizational structure. Its Euro brand teams, which analyze opportunities for greater product-market combinations, are chaired by brand managers from major markets according to country. Each team includes brand managers from the European subsidiaries that market the brand, managers from the company's European technical center, and one of P&G's European division managers. P&G's division managers are responsible for a portfolio of brands and a group of countries simultaneously.[11]

Dow Chemical uses a three-dimensional matrix organization. It is composed of 6 geographic areas, has 3 major functions (which are marketing, management, and research), and more than 70 product groups.

IBM uses a two-dimensional matrix. One dimension is profit centers, such as the information systems and technology group. The second dimension is related to various business areas, such as typewriters.

Matrix-based organizations also have some problems. The most obvious problem is that of organizational conflict stemming from imbalances in the geographic and product structures. Where products really need special attention, the regional manager may have too much power, or where local markets require additional marketing effort, the product-line manager may have too much power. In both cases, the prevailing organizational conflicts weaken the firm's efforts. In fact, because of such organizational conflicts, some firms, having experimented with matrix structures, have switched to one of the other organizational structure options.

STRUCTURAL EVOLUTION OF MULTINATIONAL FIRMS

As long as foreign sales are low, most companies handle foreign operations merely as an appendage to the existing product or functional division. The next stage is a simple export organization. A functional organizational structure follows this simple export organization as the firm's international involvement increases. The functional structure then starts developing into one or the other of two options, becoming either a geographic organization or a product organization. Finally, the most advanced stage is the matrix-based organization.[12] Although there are exceptions to this progression, the typical movement is from centralized to decentralized organizational forms (see Figure 19–6).

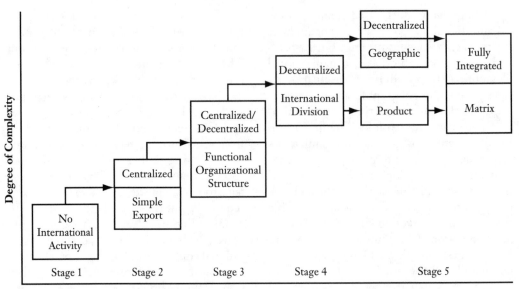

FIGURE 19-6 *Structural Evolution of Multinational Firms*

THE CONGRUENCE BETWEEN STRATEGY AND STRUCTURE

The organizational structure should support the marketing strategy. Congruence between organizational structure and marketing strategy is extremely important to the realization of optimum results. Figure 19–7 illustrates how congruence works. If the firm successfully internationalizes its strategy and its structure, it moves out along the "contract curve," which yields the best results in every stage. Note, however, that possibilities exist for the firm to go off on a tangent either horizontally (over-structured) or vertically (over-strategized). Thus, a big challenge is to keep both structure and strategy in *balance*.

Consider the following example: A southern-California-based conglomerate had several divisions engaged in exporting. When these activities reached the magnitude of about stage 2 (Figure 19–7), a vice president of international operations was hired to coordinate the foreign activities. The magnitude of the overseas operations increased through stage 3 because of certain foreign acquisitions and joint ventures. An international division, functionally organized, took over. Finally, because of the variety of products and diversity of the markets, the company proceeded to stage 4 with a matrix-based organization based on product-market combinations, at which point the company formulated a multinational marketing strategy to match the structure.

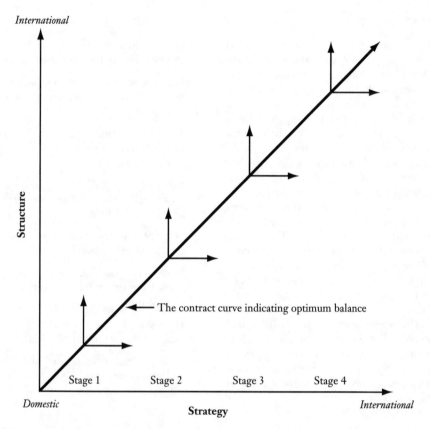

FIGURE 19–7 *The Strategy-Structure Contract Curve*

SUMMARY

The implementation of marketing strategy requires an appropriate organizational structure. As American firms became more involved in international markets, they organized their international structures differently from their domestic structures and created a structural gap. Both internal and external factors influence the choice of the appropriate organizational structure. Among the internal factors are: (1) magnitude of international business volume, (2) diversity of the firm's international markets, (3) commitment to international operations, (4) availability of manpower resources, (5) desired organizational flexibility, (6) management style, and (7) corporate goals. The external factors influencing organizational structure include: (1) geographic distance, (2) level of economic development, (3) type of consumers, and (4) government regulations. The existence of these internal and external factors results in four basic types of organizational structures: (1) functional, (2) geographic, (3) product, and (4) matrix. There is an organizational structural evolution in multinational firms that moves from centralized to decentralized structures. Organizational structure and marketing strategy must be congruent for optimal company performance.

DISCUSSION QUESTIONS

1. Discuss the differences between domestically versus internationally oriented structures.

2. Under what circumstances should the international structure be made more complex? More simple?

3. What key internal factors influence the organizational structure? Can you think of additional factors? Explain.

4. What key external factors influence the organizational structure? Can you think of additional factors? Explain.

5. What are the key bases for international organizational structures?

6. How would you differentiate matrix organizations from others? Is this difference important? Why?

7. Discuss and explain the structural evolution experienced by multinational firms.

8. Why is congruence needed between strategy and structure? Discuss.

Siemens U.S.A.

Siemens AG had its headquarters based in West Germany. The company planned and managed a $3.4 billion R&D operation in a variety of electrical and electronic fields to support its $34 billion product sales in 1988, which came from more than 170 factories in 35 countries. Siemens maintained 23 laboratories in the United States that were oriented toward specific product/system development. Historically, the bulk of the company's R&D funds have been expended in its central manufacturing and R&D complexes in West Germany. This is a classical view of centralized R&D activity. Exhibit 19–1 illustrates this portion of Siemens organization. The company's basic position was that R&D is a strategic tool in global competition.

More than 10 years ago, Siemens established an American enterprise, a "Corporate Research and Technology Laboratory," with the intention of conducting exploration and applied research in the United States. This enterprise, directed and staffed mainly by U.S. professionals, provides research support to the Siemens manufacturing companies in the United States. For its applied research inputs, the U.S. laboratory relies on both the corporate laboratories in West Germany and on its professional ties and cooperative programs with a number of U.S. universities. Product development and engineering are independent activities within the Siemens U.S. operations, 23 of which have ongoing development activities in their own product areas.

Questions

1. From this brief description and the organizational chart, what do you think are some of the basic problems that Siemens may be facing? Discuss.

2. What kind of changes can you suggest that would eliminate these problems?

3. Review Chapter 19. What kind of feedback and feedforward efforts could you put forth to make Siemens U.S.A. more effective? Discuss.

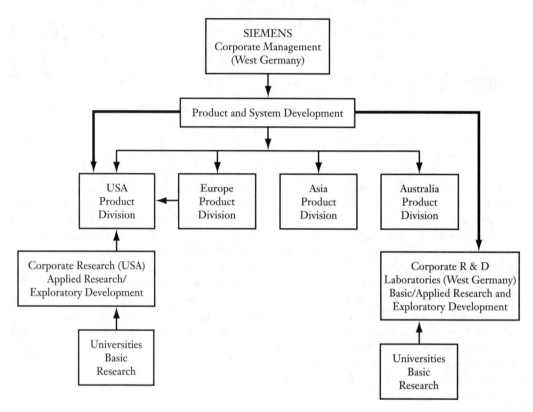

EXHIBIT 19-1

ENDNOTES

1. Raymond Vernon, "Gone are the Cash Cows of Yesteryear," *Harvard Business Review*, November–December 1980, 150–55.

2. Ibid.

3. Jean-Pierre Jeannet and Hubert D. Hennessey, *International Marketing Management* (Boston: Houghton Mifflin Co., 1988), 511–12.

4. A. Coskun Samli, James Wills, and Kamal Ranadireksa, "International Cultural Congruence and Acculturation," in *Proceedings of the Fourth World Marketing Congress*, ed. W. Lazer and E. Shaw (Miami, Fla.: Academy of Marketing Science, 1989), 133–36.

5. Stephen H. Rinesmith, "Open the Door to a Global Mind Set," *Training and Management*, May 1995, 34–35.

6. C. K. Prahalad and Yves L. Doz, *The Multinational Mission* (New York: Free Press, 1987), 178–79.

7. Prahalad and Doz, *The Multinational Mission*, 179.

8. John A. Quelch and Edward J. Hoff, "Customizing Global Marketing," *Harvard Business Review*, May–June 1986, 59–68.

9. Jeannet and Hennessey, *International Market Management*, 511–12. See endnote 3.

10. Quelch and Hoff, *"Customizing Global Marketing,"* 66. See endnote 8.

11. Ibid.

12. John D. Daniels, Robert A. Pitts, and Marietta J. Tretter, "Strategy and Structure of U.S. Multinationals," *Academy of Management Journal*, June 1984, 292–307.

20

Control Feedback and Adjustment

Chapter Outline

Learning Objectives

When you have mastered the contents of this chapter, you will be able to do the following:

1 Explain the meaning of international control and discuss how it is developed.

2 Demonstrate the need for international controls.

3 Discuss the various global feedback criteria and show how they are used in control.

4 Define the strategic-business-unit concept and demonstrate its use in control.

5 Show how feedback inputs fit into control, redirection, and changes in plans.

6 Explain the meaning of common-denominator management.

Effective management succeeds in implementing the organization's strategic plans. Successful implementation requires all managerial personnel to know and understand the company's strategic posture. Managers must share a common worldview and must agree upon the tasks to be performed.[1] Thus, the successful implementation of strategic plans relies heavily on a good control mechanism that provides managers with a common worldview and a uniform priority of the organization's missions and tasks.

International markets are heterogeneous. Each market differs from every other market. The differences are in distance, size, values, language, behavior patterns, and other factors. Many multinational firms have branches, subsidiaries, or other close relationships with many different markets worldwide. Consider, for instance, Xerox Company in the United States and its relationship to Fuji Xerox in Japan, Modi Xerox in India, Xerox Brazil, Xerox Mexico, and Xerox Canada. Each location has production, distribution, and service facilities, and all require coordination and control of overall international strategic plans and their implementation.

The discussion in this chapter covers the control function in international marketing. After establishing the conceptual foundation, the analysis focuses on the interface between the marketing process and implementation of the international marketing strategy. The key question is to determine how to establish a control mechanism capable of early interception of emerging problems. Considered here are various criteria appropriate for the evaluation process, control styles, feedback, and corrective action. These concepts are important for all businesses; in the international arena, they are vital.

THE CONCEPT OF CONTROL

Theorists and practitioners agree that effective management requires effective control. For the combination of well-planned objectives, strong organization, capable direction, and motivation to succeed, there also must be effective control.[2] Control has been defined as "the process of taking steps to bring the actual and desired results closer together."[3]

In international marketing, management control relates to the variance between planned and actual outcomes. In multinational companies, administrative orientations may show variations in management approaches across business units. These variations sometimes reflect decisions made by senior management on the focus and location of responsibility for organizational units. These are planned and deliberate variations. Other variations occur unintentionally. Variations, therefore, may be either expected or unexpected. If they are expected, they are *engineered* variations; that is, they are engineered by the management for specific purposes. If they are unexpected, they are *autonomous* variations; these variations surface because of the nature of the organization and international markets.

The Beckton-Dickinson Company has a system in which each of its business units has a unique set of objectives, compensation system, planning format, control system, and organizational structure. As a result, each unit has its own autonomous variations deriving from the company's overall management philosophy.

For more than 30 years, Corning followed an autonomous administrative orientation in order to generate rapid international growth. This orientation led to problems of product-line proliferation, manufacturing inefficiency, ineffective marketing coordination, and weak strategic control. Recently, Corning has been moving away from autonomous flexibility and toward engineered flexibility.

Westinghouse also once had a flexible and autonomous approach to international operations, but it replaced this system several years ago with a more centrally engineered control approach. The company has succeeded in reducing the risks of autonomous variations in selected areas of international management responsibilities.[4]

These and other companies have been moving from situations that generate autonomous variations in management practices to situations that generate engineered variations. However, autonomous variations do emerge in both totally centralized and totally decentralized situations. Under totally decentralized conditions, autonomous variations are expected; however, the reasons that they occur in centralized management situations are not so obvious. Therefore, let us examine the causes of autonomous variations in international organizations.

Autonomous Variations

The existence of autonomous variations implies ineffectiveness in the international control mechanism. Three factors cause autonomous variations: (1) size, (2) external conditions, and (3) human resources.

SIZE ■ As organizations grow, they tend to develop internal differences because various organizational components start adjusting to unique conditions. As the multinational corporation grows larger, its units (also growing larger) start reacting to conditions and problems in distinctive ways. Because changes in the size of various units occur unevenly and different units grow at different rates, the result is autonomous variations.

EXTERNAL CONDITIONS ■ Markets, customs, and many other external variables affect marketing decisions. These factors differ markedly in various parts of the world. Thus, the international firm requires a certain flexibility to enable its different subsidiaries to cope with their unique variations. Imperial Chemical Corporation's Turkish subsidiary, for example, develops variations in its management practices differently from those of the Pakistani subsidiary or the British parent company. Unless specified and controlled, such variations are autonomous.

HUMAN RESOURCES ■ Human resources also account for the emergence of some autonomous variations. Many countries' educational systems do not generate sizable pools of managerial talent, and company training and development programs cannot always compensate for these deficiencies. Hence, autonomous managerial variations are inevitable. If different existing talents in different subsidiaries are trained dissimilarly, then the decisions of executives will tend to vary from country to country, even under similar circumstances.

To avoid autonomous variances and to implement engineered variances requires effective control over managerial actions. In the classical, bureaucratic model of organization, control is based on explicit rules and regulations, so power and authority therefore have a rational-legal base.[5] In international circles, however, this sort of tight control is nearly impossible. The alternative is to have an organization with informal corporate-culture-based controls. Reliance is then placed upon an implicit, worldwide organizational culture, one of whose major functions is to control the organization's members. In such an organizational cultural control, power and authority are grounded in the customs and traditions inherent to the organization's culture.

Three types of controls used by multinational firms, all of them related to persons and/or corporate cultures, are: (1) personal control, (2) bureaucratic control, and (3) control by socialization.

Personal control is direct and is effected by assigning trustworthy personnel from headquarters to key positions in the subsidiaries.

Bureaucratic control is indirect and is implemented through an extensive set of rules, regulations, and procedures that limit managerial roles and authority in the subsidiaries.

Control by socialization is indirect and works through assigning significant proportions of expatriates in upper and middle management positions throughout the subsidiaries. It thrives on frequent information exchanges between headquarters and subsidiaries, and it de-emphasizes formalization of rules and procedures.

This classification does not cover the more formalized control processes. Table 20–1 illustrates the two types of controls and their uses in multinational situations. In the real world, or course, control processes are hybrid rather than pure.

Control processes used by multinational firms change over time. Many multinational firms have moved from formal controls to cultural controls. Both types can give rise to engineered variations among management practices; cultural controls provide more flexibility in customizing the control process. The customized approach provides opportunities to combine corporate culture and host-country characteristics into an effective control system. Some Swedish companies have moved in the opposite direction, however, and formulate goals for their foreign subsidiaries at their central headquarters. Follow-ups and performance evaluations in these firms have moved toward the use of financial data and away from personal contacts and assessments.

Using Controls

As indicated in Table 20–1, the control function has numerous objectives. It may involve monitoring the overall outputs or behavior patterns in subsidiaries, checking on prevailing attitudes and values of subsidiaries in general, or evaluating personnel in particular. Well-designed control systems ignore autonomous variations in performance (because they indicate lack of formal control) and emphasize the achievement of a minimum amount of engineered variation.

Corporate cultural controls are more likely than formal, rule-based controls to incorporate engineered variations. Ciba

TABLE 20–1 ▪ *Various Multinational Control Types*

	Types of Control	
Levels of Control	**"Pure" Formalized Control**	**"Pure" Corporate Cultural Control**
Output	Formal performance reports	Shared norms of performance (personal)
Behavior	Company manuals	Shared philosophy of management (bureaucratic)
Attitudes and values	Company training programs	Shared values of management with local cultural inputs (socialization)

Geigy and companies with similar control systems devote most of their attention to pure informal control (through relying on their managers interpersonal management mechanisms).[6] In marked contrast, Rank, Xerox, and companies with similar control systems emphasize data management in formal control systems.

Levels of Control

There are three main levels of control (see Table 20–1). Therefore, "pure" formal control and "pure" corporate cultural control differ not only generally but also at specific levels. The three levels of control (identified by their objectives) are output, behavior, and attitudes and values.

OUTPUT ■ In situations involving pure formal controls, formal performance reports (more often quantitative than qualitative) show measures of productivity. By contrast, in situations where pure informal controls predominate, the focus is on appraisals of personal performance norms; many scholars, including the authors, regard this focus as the highest expression of corporate philosophy.

BEHAVIOR ■ In pure, formalized control situations, behavior is controlled using company organizational and other manuals, job descriptions, and other materials detailing the specific functional aspects of each position. This approach contrasts with the situation in which pure, informal, social controls predominate; that is, where a shared management philosophy is inculcated in key personnel and passed on to everyone in the organization. General tenets of behavior, which are prone to generating engineered variations, are more likely to appear in MNCs with a global corporate outlook than in those emphasizing pure formalized controls.

ATTITUDES AND VALUES ■ Although attitudes and values stand behind general patterns of behavior, many companies use controls to deal directly with these cognitive phenomena. Where the emphasis is on pure formalized control, management attempts to control attitudes and values through tightly administered company training and development programs. The aim is to mold all company personnel throughout the entire world so that they share substantially the same attitudes and values. Other companies claim that the same results are achievable through assigning personnel from the home country (who are extremely familiar with home-office corporate procedures) to key positions in overseas subsidiaries.[7] Unilever is one company that uses both methods to create an identifiable and unique "Unilever culture."

In situations involving pure social control, interpersonal interactions provide the control mechanisms through which values leading to certain attitudes are inculcated. Socialization processes, in time, are instrumental in building these values and attitudes into all members of the corporation. In effect, international interpersonal networks are established and used throughout all organizational units for control purposes. These networks facilitate the socialization processes necessary for effective social control.

Control is important to improvement and/or continued success in international marketing. Inasmuch as variations in international operations are more likely to occur than not, engineering them through an appropriate control mechanism makes good sense. Neither 100 percent formal control nor 100 percent informal control are advisable in international marketing operations. Both styles of controls are useful in given circumstances. Identifying these circumstances is a major challenge for the international marketing executive.

INTERNATIONAL MARKETING CONTROLS

International marketing controls are important for a number of reasons; they must overcome the problems of (1) organization size, (2) distance between units, (3) information needs, (4) environment, and (5) culture.

- **Organization Size.** As multinational companies grow larger both in sales volume and in the number of their subsidiaries and branches, the necessity for effective control also increases. MNCs, such as Unilever and Colgate-Palmolive, not only want each of their subsidiaries to perform in line with their strategic plans, they also want to achieve optimum performance of the overall international marketing operation. The greater the global spread of company subsidiaries, the more need there is for cultural control rather than formal control. Consider the control mechanism for organizations like Club Med; while some level of formal control remains essential, the behavior patterns and service characteristics differ greatly in different parts of the world, and cultural controls become not only appropriate but inevitable.

- **Distance.** Typically, large MNCs have branches or subsidiaries scattered throughout the world. Many subsidiaries operate in markets geographically far removed from the parent company's offices. The more widespread the operations of the multinational firm become, the greater the need for effective control.

- **Information Needs.** Multinational companies with large numbers of subsidiaries scattered throughout the world and with wide and diverse product lines have substantial needs for control information. These companies need certain information on a regular basis in order to measure the performance of individual operations, of product groups, and of the multinational firm as a whole.[8] For these companies, control has two stages: (1) control of incoming information, and (2) control of operations.

- **Environment.** Some countries are high-risk markets, and in them, economic, social, and political changes occur abruptly and rapidly. These changeable environments require an effective monitoring mechanism capable of triggering quick and appropriate corrective responses. Many Latin American and African countries are high-risk markets.

- **Culture.** The cultural characteristics of world markets vary dramatically. Values, behavior patterns, individual motivational profiles, and communication patterns can differ greatly in different parts of the world, resulting in quite dissimilar management styles. Hence, in the absence of deliberate action by MNCs, unengineered autonomous variations in managerial practices throughout their worldwide operations are bound to appear. Consequently, companies with subsidiaries, branches, and other operations have strong needs for effective control mechanisms. Most often, this control stresses the maintenance of a worldwide, uniform, corporate culture. For example, one company using this approach made certain that its Brazilian sales office was an exact replica of its offices elsewhere. The Brazilian operation used standardized corporate typefaces and logos in all of its advertising and signs. The Brazilian office, like those elsewhere, had expatriates staffing key positions—all of them trained according to company standards and thoroughly indoctrinated with the company's managerial philosophy.

INTERNATIONAL MARKETING CONTROL MECHANISM

Establishing an effective international control mechanism requires the development of a multinational marketing strategy. This process sets forth not only the overall strategy but also the implementation methods and performance standards. Figure 20–1 is a schematic diagram showing how an overall international marketing control mechanism functions. Development of the multinational marketing strategy is the starting point. An automobile manufacturer such as Toyota, for example, wants to become the largest automobile marketer in the world. The first step is for the company to devise its multinational marketing strategy. The next step is to develop specific plans for implementing this strategy and to establish standards for evaluating marketing performance.

In international marketing, both purely formalized and purely cultural controls are important. As the automaker establishes standards to evaluate its marketing performance throughout the world, it must establish purely formalized criteria for each market: market share, dollar sales volume, unit sales volume, revenue per car sold, revenue per dealer, maximum price discounts, trade-in values, and the like. Similarly, the automaker establishes purely cultural controls in terms of the overall quality of its corporate service. It may strive to achieve the same type of customer satisfaction that Mercedes-Benz enjoys practically everywhere in the world.

As Figure 20–1 shows, standards are established for the components of the marketing mix as well as for the overall marketing performance. While an international company uses purely formalized control measures for appraising the performances of product, price, and distribution elements, it may use cultural controls for appraising promotion and overall marketing performance. Product, price, and distribution activities require quantitative performance measures for control. Performance appraisals of advertising and personal selling efforts require consideration of cultural criteria and the corporate culture. Overall marketing performance of overseas subsidiaries is best assessed through cultural controls. Shared norms of performance (see Table 20–1) are appropriate. Pure formal control is inappropriate because of *environmental discontinuities*.[9]

International markets are plagued with fundamental discontinuous changes, such as emergence of powerful cartels, rapid changes in technology, and sudden economic realignments.[10] Furthermore, from time to time, countries involve themselves in disruptive international political activities. These environmental discontinuities necessitate engineered variations, some of them impromptu, in management practices. Multinational companies exercise personal and socialization marketing controls (see Figure 20–1) in dealing with their overseas strategic business units (SBUs). The greater the environmental discontinuities, the greater the probabilities of actual activities not conforming to planned activities.[11] The discrepancies between actual and planned activities necessitate corrective actions through control. Feedback facilitates the control mechanism and corrective action.

When Nestle developed a baby formula and marketed it in remote parts of Latin America and Africa, the results did not materialize as planned. Thousands of babies died because the mothers did not have clean water, did not use proper measurements, or

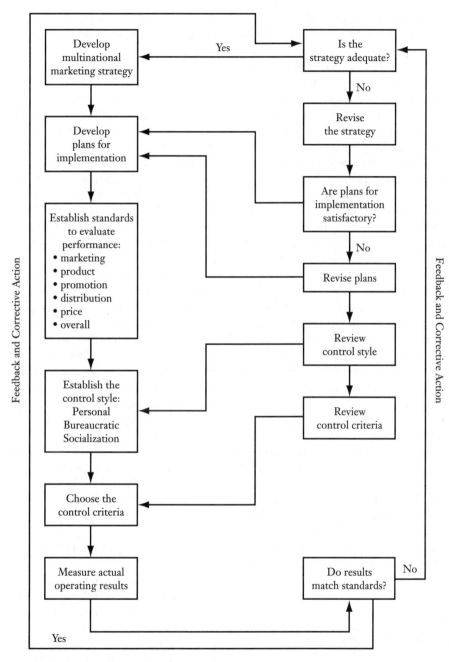

FIGURE 20–1 *International Marketing Control Mechanism*

did not have clean bottles. Nestle (and other baby formula marketing companies) should have been aware of these problems and should have adjusted its product and its marketing practices. After boycotts against Nestle products, corrective action was taken, but it was too late for thousands of families.

Nestle should have established certain control criteria. These criteria would have included such questions as: (1) How easy are the instructions to follow? (2) Can product quality be maintained in rural areas? (3) Is the product's price feasible for the lower classes, who represent the majority of the population? (4) Would the acceptance or rejection of baby formula have any connection to other Nestle products?

These controls would have provided the necessary feedback and would have indicated early on that there was a discrepancy between the plans and actual market performance. As can be seen in Figure 20–1, as a specific step is taken in an effort to establish a good control system, each step is questioned before it is accepted or revised. However, the most important component of Figure 20–1 is the comparison of market results with the established standards. If there is a significant discrepancy, the overall strategy is deemed inadequate, and it is revised, or a new strategy is planned. The crux of this activity is related to measuring actual operating results and using them as feedback. It is therefore necessary to review some of the kinds of feedback that can be used in international marketing.

THE GLOBAL FEEDBACK SYSTEM

Multinational corporations and other international marketers have feedback systems to assess marketing performance and trigger

needed corrective action. A global feedback system is designed to evaluate performance in each and every strategic business unit throughout the world. Two examples illustrate the importance of feedback mechanisms. Audi 5000 had some serious problems in the U.S. market. Instead of acknowledging that there may have been an engineering flaw in the engine, the president of Audi of North America appeared on U.S. TV and claimed that those who had problems with the car did not know how to drive. Consumer complaints in this instance were not used as feedback that could have led to corrective action. Audi's sales and reputation suffered as a result.

The second example was Perrier's misfortune during 1989–90. Traces of benzine, a highly toxic substance, were found in the water. Although the company quickly recalled existing bottles on the market, it should not have allowed this incident to take place. The company should have had closer quality control because the water itself was the basic product ingredient, and impurities in the major ingredient should have been quickly spotted.

A global feedback system has four key components: (1) early-performance indicators, (2) overall image, (3) market position, and (4) performance analysis.

Early-Performance Indicators

Early indicators of performance in the world market come in different forms and from different sources. Performance needs to be evaluated early on so that corrective action can take place in time. Early-performance indicators are oriented more to the short run than are the performance analysis criteria. Performance analysis criteria provide information as to the firm's performance in different markets for longer periods of time, such

TABLE 20–2 ■ *Some Key Indicators of Early Performance*

Early Performance Indicators	Market Implication
Sudden drop in quantities demanded	Problem in marketing strategy or its implementation
Sharp decrease or increase in sales volume	Product gaining acceptance or being rejected quickly
Customer complaints	Product not debugged properly
A notable decrease in competitors' business levels	Product gaining acceptance quickly or market conditions deterioriating
Large volumes of returned merchandise	Problems in basic product design
Excessive requests for parts or reported repairs	Problems in basic product design; lacking standards
Sudden changes in fashions	Product (or competitors' product) causing a deep impact on the consumers' lifestyles

as a year, two years, or even longer periods. A list of early-performance indicators and their market implications is presented in Table 20–2 and is discussed below.

SUDDEN CHANGES IN DEMAND

■ A significant early indicator is a sudden change in the quantities demanded. If a drop or increase is in the industrial area, the amount will be more readily detectable by examining factory orders or inventory levels.[12] When Coca-Cola sales plunged in Afghanistan, for example, the company understood that the negative reaction was to the reddish color, which was associated with the Soviet Union. At that time, Afghanistan had an ongoing military conflict with Soviet Russia. Coca-Cola changed the color of its labels to green (the color of Islam) to make the product acceptable to this market. Because each world market functions quite independently from other world markets, the multinational firm has to keep track of each market and each strategic business unit (SBU).

A sudden drop in quantities demanded is very closely related to the first indicator, a sharp increase or decrease in sales volume. In the continental United States, major companies such as Sears have developed computer networks that provide information on a daily basis. At the end of each working day, company headquarters knows whether merchandise is fast moving or slow moving, regional sales volumes, each individual business unit's sales volume, and the like. Although similar systems are not quite developed yet in the international scene, the Japanese, for instance, are known to have very good communications networks through worldwide telex and fax systems. Such information is extremely important, particularly for companies selling many products in multiple countries where relative performance must be closely checked.

CUSTOMER COMPLAINTS

■ A performance indicator used in U.S. domestic businesses is customer complaint. This type of information is not as readily used internationally. However, if a certain appliance manufacturer had occasion to note that its newest model had created a disproportionate amount of consumer complaints, particularly in an area where consumers typically are not too vocal, this type of information would certainly cast doubt on the performance of the new model.

COMPETITORS' BUSINESS LEVELS ■ Another early-performance indicator is the observation of competitors' business levels. A notable increase or decrease in the competitor's business may indicate how the observing company's product is performing. If competitors are doing very well, a company would want to know why. American auto manufacturers upgraded product quality and styling as they noted steadily mounting imports.

RETURNED MERCHANDISE ■ Closely related to customer complaints as an early-performance indicator is "returned merchandise." Again, if an appliance manufacturer noticed an excessive number of returns, that company could conclude that its performance at that time and in those markets needed to be improved.

EXCESSIVE REQUESTS FOR PARTS ■ Still another early-performance indicator is an excessive request for parts, or excessive amounts of reported repairs. For examples, when Jaguar developed a customer emergency-service network worldwide because of the excessive number of requests, the company was responding to feedback about its market performance.

RAPID CHANGES IN FASHION ■ Finally, in certain parts of the world, fashions and styles change rather fast. If a manufacturer of swimwear detects the unpopularity of, say, bikinis at an early stage in the game, the company can easily foresee a declining performance in its markets later on.

Overall Image

The overall image of a company, and any changes in it, is one of the most important components of a feedback system in helping the company decide whether to maintain or change its international marketing strategy. There are numerous global products, such as Mercedes Benz, Ferrari, or Rolls-Royce, which are regarded as high-class throughout the world. Many global products, however, do not enjoy such a uniformly favorable image. Furthermore, many products have a changeable image in various world markets. Frigidaire, for instance, has been so popular in many parts of Europe that its name has become generic; refrigerators in those countries are called frigidaires. The brand does not enjoy the same image in other parts of the world. Similarly, the Volkswagen Golf has been a very popular car in Europe, but it has not been equally successful in the United States. The overall image of a company's products and, in particular, sudden changes in their image indicate changes in those products' performance in world markets. Image feedback can easily trigger the control function and encourage corrective action as needed.

Market Position

Performance of products in various world markets can be measured by examining their market position. For example, if a certain headache remedy moves up from third place to first place in Europe, that move is indicative of the effectiveness of the company's marketing practices in that part of the world. Nielsen's international pharmaceutical data, which can be acquired from the company on a syndicated basis as described in Chapter 17, is a useful source of data in this area. Similar data may not be available for many other products in many parts of the world.

In addition to the above feedback criteria, other types of performance analyses are also needed. These analyses enable the multinational company to make more critical and longer-range decisions.

Performance Analyses

In addition to early-performance indicators, there are a number of performance analysis tools. These tools provide the criteria for a more complete picture of overall international performance. Four performance analysis tools are discussed in this section. It must be emphasized that these tools can be used for planning as well as control. These tools are: (1) product portfolio, (2) profit picture, (3) competitive edge, and (4) growth.

PRODUCT PORTFOLIO ▪ Product portfolio analysis, as first developed by Boston Consulting Group, is applicable to international as well as domestic situations.[13] For multinational companies that have many products and multiple strategic business units (SBU), it is reasonable to develop a portfolio analysis for each SBU. However, if the company has multiple products but only a few or almost no SBUs, then one general portfolio analysis may be sufficient.

As discussed in Chapter 11, product portfolio analysis has four categories: stars, cash cows, problem children (also called question marks), and dogs. Stars are products that capture a large share of a high-growth market. Cash cows, as the name implies, bring in a lot of revenue, but typically, their future is not very bright because they have a large share of a low-growth market; they may have reached their peak and are not likely to go any higher. Problem children have a small share of a high-growth market. They deserve a change in strategy to help them perform better, perhaps to become stars. Least desirable are dogs, which have a small share of a low-growth market. It is quite likely that taking a chance on any other product (or products) on the portfolio would yield better overall profits than would a dog.

The control function is triggered by periodically classifying the company's products into these four categories. Table 20–3 illustrates one such attempt by one company in one SBU. As can be seen, some stars

TABLE 20–3 ▪ *Changing Product Portfolio of XYZ Company, SBU 1*

	Period	
Product Lines	**1991**	**1997**
Product A	Star	Cash cow
Product B	Star	Star
Product B1–5	Star	Star
Product C	Cash cow	Cash cow
Product D1–3	Cash cow	Dog
Product E	Problem child	Star
Product F	Problem child	Star
Product G	Problem child	Dog
Product H1–6	Dog	—
Product I1–4	—	Problem child

remained stars, and some stars became cash cows; some of the cash cows remained cash cows, and others became dogs; some of the problem children became stars, and the others became dogs. Because the dogs of 1991 were eliminated, there are no such products displayed in the table for 1997.

Assume that the SBU had put its emphasis and its cash resources into the stars and problem children by taking them away from the cash cows and by eliminating the dogs. The portfolio analysis of 1991 triggered the control and corrective-action mechanisms. The situation created at least two new stars and two problem children. Once again the SBU, because of the control function, was in a position to decide how its resources should be allocated among these products.

PROFIT PICTURE ▪ Although each product in a portfolio can also be analyzed in terms of its contribution to the profit picture, for a multinational company it may be more realis-tic to assess the performance of each SBU. Assume a company has eight SBUs. Figure 20–2 illustrates the profit positions of these eight SBUs. SBU 6 has the highest increased sales from the last analysis and a commensurate increase in profits. Under normal conditions, it is performing the best of all the SBUs. However, the most unusual performance is that of SBU 8. While this unit barely increased its sales volume, its profits went up almost as high as those of SBU 6. Obviously, SBU 8 has done something that needs to be analyzed. It may have improved its efficiency, or it may have created more cash cows and stars; it may, however, have raised prices too high, a policy that may back-fire later on. The reason for this performance must be determined, and the company must consider if it can be used in other SBUs also.

COMPETITIVE EDGE ▪ Profit-picture analysis of SBUs is likely to indicate the competitive edge of each of the SBUs as well as of the

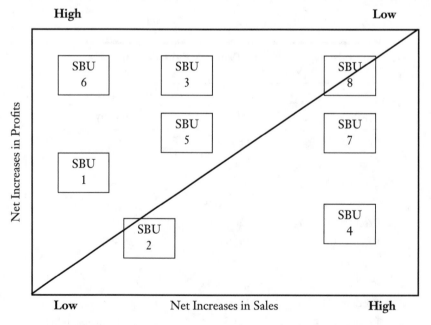

FIGURE 20–2 *Profit Picture Analysis*

multinational company as a whole. Determining the competitive strengths of these SBUs can lead in the direction of improving the multinational firm in the world. The competitive edge of each SBU (if any) must be examined so that the multinational company can understand its strengths and develop or revise its marketing strategies accordingly. Realistically understanding its competitive edge is perhaps one of the most important bits of information that a multinational company can use in its strategic decisions. BMW is a global product whose competitive edge cannot be its price; likewise, Kodak Company does not have a competitive edge based on its prices. Volkswagen and Honda are also global products, but their competitive edge, among other features, is quite likely to be the price.[14]

After receiving the feedback, part of the control function is considering whether adjustment or corrective action is appropriate. If Nissan decides that its competitive edge should no longer be price, then the company may change its strategic points of emphasis and emphasize other features of its products such as engineering and design.

GROWTH ■ As seen in Figure 20–2, in analyzing performance, growth is an important criterion. Companies evaluate SBU growth and

allocate corporate resources accordingly. In Figure 20–2, SBUs that are above the norm (the low-low line)—that is, SBUs 6, 1, 5, and 3—are growing faster than those that are below the low-low line. This distinction again may be critical in terms of managing the company's international growth. The SBUs that are growing faster may be emphasized to accelerate the future growth even further.

The discussion thus far has been on feedback components after the fact. They reflect information about past performance. However, some of the indicators are feedforward rather than feedback.

International Symptomatology

The *feedforward* concept in the control functions is related to international symptomatology, the study of symptoms. Unlike feedback, feedforward facilitates corrective action or change in the strategy before the fact.[15] Feedforward controls are designed to detect deviations from a standard goal. Generally, there are early symptoms of success and failure. If these symptoms can be detected early on, they will facilitate revisions in the strategy before it is totally implemented. Figure 20–3 displays this process. By revising the marketing strategy at an early stage, it is possible for

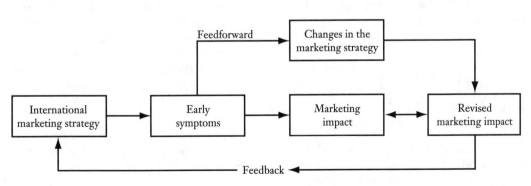

FIGURE 20–3 *Adjustment of International Marketing Strategy*

the multinational company to change the marketing impact of that strategy. For example, when Mazda entered the American market, it realized that too many cheap and well-built Japanese cars had taken up much of the lower end of the market. Mazda had enough good product features to distinguish itself from Nissan, Honda, and Toyota, and to position itself closer to the medium-priced rather than the low-priced end of the market without consumers noticing the repositioning. The strategic adjustment took place early in the game.

Figure 20–3 illustrates the importance of early symptoms as components of feedforward, and how feedforward facilitates the change in marketing strategy. The Campbell Soup Company, which had not done too well in world markets, particularly Australia, Great Britain, and Brazil, could have emphasized early symptoms and either pulled out of these markets or changed the marketing strategies originally used in these countries. Campbell Soups did not do well in the United Kingdom because British women are not used to adding water to canned soups. Brazilians preferred dehydrated soups. Brazilian housewives did not feel that they were fulfilling their role as homemakers when using the product. If these problems had been noticed early enough, they could have been used as feedforward to revise marketing strategies. Every multinational company, even every SBU, is likely to have certain early indicators or symptoms that can be used as feedforward.

UTILIZATION OF FEEDBACK INPUTS

Feedback inputs in the international scene are particularly important for at least three different purposes: (1) control, (2) redirection, and (3) change in plans.

CONTROL ■ As was discussed earlier in this chapter, control implies bringing the planned and actual performance closer together. If early symptoms indicate an expected gap between planned and actual performance, the control mechanism is activated. The control mechanism either indicates corrective action or changes the values and expectations to bring the planned and the actual together. National Office Machines entered into a joint venture with Nippon Cash Machines and started competing in world markets with multinational giants such as IBM, National Cash Register, and Burroughs. The company's positioning of its products vis-à-vis other international giants was monitored, and a combination of feedback and feedforward information dictated that the newly established joint venture should position its products below the well-established multinational competitors and enter world markets through a carefully orchestrated penetration strategy, particularly in those relatively small and medium-sized markets where the existing giants were not very strong. The original plan was to position products to compete head on with the multinational giants.

REDIRECTION ■ As indicated in this example, the control mechanism created a redirection in the overall marketing strategy. The speed and accuracy of this redirection process plays a critical role in the market success of multinational firms. It must be reiterated that control and redirection are not separate options. Rather, redirection is the outcome of the control function. Differences between planned and actual performances ideally redirect the overall marketing strategy. For example, when H. J. Heinz entered the Japanese market through a joint venture, it found that acceptance of ketchup was quite limited. Accordingly, the company reduced its sales network commensurate to the reduced size of operations.

CHANGE IN PLANS ■ Redirection, as seen in the two previous examples, was the outcome of a triggered control mechanism. The same mechanism can also bring about a complete change in plans. General Mills, for instance, established a joint venture to enter the Japanese market. The joint venture did not succeed in popularizing cornflakes and other breakfast cereals in that country, where people are accustomed to a very different morning diet. The joint venture had to change its marketing plans almost completely and turn toward other food products, including a rice-based cereal, a change that subsequently improved its profit picture substantially. This kind of change in plans as a result of the control mechanism can be quite desirable.

In dealing with feedback and adjustment-related areas, one point must be particularly noted—the benefits to the host country. If the multinational company's activities generate an adverse impact on a country's economy, the feedback inputs must state it clearly. Thus, the international firm must understand that what is good for it must be good for the host country's economy as well. Instead of pursuing its selfish, short-run interest, the multinational firm must make sure that its benefits are not conflicting with economic benefits to the host country.

A KEY FACTOR: FLEXIBILITY

The discussion thus far posits one single rule above all: Survival and success in international marketing is very closely related to flexibility, and flexibility can be assured by an effective control mechanism that always triggers proper corrective action. Decentralized organizational structures based on geographic or matrix patterns (see Chapter 19) typically have a quick response time.

With constantly changing competition in the international arena, the feedback function

provides the necessary ability to adjust. As the multinational firm adjusts, it shows evidence of its flexibility. Over the years, the American auto industry did not show enough flexibility, and as a result, it lost many lucrative world markets. The Japanese electronics industry, which showed a substantial degree of flexibility, competed successfully with the American and European electronics industries. More specifically, John Deere and International Harvester did not exercise the necessary flexibility in the world markets, and therefore, they did not perform anywhere near their potentials. By contrast, companies such as Ciba Geigy, Bristol-Myers, and Nestle have done well by maintaining a substantial degree of flexibility and by responding to local or regional needs, reactions, and objections.

The future in international marketing, if anything, lies in accelerated change and intensified competition. Thus, those who have effective feedback and adjustment mechanisms and a high degree of flexibility in international markets will improve their probabilities of survival and success.

THE NEED FOR FUTURE PLANNING

One aspect of overall flexibility is related to planning for the future. In recent years, management theory has maintained that in business, there must be contingency plans so that if the actual plan does not succeed, there is another plan to fall back on.

Such plans are equally important for international marketing. Because of their complexity and changeability, international markets require carefully prepared plans mapping out the future activities of the multinational firm. Such plans must be prepared on the basis of future opportunities and market attractiveness. It has been suggested that in addition to an operational budget, there should also be an opportunities budget. Such a budget would account for proposed new and different ventures.[16]

Thus, an opportunities budget is the essence of an effective future plan. Although such a plan is not part of the standard operating procedures, it gives management resources to take advantage of new opportunities that could unfold or arise in a dynamic global marketplace. Budgetary rigidity should never limit a company's ability to respond to new opportunities.

SUMMARY

International marketing control, which is triggered by feedback information, is important because it facilitates corrective action. Because control is related to bringing together the planned and the actual, deviations from the planned results must be explored. There are three types of controls: (1) personal control, (2) bureaucratic control, and (3) control by socialization.

A global feedback system is necessary if a company's planned and actual performances are to be very close together. Such a feedback system is composed of four key components: (1) performance indicators, (2) overall image, (3) market position, and (4) performance analysis. Four tools of performance analysis are: (1) product portfolio, (2) profit picture, (3) competitive edge, and (4) growth.

Feedback leads to at least three related types of corrective actions: (1) control, (2) redirection, and (3) change in plans.

In essence, the multinational firm must make decisions that will benefit not only the company but the economy of the host country as well.

Flexibility is an important key to international viability. One way of maintaining flexibility is developing contingency plans. Although they are not widely utilized at the present time, their importance cannot be overstated.

DISCUSSION QUESTIONS

1. What does control mean in the context of international marketing?

2. What are the key factors that cause autonomous variations from the intended changes that are expected to take place? Discuss.

3. What types of controls are related to corporate philosophy and local views?

4. Why do firms need international marketing controls? Discuss.

5. Put together the key elements of an international marketing control mechanism. Discuss.

6. What is meant by performance indicators? What are they? Why do we need them?

7. As CEO of an international firm, what key tools for performance analysis would you be inclined to use? Why?

8. How should a CEO use feedback? Why?

The IKEA Story

IKEA, a Swedish retailer that operates one of the largest (if not the largest) furniture chains in the world, entered the American market through its mammoth store near Philadelphia. It then moved to three more cities, Washington, Baltimore, and Pittsburgh. The company is expanding slowly in the United States because of problems with distribution, particularly in terms of finding warehouses and setting up a distribution network. IKEA is coping with this problem by building very large distribution centers. Two such centers are located in Philadelphia and Montreal to serve Eastern stores. It is also planning to build a distribution center near Los Angeles to serve Western stores. The company expects to open two or three stores a year.

IKEA has attracted a lot of attention from the retailing sector. IKEA stores are doing well, with an increase in U.S. sales of 40 percent. Their stores handle sleek, inexpensive furniture that appeals to young adults and families, who compose the market segment that buys most furniture. A number of competitors and other retailers have been experimenting with IKEA's practice of offering child care while parents shop. When the company enters an area, it blitzes the area with catalogs and billboards. About 50 percent of its promotional budgets goes into its annual catalog. This very attractive publication goes to the population located within an hour's drive from an IKEA store.

Once IKEA attracts customers to one of its 200,000-square-foot stores, it uses numer-ous creative merchandising techniques. The store provides shoppers with tape measures, catalogs, paper, and pencils. Child care, strollers, and free diapers are made available. Each store has a restaurant featuring Scandinavian delicacies. Customers can borrow automobile roof racks to carry furniture home. The company's sales per square foot in 1988 were about $350, which is three times higher than the industry average.

IKEA keeps its prices low by making customers do some of the finishing work. The company has developed many of its marketing techniques in Europe, where more than half of its stores are located. U.S. management is thinking of introducing another European innovation, the Family Membership Club. Customers who become members receive discounts in stores and at gas stations located nearby.

QUESTIONS

As a consultant to the IKEA world organization, establish a feedback and control system for the company.

1. To what extent should the control be global?

2. What specific early indicators can you identify?

3. Present an overall feedback system to the company's top management.

Source: Case based on "IKEA Appears to Mean Smart Retailing," *Business Week*, 9 October 1989, 88.

ENDNOTES

1. 1. C. K. Prahalad and Yves L. Doz, *The Multinational Mission* (New York: Free Press, 1987).

2. Earl P. Strong and Robert D. Smith, *Management Control Models* (New York: Holt, Rinehart and Winston, 1968), 1–2.

3. Philip Kotler, *Marketing Management* (Englewood Cliffs, N.J.: Prentice-Hall, 1988).

4. William Davidson, "Administrative Orientation and International Performances," *Journal of International Business Studies*, Fall 1984, 11–23.

5. Alfred M. Jaeger, "The Transfer of Organizational Culture Overseas: An Approach to Control in the Multinational Corporation," *JIBS*, Fall 1983, 91–103.

6. Yves Doz and C. K. Prahalad, "Patterns of Strategic Control within Multinational Corporations," *JIBS*, Fall 1984, 55–72.

7. B. R. Baliga and Alfred M. Jaeger, "Multinational Corporations: Control Systems and Delegation Issues," *JIBS*, Fall 1984, 25–40.

8. Warren J. Keegan, *Global Marketing Management*, 4th ed. (Englewood Cliffs, N.J.: Prentice-Hall, 1989).

9. R. A. Stephens and Yao Apasu, "Strategic Marketing Implications of Responses of Multinational Corporations to Environmental Discontinuities," in *Proceedings of Second World Congress*, eds. Susan Show, Leigh Sparks, and Erdener Kaynak (Miami, Fla.: Academy of Marketing Science, 1985).

10. Lawrence Chimerine, "The New Economic Realities in Business," *Management Review*, January 1997, 12–18.

11. James A. F. Stoner, *Management*, 2nd ed. (Englewood Cliffs, N.J.: Prentice-Hall, 1982).

12. A. Coskun Samli and Tansu Barker, "Early Diagnosis of Marketing Problems," *Management Forum*, March 1984, 22–26.

13. James C. Leontiades, *Multinational Corporate Strategy* (Lexington, Mass.: Lexington Books, 1985).

14. Kenichi Ohmae, *The Mind of the Strategist* (New York: Penguin, 1983).

15. Harold Koontz and Robert W. Bradspies, "Managing through Feedforward Control," *Business Horizons*, June 1972, 25–36.

16. Peter F. Drucker, *Managing in Turbulent Times* (New York: Harper and Row, 1980).

C H A P T E R **21**

What the CEO Should Know about International Marketing

Chapter Outline

Learning Objectives

When you have mastered the contents of this
chapter, you will be able to do the following:

1 Explain the tasks confronting CEOs as
they move their organizations abroad
and instill global philosophies into
home-market executives.

2 Recognize when adjustments need to be
made to organizational structures, and
how change can make companies more
competitive.

3 Know what elements comprise a basic
international SWOT analysis.

4 Have a framework for understanding
how today's trends may impact tomorrow's international marketing strategies.

For CEOs it is one thing to talk about making the big international move, quite another thing to make it successfully. That requires a special kind of leadership. The effort is tough on organizations, tough on people. But it may be the only way for. . . companies to survive in a competitive world.[1]

Today, all major companies are internationally competitive. Trade and investment linkages among them are at all-time highs, as American, European, Japanese, and developing-country MNCs compete for the patronage of international customers. The key role of chief executive officers (CEOs) is to steer their companies profitably through world markets, organizing corporate resources to meet the needs of customers in an ever-more-competitive global economy.

Today's CEOs command vast commercial empires. In terms of sales, the U.S.'s General Motors, at $169 billion annual sales turnover, was tops in 1995. Of the top 10 companies, 6 were Japanese (including 5 of the top 6), 3 were American, and 1 was European.[2] These companies became successful by giving customers what they wanted at attractive prices and by responding quickly and efficiently to opportunities and threats in the global marketplace.

Global competition has transformed and reoriented many industries. In automobiles, GM, Ford, and Chrysler held down two-thirds of the U.S. car market in 1990, but this was a 10 percent drop from their 1980 position. Quality products from Japanese competitors have brought down the average number of defects per car in American cars— from GM, 7.4; Chrysler, 8.1; and Ford, 6.7 in 1980; to GM, 1.7; Ford, 1.5; and Chrysler, 1.8 in 1990. The Japanese, however, also improved their product quality and had only 1.2 defects per car.[3]

Japanese and European competition has caused the U.S. auto industry to rethink its strategies. In doing so, U.S. managements have realized that Detroit does not have all of the answers. In response, they have gone abroad to bolster their foreign-market positions and to gain some new perspectives on auto design and manufacturing. Many aspects of the award-winning Ford Taurus were reverse-engineered from Europe and Japan. Ford purchased Britain's Jaguar and Aston Martin Lagonda companies to gain entry into the European luxury car market. GM bought Britain's Lotus and a half share in Sweden's Saab. Chrysler paid $25 million to obtain Italy's Lamborghini and, with it, the world's fastest factory-built car, the Diablo, which can reach a speed in excess of 200 mph.[4]

What must a CEO do to maintain and improve an organization's competitive standing in world markets? While there is no one answer to this question, there are certain steps that all CEOs can take to gain and maintain competitive global postures:

1. Recognize the importance of and make commitments to world markets.

2. Become globally minded and recognize that profitable business ideas can originate anywhere. Similarly, recognize that marketing innovations and executive talent are not just to be found in the home market.

3. Build organizational structures to sustain the enterprise's global competitive position.

4. Identify corporate strengths and weaknesses worldwide. Perpetuate and consolidate strengths and eliminate or minimize weaknesses.

5. Maintain a global watch for opportunities and threats.

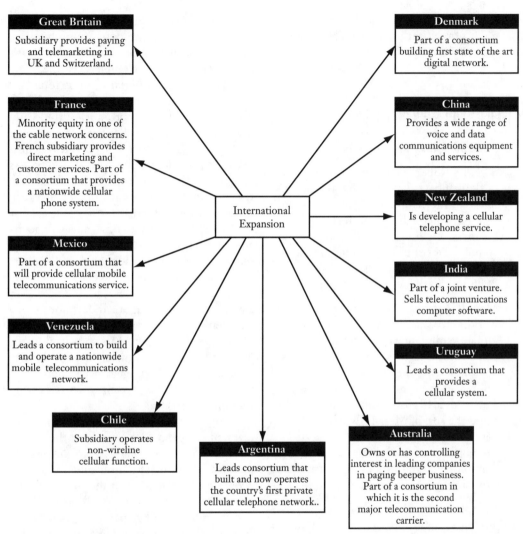

Great Britain
Subsidiary provides paying and telemarketing in UK and Switzerland.

France
Minority equity in one of the cable network concerns. French subsidiary provides direct marketing and customer services. Part of a consortium that provides a nationwide cellular phone system.

Mexico
Part of a consortium that will provide cellular mobile telecommunications service.

Venezuela
Leads a consortium to build and operate a nationwide mobile telecommunications network.

Chile
Subsidiary operates non-wireline cellular function.

Argentina
Leads consortium that built and now operates the country's first private cellular telephone network..

International Expansion

Denmark
Part of a consortium building first state of the art digital network.

China
Provides a wide range of voice and data communications equipment and services.

New Zealand
Is developing a cellular telephone service.

India
Part of a joint venture. Sells telecommunications computer software.

Uruguay
Leads a consortium that provides a cellular system.

Australia
Owns or has controlling interest in leading companies in paging beeper business. Part of a consortium in which it is the second major telecommunication carrier.

- Like other phone companies, BellSouth has ambitions to go abroad.
- The incentives are enormous. Governments around the globe plan to spend $100 billion in the next 10 years to upgrade their telephone systems.
- Venturing overseas also allows BellSouth to delve into businesses that it is not allowed to offer in the United States.

- BellSouth officials argue that telecommunication is increasingly a global business and that their future lies in learning how to do business abroad. Even though overseas operations are only a small portion of the company's business, it is engaged in different projects in some 15 countries. The company has activities in the countries listed above.

Source: Information based on data supplied by BellSouth.

FIGURE 21–1 *BellSouth Ventures Abroad*

6. Anticipate future trends and shape today's organization to deal with emerging and future problems.

GOING INTERNATIONAL

Consider the following companies:

- AT&T's Robert E. Allen and the CEOs of Bell affiliates have realized the potential that international markets represent and have been busy mastering global business techniques and establishing commercial contacts in foreign markets. Figure 21–1 chronicles the efforts of BellSouth in the world marketplace.

- Merrill Lynch's William Schreyer is working to establish his company in the global capital markets arena. A major competitor is Japan's Nomura Securities, a company whose executives were trained in the United States during the 1940s and 1950s. Nomura is now 15 times the size of Merrill Lynch.

But going international requires resources and commitment, and it does not always pay off in the short term. For example:

- Campbell Soups have found internationalizing soups to be a hazardous undertaking. In particular, they found that European biases toward dry soups were an obstacle; that canned soups were too expensive in China; and that their American soup line (with the exception of mushroom) was not well received in Poland.

- Whirlpool similarly found weak demand for consumer durables in Europe, high start-up costs in Asia, and ferocious attacks by rivals in the U.S. market to be tremendous distractions to its overseas push.[5]

Going abroad for the first time makes CEOs and shareholders apprehensive. Historically, world business academicians and practitioners have emphasized the many social and market differences to be found on the international scene. The social and economic commonalities promoting trade and investment among countries have been downplayed. In many cases, only heavy competitive pressures have forced companies abroad. But as most corporations find, once they commit resources to foreign markets, success has often followed.

Being first overseas has always had its advantages. Coca-Cola first went abroad during World War II after CEO Robert Woodruff patriotically declared that he would make Coca-Cola available wherever American troops fought. Today, both Coke and Pepsi are in more than 150 markets, but Coke gets 80 percent of its soft-drink earnings and 66 percent of its soft-drink sales abroad, whereas Pepsi gets just 15 percent of its earnings and 50 percent of its sales from foreign markets.[6]

To turn this relationship around, Pepsi planned to spend $1 billion over the period 1990–1995 to upgrade its foreign-based plants and its distribution and marketing programs. Sales pushes in the former Soviet Union (where Pepsi used to outsell Coke) and in India were key parts of a new global strategy designed to erode Coke's two-to-one market share lead in foreign countries and to boost Pepsi's soft drink volume abroad from 2 billion to 5 billion cases by 1995. The latest battleground for the two soft-drink rivals in the mid-1990s has proved to be Central and Eastern Europe, where they are engaged in a fierce fight for market leadership in these newly emerging markets.[7]

In the early 1980s, it was Atlanta-based telecommunications magnate Ted Turner's dream to create a news network accessible to the entire world. Today, his foresight has been realized, and Cable News Network (CNN) reaches 68 million homes in the United States and 107 million customers internationally in over 100 different countries. In effect, Turner did for television what Reuters and the Associated Press had done many years before for print—he internationalized a new medium. He did this by creating a comprehensive worldwide network of bureaus and correspondents. Most of the network's overseas viewers are in Europe, but millions of tourists and business travelers every year keep themselves current with CNN news in hotels from Buenos Aires to Budapest. Many Japanese banks and securities companies subscribe to CNN to keep touch both with the U.S. economy and with news events worldwide. CNN has become a valuable tool for international executives as well as being a prime example of premeditated international expansion.[8]

BECOMING GLOBAL

Taking a company international is one thing; transforming it into a global corporation is another. This process occurs when companies lose their home-market orientation and become world-oriented enterprises. That is, they choose markets, manufacturing sites, personnel, and raw-material sources without regard to national prejudices. Research and development facilities are located where there are suitable market conditions and talented personnel. Financial resources are drawn from countries with the lowest capital costs. Manufacturing is based where companies obtain optimal cost-quality combinations. Figure 21–2 discusses the steps ASEA-Brown Boveri, BASF, Xerox, Otis, and Hewlett-Packard have taken to improve their global statures. CEOs play big roles in inculcating this non-nationalistic philosophy

into executives and workers. Ted Turner pioneered this approach in CNN by forbidding use of the word *foreign* within his company.[9]

Of course, some companies gain little from being truly global. Firms using multilocal strategies (for example, those selling mainly services) and those producing certain kinds of consumer products (for example, food and drink) gain their competitive advantages by tailoring products to local tastes. Others have built-in advantages from manufacturing in the home country. French perfumes, Spanish sherries, and Belgian and Swiss chocolates would all lose some of their allure if they were marked "Made in the USA."

For most companies, however, going global makes sense. It enables them to manufacture and market on a large scale. For example, many high-tech products must be mass-marketed at competitive prices to match rivals pursuing the same strategies. Cornelius J. Van der Klugt, CEO of Philips, the Dutch electronics giant and producer of Magnavox, overhauled his $29 billion organization because of pressures from Japanese competition. He narrowed the company's focus to just four main businesses—consumer electronics, lighting, computers, and chips. Noncompetitive European plants were closed, and 24,000 workers were laid off. Major manufacturing and assembly operations were moved to cheap Far Eastern locations.

On the marketing side, Philips took on the Japanese consumer-electronics giants Sony and Panasonic. Philips, which invented the VCR and pioneered compact discs (and still collects royalties from Japanese licenses), revamped its R&D to move products from laboratories to markets more speedily. Aggressive marketing of its Magnavox name resulted in its share of the CD market increasing in the late 1980s. New technologies in the 1990s have pushed the Philips Magnavox television brand toward Internet TV terminals and digital TV.[10]

The multinational of the 1970s is obsolete. Global companies are groups of overseas subsidiaries that execute decisions made at headquarters. A new type of company is now evolving. It does research wherever necessary, develops products in several countries, promotes key executives regardless of nationality, and even has shareholders on three continents.

The Swedish-Swiss conglomerate ASEA-Brown Boveri has sales of $30 billion. In 1989, it acquired the U.S. firm Combustion Engineering. Its headquarters are in cosmopolitan Zurich, Switzerland, where business is transacted in English and the books are kept in dollars.

Germany's BASF shifted its cancer and immune-system research to Cambridge, Massachusetts, because of problems with safety, animal rights, and environmental activists in Germany. The attraction was not only a skilled labor pool but the fact that there were fewer controversies about the type of research (for example, use of animal experiments) in the United States than in Germany.

Xerox moved some of its copier rebuilding work to Mexico, an example of operational flexibility that allowed it to change work styles and improve productivity at its New York facility. Dow Chemical was able to avoid layoffs by shifting production around when European demand for a popular solvent decreased.

Fuji-Xerox has engineered some 80 office copier models in Japan, which have been introduced into the United States, showing that innovations can occur anywhere.

Otis Elevator, a division of United Technologies, developed its new Elevonic 411 in six research centers in five countries, saving an estimated $10 million in design costs and cutting the development time in half.

In Asia, Hewlett-Packard affiliates working closely together rolled out a new line of graphics terminals in 18 languages, complete with equipment and documentation. The company had previously been "beaten to market" by competitors in locally oriented new-product introductions.

Source: Adapted from William J. Holstein, "Stateless Corporation," *Business Week,* 14 May 1990, 98–105.

FIGURE 21-2 *The Stateless Corporation*

MAKING ORGANIZATIONAL ADJUSTMENTS

Organizations run smoothly when there are orderly flows of information and definite lines of authority and responsibility. One of the CEO's most important roles is to realize when there have been sufficient changes in the marketplace or in company strategies to warrant organizational adjustments. Growth causes most organizational changes. For example, geographical diversification into new markets strains product structures that function best over relatively few markets. Similarly, product-line extensions and acquisitions tax geographic structures that work well with smaller product lines. CEOs alone are in the best position to know when organizational overhauls are needed.

Global representation at the highest corporate levels facilitates organizational adjustments. The Japanese realized a need to hire non-Japanese managers to help them run their worldwide organizations. Honda appointed non-Japanese to its major boards in the late 1980s and has attempted to create a more entrepreneurial corporate culture to cope with the globally turbulent marketplace.[11]

ICI, a British firm that is in the world's top 50 corporations and a $16 billion-a-year producer of pharmaceuticals, film, polymers, agricultural chemicals, and explosives, moved away from its country-oriented structure by establishing 13 worldwide business units. Their new focus on products rather than areas reduced decision-making time, quickened new-product introductions, and decreased administrative overlaps between countries. With the global focus came global management. Four of ICI's nine worldwide business units were headquartered outside the United Kingdom. ICI's Board, previously all British, now included two Americans, a Canadian, a Japanese, and a German, and one-third of 180 top executives were non-British.[12]

In the late 1980s, Ford Motor Company began to unify its foreign and domestic auto operations with the objective of developing global products. Follow-ups to the Tempo, Topaz, and Sierra cars were designed in the United States and Europe. Five global product-development centers were established under the company's Ford 2000 globalization plan: small cars, front-drive cars and trucks, rear-drive cars, light trucks, and commercial trucks. New communications methods, featuring computer-aided design and manufacturing and teleconferencing, facilitated the process.[13]

Communications technologies similarly enabled Citicorp to link its 90-country network into an efficient, competitive organization. Instead of borrowers doing business with just one office, clients were able to obtain competitive bids from any number of foreign locations.[14]

Increasingly, international companies are allocating resources without regard to national boundaries. Further examples of the "stateless corporation" trend are shown in Figure 21–2.

MAINTAINING THE GLOBALLY COMPETITIVE ORGANIZATION: THE INTERNATIONAL SWOT ANALYSIS

The CEO has global responsibilities for maintaining and improving the company's competitive position worldwide. This task involves evaluating the corporation's strengths and weaknesses, the opportunities it faces, and the threats confronting it. To help identify these, companies do SWOT (strengths, weaknesses, opportunities, and threats) analyses.

Strengths and Weaknesses

Few companies lack weaknesses. As noted in Chapter 10 on marketing strategy, firms with extensive R&D facilities, full product lines, and full services are vulnerable to low-cost competitors that "cherry pick" and use guerrilla tactics on selected product lines. Globalization has upped the stakes in many industries. New-product development costs are so high for some industries (such as pharmaceuticals and aerospace) that worldwide marketing is the only way to recoup costs.

Today's CEOs are concerned about worldwide performance in three critical areas—research and development, manufacturing, and marketing. Their aims, given limited resources, are to maintain technological competitiveness, lower manufacturing costs, create effective product-delivery systems, and achieve good reputations.

RESEARCH AND DEVELOPMENT ■ Efforts in

R&D determine the technical competitiveness of company products and services. But R&D is costly. New-product-development costs for pharmaceuticals use about $16 million spread over five years. By the 1990s, costs were estimated to be $250 million per new product spread over 12 years.[15]

Firms reduce risks through careful market research (to ensure that R&D is customer oriented) and through consortia (for example, in the aerospace industry as described in Chapter 12) and joint ventures. In the pharmaceutical industry, Bristol-Myers and Squibb merged to give both companies the necessary critical mass for R&D and global competitiveness.[16] Mergers and joint ventures ideally capitalize on each partner's strengths and help eliminate weaknesses. Similarly, global alliances often have R&D as their centerpieces. Siemens and IBM (chip development), Rolls-Royce and Snecma (aero engines), AT&T and Mitsubishi (SRAM chips), and GE and Toshiba (home appliances) are all examples of alliances that were formed to take advantage of different expertises and to get products to market quickly.[17]

Companies realize the importance of R&D, and most commit substantial resources to maintain technological leadership. Philips's work on VCRs and compact discs is an example. Sony's new pocket copier scans, picks up, and prints lines of a book or magazine. It is 4 inches by 2 inches by 1 inch, and it weighs 4 ounces (about 120 grams).[18]

MANUFACTURING WEAKNESSES ■ Marketing

strategy is adversely affected by high costs (which raise prices) and poor-quality products (which lowers company reputation). CEOs combat high costs in two ways. First, they encourage the use, where possible, of robotics and computer-aided manufacturing. Second, they shift production to offshore units to decrease labor costs (as Philips did).

Problems in quality give marketers unreliable product images. The Japanese improved manufacturing quality through use of quality circles (QCs), which are groups of employees acting in concert to improve quality and productivity,. Motorola initiated a top-to-bottom reform of its manufacturing processes. Advanced production techniques, massive employees retraining, and a goal of 99.9997 percent error-free manufacturing transformed the company into a world-class competitor in both the consumer and industrial electronics fields.[19]

MARKETING WEAKNESSES ■ Weaknesses can

occur in any of the product, pricing, distribution, or promotion areas. Distribution and promotion are usually the chief problem areas. Establishing dealer and distributor networks is expensive. Hence, as occurs in the industrial products sector, companies form consortia and global alliances to strengthen distribution in countries where they lack adequate representation. Nestle formed alliances with General Mills to sell GM's breakfast cereals throughout the world, except in North America. Nestle created another alliance with Baxter Healthcare to develop and distribute a nutritive products line.[20]

CEOs are aware that favorable corporate images aid worldwide sales. Some companies (IBM, Sony, NCR, and Toyota) have global reputations. Others have identity problems when moving to new markets and must advertise to make people aware of their corporate existence. Figure 21–3 shows a Mitsubishi Electric advertisement promoting its American presence.

Source: Courtesy of Mitsubishi Electric America. Reproduced with permission.

FIGURE 21-3 *A Mitsubishi Advertisement*

Opportunities and Threats

The global marketplace, because of its turbulent nature, presents companies with an abundance of threats and opportunities. Analyses of them are performed at industry and geographic levels. Both involve monitoring, anticipating, and responding to environmental change.

INDUSTRY ANALYSIS ■ Industries globalize at varying rates. The retailing industry did some early globalizing under the F.W. Woolworth name many decades ago. Then came the 1960s and 1970s flood of U.S. franchisers into world markets, as McDonald's, Kentucky Fried Chicken, Pizza Hut, and so on sprang up around the world. In the 1980s and 1990s, large general stores such as France's Carrefour, Holland's Makro, and Britain's Marks and Spencer have joined the U.S.'s Kmart and Wal-Mart in increasing numbers of foreign ventures. Then there are the "category killers" and specialty retailers, such as Toys R Us, Laura Ashley, The Body Shop, and IKEA that have come to realize what opportunities there are in world markets.[21] It is estimated that by the year 2000, 90 out of the top 100 largest retailers in the world will be global.[22]

GEOGRAPHIC ANALYSIS ■ Analysis of geographic regions also uncovers opportunities and threats. Consider for example, four events discussed earlier in this book—the 1990s economic and political unification of Western Europe, the economic revival of Latin America and of Eastern Europe, and the emergence of China as a dominant force in the world economy. All of these events have opened up opportunities for international firms and posed problems.

Western Europe's EC '92 economic unification package has pushed firms toward harmonization of both their products and corporate images across the region (with extensions, in many cases, to world markets generally). The new marketing emphasis is on similarities rather than differences within Europe. During the 1980s, Birds Eye Walls (a Unilever subsidiary) twice tried to transplant its frozen fish meal from Germany to the UK, and twice it failed. Finally, the company tried the same recipes and packaging across both markets. The new strategy was a success.[23] Nestle's traditional policy of geographic decentralization was challenged as the company sought to consolidate its diverse country activities into more unified strategies. Nestle's approach was to rationalize its European supply chain and create a Europe-wide information system to manage the increasing complexity of its logistics function.[24]

The impending political unification of Europe through a common "Euro" currency is a problem that firms are anticipating and for which they are proactively preparing. A common currency is likely to impact financial and treasury management (foreign-exchange exposures, simplified cash-management policies); legal issues (dual-pricing problems, contract continuity); information systems (conversion of historic cost data and data comparability between Euro and non-Euro participants); and corporate communications (transferability of data within and outside of Europe).[25]

Latin America's economic and political rejuvenation has caused companies to tackle many new problems as they seek to harvest the region's business potential. Citibank spent five years building up its branch network distribution in Venezuela to exploit the surging credit card market (Venezuelans hold over 2 million credit cards over its 21 million population). The company faces significant problems, however, because of poor credit bureaus and a lack of credit risk information. This has caused high default rates on card balances and substantial cost escalations.[26]

While physical infrastructures and distribution systems are well established in urban areas, problems moving goods continue in rural parts. In Colombia, companies must use many warehouses across the market to serve the "mom and pop"–dominated retail system. Rural-based guerrilla groups pose problems and many of the more than 1,000 transportation companies use convoy systems with armed guards as countermeasures.[27]

Nevertheless, international marketers see potential in the region, and they have instigated pan-regional strategies to take advantage of common Latin cultures and themes. Consolidation of regional manufacturing, distribution, and promotional activities into coherent regional strategies are occurring at increasing rates.[28]

After some hesitation, international firms have begun to make serious commitments to Eastern Europe as the seeds of democracy and capitalism are beginning to bear fruit. Baskin-Robbins ice cream completed a $30 million greenfield factory in Moscow to service its 200 supermarket and kiosk outlets. Coca-Cola airlifted an 81 ton bottling line to Russia and created an entirely new distribution system to attack Pepsi and to overcome a 5:1 sales deficit that has existed within the region since 1991. Coke and Pepsi were roughly equal in 1996 but with momentum in world leader Coca-Cola's favor.[29]

China's emergence onto the world marketing scene has sent tremors throughout both developed and developing nations. On the one hand, the limitless labor supply keeps wages low and competitive at about $100 a month (a worry to competing developing economies); on the other hand, China's constant demands for high-technology transfers and its known pirating habits have caused trade and political frictions with developed nations. Protectionist tendencies and human rights problems have also persisted. But the lure of the 1.2 billion consumer market has caused many governments and companies to overlook these problems in order to prevent being shut out of one of the major world markets.[30]

As CEOs survey the world's 200-plus markets, they see opportunities as far as the commercial eye can see. But so do other CEOs. The rush is on to gain access to worldwide markets to forestall threats from industry competitors with the same global pretensions. In many countries, though, circumstances cloud judgments about market opportunities. For example:

- While Boris Yeltsin has been reelected in Russia, what are the prospects after the year 2000, when new leadership is necessary?

- Will the fledgling democracies now emerging on the African continent take hold and enable the region's vast mineral resources to be leveraged into economic development? Similarly, how will South Africa fare after Nelson Mandela's scheduled step-down in 1999?

- How will the resurgence of Islamic fundamentalism affect the politics of North Africa and the Middle East?

- To what extent will Japan's and China's combined $100 billion trade surplus with the United States affect commercial and diplomatic relations among these nations?

- As countries modernize and continue to increase their use of the world's resources, how soon will it be before material shortages become major factors in world marketing?

The answers to these and other questions depend on predicting tomorrow's events. However hazardous it may be to prophesy about the future, it is necessary to define future opportunities and threats and to equip the international corporation to meet those challenges.

GAZING AT THE CRYSTAL BALL: PRESENT AND FUTURE TRENDS

Time present and time past
Are both perhaps present in time
    future,
And time future contained in time
    past.

T.S. Eliot, Four Quartets

It is the task of CEOs to equip their organizations to deal with the future. However, predicting the future is not easy. Most executives extrapolate past trends to envisage tomorrow's world. For international marketers, the process involves monitoring world trends and evaluating their effects on marketing strategy.

World Marketing Environment: "The Global Village"?

There is little doubt that globe-shrinking technologies and communications will continue to bring countries closer together. In the process, world trade and economic interdependencies will increase. Trade barriers will fall, and more countries will depend on free trade and global market forces to allocate world resources. The economic unification of Europe and the movement of Eastern Europe away from government-dictated resource allocations make certain the prospect of a more competitive world marketplace.

ECONOMIC INTEGRATION ■ In 1980s and the 1990s have seen significant integrations within and between major regions of the world. The Free Trade Agreement of the Americas aims for total integration of North, Central, and South America by 2005. Talks have been held between the European Union, NAFTA, and MERCOSUR trade groups with a view toward establishing a transatlantic free trade area (TAFTA). Similarly, the EU has taken the initiative in considering the Visegrad countries (Hungary, Poland, and the Czech and Slovak Republics) for membership around the year 2000. Further pushes to the east have resulted in speculation about a 44-country greater European Union in the future.[31] Talks have also been held between 15 EU and 12 Mediterranean countries about extending the European Union southward to include selected nations in North Africa and the Mediterranean. The year 1995 also saw the EU ratify the Lome convention governing its trading relations with over 70 African, Pacific, and Caribbean markets.[32] With Russia an eventual entry into the EU, free trade areas could stretch from Anchorage, Alaska, in the U.S. all the way around the world to the Bering Strait between Russia and the U.S.

FINANCIAL INTEGRATION ■ World financial markets are already integrated in that what happens in New York, London, or Tokyo affects world traders elsewhere. The dollar has been the key currency since 1945. In the 1980s, the rise of Japanese financial institutions made the yen a major world currency. Further economic and political integration in Europe is likely to produce a European currency by the year 2000. This development would strengthen the world economy, which would then be based on not one but three major currencies—the dollar, the yen and the Euro. Similarly, over time, common Asian, Middle Eastern, African, or Latin American currencies should emerge.

POLITICAL DEVELOPMENTS ■ The 1980s was a decade of great political change, the consequences of which have stretched into the 1990s. East-West tensions have decreased, with "peace dividends" accumulating both in Eastern Europe (where there is a pressing need to boost industrial investment, especially in consumer goods) and in the United States (where social programs such as education could benefit). One cloud on the horizon is that trade or commercial wars (for example, between China/Japan and the EU/U.S.) may replace military conflicts as sources of world political tension.

The emergence of the Eastern European, Latin American and Asian markets, together with free-market movements in Western Europe (with privatization and deregulation), should promote international competition. It is also only a matter of time before 100 percent foreign ownership is allowed throughout all major world markets, and emerging market currencies become fully convertible.

As technologies become more refined and flexible, manufacturing should become more evenly split between developed countries (through robotics and computer-aided production) and developing countries. Trends in the United States, Canada, and Western Europe suggest that developed markets will become research and development centers and be oriented more toward distribution and service.

RESOURCE AND ECOLOGICAL CONCERNS ▪

Commercialization and industrialization take their tolls on the world's resources and its ecological environment. As countries develop, the demand for minerals and metal increases. Sooner or later, world reserves will run out. If production is maintained at 1988 levels (which is highly unlikely) and world prices remain constant (which affects the reserves economically obtainable), estimates are that there are about 224 years of aluminum left and 167 years of iron ore. Minerals in shorter supply include nickel

(65 years); copper (41 years); and cadmium, lead, mercury, tin, and zinc, all with less than 25 years of reserves.[33]

Mineral shortages affect corporate strategies. The prices of commodities must eventually rise, forcing up user costs. Countries with mineral reserves will become economically more powerful and, where necessary, control the extraction of materials (just as the Middle East has done with its oil). Companies using these materials will look for substitutes, either natural or synthetic.

Ecological concerns center around pollution and environmental problems. In the United States, lobbies such as the Sierra Club maintain public awareness of environmental issues. In Europe, the Green Party monitors and publicizes ecological concerns. In other countries, there are no such groups. In Eastern Europe, industrial pollution has caused extensive forest damage in Bulgaria and in the Czech and Slovak Republics. Rivers and reservoirs are contaminated. Air pollution was found to be 50 to 100 times "tolerated" levels, and high percentages of children suffer from pollution-related illnesses.[34]

International projects and investments have come under ecological scrutiny as governments seek to limit foreigner-initiated damage to domestic and international environments. Resource-poor Japan has been criticized for its drift-net fishing techniques, which kill dolphins. Japan has also come under fire for using other countries' timber reserves (for example, in Malaysia and Brazil) and for exporting its most-polluting industries to developing countries.[35]

Perhaps the most serious long-term problem is global warming. While some countries (including the United States) are skeptical of the overall "greenhouse effect," others (including Western Europe) are taking the problem seriously. A worst-case scenario has the world's average temperature rising by 8 degrees Fahrenheit (about 5 degrees

Celsius) over the next 60 years. If this occurs, it would shrink some of the world's major rivers, melt part of the polar icecap, and redefine national coastlines.[36]

Company responses to resource and ecological concerns vary. Heinz took advantage of the drift-net fishing controversy by stating that it would not purchase tuna from companies using harmful fishing techniques. Other companies advertise the biodegradability of their products (for example, rubbish bags and diapers) or of their packaging.

Resource shortages also affect corporate strategies. Dimmed prospects for river transportation caused Archer Daniels Midland Company to purchase a stake in Illinois Central Transportation Company, a large U.S. railroad group. Weyerhaeuser, a Tacoma, Washington–based lumber company, is developing trees that are more drought resistant. Other ramifications of a possible greenhouse effect include rising demands for utilities and insurance claims for an extended hurricane season.[37]

Trends in International Marketing Management

CUSTOMER TARGET MARKETING AND PRODUCT STRATEGY ■
The liberalization of trade restrictions and advances in communications will affect target marketing. The growth of international direct marketing should increase as companies develop cross-national customer lists.

As countries develop, trade barriers fall, and international communications increase, more products should acquire global status (that is, they can be marketed in similar fashions in several or all countries). At present, industrial products, luxury autos, and certain consumer durable goods are globally oriented. As living standards rise and produc-

tion costs fall, more products should attain global identities.

Advances in product design methods and decreasing national differences should facilitate the movement toward global products. Goods can be engineered to satisfy multiple market requirements simultaneously and to be mass-produced at low cost.

MANUFACTURING AND DISTRIBUTION ■
Advances in communications (for example, teleconferencing, fax machines, and automatic translators) should enhance the coordination efforts of multinational corporations. During the 1980s, offshore sourcing became popular as companies took advantage of low labor costs and favorable exchange rates. This trend should continue, with companies shifting sources to obtain the best combinations of product, price, and quality.

Different developing countries should become sources of offshore products. Taiwan, Hong Kong, South Korea, and Singapore were competitive suppliers during the 1980s. The 1990s is seeing the emergence of the People's Republic of China, India, Malaysia, Philippines, and Thailand as suppliers. Beyond the year 2000, perhaps Chad, Ethiopia, Sudan, and other African states will become the world's low-cost producers and the sites for assembly operations.

As manufacturing becomes more competitive, power will shift toward the channels of distribution. In all markets, distribution exposure is finite—there is only so much space for retail outlets. There is also only so much time that consumers are willing to devote to shopping and catalogue browsing. As competition increases, retailers and distributors will exert greater control over product destinies. International companies have already recognized the importance of foreign channels. U.S. investment in foreign distribution in 1995 was $71.3 billion, or 10 percent of the $711 billion total. In contrast, foreign investments in U.S. channels was $85 billion, or about 15 percent of the $560 million total.

PROMOTIONAL STRATEGIES ▪ As satellite

technologies improve, television and radio programming capabilities are upgraded. International media became common in the 1980s. *Reader's Digest*, *The Wall Street Journal*, the *Economist*, *Cosmopolitan*, and the *Financial Times* all have multicountry distribution. Television programs such as "Dallas," "Dynasty," and "Miami Vice," and sports events such as the Superbowl and the Olympic Games are carried by networks worldwide. Europe-wide programming with Sky Channel is already operational, and CNN has demonstrated the potential for international programming.

As trade barriers have fallen, more companies are promoting products directly to customers. International toll-free telephones, sophisticated mailing lists, and in-home television shopping systems (such as Videotext in France) have all made consumers more accessible to direct response promotions (that is, customers see or read a sales pitch and respond instantaneously). Global availability and acceptability of credit cards such as American Express, Visa, and Mastercard have made international consumer transactions easy.

The availability of international broadcast and print media, the upsurge in international direct marketing, the emergence of global consumers (such as the Triadians), and the internationalization of the advertising industry have all made standardized promotions more likely in the future.

PRICING STRATEGIES ▪ Currency inconvertibility (not being able to convert soft currencies such as Indian rupees into hard currencies such as U.S. dollars or British pounds) is slowly becoming less of a problem.

As more countries trade in larger volumes, the currencies of developing-country traders will slowly become convertible, as soon as their inflation levels subside. In the meantime, barter expertise is well developed and there should be fewer payment problems among countries. Electronic money and document transfers are becoming increasingly commonplace as global financial systems develop and as fraud-prevention methods improve. Consequently, barter will increase. Countries with soft (inconvertible) currencies will move toward an increased use of convertible currencies in trade with other soft-currency countries. For example, a 1990 protocol between the U.S.S.R. and Hungary opted for dollar-based trade between the two countries beginning in 1991. This agreement replaced the impractical ruble-based trade. [35]

THE INTERNATIONAL MARKETING MANAGER'S CONTRIBUTION TO GLOBAL STRATEGY

Marketing managers play vital roles in formulating and executing global strategies. Figure 21–4 shows how managers affect company strategies worldwide. First, the strengths of international managers depend directly on their understanding of local market conditions, including not just market sizes, segments, and competitor strategies but also political, legal, economic, and other environmental factors. Also, the better able they are to relate strategies to other market conditions, the more inputs they will have into corporate strategies worldwide, including the assessment of commercial threats and opportunities. These must be compared to firms' strengths and weaknesses in order to establish viable corporate objectives and strategies.

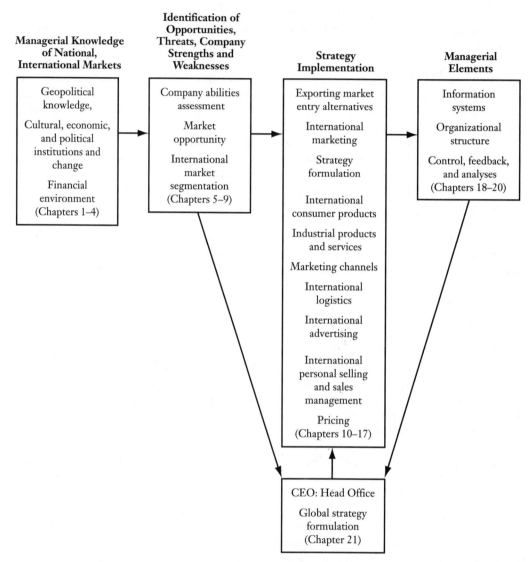

FIGURE 21-4 *International Marketing Manager's Inputs into Global Strategy*

Once strategies are formulated, market managers play key roles in implementation. In smaller companies, export managers maintain flows of goods and services to foreign markets. In multinational corporations, export-import trade is often part of complex manufacturing and marketing logistics systems enabling companies to service countries with low-cost, high-quality merchandise. In all cases, the most important managerial task is molding product, promotion, distribution, and pricing components into distinctive profit-producing marketing mixes.

Strategy implementation is ongoing in corporations, as are the systems that support and nurture corporate activities. International marketing information systems provide data for managerial decision making and help to maintain corporate alertness to opportunities and threats in all markets. Where firms make significant strategy shifts (such as taking on new products businesses or expanding their market base), organizational structures often need adjustment. Finally, and most importantly from a managerial viewpoint, control mechanisms must be effective in detecting early problems and ensuring that executives have sufficient time to amend strategies.

SUMMARY

Today's CEOs oversee large commercial empires. It is the task of the top company executive to marshal corporate resources to meet customer needs in an increasingly competitive global marketplace. In particular, CEOs are instrumental in taking their corporations into foreign markets and instilling global orientations into corporate executives. One major concern is maintaining a fit between the strategies companies pursue and the organizational structures needed to execute those strategies. Adding products and markets imposes strains on existing structures, and CEOs constantly monitor world markets to eliminate or minimize weaknesses in research and development, manufacturing, and marketing, or to capitalize on their strengths in these areas. Additionally they are active in initiating or reducing activities in those parts of the world that represent opportunities or threats to their companies.

Finally, a major role of CEOs is to anticipate global developments and to equip their companies to deal with them. One such movement is toward the "global village," with economic, political, and financial forces bringing countries closer together and establishing increasing interdependencies between them. All such factors require monitoring, and their effects on corporate marketing mixes must be analyzed. Marketing managers play critical roles in all aspects of global strategy—its planning, implementation, and control.

DISCUSSION QUESTIONS

1. You are the CEO of an international consumer-electronics company. Review the questions raised under "geographic analysis" and indicate how you would approach those situations (for Eastern Europe, Latin America, Africa, and China).

2. Given that international corporations are likely to expand their commercial interests into more and more markets, how do you expect CEOs to react? Think of the strategy and then the organizational structure implications of expansion.

3. As more countries become industrialized and market blocs form, do you think the CEO's job will become easier or more difficult?

Mercedes Goes Global: A Merc in Every Driveway?

By the late 1980s and early 1990s, Mercedes knew it was in a competitive dogfight to maintain its position in the world auto market.

- Labor costs in Germany were among the highest in the world at about $30 an hour (including indirect government payroll taxes). The German mark had appreciated over 15 percent against major world currencies between 1986 and 1991, forcing export costs to rise.

- Lexus and Infiniti were challenging Mercedes (and BMW) in the world luxury automobile market.

- BMW's international growth had put its sales on a par with those of Mercedes.

- Mercedes luxury cars had come under pressure from environmentalists in Europe and from an aging European clientele now looking for smaller luxury cars.

The giant automaker sprang into action under CEO Helmut Werner. In 1993, the company announced plans to compete in the 1 million-unit sports-utility-vehicle (SUV) market in the U.S. and established a plant to produce it in Tuscaloosa, Alabama. The first SUV rolled off the line in mid-1997.

In addition, Mercedes' fully loaded SLK convertible sports car was introduced and priced at $40,000 to compete with BMW's Z3 sports vehicle. A minivan was to be produced in Spain; and the smallest Mercedes A-class (at 11 feet long) debuted at the 1997 Frankfurt Motor Show, with a projected price tag of about $15,000. Offshore sourcing was selectively used in Mexico and Eastern Europe to contain costs. Distribution was upgraded worldwide to cope with the greater variety of Mercedes models.

QUESTIONS

1. Would you say that Mercedes was internationalizing or globalizing? What is the difference between these two corporate strategies?

2. Which do you think is the primary factor contributing to the change now occurring at Mercedes? Why?

3. How else can Mercedes capitalize on its global brand image? More automobiles? Non-auto products? Why?

Source: Adapted from John Templeman, "A Mercedes in Every Driveway?" *Business Week*, 26 August 1996, 38–40; and John Still, "Mercedes: Why They're Here, What They Want," *Tuscaloosa News*, 3 October 1993, 9A.

H.J. Heinz:
International Expansion

Anthony J. F O'Reilly is chairman of H. J. Heinz, the multi-billion-dollar food conglomerate. He decided that in spite of a 6 to 8 percent sales growth and healthy profit margins, organizational changes were necessary. He informed top executives that the formula Heinz had used so successfully throughout the 1980s—fanatical attention to lowering costs, decentralized structure, and aggressive marketing—would not be enough to cope with the more turbulent and competitive international marketplace of the 1990s.

During the 1980s, Heinz diversified geographically by going into Africa and Asia. In some countries, the company capitalized on local crops to custom-manufacture new products. Its joint venture with a Chinese food manufacturer resulted in a Western-style banana-flavored rice cereal for infants. In Africa, Heinz introduced new crops, such as beans and tomatoes, and made Heinz expertise available to local agriculturists. In Asia, Heinz tried to introduce more modern products to take advantage of Westernization tendencies.

Following O'Reilly's program, Heinz switched its production focus from cost cutting to improving quality. Then, it went on an acquisition spree, buying up $500 million worth of new companies and products. On the marketing side, Heinz elected to exert more centralized control over previously autonomous subsidiaries. Said O'Reilly:

"The petty privilege of individual managers protecting their turf is no longer tolerable," and Heinz's 44 subsidiaries worked toward sharing some production, purchasing, and marketing ideas. Initial savings from the centralization move were estimated at $50 million. Marketing emphases were placed on ketchup and Weight Watchers diet meals, and efforts were made to transform these into "global brands."

QUESTIONS

1. What sort of organizational structure would you expect Heinz to have? (Check Chapters 19 and 20 on organization and control.)

2. What strains and stresses will O'Reilly's actions have on that organizational structure (that is, acquisitions, geographic diversification, and increased centralization)?

3. Toward what form of organization should Heinz contemplate moving? Why? What sorts of problems might the company experience with its new organizational format?

Source: Based on Carol Hymowitz, "Heinz Sets Out to Expand in Africa and Asia, Seeking New Markets, Sources of Raw Materials," *The Wall Street Journal*, 27 September 1983, A1, A10; M. X. Pei, "Heinz Gets a Foothold in China," *Birmingham News*, 29 August 1986, Al 8; and Gregory L. Miles, "Heinz Ain't Broke, but It's Doing a Lot of Fixing," *Business Week*, 11 December 1989, 84–88.

ENDNOTES

1. William J. Holstein, "Going Global," *Business Week*, 20 October 1989, 9.

2. William C. Symonds, et al., "The Globetrotters Take Over," *Business Week*, 8 July 1996, 46.

3. Anneta Miller and Frank Washington, "Japanese Cars: Born in the USA," *Newsweek*, 9 April 1990, 36–37.

4. John Rossant and Wendy Zellner, "The World's Fastest Car is Now—a Chrysler?" *Business Week*, 12 February 1990, 44.

5. William J. Holstein, "Going Global"; Joseph Weber, "What's Not Cooking at Campbell's," *Business Week*, 23 September 1996, 40; and Bill Vlasic and Zachary Schiller, "Did Whirlpool Spin Too Far Too Fast?" *Business Week*, 24 June 1996, 135–136.

6. Subrata N. Chakraverty, "How Pepsi Broke into India," *Forbes*, 27 November 1989, 43–44.

7. Michael J. McCarthy, "PepsiCo Plans Extensive Ad Campaign to Contest Coke's Overseas Dominance," *The Wall Street Journal*, 2 April 1990, 2b; and Dana-Nicoleta Lascu, "The New Front for the Battle of the Cola Brands: Central and Eastern Europe," *Journal of Global Marketing* 10, no. 2 (1996): 97–99.

8. Marc Gunther, "CNN Envy," *Fortune*, 8 July 1996, 120–126.

9. "Ted Turner, the Sequel," *The Cable Guide*, 17 April 1989.

10. Jonathan Kapstein and Thane Peterson, "Look Out, World, Philips Is on a War Footing," *Business Week*, 15 January 1990, 44–45; and Joshua Piven, "The PC's Bells and Whistles Could Be Playing a Swan Song," *Computer Technology Review*, December 1996, 1, 18.

11. Jeremy Main, "How to Go Global—and Why," *Fortune*, 28 August 1989, 70–76; and Akihiro Okumura, "Corporate Restructuring at Japanese Companies—Lessons from Global Restructuring," *Management Japan*, Autumn 1996, 3–8.

12. Jeremy Main, "How to Go Global"; and Patricia Layman, "Customer Awareness Becomes a Byword at Rapidly Internationalizing ICI," *Chemical and Engineering News*, 3 June 1996, 14–19.

13. Jeremy Main, "How to Go Gobal"; and David C. Smith, "How Ford's New Brand Strategy Works," *Ward's Auto World*, October 1996, 40–41.

14. Ibid.

15. Ibid., 70.

16. Ibid., 70.

17. Philippe Gugler, "Building Transnational Alliances to Create Competitive Advantage," *Long Range Planning* 25, no. 1 (1992): 90–99.

18. "The Smallest Copier Yet Prints on Just about Anything," *Business Week*, 3 July 1989, 48.

19. Thomas J. Murray, "How Motorola Builds in Speed and Quality," *Business Month*, July 1989, 36–37.

20. Gugler, "Building Transnational Alliances."

21. Alan Treadgold, "The Emerging Internationalization of Retailing," *Irish Marketing Review* 5, no. 2 (1990): 11–27.

22. Thomas P. Conley, "U.S. Retailers Must Global-Trot Too," *Discount Merchandiser*, March 1996, 68.

23. "Design for Europe," *Business Europe*, 9 October 1996, 9–10.

24. "Information Drives Nestle Supply Chain," *Crossborder Monitor*, 7 August 1996, 8.

25. "Europe's MNCs Take Steps toward Single Currency," *Crossborder Monitor*, 3 July 1996, 1, 3.

26. "Citibank Pushes Plastic in Venezuela," *Crossborder Monitor*, 27 November 1996, 9.

27. "Colombia's Chain of Distribution Rattles MNCs," *Crossborder Monitor*, 4 December 1996, 1.

28. John S. Hill and Giles D'Souza, "Strategies for the Emerging Americas Market," *Journal of Business Strategy* (forthcoming).

29. "Baskin Robbins Finds Russian Market Sweet," *Crossborder Monitor*, 2 October 1996, 8; and "Coke in Russia: Coming on Strong," *Crossborder Monitor*, 4 September 1996, 8.

30. Pete Engardio, "Global Tremors from an Unruly Giant," *Business Week*, 4 March 1996, 59–64.

31. "Greater Europe: Moving the Goalposts," *Business Europe*, 20 November 1996, 9–10.

32. "External Relations," *European Trends*, fourth quarter 1995, 46–54.

33. World Resources Institute, *World Resources 1990–91* (New York: Oxford University Press, 1990), 322–332.

34. Mark Maremont "Eastern Europe's Big Cleanup," *Business Week*, 19 March 1990, 114–115; and Associated Press: Moscow, "Gorbachev Hears about Pollution," *Birmingham News*, 28 April 1990, 3A.

35. Neil Gross, "Charging Japan with Crimes against the Earth," *Business Week*, 9 October 1989, 108–112.

36. Vicky Cahan and Brian Bremner, "When the Rivers Go Dry and the Ice Caps Melt," *Business Week*, 13 February 1989, 95–98.

37. Ibid.

Subject Index

▪ F ▪

Name Index

Product Index

A

Abrasive Distributors Corp., 175
Acorn Computers, 273
Air Canada, 322
Air France, 322
Ajax, 252
Akzo Nobel Chemicals, Inc., 175
American Express, 270
American Motors, 207
American President Lines, 322
Amnesty International, 284
Analog Devices, 130
Anderson and Lembke, 279
Anheuser-Busch, 210
Apple Computers, 170, 278
Archer Daniels Midland Co., 486
Arrow Shirt, 304
Arthur Young, 281
Asea-Brown-Boveri, 11, 12, 18, 171, 477, 478
ASKO washers and dryers, 265
Aspirin, 243
Aston Martin Lagonda, 474
Atari, 166
AT&T, 270, 272, 273, 277, 287, 288, 306, 476, 480
Atwood Richards, 404
Audi, 261
Australia Telecom, 288
Avis, 235

B

Banana Republic, 292
Bankers Trust, 233, 284
Bank of America, 177, 281
Bany Pharmaceutical Company, 207

BASF, 13, 477, 478
Bayer aspirin, 13, 340
BBDO, 279, 342
Becton-Dickinson Company, 318, 455
BellSouth, 475
Benetton, 292, 304, 330
Birds Eye Walls, 482
BMW, 10, 13, 171, 248, 392, 467, 490
The Body Shop, 482
Boeing Co., 175, 272
Boveri, 12
Breckhill Ltd., 276
Bristol-Myers, 469, 480
Bristol Sidderley, 277
British Airways, 322, 323
British Broadcasting Corporation, 335
British Petroleum (BP), 12, 279
British Rail, 13
British Telcom, 288
Brown-Forman, 130
Burger King, 235
Burroughs, 468

C

Cable News Network (CNN), 477
Cadillac, 249
California Coolers, 130
Campbell Janan, Inc. (CJI), 297
Campbell Soup, 245, 468, 476
Canada Dry, 226, 252
Canadian Airlines, 322
Canon, 27, 231, 234, 236, 278, 292

Caprock, 312
Carnation, 338, 413
Carrefour, 482
Casio Company, 236, 263
Caterpillar, 175, 199–200, 207, 233, 272, 275, 276, 313
CDC, 379
Central Transportation Co., 486
Cesna Aircraft, 17
Chanel No. 5, 167, 348
Charles of France, 390, 398
Chase Manhattan, 233, 270, 281
Chesebrough-Ponds, 253
Chin Chee Tea, 355
Chiyoda, 272
Christian Dior, 390, 398
Chrysler, 233, 235, 319, 341, 474
Ciba Geigy, 412, 469
Citicorp, 171, 177, 233, 270, 281, 482
Citizen, 27
CKD, 133
Coca-Cola, 17, 123, 126, 170, 205, 224, 226, 227, 235, 243, 244, 248, 252, 297, 304, 335, 337, 340, 346, 349, 371, 402, 463, 476, 483
Colgate-Palmolive, 168, 226, 227, 231, 250, 252, 253, 434, 444, 459
Compaq, 278
Concert, 272
Conoco, 17
Control Data, 233
Cool Whip, 354
Cooper Industries, Inc., 175
Corning, 249, 455–56
CPC International, 175, 444
Cray Supercomputers, 129
Credit Lyonnais, 281
Creole Petroleum Company, 390
Cross Pens, 129